Craftsmen
of the Army

Craftsmen of the Army

The Story of the Royal Electrical
and Mechanical Engineers
Volume III 1993–2015

Compiled by

Colonel R B Peregrine
(late Corps of Royal Electrical and Mechanical Engineers)

Brigadier R J Croucher CBE
(late Corps of Royal Electrical and Mechanical Engineers)

Pen & Sword
MILITARY

First published in Great Britain in 2017 by
Pen & Sword Military
an imprint of
Pen & Sword Books Ltd
47 Church Street
Barnsley
South Yorkshire
S70 2AS

Copyright © Corps of Royal Electrical and Mechanical Engineers, 2017

ISBN 978 1 47389 988 9

The right of the Corps of Royal Electrical and Mechanical Engineers to be identified as the Authors of this Work has been asserted by them in accordance with the Copyright, Designs and Patents Act 1988.

A CIP catalogue record for this book is available from the British Library

All rights reserved. No part of this book may be reproduced or transmitted in any form or by any means, electronic or mechanical including photocopying, recording or by any information storage and retrieval system, without permission from the Publisher in writing.

Typeset in Ehrhardt by
Mac Style Ltd, Bridlington, East Yorkshire
Printed and bound in Malta by Gutenberg Press Ltd

Pen & Sword Books Ltd incorporates the imprints of Pen & Sword Archaeology, Atlas, Aviation, Battleground, Discovery, Family History, History, Maritime, Military, Naval, Politics, Railways, Select, Transport, True Crime, and Fiction, Frontline Books, Leo Cooper, Praetorian Press, Seaforth Publishing and Wharncliffe.

For a complete list of Pen & Sword titles please contact
PEN & SWORD BOOKS LIMITED
47 Church Street, Barnsley, South Yorkshire, S70 2AS, England
E-mail: enquiries@pen-and-sword.co.uk
Website: www.pen-and-sword.co.uk

CONTENTS

Acknowledgements ix
Foreword x
Preface xi

Chapter 1 Introduction 1
Overview of events covered by Volumes 1 and 2 of Craftsmen of the Army and general introduction.

Chapter 2 The Fundamentals and Organisation to 2010 7
Explains in simple terms what REME does, and how it was organised (to 2010) with a view to making the chapters that follow understandable by those without current knowledge of the Corps.

Chapter 3 Strategic Defence and Security Review 2010 and Army 2020 26
Effectively an update on the previous chapter, including changes still in the process of implementation at the time of writing.

Chapter 4 Collective Training for Operations 34
Readiness requirements and how collective training was structured to meet them.

Chapter 5 Operations General 46
REME's involvement in operations other than those covered in other chapters. These included operations in Northern Ireland, Rwanda, Sierra Leone, Darfur, Libya, Cyprus and UK (including those related to foot and mouth disease and the firemen's strike).

Chapter 6 Operations in the Balkans 1 – Bosnia 56
Operations in the region including Operations GRAPPLE 1–6, which developed into Operation RESOLUTE with the arrival of the Implementation Force, and subsequently developed into the Stabilisation Force and Operation LODESTAR and Operation PALATINE.

Chapter 7 Operations in the Balkans 2 – Kosovo 75
Operation AGRICOLA, the invasion of Kosovo in 1999 and subsequent peacekeeping operations including Operation BESSEMER (Macedonia) leading to the merging of UK operations in the Balkans into Operation OCULUS and the withdrawal of the last UK battlegroup in 2003.

Chapter 8   The Invasion of Iraq (Operation TELIC 1)   91
The invasion of Iraq in 2003.

Chapter 9   Iraq – Aftermath of the Invasion (Operations TELIC 2–13)   118
Subsequent operations in Iraq (Operations TELIC 2–13) culminating in the withdrawal of combat forces in 2009 (Operation BROCKDALE).

Chapter 10   Afghanistan – The Prologue (2001–March 2006)   157
The background to the UK involvement in Afghanistan, including Operations JACANA, FINGAL, TARROCK and HERRICK 1–3, none of which involved significant combat activity.

Chapter 11   Afghanistan – The Long Haul (Operations HERRICK 4–14)   167
The deployment of a UK brigade on Operation HERRICK 4 in mid-2006. The bloody fighting that followed, and the subsequent build-up of forces, which led to a much more stable situation by the end of Operation HERRICK 14 in September 2012.

Chapter 12   Afghanistan – Drawing Down   220
Operation HERRICK 15 to the end of 2014, further operations and the plan that saw the withdrawal of the UK combat force in Helmand Province by the end of 2014.

Chapter 13   REME in the UK – Structure and Organisation   252
REME's activities and changing organisation in the UK, in the context of wider changes within the Army and Defence.

Chapter 14   REME Overseas   264
Non-operational overseas commitments, including those in Germany, Brunei, Canada, Cyprus, the Falkland Islands, Kenya, and on loan service.

Chapter 15   REME Aviation   280
The evolving world of Army aviation, including the introduction of the Apache attack helicopter, and REME's role in supporting it.

Chapter 16   REME and the Reserve Army   300
The change of REME Reserve Forces from an organisation primarily intended to be used as a 'force of last resort' to one that routinely made a significant contribution to ongoing operations. The need for increasing reliance on the Reserve Army, and some of the issues and consequences for REME.

Chapter 17   REME Equipment and Technology   334
Changes to equipment used by REME, and the technology involved.

CONTENTS

Chapter 18   Support for Army Equipment – An Overview   349
The changing higher organisation for managing Defence procurement and support within which REME operated. The formation and role of the Defence Logistic Organisation and Defence Equipment and Support.

Chapter 19   Technical Support and Base Repair Agencies   379
The history of these formerly REME organisations that became agencies, and which provided technical support and base repair.

Chapter 20   Army Equipment and its Management   394
An overview of changes to the inventory that REME had to support and evolving ideas on (whole) fleet management.

Chapter 21   HQ DEME(A) and RHQ REME   427
The history of HQ DEME(A) from its formation in 1999 until it was dismantled in 2012. The role of RHQ REME before its incorporation in HQ DEME(A), during that time, and the role that it played thereafter.

Chapter 22   REME People   444
Recruitment, selection, individual training and career paths of officers and soldiers.

Chapter 23   Individual Training Organisations   459
The REME training organisations at Arborfield and Bordon, and their evolution in the context of a wider Defence training strategy.

Chapter 24   Corps ('Regimental') Matters   482
An introduction and overview of governance issues, the role of the Colonel in Chief, and the evolving Corps committee structure.

Chapter 25   The REME Association and Veterans   487
The continuing history of the REME Association, and matters related to former members of the Corps.

Chapter 26   REME Charities and the REME Museum   495
The REME Central Charitable Trust and the pattern of its income and expenditure, the REME Institution, and the success story of the REME Museum.

Chapter 27   Other Corps Institutions, Facilities and Activities   505
Officers' and Sergeants' Messes, the role of the Corps Regimental Sergeant Major and Corps Artificer Sergeant Major, the REME Hotel Bavaria, St Eligius Church, the REME Band, the Bloodhound Supersonic Car project, 'naming the train', Corps publications and the evolving communications strategy.

Chapter 28   The Plan for Lyneham   523
The organisation being set up to provide REME technical training. The moves from Arborfield and Bordon to Lyneham, and its establishment as the new 'Home of the Corps', including Corps Messes, the REME Museum, Corps Church, 8 Training Battalion REME and RHQ REME.

Chapter 29   Corps Sporting and Adventurous Activities   532
A summary of REME's achievements in these fields, including a list of winners of the Rory Cape Memorial Award.

Appendix A: Key Corps Post-Holders and Awards   607
Appendix B: Terminology and Acronyms   616
Index   636

ACKNOWLEDGEMENTS

This book has been completed with the assistance of many members of the Corps of Royal Electrical and Mechanical Engineers. The Corps Regimental Headquarters has played an important role in coordinating contributions and allowing use to be made of Corps publications including The Craftsman magazine and the REME Journal. The help of all is gratefully acknowledged.

FOREWORD

BUCKINGHAM PALACE

It is not surprising that accounts of military campaigns tend to concentrate on battles. Those are the defining moments of a campaign. The mundane business of providing the armies with food and appropriate equipment is usually ignored. The fact is that no army has been able to fight effectively without adequate weapons and equipment. What has changed in modern warfare is the complexity of modern weapons systems and the wide range of specialist vehicles.

Military engineers have always been essential components of armies, but they were 'combat engineers'. It was the introduction of these more complex weapons and equipment which created the need for a specialised corps to maintain and repair this equipment. The introduction of tanks in World War I is a classic example. The establishment of the Corps of Royal Electrical and Mechanical Engineers was the British response to this new feature in land warfare.

This third volume covers the transition from mechanisation to digitisation and tells the story of the creation and development of what has become one of the essential 'sinews of war', and how the Corps has responded to the task of maintaining the Army's ever more sophisticated fleet of fighting vehicles, weapons systems and equipment ranging from the optical sights on the basic rifle to the Apache helicopter.

Colonel in Chief

Field Marshal His Royal Highness The Prince Philip, Duke of Edinburgh
KG KT OM GBE AC QSO

Colonel in Chief the Corps of Royal Electrical and Mechanical Engineers

Lieutenant General A C Figgures CB CBE
Master General Royal Electrical and Mechanical Engineers

PREFACE

Volume 1 of Craftsmen of the Army, the story of the Corps of Royal Electrical and Mechanical Engineers (REME), was first published in 1970 and covered the period from its formation in 1942 in the middle of World War 2. Volume 2 was published in 1996 and covered the period from 1969 to principally 1992, the 50th Anniversary of the formation of the Corps, although to complete some story threads it overran to 1994. This is the third Volume and covers the period from the early-1990s to 2016. Like its predecessors, Volume 3 is intended to be both an historical reference book and a tribute to the men and women of REME, both regular and reservist, and their remarkable success in keeping the Army's equipment operationally fit, sometimes under very challenging circumstances.

To set the book in context, in the early-1990s the Army was beginning to adjust to the end of the Cold War. Until then, despite the Falklands War and continuing operations in Northern Ireland, most training and planning focused on repelling a Soviet invasion in Germany. This 'high-intensity warfare capability' proved invaluable in prosecuting the first Gulf War in Iraq (Operation GRANBY). However, the nature of operations was about to change very rapidly. Peacekeeping operations in the Balkans, a second high-intensity operation in Iraq (Gulf War 2), lengthy and bloody counterinsurgency operations in Iraq and Afghanistan as well as other small operations elsewhere in the world required the Army, and the Corps of REME, to rethink its organisation, tactics, training and equipment requirements very rapidly. The emphasis moved from units that were broadly single-role and single-purpose to flexible building blocks that could be 'mixed and matched' to meet a specific operational requirement. Inevitably, this would have to be done against a backdrop of tight financial control.

If there is one overwhelming thread that runs through this book it is the story of continuous and rapid change. In the early-1990s, the 'Head of the Corps of REME', the Director General Electrical and Mechanical Engineering had just taken responsibility for Army Equipment Support and become the Director General Equipment Support (Army). However, within the decade, management of the Corps was separated from equipment support, which itself was rationalised on a tri-Service basis with the formation of the Defence Logistics Organisation (DLO) which, in turn, would subsequently merge with the procurement organisation to form Defence Equipment and Support (DE&S). REME units restructured and relocated, some from Germany. Latterly, dependence on Reserve Forces substantially increased. REME's technical training was rationalised and put under tri-Service management and financial control. As part of this, the REME technical training schools, and its 'Home of the Corps', which had been in Arborfield and Bordon for over 60 years were rationalised and relocated to the former RAF base at Lyneham. As described in the early chapters, there was an ebb and flow of other responsibilities with consequent changes to the management structure of the Corps. Fortunately, the fundamental concept of REME lines of support together with the quality and ethos of REME officers and soldiers meant that the combination of budgetary pressures with the demand to provide more capability could be, and was, met with innovative and creative solutions.

In 2005, the then Corps Secretary proposed to the Corps Committee that the scale and pace of change as well as recent operations suggested that it would be timely to begin compiling Volume 3 of the history of the Corps. The Committee agreed and so he contacted Colonel Richard Peregrine (a former Regimental Colonel) and asked if he would undertake the work. This book is the result of his hard labour and research. He authored most of the content based on contemporary documents, internet searches and personal recollections and anecdotes. All of the chapters have been scrutinised and, where appropriate, contributed to and edited by a significant number of serving and retired members of the Corps. Particular thanks is due to Brigadier Rod Croucher (a former DEME(A)) for his meticulous proof-reading and final editing of the draft manuscript. This final version should therefore represent an authoritative account of both what actually happened and how things were perceived at the time.

Shortly after the formation of REME, Field Marshal the Viscount Montgomery of Alamein pithily described its role as 'keeping the punch in the Army's fist', a phrase he reiterated in the Foreword to Volume 1. The strength of the Corps undoubtedly lies in its officers and soldiers, in their ingenuity, resourcefulness, and their engineering and military professionalism. The ensuing pages illustrate just how successful they have been in keeping the Army's equipment fit for purpose despite some considerable challenges and turbulence. I hope that the reader will find the book of great interest.

MGREME

CHAPTER 1

INTRODUCTION

When World War 2 started in 1939, the British Army was going through a process of rapid expansion and unprecedented mechanisation. The cavalry fought from armoured vehicles and even the infantry used tracked, lightly-armoured carriers. The Army's ability to counter, and even engage in, fast-moving operations of the 'blitzkrieg' type therefore depended on its ability to keep fleets of wheeled and tracked vehicles operationally fit.

Early on in World War 2, during the operations prior to the evacuation of Dunkirk, the Army found that many of its tanks, trucks and other equipment did not work when they were most needed. Specifically, a counterstroke by a whole British armoured brigade, which was designed to scythe through the German lines of communication, resulted in only one working tank making it to the start line (and this promptly broke down). Such experiences taught the hard lesson, no less relevant today than it was then, that equipment itself does not deliver military capability; to do that, it must work properly when and where it is needed. It became clear that fast-moving armoured operations of the 'blitzkrieg' type involved a high degree of attrition from mechanical failures, on top of any battle casualties. The side that proved best at sweeping up casualties, repairing them and feeding them back into the battle would thereby gain a cumulative advantage in the numbers game, which could make the difference between success and failure on the battlefield. This was an area in which the British Army was initially at a distinct disadvantage against the German forces.

The Army started World War 2 with a fragmented system for maintaining equipment. The Royal Army Ordnance Corps (RAOC) had a large engineering organisation (RAOC(E)). It had experience from World War 1 of setting up major base workshop facilities in operational theatres abroad; it also had mobile workshops, which could deploy to support formations in the field. Regiments and Corps generally had their own armourers and fitters who operated at unit level but in order to make a unit combat ready it was generally necessary to supplement them with a Light Aid Detachment (LAD) from RAOC(E) units. As the scale of the technical challenge became apparent, the Army decided that it needed a new engineering Corps. This would be responsible for pulling together all aspects of the repair and recovery of mechanical equipment, and also of electrical and electronic equipment (such as radio and radar that were increasingly important). The Corps of Royal Electrical and Mechanical Engineers (REME) was formed on 1 October 1942. Its purpose was '*to keep fit equipment in the hands of troops*' – and that has not changed since then.

The new Corps earned its spurs quickly, and after the battle of El Alamein, which began in October 1942, General Viscount Alexander paid the following tribute:

> 'It was very largely the high efficiency of the repair and recovery organisation which enabled us to retain our superiority in armour throughout the fighting. In 10 Corps alone, of 530 tanks received into workshops, 337 were put back into service again in the first 11 days of the battle'.

By the end of the War, REME had taken control of virtually all Army static workshops (including those formerly under the Royal Engineers (RE) and the Royal Army Service Corps (RASC)). Its well proven systems for operating in the field were supported by substantial training and technical organisations giving it a peak strength of around 45,000 towards the end of World War 2. At this stage, many unit level fitters still wore their parent unit capbadge. This changed shortly after the War with the 'Phase 2' restructuring exercise, which resulted in almost all being absorbed by REME, thereby producing a rationalised trade structure that offered much broader career opportunities for those in technical specialisations.

CRAFTSMEN OF THE ARMY – VOLUME 1

These early developments are covered in Volume 1 of Craftsmen of the Army, the history of REME up until 1965. Volume 1 includes the period of conscription, the Korean War, Suez, the small colonial/post-colonial wars and REME's contribution to the British Army of the Rhine (BAOR), which was to become by far the Army's biggest single commitment. It also explains how REME increasingly provided technical support to the procurement of equipment, as the need for a 'through-life' approach to managing equipment became ever more apparent. REME, as a technical organisation with unparalleled experience of repairing and maintaining

Army equipment, was extremely well placed to help ensure that reliability and maintainability were built into equipment right from the start of the design process.

CRAFTSMEN OF THE ARMY – VOLUME 2

Volume 2 covers the history of the Corps from 1965 to 1992. It deals with the period during which the perceived importance of BAOR increased, then waned, as the Cold War came to its end and the Berlin Wall came down. Operations in Northern Ireland started in the late 1960s and continued throughout, with many BAOR units doing 'roulement' operational tours. The Falklands crisis blew up in 1982 and was quickly resolved with a brilliant campaign.

As the Cold War wound down, western governments were keen to find a 'peace dividend' in the form of reduced expenditure on defence. In UK, this resulted in an 'Options for Change' study. Whilst this was still under way, Saddam Hussein invaded Kuwait. The UK was a major participant in the coalition set up to eject him. It deployed 46,000 personnel (with a peak REME component of 3,700) to the Gulf. These played an important role in the outstandingly successful operations that followed in 1991. The 'Options' process resumed thereafter and, broadly speaking, REME was reduced in line with reductions to the organisations that it supported.

Volume 2 also covered the changes which resulted from the Logistic Support Review (LSR) that was initiated in the late 1980s. As it had a profound effect on REME's business, a brief explanation may be useful. At the time REME was formed there were three main logistic Corps. First, the RASC, which was primarily concerned with transport (and was to evolve into the Royal Corps of Transport (RCT) in 1965). Second, the RAOC was responsible for provisioning and storing pretty well everything, including large volumes of combat supplies (such as ammunition and fuel), as well as spares for equipment maintenance and repair. Finally, REME was responsible for equipment-related engineering and for equipment recovery. The relationship between REME and RAOC was obviously crucial because, as a distinguished REME officer was wont to say, '*spares and repairs go together like eggs and bacon*'. Spares for tanks, guns and complex military electronic systems cannot simply be bought off the shelf, and engineering input is required to ensure that enough of the right spares are available when and where they are required. The relationship between REME and RAOC was generally close and constructive at all staff levels, and also at unit level (with RAOC stores sections embedded in larger REME workshops). Ultimately, however, when equipment availability was unsatisfactory, allocation of responsibility between the two large organisations was not always easy to pin down.

The broad conclusion of the LSR was that the Army's three logistic Corps should be reconstituted as two, each headed by a two-star (Major General) Director General (DG). In essence, RAOC and RCT merged to form a new Royal Logistic Corps (RLC). REME retained its name, and at unit level things were essentially unchanged except that RAOC personnel within REME units rebadged as RLC. Within the staff chain, however, there was a major change in that RAOC's former provisioning and purchasing responsibilities for technical spares were added to those of the old REME management organisation, thus at last bringing together 'spares' and 'repairs' under one organisational chain. This new enhanced structure was clearly about more than just 'electrical and mechanical engineering' (EME) and in view of its wider remit the 'EME' label was dropped in favour of 'Equipment Support' (ES). This applied all the way up the staff chain to Director General (DG) level, where the former DGEME became the DG Equipment Support (Army) (DGES(A)). He took on additional staff and responsibilities at his HQ at Andover to enable him to run the entire ES organisation whilst still managing the Corps of REME, and remaining its corporate head.

Although the new ES directorates at Andover were based on their EME forebears (plus a directorate inherited from the RAOC that had responsibilities for wheeled vehicles and supply management, and an RE branch concerned with RE equipment and plant), changes were much more than cosmetic. The new equipment branches moved in a multidisciplinary direction with responsibilities for spares, finance, and in-service modifications being added to their original engineering management role. This was eventually to lead to their transformation into Integrated Project Teams (IPT). The ES organisation at this time was very aware of the importance of planning equipment support on a 'through-life' basis. It sought positive engagement with the Ministry of Defence's (MoD) procurement organisation and supported the use of recognised analytical techniques such as Integrated Logistic Support (ILS) from the start of procurement. It was also very outward looking. It embraced the Total Quality concept, and it played an active role in changing some of its organisations into 'agencies' with greater autonomy and freedom to manage the way in which they provided their outputs. The continuing need to find 'efficiency savings' meant it was also active in looking for ways in which support costs could be reduced by market testing, outsourcing or contractorisation.

In short, by the end of 1992 (the period covered by Volume 2), the REME organisation in the field had come through the period after the Cold War more or less unchanged (beyond a pro rata reduction in size reflecting the reduced size of the Army). It had a two-star 'Head of the Corps' who also had direct responsibility and authority over a base workshop organisation, a spares procurement organisation and a group of technical organisations that provided specialist support and advice. He also had substantial responsibility for running the large REME training organisation. DGES(A) had overall responsibility for managing the Army's ES organisation, with his HQ at Andover to help him do this. In fact, from a purely Army perspective, it seemed that the management and support of its equipment had never been so coherent, with responsibility, accountability and budgets for personnel, training, engineering support equipment and policy, and spares provision well aligned.

CRAFTSMEN OF THE ARMY – VOLUME 3

Volume 3 tells REME's story from 1993 to 2015. The period has been extraordinarily eventful for REME, with the Army more operationally stretched than at any time since World War 2. Changes linked to the LSR (and some later ones) had the effect of opening up many equipment-related jobs, formerly tied to REME, to competition from other military capbadges or suitably qualified civilians. The other side of the coin was that REME officers were freed up to use their talents in a wider arena. REME officers served in a variety of command and staff appointments and the glass ceiling at two-star level was broken. At the time of writing, there were four serving late-REME Major Generals, including both the General Officers Commanding Support Command and British Forces in Germany. Key Corps post-holders and awards are at Appendix A.

The Strategic Defence Review 1998 (SDR 98) resulted in responsibility for logistics (including ES) outside the Field Army being taken away from the Army and given to a newly-formed Defence Logistic Organisation (DLO) in 2000. The underlying idea was that the tri-Service rationalisation of the Services' logistics could yield significant savings. This meant that HQ DGES(A) had to be dismembered. The Directorate that had been responsible for managing REME (as a Corps within the Army) was extracted from Andover and moved to Arborfield where its one-star (Brigadier) head became the Director of Electrical and Mechanical Engineering (Army) (DEME(A)). He also became the 'Head of the Corps of REME', and was essentially responsible for ensuring that REME first and second line units (which remained firmly part of the Army) were properly organised, trained and manned.

The former DGES(A) (with the rest of his HQ) went into the newly-formed DLO, and he became the Director General of Equipment Support (Land) (DGES(L)). His HQ and the organisations that came under him underwent numerous changes in the years ahead. An overview of the changing structure for managing support for Army equipment is at Chapter 18 ('Support for Army Equipment – An Overview').

The financial crash of 2008 was followed by a change of Government, which led to the Strategic Defence and Security Review of 2010 (SDSR 2010) and resulted in yet further change. The post of DEME(A) was cut and his HQ was dismembered, with many of its staff joining the relatively new Army HQ at Andover. This effectively left the Regimental Colonel (who was renamed Colonel REME) as 'Head of the Corps'. To support him, the post of Master General REME (MGREME) was created and approved by the Queen on 1 April 2012. The first incumbent was Lieutenant General Andrew Figgures CB CBE, a retired REME officer able to act as advocate and adviser on REME matters at senior level. SDSR 2010 was also linked with a plan to close REME technical training at Bordon and Arborfield, and move it to a new Defence Technical Training College (DTTC) at Lyneham along with REME's Regimental HQ and Museum.

This Volume covers a period of almost continuous upheaval, with changes in terminology, structure and organisation, which may seem bewildering to those who have been away from REME for even a few years. This may give an initial impression that nothing about REME is the same as it was. Hopefully, this idea will be dispelled as you read about what REME has actually done. Look behind the new acronyms (helpfully listed at Appendix B) and you will see REME men and women performing much the same functions as their predecessors, and showing much the same ingenuity, flexibility, technical skill and fortitude under pressure whilst *keeping fit equipment in the hands of troops*.

CHAPTER 2

THE FUNDAMENTALS AND ORGANISATION TO 2010

The purpose of this Chapter is twofold. First, it is to explain to the general reader enough about REME to make the chapters that follow intelligible. Second, it is to update those who have served in the Corps on the terminology and outline structure up until 2010 when REME had an overall strength of around 9,500 in the Regular Army (9% of the Army) and some 2,000 in the Territorial Army (TA). Subsequent changes were linked to the Strategic Defence and Security Review of 2010 (SDSR 2010) and, as some have not been fully implemented at the time of writing (and there was an element of uncertainty about certain aspects), they are covered separately in Chapter 3 ('Strategic Defence and Security Review 2010 and Army 2020').

Military terminology, acronyms (there is a useful list at Appendix B) and organisations seem to be ever-changing, but baffled old REME hands should be reassured that the way in which REME does its business in the field has stood the test of time, and is based on principles that have changed remarkably little.

Underlying all the other fundamentals is the principle that uniformed REME personnel are trained as both soldiers and engineers, and may need to switch rapidly between military and technical roles. The validity of this 'soldier-tradesman' concept was amply proved in World War 2. Interestingly, the German Wehrmacht initially believed that the contractors who had manufactured their tanks and vehicles would also be able to repair them in the field, but quickly learned they needed an organisation, which was similar in principle to REME. Recent REME operational experience has served to reaffirm the validity of the concept.

FIRST LINE

Roughly two-thirds of REME soldiers serve at 'first line' and this split has changed little over time. The term collectively refers to REME personnel embedded in non-REME units to provide immediate technical support. Virtually every unit in the Army has some form of integral REME support. The level of support is tailored to the organisation being supported. Smaller units, or those which hold little complex equipment, simply have 'attached tradesmen' (for example, a Royal Military Police detachment with light wheeled vehicles and a few trucks might have a pair of REME Vehicle Mechanics attached to it). Major units, which hold a significant amount of complex equipment (such as a tank regiment or an armoured infantry battalion), would have an integral 'Light Aid Detachment' (LAD). LADs vary greatly in size, and are typically anything from 22 to 100+ strong. They provide both repair and recovery support, and are often organised into an HQ element and fitter sections attached to sub-units. Figure 2.1 (at the end of this Chapter) shows a typical LAD of this type (commanded by a REME Captain) for a Type 38 armoured regiment.

Finally, just to make things more confusing, there is another type of first line unit, the 'Regimental Workshop'. To all intents and purposes these are large LADs, but they are not called that because they carry out 'second line' repairs on their specialist vehicles and equipment.

First Line Unit – 1 Royal Horse Artillery LAD Iraq 2007

LEVELS OF REPAIR AND LINES OF SUPPORT

That last sentence leads neatly to the topic of 'levels of repair' and 'lines of support' (familiar to old REME hands). The terminology may have changed over time, generally to adopt standard NATO definitions, but the basic principles have not. The key point to appreciate is that the terms first line and second line support do not necessarily relate to how close REME is to the front line. They relate to the level of repair support provided. NATO defines four levels of support tasks.

Level 1. These are user tasks, such as changing tyres, topping up the oil, doing user functional tests and the like. In theory, this is not a REME responsibility, except for its own equipment, but, in practice, REME personnel frequently mentor and advise the users, particularly young soldiers who have little general technical understanding, but are required to operate and maintain some very complex equipment.

Level 2. Essentially these are tasks carried out by REME at first line. They include providing immediate repair and recovery support when equipment fails for technical reasons or through enemy action. Also, undertaking routine maintenance beyond the user's capability as well as minor repairs (such as fixing the brakes or exchanging components), but not major repairs (such as completely replacing the engine of a large truck).

Level 3. These are tasks that are beyond the capability of first line REME units to deal with (for operational or technical reasons) but can be carried out by second line REME organisations. Second line REME organisations are essentially deployable workshops that now generally come in the form of REME battalions, but can be REME companies embedded within logistic support battalions. Notwithstanding NATO terminology, 'Level 2/Level 3 repairs' are still often colloquially (and confusingly) referred to as 'first/second line REME jobs' respectively.

Level 4. These are tasks that are most sensibly done in a factory-type environment. Typically, these would include complete equipment overhaul/refurbishment programmes or the stripping down and rebuilding of assemblies such as engines or gearboxes. At one time, they would generally have been carried out in REME base workshops (which might be in the UK or deployed in an operational theatre) and this level of repair was referred to as 'base repair'. These days, such repairs would be carried out either by the Defence Support Group (DSG), which grew from the Army Base Repair Organisation (ABRO), or a contractor with relevant expertise.

REME Equipment. Chapter 17 ('REME Equipment and Technology') describes some of the repair and recovery equipment used by first and second line REME units. One of the points that emerged clearly from operations in Iraq and Afghanistan was the need for REME vehicles to have levels of mobility and protection matching those of the equipment they need to support.

FIELD REPAIR PRINCIPLES

Before describing REME's second line organisation, it is useful to explain two underlying principles that drive it. The first is that equipment support processes must be broadly the same during peacetime training as they are on operations. Unless processes are practised in peacetime it is unlikely that they will work effectively in war, or allow a smooth transition from a peacetime to an operational footing.

The second is the requirement to make equipment fit and get it back into the user's hands on the battlefield as quickly as possible. This dictates a 'repair forward' policy, which has always been REME doctrine and remains so today. This policy begs the question as to what 'forward' really means in this context. In reality, it means 'repair as far forward as is sensible', which leads to the further question of how to determine what is 'sensible'. The answer is simply that there isn't a simple answer. Judgments have to be continuously made at all levels based on the interplay of operational, technical and even economic factors. Deciding where REME units should be based in the field, when they should move and what tasks they should be loaded with is core business for ES commanders and staff. Broadly speaking, in the field there are often trade-offs to be made between moving units to where they can provide the most immediate support, or leaving them in more stable and secure environments where they can maximise their productive output. It is a truism that REME units can move or work, but they cannot do both at the same time. Also, the more effort a REME unit has to expend on protecting itself, the less effort is available for production. A key implication of the repair forward policy is that REME units must be able to deploy into the operational area close to the units they support, and be capable of moving on the battlefield and defending themselves against local threats.

SECOND LINE – TYPICAL TASKS

Before outlining the second line organisations, it is also useful to have an idea of the tasks that are typically carried out by second line REME units.

Forward Repair of Armoured Fighting Vehicles. Armoured Fighting Vehicles (AFVs) generally have their engines, gearboxes and cooling groups built into an easily replaceable power pack (PP). If a tank has a serious problem affecting any of these assemblies the quickest way to fix it will often be simply to change the complete PP in situ, which might be done in an hour or two. Forward Repair Teams (FRT) from second line REME units do just this. They are tasked to go forward in their tracked vehicles to specific casualties, carrying the required replacement assembly (which is not necessarily a PP). They carry out the repair (only moving the casualty if they need to) and return to their unit with the faulty assembly, leaving a happy customer with a vehicle ready to fight.

Power pack exchange at night on a training exercise in Canada

AFV Power Pack Repair. A successful forward repair system requires the availability of fit PPs. These assemblies are large (a tank PP weighs about six tonnes), expensive and if vehicle activity rates are high a lot of them may be needed quickly. Running a repair loop back to contractor facilities in UK would require an enormous pool of assemblies, and would involve potential risks and difficulties with a long supply chain. The PPs are therefore repaired at second line in Power Pack Repair Facilities (PPRF). These require cranes, jigs to allow engines and gearboxes to be split, and facilities to run up and test systems. Ideally, the work is done in a factory-type environment but all the necessary facilities to do the work can be packed into demountable containers, which can be used to support repair operations on any reasonably flat and firm terrain. PPs are generally repaired by replacing an engine or gearbox (with the dead assembly being returned for base repair), but this is not always the case. The PPRF also has the capability to cannibalise assemblies; that is, to make one good PP out of two defective ones – a capability that can be of key operational importance in a crisis.

Power pack repair in Iraq 2003

Optronic Repair. Serious faults with optical or electronic systems are usually repaired at first line by identifying a faulty 'black box' (called a line replaceable unit (LRU)) and exchanging it for a good one. The faulty LRU goes back to second line where it can be tested to a greater depth and usually repaired by replacing a faulty circuit board or other component. The repairs may be done in container bodies, which contain the necessary test and repair facilities and are generally vehicle mounted, or in suitable 'clean' facilities in barracks.

Vehicle and General Repair. Vehicle and General (V & G) repair embraces the repair of wheeled vehicles of all types, weapons and almost anything that needs welding, patching up or modifying. Alternatively, vehicle repairers may be sometimes put into their own dedicated Vehicle Platoon(s), with welders, armourers and other trades being put into a separate Armament and General (A & G) Platoon.

Recovery. Recovery has always been a key REME function. It involves more than providing a simple 'green flag' recovery service for vehicles that have broken down. There is a requirement to recover battle damaged vehicles and deny them to the enemy. On operations, keeping a main supply route open during an advance or withdrawal (or to sustain ongoing operations) can be critical, particularly if it has potentially vulnerable choke points. Units will frequently move on bad roads or cross country. It is not only wheeled vehicles that can get stuck, as whole squadrons of tanks may become bogged down and require REME assistance to get them out. REME first line units generally have some form of recovery capability (often a single recovery vehicle) but they will not always be able to cope either with the number of vehicles or the scope of a complex individual task. Recovery resources are therefore also held at second line to be deployed where they are needed under the control of a REME recovery officer responsible for coordinating the recovery effort.

Stricken Mastiff vehicle being winched clear of an obstacle in Afghanistan 2012

SECOND LINE ORGANISATION

Although the tasks carried out at second line have remained much the same over the years, the way in which units have been organised and titled has not. Prior to 1992, all second line units were called 'X Workshop REME' with a number plus a name to indicate the nature of their role, for example 'Field' (for a non-armoured role) and 'Armoured' (for an armoured role). The name would be abbreviated in the format, for example, of 4 Armd Wksp REME. Units varied considerably in size. For example, there were 'small' armoured workshops. These were substantial independent sub-units (over 200 strong) but were rated as a 'company equivalent', and were therefore commanded by a Major.

There were also 'large' armoured workshops, which were really two small armoured workshops bolted together. These were seen as a 'battalion equivalent' and were therefore commanded by a Lieutenant Colonel. They enjoyed 'major unit' status (and the infrastructure that went with it) and could take on general battalion-type duties (which smaller second line workshops could not). REME personnel may have had no difficulty understanding the difference between a 'small' armoured workshop, a 'large' armoured workshop, a field workshop, a base workshop, a regimental workshop, or any other type of workshop. But the structure was utterly confusing to the rest of the Army, which called major units 'battalions' (or 'regiments'), and called sub-units 'companies' (or 'squadrons' or 'batteries'). Inevitably, this caused problems and misunderstandings.

As REME (and the Army) drew down in size in the early 1990s, there was hot debate as to how REME should be organised at second line in Germany. The forces there were being drawn down into one large armoured division (1 (UK) Armoured Division) comprising three armoured brigades plus divisional troops. As ever, choices were constrained by the manpower and resources available, and boiled down to this organisation structure:

- lots of independent workshop companies commanded by Majors (similar to the old 'small' armoured workshops)
- two large REME battalions, which would be controlled at divisional level – one of these would be designed for forward repair, able to allocate a forward repair company to each brigade and, the other, would operate further to the rear and would focus on tasks such as PP repair, which are best done in a more stable working environment
- three smaller REME battalions, which could be loosely affiliated to brigades and which would all have the complete range of capabilities.

Eventually, the third option was chosen, giving a REME battalion of 28 + 428 (military). [By convention, 28 + 428 means 28 officers and 428 other ranks.] This comprised HQ, General Support (GS) and Close Support (CS) companies plus a non-deployable Garrison Workshop (Gar Wksp) (manned by civilians). This was an organisation the rest of the Army understood, and which produced numerous benefits, not least that the best Lieutenant Colonels 'in command' actually commanded soldiers rather than directing workshops from divisional HQ. CS companies were intended generally to operate further forward than GS companies and included the FRT element. The battalions were organised and affiliated as shown in Figures 2.2 and 2.3 (at the end of this Chapter).

A similar approach was adopted for UK, a decision having been taken in principle that all REME major units would be called 'battalions' and their sub-units 'companies'. Initially, two Regular Army REME battalions were formed in the UK, 4 and 6 Battalions, based respectively at Tidworth and Bordon. These were larger than the REME battalions in Germany, having two GS companies each. In 1998, a new REME battalion was formed, 5 Battalion, with resource headroom being created by removing a company from each of the UK battalions.

This provided a degree of symmetry. Both UK deployable divisions, 1 (UK) Armoured Division in Germany and 3 (UK) Division in UK, had three combat brigades and three REME battalions with similar capability. The affiliations of the REME battalions in UK are shown in Figure 2.4 (at the end of this Chapter).

Second line support for helicopters in 16 Air Assault Brigade was provided by 7 Air Assault Battalion REME based at Wattisham. This unit incorporated 8 CS Company based in Colchester to provide an airborne second line REME capability to support airborne land operations.

Although the bulk of REME's second line Regular Army manpower was in these battalions, there were also REME second line companies embedded within composite Combat Service Support (CSS) units. These were essentially logistic battalions (sometimes called that) comprising a REME workshop company plus RLC companies that provided a supply, storage and transport capability. The Commando Brigade, as well as 101 and 102 Logistic Brigades, had units of this type. Five TA REME battalions were also formed. More details are in Chapter 16 ('REME and the Reserve Army') but, in essence, one of them provided a national pool of specialist reinforcements. The others were designed to provide deployable second line recovery and general support in the event of mobilisation, with their likely roles being support for lines of communication (L of C) and for thickening up Regular Army second line support.

SECOND LINE REORGANISATION

This second line organisation was what REME had in place for the invasion of Iraq and the subsequent period when it faced intense multiple operational demands in Iraq, Afghanistan and elsewhere. The structure proved flexible and able to cope with all the demands placed on it, but in the light of operational lessons and the continuing squeeze on manpower and resources, significant changes were made. At the time, the idea of 'rapid effect' was very much in vogue; that is, the idea that intervention should be as rapid and potent as possible to minimise an opponent's scope for organising resistance or countermeasures. This was linked to two ideas.

First, an overall shortage of manpower created the need to make better use of REME TA in roles that played to their strengths. Second, the concept of 'off platform repair' (OPR). This terminology will be new to many REME readers but the concept will not be. The second line forward repair of a 'platform' (such as a tank) will often involve diagnosis followed by the replacement of an assembly, which might be mechanical (such as a PP) or electronic (such as a 'black box'). This 'on platform' repair has to be carried out on the tank, but the subsequent second line repair of the assembly will be carried out 'off platform' in a second line facility, perhaps much further back. Hitherto, all REME battalions had integral OPR capability within their GS companies (and had the same generic capabilities). It was argued, however, that in a 'rapid effect' scenario the OPR capability would usually be best centralised and deployed in a force support area. This would probably be the base area at the rear of the theatre L of C, where greater stability, better infrastructure and the potential to interact more easily with the supply chain would enable these deeper repairs to be carried out more efficiently. This led to the concept of two different types of REME battalion – Close Support (CS) and Force Support (FS). The idea behind this was very similar in principle to the 'two large battalions' option considered for Germany around 1990, as previously described.

Close Support Battalions. These had lost their OPR capability, and were designed to provide intimate repair and recovery support to armoured or mechanised formations. Their organisation, set out in

DEME(A) Battlefield ES Doctrine April 2008, was to be as in Figure 2.5 (at the end of this Chapter).

Force Support Battalions. OPR capability would be centralised in two integrated Regular Army/TA FS battalions that would be affiliated to the logistic brigades and responsible for logistic support at force level. As well as carrying out OPR, these battalions would provide repair and recovery support along the L of C and also second line support for units and organisations (particularly in support areas) with no other second line support affiliation. The new battalions were organised as in Figure 2.6 (at the end of this Chapter) [from DEME(A) Battlefield ES Doctrine April 2008].

SECOND LINE ORGANISATION AS AT 2009

By 2009, the reorganisation had taken place, and 4 Armoured Brigade had by this time moved from Germany to Catterick and become 4 Mechanised Brigade. The affiliations of the reorganised REME battalions are shown in Figure 2.7 (at the end of this Chapter).

11 Armoured Company, 2 Close Support Battalion REME Canada 2012

RECRUITING AND INDIVIDUAL TRAINING

REME is only as good as its people. Its success depends on recruiting and training people with the right potential. They are normally untrained when they join the Army and the process of providing the military, technical and management skills they require is a long and complex one. Recruiting, individual training and REME's trade structure is covered in Chapter 22 ('REME People').

The story of the organisations that provide individual training is told in Chapter 23 ('Individual Training Organisations'). This starts at a time when the technical training schools at Bordon and Arborfield were part of REME Training Group. These later came under the umbrella of the Army Training and Recruitment Agency (ATRA), and subsequently became part of a Defence technical training organisation.

READINESS AND COLLECTIVE TRAINING

During the Cold War era most of the Army was continuously at high readiness. This implied that units needed to hold most of their equipment all the time. It also required an annual training cycle. In principle, this meant that units started their year with individual training (refreshing and upgrading skills). They then moved on to progressive collective training at platoon, company and unit level, before going on to formation level collective training (at brigade, division and sometimes even Corps level).

Early in the post-Cold War era, it was recognised that the collective training required to achieve high readiness was expensive, and that not all the Army would need to be at high readiness the whole time. This led to the concept of a three-year 'Formation Readiness Cycle' (FRC) being formally ushered in by the Strategic Defence Review (SDR) of 1998.

This concept had to be somewhat modified in the light of events in Iraq and Afghanistan, but the basic concept, somewhat modified, is planned to continue in the post-Afghanistan era. The topics of collective training and readiness are covered in more detail in Chapter 4 ('Collective Training for Operations').

The fact that some units were not at high readiness also meant that they did not have to hold as much equipment as they formerly did in the Cold War era. This led to new thinking on the way in which equipment could be more economically and effectively managed, and ideas about Whole Fleet Management (WFM) emerged. These are explained in Chapter 20 ('Army Equipment and its Management'), which also outlines the major changes in REME's equipment dependency.

DELIVERING CAPABILITY – MATCHING ORGANISATIONS TO TASKS

It would be wrong to imagine that the actual strength and organisation of REME first and second line units always match their paper organisation.

In fact, unit strengths are continuously manipulated by posting people in or out with a view to matching REME strengths as fairly as possible to known unit commitments (taking account of REME's overall manpower availability in various ranks and trades). For example, a unit deploying on operations would expect its REME component to be brought up to full strength (or even above it), which would inevitably result in other units being undermanned.

REME units deploying on training or operations expect to have their organisation configured to the task they have to take on. This 'task organisation' may see them with a radically different configuration from their normal peacetime organisation. REME's first and second line organisation may therefore be seen as providing a flexible framework, which needs to be actively managed to ensure that REME organisations on the ground are tailored to support the tasks the Army is committed to. The process of 'task organisation' may be deliberate (for example, to last for a complete operational tour) or it may have to be done on an ad hoc basis to deal with rapidly changing situations. There are well-established mechanisms for doing this at all levels.

First Line Operations and Training. Combat arms tend to work in battlegroups (BG). These are battalion-sized all arms groups based on a parent unit, such as an armoured regiment (perhaps the 'X Lancers'). This might, for example, lose two squadrons of tanks and gain two companies of armoured infantry plus other supporting elements, such as an armoured reconnaissance platoon (it would then become the 'X Lancers BG'). The groupings can change at short notice. This has major implications for ES arrangements, which must provide seamless support. The Officer Commanding (OC) the LAD of the parent unit of a BG (normally referred to as the 'EME') should achieve this by taking under his wing the fitter sections that support the sub-units joining his BG (and making sure that any detached sub-units go with the right REME elements). The original unit LAD has thereby transformed itself into a task-oriented BG LAD, with the EME acting as the functional adviser on all ES matters to the BG commander.

Second Line. REME second line units are normally commanded and controlled at brigade, division or force level. As such, they provide a pool of ES resources that can be managed to meet higher level priorities, and apply ES effort where it is most needed. Second line units can be configured to match whatever missions they are allocated. They may operate and deploy as battalions, or deploy independent companies, or even platoons/detachments organised to carry out specific roles. A specific commitment may also result in the formation of an Intimate Support Team (IST). This is a bespoke grouping of ES personnel set up to do a particular task and exists only until the task has been completed. The manpower will generally be drawn from REME battalions but could also come from first line REME units. IST is a relatively new term, but reflects something that has always happened to some extent or other – REME has always been an extremely flexible organisation.

Operations – Theatre Organisation. REME's organisational structure for any operation reflects the particular circumstances that apply, and is not constrained by doctrinaire divisions between first and second line. Counterinsurgency operations, for example, tend to involve troops operating from major bases, Forward Operating Bases (FOB) or Patrol Bases (PB) with movement between bases involving significant risk. This tends to lead to first and second line organisations being functionally integrated within secure base areas, and much use made of ISTs and FRTs pushed to forward locations to 'repair forward'. The REME structure copes comfortably with this, as it always has, and units easily revert to their normal first and second line roles once they return from an operational theatre.

PULLING IT ALL TOGETHER – ES COMMAND AND CONTROL

It should be clear from these fundamentals that the overall task of managing the ES effort is an extraordinarily complex multidimensional one, which needs to be integrated from the strategic level downwards. All aspects of the organisation need to be coherently led and managed at every level, and repair processes have to be designed to work effectively and economically 'from factory to foxhole' without a hiatus that could have a knock-on effect on user equipment availability.

The higher level management of ES has changed radically throughout the period covered by this book. At the start, it was fundamentally an Army responsibility and the Army had a two-star DGES(A) to lead on it. The formation of the DLO following SDR 98 led to top-level responsibility for ES moving into the Defence domain, and the formation of one-star HQ DEME(A). It is beyond the scope of this Chapter to describe the changes to the higher management of ES but the essentials are covered in Chapter 13 ('REME in the UK – Structure and Organisation') and Chapter 18 ('Support for Army Equipment – An Overview').

Within the Field Army, the well proven ES functional chain of command from divisional level downward (that grew from the REME system) has not greatly changed in its essentials. Although 'ES' does not equal 'REME', in practice all operational ES commands at Colonel level and below have been filled by REME people.

Divisional Level. Divisions have a Colonel with responsibility for all ES matters (sometimes titled 'Colonel Equipment' and sometimes 'Commander ES'). They have functional responsibility for all ES matters in their formation (or force) and may have direct command of second line REME units. As a variation, a deployed operational force (such as that sent to Afghanistan) may have a Colonel with a title such as 'Colonel Equipment Capability' with overarching responsibility for ES in the theatre of operations.

Brigade Level. At brigade level there is a Staff Officer Grade 2 (SO2) ES (Major), still generally referred to as the 'BEME' (Brigade Electrical and Mechanical Engineer), responsible for dealing with all ES matters at his level, overseeing first line REME elements as necessary and acting as the brigade commander's functional adviser on ES.

Battalion Level. Commanding Officers (COs) of REME battalions (Lieutenant Colonels) frequently have the dual task of commanding their units, and providing an additional link in the ES chain. They have the technical and operational management capability to take on such tasks as coordinating recovery and backloading operations (for which they would provide the Divisional Recovery Officer (DRO)), or organising modification programmes. They may therefore be double-hatted as Commander ES as well as unit CO. During operations in Iraq and Afghanistan especially, the rapidly changing threat spectrum meant that the introduction of equipment procured as an Urgent Operational Requirement (UOR) became a key feature. It meant that the integration of new systems into complex platforms, often concurrently with training, and often in theatre, became a major additional technical challenge for REME.

First Line. At first line, the Officer Commanding (OC) the LAD (still often called the 'EME'), comes under the direct command of his unit CO (his 'line manager') but comes under the functional control of the ES chain. This sort of situation applies across the board at first line, which is one reason why REME people tend to be very comfortable working within 'matrix' organisational settings.

SUMMARY

REME is deployed wherever the Army is deployed. It has responsibility for repairing and recovering the Army's full range of equipment, ranging from relatively straightforward equipment such as trucks, through all types of weapons, sensors and communication systems, through to advanced attack helicopters fitted with state of the art weaponry and surveillance systems. It is staffed with military personnel who are trained as soldiers as well as engineers. Its aim remains *'to keep fit equipment in the hands of troops'*, which still requires it to be able to 'repair forward'.

Some two-thirds of its strength is at first line, embedded within Army units of all types. These are backed up by second line REME units (largely in the form of battalions), which are capable of taking on more demanding (or time consuming) repair and recovery roles.

REME is a key enabler of the Army's ES system. The overall system is hugely complex, and requires REME's activities to be integrated with those of contractors and equipment suppliers. They also need to be planned and managed in conjunction with Defence staff responsible for operations, logistics, procurement, training and personnel.

THE FUNDAMENTALS AND ORGANISATION TO 2010 23

Unit/Unit LAD	Unit/LAD Structure	
Parent unit Type 38 Armd Regt (30 + 363)	Regimental HQ (RHQ) and Echelon (including two RHQ tanks)	3 x Squadrons (12 tanks and support vehicles)
LAD REME (2 + 71)	HQ LAD (2 + 30) Technical control and support of fitter sections – repairs Echelon vehicles and electronic equipment (has own wheeled recovery vehicle)	3 x Squadron Fitter Sections (0 + 13) Equipped with armoured repair and recovery vehicles

Figure 2.1: Organisation of a Type 38 Armoured Regiment LAD (from the Staff Officers Handbook 1997)

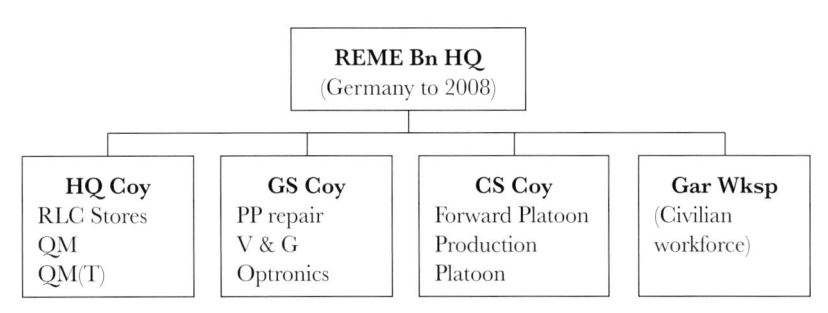

```
                    REME Bn HQ
                  (Germany to 2008)
    ┌──────────┬──────────┬──────────┬──────────┐
    HQ Coy     GS Coy     CS Coy     Gar Wksp
    RLC Stores PP repair  Forward Platoon (Civilian
    QM         V & G      Production      workforce)
    QM(T)      Optronics  Platoon
```

Figure 2.2: Organisation of a REME Battalion in Germany to 2008

REME Battalions in Germany as at 2007 (1 (UK) Armd Div)		
4 Armd Bde	1 Bn REME Osnabruck	4 CS Coy
		12 GS Coy
		1 Gar Wksp
7 Armd Bde	2 Bn REME Fallingbostel	7 CS Coy
		11 GS Coy
		2 Gar Wksp
20 Armd Bde	3 Bn REME Paderborn	5 GS Coy
		20 CS Coy
		3 Gar Wksp

Figure 2.3: Affiliation of REME Battalions in Germany as at 2007

REME Battalions in UK 1998–2006 (3 (UK) Div)

12 Mech Bde	4 Bn REME Bordon	9 GS Coy
		10 CS Coy
19 Lt Bde	5 Bn REME Catterick	6 GS Coy
		15 CS Coy
1 Mech Bde	6 Bn REME Tidworth	3 CS Coy
		14 GS Coy

Figure 2.4: Affiliation of REME Battalions in UK 1998–2006

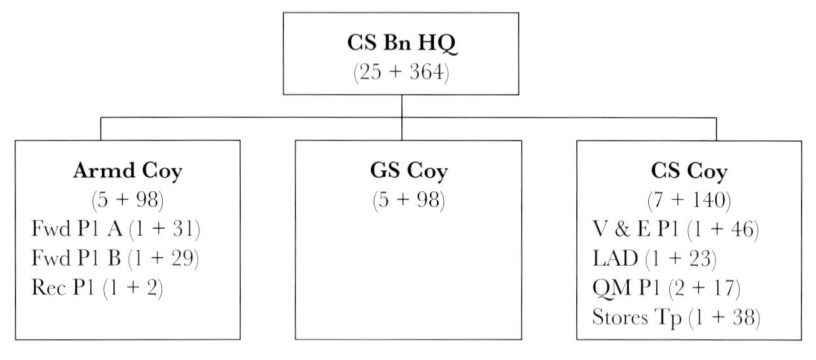

CS Bn HQ
(25 + 364)

- **Armd Coy**
  (5 + 98)
  Fwd Pl A (1 + 31)
  Fwd Pl B (1 + 29)
  Rec Pl (1 + 2)

- **GS Coy**
  (5 + 98)

- **CS Coy**
  (7 + 140)
  V & E Pl (1 + 46)
  LAD (1 + 23)
  QM Pl (2 + 17)
  Stores Tp (1 + 38)

Figure 2.5: Organisation of a REME CS Battalion 2009

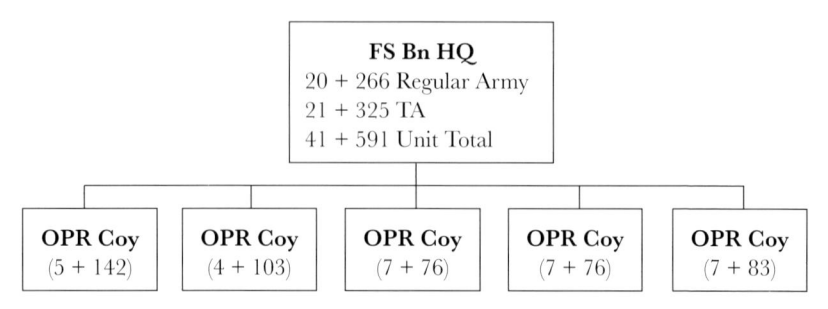

FS Bn HQ
20 + 266 Regular Army
21 + 325 TA
41 + 591 Unit Total

- **OPR Coy** (5 + 142)
- **OPR Coy** (4 + 103)
- **OPR Coy** (7 + 76)
- **OPR Coy** (7 + 76)
- **OPR Coy** (7 + 83)

Figure 2.6: Organisation of a REME FS Battalion 2009

REME Battalions as at 2009

Unit	Supporting	Location	Companies
Regular Army			
1 CS Bn REME	4 Mech Bde	Catterick	24 Fd, 4 & 12 Armd
2 CS Bn REME	7 Armd Bde	Fallingbostel	22 Fd, 7 & 11 Armd
3 CS Bn REME	20 Armd Bde	Paderborn	18 Fd, 5 & 20 Armd
4 CS Bn REME	12 Mech Bde	Bordon	15 Fd, 9 & 10 Armd
6 CS Bn REME	1 Mech Bde	Tidworth	13 Fd, 3 & 14 Armd
7 Air Asslt Bn REME	16 Air Asslt Bde	Wattisham	8 CS(AB), 71/72/73 CS
Integrated (mixed Regular Army and TA) FS Battalions			
101 FS Bn REME	102 Log Bde	Wrexham	50 OPR, 20 Fd, 126 & 127 Fd (V), 119 Rec (V)
104 FS Bn REME	101 Log Bde	Bordon	55 OPR, 146 & 147 Fd (V), 118 Rec (V)
TA			
102 Bn REME (V)	Regional Forces	Newton Aycliffe	186 & 153 Fd, 124 Rec
103 Bn REME (V)	Regional Forces	Crawley	201/207/210 Incr, 128 & 133 Fd, 150 Rec

Figure 2.7: Affiliations of REME Battalions as at 2009

CHAPTER 3

STRATEGIC DEFENCE AND SECURITY REVIEW 2010 AND ARMY 2020

When a Labour Government came to power in 1997, it carried out a Strategic Defence Review (SDR) that was completed in 1998. Its theoretical start point was to define what the UK might want its Armed Forces to do in the world after the Cold War, from which the size and structure of each of the Services could be deduced. In practice, a lot of preliminary work had already been done and the MoD more or less had a plan up its sleeve to meet the stated requirements, and which matched the finance likely to be available. The Labour Government effectively adopted these ideas. The SDR was completed with few surprises, and little controversy, at a time when military peacekeeping operations had been going well, and the economy seemed to be on a healthy track.

The next strategic study, the Strategic Defence and Security Review (SDSR), was presented to Parliament by the Prime Minister in October 2010. Its tone was very different. It lamented:

> 'Our Armed Forces – admired across the world – have been overstretched, deployed too often without appropriate planning, with the wrong equipment, in the wrong numbers and without a clear strategy. In the past, unfunded spending pledges created a fundamental mismatch between aspiration and resources'.

It made no bones about the need to save money in view of the dire state of public finances following the financial crash of 2008. The size of the Regular Army was to reduce to 82,000 and the Reserves were to be increased to 38,000 (this figure was subsequently reduced to 30,000). In outline, the plan was that all soldiers would be withdrawn from Germany and the predominantly UK-based Army would be restructured. The reorganised Army was to comprise Reaction Forces (around 90% Regular Army) and Adaptable Forces (with a larger Reserve Army component).

These were to be backed up by Force Troops, which would provide support for both the Reaction and Adaptable Forces. The outline organisation (including the second line REME element) is shown in Figure 3.1 (at the end of this Chapter).

This new structure, sometimes referred to as 'Army 2020', was to involve a lot of relocating and reorganising of units. The overall plan for achieving this, the Regular Army Basing Plan is outlined in Chapter 13 ('REME in the UK – Structure and Organisation'), and the plan for REME Reserve units is outlined in Chapter 16 ('REME and the Reserve Army'). Some of the major unit changes outlined for REME were to be:

- the formation of 5 Force Support (FS) Battalion REME – initially at Tidworth and Bielefeld until Cottesmore became ready (not before 2015)
- 2 Close Support (CS) Battalion REME – to change structure in Fallingbostel before its move to Leuchars (not before 2015)
- 3 Close Support (CS) Battalion REME – to re-role in Paderborn before its move to Tidworth (not before 2017).

THE PLANNED REME ORGANISATION AND ITS JUSTIFICATION

The numerous 'savings' and 'efficiency' measures that arose during the 1990s and the years thereafter often included an underlying idea that *cutting the tail whilst preserving the teeth* was an inherently good way to get more capability for less money. Such amateur strategic thinking fails to recognise that the capability of a force is actually reduced if it cannot be optimally deployed and sustained.

This was not the case with SDSR 2010. Although the Army was significantly reducing in size, it was recognised in the Annual Report to the Colonels Commandant REME 2012 that:

> '… the march of technology coupled with multiple platforms coming from UORs (Urgent Operational Requirement) into core meant that the Army would be equipped with a greater complexity and diversity of equipment than before. In this context the Army Command Group invested significantly in REME to deliver LADs, workshops, and battalions matched to the operational roles of the equipment they support'.

Put simply, the operational experience of recent years convinced equipment users that they needed proper REME support at first line, which needed to be backed by proper REME support at second line. REME tactical doctrine was still considered 'fit for purpose', as recognised in the Annual Report to the Colonels Commandant REME 2012:

> 'Battlefield Equipment Support Doctrine (BESD(A)) remains a highly regarded example of doctrine best practice, succinctly presenting as it does the overview of Equipment Support'.

The idea of the REME 'soldier-tradesman', that grew out of the experience of supporting mechanised forces in World War 2, has been revalidated in every major Army operation since then, and is now implicitly accepted.

What emerged was a sound organisational solution for REME. First line establishments would be reviewed but, in general, it was intended that reductions would be in line with reductions in supported units, and that first line units would be properly manned. The second line structure is outlined in Figure 3.1 (at the end of this Chapter), and the planned structure for the Reserves is given in Chapter 16 ('REME and the Reserve Army').

This organisation needed to be well equipped. It is encouraging that the principle seems to have been generally accepted that REME support vehicles need to be as well protected as the equipment they support. This is explained in Chapter 17 ('REME Equipment and Technology').

MOVE FROM ARBORFIELD AND BORDON TO LYNEHAM

Delivery of individual technical training had already become a Defence responsibility and, at the time of SDSR 2010, it was intended to move REME technical training to a Defence Academy at St Athan (South Wales) as part of a complex Private Finance Initiative (PFI) deal. This collapsed in 2010 and led to the setting up of the Defence Technical Training Change Programme (DTTCP). This had the long-term aim of developing a Defence Technical Training College (DTTC) at Lyneham eventually to provide nearly all technical training for the three Services. The first stage, Tranche 1, involved the closure of Arborfield and Bordon, and the migration of the Defence training facilities from there to Lyneham. This was fully funded and the move was underway in 2015. It was recognised that there were elements housed at Arborfield and Bordon, which were

'REME' rather than 'Defence'. Also, that these play an important part in the life of the Corps, the development of its ethos and special-to-REME training, as well as the well-being of current and former members of the Corps. The umbrella phrase for all this is 'Home of REME'. The argument that 'Home of REME' facilities should move to Lyneham, or be replicated there, was made and accepted. All this is explained in more detail in Chapter 23 ('Individual Training Organisations') and Chapter 28 ('The Plan for Lyneham').

Although the move was to involve leaving behind things dear to REME hearts (not least the magnificent Officers' Mess at West Court), it would seem on balance to be potentially a very good thing for REME. For the first time, all REME technical training would be collocated at a single site along with the 'Home of REME', plus a REME training battalion to support military and adventurous training, personnel administration and 'duty of care'. The REME Arms School and Regimental Headquarters (RHQ) REME will also be based in the complex. The other 'Home of REME' elements include a museum, Corps Officers' and Sergeants' Messes, a church, and provision for the Band. More information is provided in Chapter 28 ('The Plan for Lyneham').

Whilst the plans for Tranche 1 were well in hand at the time of writing, it was not clear when (or if) further tranches would happen. MoD policy appeared to be that each case will be looked at on its merits (with the availability of funding a key pre-requisite).

MANAGEMENT OF THE CORPS OF REME

One of the outcomes of SDSR 2010, was the decision to cut the posts of eight individual Arms and Services Directors, and merge and re-model some of their organisations in the form of four Capability Directorates (CD):
- Combat Capability (infantry and armour)
- Combat Support Capability (Royal Artillery and Royal Engineers)
- Information Capability (Royal Signals and Intelligence Corps)
- Combat Service Support Capability (REME and RLC).

This meant that the post of DEME(A) was cut, and REME lost its one-star 'Head of the Corps'. The incumbent, Brigadier Martin Boswell (late REME), ceased to be DEME(A) in 2012 and moved on to the recently re-named Army HQ (formerly HQ Land Forces) at Andover to take up a post as the Capability Director for Combat Service Support (CSS) (a rotational post with responsibilities embracing both REME and RLC) (see also Chapter 21 ('HQ DEME(A) and RHQ REME')).

The Regimental Colonel was retitled 'Colonel REME' and, whilst his RHQ continued to have largely the same functions, he had certain additional ones as he had become, de facto, the senior REME officer dedicated to the management of the Corps of REME.

The demise of DEME(A) involved the loss of part of the mechanism used to control REME manning. This was replaced by creating a 'REME Manning Brick' within Army HQ at Andover. It comprised a team of four, headed by a Staff Officer Grade 1 (SO1, Lieutenant Colonel), and its function was explained in The Craftsman magazine (August 2013):

> 'Our role is to sustain the REME manning plan by supporting and synchronising across the 'Four Balls'. We take the unit structures demanded (liability) by the Capability Directorates; particularly CD Combat Service Support in our case; generate the manning supply to meet the demand through the Directorate of Manning (Army) (DM(A)); provide the Army Personnel Centre (APC) promotion quotas and manning priorities to ensure people are assigned where they are needed; and oversee wider trade and manning issues in conjunction with the Colonel REME. In short, we work with CD CSS, DM(A), APC and the Colonel REME (the 'Four Balls') to ensure that REME has the right amount of people, with the right competence, provided to the right unit at the right time'.

For those who find such things easier to absorb in a picture format, this model is shown at Figure 3.2 (at the end of this Chapter).

In order to get all these changes into context it is perhaps worth remembering that, at the start of the period covered by Volume 3 of Craftsmen of the Army, the Equipment Support (ES) function was primarily an Army responsibility and came under its Quartermaster General (QMG). Whilst QMG himself was not an equipment professional, he had a two-star 'subject matter expert' in the form of DGES(A) who was an expert. DGES(A) headed an integrated functional ES organisation, which embodied a wealth of technical expertise and practical experience of ES at every level. The nature of his organisation meant that DGES(A) was well placed to identify tricky ES problems (and unworkable notions masquerading as their solutions) and offer timely advice on them.

In contrast, in 2012, top-level responsibility for managing ES rested within a large Defence Equipment and Support (DE&S) organisation headed by a civilian, largely manned by civilians, and with no tied senior REME posts in it. From an Army HQ perspective, if the CD CSS did not happen to be a REME officer, the most senior person offering ES advice would be a Colonel briefing through a one-star who would be unlikely to be an equipment expert himself. It is not hard for those who have wrestled with urgent or intractable ES problems at critical times to imagine circumstances in which this might prove not to be a good thing.

Against this background, REME gained a new appointment in the form of a Master General REME (MGREME), which was approved by The Queen with effect from 1 April 2012. This put a senior late-REME officer in a position where he would be able to feed in 'words of wisdom' at an appropriate level if and when they were required. Lieutenant General Andrew Figgures was appointed the first incumbent in 2012.

LOOKING AHEAD

This book covers two decades of almost continuous change for REME. At various points along the way, it seemed that the pattern for the future was settled. At each of these points, something new arose that resulted in further change. Inevitably, some of the change has been wholly beneficial; some had been partly beneficial but came with a significant downside; and, with hindsight, some has not proved a good idea.

The book ends with further change on the way, the perceived end state of which will be an Army primarily based in the UK with no major operational commitments on its books. The new concept is therefore that the Army is to be 'contingency' based.

This Chapter was written in 2015 shortly after a general election, which resulted in an overall Conservative majority that few had anticipated. This followed a campaign during which the Prime Minister made it clear that he was not keen for Defence to become a major election issue. Public attitudes to Defence had clearly changed over the years. The Cold War was a distant memory, and pride in our Armed Forces and confidence in their political and military leadership (that had been high in the 1990s) had been tempered by events in Iraq and Afghanistan. This happened against the background of serious public sector deficit and ongoing efforts to find politically acceptable budget cuts. There was no longer quite the same consensus (within or between political parties) that the UK should fund a highly capable professional Army, which would allow it to 'punch above its weight' and intervene in the international arena. Therefore, there seemed a real prospect that Defence would have to absorb further funding cuts and make further changes in the years ahead, despite an international environment that seemed increasingly dangerous and unstable.

One factor that has been constant throughout the period covered by this book has been the adaptability, commitment and professional skill of the Corps of REME. This has enabled it to ensure that the Army has always had *'fit equipment in the hands of troops'* when it was really needed. There is good reason to hope this will continue to be the story as the Army faces the new challenges in the future.

REACTION FORCES	
Two-star Divisional HQ (3 (UK) Div – Bulford)	
Formation	Second Line REME Element
1 Armd Inf Bde (Tidworth)	6 Armd CS Bn REME (Tidworth)
12 Armd Inf Bde (Bulford)	4 Armd CS Bn REME (Bulford)
20 Armd Inf Bde (Tidworth)	3 Armd CS Bn REME (Tidworth)
16 Air Assault Bde	7 Air Assault Bn REME (Wattisham)
Cdo Bde – not part of the Army	REME elements in Cdo Bde
101 Logistic Support Bde	5 Force Support Bn REME (Cottesmore)

ADAPTABLE FORCES	
Two-star Divisional HQ (and capability to form a two-star Support Command HQ)	
Formation	Second Line REME Support
7 x Inf Bdes 102 Logistic Support Bde 3 x Light Cavalry Regts Inf Bns on standing tasks (Cyprus, Brunei, Falkands etc)	1 CS Bn REME (Catterick) 2 CS Bn REME (plus 2 x FS Coys (V)) (Leuchars)

FORCE TROOPS (to support Reaction and Adaptable Forces)	
Formation	Second Line REME Support
Artillery Bde Engineer Bde 2 x Signal Bdes Intelligence and Surveillance Bde Logistic Support Bde Medical Bde Security Assistance Group MP Bde (Joint) Two-star Joint Helicopter Command	6 x REME Bns (V) – See Chapter 16 ('REME and the Reserve Army')

Figure 3.1: SDSR 2010 plan for Army reorganisation

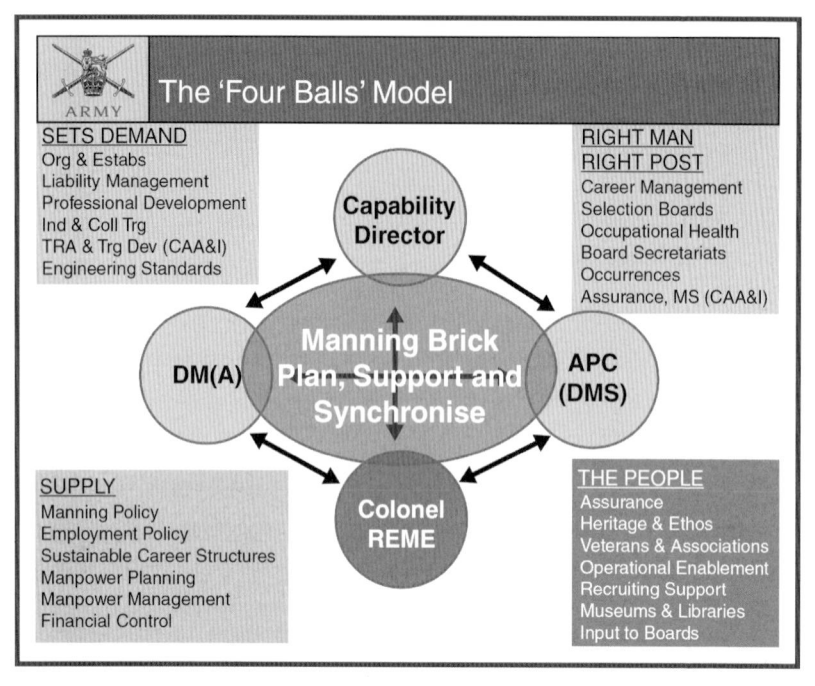

Figure 3.2: 'Four Balls' Model

CHAPTER 4

COLLECTIVE TRAINING FOR OPERATIONS

The British Army is now relatively small, and an internet search suggests that in terms of size it comes in at about number thirty-five (approximately the same size as the Democratic Republic of the Congo). During the past couple of decades, however, it has contributed more to international military operations than any other European country and it remains a significant global military player.

Two factors make it much more effective than many larger armies. The first is its ability to project power, which depends in turn on having effective and deployable systems for supporting equipment. The second is its ability to engage in the full spectrum of military operations, including high-intensity (armoured) operations at formation level. Few armies have this range of capability, which depends critically on being able to field appropriately trained forces quickly enough.

Training may be broadly divided into individual training and collective training. In the case of REME, individual training embraces military training, technical training (both general engineering training and special-to-equipment training) as well as training in leadership and management. Much individual training is carried out at training establishments, but this is complemented by 'on-the-job' training and upgrader courses for more junior staff, which are run at unit level. Individual training (and the organisations that deliver it) are covered in Chapter 22 ('REME People') and Chapter 23 ('Individual Training Organisations').

Collective training is the term used to cover all the further training needed to get sub-units, units and formations trained to the state where they are ready to carry out the types of operation that they may expect to be engaged in. As a prelude to reviewing REME's involvement in operations, it is worth looking at collective training and its relationship to readiness.

Collective training must be carefully organised, and has to be progressive and cyclical. It must be cyclical not only because of skill fade, but also because of the turnover of personnel. Typically, officers in key command

and staff posts move on every two or three years. This high turnover of staff being the price paid for keeping leaders young and for providing them with a breadth of experience. Teams therefore continuously change as individuals leave, arrive, get promoted or moved sideways to other jobs.

In the days of the Cold War, the British Army was faced with the threat of a 'short warning scenario' attack on Germany by the Warsaw Pact forces. The bulk of the Army with its heavy equipment was based in Germany in the form of the British Army of the Rhine (BAOR) where it needed to be at a state of continuous high readiness, as did forces earmarked to reinforce it (much of the rest of the Army).

In practice, this Cold War readiness requirement translated into the requirement for a busy annual training cycle. Around the beginning of any year many key jobs would be handed over, which was partly triggered by the arrival of the latest graduates from Staff College. The emphasis in the early part of the year was on individual training, done both on short courses organised at unit level, and by getting as many people away as possible on external courses. It would later shift to low-level sub-unit training, with platoon commanders having the opportunity to exercise their teams, and to enjoy the benefit of the wisdom and guidance of their company commanders. This would be followed by company-level training (with company commanders benefiting from the wisdom of their COs), and on to unit-level training. This training was carried out largely on military training areas – both small local ones and the major NATO training areas in Germany, such as the Bergen-Hohne ranges and the Sennelager complex. This training would involve both 'dry' exercises and live firing.

By the autumn, formations would be ready to emerge from barracks on manoeuvres around the German countryside at divisional or even Corps level on the great 'autumn exercises' (fondly remembered by those who took part in them). These Field Training Exercises (FTX) were not always as fondly remembered by the German farmers whose fields had been torn up by tanks, or by German motorists stuck behind British Army convoys. By the end of the process, the different Arms and Services understood how to work together, numerous practical lessons had been learned (or re-learned) at every level, teams had gelled, and units and formations were ready for war. It was then time to look ahead to Christmas, and to start the process again the following year.

Collective training for non-BAOR units took place in the UK and elsewhere – sometimes in interesting places such as Norway, Cyprus or

Belize. There was also a major Army training facility on the Canadian prairie, in the form of the British Army Training Unit Suffield (BATUS). This was established in 1972, and was still going strong at the time of writing. This provided the opportunity for all Arms to carry out progressive 'fire and manoeuvre' exercises up to battlegroup level. Around six battlegroups (normally from Germany) would be programmed into the training season. These exercises provided excellent training for the first line REME personnel integral with the battlegroups, as well as those supporting exercise 'enemy forces'. Additional REME backup was provided during the training season, and also 'off season' when the Winter Repair Programme was run to refurbish equipment prior to the next training season.

Once the Cold War ended, two issues became clear. The first was that FTX training would never again be allowed in Germany on the scale that had happened in the past, and that it was necessary to look for different solutions to the problem of collective training in manoeuvre at brigade level and above. The second was that readiness costs money, and it was not long before financiers became aware that training (individual and collective) represented a substantial component of the cost of Defence. In an era in which a 'peace dividend' was being sought, a balance had to be struck by delivering enough training of the right sort, whilst avoiding unnecessary expenditure on training facilities and mimising overall equipment operating costs.

The problem of providing formation-level training for forces in Germany was solved by an agreement with the Polish Government that allowed British forces to use the Drawsko Pomorskie Training Area (DPTA) in western Poland. The first use of the training area was in 1995, with the overall name for the exercise being ULAN EAGLE. This was followed by further ULAN EAGLE exercises at brigade level for the next 10 years. The area allowed the deployment of a complete brigade-sized formation. The training area provided a break from Germany and was described by one British user in this way:

> 'The training area of Drawsko Pomorskie is a mixture of rolling hills, tended woodland and large expanses of open areas. The area is strewn with old Soviet training systems, burnt out hulks of tanks and mobile guns some dating back to the Second World War which adds a realism effect that is found in only a few areas'.

REME vehicle on Exercise ULAN EAGLE 2000 in Poland

This training provided a useful opportunity not only to deploy a complete brigade (the move to Poland itself providing some useful training) but to deploy a slice of second and third line Divisional Combat Service Support (CSS) assets. An article in The Craftsman magazine (January 2001) describing the involvement of 2 Battalion REME in Exercise ULAN EAGLE 2000 explains:

'1 (UK) Division's exercise in DPTA during September and October consisted of three phases designed to practise war-fighting operations: namely Ex ULAN BARBERA involving the Divisional Offensive Support Group, Ex PRAIRIE EAGLE involving 20 Armoured Brigade, and Ex ULAN LIFELINE involving 2nd and 3rd line Div CSS assets. 2 Bn REME was directed to provide equipment support to exercising units, but more importantly, it was to train in individual and low-level special-to-arm skills in order to achieve desired levels of readiness. This exercise was one of the few opportunities to exercise the 'repair loop' between the General and Close Support Companies and to examine the planning and operational functions of Battalion HQ. Sub-units deployed in urban and field environments and maintained a loop between a former Russian barracks, Stargard, and the DPTA, a distance of around 60km'.

Meanwhile, the question of how much collective training needed to be done had been addressed by planning and finance staff. By the mid-1990s, a stable pattern of operational commitments seemed to have emerged, with the UK having a force of around brigade size committed to peacekeeping operations at any one time. This allowed an elegant solution to the training/readiness problem to emerge, based on a 3-year Formation Readiness Cycle (FRC) through which units and formations would rotate. The FRC was facilitated by the Army moving to a structure based on two deployable divisions, each with three general purpose brigades. The first year of the FRC was the 'high readiness year' – units started at high readiness and during this year they could expect to deploy with their formation on a 6-month operational tour. The second year was the 'other tasks year' – during which they needed only to do individual training, which freed them up for 'other tasks'. The third year was the 'training year' – during which they underwent progressive collective training up to formation level, which got them up to 'high readiness' ready to start the cycle again. The FRC is illustrated diagrammatically at Figure 4.1 (at the end of this Chapter).

This concept, which had been maturing within the MoD for some time, was elaborated and formally embraced in the Strategic Defence Review of 1998 and presented to Parliament in July 1998. Provided the assumptions on which it rested were valid, it would provide sufficient fully trained forces to go on operations and would give soldiers a slightly less disrupted lifestyle. It also met the requirement to justify to HM Treasury that soldiers were receiving enough training, but no more than enough.

The FRC concept went with a whole new calculus of readiness and training, and a new language to go with it. NATO readiness requirements were translated into UK definitions of readiness; for example, R1 allowed 2 days to deploy, R6 allowed 60 days to deploy, R8 allowed 180 days to deploy. Along with these went specified levels of manning, equipment availability and the amount of collective training required (including special-to-arm training) associated with each level of readiness [as set out in LAND G3/G8 335/13 dated 21 July 1997]. These were linked to the FRC and were meant to be auditable back to the Military Tasks (MT), which the Government had allocated the MoD.

One of the capabilities required in SDR 98 was for a Joint Rapid Reaction Force (JRRF). This could be deployed as a national force, or as part of a multinational force. It would be controlled by the Permanent Joint Headquarters (PJHQ) – established at Northwood in 1996. The land component provided for a spearhead element (special forces and/or battalion-size infantry group at light scales), a Joint Landing Force (3 Commando Brigade or 16 Air Assault Brigade) followed by a second echelon, which would include much more heavily armed forces from 1 (UK) Armoured Division and/or 3 (UK) Division.

This concept was tested on a major deployment to Oman from September to November 2001 called Exercise SAIF SAREEA 2. It was the largest single deployment of UK forces since the first Gulf War with over 22,500 personnel, 6,500 vehicles, 21 naval vessels, 49 fixed wing aircraft and 44 helicopters being deployed. 1 Battalion REME deployed in support of 4 Armoured Brigade Group (the major contributor to the Land Component), as part of training the Group to Collective Performance Level 5 in anticipation of it becoming the High Readiness Brigade.

Its CO (Lieutenant Colonel Martin Boswell REME – later to be DEME(A)) provided a useful post exercise report. He rated it a great training experience and concluded that the REME battalion structure had worked – but had been extremely stretched. Lack of spares was identified as a major problem, and his remarks provided a useful injection of reality into ideas about 'just-in-time' spares and logistics, which had rather been in vogue. He commented:

> 'The impression was that we were provided with 'not enough, just too late' as a consequence of financial capping'.

He pointed out that the maintenance of tempo in warfighting operations depended on sound logistic planning and the availability of adequate ES resources. He explained the need for an external link back to HQ LAND ES, equipment branches and others in the ES system as well as contractors. The National Audit Office (NAO) also ran a rule over the exercise, and its report [Report by The Comptroller and Auditor General, HC 1097 Session 2001–2002, 1 August 2002] is consistent with Lieutenant Colonel Boswell's, although he did not mention the need further to develop Resource Accounting and Budgeting (RAB), which they clearly saw as important! Having got its teeth into readiness issues, the NAO was unlikely to let the subject go and, in 2005, there is a report from them in which they see readiness as being linked with Public Service Agreements [NAO Report HC72 Session 2005/6 dated 15 June 2005].

Meanwhile, during the early stages of Exercise SAIF SAREEA those involved were shocked to learn of the '9/11' attacks, and there was

Warrior vehicle on Exercise SAIF SAREEA in Oman 2001

considerable concern by troops about the safety of their families, and vice versa.

The '9/11' attacks triggered a chain of events that was to change the nature of UK military commitments radically over the next decade. Within months, the Army was to start extricating itself from its commitments in the Balkans, and to prepare for the invasion of Iraq in 2003. The invasion itself represented one of the kinds of operation the Army had been preparing for (and for which Exercise SAIF SAREEA had provided useful preparation), and its execution was, in general, very successful. It was hoped, and expected, that the invasion would transition into the sort of peacekeeping operation that the Army had proved so adept at in the Balkans and elsewhere. Instead, it soon found itself involved in a bitter counterinsurgency operation of a type that it had not been involved in for a very long time, and for which it was not fully prepared or equipped.

The involvement in Iraq lasted from 2003 to 2009 in the course of which some very fierce combat took place, as outlined in Chapter 8 ('The Invasion of Iraq (Operation TELIC 1)') and Chapter 9 ('Iraq – Aftermath of the Invasion (Operations TELIC 2–13)'). In 2006, the UK's previously small commitment to Afghanistan was increased when 16 Air Assault Brigade was deployed to Helmand Province, on what was hoped to be a fairly benign peacekeeping operation. It soon proved to be anything but that, and required a significant presence until 2014. With two simultaneous major operational commitments, the overriding priority became to tailor training to the needs of the operational theatres.

As the pattern of operations changed, and as new equipment came into use, training had to change as well. It was realised that Combat Service Support (CSS) units needed specialised training advice, so a CSS Training and Advisory Team (CSSTAT), which always included a REME representative, was set up to support training in both Germany and UK. As operations in Afghanistan continued, training was changed to a new progression, which involved: Hybrid Foundation Training (HFT), Mission Specific Training (MST) (which would include an element of specific-to-REME training), and a Confirmatory Field Exercise (CFX) FTX. An in-theatre training centre was set up in Afghanistan. The Reception Staging and Onward Integration package (RSOI), which was designed to ensure that individuals were up to date in all the skills they required for their particular roles, is described later in the chapters on Afghanistan. The phrase 'Contemporary Operational Environment' (COE) gained currency as a way of referring to operations in Afghanistan, or those like them.

The cost of operating equipment for training, combined with the limitations of training areas and environmental issues related to their use, led the Army to make a substantial investment in synthetic training. This led to the development of the Combined Arms Tactical Trainer (CATT), a synthetic training facility (the largest virtual training system of its type in the world). It was developed, staffed and run jointly by the MoD, Lockheed Martin and BAE Systems.

CATT was intended to provide HFT and MST at two sites – one in UK (Warminster) and one in Germany (Sennelager). Originally designed as a high-intensity battlefield manoeuvre warfare trainer, it was expanded to accommodate the changing nature of operational requirements. This facility:

- could link 140 manned simulators and up to 450 participants – so all elements of the battlegroup could practise individual and collective skills
- could support one full battlegroup, four sub-units, or one brigade headquarters

- allowed training crews to operate simulated vehicles and aircraft, and to interact with computer-generated civilians as well as friendly/enemy forces
- had 70 vehicle-specific simulators, including Challenger tanks, Warrior infantry vehicles, Scimitar reconnaissance vehicles, and Warrior observation posts – these provided high physical and functional fidelity for training crews
- hosted an additional 70 generic vehicle simulators, desktop devices that replicated surface and air vehicles (from engineer and air defence systems to attack helicopters and fast jet air support)
- drew from highly detailed geographic databases for maximum realism
- offered full after-action review, even of individual incidents, so that participants could get the full learning experience.

Additionally, a Combined Arms Staff Trainer (CAST) was also located within the Land Warfare Centre at Warminster. In total, three CAST sites were set up at Warminster, Catterick and Sennelager. These facilities provided collective training for British Army and NATO units at levels from battlegroup up to corps level. Raytheon personnel operated the facility, providing engineering support and system advice to the military. (**See Plate 1**)

The winding down of operations in Afghanistan, and the Strategic Defence and Security Review of 2010, which envisaged a reduction in the size of the Army and a withdrawal of forces from Germany, meant that the Army needed to look at its requirement for collective training in the future. The investment in synthetic training looked a wise one, given the pressure on training real estate in the UK, especially once all forces have returned from Germany. With training no longer driven by the demands of Afghanistan, it became possible to look at collective training in a more measured way, and the idea of the 3-year readiness cycle came back into its own.

Battlegroup level training seems set to continue at BATUS, where the freedom to engage in fire and movement provides an ideal environment for the collective training of armoured forces. During operations in Afghanistan, increased use was made of training facilities in Kenya, which were well suited to collective training at up to battlegroup level for less heavily armoured forces. Training in Kenya therefore nicely complemented training at BATUS on which there is more information in Chapter 14 ('REME Overseas').

Support for training in Kenya – Exercise ASKARI THUNDER 2011

Collective training is expected to continue to be delivered in training areas in UK, including the use of synthetic trainers, complemented by routine overseas training at up to battlegroup level in BATUS and Kenya. Doubtless there will be further major overseas deployment exercises in the future but, at the time of writing, plans are not firm.

COLLECTIVE TRAINING FOR OPERATIONS

3-Year Formation Readiness Cycle for a Brigade	
Year	Activity
1 – High Readiness	Formation starts fully trained. Many units would expect to go on a 6-month peacekeeping tour, which with pre-tour training and post-tour leave would take up most of a year.
2 – Other Tasks	Individual training, but limited collective training and no formation-level training. Units are free to do 'other tasks'.
3 – Training	Full progression of collective training up to brigade level, allowing the brigade to start the next High Readiness Year fully trained.

Figure 4.1: Formation Readiness Cycle

CHAPTER 5

OPERATIONS GENERAL

Following the overwhelming success of the Coalition forces in the Gulf War of 1991, the demise of the Warsaw Pact, and the relatively subdued state of affairs in Northern Ireland, there were some, in around 1992, who were concerned whether the Army would have enough operational commitments to keep it busy over the next couple of decades. They need not have worried.

The Army was soon engaged in peacekeeping in the Balkans, followed by peace enforcement, and culminating in the invasion of Kosovo. Not too long after this, the '9/11' attacks on the USA set off a chain of events that resulted in the British Army being involved in operations in Iraq from 2003 to 2009, and in Afghanistan until the main withdrawal from there in 2014. These were all major commitments and are covered in some detail in the relevant chapters that follow.

In addition, during this period the Army carried out a wide range of activities, which it classified as 'operations'. Some were enduring, some were short 'one-offs', some were 'operations within operations', which could be generic (for example, Operation MUBAREZ was the name given to Combat Logistic Patrols within Afghanistan) or 'one-offs'. Some were 'kinetic' and others involved providing support of a nature that did not require weapons to be drawn. REME personnel were involved in almost all of these. In some cases, they were acting in a non-technical role. For example, REME supplied a good proportion of the security personnel that the Army had to provide at short notice for the 2012 London Olympics, to cover for the failure of the security contractors to provide the staff required.

In most cases when REME personnel were involved in the operations, however, their primary role was usually to ensure that vehicles, weapons and other equipment worked properly when they were needed. The problem from the narrator's point of view is that they consistently did this successfully without great fuss, which makes for less exciting tales than if they had failed to do so. It is not, therefore, intended to list every operation with REME involvement in this chapter, but to pick out enough to give an idea of the range and extent of the 'secondary' operations REME was involved in during this period, and then later look at those 'primary' operations, which deserve their own chapter.

OPERATION BANNER NORTHERN IRELAND 1969–2007

The Army deployed in 1969 into a volatile situation in Northern Ireland. This was followed by a long and bloody campaign of terrorism and public disorder, which resulted in the death of 736 members, and former members, of the Armed Forces, and a peak deployment of around 25,700 soldiers in 1972 (reported by Colonel Peter Brown (late REME) in his article in The Craftsman magazine (August 2007)). The security forces endured and created the conditions that allowed a political solution to be worked out. The so-called 'Good Friday Agreement' of April 1998 resulted in the formal decommissioning of IRA weapons, and the formation of the Northern Ireland Assembly in 1999. Low-level violence by dissenting factions, and those with a criminal agenda, continued but declined to the point where it could be controlled by the police without military assistance.

'Normalisation' was announced in August 2005, and roulement tours, which had always been a drain on units, were reduced in 2006 and stopped in 2007, when infantry battalions were taken off operations and withdrawn. This was a welcome development for the Army, as it was very stretched by the need to support operations in both Iraq and Afghanistan at this time. The Royal Irish Home Service Battalions were disbanded, with some of their former members joining the Territorial Army. The REME commitment to Northern Ireland had included the Northern Ireland Roulement Workshop, which was set up in 1973 and, in due course, was to be transformed into 46 Northern Ireland Workshop (commanded by a Lieutenant Colonel). In 1999, this reduced to a sub-unit (commanded by a Major) and was incorporated as 46 Workshop Company within a newly-formed Northern Ireland Combat Service Support Regiment. This Regiment was disbanded on 20 July 2007. On 30 August 2007, HQ Northern Ireland was replaced by, or one might say transformed into, 38 Irish Brigade. This gave it essentially the same role as other regional brigades at the time, but with some additional autonomy and reinforcement because of its special circumstances. Thus ended, with a welcome whimper rather than a bang, an operation on which many thousands of REME soldiers had served. It would be wrong to imagine that they had all been completely (or even partially) involved in REME's normal repair and recovery functions. They had taken on many additional tasks – frequently 'downing spanners' to man sangars or checkpoints, some had secondary (or even primary) roles as members (or leaders) of vehicle crews or patrol 'bricks', and some worked in operations rooms or intelligence cells.

OPERATION GABRIEL RWANDA 1994

Civil war and genocide were triggered in Rwanda in 1994 by an incident that led to 100 days of fighting and murder involving Hutu and Tutsi tribespeople. It led to the death of around one million Hutu people. The end of the fighting was followed by a humanitarian crisis, which was exacerbated by cholera and dysentery epidemics. UNAMIR (United Nations Assistance Mission in Rwanda), which was in due course to grow to around 5,000 strong comprising British, French, Canadian, Ethiopian and other African Contingents, was initially unable to cope. A British Contingent had therefore been dispatched to provide humanitarian and logistic support. A major element of this was 5 Airborne Logistic Regiment, which normally provided logistic support to 5 Airborne Brigade and included 10 Airborne Workshop REME, then commanded by Major Ian Duncan REME.

Operation GABRIEL Rwanda 1994

Around 600 all ranks from this unit deployed from Aldershot after five days of preparation. Great work was done during the following four months before the British Contingent withdrew. 23 Parachute Field Ambulance RAMC dealt directly with around 125,000 people needing treatment, 9 Field Squadron RE contributed to the repair of roads and facilities, and essential transport support was provided. The CO of 5 Airborne Logistic Regiment (Lieutenant Colonel Mike Wharmby RLC) described the REME role thus:

> 'By the time the British Airborne contingent arrived, the war and the roads had already taken a toll of UN's equipment, and the highest priority for 10 Airborne Workshop REME was to recover the UN's diverse fleet of armoured, utility and transport vehicles and equipment which had been abandoned the length and breadth of Rwanda. As with everything else, repair parts were cannibalised or improvised and a remarkable range of hitherto unfamiliar equipment was soon back in UN hands, enabling the UNAMIR force commander to regain control of his mission'.

A REME subaltern (Lieutenant Whittle) wrote an interesting personal account of this deployment in The Craftsman magazine (February 1995), which explained in rather more technical language that the role of 10 Airborne Workshop REME was to provide both first and second line repair and recovery support for British elements, and second line repair and recovery support for the UN force as a whole.

OPERATION SIBELLIAN UK 2000

In 2000, there was the threat of a major strike by fuel tanker drivers. In October 2000, the Army deployed a number of units (complete with their first line REME complement) to provide tanker drivers for the supply of fuel to the emergency services during the tanker drivers' dispute.

OPERATION PALLISER AND OPERATION SILKMAN SIERRA LEONE 2000–2001

In 2000, Sierra Leone was racked by civil war. One of the parties, the Revolutionary United Front (RUF), seemed intent on taking the capital Freetown. UK initially sent an 'operational reconnaissance and liaison team' (Operation PALLISER) with a view to protecting besieged ceasefire observers. The commitment grew, and included Operation SILKMAN, as British troops became active in encouraging the RUF to disarm. The capture of British soldiers by the 'West Side Gang' led to a spectacular special forces rescue supported by a company of the Parachute Regiment. In due course, the situation stabilised and for a while UK provided a military presence to assist the Sierra Leone Government.

REME elements were embedded in all the UK forces involved, but got little mention, essentially because they achieved what they were expected to achieve. The intervention in Sierra Leone was seen as very successful from a UK perspective but, with higher priority demands on resources after '9/11', the presence in Sierra Leone was withdrawn other than as a training mission.

Sierra Leone Vehicle Park – a familiar sight in the early days

OPERATION PENINSULAR UK 2001

An outbreak of foot-and-mouth disease in UK in 2001 caused a crisis in British agriculture and tourism. This epizootic saw 2,000 cases of the disease in farms across most of the British countryside. Over 10 million sheep and cattle were killed in an eventually successful attempt to halt the disease. Attempts by the Ministry of Agriculture, Fisheries and Food, which was shortly thereafter renamed the Department for Environment, Food and Rural Affairs, to dispose of the carcasses floundered until it was decided to call in the Army, which rapidly sorted things out.

Inevitably, REME played its part, and the following is extracted from an account in The Craftsman magazine (August 2001) by REME soldiers supporting 101 Regiment RA (V):

> 'Sgt Dave Ellis and WO2 Kev McLoughlin received the first case for the regiment, a pig farm where the animals had already been slaughtered for four weeks. As you can imagine this was not a pleasant experience, but with the usual REME 'let's get the job done, and do it well' spirit, the task was completed in quick time and in a very professional manner. Meanwhile the rest of the Workshop was busy dealing with numerous and at times extremely stressful cases, working a minimum of 12 hours a day, and often up to 18 or 20 hours … The only plus side from this was the fried breakfast 'all you can eat' policy provided by the numerous hotels that the Workshop personnel stayed at during the operation'.

OPERATION FRESCO UK 2003–2004

Operation FRESCO was to provide support in UK during the period of the firemen's strike. All three Services were involved, and in all some 18,600 Services' personnel were deployed. As the Services did not have anything like the required number of modern fire engines, the Army had to resort

Operation FRESCO 1 Royal Welch Fusiliers LAD with 'Green Goddesses'

to using 'Green Goddess' fire engines, which had been stored in depots. In all, 827 of these machines were deployed by the Army. Much of the job of inspecting these equipments, preparing them for operation and maintaining them thereafter fell to REME. Although the fire engines were antiquated, REME was able to keep them operational and they proved capable of doing what was required, with REME battalions taking responsibility for areas of the country. This operation represented a major nuisance for REME, as it coincided with a period of intense activity related to the invasion of Iraq.

OPERATION ABELLIAN DARFUR 2005

REME personnel are often required to deploy on operations as individuals, or in small teams, because of the technical skills and understanding they are able to offer. In 2005, there was a humanitarian crisis in the Darfur regions of Sudan. Major Peter Brierley REME explained in his article in The Craftsman magazine (February 2006) that the region, around the size of France, was over populated and desperately poor. It had been marginalised by the north-south conflict in Sudan. Warfare between settlers and nomads, as well as conflict between the Government of Sudan and its sponsored militia (the Janjaweed), the Sudanese Liberation Army and the Justice and Equality Movement had resulted in some 1.6 million people being displaced and 300,000 killed.

The African Union (representing 52 African nations) set up the African Mission in Sudan (AMIS), which provided troops or other assistance.

Operation ABELLIAN newly-delivered vehicles in the vehicle park

Various other nations provided assistance, including those in the European Union. The UK contribution at this stage being about £20m, largely spent on providing vehicles. It was essential to have someone who understood vehicles (and how to support them) to ensure this effort bore fruit. Major Brierley was therefore selected for the job of Staff Officer Grade 2 (SO2) (Maintenance) on a multinational logistic support staff. He had a fascinating and productive time before handing over to his replacement, Major Gary Holden REME.

OPERATION ELLAMY LIBYA 2011

Operation ELLAMY was the name for the UK participation in the 2011 military intervention in Libya. The operation was part of an international coalition aimed at enforcing a Libyan no-fly zone in accordance with the UN Security Council Resolution 1973. The operation mostly involved attacks by cruise missiles or fixed wing aircraft, but four British Army Apache attack helicopters were deployed on HMS Ocean, an amphibious assault ship. This provided the challenge of 'marinisation' of the aircraft, which was successfully overcome with REME support. These helicopters were used to powerful effect in the late stages of the operation. REME soldiers provided support from HMS Ocean and were able to integrate effectively with RN and RAF technical staff to keep the aircraft operationally available.

Operation ELLAMY Apache helicopters with HMS Ocean near Libya 2011

OPERATION TOSCA 17 CYPRUS 2012

Operation TOSCA was the name for the UK contribution to the United Nations Forces in Cyprus (UNFICYP). 101 Battalion Group REME took over the task of the Sector 2 Roulement Regiment for a 6-month tour starting 1 October 2012, as described in an article in The Craftsman magazine (February 2013). This was the first time a REME battalion led the UK contribution since the formation of UNFICYP in 1964. The task of the Battalion Group was to monitor the Buffer Zone (BZ) between the Republic of Cyprus and the Turkish Republic of Northern Cyprus. The strong contingent of 263 personnel was based around 101 Force Support (FS) Battalion REME (a hybrid unit), but included contributions from 23 units in all (eight of them Territorial Army). The role of the force was:

> '… in the best interests of preserving international peace and security, to use best efforts to prevent a recurrence of fighting and, as necessary to contribute to the maintenance and restoration of law and order'.

In practical terms, this meant setting up a Battalion Group HQ in the Ledra Palace Hotel, largely unchanged since the 1974 war, putting lots of patrols on the ground to promote harmonious relations, and backing this up with a Force Reserve capable of dealing with rioting or other contingencies if things started to get out of hand. This was based on the UN Protected Area around the old Nicosia Airport. Naturally, it required a programme of training and preparation to put all this in place.

The first stage of Mission Specific Training was carried out at the Sennelager Training Centre, with the Regular Army and Reserve elements of 101 FS Battalion exercising together along with elements joining from other units. This led to a Mission Rehearsal Exercise, and a Mission Specific Assessment carried out at Nesscliffe Training Centre (Shropshire). Given the combination of the command and leadership skills within a REME battalion, and the fact that REME personnel tend to make good soldiers as well as tradesmen, it is no surprise that the training was completed successfully, and that the deployment and 6-month tour that followed was a complete success.

The tour gave an opportunity for REME soldiers to do something very different from their normal work, and to demonstrate their versatility. Craftsman Lihou (50 OPR Company) found the tour to be a good challenge, as he described in an article in The Craftsman magazine (April 2013):

'My role within the Section is more daunting than most. As a patrol commander it's my job to plan patrol routes through the BZ ensuring that as much ground as possible gets covered. I am also responsible for dealing with any and all violations I come across in the BZ, relaying as much information as possible to the S2 Joint Ops Cell (JOC) allowing them to get a picture of what we are dealing with and also advise what further action should be taken. I have dealt with a number of incidents within the BZ, many of which were within the first few weeks of the tour. I felt that we were thrown into the deep end but immediately rose to the challenge, getting into our stride in the first few days'.

Operation TOSCA 17 REME soldiers working with the
UN Police and civilian agencies

CHAPTER 6

OPERATIONS IN THE BALKANS 1 – BOSNIA

In the aftermath of the Cold War and first Gulf War, with the USA being widely seen as an invincible superpower, many in REME were wondering what challenges the new world order might bring. The first new major operational commitment was not long in materialising, and by late-1992 UK forces had deployed into the Balkans.

HISTORICAL BACKGROUND AND POLITICAL OVERVIEW

The Balkans has been an unstable part of the world for centuries, as many ethnic, religious and political fault lines run through it. It also has a history of particularly brutal conflicts.

At its peak, the Ottoman Empire (Muslim) ruled much of the southern area, but by the time of World War 1 the Austro-Hungarian Empire had rolled back its advance, and controlled most of the Balkans. That War proved to be a disaster for the Austro-Hungarian Empire, which was broken up into its constituent states as a result. The former kingdoms of the Croats, Slovenes and Serbians broke away, and were united in a single kingdom known as Yugoslavia from 1929. During World War 2, it was invaded by the Axis Powers in 1941. Although the country was quickly overrun, the various Yugoslav factions fought a fierce guerilla war against the forces of the Axis Powers, which were eventually expelled. An internal power struggle ensued, in which the communists came out on top, and a socialist Federal Republic of Yugoslavia was set up in 1943 under Josip Broz Tito, a former partisan leader. The federation comprised: Bosnia, Herzegovina, Croatia, Macedonia, Montenegro, Serbia, and Slovenia. Tito was a forceful and canny leader. Although he was a communist, he had no wish for Yugoslavia to become part of the Soviet Union and he managed to resist this. He carved out a role for Yugoslavia as a leading non-aligned socialist nation, which was neither controlled by the Soviet Union nor dominated by western capitalism.

Tito's death, as well as turmoil in the region associated with the end of the Cold War, led to Yugoslavia starting to unravel. Underlying ethnic, political and religious differences, which had been suppressed under Tito's regime, re-emerged and were to tear apart the Yugoslav state. The first element to break away was Slovenia (the northernmost part of the country). Following a referendum in December 1990, it declared independence in 1991. A 10-day war followed, which resulted in the international acceptance of Slovenia as an independent state.

The further break-up of Yugoslavia was to prove a much more protracted and very unpleasant process. Serbia was the biggest state in the federation (with many ethnic Serbians living outside Serbia), and central control within the federation passed increasingly to Serbian military and political leaders with a Serbian nationalist agenda. Their interests were, first, to retain power and, second, to ensure that all ethnic Serbs would be subject to a pro-Serbian government. Not surprisingly, this encouraged those who were not Serbian to seek independence as ethnically-based states. Given the long Balkans history of brutal inter-ethnic conflict, the process of 'ethnic cleansing' this implied, proved bloody and ruthless.

Bosnia-Herzegovina (which had a mixed population of Serbs, Croats and Bosnian Muslims) declared independence in 1992. This triggered a complex and bloody three-way conflict between Serbs, Bosnian Muslims and Croats. Croatia had already declared independence and, at times, fought against Bosnian Muslims to gain territory for Croats, and at other times fought with them to expel Serbs from Croatia and parts of Bosnia.

The international community (and the western world in particular) was appalled at the vicious conflict that had broken out in what was seen as Europe's backyard. The UN tried, while remaining impartial, to assist those in the greatest need by providing aid coordinated by the UN High Commission for Refugees (UNHCR).

THE DEPLOYMENT OF UNPROFOR – OPERATION GRAPPLE 1

By August 1992, it was clear that thousands would die unless action was taken to improve the flow of humanitarian aid to various parts of Bosnia before winter. The UN therefore passed a motion to sponsor the deployment of an extra 8,000 troops made up from five countries to escort UNHCR aid convoys into Bosnia. This force, the UN Protection Force (UNPROFOR), was to be commanded from a composite HQ in Kiseljak (west of Sarajevo). Its mission went beyond a purely passive peacekeeping role, and orders for opening fire were issued that allowed the proper protection of UNHCR drivers and UN personnel in hazardous areas.

The initial UK contribution to this force was the 1 Cheshire Battlegroup (BG), plus a National Support Element (NSE) under a one-star UK BRITFOR HQ. A task-organised workshop company of 6 + 134 from 7 Armoured Workshop REME was formed up under Major Mike Heelis REME, and became one of the three main pillars of the NSE. The composite NSE HQ was set up under the CO of 5 Ordnance Battalion, which duly set about devising procedures to support 1 Cheshire BG, which before long was to be very much in the public eye. Its CO, Lieutenant Colonel Bob Stewart, who was later to become a Member of Parliament, frequently appeared on television.

Major Heelis described his experiences after arriving in Split in October 1992 in this extract from his article in the REME Journal 1993–1994:

'It was my task as OC Workshop to assist with the opening up of the Main Supply Route (MSR) from Split in Croatia to Vitez in Bosnia. I was also to set up the Workshop in Gornji Vakuf, Bosnia, which would be known as Log Base Charlie. The overall length of the MSR from Split to Vitez over the Dinaric Alps was approximately 240km which later was to be extended a further 160km to Tuzla. Without delay we set off to explore the Split area and then the MSR into Bosnia. The first section of the road to Tomislavgrad is 90km of good quality tarmac road climbing up from sea level to 1,000m.

… Tomislavgrad, which is predominantly Bosnian Croat and had been recently shelled by Bosnian Serb artillery, was to be our first experience of the conflict, with boarded up shops and night time curfew within the town. A short distance down the road from Tomislavgrad the tarmac ends and is replaced by very narrow single track dirt road which winds its way across a mountainous route. This had been an old logging trail and was now being used as one of only two main routes into Bosnia due to the closure of the Mostar road to the south. The other route was a similar standard track slightly further south via Jablanica. Many of the numerous hairpin bends upon the first section needed to be shunted around by anything larger than a Land Rover. Later on Recovery Mechanics were to carry out a spectrum of difficult tasks upon both military and civilian vehicles sometimes in appalling weather conditions on these essential routes to keep the flow of traffic moving. The Engineers also did a superb job of widening and improving the surface quality. The scenery along the way was quite breathtaking in what is indeed a beautiful country'.

The Workshop was duly set up in Gornji Vakuf, and shared a factory site with a company of 1 Cheshire BG. Major Heelis continues his report:

'On 25 October in a mainly Croat town called Prozor some 25km south of Gornji Vakuf ethnic cleansing was carried out on the Muslim families living there. It was on that particular day that I was heading for Gornji Vakuf in command of a small Land Rover packet. What we witnessed as we passed through the town where the looting and destruction was still going on was frightening with dead bodies in the road and many houses burning fiercely. Fortunately, the drunken troops who perpetrated this destruction were so surprised to see us that we passed through the town unchallenged and continued on our way. In Gornji Vakuf it was obvious that the town had adopted a defensive posture with the expectation that they would be attacked next. The BIH (Bosnian Army – largely Muslim – which had a presence in the town) quickly signed up to leasing us the factory as, clearly a UN presence would be highly beneficial to the town'.

THE FIRST WINTER AND THE WORKLOAD INCREASES

As winter set in, the icy conditions posed problems, not least for the Warrior vehicle, a heavy tracked armoured personnel carrier. 7 Armoured Workshop REME reported:

'The performance of Warrior on ice even with crampons fitted to the track proved inadequate. Once adhesion with the surface had been lost the vehicle (and in some instances the trailer) adopted a mind of its own and luck took a hand as to where they would come to rest. Considering the sheer drops and dangerous hazards in the mountains it was in many instances white-faced and nervous drivers who eventually arrived at Gornji Vakuf after a BG deployment. As the operation developed and weather conditions worsened we carried out recovery tasks on Warriors which had overturned or come to on their sides. Once recovered the movement of casualties proved extremely difficult as traction on the icy surfaces was poor and in one instance a BG LAD recovery task took five days'.

The Workshop was soon busily productive in the excellent factory location, and with a steady workload of electronic tasks, B Vehicle (wheeled vehicle) repair and A Vehicle (armoured vehicle) power pack repair. Two Forward Repair Teams (FRT) were initially collocated with the BG Echelon in Vitez. Junior Non-Commissioned Officer (NCO) crew commanders thrived upon the challenges presented to them and gave an excellent account of themselves, particularly at the numerous, often hostile and uncooperative, road blocks. The accident rate soared especially for wheeled vehicles where the late arrival of snow chains into theatre, and reluctance to use them when they did, had its effect. It was therefore necessary to carry out Level 3 repairs (see definition in Chapter 2 ('The Fundamentals and Organisation to 2010')) to make one good vehicle out of two in order to maintain a sufficient number on the road. A high percentage of recovery tasks required cranage, and the value of having recovery vehicles fitted with cranes was very evident. The weather worsened and temperatures plummeted to –20°C in still air and down to –56°C (with wind chill) on the mountain as winter approached. The cold weather froze pretty well everything that could freeze, and the 'waxing' of diesel fuel became a major problem.

ATTACKS INTENSIFY

Early in January 1993, the HVO (Croatian Defence Council – a military force) demanded that the BIH hand over Gornji Vakuf to them, as under the Vance/Owen Peace Plan it was to be administered by Bosnian Croats rather than Muslims as it was at the time. Not surprisingly, the BIH refused and after a period of tension the town was attacked with tank, mortar, artillery and small arms fire by the HVO. As the Log Base location was only 1km from the town centre (and also adjacent to the local HVO barracks) it was at high risk from the persistent ongoing barrage. Much time was therefore spent under the limited hard cover available, with manned Warrior vehicles covering defensive arcs. Fortunately, although the base was hit by one or two mortar rounds and a lot of small arms fire, there were no UN casualties. After some three weeks, the local BG Company Commander was able to negotiate a ceasefire that reduced the intensity of the conflict. Although the BIH had retained control of the town, it was substantially damaged and many surrounding villages were destroyed. The resulting human suffering and misery witnessed by the troops patrolling from the Log Base was sickening. As almost all able men were involved in the fighting, it was the women and children who were seen to be suffering the most in situations of appalling deprivation.

Recovery of a UN vehicle

A CHANGE OF LOCATION

Partly as result of the continuing poor security situation, it was decided to move the main workshop site to a factory in Split on the Croatian coast that had good working facilities, including a swept overhead gantry 7-tonne crane. The main move took place in February 1993, with the Forward Repair Group (FRG) command element and all FRTs being deployed to Vitez, except for two crews continuing in Tuzla. An assembly and power pack exchange point was established at Gornji Vakuf together with a Foden recovery vehicle and crew.

The REME Workshop shop floor Koncar Factory Split 1994

SUMMARY OF OPERATION GRAPPLE 1

The small British force initially deployed on this UN operation acquitted itself with distinction, showing courage, restraint and professionalism in trying and distressing circumstances. Specifically, REME came through with flying colours and was able to maintain excellent levels of equipment availability throughout, despite extreme cold and some extraordinarily difficult terrain.

OPERATION GRAPPLE 2 – APRIL TO NOVEMBER 1993 – A REME FIRST LINE PERSPECTIVE

1 Prince of Wales Own BG (1 PWO BG) relieved 1 Cheshire BG in April 1993, and a company from 4 Armoured Workshop REME took over the second line support role. As the narrative thus far has tended to focus on second line it is useful to get a complementary view from first line. This is provided by the extracts that follow from an article in the REME Journal 1993 – 1994 by Captain Tim Sayer REME who was the Officer Commanding the 1 PWO LAD REME:

> '… suffice it to say that the war in Bosnia had left the country broadly divided into two tranches of Serb held land in the northwest and east, with the remaining area mostly consisting of Croats in the south and Muslims in the north. That simplistic explanation belies the fact that the ethnic population of all areas is not homogeneous and it was in the areas of Vitez and Gornji Vakuf that the flashpoints were at their worst. It was always difficult to define the mission of the British Battalion precisely, but it was something akin to 'creating the conditions whereby humanitarian aid can be delivered', a loose definition which could be interpreted in different ways. Thus the Bn HQ and two of the four sub-units moved into Vitez, with Gornji Vakuf and Tuzla in the north as the locations for the other detached sub-units. The LAD was located in an old Renault commercial vehicles garage about a mile away from the main location at Vitez.
>
> After only a few weeks of the tour, the nature of the conflict changed significantly and we found ourselves performing fewer tasks of directly supporting aid lorries, and more often trying to prevent bloodshed in the area getting out of hand. The Muslims had retaken Travnik, Bugojno and Kakanj in a series of bloody encounters, and the destruction of Travnik and the dramatic evacuation of Guca Gora being two notable instances when the Battalion was severely stretched for several days. The emphasis had become, of necessity, one of physical separation of the Muslims and Croats in order to give the convoys of the UNHCR a chance of delivering aid. Clearly the task of the LAD was made more difficult by the intensive use the vehicles were receiving, particularly the Warrior, whose impressive firepower and presence was greatly respected by the local militia, and perceived as invaluable protection by the unprotected aid workers. At the height of the operation some of these vehicles

CROATIA AND BOSNIA AND HERZEGOVINA
Spring 1993

– – – – – – – – Bosnian Serb Front Line

CROATIA

BIHAC

BOSNIA
BANJA LUKA
AND
HERZEGOVINA
SIPOVO
VITEZ
GORNJI VAKUF
KISELJAK
TUZLA
SARAJEVO

SERBIA

CROATIA
TOMISLAVGRAD

SPLIT

MOSTAR

MONTENGRO

ADRIATIC SEA

were completing up to 800km a week, with the corollary being a greater amount of repair work was required. Indeed, the LAD was having to work phenomenally hard at a rate that would have been unsustainable for a longer period. Normally availability would average between 88 and 94%, with that for Warrior staying higher. At one point, it looked as if the equipment support would not be able to keep up with the pace of the sustained activity which had expanded to take advantage of the long summer days; fortunately, the bitter fighting started to subside and the pressure on REME was reduced'.

Captain Sayer describes a number of factors that affected the LAD's work. They had to implement a number of modifications, including uparmouring Warrior vehicles and fitting global positioning systems (GPS) to some of them. The previous LAD had suffered from extreme low temperatures in winter, their replacement had to cope with problems of high temperatures and fine dust (which became ingested into engines), with mountainous roads causing frequent failures to running gear. To the problems of recovery on mountainous roads was added the growing menace of mine attacks, including seven incidents involving armoured vehicles. The LAD was lucky to get through the tour with no fatalities despite soldiers often having to complete their jobs under fire. One Lance Corporal Recovery Mechanic experienced seven rounds striking his Samson vehicle three inches above his head, was six feet away from an anti-tank mine when it blew up, and was surrounded in his vehicle by armed militia. Captain Sayer concludes his article by saying:

> 'The political arguments as to the viability of the Army's presence in the Former Yugoslavia will be contended for years to come. However, from the REME point of view, it has been a success story throughout the Equipment Support organisation, and one which the Corps should not allow itself to play down'.

OPERATIONS GRAPPLE 3–5 (NOVEMBER 1993–APRIL 1995)

The lull at the end of Operation GRAPPLE 2 did not, sadly, presage the end of the troubles in Bosnia, and ethnic violence was to continue to flare up in different areas at various times. From the point of view of the British forces in Bosnia the period of Operations GRAPPLE 3–5 could largely be seen as one of stable confrontation.

This did not mean that they always enjoyed a safe or comfortable time. The majority of REME personnel were serving at first line, each unit deploying with its organic REME element, and risk was ever present. Although there were never large-scale organised attacks on UN forces, there were mines to contend with, isolated attacks, dangerous 'stand-offs' at checkpoints, and in certain areas at certain times there was the danger from indirect fire. The range of working conditions varied from the almost luxurious in Koncar and Zepce, where factory sites had been taken over, to the positively spartan facilities in some of the outlying stations. In general, those in Split in Croatia had a more comfortable time with those up country having to cope with appalling winters, down to $-26°C$ with deep snow on the roads.

By the time of Operation GRAPPLE 5, it was clear that those previous attempts to achieve a ceasefire and settlement had proved false dawns, and that things were heating up rather than cooling down. The British presence in theatre had been building up, and the supporting ES Company from 2 Battalion REME (158 strong in eight locations) had to support 340 A Vehicles and 1,100 B Vehicles, as described in The Craftsman magazine (April 1995).

By Operation GRAPPLE 5, the British presence comprised: two infantry battalions (BRITBAT 1 and 2), an armoured reconnaissance unit (BRITCAVBAT), an engineer battalion (BRITENGBAT), a logistic battalion (BRITLOGBAT), as well as smaller supporting organisations such as a Cymbeline mortar locating troop and a signals squadron. There were four Lynx helicopters of 664 Squadron AAC, collocated with French helicopters and 845 Naval Air Squadron, which had been there for over two years and was well established – unlike 664 Squadron Workshop that lacked hangar space. The resident REME Battalion CO was based in Split, and double-hatted as the Theatre Commander ES.

All trades contributed successfully maintaining high equipment availability, but the performance of REME Recovery Mechanics under the most demanding conditions proved an outstanding advertisement for the qualities of the British Army and REME in particular. (**See Plate 2**) Their support was not limited to the British forces. As a REME Recovery Mechanic Senior NCO on Operation GRAPPLE 5 described the situation:

> 'And here we are with the platoon spread far and wide with the FRG HQ in Vitez and detachments in Gornji Vakuf, Bugojno, Zepce, Sarajevo, Gorazde and just south of Prozor in Fort Invicta. We are now providing support to anyone and everyone connected with the UN's efforts in the Former Yugoslavia. 'No job is too big, no job too small', living by the motto provided by our predecessors 'flexible is too rigid, fluid is the word''.

Although UNPROFOR was not an unqualified success, it was undoubtedly instrumental in deterring violence to an extent, and thereby saved many lives. Importantly, it also allowed aid convoys to get through to those who were in desperate need, particularly in the harsh winters of the Balkans. It provided a beacon of hope and civilisation in a country in which barbaric behaviour was all too often instigated or condoned by those in authority.

OPERATION GRAPPLE 6 – SUMMER 1995 – EVENTS COME TO A HEAD

In the summer of 1995, a number of events conspired to come together, to bring matters to a head and fundamentally change the situation.

First, there were the events at Srebrenica, which had been declared a UN 'safe haven'. In July 1995, a Serbian column forced its way into the area, under the eyes of the appalled Dutch UNPROFOR troops, and proceeded to capture the town with a population of some 40,000. They stripped all the male Muslim prisoners, military and civilian, elderly and young, of their personal belongings and identification, and deliberately and methodically killed them. The remaining population of some 30,000 was displaced.

Second, Sarajevo (the host to a Winter Olympics in happier times) had been besieged since 1992 by Serbian forces including artillery based on the high ground around the town. By 1995, this situation was the focus of world media attention, and the sight of innocent civilians being sniped at, or being killed by shells hitting the market place fuelled the feeling in the international community that 'something must be done'.

Third, in August 1995, the Croatian Army supported by the Bosnian Muslims attacked the separatist enclaves claimed by Serbs in the Krajina region. The four-day campaign was a complete military success and some 150,000–200,000 Serbs were displaced. By now, the international community had little sympathy for the Serbs. US contractors had assisted the Croats, and a senior US official had commented that the Serbs needed to suffer some serious casualties to bring them to the negotiating table in the right frame of mind.

Meanwhile, a steady build-up of UN forces had started. The taking of UN hostages led to the formation of a UN Rapid Reaction Force (RRF). The UK was a major contributor to this, its contribution including the deployment of 24 Airmobile Brigade to Ploce (in Croatia on the coast south of Split). They made only limited air and ground forays into Bosnia, but were clearly capable of serious intervention at short notice if required. The UK also provided an infantry battalion, 1 Devon and Dorsets (1 D&D), and 19 Regiment RA with its AS90 guns (155mm self-propelled gun) as part of a French-led Multinational Brigade (MNB). This deployed in the Mount Igman area where it was capable of striking at the Serbian artillery threatening Sarajevo. More heavy armour arrived in theatre with 31 Engineer Squadron, which deployed with AVLB (Armoured Vehicle Launched Bridge), AVRE (Armoured Vehicle Royal Engineers) and ARRV (Armoured Repair and Recovery Vehicle). Logistic support was coordinated by the RRF Logistic Group (RRFLG) based on the UK Combat Service Support Group (CSSG(UK)), which had deployed in June 1995.

The international community, having lost patience with Serbia, decided to start using some of the considerable military capability available to it. The Serbian positions around Sarajevo were pounded from the air, and British artillery gave them a taste of what AS90 could do. This was the first use in action of this very successful British gun.

At some point the Serbians got the message. Their impotence in the face of NATO air power and heavy forces was almost total, they were short of friends in the international community and they had lots of enemies who were all too keen to settle scores with them. They realised that it was in their best interests to negotiate before their situation got any worse. This led to negotiations in Dayton Ohio (USA), which resulted in a Serbian acceptance of Bosnian independence within agreed boundaries, which was to be policed by a powerful international military force.

The peace was still, however, fragile on the ground. A REME officer working as a G5 (civil affairs) liaison officer with 1 D&D outlined the problem vividly:

> 'Due to previous fighting 'The Federation' between Muslims and Croats remains fragile. Local prejudices mean there are no simple solutions to problems that arise between villagers of different ethnic origins. My first experience of village politics was when a nearby village sent a gang of heavies down to one of our checkpoints to protest that their water had been cut off. The heavies were village women and they struck fear into the heavily armed troops. The water supply that had been 'ruthlessly sabotaged' came from a Muslim area and they were, of course, Croat. The ladies were persuaded to go home and upon investigation it was found that the water system was just very old and required rebuilding. It showed how an everyday occurrence could degenerate. All problems became interlinked: a village couldn't be connected with electricity because the power was Croat going to the Muslims, who hadn't paid their phone bills. The Muslims hadn't paid for their water etc … Meeting the local people and listening to their problems, was however, extremely interesting. Most business was conducted in cafes and the local brandy seemed to help negotiations go smoothly. Being forced to drink brandy at 1000hrs while sitting

in the sun listening to the local people telling you war stories was an excellent way to make a living. I realised this simplified the whole problem and understood why the locals drank so much'.

OPERATION RESOLUTE – ENTER THE IMPLEMENTATION FORCE

The military operation to implement the Dayton Agreement was of a different order from the initial deployment of UNPROFOR, and it was clear that the UN did not have the military expertise or infrastructure to handle the deployment of a force of some 80,000 in all, around 54,000 of whom would be deployed in Bosnia. Realistically, the only organisation that did have it was NATO, and so on 19 November 1995 responsibility was passed to NATO by the UN. This was effectively the end of Operation GRAPPLE, and British soldiers took off their blue UN helmet covers and replaced them with their normal ones as they became part of Operation RESOLUTE.

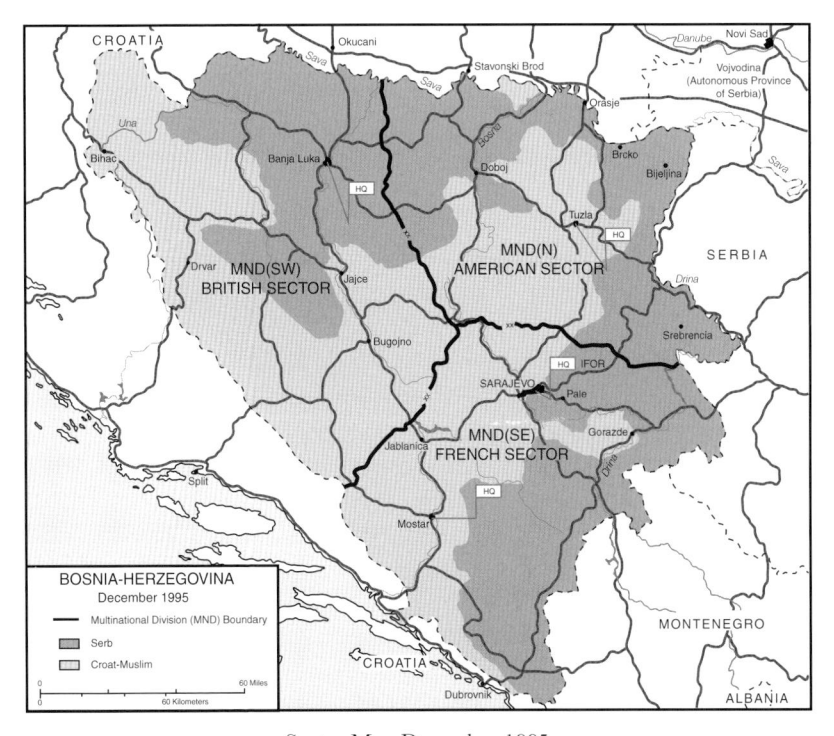

Sector Map December 1995

This was NATO's first major out-of-area deployment, and the first operational deployment of its Allied Rapid Reaction Corps (ARRC) HQ. This HQ had been set up in Bielefeld (Germany) following the end of the Cold War, as NATO worked out its role and purpose in the new strategic landscape.

HQ ARRC deployed in December 1995 with its land forces under a British commander, Lieutenant General Michael Walker. It had three major components. The first was a French-led Multinational Division in the southeast (MND(SE)), which included Sarajevo, Mostar and the south. The US led a MND in the north (MND(N)), and the British led a MND in the southwest (MND(SW)). Its HQ was in Banja Luka, and its main components were initially 4 (UK) Armoured Brigade, which included a Dutch battlegroup, and 2 Mechanised Brigade Group (Canadian).

By 31 January 1996, the British contribution to the Implementation Force (IFOR) was complete, with 11,500 ground troops in theatre. This force was widely spread around the Former Republic of Yugoslavia (FRY). The deployment involved:

- support for the HQ ARRC group, which was initially based in Kiseljak, and had its own Brigade Electrical and Mechanical Engineer (BEME)
- MND(SW) Divisional units, many including 4 General Support Regiment RLC were based at Kupres (with a BEME Divisional Troops to support them)
- 4 Armoured Brigade was based at Sipovo (with the Battalion HQ and CS Company of 3 Battalion REME)
- power pack repair and general second line support was provided at Split by the GS Company of 3 Battalion REME (which deployed as a complete unit for the IFOR mission with 111 augmentees from a number of Regular and TA REME units).

From the REME perspective, enemy action was one of the lesser problems causing concern. Hostile locals who had been somewhat intimidated by Warrior vehicles, found AS90 even more worrying, and, frankly, when they discovered that it had a big brother in the form of the Challenger 1 main battle tank they felt even less inclined to cause trouble. Aggressive and frequently drunk soldiers at checkpoints had largely become a thing of the past.

The weather was, however, a major problem, and a shock to those who had not encountered it before. This was combined with the problem that activity levels shot up from early December 1995. The most problematic time was over the Christmas/New Year period, prior to the deployment of the bulk of the reinforcements. According to Brigadier Nigel Williams (late REME) in conversation in March 2015, 3 Battalion REME just managed to cope with the workload but only because 33 TA soldiers deployed before Christmas.

Accidents on snowy mountainous roads were also a frequent occurrence, and continuously challenged REME's Recovery Mechanics. Lack of real estate and facilities also posed serious difficulties. The area was fairly backward to begin with, but years of conflict had led to many buildings being burnt down or shelled into rubble. A major movement of forces therefore took place into many areas with facilities that would have been unsatisfactory at the best of times, but posed a real challenge in a freezing winter. There was also a lot of heavily used military equipment that REME had to support. The size of the task, just for the A Vehicle dependency, is illustrated in Figure 6.1 (at the end of this Chapter).

The support system was stretched at times and the stock of A Vehicle power packs got dangerously low at times, but, true to form, REME rose to the occasion. As ever, many problems arose that typically occur when a new deployment takes place (and new equipments are deployed), before new supporting systems and supply chains are fully bedded in. As usual, REME found solutions that drew on its technical ability to innovate and improvise as well as the sheer determination and 'can do' attitude of its soldiers.

ES challenges were not confined to A Vehicles. As recorded in The Craftsman magazine (March 1997), the Commander ES at the time pointed out that the 1,600 Land Rover vehicles deployed were of 250 coded types. He lamented the lack of effective ES IT systems, and that a lot of time and money had to be spent repairing elderly B Vehicles (notably fuel tankers and tank transporters).

IFOR proved to be able to do exactly what it was supposed to do. It implemented an agreement, which is essentially still in place, and it put an end to the years of bloodshed in Bosnia. The weather started to improve and, in April 1996, 6 Battalion REME came out to replace 3 Battalion REME (Operation RESOLUTE 2). With equipment activity reduced, the Battalion had the capacity to start making a contribution to the local community, including helping to restore a church and to build a swimming pool. The situation gradually settled down, and the process of sorting things out to make operations more efficient and comfortable steadily got under way.

OPERATION LODESTAR – IFOR BECOMES THE STABILISATION FORCE – DECEMBER 1996

Although IFOR had succeeded in its aim of implementing the Dayton Accord, it was recognised that a substantial international military presence would be needed for a long time to minimise the risk of trouble flaring up in the region again. IFOR was therefore given a new mandate and transmuted into the Stabilisation Force (SFOR) with the UK commitment being renamed Operation LODESTAR. This was accompanied by a steady winding down of force levels. From the REME point-of-view, one of the early changes was the return to Germany of the Commander ES of 1 (UK) Armoured Division (Colonel Ken Ferguson (late REME)) who handed over the role of Theatre Commander ES to the CO of 1 Battalion REME who was to be based at Sipovo with his team. The GS Company was based in Split, and much of the CS Company was based in Sipovo, but with the Battalion providing the mainstay of recovery for MND(SW), including cover for the MSRs into Croatia, there were widely-spread REME detachments.

Queen's Royal Hussars LAD power pack exchange in the snow Bosnia 1996

CONTINUING OPERATIONS – OPERATION PALATINE

Although there was to be a significant UK commitment to Bosnia for several years, the broad pattern was now set. There was general pressure to reduce numbers, and by the year 2000 there were only 2,230 British troops in Bosnia (of which 209 were REME – 144 of them at first line). The winters continued to be extremely hard, with challenging recovery tasks in mountainous terrain. Ethnic tensions continued (and it would be optimistic to assume that they will not continue for generations to come) and the presence of armed, neutral soldiers was required to prevent trouble, or to contain it locally. The REME support system was well bedded in, and although there was much work to do, there was also time to perform tasks in support of local communities.

When SFOR's mandate was updated in 1998, the UK commitment was renamed Operation PALATINE. When events in Kosovo got out of hand in 1998, the situation in Bosnia remained generally quiet. Once the situation in Kosovo had been brought under control, it was decided that ES in the Balkans needed to be managed on a Pan-Balkans basis, and the first Pan-Balkans REME Battalion deployed in August 1999. The story of what happened after that is covered in the next Chapter ('Operations in the Balkans 2 – Kosovo').

Equipment	Fleet size	Average distance (km)
AS 90	18	521
CET	7	58
Challenger	38	398
Chieftain	14	27
CVR(T)	135	850
FV430	180	149
Saxon	73	392
Warrior	89	758
Total	554	475

Figure 6.1: Equipment use in March 1996

CHAPTER 7

OPERATIONS IN THE BALKANS 2 – KOSOVO

By 1997, it was clear that a new arena of conflict was developing in the Balkans. Kosovo is in the south of Serbia and is bordered on the southeast by the Former Yugoslavia Republic of Macedonia (FYROM), which managed to secede peacefully from Yugoslavia in 1991. It is bordered on the southwest by Albania. Kosovo has a complex history of bloody ethnic conflict under different rulers including the Ottoman, Serbian and Austro-Hungarian Empires, with the added factor of being the place of a battle of great Serbian significance (The Field of Blackbirds). It is a mountainous region and in 1999 its population was estimated at 1.8 million of whom around 300,000 lived in its largest city Pristina.

The settlement at the end World War 2 saw Kosovo as part of Serbia, but Tito, who believed in 'weak Serbia – strong Yugoslavia', made it a nearly autonomous state. Over the years, the ethnic Albanian population grew much faster than the Serbian. By 1989, the Serbian leader, Slobodan Milosevic, who achieved power by exploiting Serbian nationalist sentiment, brought about constitutional changes that effectively ended Kosovo's autonomy. In July 1990, Kosovo's parliament adopted a declaration of independence. This was followed by a referendum in which 99.7% of those voting (with a turnout of 87%) favoured independence. This was not accepted by Belgrade, and the scene was set for future trouble. Between 1991 and 1995, while Belgrade focused on events in Croatia and Bosnia, attacks on police units by Kosovar Albanian guerilla increased.

The Kosovo Liberation Army (KLA) emerged as the leading power amongst anti-Belgrade forces and began to threaten government control of the region. In 1996, the violence escalated. In 1997, Albania collapsed into chaos as the people rebelled against the Government, and law and order broke down. Military stockpiles were looted with impunity by criminal gangs, with much of the hardware ending up in western Kosovo and so boosting the growing KLA arsenal. By 1997, the KLA was using anti-tank weapons and launched up to 10 coordinated attacks against police forces in the province. In March 1998, the UN Security Council

Map of Serbia, Montenegro and Kosovo

in its Resolution UNHCR 1160 urged political compromise through dialogue, and condemned the excessive use of force by Serbian police and terrorist acts by the KLA. It had little appreciable effect. In the summer of 1998, the KLA made the tactical error of attempting to occupy several villages and key areas. Yugoslav Army and police units responded quickly, isolating major border points and launching a series of attacks against villages held by the KLA.

The international community became increasing concerned that another genocidal conflict was about to start. A new UN Resolution (UNHCR 1199) expressed grave concern over the intense fighting in Kosovo and, in particular, the excessive and indiscriminate use of force by the Serbian security forces and the Yugoslav Army. According to UN estimates, the fighting had displaced over 230,000 people from their homes. In October 1998, a ceasefire agreement was negotiated. This collapsed during the winter of 1998.

During February 1998, the threat of international air strikes forced the Yugoslav officials to attend negotiations with a Kosovar Albanian delegation in Rambouillet (France). The successful conclusion of these negotiations envisaged an international force of 12,000 troops (from Britain, France, Germany and Italy) being deployed into Kosovo from FYROM to help implement a peace agreement. For this reason, 2 Battalion REME was warned for a short notice deployment to FYROM on 1 February 1999.

OPERATION AGRICOLA 1 – PHASE 1 PREPARATION

The preparation for the eventual move into Kosovo was confused at times. This was not surprising as events on the ground were changing rapidly. International military operations on this scale are also inherently complex, and new teams of staff officers have to learn old lessons. For example, that REME units cannot provide repair and recovery support before its planned arrival date in theatre, and the hardy perennial that units cannot move instantly from a low state of readiness to a higher one. The following extracts from articles in The Craftsman magazine (July, September and October 1999) by the CO of 2 Battalion REME (then Lieutenant Colonel Ian Simpson REME) are worth repeating:

> 'There was no mission at that stage, and no concept of operations. It was obvious, therefore, that at unit level things would be even more vague. Back in Fallingbostel, the Battalion 2IC started to receive conflicting information, including that the first elements of the Battalion were to be on the ground in FYROM from 18 February. There was also confusion as to the Battalion's readiness category. The Battalion's understanding for the previous 6 months was that it was at 10 days' notice to move (NTM) and with an enhanced CS (Close Support) company at 6 days' NTM. The Permanent Joint Headquarters (PJHQ) at Northwood was controlling Op

AGRICOLA. They produced a Force Equipment Table (FET), allocating forces from Land Command, 1 (UK) Armd Div and 3 (UK) Div without using either of the 2-star headquarters to coordinate the operation. As a result, there was a dearth of information at battalion level. The first FET which anyone in the Battalion had sight of showed CS Coy and Battalion HQ grouped with 4 Armd Bde (the high readiness JRRF brigade) at readiness category R3. General Support (GS) Company was included under the Combat Service Support Group (UK) (CSSG(UK)) (the force logistic enablers) grouping at readiness category R5 (30 days' NTM). The first edition of the FET was amended to show Battalion HQ chopped to the CSSG(UK) grouping at readiness category R5.

From the outset therefore, the lack of a coordinating superior headquarters made life difficult at unit level. The Battalion started to receive direction from 4 Armd Bde and from then on CS Company were kept particularly well informed. OC GS Company meanwhile managed to fit in a liaison visit in an attempt to gain some direction before the latter organisation deployed to FYROM. Once the lead elements of 4 Armd Bde and CSSG(UK) had deployed to FYROM all forms of communication back to Battalion became very difficult, and the Battalion staff were left to plan for the deployment of the unit as best they could. The CO meanwhile attempted to clarify the command status of the Battalion once deployed to theatre, along with its mission and concept of operations. There was also the issue of a Theatre ES Branch and manning of any such branch in theatre'.

Fortunately, 2 Battalion REME was a well-manned and well-trained unit (which had supported 4 Armoured Brigade on Exercise ULAN EAGLE in Poland in 1998), and the difficulties described were duly resolved. The unit's equipment was moved by ship from Emden (Germany) in mid-February and arrived in Thessaloniki (Greece) in early March. The unit's heavy equipment was either put on transporters or driven from Greece to FYROM. The Battalion duly set up a base at Kavadarci (Macedonia), and proceeded to provide very successful support for the deployed force that had commenced training in the Krivolak Training Area. (**See Plate 3**)

The CO of 2 Battalion REME was also double-hatted as the Theatre Commander ES. In addition to its technical role, 2 Battalion REME made an important contribution to the establishment of a refugee camp at Razada. By the end of March, there were 437 REME personnel in the area out of a total deployed force of 4,400.

The deployment had the full support of a relatively new Labour Government, which had declared itself committed to an 'ethical' foreign policy. The Prime Minister, Tony Blair, who was at the height of his popularity, eloquently described the difficulties in the region, and made the case for possible military intervention if other means of resolving them failed.

The peace talks at Rambouillet finally collapsed on 18 March 1999. On 22 March 1999, the North Atlantic Council granted authority to commence air strikes on an approved list of military and civil infrastructure targets in the Former Republic of Yugoslavia.

OPERATION AGRICOLA 1 – PHASE 2 FROM B HOUR TO D DAY

The NATO bombing campaign was started on 22 March 1999 (B Hour). Its proclaimed goal was summed up by its spokesman as "Serbs out, peacekeepers in, refugees back". That is, Yugoslav troops would have to leave Kosovo and be replaced by international peacekeepers to ensure that the Albanian refugees could return to their homes. It was initially expected that the campaign would last a few days and that not a great deal of damage would need to be done. The willingness of the Serbs to resist had been greatly underestimated, however, and the campaign lasted for 10 weeks until 11 June 1999. It involved up to 1,000 aircraft from many NATO nations flying over 38,000 combat missions.

On the ground, the ethnic cleansing campaign by the Serbians was stepped up and within a week of the war starting, over 300,000 Kosovo Albanians had fled into neighboring Albania and the Republic of Macedonia, with many thousands more displaced within Kosovo. By April, the UN was reporting that 850,000 people, the vast majority of them Albanians, had fled their homes. Public opinion began to waver as the range of targets being attacked widened, and mistakes happened (notably the bombing of a TV studio, of the Chinese embassy, and of an Albanian refugee column in mistake for a Yugoslav Army unit).

Eventually, NATO decided that the situation could be resolved only by a land invasion of Kosovo. In the event, the threat of invasion proved enough. On 3 June 1999, Slobodan Milosevic capitulated and accepted peace conditions. On 12 June 1999, after Milosevic accepted the conditions, the NATO Kosovo Force (KFOR) entered Kosovo.

KFOR was based on the Allied Rapid Reaction Corps (ARRC) HQ, commanded by a British officer, Lieutenant General Mike Jackson. It consisted of brigades from France, Germany, Italy, the USA as well as a substantial UK contribution, which included 4 Armoured Brigade and 5 Airborne Brigade.

The period of waiting and uncertainty leading up to the occupation is described in this report from 2 Battalion REME:

'On 7 June the Bn HQ were warned off to move at short notice to provide C2 to the multinational KFOR ECCP at Brazda Eurotrade. The location would house the KFOR Forward Assembly Area (FAA) and thus be the last staging posts for the majority of KFOR troops before entering Kosovo. CS Company and assets from 28 Engr Regt Wksp and the KRH and Irish Guards LADs would be tasked to supply the FRT, recovery support.... Ground had become at a premium due to the Kosovo refugee crises. With the nearby refugee camps of Brazda and Stenkovac only 500m and 2km away respectively, the Eurotrade site had suddenly become the home of many an aid agency with little or no concept of the economical use of ground space. Vast areas of hard standing would be littered with unwanted or damaged refugee tents. Rubb shelters and Corimec containers with food supplies and accommodation would be scattered erratically.

The exact dates and timings for D Day and H Hr were left very flexible as BHQ settled into the Eurotrade site. Finally, external events decided the outcome as several hundred uninvited Russian troops from 104 Paratroop Division headed for the airport at Pristina, the Kosovo capital, from their SFOR base in Bosnia to seize the strategic site. So began the race for Pristina. The evening of the 11th saw the arrival of the KRH battlegroup into the FAA beginning at 2130hrs and until around 0330hrs on the 12th. As the packets arrived so did the vehicles and casreps. With the only Challenger tank failing to make it under its own steam being that of the CO of the KRH!! As the morning sun crept over the FYROM/Macedonian mountain range, so the first 'official' troops deployed into Kosovo. The sky filled with rotorcraft as over a dozen Chinook and Puma helicopters alighted from the regions of Piper Camp, a few kilometres from Brazda, and began the transportation of the men from 5 Airborne Bde. Escorted by Lynx and several American

Apache helicopters the scene was worthy of any Hollywood epic. The flight of aircraft flew low over the FAA and both Brazda and Stenkovac camps, eliciting cheers of 'NATO, NATO' from the tens of thousands of Kosovar refugees; a cry that would be heard by any KFOR vehicle passing ethnic Albanians for weeks afterward'.

The move into Kosovo (near Urosevac)

THE OCCUPATION OF KOSOVO AND ONGOING PEACEKEEPING OPERATIONS

Although **KFOR** had been fully geared up to fight its way into Kosovo, the occupation was, in the event, largely peaceful. The Serbian forces were allowed to withdraw from Kosovo in relatively good order, and the degree to which its armoured vehicles and equipment had been unscathed by the Allied air offensive was something of a surprise. They had clearly been very adept at hiding military hardware in buildings, under bridges and the like, as well as setting up dummy targets, which were hard for pilots to identify without flying low enough to be vulnerable to low-level air defence.

An extraordinary chain of events unfolded at Pristina Airport. Russian paratroops arrived unannounced from Bosnia ahead of NATO troops, and claimed possession of it. For ethnic and historic reasons, Russia was more sympathetic to the Serbian cause than NATO and expected to have an independent sector of Kosovo rather than operating under the NATO command structure. The Supreme Allied Commander Europe (General Wesley Clark) ordered Lieutenant General Jackson to block the airfield runways and isolate the Russians. This he refused to do, on the grounds that he was not prepared to risk precipitating 'World War 3'. Eventually, a deal was struck whereby the Russians operated as a unit of KFOR, but not under the NATO command structure.

REME Recovery Mechanics and liaison officers from 2 Battalion REME were the first NATO troops to join the Russians on the disputed airfield. This extract from the unit article in The Craftsman magazine (September 1999) explains:

> 'The Russian Paratroops Division again displayed their lack of deployed combat service support and were suffering from a lack of logistic support. Having already required a resupply of water from British troops around the airfield, this time REME support was requested to repair a BTR-60 armoured personnel carrier. A Foden wheeled recovery vehicle crewed by Cfn McCoy and Cfn Walker were tasked to lift the engine and gearbox of the APC so Russian mechanics could fix it'.

The move of 2 Battalion REME into Kosovo was described by its Operations Officer as follows:

> 'The following day saw recce parties from BHQ and 8 Fd Wksp head north to identify appropriate real estate. As our vehicles approached the Deneral Jankovic border crossing point the roads began rapidly to choke with all manner of civilian vehicles as the exodus of refugees began their long trek home from the camps. Rapidly waved through the crossing point by the American military police our military convoy headed up the Kacanik defile. Initial views displayed why the politicians were loath to deploy troops into a semi-permissive environment. The 7km long defile consisted of a narrow winding road over bridges with vehicle and infantry bunkers still visible deployed on either side. Many darkened tunnels with empty landmine boxes still littering the tarmac were visible on road verges waiting to be cleared by Engineers. Buildings believed to have been occupied by the Serb military lay in ruins, destroyed by the precision bombing.

As our vehicles progressed back into the flatlands and through the towns and hamlets around Urosevac, evidence of the looting of buildings by Serbs became apparent. Few buildings had windows left intact, and all rooms appeared bare with soot marks betraying the evidence of torching. At this stage, few locals could be seen; the vast majority still penned in the many refugee camps or cluttering the border in their attempts to return home as speedily as possible. Unfortunately, some refugees managed to return home before their houses could be cleared and entire families were killed as they initiated booby traps left by the Serbs.

On arrival at Pristina, BHQ collocated with CS Company at their new site on Tesco's car park complex whilst 8 Fd Wksp would relocate onto some adjacent real estate to see out their 30 days in theatre. Shortly afterwards, GS Company would also relocate to the fruit factory site at Morane, just SE of the FROY capital of Skopje. Production again became hectic after the move of the BRITFOR troops into the Kosovo Province. None more so than the Recovery Mechanics who not only had to recover BRITFOR vehicles, but also Serb Army and civilian wrecks'.

Whilst a REME history will tend to focus on what happened at second line, it should be remembered that most REME personnel were serving at first line and sharing the experiences of their parent units as they repair and recover their equipment. This extract from an article in The Craftsman magazine (November 1999) from a fitter section of 4 Regiment RA paints a typical picture:

> 'Our arrival at the border was an anti-climax. The next 10km were strange, with an eerie feel due to the complete lack of local population. We passed our fitter section CRAARV, located on a bridge. The weather on D Day was scorching; it was a glorious day to liberate an occupied territory. Our first night in Kosovo was spent in troop locations north and south of Urosevac where once again we were given a hero's welcome, a far cry from what we had been expecting. We deployed to a grain mill at Gadmsko Blato, where we stayed for three full days. The obvious sleepless nights for essential maintenance ensued. Whilst at the mill we watched as the Battle Group passed us interspersed with Serb convoys of stolen cars displaying Yugoslav flags leaving the country. We deployed to three

distribution warehouses at Lebane. NATO's bombing had left these in a state of indescribable destruction. On arrival we had an eyeball competition with Serb troops who were in a convoy of 25 T55s. It would appear that our six AS90s won and by the following morning they were gone. Our two gloomy nights here were disturbed by the sound of gunfire coming from withdrawing Serb forces that were also torching houses on the way. We finally made it to the polyester factory in Podujevo, our new home, with a 432 in tow. Since arriving we have been kept busy with an active patrolling programme in support of the KRH and IG, and one gun troop is deployed in Obilic, NW of Pristina providing patrols to reassure the local Serb community'.

The occupation of Kosovo having gone fairly smoothly, British forces started thinning out, and 5 Airborne Brigade was soon heading back to the UK along with 8 Field Workshop. 2 Battalion REME moved to the Kosovamont factory site north of Pristina. This factory site, complete with overhead cranes, was near a large power station and was an acceptable working site, except for the acrid smell of lignite from the local mine. It was to become REME's main second line base in Kosovo. Overall, the REME side of Operation AGRICOLA 1 went very much to plan.

With KFOR fully in place the immediate priority was to get Kosovo back on its feet again, to keep the peace by getting the KLA under control, and prevent the various ethnic groups from attempting to settle old scores. This grew into an ongoing Balkans peacekeeping commitment of a type already all too familiar to the British Army at the time.

OPERATION AGRICOLA 2 – THE PAN-BALKANS REME BATTALION AUGUST 1999–MARCH 2000

REME now had battalions in both Bosnia and Kosovo. With only six battalions available the maintenance of this level of commitment would have resulted in tour intervals of around six months, for something that was clearly unsustainable in the long term. Given that the operational situation in the Balkans was fairly stable, the decision was taken to replace the two REME Battalions with the Pan-Balkans REME Battalion. This was considered workable by cutting to the minimum the number of 'just-in-case' military personnel and by making good use of locally employed

civilians (LEC) to carry out routine repair work. 6 Battalion REME duly took on this role in August 1999. The CO alternated between theatres as overall Commander ES. The Second-in-Command was deployed to Banja Luka to provide the basis of the ES Branch of the HQ (UK) NSE (National Support Element), which was collocated with the deployed British Brigade HQ. A small detachment was based in Split with the Regimental Admin Officer, Quartermaster, Regimental Quartermaster Sergeant, and Air Liaison Officer with a link back to Tidworth and a fitter section to support the 'garrison'. The main company deployments were to:
- Sipovo in Bosnia – where a composite ES company deployed – initially 126 strong, this was reduced to 60 and subsequently incorporated into a specially configured UK CSS Battalion (with HQ and Logistic Support Company collocated) the command of which was to alternate in due course between REME and RLC
- Obilic in Kosovo – where a 100-strong composite ES company took over the Kosovamont factory site (which was less than ideal as access was limited, machinery was in the way, and accommodation was primitive until developed) from 2 Battalion REME at the end of their eventful and tiring tour.

Members of 11 GS Company leave the ES Squadron Base on patrol 2001

FURTHER OPERATIONS IN THE BALKANS

With stability restored to the Balkans, the UK Government's interests lay in reducing its commitment (and their cost) by rationalising, outsourcing/civilianising, and withdrawing as many forces as possible, with the impetus behind this increasing as the need for British forces to be deployed elsewhere became ominously apparent. By 2001, the British commitment to Kosovo involved providing two battlegroups with second line support, which provided the framework for a multinational brigade.

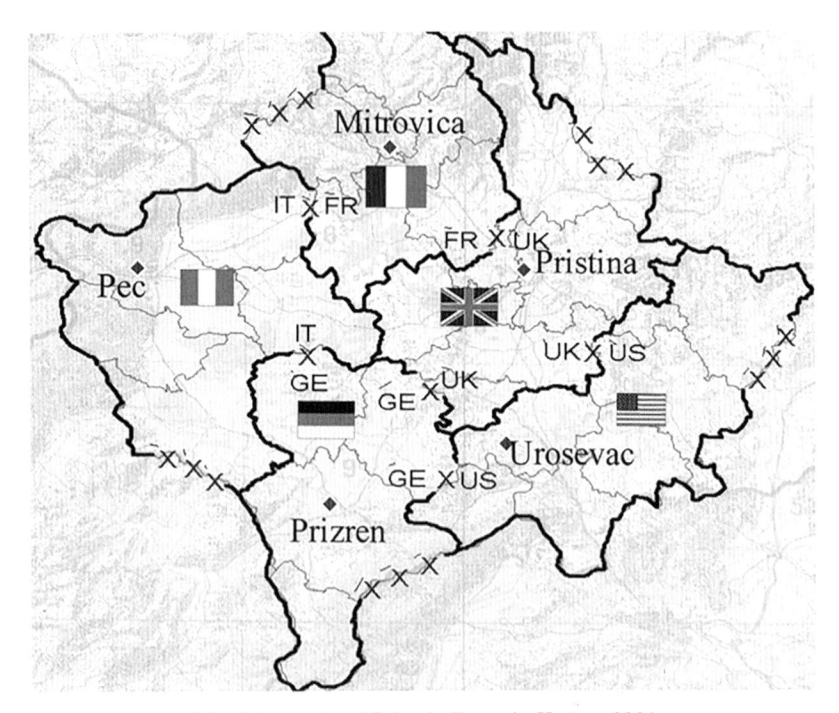

The Multinational Brigade Zones in Kosovo 2001

As in Bosnia, a composite ES company from the Pan-Balkans REME Battalion was embedded within the second line Combat Service Support Battalion, the command of which alternated between REME and RLC.

There was an interesting adjunct to the peacekeeping operations in July 2001 when many of the non-aviation elements of 16 Air Assault Brigade deployed to Macedonia on Operation BESSEMER. There had been significant unrest within Macedonia, triggered by events in Albania/Kosovo in 1999. By 2001, this had been largely resolved but a neutral force was required to collect the weapons held by the so-called National Liberation Army – the purpose of Operation BESSEMER. Second line REME support was provided by 8 CS Company (from 7 Air Assault Battalion REME), which successfully dealt with all the problems that arose, including all too frequent road traffic accidents. Not everyone was pleased to see foreign troops in Macedonia, and some of the locals had taken to stoning NATO vehicles, resulting in the death of a Sapper from 9 Squadron RE. 8 CS Company therefore set about fitting vehicle windscreen protection kits, thus complying with the pattern that on operations REME is almost invariably required very quickly to fit some form of modification/protection package, which usually involves metalsmiths and welding equipment.

Bus repair in the REME Workshop in Kosovo 2001

By 2003, there had been a further drawdown in the Balkans and the two theatres became a single Joint Operational Area. The reorganisation was reflected in a new generic name Operation OCULUS (for operations in both Bosnia and Kosovo). By this time, the UK commitment was a single battlegroup in Bosnia and a company-sized force in Kosovo plus a NSE element. Total REME involvement at both first and second line was 91.

In March 2007, the Welsh Guards Battlegroup left Bosnia. It was not replaced and the British military commitment to Bosnia effectively ended. In 2009, it was announced that all but three of the 167 British military personnel would leave Kosovo, marking the end of British operations in the Balkans.

OPERATIONS IN THE BALKANS IN PERSPECTIVE

After the end of the first Gulf War, the Cold War having finished, frankly, most people were unsure what would lie ahead for the British Army. After the 10 years of involvement in the Balkans that followed, many writing at the time felt that a likely pattern for the future had been set. It seemed that the use of overwhelming allied airpower, plus the threat, at least, of intervention by forces capable of high-intensity operations using modern weaponry could be used to force errant states to the negotiating table in order to find peaceful solutions to their problems, which could be underwritten by peacekeeping forces put in place by the international community. The Strategic Defence Review of 1998 was certainly consistent with this line of thinking, and it envisioned a British Army that was capable of periodic large-scale high-intensity operations of limited duration, and of maintaining a continuous peacekeeping presence overseas of at least brigade strength.

Undoubtedly, the British Army's performance in the Balkans had been superb. It followed a string of successes going back to the stunning victory in the Falklands two decades before. Although small in size, it was one of the few armies in the world that could claim to be in the 'premier league' in terms of its ability to deploy and sustain expeditionary forces capable of operating at all levels of operational intensity. It is easy to forget that REME represents a key enabler in this, and that without its ability to keep returning *'fit equipment to the hands of troops'* the Army's combat capability can all too quickly wither on the vine. There were some key lessons learned or reinforced in the process.

The need for good CSS systems to manage spares and production, with appropriate connectivity within theatre and back to UK, was reinforced, as well as the need for deployable technical infrastructure to enable repair in extreme conditions and at night. This campaign highlighted the disconnect between in-barracks and operational technical management systems.

The importance of 'expedient' or 'battlefield' repair was demonstrated, because without it 'no spare' was very likely to translate into 'no repair'.

REME was actively engaged in all elements of the Balkans campaign from supporting manoeuvre to delivering bespoke modification to battlegroup equipment. Throughout, the tenet of repair forward was reflected in REME disposition with second line units based at key CSS nodes.

The end of this campaign saw the move to CSS groupings as force levels drew down to below brigade size with either a REME or RLC CO.

The technical competence and ingenuity of REME tradesman was tested in extreme climatic conditions with winter proving the most challenging.

Operations in the Balkans had given the British Army a chance to demonstrate its particular skill in peacekeeping situations, which reflected a combination of its breadth of experience and the humanity, humour and professionalism of its soldiers. It was quite clear that the Kosovan authorities shared this view. In September 2003, the Kosovan authorities were not so much concerned about the overall drop in KFOR numbers, but that the British force was being reduced to 200 strong. The following was reported in the press at the time by Ramush Tahiri, an adviser to a leading Kosovan politician:

> 'We feel a big handicap that the British troops have left Kosovo because their experience with similar missions is far beyond that of many armies that are now in charge of security in Kosovo, perhaps for the first time out of their country.
>
> The British troops dealt with the tense situation immediately after the war very well and they did this by establishing excellent co-operation with the population, while still being firm. Their experience from Northern Ireland was a valuable asset because it made the Brits one of the rare armies that had experience of how to operate in an unconventional conflict'.

British politicians had accepted that the exceptional quality of Britain's small armed forces had allowed the UK to 'punch above its weight' in the international arena. This perception was a great compliment to the Services, but such an approach carries risks. The assumption that the Armed Forces will always be able to 'punch above their weight' carries risks, not least the notion that there is always scope safely to cut resources. The Defence Costs Study of the mid-1990s, predicated on the idea that is was both possible and desirable to 'cut the tail without cutting the teeth', reflected this view.

The Balkans was still the British Army's major operational preoccupation in mid-2001. Then, on 11 September 2001, Al Qaeda terrorists crashed aircraft into the World Trade Centre in New York – and the world changed forever.

CHAPTER 8

THE INVASION OF IRAQ (OPERATION TELIC 1)

After a decade during which its operational focus had been primarily on the Balkans, the British Army's interest shifted in 2002 to the Middle East and, specifically, to Iraq and Saddam Hussein. Saddam Hussein had invaded Kuwait in 1990, and the British Army had been a major contributor to the Coalition forces that, in early 1991, inflicted a rapid and crushing defeat on the Iraqi forces leading to their headlong retreat from Kuwait. The Coalition forces did not follow up their victory by invading Iraq, but there was some optimism that the Iraqi people themselves would rise against Saddam Hussein and remove him. In the event, the wily dictator consolidated his control of the country soon after his defeat, putting down a Shia uprising in Basra with great brutality, dealing ruthlessly with Kurds in the north of Iraq, and anyone else who opposed him.

The international community's response was, for several years, one of containment. It imposed 'no fly' zones to protect 'safe havens' for Kurdish and other opponents of the regime. It demanded that Iraq give up any Weapons of Mass Destruction (WMD), and the capability to develop them. Saddam Hussein actually did this, but he also obstructed the process of verification; presumably, on the grounds that he wished to enjoy the benefits of 'the deterrence of doubt', and felt that he would be safer if opponents thought he might have WMD. This proved a fatal miscalculation. By the time he was prepared to allow international inspectors free rein to look for WMD, the international climate had changed. The events of '9/11' persuaded the USA President, George W Bush, that he could not take chances, and that Saddam Hussein's regime needed to be toppled by military force at an early date. In this, he was fully supported by the UK Prime Minister, Tony Blair.

The invasion of Iraq was essentially an Anglo-American operation, with the bulk of the forces (some 248,000) being provided by the USA and some 46,000 being provided by UK. Although many countries contributed troops to the stabilisation of Iraq later, the only other countries who contributed regular forces to the invasion were Poland (200 special forces, some of whom worked with 3 Commando Brigade) and Australia (around 2,000 troops).

The Iraqi Army, some 375,000, was much smaller than it had been in 1991. It was of very varied quality, but even its best formations (the Republican Guard and Special Republican Guard) were at a marked technological disadvantage to the Coalition forces. There was also a substantial Fedayeen (militia) force, as well as police and security forces, some of whom had a vested interest in the survival of the regime. Despite having plenty of aerial and electronic intelligence, the Coalition was remarkably light on human intelligence (HUMINT), and there was a good deal of uncertainty about how much resistance would be encountered.

Some US defence planners considered the Iraqi regime to be a 'balloon' that would collapse with the first 'prick' of military force – and the invading force would be treated as liberators by cheering crowds. Others questioned the wisdom of making this assumption, and highlighted the risk that Saddam Hussein would make successful use of WMD. Planning was driven by the USA Secretary of Defense, Donald Rumsfeld, who believed that speed and superior technology were a substitute for large numbers of 'boots on the ground'. He required the operation to be very swiftly mounted (he was not prepared to allow the sort of lengthy build up that had preceded the war in 1991), and the US force to be deployed was substantially smaller than the one that US military planners had originally felt necessary.

CONCEPT OF OPERATIONS

At one time, planners considered an attack from two directions, from the north going through Turkey, and from the south from Kuwait. In the event, Turkey was not willing to offer the Coalition the right of transit for an attack. So the invasion had to be essentially mounted from Kuwait, less an airborne operation by the US 173 Airborne Brigade, which linked up with rebel Kurdish militia forces in the north of Iraq.

The first Gulf War had commenced with an aerial onslaught on Iraqi forces and key military facilities, which had lasted several weeks. This time, the initial aerial attack was short and sharp, almost concurrent with the land attack, and aimed at shattering command and control systems. This reflected both a desire to minimise civilian casualties, and also that the Iraqi air power and air defences had been extensively attacked in the course of enforcing 'no fly' zones. Coalition air superiority was overwhelming.

Both the US and UK land forces were to break into Iraq from Kuwait. The US forces would drive rapidly north towards Baghdad, with broadly parallel thrusts to the east and west of the Rivers Tigris and Euphrates. The UK forces were to drive east, and take control of Basra (Iraq's second largest city) as well as strategic oilfields to the north and south of it, exploiting from there to take control of the southern part of Iraq, including Maysan Province that borders on Iran.

The operation comprised four phases. Phases 1–3 of the operation were planned in detail, and were designed rapidly to crush military resistance, creating such 'shock and awe' that Saddam Hussein's regime would collapse and allow the Coalition to establish military control over the whole of Iraq. Phase 4 was about what would be put in place of the regime that had been brought down and is covered in Chapter 9 ('Iraq – Aftermath of the Invasion (Operations TELIC 2–13)'). The text that follows in this Chapter is based on a document from 1 (UK) Armoured Division ES Branch (Electronic Post Operational Report Version 1.0 (Restricted)). This was a CD that included post operational reports from many of the first line REME units involved, and all the second line major units, as well as divisional-level material, which provided most of the technical and operational data.

THE UK CONTRIBUTION

The UK land component was based on 1 (UK) Armoured Division, which had under command Divisional units and:
- 3 Commando Brigade – with a second line REME company within its logistic regiment
- 7 Armoured Brigade – to be supported by 2 Battalion REME
- 16 Air Assault Brigade – to be supported by 7 Air Assault Battalion REME
- 102 Logistic Brigade – to be supported by 3 Battalion REME.

Its equipment inventory included over 16,000 vehicles. These were categorised as follows:
- 26 variants of A Vehicles
- 19 types of artillery equipment
- 6 variants of helicopters
- 34 variants of general service wheeled vehicles
- 19 variants of generators/motorbikes/other wheeled vehicles

- 26 variants of other general service equipment, such as plant
- 12 variants of Commando BV vehicles (articulated, tracked, all-terrain)
- 13 variants of box body vehicles.

Looking after this miscellany of equipment were 3,069 REME tradesmen, of whom about two-thirds were at first line, and one-third at second line.

The challenge to the UK forces was no easy one. The Army had many other commitments; some of the units that deployed to Iraq had only just finished providing support during a firemen's strike, which had involved some 19,000 Services' personnel. It had to deploy a high proportion of its strength at short notice by sea and air over a distance of some 3,400 miles and had to be capable of supporting it on intensive operations. To achieve this, many difficult logistic and equipment support problems had to be solved quickly. Whilst such problems tend not to catch the media headlines unless things go obviously wrong, knowledgeable people realise their criticality. The expression 'amateurs talk tactics, professionals talk logistics' overstates the case, but reflects an element of truth. Interestingly, an account of the British invasion of Iraq in World War 1 (initial tactical success leading to humiliating surrender in Kuwait as a result of the complete failure of the logistic support system) was required reading for US staff planners.

PREPARATORY PLANNING, PRE-DEPLOYMENT TRAINING AND DEPLOYMENT

From mid-2002, as the possible requirement to invade Iraq began to take shape, a number of contingency planning exercises took place, involving both UK and US staff. Early in January 2003, things began to move rapidly. Pre-deployment training started on 6 January, and on 10 January HQ LAND issued the force generation order for the Land Contingent. A period of tactical planning followed, after which key staff and advance parties moved to Kuwait, the main body of 1 (UK) Armoured Division being in place by 7 February.

Thereafter, units began to arrive in theatre. 3 Commando Brigade was fully operational by 15 February, as was 3 Battalion REME by 24 February, the Royal Regiment of Fusiliers Battalion (1 RRF) was complete by 1 March, the Black Watch Battalion (1 BW) by 4 March, the Royal Tank Regiment (2 RTR) by 8 March, and the Royal Scots Dragoon

THE INVASION OF IRAQ (OPERATION TELIC 1)

Guards (SCOTS DG) by 12 March. By 18 March, REME had completed a Challenger 2 modification programme, the theatre painting programme had finished, and the 7 Armoured Brigade in-theatre training programme was complete. All was ready for the commencement of operations the following day.

The overall deployment time frame was 10 weeks. This was a very tight programme, and meeting it was a considerable achievement. The comparable deployment time for Operation GRANBY, the invasion of Kuwait for the first Gulf War, was 22 weeks.

CHRONOLOGY OF THE UK OPERATIONS IN 2003

19 March. Operation RESOLUTE in the Balkans ended at 1900Z and Operation TELIC 1 began. Incidentally, the rumour that 'TELIC' was an acronym for 'Tell Everyone Leave Is Cancelled' was false – UK operational names are selected by computer, unlike US names that are intended to be meaningful.

20 March. There were three separate operations.
- 3 Commando Brigade with the US Marines under tactical command attacked and seized the Al Faw peninsular and blocked its strategic oilfields. It went on to seize Um Qasr, which was important as it was an Iraqi naval base, and as Iraq's only deep-water port needed to be opened so that it could provide a route for supplies and humanitarian aid. It met with significant resistance.
- 7 Armoured Brigade deployed into Iraq with the intention of capturing Basra from the west. Armoured Engineer Squadrons breached the Kuwait/Iraq border berms, providing breaches for US forces, which needed to push rapidly northwards to capture Baghdad.
- 16 Air Assault Brigade began its deployment with the intention of protecting the key Rumaylah oilfield installations to the northwest of Basra, relieving US forces that had briefly occupied them before continuing their push to Baghdad.

21 March. Operations continued, with 7 Armoured Brigade launching a limited attack at 0300Z to protect the flank of the US Marines.

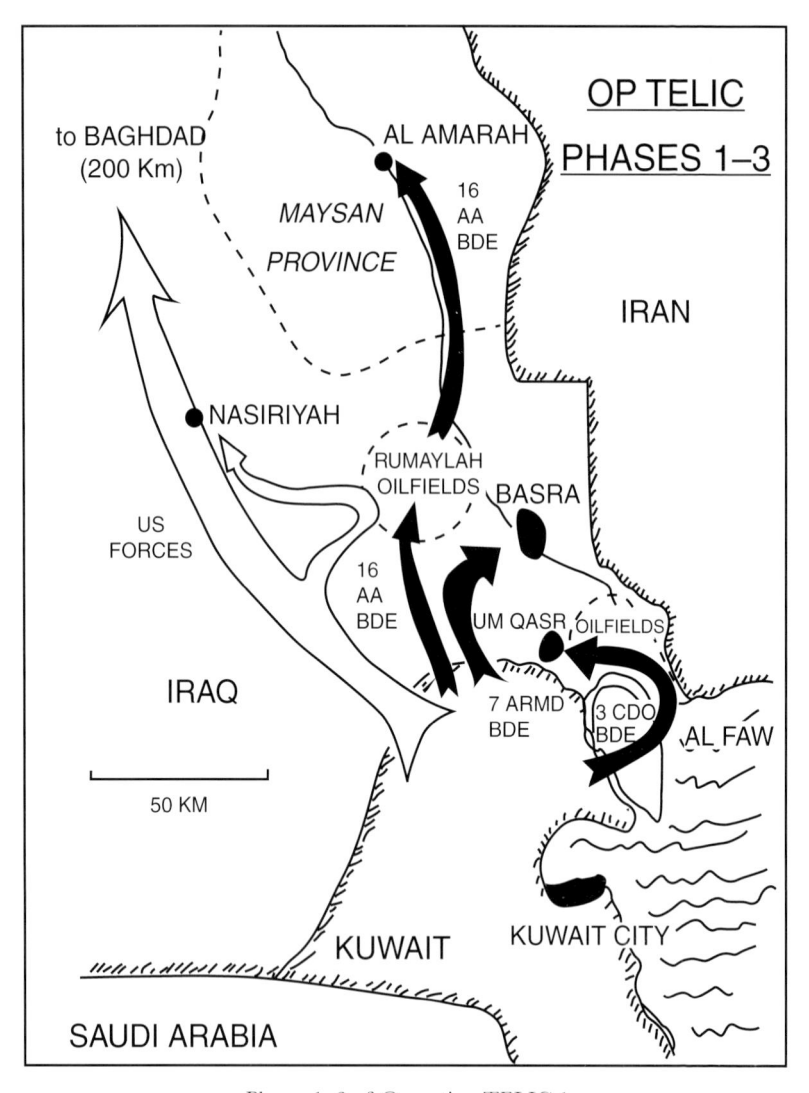

Phases 1–3 of Operation TELIC 1

22 March. 7 Armoured Brigade creates 'blocks' around Basra and the port of Az Zubayr meeting with limited resistance. 16 Air Assault Brigade is established in the Rumaylah oilfields.

23 March. 3 Commando Brigade secures Az Zubayr (just southwest of Basra).

THE INVASION OF IRAQ (OPERATION TELIC 1)

25 March. 16 Air Assault Brigade expands north of Rumaylah.

28 March. 7 Armoured Brigade gains lodgements in Az Zubayr, aid is distributed to locals.

29 March–5 April. Further operations to close in on Basra.
- 3 Commando Brigade moving in from the south meeting sporadic resistance.
- 7 Armoured Brigade moved in from the west, encountering resistance both from Fedayeen and the Iraqi Army (14 Iraqi tanks were destroyed without loss in an engagement with tanks from 7 Armoured Brigade).
- 16 Air Assault Brigade moving in to occupy Ad Dayr immediately to the north of Basra.

6 April. The formal entry to Basra commenced, with 7 Armoured Brigade securing key objectives and linking up with 3 Commando Brigade (which seized Basra Palace).

7 April. There is widespread looting across Basra, whilst isolated and limited resistance to the UK forces continues. A battalion of the Parachute Regiment (3 PARA – the Divisional Reserve) is committed to the clearance of 'Old Basra'. 16 Air Assault Brigade occupied Al Dayr.

8–10 April. 16 Air Assault Brigade secures bridges over the River Euphrates, A Squadron the Queens Dragoon Guards (QDG) crosses the Shatt Al Arab Canal. Looting continues and there are isolated attacks on the SCOTS DG and RRF battlegroups. HQ 7 Armoured Brigade sets up in the Basra presidential palace.

11 April. 3 Commando Brigade takes over responsibility for key oil installations from 16 Air Assault Brigade, allowing it to concentrate before moving north into Maysan Province.

12 April. 16 Air Assault Brigade enters Al Amarah (in Maysan Province). Joint patrols start with local police in Basra.

14 April. NBC (Nuclear Biological Chemical) state lowered, respirators no longer required to be carried. Incidents continue, but they are considered to be 'turf wars' and not directed at the Coalition forces.

19 April. UK MoD declares Recovery Day (R Day), the end of warfighting operations in the UK area of operations and the start of Phase 4. The Royal Irish Regiment (1 RIRISH) is taken off task and starts to recover back to their peacetime location.

5 May. President Bush announces 'hostilities officially over'.

6 May–3 July. This was a period of thinning out troops and reallocating operational responsibilities. 3 Commando Brigade handed over most of its responsibilities to 7 Armoured Brigade, and was clear of the operational area by 13 May. 16 Air Assault Brigade handed over Maysan Province to 1 PARA who became an independent battlegroup reporting directly to Divisional HQ.

4–12 July. Operation TELIC 1 effectively ended as 7 Armoured Brigade handed over Basra Province to 19 Mechanised Brigade (4 July) and HQ 3 (UK) Division relieved HQ 1 (UK) Armoured Division.

THE PROOF OF THE REME PUDDING

To answer the question 'how did REME do in all this?', one must look first at the force availability statistics. The operational availability statistics at Figure 8.1 (at the end of this Chapter) cover the period building up to the start of operations, and the period of major operational activity.

The story the figures tell is unequivocal. The force had deployed at short notice with a large amount of equipment, much of it highly complex, and had to train, then fight in a harsh and unfamiliar environment. It started operations with 94% of its equipment operational, and the average availability during the most active period of operations was 90%. The availability figures for Challenger 2 will warm the hearts of readers who recall the Chieftain tank era, with training areas in Germany and Canada being littered with broken down tanks. In short, these excellent availability figures would not have been possible unless REME had done an excellent job.

Expeditionary operations on the scale of Operation TELIC 1 produce a set of logistic and equipment support problems, which are different from those on other types of operation. The UK forces were fortunate that they had experience of a similar type of operation a decade before. They were also very lucky to have carried out a major exercise, Exercise

THE INVASION OF IRAQ (OPERATION TELIC 1)

SAIF SAREEA, in 2002, which involved the deployment of an armoured force to Oman. This taught many lessons, and reminded a new generation of staff officers of the lessons learned in 1991. In order to understand how the overall ES system worked in its entirety, it is useful to view what happened from various perspectives.

SECOND LINE SUPPORT – THE ROLE OF 3 BATTALION REME

One of the key lessons learned on Exercise SAIF SAREEA was of the importance of getting a second line ES capability in place right from the start to support the Reception Staging and Onward Movement (RSOM) of an expeditionary force. Fortunately, this helped 3 Battalion REME get a high priority on the Desired Order of Arrival Staff Table (DOAST). Its advance party arrived in theatre on 4 February 2003, and it declared an initial operating capability on 15 February. It was fortunate to get excellent real estate in a Kuwait Army barracks, named Vitruvius Lines. **(See Plate 4)**

The Battalion's long-term role was primarily to provide second line support for the deployed force's logistic component, but as the first REME 'foot on the ground' it also had a crucial Theatre ES role. Tasks that fell to it soon after deployment included:
- providing a recovery system
- carrying out a range of modifications and tasks related to Urgent Operational Requirements (UOR), notably uparmouring and modifying all Challenger 2, uparmouring many Combat Vehicle Reconnaissance (Tracked) (CVR(T)) variants, making environmental modifications to AS90 (tracked 155mm self-propelled artillery system) and applying combat identification modifications to all fighting echelon vehicles
- organising and carrying out a vehicle painting programme (over 7,000 vehicles were painted)
- providing 'fallback' repair support for immediate problems that arose before the ES system was fully established in theatre
- linking in with local and US sources of technical support, and taking contract support staff under its wing.

3 Battalion REME had to take on its role at exceptionally short notice, and had to undergo a major reorganisation in a matter of a few days in order to do so. It had to provide three War Fighting Increment (WFI)

platoons for 2 Battalion REME, as well as absorbing both regular and reservist staff to bring itself up to strength for deployment – no mean task for the CO, Lieutenant Colonel John Abbott REME.

The peak of the Battalion's activity was in the period up to the start of decisive combat operations. As activity reduced, the Battalion was able to move its CS Company to excellent facilities in the port of Um Qasr, where it was able to recruit a civilian workforce component. As the operational use of equipment decreased, its workload diminished and in due course it was able to hand over to 2 Battalion REME to absorb its second line support responsibilities.

Power pack repair Vitruvius Lines

This was the first time a REME battalion had been used in a Joint Force Logistic Component (JFLogC) support role. The concept proved to work, but key points emerged from post-operational reports.

Spares were a problem, and were generally the limiting factor (rather than manpower or facilities). Some 54% of the unit's Priority 01–04 spares demands were not met. This was partly because of imperfections in the supply chain and its asset tracking systems, but also because operational spares' holdings had been skewed by the use of contractor repair and low peacetime usage rates. For example, 54% of Priority 01–04 spares were not scaled.

Spares problems therefore had to be overcome by the ingenuity of REME tradesmen and by salvage, and in some cases cannibalisation. 3 Battalion REME was responsible for managing the force's pool of unrepairable vehicles, and for controlling salvage.

ES is a key enabler in the RSOM process, and many of the tasks were not directly related to routine first and second line support of logistic

THE INVASION OF IRAQ (OPERATION TELIC 1) 101

component equipment. Getting a REME unit deployed early in a suitable location is vital, as REME units required to move or to be deployed tactically will inevitably be less productive.

Uparmouring and modifications to Challenger 2 tanks

SECOND LINE SUPPORT – THE ROLE OF 2 BATTALION REME

The role of 2 Battalion REME (CO, Lieutenant Colonel John Henderson REME) was to provide second line support for 1 (UK) Armoured Division, with special emphasis on the support of 7 Armoured Brigade, the force's 'heavy metal'. It had undergone a period of collective training during 2002 and assumed the role of High Readiness REME Battalion in November 2002. In early January 2003, it was formally warned for operations to be carried out at war fighting establishment. It deployed by air on 20 February, less its WFI platoons (that were from 3 Battalion REME and which deployed early with that Battalion), and its vehicles and equipment came by sea and were unloaded in Kuwait by 1 March.

The Battalion CS Company (7 CS Company) was deployed with 7 Armoured Brigade, and following the start of operations deployed across the Iraqi border on 22 March. **(See Plate 5)** Two days later the Battalion

HQ and its GS Company (11 GS Company) moved to the Abdali Farms complex, the occasion being marked by their twenty-fourth alert for Scud missiles. On 11 April, the HQ and 11 GS Company moved again, this time to Shaibah Airfield some 30km southwest of Basra. From 29 April, the Battalion started to lose its WFI platoons and augmentees, and continued at reduced strength until around the end of June when it drew down to a company-size organisation tailored to support anticipated second line needs.

Overall, its ES arrangements were highly successful. 7 Armoured Brigade started operations with 98% availability and, after three weeks of intensive operations, availability was at 95%, 10% above target. Highlights of support included the regeneration of 310 A Vehicle power packs in less than three months, as well as the repair of 2,400 items of telecommunications equipment. The criticality of the power pack repair effort is evidenced by the note in the post-operational report that on 21 March there was only one fit K60 power pack available to support the force's large fleet of FV430 series A Vehicles.

Power pack exchange by 2 Battalion REME

A friendly reception

Major David Edmondson REME, who commanded 7 CS Company, helped to bring the realities of the operation to life with this extract from his article in The Craftsman magazine (March 2004):

> 'At full War Fighting Establishment with an additional Fwd Platoon from 3 Bn REME, backfill from 1, 4 and 6 Bns as well as TA the Coy comprised 7 + 229 with 110 vehicles of which 32 were A Vehicles ... I got back to the Company in time to give my 'going into battle' speech; it was not a 'Tim Collins' Henry 1V theatre production, but a simple promise not to put the soldiers into any unnecessary danger by ensuring that we got the most up-to-date information/intelligence regarding cleared routes, and that if possible all CASREPS (Casualty Reports) would be conducted in ECCPs (Equipment Casualty Clearing Points).
>
> ... We crossed the breach on 22 Mar 2003 with Sgt Breen's Foden being the first B Vehicle into Iraq and Fwd 7 established an ECCP at Safwan. We were on radio silence so I was able to listen to the Six Nations England versus Scotland match on my long wave radio – another fine victory. We bypassed Safwan and established another

ECCP at the Coy location within the BSG (Brigade Support Group) where we were supposed to be for 24 hours, but in fact remained for eight days. Our mobile hard standing, Class 70 trackway proved invaluable for conducting heavy B Vehicle repairs in the desert. We closed the Safwan ECCP and temporarily moved Fwd 7 to the BSG before moving them to Shaibah Airfield, maintaining two separate ECCPs at all times. It was in the first two days after crossing the breach that we were at our busiest, with 19 crews on CASREPS simultaneously. This was when the Power Pack/E&MA/LRU loop was fully utilised and proved to be most successful due to the excellent working relationship between ourselves and 11 GS Coy. This enabled the Power Pack repair to be prioritised in accordance with usage and future plans; as such only one vehicle ever waited for a power pack (this was a **BG CRAARV** so we loaned one until it was repaired).

When we eventually moved out we joined Fwd 7 in Shaibah Airfield, and sent Fwd 20 to establish another ECCP, again keeping two feet on the ground. … By now the war was hotting up and we sent various teams to support BG tasks. … As 7 Armd Bde waited outside Basra it was enthralling to watch the bombardment of Basra and Az Zubayr in the evening, thankful we were not on the receiving end. The plan to enter Basra involved a number of the Coy CRARRVs being detached to BGs with an ECCP by Bridge 3.

During March and April 2003 the company completed: 393 A Vehicle CASREPS, 254 LRU CASREPS, 118 Production Platoon tasks and 1,918 Tels tasks. I would like to pay tribute to all members of 7 CS Coy for their hard work, dedication and professionalism. This recognition is also deserving of the members of 11 GS Coy for without their tireless production 7 Armd Bde would not have remained in such a good state. I was particularly impressed with the quality of the REME Young Officers who demonstrated the confidence and ability to make military and engineering decisions – the future of our Corps is in good hands.

I am pleased to say that I managed to keep my promise to the Company, as all returned home from the war safely'.

Summing up, the Battalion CO's report concluded that his REME battalion organisation (at warfighting strength) worked exceptionally well. Many of its comments mirrored those in the report from 3 Battalion

THE INVASION OF IRAQ (OPERATION TELIC 1)

REME, but it also emphasised the need for REME second line units to have adequate scales of night vision equipment. It explained that the availability, and lack of visibility, of spares had been a major problem and sounded the cautionary note that:

> '… the skill level of REME tradesmen in 2 Battalion REME compensated for a lack of spare parts in all areas. Soldiers were able to repair by repair, using skills which would not be taught were the engineering content of training courses to be reduced'.

SECOND LINE SUPPORT – THE ROLE OF 7 AIR ASSAULT BATTALION REME

Basically, the Battalion had two roles. The first was to support deployed helicopters and, the second, was to provide second line support for 16 Air Assault Brigade's ground forces, which deployed with wheeled vehicles and light armour. As the roles are very different it is useful to look at them separately.

AVIATION SUPPORT – DEPLOYMENT

Divisional aviation assets comprised the Commando Helicopter Force (847 Naval Air Squadron with Lynx and 845 Naval Air Squadron with Sea King, both largely supported from HMS Ocean), Chinook and Puma squadrons from the Joint Helicopter Force (18 and 33 Squadrons RAF respectively), and the Lynx and Gazelle helicopters of 3 Regiment AAC, which were 7 Battalion REME's primary concern. Second line forward support for Army helicopters was provided by Forward Repair Teams (FRTs) of 71 CS Company. Further second line support was provided in a facility at the Ali Al Salem Air Base in Kuwait where 73 GS Company (from 7 Air Assault Battalion REME) was collocated with the Battalion's supply squadron, and RN and RAF technicians.

AVIATION SUPPORT – SUPPORT FOR OPERATIONS

ES for helicopters was a challenging area, due in a considerable degree to operating in a hot and sandy environment. At one point, the availability of 16 Air Assault Brigade's helicopters had dropped to 27%. Sterling work by REME got availability back to an acceptable level for operations. The key element in this was the capability of 7 Battalion REME's GS Company. The CO, Lieutenant Colonel Mark Armstrong REME, commented after the operation:

> 'One of the major successes of the Op has been the confirmation of the worth of a deployable GS Coy and its ability to integrate its attached RAF tradesmen … 73 GS Coy repaired and overhauled 85% of repairable Lynx Composite Main Rotor Blades. Had they not done so then the availability of Lynx would have been severely hampered'.

SUPPORT FOR GROUND UNITS

Support arrangements for ground units were put under a lot of pressure but worked very well. The CO commented shortly after the operation:

> 'On OP TELIC we were very busy at both first and second line as a result of the significant mileage covered and the effect of the demanding terrain and environment (over 60 E&MA were replaced in 8 weeks). Spares supply for both first and second line tasks was very poor. The VMs themselves performed extremely well and their training at every trade class level is clearly well focused. Shortage of spares meant that 'adapt, improvise and overcome' was very much the order of the day and this was only achievable by a thorough understanding of basic engineering principles.
> … This brings me back to my main Op TELIC theme 'the need to maintain second line GS capability'. CS speaks for itself, Smart Procurement, CLS, Direct Delivery etc may all look to be cheaper, however contractors have been conspicuous by their absence. There are no 'specialist dealers' in the Maysan Province and the supply chain from the UK did not cope with the demand. Without deployed GS, 16 Air Asslt Bde would have lost a significant amount of warfighting capability'. (**See Plate 6**)

REME AT FIRST LINE

With REME personnel spread around every Army unit deployed on the operation it is obviously not possible to describe in detail what happened to every REME first line unit. The following accounts by REME soldiers with D Squadron Household Cavalry Regiment have been extracted to give a feel for what happened.

This account was written by Sergeant John Bradley in an article in The Craftsman magazine (November 2003):

> 'Gav Shaw was there to meet us and we proceeded to Camp Eagle 1 built by the Americans. The next few weeks were madness. We were constantly training, the most important training being navigation as the desert was featureless. We also did NBC training which at the time was thought to be our biggest threat. During this period, Capt Carney managed to get our comfort boxes to us and set up welfare phones so we could phone home, which was important. A completely new experience to us was loading up our CVR(T)s with as many rations and ammo as possible, not knowing how long we would be in action.
>
> Now it was just a matter of waiting. Two or three days before we moved into Iraq we were told to sanitise our kit which meant burning all our personal letters and photos which was a difficult thing to do. We were also allowed one phone call home, which for the first time ever rendered my wife speechless!
>
> Twelve hours later we crossed the border. The first thing we came across was a UN compound that had been evacuated a few days earlier. We then moved to our first location which was one of the GOSPs (Gas Oil Separation Plants) where the squadron completed its first task of the war by making it secure. From this point we continued north for three or four days.
>
> The squadron then leaguered up, and the faults kept flooding in thick and fast, we worked through the nights to complete them. At this stage there seemed to be a hitch in the big plan as we stayed in this position for two days longer than we expected.
>
> We continued north to the Rumaylah oilfields which was a key objective for the Squadron. At this stage, things kicked off and we watched tracer and missiles being fired in all directions. We had little sleep and time seemed to pass quickly as so much happened in such a short space of time. During this period of time three members of the Squadron were killed, we had no time to grieve, but were still shocked by their loss.
>
> The Squadron performed above and beyond what was expected by the brigade and I was proud to be part of it. The war was an

experience I will never forget, and one I hope no one else has to go through'.

A second account written by Lance Sergeant Vinny Morelli:

'On 15 Feb 2003 D Sqn arrived in Kuwait at Camp Eagle 1. The vehicles arrived, were MSF'd, painted then straight onto Udairi ranges for further training/exercises, and, on our daily briefings the words 'Northern Option' were repeated at least seventy times a day. The LAD knuckled down to it as the squadron hammered the vehicles, managing to use two years' worth of track mileage in ten days!

… On the night of 21 Mar 2003 the Squadron entered Iraq. 'A night in hell' is how some people described it, surrounded by burning oil heads gas pipes and US Marine Corps troops. D Sqn's task was to provide relief in place for the USMC so they could be freed to push on further NW. We would then hand over to 1 R IRISH, freeing us up for taskings further north if required.

As the LAD moved north to marry up with the remainder of SHQ the OC almost inadvertently ended our whole campaign by taking us into a minefield. Luckily we managed to safely extract and as we were about to move off, several Iraqis emerged from previously unseen positions. The fitter section, less Sgt 'top cover' Bradley, debussed and rounded up the prisoners until they could be taken to the PW camp. There was a myriad of bunkers in the area, all of which had to be cleared. Once this was accomplished the REME call signs quickly linked up with the rest of the squadron waiting further tasking.

All tradesmen excelled, mainly through necessity as spares were still non-existent. The Squadron were all battleworthy less one Scimitar, as we seemed to bounce from one drama to another, employing only the best BDR (Battle Damage Repair) techniques. All of a sudden the Northern Option was back on, so north we went. Still no spares, so C/S 13 became a (not so) mobile spares pack with no system remaining unscathed. During the period 24 Mar to 2 Apr the squadron was in constant contact with the enemy who used vehicles ranging from MBT (T55) to arty spotters using Isuzu pick-ups and motorbikes. The area in which we were now operating was a series of levees and water filled relief ditches and some of the Squadron managed to find themselves in them at irregular intervals, so the Samson (CVR(T) recovery variant) was used several times. Most of the recovery tasks would take place after a few hours digging as the Samson was found not to be really man enough for the job in the terrain we were operating in. On 2 April the decision was taken to pull back to 8 CS Wksp's location at area 'Manchester' some 35km to the south for 36 hours of rest and essential maintenance, assisted gratefully by the tradesmen at that location.

The time soon passed and we headed back north again. Operations with 1 PARA and 1 R IRISH passed quickly and we swiftly married up with the QDG north of Basra, tying up the whole area under British control. The Iraqis had deserted their posts in numbers, so there was no enemy to fight. We spent the next four days in an abandoned school near Al Qurnah in Medina listening to a constant cry of 'Mister, Mister, water, water'. The squadron was then tasked to lead the brigade 100km north to Al Amarah, this was to be our home until returning to the UK. Finally, the RLC produced some results by way of 20 pallets of track. This enabled the squadron to carry out its next task; Iran/Iraq border overwatch and oil head protections. The fitter section has been kept constantly busy supporting this and various range packages.

We all returned in June. A challenging time was had by everyone of the fitter section, a lot of weight had been lost, but no doubt most will be regained in the bars around the UK on return'.

THE REME TA PERSPECTIVE

REME TA had first earned its spurs during the Gulf War of 1991, and was well represented on Operation TELIC 1. In his book 'Weekend Warrior – A Territorial Soldier's War in Iraq', Corporal Kevin Marven gives an unvarnished and amusing account of his experience as a Recovery Mechanic in the thick of things. He had his first excitement before the war actually started.

Having been sent to recover a CVR(T) in a Foden recovery vehicle, he and his crewman realised that they had strayed across a badly marked part of the border and were over 1km into Iraq in an area of soft sand, which made progress difficult. An Iraqi military vehicle followed them,

Foden recovery vehicle (without the protection kit later fitted) recovering Land Rover

closed up to around 400m from them before a soldier with an RPG dismounted, and took aim at them. Corporal Marven debussed and, after a brief discussion with his crewman on their relative scores on the rifle range, came up with a plan. There were five Iraqis and he lined up his rifle sights on the one with the RPG, and his crewman (Stuart) then said:

> 'Should we wait until they fire the first shot? Otherwise we would be responsible for starting the war. And do you realise that, by rights, they're not the enemy, not yet, anyway. Rules of engagement and all that' … a discussion ensued on which Corporal Marven commented … 'also I couldn't believe we were having an argument as we faced our first actual life-or-death situation.… This wasn't how I thought I would react to my first fire-fight – arguing over grouping scores and the politics of our position while desperately trying to think of a diplomatic solution to our crisis'.

Fortunately, the Iraqis drove away and the Foden recovery vehicle was able to get back into Kuwait and pick up its casualty and head back for his base. That was not the end of his problems for the day, as once it was dark he found himself passing some apparently derelict Iraqi armoured vehicles. There was suddenly a massive explosion nearby. In due course, the crew of the CVR(T) he had in tow managed to contact him and say that they had been in touch with their unit who told them that they were in the middle of an American artillery range, not shown on Corporal Marven's map.

THE INVASION OF IRAQ (OPERATION TELIC 1)

Corporal Marven carried out numerous recovery tasks over the next couple of weeks, being under fire and returning fire on several occasions. Some of his tales reflect the sometimes bizarre reality of war. He says (when there was apparently an attempt to attack his location):

> 'My attention was drawn to the alleyway to my right. Of course, I thought, the road at the end of the alleyway. They must be heading towards the road that ran parallel with the back of the bus station. Sure enough the vehicles passed the other end of the alleyway. The exit was narrow but I managed to catch a fleeting glimpse of a municipal refuse truck with automatic fire coming out of the back. A few seconds later a Challenger 2 rumbled past in hot pursuit of the truck. I couldn't believe what I was seeing; they were firing at the Challenger with automatic rifles. If they were lucky they might have scratched the paintwork.
>
> … A report of a shell leaving the barrel of the Challenger, quickly followed by an explosion, soon filled the air, creating a fireball which rose above the north of our location. A few seconds later bits of refuse truck came raining down on the bus station'.

Corporal Marven's escapades are entertainingly related, but the underlying reality that comes across is that, as a REME TA soldier, he was doing a very difficult and extremely dangerous job in an unarmoured recovery vehicle, travelling extensively in territory still alive with Fedayeen and other hostile armed elements.

OPERATIONAL HONOURS

As an organisation REME is not much given to blowing its own trumpet, so it is always nice when its efforts are recognised by others. The following three abridged citations from The Craftsman magazine (December 2003) indicate how REME's contribution is seen by our 'customers', as well as painting a picture of some of the more dangerous moments for REME at first line.

Corporal Craig Comber – Military Cross

> 'Corporal Comber was the Recovery Mechanic in C Squadron, the Queen's Royal Lancers, part of the First Fusiliers Battlegroup for

Operation Telic. C Squadron was in contact with the enemy from 21 March to 6 April 2003 before the final attack into Basra. During this period Corporal Comber selflessly and repeatedly put himself in danger to assist others. On 22 March the Squadron moved north towards Basra. One of the Squadron's Challenger 2 tanks struck a mine en route and was disabled. The minefield was unmarked and had been placed around a culvert on a main supply route for forces moving north into Iraq. Acting quickly and realising the danger, Corporal Comber attempted to recover the tank and bring the crew to safety outside the minefield which he did once Royal Engineers had cleared a route through the minefield.

On 24 March, 3rd Troop from C Squadron was attached to Z Company to maintain the block on the southern road bridge over the waterway onto the main route into Basra. The assault aimed to expand the bridgehead and remove the enemy. As the attack began, one of the Challenger 2 tanks had a mechanical failure and became the focus for sustained direct and indirect enemy fire. Corporal Comber immediately and of his own volition, took his recovery vehicle forward and under fire recovered the stricken tank. Undoubtedly this action saved the crew and tank from further exposure and danger. On 4 April, Comber once again fearlessly recovered a tank that had been immobilised by a mine strike in an unmarked minefield. However, Corporal Comber reacted immediately and with such calmness that his crew was swiftly able to recover the vehicle to safety.

On 6 April, the Squadron advanced into Basra, the route was mined with plastic anti-tank mines which were initially engaged by main armament and machine gun fire from a tank. Engineer assets were not with the Squadron for this attack and momentum had to be maintained, so Corporal Comber was tasked to plough a route through a minefield. This is a particularly dangerous task for an armoured recovery vehicle. Without hesitation, Corporal Comber moved forward and cleared the route through the mines. Momentum was re-established and the Battlegroup were able to continue their advance, ultimately resulting in the capture of Northern Basra.

All of these acts displayed continued and sustained courage by Corporal Comber. He without doubt saved lives and key equipment for future operations. This was all done in a recovery vehicle armed only with a machine gun for close protection'.

Corporal James Garrett – Mention in Despatches

'Between 27 March and 4 April 2003, C Squadron the Royal Scots Dragoon Guards was attached to 40 Commando Royal Marines. Corporal Garrett was employed throughout as the commander of the Squadron's organic Challenger Armoured Repair and Recovery Vehicle (CRAARV).

On 30 March 2003, 2nd Troop C Squadron was providing intimate support to a Royal Marines Company clearance operation West of Abu Al Khasib. At approximately 1400hrs its point tank became decisively engaged by the enemy armed with Rocket Propelled Grenades, machine guns and mortars. As a result, the tank became disabled to the side of a narrow causeway and attracted concentrated fire. Another CRAARV was initially tasked to recover the stricken tank and did so successfully before its winch became inoperable. Corporal Garrett, in command of the Squadron CRAARV, was tasked to complete the recovery. In near total darkness, enemy action and confusion of the situation the tank again became stuck, in an even more difficult position.

For the next six hours, Garrett's CRAARV struggled to complete the recovery. Throughout Corporal Garrett remained in command of the CRAARV, providing close protection to the recovery mechanic on the ground with machine gun fire from his turret. This was at considerable and sustained risk to himself, for it involved exposure from the waist up out of the turret whilst the enemy mounted numerous attacks until recovery was effected.

Corporal Garrett's calmness under pressure during his coordination of the recovery operation, as well as provision of close protection, was fundamental in ensuring the successful recovery of the tank. He acquitted himself with complete disregard for his own safety and provided a reassuring presence to the recovery team on the ground. His concern for the safety of his colleagues and the successful completion of the mission was uppermost in his mind at all times. His bravery was evident to all, as corroborated by the Commanding Officer 40 Commando Royal Marines, and his professionalism a credit to his Corps and the Service'.

Corporal Justin Simons – Mention in Despatches

'Between 27 March and 4 April 2003, C Squadron the Royal Scots Dragoon Guards was attached to 40 Commando Royal Marines on the Al Faw Peninsular and for the entire period Corporal Simons was employed as the Squadron's recovery mechanic. At dusk on 29 March 2003 the Squadron was committed on Operation JAMES, a 40 Commando clearance operation in the area of Abu Al Khasib to the South East of Basra.

During the late afternoon of 30 March 2003, during a Coy/Tp clearance operation a C Squadron Challenger 2 tank became decisively engaged and disabled to the side of a narrow causeway in close country. The vehicle was being actively targeted but recovery was successfully achieved by an attached CRAARV, however this vehicle became inoperable and Corporal Simons was tasked to complete the recovery. As darkness fell, and under continued attacks by the enemy from Rocket Propelled Grenades, small arms and mortar fire, Corporal Simons took charge of the recovery situation. Due to the poor light, enemy action and confusing situation the tank again became stranded in an even more difficult position from which to recover it. For the next six hours Corporal Simons struggled to break both the tracks conventionally before resorting to arc welding equipment, which was an incredibly brave decision as the light given off certainly attracted the enemy's furious attention. Unfortunately, this did not work, and Corporal Simons decided to try the unorthodox by organising a CRAARV on CRAARV recovery in an attempt to drag the tank back to safety. This audacious and intelligent move was successful, and some nine hours after the tank was initially disabled it was dragged back to friendly lines.

Through his devotion to duty, at considerable risk to himself and his crew, Corporal Simons that night ensured the recovery of a badly damaged tank, the destruction or capture of which would have had far-reaching consequences for C Sqn and 7 Armd Bde. During this action, Corporal Simons showed no regard for his own safety and was totally focused on the task in hand. His leadership, calm decision-making under enemy fire and intelligent use of unorthodox methods proved an inspiration to all. His actions were in the finest traditions of his Service and Corps'.

A painting of this incident, titled 'Thrown Tracks', was unveiled in the Corps Sergeants' Mess as reported in The Craftsman magazine (November 2007). (**See Plate 7**)

THE VIEW FROM HQ 1 (UK) ARMOURED DIVISION

The REME officer responsible for managing the REME effort in theatre was Colonel John Rouse (late REME), the Commander ES of 1 (UK) Armoured Division. Shortly after the operation, he wrote the following in the REME Journal (Winter 2003):

> 'At each level of command there will be key ES lessons learned which need to be recorded and taken forward, with action where necessary. Indeed, there are so many lessons that it would be impossible to list them all in one document.
>
> In therefore trying to identify key lessons, I have had a great deal of difficulty – every lesson is key to somebody somewhere. Therefore, I have selected, at my level, general lessons which, if actioned or respected (as appropriate) will make future operations more effective from an ES point of view. They are listed in no particular order of priority.
>
> There is a need for better visibility of spares availability both in depots and in transit. Moribund, unreliable and sometimes non-existent information systems made it difficult to identify whether spares were available and if they were, where they were held or where they were in the supply chain. Much effort was expended in searching for spares that had been lost in the system and there was wasteful re-demanding of spares that had already been issued and lost.
>
> **The training of our soldiers and ES staff is correct.** During periods of spares paucity our tradesmen were required to improvise. This involved such activities as repair by repair, compromising accepted standards of engineering integrity and hygiene, safety and performance. That these compromises were always effective and achieved with good military and engineering judgement is testament to a sound and robust training system that gives our REME tradesmen excellent theoretical engineering training (on the various trade courses) and sound engineering practice in the training required of the Formation Readiness Cycle. Reduction of any of this training

will remove the key tool that is in the REME toolbox – that of the engineering ability and professionalism of our soldiers.

ES doctrine and structures work. Many untried structures (such as the war fighting ES Battalion structure) and new doctrine (such as ES to the JFLogC) was tried and tested on this operation along with some more traditional aspects of ES operations and all were proved to be effective, robust and able to deliver what was required.

REME equipment is good but needs modification to suit the operation. Generally, REME repair equipment did what it was designed for. However, in order to respect the moral component, REME must insist that REME variants of equipment get the same modifications as the main equipment type. On this operation, Challenger 2, Warrior and CVR(T) were all up armoured, but none of the REME variants were. If our soldiers take the same risks, then they deserve the same protection.

There is a need for a dormant enabling contract. One of the continual frustrations was the difficulty in setting up contracts for repairs or facilities not available through the military chain. This included such areas as windscreen manufacture, tyre changing, radiator repair, hose manufacture, motor and generator rewinding, FIP repair etc. This was not helped by a contracts process, run by experts in contracts but not engineering, that is so scrupulously fair and protected against abuse as to be totally unresponsive to the needs of the military. We need a permanent contractor, along the lines of the US Brown & Root organisation, to be available that, with an enabling contract, can produce all of the standard contract items, anywhere in the world, either for exercise or operation'.

SUMMARY

Notwithstanding the problems that arose later, the invasion of Iraq must get a big tick in the box for the British Army as a whole, and a very big tick in the box for REME. A large expeditionary force capable of high-intensity warfare had been deployed at exceptionally short notice. It did everything that it was required to do rapidly, and operational availability of the force's equipment was excellent throughout.

Period in 2003	13 February to 18 March	19 March to 30 April
Number of vehicles and equipments reported on	7804	8513
Overall average availability	94.28%	90%
A Vehicles overall	91.8% (1108 vehicles)	84% (1149 vehicles)
of which Challenger 2	99%	95%
Artillery overall	96.5% (341 equipments)	97.5% (400 equipments)
of which AS90	88%	95%
Helicopters	79% (62 aircraft)	63% (78 aircraft)
GS Vehicles	94.1% (4894 vehicles)	91% (5340 vehicles)
General vehicles	92% (887 vehicles)	97.2% (974 vehicles)
Engineer equipments	84.2% (311 equipments)	86.4% (359)
Commando equipments	87.4% (151 vehicles)	95.4% (154 vehicles)
Box body vehicles	100% (50)	96.4% (50)

Figure 8.1: Operational availability

CHAPTER 9

IRAQ – AFTERMATH OF THE INVASION (OPERATIONS TELIC 2–13)

This Chapter covers events in Iraq from the withdrawal of most of the original invasion force and the arrival of new units in July 2003, on Operation TELIC 2, through successive roulement tours, until UK operations ceased on 31 July 2009 when Operation TELIC 13 merged into Operation BROCKDALE (the drawdown from Iraq). In order to understand what happened to the UK force during six years of operations, it is important to have an overview of what happened in Iraq as a whole.

OVERVIEW OF EVENTS IN IRAQ 2003–2009

Phases 1–3 of the invasion of Iraq had been planned in detail and, overall, had worked out very well indeed. Lead responsibility for Phase 4, which was essentially 'getting Iraq on its feet again', remained with the US Department of Defense. It had not been planned in any depth for a number of reasons. First, the USA President (George W Bush) and Secretary of Defense (Donald Rumsfeld) were not keen in principle on the idea of lengthy peace support or nation-building operations. They were, naturally, still deeply affected by the events of '9/11' and were prepared to use overwhelming military force to create 'shock and awe', with a view to deterring further attacks on the USA and its vital interests.

Secretary of Defense Rumsfeld had insisted, against professional military advice, that fewer troops would be needed to stabilise Iraq than to invade it. He hoped that the US involvement would be as short as possible, and that once Al Qaeda had been rooted out, and weapons of mass destruction (WMD) disposed of, he was keen to disengage US forces as quickly as possible, and to call in help from the international community, including the UN, to facilitate the peace support operations. In short, the result was that much of the plan for Phase 4 had not been worked out in any detail. It was assumed that once Phases 1–3 had succeeded, the plan for Phase 4 could be worked out in detail in the light of the situation on the ground.

Initially, there were grounds for optimism. The world saw pictures of cheering crowds toppling a statue of Saddam Hussein. His regime was unpopular and, although not all Iraqis were happy to have their country invaded by foreign troops, there was initially a fair reservoir of goodwill for the Coalition forces who had freed the land from the grip of a brutal dictator. Countries that had been conspicuously unwilling to join in the invasion of Iraq were prepared to provide troops to help stabilise the country.

The UK, whose armed forces had a highly successful track record in peacekeeping and low-intensity operations, was given responsibility for the South Zone, and provided a divisional headquarters to run a multinational division. This was called the Multinational Division (South East) (MND(SE)) and soon included an Italian brigade and a Dutch battlegroup.

Much of the population in southern Iraq was Shiite, had been ruthlessly repressed by Saddam Hussein, and might be expected to be particularly grateful for his removal. From the UK point of view, it was not unreasonable to assume at the time that its area of responsibility would gradually quieten down and become a peacekeeping operation similar to that in Kosovo, before responsibility was gracefully handed over to a new Iraqi regime. That this did not happen was due to factors outside the British Army's control.

The warning signs that things would not be as easy as expected began to emerge early on. The first shock to the Coalition forces was the poor state of the infrastructure. In many cases, decay to the infrastructure that had been assumed to be the result of Coalition air attacks proved to be due to simple neglect, or lack of investment. The country was also awash with arms and munitions. Saddam Hussein had set up numerous large decentralised stocks of weapons intended to arm militia forces in the event of an invasion. Initially, the US forces were only interested in finding WMD and failed to secure, or put out of use, weapon dumps that contained no WMD.

Immediately after the invasion, security broke down in many areas, with widespread looting in Baghdad and elsewhere. The US forces had been configured for a warfighting operation. Their training and doctrine had not prepared them well for a rapid change to a peacekeeping operation. Their early response to the deteriorating security situation was to take no chances, with some units gaining an unfortunate reputation for being 'trigger happy'. They tended to patrol in heavily armed vehicles, often

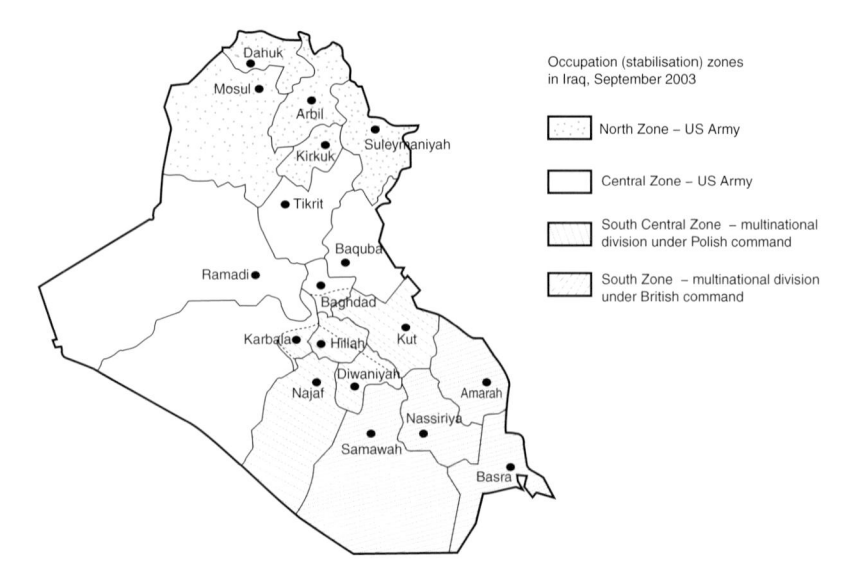

Map showing occupation zones in Iraq in September 2003

pointing weapons at the local population, without realising the impact this had. This approach, combined with a failure to control the security situation or deliver improvements to the infrastructure, led to the steady draining of the reservoir of goodwill.

The essentially tribal nature of Iraq, linked with religious affiliations and lack of experience of democracy, posed a fundamental political problem. The Baathist regime, that had ruled Iraq for several decades, was theoretically secular, but in practice it provided the vehicle whereby a Sunni minority was able to dominate a Shiite majority. Ethnic, tribal and religious influences were also strong. Many of the Kurds in northern Iraq aspired to independence as part of a Kurdish state. The Shiites, perhaps understandably, were less interested at that time in making a fair and generous accommodation with their former Sunni overlords than in settling old scores and ensuring that they had full control of the levers of power. The Shiites were, anyway, far from being a homogeneous grouping. One of their firebrand clerics, Muqtada al-Sadr, began recruiting a large militia with a fundamentalist Islamic agenda.

The US administration in Washington was slow to appreciate what was happening. Publicly throughout 2003, they were talking in terms of dealing with 'terrorists' and regime 'dead enders'. When Saddam Hussein was captured in December 2003 there was much optimism that troubles in Iraq would soon be at an end.

In fact, by the summer of 2003 Iraq was on the brink of an insurrection, and soon the newly-formed Coalition Provisional Authority (CPA) had a far bigger security problem on its hands than it had foreseen. The first person put in charge of the CPA had been retired US officer, Lieutenant General Jay Garner. He did not last long in the post before being replaced by Paul Bremer, a former US diplomat in whom Secretary of Defense Rumsfeld had confidence. One of Paul Bremer's early decisions was to disband the Iraqi Army and embark on a radical de-Baathification policy (despite being advised by the UK, the US military and others of the dangers involved). This effectively decapitated the police and much of the administration. It also had the effect of sacking around a half a million public servants, many with badly needed skills, and sending them home humiliated, without any income, many taking weapons and military skills with them. This move had hit the Sunni community disproportionately, and it was not long before serious trouble started in the 'Sunni triangle' near Baghdad. The US administration's lack of 'boots on the ground' now came back to plague it. It lacked the forces to seal off Iraq effectively, particularly the borders with Syria (a Sunni state) and with Iran (a Shiite state). This was important, as Iraq had become a magnet for Al Qaeda and others whose Islamic views persuaded them that they should fight against 'The Great Satan'.

By early-2004, the extent of Iraq's security problems had become manifest. US forces fought the first battle of Fallujah in March 2004, without the aid of a newly-trained Iraqi battalion that refused to fight and simply melted away. The second battle of Fallujah was in September 2004. All but an estimated 400 of the town's 250,000 occupants had fled as a force of 10,000 US troops and 2,000 Iraqi forces fought a bitter and prolonged house-to-house battle with local Sunni insurgents as well as Al Qaeda and other foreign fighters.

Trouble was not restricted to the Sunni areas. There was a general breakdown of security in much of Baghdad and elsewhere, with car bombings, suicide bombings, and various Sunni and Shia militias. Death squads operating against each other and the US forces stirred up sectarian strife. The dire security situation hamstrung attempts at reconstruction, with US officials increasingly being isolated within the high security 'Green Zone' in Baghdad. The UN withdrew from Iraq after losing many staff in a devastating bomb attack on its headquarters. Many of the nations who had contributed troops for the stabilisation of Iraq began to set about withdrawing them.

The CPA also had difficulty forming an Iraqi Government and, eventually, following elections, a predominantly Shiite Interim Iraqi Government was formed under Ayad Allawi at the end of June 2004. By no means all Shiites approved of the Government and, shortly after the Government was formed, Muqtada al-Sadr called his Mahdi militia to arms.

Meanwhile, although the British sector had been spared the sort of sectarian carnage that had happened in Baghdad, the security situation had been slowly deteriorating in that area despite efforts to train Iraqi security forces. When the Mahdi militia took up arms, it did so in the British areas as well as the north, and there was serious fighting both in Basra and Amarah (Maysan Province). The UK and US forces fought back strongly against the militias, who were persuaded to agree to a ceasefire. This lasted until the US/Iraqi forces decided to arrest Muqtada al-Sadr, who fled to the Imam Ali Mosque in Najaf. This was the holiest of Shiite places. Muqtada al-Sadr claimed that the US forces intended to destroy it and called for a jihad. Trouble erupted in the south again, and there was further serious fighting in both Basra and Amarah. The uprising ended when the Grand Ayatollah Ali al-Sistani, the Shiites most senior religious leader, sided with the Interim Government and brokered an end to active hostilities (the US and UK forces having taken a considerable toll of the Mahdi militia before this happened). Although the British Sector quietened down, thereafter it was clear that underlying conflict between the militias, the Interim Government and Coalition forces had by no means been resolved.

In the months that followed, security in the US Sector steadily deteriorated. News reports told a daily tale of attacks on convoys, suicide bombs, tit-for-tat killings and other horrors. The US forces were in no danger of losing any military battle, but they did not seem to be winning either, and it became clear that US public opinion would not accept the high US casualty rate indefinitely. By mid-2006, the extent of the problem had become clear to President Bush, who was faced with some tough choices. The option he eventually selected was recommended by Lieutenant General David Petraeus, who advised that the combination of a 'surge' of additional forces, and a change of tactics might turn around the situation. Lieutenant General Petraeus had proved his ability in Iraq when in command of 101 Airborne Division, and had been the only US divisional commander who managed to get his operational area under control in the period after the invasion.

The 'surge' option involved putting a further 28,000 troops into Iraq to bolster the 140,000 already there, increasing the US strength from 15 to 20 combat brigades. As predicted, casualties initially got worse as the 'surge' took place but the combination of additional forces and new tactics achieved the desired results. The security situation improved, and US casualties started to fall dramatically as shown in Figure 9.1 (at the end of this Chapter).

Whilst the US was applying its 'lessons learned' and benefiting from the 'surge', the UK was in no position to match the US increase in resources. It had fairly quickly cut its forces from divisional to brigade group size after the invasion and, by 2006, had only some 5,500 troops in theatre. Rival militias and criminal gangs controlled many parts of Basra and the surrounding area. The new police force proved a disappointment, with many of its members owing loyalty to the competing local warlords. UK forces patrolling of Basra became counterproductive, as it caused resentment by attracting attacks (including mortar fire), which alienated the locals without being able to neutralise the troublemakers. In September 2007, the UK withdrew from its bases in Basra. It concentrated its forces on a Contingency Operating Base (COB) at Basra International Airport. This allowed it an 'overwatch' capability to intervene if it had to, and the UK continued to train and mentor Iraqi security forces. Its operational activity from this point proved to be largely confined to local protection.

By early-2008, the 'surge' had succeeded in the north of the country and the Iraqi Government decided that the time had come to get Basra back firmly under control. They launched Operation 'Charge of the Knights' on 28 March 2008 deploying the Iraqi 1st Division and 14th Division with US and UK support in a deliberate attack on the criminal militia strongholds. This had the desired effect and security in Basra improved dramatically. This paved the way for the UK forces to withdraw from Iraq in July 2008.

REME SUPPORT FOR UK OPERATIONS – DEVELOPMENTS AFTER THE INVASION

Operations were overseen by HQ MND(SE) based at Basra Airport. This was initially very much a UK organisation (1 (UK) Armoured Division setting it up and 3 (UK) Division taking over from them), but fairly soon it became genuinely multinational. Two of the provinces it covered remained controlled by the British (Basra and Al Amarah), and two were taken over by the Dutch (Al Muthanna) and Italians (Dhi Qar) respectively. For Operation TELIC 2, the main UK manoeuvre force was 19 Mechanised Brigade. The Brigade order of battle comprised: the Queen's Lancashire Regiment (1 QLR), the King's Own Scottish Borderers (1 KOSB), the King's Regiment (1 KINGS), the Light Infantry (2 LI), the Royal Green Jackets (1 RGJ), elements of the Queen's Royal Lancers (QRL), the Light Dragoons (LD) and the Royal Tank Regiment (2 RTR), 40 Regiment RA and 38 Engineer Regiment. This Brigade had to cover both UK provinces comprising an area the size of Northern Ireland with a population of approximately two million. There was also a UK National Support Element (UK NSE) consisting of a miscellany of support units ranging from a large logistic regiment to a 15-strong working dog unit. The UK NSE provided second and third line support for the UK force from the

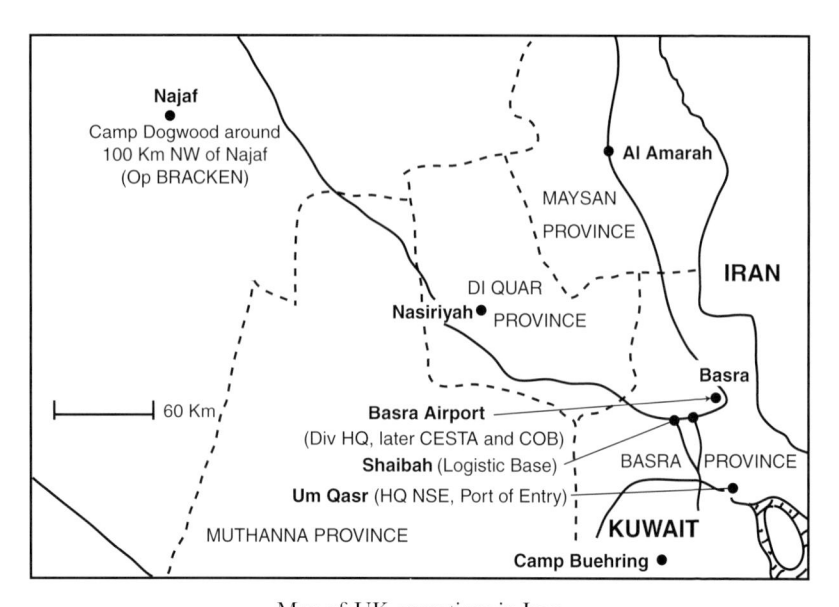

Map of UK operations in Iraq

theatre entry point to the battlegroups. HQ UK NSE was formed from a reinforced HQ 102 Logistic Brigade and was based in the port of Um Qasr. During the summer of 2003, Commander UK NSE was reduced from a one-star appointment held by Brigadier (later Major General) Ian Dale (late REME) to an OF5 (Colonel level) appointment initially filled by a RAF Group Captain.

The two REME battalions that conducted the manoeuvre campaign on Operation TELIC 1 (2 Battalion REME in the divisional support role and 3 Battalion REME in the force support role) were replaced at the start of Operation TELIC 2 by a single REME battalion, 5 Battalion REME, commanded by Lieutenant Colonel John Power REME. The Battalion was based in a tented camp in Shaibah Logistic Base (SLB), previously a disused and derelict World War 2 RAF air station. As 5 Battalion REME was a 'cadreised' battalion, it deployed with a sizeable REME TA contingent employed as individual reinforcements. The Battalion's technical facilities in SLB were based in and around a large derelict World War 2 RAF aircraft hangar which, at least, provided some shelter from the burning sun. About two months into Operation TELIC 2, the REME second line presence was reduced again to a composite ES Company drawn from 15 CS Company and 6 GS Company. Detachments of the ES Company were deployed forward to Al Amarah and Um Qasr. OC 15 CS Company, Major Mike Pendlington REME, stepped up on promotion to be Commander ES for the theatre, based with HQ UK NSE.

Old aircraft hangar in Shaibah Logistic Base

As things moved from a war of manouevre to a peacekeeping/ counterinsurgency situation the pattern of deployment and operations changed. The manoeuvre brigade was split up and deployed to bases from which they operated, and logistic units in Basra were eventually largely collocated at SLB. In this situation, it made sense to 'mix and match' first and second line REME units to produce optimum working solutions on the ground. As REME is a pragmatic and flexible organisation, this solution worked very well. In later roulement tours, the second line REME Company was always based on a CS or GS company in a REME battalion, but it deployed with a bespoke organisation tailored to its deployment role. In due course, it was decided that the REME Company should operate as a sub-unit of the Theatre Logistic Regiment (combining with the Regiment's LAD). Second line resources provided elements to bolster support at first line where necessary, and were often referred to as Intimate Support Teams (IST). Whilst the terminology was new, the concept of pragmatically moving resources between first and second line was as old as REME itself. Senior members of the Corps played a key role in making this work. (**See Plate 8**)

The 'honeymoon' period lasted for about six weeks after the end of the warfighting campaign and the support of the local people began to diminish, primarily due to lack of progress by the CPA in delivering improvements to the lives of the local people. It was soon clear that the local populace did not want the presence of Coalition security forces in Iraq and attacks by local Shia militias multiplied in the two UK-controlled provinces.

Particularly noteworthy in the attacks on Coalition forces was the increasing use of remotely-operated roadside improvised explosive devices (IED). The problem with the UK military equipment deployed to Iraq was that it was based on warfighting in a linear battle; that is, with armour at the front and 'soft-skinned' vehicles following behind. In 2003, the British Army was not equipped for fighting a counterinsurgency involving asymmetric warfare. In a scramble to provide better protection, the only Urgent Operational Requirement (UOR) Protected Mobility (PM) vehicle available was the Snatch Land Rover, designed for crowd control in Belfast. These were quickly fitted with Clansman tactical radio by a REME team and shipped to Iraq towards the end of Operation TELIC 2.

The use of sophisticated remotely-initiated devices pointed to outside technical assistance and training (likely Iran) and the technical development of these devices was breathtaking and faster than anything experienced in Northern Ireland, all of which came as a shock to Coalition commanders. From its lengthy security operation in Northern Ireland, the British Army had the most experience of all Coalition forces in electronic counter measures (ECM) used to counter the IED threat. At the beginning of Operation TELIC 3, in response to the deteriorating security situation and the increasing IED threat, British forces deployed a family of ECM devices called the Locksmith Suite. This was fitted to British military vehicles (initially Snatch Land Rovers) by a REME team. REME drew on its extensive experience of supporting ECM in Northern Ireland, from the Optronics Platoon based in Kinnegar, to provide in-theatre second line support for the Locksmith Suite.

UK operations were to continue in Iraq for a further five years with REME involved at both first and second line in most of what happened. It was felt that it was not sensible to try and compress a detailed account of everything that occurred into this single Chapter. The approach adopted has therefore been to provide a series of snapshots that draw heavily on the accounts of REME people present, and which are intended cumulatively to give the reader a clear picture of the way in which events unfolded and of the lessons learned.

REME SUPPORT FOR UK OPERATIONS – AL AMARAH AND MAYSAN PROVINCE

Maysan Province is a Shia province, which borders Iran. The provincial capital, Al Amarah, is located beside the River Tigris. It does not have a happy recent history. It suffered greatly during the Iran/Iraq War, and also after the Shia uprising, which followed the first Gulf War. It was the traditional home of the 'Marsh Arabs', who were a thorn in the side of Saddam Hussein, so he displaced many of them and drained some of their wetlands. It has a history of being a lawless province, with many tribes and factions (some aligned to Iran) having a long history of conflict with each other and with the Government.

It did not take long for it to be clear what a dangerous place it could be for Coalition forces. In June 2003, six military policemen were attacked and killed by a mob in a police station in Majar al-Kabir, the second city of Maysan, whilst a nearby patrol of paratroopers was being stoned.

The UK battlegroup in Maysan was based in Camp Abu Naji, a former military base outside Al Amarah, with a company group located in the Civil Military Cooperation (CIMIC) House (CIMIC – effectively the local UK HQ) in the centre of the town. The security situation changed dramatically for the worse in the summer of 2004 when the Mahdi militia tried to take over Al Amarah, and attacked the Princess of Wales's Royal Regiment (PWRR) Company located in the CIMIC House. A short ceasefire followed, which ended when the US forces threatened the arrest of Muqtada al-Sadr, after which all the Shiite militias joined to attack the British forces, and a serious attempt was made to overwhelm the PWRR Company in the CIMIC House. It was during this period that Private Beharry (1 PWRR) won his Victoria Cross.

The intensity of the fighting and the realities of the situation received little exposure in the UK and world media. This was because Al Amarah and Basra had become very dangerous places for reporters, and their inhabitants were well aware that full and frank criticism of the militias or criminal gangs could have fatal consequences. An idea of the intensity of the conflict from the records of the PWRR Company based in the CIMIC House, show that during a 23-day period there were 595 incoming mortar rounds, and 57 RPG (Rocket Propelled Grenade) attacks. The traffic was not all one-way and 1 PWRR inflicted heavy casualties on the attacking militia, who were arguably quite relieved when a second ceasefire was negotiated. Although the militias had been badly hurt, they had not been put out of business, and attacks on the British and Iraqi forces, as well as fighting between themselves, continued until the British forces finally withdrew.

Warrior vehicle and Challenger 2 tank in Al Amarah on Operation TELIC 4

4 Regiment RA LAD, part of which was attached to the Welsh Guards (WG) Battlegroup in Al Amarah, reported on their tour on Operation TELIC 5 in The Craftsman magazine (June 2005):

'Spares are supplied to us via the logistical chain using a long MSR (Main Supply Route) from Shaibah. This usually involves a company of Warriors and a squadron of CR2 tanks having to escort the convoy through some pretty hostile areas ('IED Alley'). Of course, when these are deployed the inevitable REME cover has to be supplied, which generally means 'spannering' during the day and swapping spanners for SA80s and GPMGs for the night time activities. The Rec Mechs are constantly on 30 minutes notice to move, the team headed by Sgt Chris Whittle. With one CRARRV, two Fodens, two WR512s and one WR513 and a Samson, the section has a wide array of assets at their disposal.

During the various tasks to date the crews have managed to be blown up, shot at and bricked, with an IED nearly removing Sgt Sapsford from the comfort of his cab. … The tour so far has not been as comfortable as at first expected. The facilities are poor compared to Shaibah. The water is regularly turned off and CBA and helmets are part of the daily routine due to the regular attacks on the camp by mortar, rocket and RPG from the locals (what a pleasant bunch!). The welfare facilities are slowly arriving. You get twenty minutes a week on the phones and there is an internet suite which is very busy. The LAD are now supporting in excess of 290 vehicles from such regiments as the RDG, 1 DWR, 1 WG and attachments from other units including SG, QDG, P Bty, 18 Phoenix Bty, 40 Cdo, ATO, EOD, Med Regt, RMP and the force handling team'.

The Royal Regiment of Wales (1 RRW) deployed a fitter section to Camp Abu Naji. **(See Plate 9)** As the following report explains, the work might have been hard, but was often professionally rewarding:

'The fitter section deployed to Camp Abu Naji at Al Amarah. This was in support of a full company of Warrior. It became apparent on arrival that the company's Warrior fleet was the least of the section's worries. Due to the massive amount of vehicles within the Battlegroup (Warrior, CR2, CVR(T), 432) the Fitter Section was

Burnt Snatch Land Rover recovered in Al Amarah on Operation TELIC 4

quickly amalgamated into a central pool of manpower. LCpl Penrose and Cfn Rodolfo were seconded to the recovery section, providing 24-hour assistance to patrols leaving the base. LCpl Sykes was swallowed up by the black hole that is the Armourers Repair Shop, while the remainder of the section worked from a central 'A' repair line.... Constant patrols and breakdowns within the Battlegroup meant that 24-hr crews were commonplace. Tradesmen quickly found themselves having to learn the 'ins and outs' of vehicles that up to now they had only seen driving past. Now they were expected to diagnose faults and repair them. Although the work was extremely hard, it was very rewarding. The time in Abu Naji passed quickly, and the tradesmen developed confidence and ability far in excess of what was expected in such a short time'.

Staff Sergeant Christopher Lyndhurst – Military Cross

Staff Sergeant Lyndhurst was awarded the Military Cross for his actions in Al Amarah. His citation (abridged) reads:

'SSgt Lyndhurst is employed as a Recovery Mechanic SNCO in the Light Aid Detachment serving with the Queen's Royal Hussars Battlegroup on Operation TELIC 8. At approximately 0215 hrs on 22 August the Battlegroup were recovering from an operation in Al

Amarah, Maysan Province when a Challenger 2 tank was struck by a rocket propelled grenade, left a raised earthen track and became stuck in a semi-dry lakebed. A Challenger Armoured Repair and Recovery Vehicle (CRARRV) was escorted to the site, under small arms and rocket propelled grenade fire, to drag the stricken vehicle clear. This vehicle also became stuck in the mud, and a second recovery vehicle commanded by SSgt Lyndhurst was deployed.

SSgt Lyndhurst immediately took charge of the situation as mortar bombs fell around him. Faced with the task of recovering two vehicles, he quickly organised the recovery of the first CRARRV before commencing the extraction of the Challenger. One of the Challenger crew had sustained minor wounds and was unable to assist, so SSgt Lyndhurst operated only with Sgt Logan, the commander of the first CRARRV. They worked in the open, exposed to enemy fire so great that the vehicles protecting them were forced to close down. Together they pulled the tank to firmer ground and then under accurate and inexorable sniper fire proceeded to prepare the vehicle for towing. Sprinting from the towing vehicle to the casualty vehicle, SSgt Lyndhurst discovered that both tracks had jammed against the hull, and after repeated attempts to split the tracks called for Ammunition Technical Officer assistance to cut them. Fire, now including rockets, small arms and mortars, was unrelenting, but did not deter him from crossing open ground in excess of twenty metres more than fifteen times in the course of his task. Bullets were observed striking the vehicles around him as he worked, and at one point he was blown completely off his feet into a bog by a mortar round which exploded less than five metres from him. He got up miraculously unhurt, and took cover under the tank, only to emerge in seconds to continue his task. When the Ammunition Technical Officer arrived he assisted him in placing charges and finally freed the vehicle. After eight hours of toil, during which the incoming fire never let up for more than two or three minutes at a time, SSgt Lyndhurst and Sgt Logan managed to extricate the tank and recover it to safety.

SSgt Lyndhurst showed outstanding leadership and repeated conspicuous gallantry in his efforts to extract both vehicles. He knew in particular that the loss of a Challenger 2 would have had a strategic impact and was willing to risk his life repeatedly and in full understanding of the danger, to ensure it was recovered. His actions were beyond the call of duty, and are hugely deserving of formal recognition. Without him a Challenger 2 would have been lost'.

REME SUPPORT FOR UK OPERATIONS – FALLUJAH/KARBALA AREA – OPERATION BRACKEN

Operation BRACKEN (27 October–4 December 2004) was a 'one-off', and represented the only significant combat outside Maysan and Basra Provinces. The background was that US forces had to throw additional forces into fighting at Fallujah, which left gaps elsewhere. The British Government decided to send a force to support them. This was the Black Watch (1 BW) BG, which was the Land Warfare Centre (LWC) resident unit based in Warminster and was designated as the MND(SE) Divisional Reserve, in addition to its normal training support role. It had to be mobilised at relatively short notice, and its REME support was provided by the LWC LAD. The plan was for a 30-day, largely unsupported, operation based on the US Camp Dogwood, which had previously earned the unhappy sobriquet 'Camp Incoming'.

1 BW BG LAD replace a turret ring in Camp Dogwood

The Battlegroup had a fairly torrid tour during which it lost five soldiers killed. Its story is perhaps best told by REME people who were there and was reported by the LWC LAD in The Craftsman magazine (July 2005):

'From Shaibah Logistics Base we moved to 40km southwest of Baghdad, an area that had seen no Coalition forces since the end of the invasion, and had seen its last Iraqi policeman murdered some five months before. A lawless area where once rich and powerful Baath Party faithful and senior Army commanders lived, now financed and housed highly trained former Republican Guards and foreign insurgents in their fight for control of the country. The presence of the insurgents did mean the people lived relatively unaffected by the chaos across the rest of the country. Camp Dogwood was in a former chemical factory with scars of bombed out buildings and the carnage of conflict very evident. Part of the 6km square area had been occupied by an American force for four days until they could remain no longer due to constant attack by indirect fire.

D Coy Fitter Section. We had been tasked with crossing the River Euphrates to the east in order to show a presence in an area that had not been patrolled by Coalition forces for the best part of 18 months. The great British press pack were up to their usual tricks of announcing our plans to the rest of the world, at least the lads didn't have to wait for me to come back from the O Group to find out what was going on! Within hours of crossing the river we had our first major job when an IED detonated directly under one of the Warriors throwing it into a ditch. Miraculously there were only a few minor injuries so we set about the recovery task.

All was going well until the local militia, who just happened to be led by some bloke called Al Zarqawi, decided to have a pop at us with RPGs and mortars – who said life in REME was dull! Luckily for us we again took only minor casualties and some nine hours later managed to recover the vehicle; even with its front three road stations missing.… Little did we know that it was at this point that the luck of the Company had finally run out.

The next day whilst recovering back to Dogwood the Company was hit by a suicide bomber resulting in three deaths and eight major casualties. The loss of life hit us hard, and it was at this point we knew that we had a fight on our hands. However, it didn't end there as just a few days later another IED detonated underneath one of the Warriors killing the driver instantly. The Section 512 was only some 30m behind when the device went off. Its commander, Jay Fordham, showed excellent composure under extreme pressure, taking control of the situation and managing to get the disabled vehicle back to Dogwood.

During the next three weeks our tactics were constantly changing in order to counter the enemy threat, which was far greater than we at first realised. We started to do more large-scale search ops involving the Battlegroup as a whole, which started to pay off instantly with a drop in the attacks.

'Final Thoughts' by WO1(ASM) Farley. The time in Dogwood was hectic with a considerable number of rocket attacks and incidents. The deployment was a very trying time and called for individuals at all levels to show resilience, leadership and courage in the face of the unknown. I feel privileged to have been part of a team that returned to basic engineering skills and showed resourcefulness and ingenuity, it is not every day that you are given the order to 'keep the kit on the road, whatever it takes'. After 19 years' service nothing had prepared me for the violence that was directed against us. Op BRACKEN will remain with all those who deployed but we must be thankful for one thing and that is we survived. Our thoughts are with the families of those who died and those who are now recovering from their injuries'.

REME Warrior vehicle on overwatch Operation BRACKEN

The LAD staff gained one Mention in Despatches and three Joint Commander's Commendations following this operation.

REME SUPPORT FOR UK OPERATIONS – MUTHANNA PROVINCE

By 2005, UK forces were back operating in Muthanna Province before control was handed back to the Iraqi Government in 2007. These two reports from The Craftsman magazine (December 2005) by the LAD of the Light Dragoons on Operation TELIC 6 suggest that their tour was entertaining as well as quite hard work.

Staff Sergeant Garson – Light Dragoons C Squadron Artificer:

'The Squadron has the enviable task of monitoring and mentoring the Iraqi Border Police as well as providing the level of training required in order to ensure effective control of the border. As a result, there is a need to provide long range desert patrols which are supported by members of the fitter section, typically distances of up to 1,000km and lasting up to 10 days. During these patrols the lads double up as members of the Troop on task, displaying the infinite flexibility of the REME soldier. Breakdown in the desert raised the question of how we go about recovery and how we were going to go about it, resulting in Land Rovers being underslung by Merlin helicopters on two occasions for the first time on Op TELIC. … The patrol matrix is hectic, but we all continue to work hard, and we manage to maintain high equipment availability'.

Second Lieutenant Gowlett REME, fresh from his REME Platoon Commanders' Course, was given command of an ad hoc troop comprising some Royal Engineers and Light Dragoons:

'Another of our roles is the slightly more glamorous sounding 'long range desert patrols'. These take the form of either training the Border Police or going on desert ops. The Border Police are seen as one of the main efforts of the Task Force, as they stand between the foreign fighters and Iraq. To this end, we are doing our best to train them and supply them with serviceable kit.

Whatever the tasking, one of the guaranteed after effects is my TUM (Land Rover) being in need of some repair. To date, I have had the turbo fixed twice, the engine replaced, four new shocks, about eight tyres, the rear shock welded on twice, new number one ball joint and many more. SSgt Garson and the C Squadron fitters recoil at the sight of the 'Death Wagon' whenever it returns from patrol.

When staying in the desert visibility is good for up to about 3km and there is normally little apparent risk. Or so you think until the friendly Bedouin tribesman from 2km away boldly strides into your lay-up and invites you round for dinner. Actions on are to eat as much as you can before going round and looking apologetically stuffed on arrival. It is however a great experience and the hubus (bread) is nice as long as you don't dip it in the hairy melted goats' butter'.

REME SUPPORT FOR UK OPERATIONS – BASRA PROVINCE

The majority of REME personnel were, of course, at first line, and what happened to them very much reflected what happened to the many and varied units to which they belonged. The British forces were trying to do two very difficult things simultaneously. First, to provide security and, second, to help build up local security forces that could progressively take over from Coalition forces and allow their withdrawal.

As well as the region being awash with arms, neighbouring Shiite Iran had no interest in seeing a prosperous and secure democracy on its doorstep, and was not unhappy at the growth of Shiite militias with criminal or political agendas. One of the major problems that emerged early on was the infiltration of the new security forces by those who owed primary loyalty to sectarian militia. When the Mahdi militia took to the streets in 2004, the police proved uncertain allies in the serious disturbances that followed.

OC 1 DWR LAD Captain White patrols Basra on Operation TELIC 5

Things came to a head when British troops stormed the Jamiat Police Station in September 2005, after two members of the SAS carrying out a surveillance operation were caught and held there. A number of policemen, allegedly members of militia groups, were arrested. But it was not until December 2005, when British troops returned and blew up the building, that the militia hold on the police station was broken. That action was part of Operation SINBAD, a five-month effort finally to purge the Basra police of corrupt and murderous elements. British and Iraqi troops swooped on areas of the city in succession, and members of the Royal Military Police were placed in stations to get rid of rotten apples. This had a beneficial effect, and the murder rate in the city declined. Ultimately, however, the militias had been contained rather than eradicated, and British patrols continued to be attacked in Basra by direct and indirect fire.

Throughout all this, REME at first line was consistently successful in *'keeping fit equipment in the hands of troops'*. Recovery tasks meant that REME had to be on the streets in the thick of the action to deal with vehicles when they broke down on operations.

Lance Corporal Paul Wilson – Military Cross
The realities of what had to be faced are made clear in the (abridged) citation for the Military Cross awarded to Lance Corporal Wilson on Operation TELIC 9:

> 'LCpl Wilson, a REME Recovery Mechanic, was deployed in support of a critical logistic re-supply operation bringing in vital supplies to Basra Palace on 6 December 2006. LCpl Wilson was part of the crew of a Warrior recovery vehicle, supporting B Coy 1st Royal Green Jackets patrol providing depth protection for the insertion of the supply convoy. During this mission, his recovery vehicle was tasked to assist a stricken Bulldog armoured vehicle. On this occasion the patrol was ambushed from nearby rooftops. Unflinchingly, with sustained and heavy enemy fire hitting the vehicles, both LCpl Wilson and Cpl Brown continued to fit the recovery drawbars to the stricken vehicle. On completion of the task Cpl Brown informed B Company Sergeant Major that the vehicles were ready to move. The crew from the broken down vehicle remounted to provide covering fire, for at no time did the hail of enemy fire cease. As the vehicles moved off a ferocious attack was made with hostile fire from both sides hitting the Warrior, the enemy numbered about twenty-five men and they were firing rocket propelled grenades, machine guns and rifles from corners and rooftops on both sides of the road at close range.

After a short period, LCpl Wilson saw Cpl Brown was badly injured, he collapsed the commanders seat and dragged him down by his belt to withdraw him, as far as possible, from incoming fire and apply immediate first aid. The radio net was congested due to the ongoing contact and the driver, Cpl Ward, could not raise the patrol commander to let him know a serious casualty had been sustained. As a result, LCpl Wilson, on his own initiative, then made the extremely courageous decision to climb onto the top decks of the Warrior under fire, via the rear stable door, as it drove erratically at about thirty kilometres an hour trying to avoid enemy fire. If he were to have fallen from this vehicle during this perilous manoeuvre he would have faced certain death from either the intense enemy fire, or by being crushed by the vehicle being towed behind. The vehicle remained under enemy fire as LCpl Wilson continued to reassure and provide immediate first aid to Cpl Brown while exposed to deadly and sustained enemy fire. Throughout he used his body to shield Cpl Brown's head from further injury.

Calmly, and still under fire, LCpl Wilson removed Cpl Brown's hand and dressing to get a better look at his injuries. On removal it was evident that he had received a severe gunshot wound to the face. LCpl Wilson continued to administer excellent first aid and using Cpl Brown's headset called for medical assistance. The patrol halted briefly and still under fire LCpl Wilson remained with Cpl Brown until the medic and Company Sergeant Major Youngs jumped on the Warrior to give assistance. WO2 Youngs made the decision to extract back to Basra Palace immediately. (**See Plate 10**) LCpl Wilson, lying on the top decks of the Warrior commanded it back to the helicopter evacuation point.

LCpl Wilson, a junior rank, showed inspirational bravery during this hour long engagement with the enemy. He displayed resolute courage whilst recovering the stricken Bulldog under fire and his gallant actions, later in the engagement, in response to the injury of his commander was extraordinarily brave and probably saved the life of his comrade. Throughout he displayed a reckless disregard for his own safety. His actions deserve public recognition of the very highest order'.

Additional tasks for REME soldiers

Repairs were largely carried out in unit operating bases, which were increasingly subject to attack by direct and indirect fire.

The REME contribution was by no means confined to equipment repair, for example:

- REME soldiers were routinely involved in the guarding and protection of bases and convoys, and other operational tasks including foot and vehicle patrols (**See Plate 11**)
- a significant number of REME personnel were involved in the training and mentoring of Iraqi security forces; for example, on Operation TELIC 6, the KRH LAD not only set up and ran basic Vehicle Mechanic and Metalsmith courses, a shortage of regimental instructors meant that they instructed on the basic military training courses as well.

REME was also liable to be called on to help with all sorts of tasks that require an intelligent and flexible workforce. For example, in the 22 Engineer Regiment LAD report of Operation TELIC 4 in The Craftsman magazine (November 2004), it states:

> 'With the Regiment taking on the responsibility of supporting the Iraqi Essential Services infrastructure, the officers of the LAD were thrown down the gauntlet of looking after refined fuels. Capt Elmes took over as OIC Fuel and Lt Odling took over Liquid Petroleum Gas (LPG). Notwithstanding the decrepit refinery infrastructure and bureaucratic distribution systems, overcoming the smuggling and corruption in Iraq is the biggest problem the Fuel Team faces. It is a constant struggle to ensure that the fuel is going to the right place after it leaves the refinery; a large proportion of it disappears into the ether or is tapped from pipelines'.

REME SECOND LINE SUPPORT – OPERATION TELIC 2

Lieutenant Colonel Mike Pendlington REME was Commander ES for Operation TELIC 2, and the following extracts from his article in The Craftsman magazine (March 2004) paint a picture of the circumstances at the time:

> 'The situation in Iraq has yet to reach steady state. Towards the end of Op TELIC 1 and the early part of Op TELIC 2 the situation was

pretty calm, with UK forces moving very much towards a Balkans type scenario. The post war honeymoon period was short, and it was not long before there were terrorist attacks against Coalition forces from former regime loyalists and rioting in the streets from an easily incited local populace disaffected with the lack of fuel (and this in a country with 70% of the world's oil reserves). Strong force protection measures had to be introduced, together with reinforcements and new equipments introduced to theatre in order to stabilise the situation. Far from getting close to the local population we were taking a step back and distancing ourselves behind vehicles with protective grilles, and wearing body armour and helmets. This, and the intensely oppressive heat of an Iraqi summer, provided the backdrop against which the REME tradesman had to support his unit.

… The threat is higher in the urban areas where the battlegroups operate the Snatch armoured Land Rovers, all moves require soldiers acting as 'top cover' and helmets and body armour are worn. Whilst the security measures do not have a major impact on REME capability, it does make for interesting recovery, whilst the force protection measures required for every move out of base quickly saps up available manpower. By far the hardest challenge in the theatre has been the heat in summer. For the better part of three weeks Iraq was officially the hottest place on earth and the oven-like temperature is something REME soldiers who served on TELIC 2 will not forget.

So how did the Army's equipment perform in what can only be described as extreme conditions. Well not too badly as a matter of fact, which is particularly comforting when one considers that the outrageous heat and dust destroys equipment – grease melts, rubber perishes, engines overheat and sand gets in and grinds away anything mechanical. … Average availability was around 86–88% throughout Op TELIC 2 which can be attributed not only to the equipment but to the sterling work done by REME units working long hours in demanding conditions. … I cannot place enough emphasis on good user maintenance in conditions experienced on Op TELIC – equipment just falls apart otherwise. There were stark differences in the availability of units which were good at it and others that were not. … I am now a firm supporter of equipment rotation; that is, units bring their own equipment and depart with it at the end of the tour. … There are two major reasons why this policy has been a success. Firstly, the environment does take it out of vehicles and it was very noticeable on vehicles left over from Op TELIC 1; secondly, units look after their own kit, which they don't for OET (Operational Equipment Table) equipment which are treated like hire vehicles'.

REME SECOND LINE SUPPORT – OPERATIONS TELIC 3–4

By Operation TELIC 3, the UK deployment was down to some 6,500 troops. The UK manoeuvre force was provided by 20 Armoured Brigade, which had responsibility for both of the UK-controlled provinces. The Brigade had five battlegroups, three of which (the Light Infantry (1 LI), the Royal Regiment of Wales (1 RRW) and 26 Regiment RA) had ground-holding roles. The remaining two (the Queen's Royal Hussars (QRH) and the Argyll and Sutherland Highlanders (1 A&SH)) worked with and mentored the Iraqi Police and the Iraqi Civil Defence Corps, penny-packeted around the two UK-controlled provinces. REME second line support came under the UK NSE and, for both Operations TELIC 3 and 4, it was provided by composite ES Companies from 6 Battalion REME (14 GS and 3 CS Companies). In January 2004, Commander ES, Lieutenant Colonel Pendlington, was replaced by Lieutenant Colonel Paul Shewry REME and then by Lieutenant Colonel Graham Belgum REME, who later became Chief of Staff HQ UK NSE.

Foden vehicle repair at Shaibah Logistic Base

During Operation TELIC 3, the outlying detachments of the ES Company at Al Amarah and Um Qasr were withdrawn into the Shaibah Logistic Base, where facilities were steadily improved.

The base was subject to occasional attacks but the company was fortunate in suffering no serious injuries. Recovery was always busy, and the Production Platoon became adept at replacing Snatch Land Rover clutches (the weight of the vehicle and demanding use pattern meant that clutches had a very short life), as well as rebuilding vehicles damaged in attacks by IEDs, rockets or other weaponry.

During Operation TELIC 4 (May–October 2004), it was not only the weather that warmed up, but the operational situation, which had a significant effect on the ES Company. Major Andy Stuart REME (OC 3 CS Company) wrote in The Craftsman magazine (December 2004):

> 'It was not uncommon to have several days above 50°C and this takes its toll on those working outside. In addition to the temperatures the political situation in Iraq developed considerably during the tour, with the transition to an Interim Iraqi Government on 30 June. The political turmoil that followed the transition led to a rapidly deteriorating security situation and contacts with anti-Iraqi forces increased sharply during August. This impacted on the Company in many ways; a need was identified in theatre to increase the use of Snatch Land Rover, a vehicle that offers considerably more protection than a stripped down TUM, this involved rushing large numbers of vehicles into theatre via a hasty desertisation programme. When these vehicles arrived they needed inspection and many required subsequent in-depth repair.
>
> In addition, the battlegroups in Al Amarah and Basra were experiencing heavy and sustained contacts with the enemy. A number of Warriors were damaged by various weapon systems and the company attempted battle damage repair where possible. The nature of the threat also evolved quickly and the enemy was able to exploit perceived weaknesses in our equipment design. Whilst the procurement process moved as quickly as possible to deliver industrial solutions to these problems, the company was asked to provide a number of immediate, expedient solutions to force protection problems. This ranged from designs that allowed Snatch armoured windscreens to be fitted to Warrior driver hatches; expedient armour plates to increase RPG detonation stand-off

distances; and an additional expedient armour pack to protect the driver of Warrior from RPG-type threats. These tasks were in addition to the usual breadth of support task involved with a high mileage and arduous operation'.

During this time, recovery became an even more hazardous exercise, as was the convoy trip to Al Amarah, to which FRTs were deployed. Much greater use was made of Warrior vehicles as a means of transport as the threat increased.

REME SECOND LINE SUPPORT – OPERATIONS TELIC 5-6

Support continued in broadly the same way during Operation TELIC 5 (October 2004–April 2005), with a composite support company from 1 Battalion REME. The facilities at Shaibah continued to be improved, and the requirement to support Operation BRACKEN (for which a Vehicle and a Telecommunications FRT were provided), caused a surge of power pack repair work. The company from 1 Battalion REME handed over to 10 ES Company, a composite company from 4 Battalion REME for Operation TELIC 6 (April–November 2005). A report on the tour in The Craftsman magazine (September 2005) highlighted three new developments.

Bowman (a new communications system). 12 Mechanised Brigade was the first to deploy to Iraq with the new communications system Bowman, and 4 Battalion REME the first to develop a repair capability. The development of the Bowman repair capability was frustrating and the best solution at the time was far from perfect. Hampered by a lack of relevant spares, and inconsistent and unreliable diagnostic equipment, the repair section made the best of what they considered a bad deal. The spares situation slowly improved and, with the authority to cross service, the technicians were able to repair a lot more equipment.

ECM equipment. The repair of ECM equipment became the top priority for the ES Company. The entire theatre holding of ECM equipment was maintained and calibrated by the ES Company. The repair section worked shifts to maximise the time spent getting ECM equipment through the two fully working Second Line Test Stations (SLTS). The heat and volume of work meant that, at one point, only one SLTS was working, which was run 24 hours per day to try and meet demand. Things improved, partly as a result of close liaison between the Integrated Project Team (IPT) in UK and REME technical staff based in Iraq.

Security Sector Reform. By this time, MND(SE) was devoting a great deal of effort to Security Sector Reform, a programme to ensure that the Iraqi Army, Police Force and other security agencies would have viable and sustainable organisations. The ES Company was tasked with providing both training and repair capability as part of the overall effort. A facility was set up in the ES Company lines, which was primarily responsible for inspecting and repairing vehicles given to the Iraqi security forces. These were a mixed bag of British Land Rovers, Toyotas from the Japan, Czech jeeps; 11 makes of vehicle in all. The project was a seen as a great plus point by the ES Company, which was able to set up the facility and train Locally Employed Civilians (LEC) to start taking over the work.

REME SECOND LINE SUPPORT – OPERATION TELIC 7

The period of Operation TELIC 7 (November 2005–May 2006) saw a significant rationalisation of the ES effort with 11 ES Company provided by 2 Battalion REME. 2 Logistic Support Regiment RLC (2 LSR) formed the UK Logistic Regiment on 1 October 2005 and the ES Company was brought under its command. The amalgamation with 2 LSR meant that the structure could be streamlined and the LSR LAD brought into the ES Company. HQ and administrative manpower were saved, whilst inspection and servicing bays were combined into a single central facility within Shaibah Logistic Base. In all, 43 posts were saved with the establishment reduced to 6 + 169 with some 74 LECs. The tour was busy and successful, with the following highlights:

- the ES organisation successfully applied 'lean' techniques to production
- electronic repair remained the biggest challenge; the combination of Bowman, ECM and EOD (Explosive Ordnance Disposal) equipment repair presenting a number of problems, which had to be resolved with the relevant Defence Equipment and Support (DE&S) IPT in UK
- Security Sector Reform continued to be a commitment, with the ES Company providing staff for a Logistic Mentoring and Monitoring Team.

REME SECOND LINE SUPPORT – OPERATION TELIC 8 AND THEREAFTER

During the course of Operation TELIC 8 (May–November 2006), planning and preparation began for the move to a Centralised Equipment Support Technical Area (CESTA). The move during Operation TELIC 9 led to a closer integration between first and second line and is covered next. (**See Plate 12**)

WITHDRAWAL TO THE BASRA INTERNATIONAL AIRPORT – CONTINGENCY OPERATING BASE

By early-2007, planning had begun for a withdrawal of UK forces from Basra City. Bases were being heavily mortared, and local patrols were starting to be counterproductive as they attracted direct and indirect attacks that were, not unnaturally, resented by local people.

The Iraqi security forces were also steadily developing their capability to deal with security themselves. Bases at the Shatt al Arab Hotel and Old State Building were closed, leaving just a 500-strong battlegroup based on Basra Palace. This force was withdrawn on 1 September 2007.

Indirect fire attack against buildings on Operation TELIC 8

At this point, the UK forces in Iraq, some 5,000 strong, were concentrated at a COB at Basra International Airport. Although they no longer patrolled Basra, their work was not yet done. First, their ongoing task of training and mentoring Iraqi forces continued. Second, they were required to provide the capability to intervene if the Iraqi security forces lost control. Third, they not only had to protect themselves and their supply lines, but also provide an assurance that supply lines to US forces would be secure, and to monitor the security of the border with Iran.

The ES arrangements, as one might expect, were pragmatic and based on centralising support in the CESTA. During Operation TELIC 9 (October 2006–May 2007), the Shaibah Logistic Base and Shatt al Arab Hotel were handed over to the Iraqis and ES capability was established within the COB. Major David Worrell REME, OC of 15 ES Company outlined the situation in his article in The Craftsman magazine (October 2007):

> 'The original concept of the CESTA was to accommodate the technical workspace of four BG LADs, the UK Log Bn LAD, the ES Company, a Centralised Servicing and Inspection Facility (CSIF) and their associated stores and facilities. It was envisaged that the grouping of working areas onto one site would simplify ES Materiel provision through a Centralised Stores Accounting for first line activity, and encourage efficient ways of working through.… As with most plans the initial brainwave rarely matches the final product, and after some detailed planning for the occupation of the COB, various limitations became apparent. The immediate problem we faced, however, was the lack of the necessary real estate to allow separate ES organisations to work effectively'.

He went on to explain how a rationalised system was put in place by pooling REME tradesmen on an equipment/functional basis (electronics, power packs, light/medium/heavy lines, recovery). He commented on the recovery effort as follows:

> '… throughout the seven months there was not a single Recovery Mechanic who did not have to earn his salt in the line of enemy fire. They accompanied every convoy as part of the routine sustainment of Force Elements in all Multinational Force locations in Basra Province, and the CRARRV commanded by Cpl 'Chippie' Carpenter deployed no less than 40 times on strike operations in the City'.

The new organisation was set up quickly, ES Company production was only halted for three days whilst the new facilities were brought on line,

IRAQ – AFTERMATH OF THE INVASION

and was soon running so efficiently that it was possible to make significant reductions in REME manpower in theatre.

3 CS Company took over the ES baton from 15 ES Company for Operation TELIC 10. The level of indirect fire shaped many aspects of life. As more rocket and mortar attacks were directed at the COB, sleeping, eating, movement and repair were all affected. This period saw 3 CS Company's Power Pack Repair Facility (PPRF) destroyed by a 122mm rocket. The OC, Major Adam Fraser-Hitchen REME, was to call forward the UK's stand-by PPRF on two occasions, as the newly-replaced facility was hit less than a month later. Major Fraser-Hitchen reported in his article in The Craftsman magazine (September 2007):

> 'Fully established in the CESTA, the Company has been joined by 56 tradesmen from first line LADs and 54 LECs. Without fail, making the best use of centralised facilities and manpower has heightened the level of on-mission effect and has seen a blurring of first and second line responsibilities. This, and the obvious focus of effort in sustaining the combat effectiveness of the Brigade continues to prove the benefits of the 'One REME' ethos. … The tempo of ops and the constant threat of indirect fire (more in the past two months than in the whole of TELIC 9), pales into insignificance as I remain humbled by the courage, tenacity and good humour of the REME soldier under fire. I cannot think of a time in my career when I have been more proud to be a member of the Corps'.

Corporal Adam Miller – Conspicuous Gallantry Cross
Corporal Miller was the first member of the Corps to be awarded the Conspicuous Gallantry Cross for his actions in Basra during this period. His citation reads:

> 'On the afternoon of 21st May 2007, on the first day of 4 Rifles battlegroup's tour in Basra City, R Company was tasked with a re-supply convoy to and from the Provincial Joint Coordination Centre – an isolated base in the heart of Basra. On the return leg the convoy came under ferocious contact on a busy junction in a militia stronghold. The ambush, involving over 100 insurgents firing small arms and RPGs, destroyed a fuel tanker, caused 2 fatalities and severely damaged a civilian low-loader carrying Saxon and Land Rover, which limped to a canal crossing before breaking down

blocking the bridge. The loss of military vehicles in the centre of Basra would have allowed the militias to claim a significant victory – the decision was taken to fight to recover the vehicles.

Whilst this contact was going on, Corporal Miller, a Recovery Mechanic, was on standby in Basra Palace. The complexity and nature of the breakdown meant that the Foden (an unprotected soft-skin wheeled recovery truck) was the only recovery asset capable of performing the task, so Corporal Miller and Lance Corporal Burn (the Foden driver) were tasked to the scene. By the time they arrived, the platoon at the bridge were engaged in an intense gun battle with about 75 militia engaging from 15–20 firing points, on roofs, from alleyways, cars and from the Iraqi Police Station at ranges of 50–200 metres and in a 360° radius. The noise of automatic fire, metallic ringing of bullets striking vehicles and repeated explosions of RPG warheads on the Warriors and Bulldogs was continuous and deafening.

Into this maelstrom drove Corporal Miller in his soft-skinned recovery vehicle. Corporal Miller carefully reversed the Foden up to the disabled low-loader and then without hesitation dismounted. The soldiers, fighting for their lives from under armour watched in fear of Corporal Miller's life, as he ran forwards 50 metres across the exposed bridge, in complete view of the enemy to begin his assessment. For the next 45 minutes, with only a single Bulldog to provide a shield at the site – scant protection in a 360° and 3-dimensional urban battle – he worked on the recovery, attempting first to bleed the brakes; then to unhook the tractor unit; and then to cut the securing chains for the Saxon and Land Rover. He repeatedly ran back to the company commander's Bulldog to report on his progress. Throughout this period, he was under continuous and very heavy fire with bullets striking the road, bridge railings and vehicle he was working on, often inches from him. The militia then resorted to firing RPGs to attempt to destroy the low-loader and its high profile military cargo. In the course of 15 minutes, 5 RPGs detonated on the vehicle, no more than a few feet from Corporal Miller as he worked. It is a miracle that he survived. Despite his extraordinary and resourceful efforts, the low-loader ultimately proved too severely damaged to be towed and only at this point, with all options exhausted, did Corporal Miller return to the Palace.

In all, Corporal Miller was exposed, either in the soft-skinned Foden or dismounted, for nearly 2 hours, much of that time under constant and heavy enemy fire including over 20 RPGs. Despite these threats and the inherent danger of a fuel explosion, Corporal Miller displayed icy nerve, professional dedication of the very highest order and almost suicidal courage in an impossible situation. In a tour characterised by numerous acts of courage in heavy urban fighting, Corporal Miller's actions stand out as the defining example of bravery under fire. His premeditated and determined conduct showed conspicuous gallantry of a very high order'.

Lieutenant Colonel Bob Fram REME – Military Cross

Not every member of REME served in his primary ES role in Iraq and many served in a variety of other roles from mentoring the Iraqi Army and police to liaison. One such individual was Lieutenant Colonel Fram, then CO of 6 Battalion REME, who commanded the Provincial Joint Coordination Centre in the centre of Basra; a role for which he received the award of the Military Cross. His citation reads:

'The Provisional Joint Coordination Centre (PJCC) is situated in the centre of Basra, in the heart of the most violent and volatile area of the city. It is an Iraqi Police base, consisting of several buildings and headquarters, of which the PJCC is one. In this small, austere and isolated location, Lieutenant Colonel Fram commanded a team of 70 men for just over three months without relief. His task was to conduct liaison with the Iraqi Security Forces (ISF) in order to both influence and understand their intent. During previous tours, the PJCC had been a relatively benign location. During TELIC 10 it was attacked almost every day, and was witness to some of the most intense and prolonged fighting seen in Basra during the UK's 4 years of occupation.

Lieutenant Colonel Fram commanded in the face of continuing militia pressure. The enemy recognised that he was very isolated and heavily outnumbered and the significance of this small outpost was not lost on them. As the day and night attacks built in intensity, they were often launched simultaneously from several firing points. These were supported by 60mm mortars and RPGs. In all, the compound was attacked over 100 times. Direct hits on the building became the norm; RPG strikes penetrated the building, and mortar rounds hit the sangars on the roof. The defence of the PJCC became one of the most intense, dangerous and dramatic urban battles of the campaign.

In order to survive, Lieutenant Colonel Fram had to live by his wits. It was a lonely and demanding command. In the event of a large scale attack, he knew that immediate relief from other UK forces would be impossible. He would have to hold the ground. Operating in temperatures exceeding 50°C, the living conditions became increasingly overcrowded and uncomfortable. Everyone was moved inside what little hard cover existed. It became a day to day existence. In mid-June his second in command – Major Paul Harding – was killed by mortar fire. Despite the loss of a trusted friend and adviser, he didn't flinch in his task. A further 8 soldiers were also injured. Through all the increasing violence he continued to conduct liaison with the ISF. This often involved movement around the police base, with limited protection, in order to meet key ISF figures. His daily reports and meetings continued throughout; and remained vital intelligence for brigade headquarters.

This was leadership and command of the highest order. In contact with the enemy daily, in an isolated detached location, Lieutenant Colonel Fram led his small team with great bravery and determination. He was under constant and enormous stress and danger; but not once did he buckle or sway from his task'.

WITHDRAWAL FROM IRAQ AND OPERATION BROCKDALE

In March 2008, a large Iraqi Government force backed by US forces and supported by UK forces attacked the militia forces in Basra head on and broke their power. This transformed the situation and paved the way for the British withdrawal from Iraq. Operation TELIC 13 merged into Operation BROCKDALE, which was essentially about withdrawing British forces from Iraq safely and efficiently. Whilst the operational challenge quickly diminished, the technical and logistic challenge of withdrawing equipment and materiel in good order grew. Past experience had taught that this was a phase of operations when things easily go wrong, resulting in massive waste, and years of accounting nightmares and recriminations. It was essential that this did not happen in Iraq. First, because the Army needed the equipment coming out of theatre to be in good working order (some was urgently required in Afghanistan); second, there was a general need to conserve resources; and, finally, there were audit requirements to be met.

This time round it was therefore decided to deploy a Joint Force Logistic Component (JFLogC) HQ whose one-star Commander would take over as the Commander of British Forces (COMBRITFOR). Its Post Operational Report (POR) (JFLogC HQ/02/03 dated 11 September 2009) explains that planning started in August 2008, with the HQ deploying in March 2009. The Main HQ was in place in Camp Buehring in Kuwait by 28 March, with the HQ JFLogC Forward HQ in the COB. The process of withdrawal was phased, starting 'with aggressive housekeeping'. The main withdrawal of forces began on 1 May, and by 12 May all 'significant military equipment' was out of theatre. At this point, the Commander JFLogC took on the role of COMBRITFOR. The COB was clear of logistic activity by the end of June, and the operation was concluded by 10 September. Although the plan ultimately worked smoothly, the POR makes it clear that the overall operation was complex and there were many dimensions that had to be managed. It was dependent on agreements that had to be negotiated between the UK Government and the Government of Iraq, also between the UK and its military allies on such issues as legal status of the British force, and the handover of operational responsibility. It was complicated at a technical level as well, and success depended on getting all the right people involved including staff at the Permanent Joint Headquarters, the DE&S as well as those already in theatre. The need for adequate reserves, and for adequate training and preparation for the HQ was emphasised, as was the need for effective deployable communications and information systems.

The withdrawal of equipment and materiel was a key element of the overall plan. Although the planning and control of this came under the aegis of a 'Joint' organisation, or the ES component within it, to a very large extent it was REME personnel who actually produced the plans and subsequently executed them. Yet again, their contribution to both aspects was excellent and exemplary. (**See Plate 13**)

Much of the detailed plan for drawing down equipment was originally worked out by ES staff in theatre, and was duly agreed or modified by the various stakeholders involved both in Iraq and UK. The plan was based on a having two 'feet on the ground'; initially, one in Iraq at the COB, and another that was set up at the Kuwait Support Facility in Camp Buehring in Kuwait. 20 Armoured Company, from 3 Battalion REME, provided the basis for an ES Group, which was part of

1 Logistic Support Regiment RLC (1 LSR). The Regiment was initially split with two companies, including the bulk of 20 Armoured Company in Iraq, and one RLC Squadron with an ES Platoon in Kuwait, which endured in theatre until 24 May. The Regiment gradually morphed into a Theatre Drawdown Unit under 12 Logistic Support Regiment RLC, with elements of 9 Armoured Company, from 4 Battalion REME, deploying for the last 10 weeks of the operation, which was complete early in August 2009. The decisive act in the withdrawal of equipment was the establishment of a Theatre Equipment Returns Section, which was absolutely crucial to the development and refinement of the reverse supply chain for equipment. The development and codification of the Theatre Equipment Redeployment System (TERS) process was crucial as it re-established hitherto forgotten processes for complex equipment redeployment over a complicated joint supply chain and enabled equipment to be returned in good order by sea and air. The development of this process by Warrant Officer Class 1 More, for which he received a Commander Joint Operations Commendation, was one of REME's critical interventions, which in hindsight was a proving ground for the redeployment of equipment by air from Afghanistan. Had the withdrawal from Iraq not occurred, the redeployment from Afghanistan would not have been as smooth as it was.

The TERS process involved inspecting vehicles, removing CES items, ECM kits and UOR items as necessary, carrying out repairs and modifications (or removing modifications) as necessary. The output of these processes was equipment that was clean, certified as free from explosives and biohazards, had an in-date roadworthiness inspection, with all other inspections and essential mission maintenance completed and properly documented, and which was fully operational. As a bonus, the team was able to lay their hands on a large number of spare electronic tags (TAV bricks), with which they were able to tag not only complete equipments, but packages of CES, which could be 'asset tracked' wherever they went.

In the event, the system in which REME had played such a key role worked extremely well, and most of the problems traditionally associated with the end of a major overseas operational deployment were avoided.

EQUIPMENT AND ENGINEERING ISSUES

During the six years of operations in Iraq, the technical challenges faced by REME were ever-changing, as was its equipment dependency. After the invasion, the use of heavy armoured vehicles declined, and it seemed that operations would largely be carried out using unarmoured wheeled vehicles. The need for better protection was soon apparent and the Snatch Land Rover provided reasonable solution to the threat at the time. A new six-wheeled protected vehicle, the Vector, was also brought into service. This was based on the Pinzgauer vehicle, and its protection level, although better than the Snatch Land Rover, was of the same order as the lightly armoured Saxon wheeled personnel carrier, which it was intended to replace. As the threat became more severe, the need for even better protection became apparent.

This was achieved in the short term by making more use of heavily armoured tracked vehicles, by modifying or uparmouring existing vehicles, either on an ad hoc basis, or through a major modification programme. For example, the venerable tracked FV432 (introduced into service in the 1960s) was fitted with a new power train and armour protection and returned to service as the Bulldog. Meanwhile, heavily protected wheeled armoured vehicles were being procured and collectively termed Protected Mobility (PM) vehicles. A family of these vehicles started to become available towards the end of operations in Iraq. The Mastiff was the most important of these, and is a large six-wheeled vehicle with a high level of protection (particularly against mines and IEDs). During this period Bowman radio was introduced, as well as numerous UOR packages ranging from technically sophisticated ECM equipment through to uparmouring kits that required basic bolting and welding.

The use of JP-8 fuel was an interesting engineering issue. Directed by the US Department of Defense, the only fuel available in theatre was kerosene-based aviation fuel known as JP-8 or Jet Propellant 8. JP-8 had been used by the US military to replace diesel since the 1990s but not by the British Army. Most British Army vehicles ran pretty well on JP-8, losing about 10% of power; the only vehicle type that had some initial problems was the Leyland DAF truck, which experienced starting problems that were soon ironed out with some adjustments to the fuel system. There was some concern amongst REME engineers about longer term wear of engines due to less lubricant in JP-8 compared to diesel, and also to the higher sulphur content that causes wear to exhaust valve seats, but these proved to be unfounded.

It is beyond the scope of this Chapter to detail the many other technical issues that required in-theatre REME staff to draw on their engineering expertise. Peacetime training requirements tend to be predictable in terms of the type and amount of usage involved, and the environment in which it will take place. Planners can take account of this and decide on standard repair policies and the training and materiel requirements that stem from them. Operations tend to be inherently unpredictable, and technical challenges need to be speedily and creatively addressed to save lives and sustain operational capability. A feature of Operation TELIC was that failure rates were significantly affected by environmental factors such as heat and dust, and such things had to be factored into planning. Operations also seem invariably to result in major and urgent modification programmes, which place extra and sometimes novel demands on REME's in-theatre technical staff – and Operation TELIC was no exception. The changing operational situation also inevitably affects the nature of the support requirement and, during Operation TELIC, the use of increasingly powerful IEDs meant that REME had to take on the technical challenge of repairing or rebuilding heavily damaged PM vehicles.

Operation TELIC also provided an important insight into the use of contractors on operations. This Operation saw REME tradesmen take full responsibility for the repair of PM vehicles having initially had in-theatre training, and, later, fully established UK-based training. Whilst contractors had delivered both excellent training and repair work, the level of indirect fire on the COB saw the vast majority of repair contractors leave halfway through Operation TELIC 10. The timing of this reduction in repair capability was a close-run thing. Major Fraser-Hitchen noted:

> 'The enduring effect that long-term rocket and mortar fire has on the individual cannot be ignored. Whilst our soldiers had their training, their friends and their soldierly pride to hold together increasingly frayed nerves, the contractors became increasingly concerned over their safety. I felt we had only just managed to acquire the technical skills required to repair the PM fleet by the time the PM contractors had withdrawn from theatre. Whilst technically excellent, it was not the contractors' place to be in such a high-threat environment. Getting the right balance between military and contracted repair solutions is a key consideration now and for the future'.

One obvious lesson from the Army's six difficult years in Iraq is that new operational requirements can arrive far faster than fully supported industrial solutions can be provided. One of REME's great contributions during the campaign was its ability to make less than perfect equipment solutions work on the ground, and to feed back engineering advice from the sharp end to designers and procurers of equipment. There is clearly value for Defence in having an expert Army functional technical organisation with a thorough understanding of the problems of supporting equipment on operations, and with the ability to communicate with those in the commercial world who are contracted to design and support equipment for the Services.

Year	US	UK	Other	Total
2003	486	53	41	580
2004	849	22	35	906
2005	846	23	28	897
2006	822	29	21	872
2007	904	47	10	961
2008	314	4	4	322
2009	149	1	0	150
Total	**4,370**	**179**	**139**	**4,688**

Figure 9.1: Coalition fatalities by year

CHAPTER 10

AFGHANISTAN – THE PROLOGUE (2001–MARCH 2006)

In order to make sense of British operations in Afghanistan, it is important for the reader to have a general understanding of that country's history, geography and culture.

In the 1960s and early-1970s, Afghanistan was known as a country that was attractive to hippies, and those keen to get a break from the burden of western materialism. They found a peaceful country whose populace, though poor, was friendly and hospitable. They perhaps did not understand its violent past, and could not know that the country was about to be plunged into decades of bloodshed and turmoil.

Afghanistan is a landlocked country with an estimated population of 28 million. It is bordered by Pakistan in the south and east, Iran in the west, Turkmenistan, Uzbekistan and Tajikistan to the north, and China in the far northeast. The territories now comprising Afghanistan have always been an important geostrategic area as they connect east, south, west and central Asia. It has been the target of many invasions from the time of Alexander the Great. Afghanistan was a buffer state between the Russian and British Empires, and the British fought several campaigns there in the 19th and early-20th Centuries. These were aimed primarily at ensuring that acceptable leaders were in power, rather than at long-term occupation or rule.

Much of the population is now desperately poor (in 2006, the average GDP per capita was estimated at around £160 per annum), and poorly educated (although 28% of the population is literate, many are barely so). The harshness of their life is reflected in a life expectancy at birth of about 43 years. Afghanistan does not have a long history as a stable nation state, and most of its population sees the world through a cultural and ideological lens that is difficult for an ordinary westerner to comprehend.

Afghanistan has been essentially Muslim since it was conquered by Arabs in the 7th Century, and religion plays a central role in most Afghan lives. Religious views are far from homogeneous, however, and there is tension between those who want the country to come to terms with the

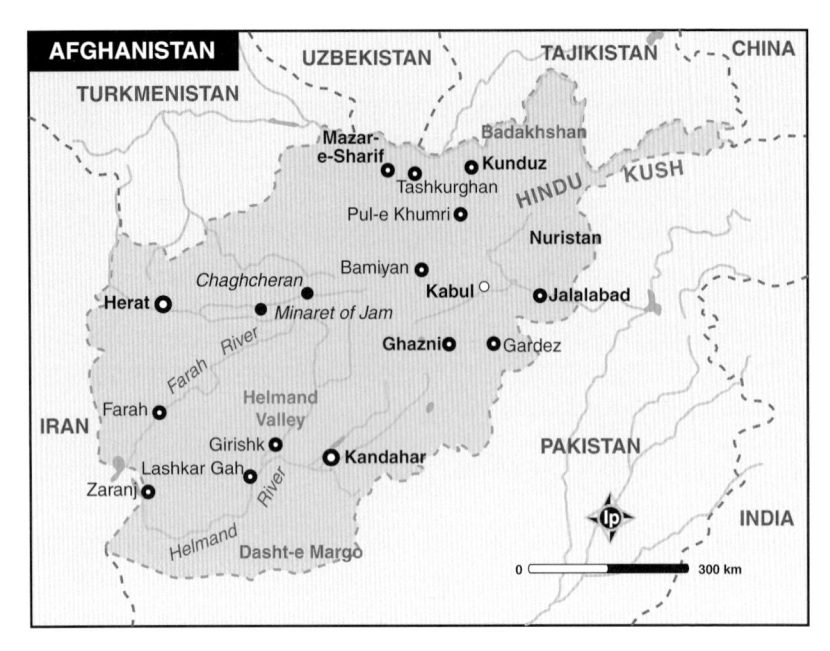

Map of Afghanistan today

modern world, and the radicals who believe that the only answer to evil and corruption in their country is a return to the ways and beliefs of the earliest Muslims. Tribal loyalties are also important. The Pashtun form the largest grouping, and are a majority in the south. The Afghanistan-Pakistan border represents something of a historical accident, with Pashtun living either side of the border. The Pashtun hold to principles of behaviour that are consistent with Islam, but to an extent pre-date it. For example, there is 'melmastia', which involves showing hospitality and profound respect to all visitors, regardless of distinctions of race, religion, national affiliation or economic status, and doing so without any hope of remuneration or favour. There are those who regard the Pashtuns as the most hospitable people in the world.

The notion of 'badal' (justice, or the taking of revenge against a wrong-doer) can seem less comfortable for a westerner. Even a mere taunt may require the shedding of the taunter's blood or, if he is not available, that of his next closest male relative. Such events may trigger blood feuds that can last generations and involve whole tribes, with the loss of hundreds of lives. Traditionally, a Pashtun male must always stand brave against tyranny, and he should always be able to defend his property, family, women and the honour of his name. Memories are long, and personal ties of loyalty or obligation, of almost a feudal nature, will often be superimposed on other considerations. With a long history of unstable government, rulers and governors at all levels have been historically prone to try and resolve internal conflicts by involving outsiders and then being prepared to switch loyalties pragmatically. Having involved outsiders, Afghans have historically tended to be all too ready to turn on them as soon as they started to be perceived as invaders or interlopers.

During the early-20th Century, Afghanistan was led by a king who embraced many western ideas and embarked on a programme of modernisation, which included developing the education system and giving greater rights to women. He pushed reform too hard, however, and was forced to flee the country as religious and political reactionaries combined against him, a reminder that Afghans tend to object to change being imposed on them, even by their own leaders. In the late-1970s, a coalition of modernisers, this time with a Marxist agenda, managed to take power, and set up a somewhat shaky, inefficient and corrupt regime. The assassination of its leader, and the ensuing turmoil, convinced the Soviet Union that it was necessary to intervene militarily to prevent a friendly communist regime from being replaced by a non-communist one. The Soviet involvement quickly escalated, until they had some 105,000 troops in the country. They never managed to subdue the entire country, and found themselves fighting a bloody and apparently unwinnable war against irregular forces, who were receiving substantial external support. They extricated themselves in 1988, essentially leaving Afghanistan to sort out its own future.

This war had a devastating effect on the country. Estimates of the number of Afghans killed range from 100,000 to one million. The population of Kandahar, the second largest city, which was 200,000 before the war, was reduced to 25,000 by carpet bombing and other military action. When the Soviets withdrew, they left a pro-Soviet government, and had helped build up the security forces to about 300,000 strong. To the surprise of some, these more than held their own until, in time-honoured fashion, internal feuding led to the downfall of the Government. The defection of one of the major warlords to the Taliban allowed this Pashtun-based fundamentalist Muslim organisation to sweep to power in 1992. The former President, Dr Mohammad Najibullah, was hung from a traffic light, a reminder that politicians who fail in Afghanistan are unlikely to be able to make a living from lucrative after dinner speeches, or from writing books.

A number of external parties had been involved, directly or indirectly, with undermining the Soviet involvement in Afghanistan. The USA provided money, specialist help and military hardware, notably Stinger hand-held anti-aircraft missiles. Pakistan has a crucial ongoing interest in having what it regards as an acceptable regime in power in Afghanistan, both from the point of view of its internal stability and regional relationships, including its historically adversarial links with India. Much western military aid to the anti-Soviet resistance was routed through Pakistan, with the Pakistan security forces playing a key role in nurturing the organisations that led to the growth of the Taliban and Al Qaeda. The Saudis, whose wealthy royal family was concerned with its legitimacy in the Arab world, were also involved. They sought to bolster their position by funding madrassas, Sunni Islamic schools. In Pakistan, these were often the only place to which poor families could send their sons. Saudi-funded madrassas taught Wahhabism, a particularly austere fundamentalist form of Islam, with many becoming indoctrination centres for jihadism (holy war against infidels). These provided a fertile recruiting ground for terrorist and extremist groups. The Saudis also provided money to support the insurgency in Afghanistan, as did many wealthy Gulf States. Others with an interest, or involvement, included Egypt, Iran (a Shia state with a long border with Afghanistan) and India.

Around 1996, the Taliban Government of Afghanistan agreed to let an organisation called Al Qaeda, which had been previously based in Somalia but had been invited to leave by its hosts, to base itself in Afghanistan. It was to be centred in and around Tora Bora, which included a cave complex in a mountainous area not far from the border with Pakistan. Relationships were not entirely harmonious. The Taliban were primarily interested in what happened in and around Afghanistan, and many of its leaders had a very narrow understanding of the wider world. Al Qaeda was headed by a sophisticated and wealthy ex-Saudi businessman, Osama bin Laden, whose organisation proved a magnet for several thousand radicalised Muslims, many with experience of fighting in Afghanistan, Chechnya, Bosnia or elsewhere. They had a vision of global jihad. They saw all things western, and particularly American, as their legitimate target. The Taliban Government was concerned that their guests, whose perspective on the world was very different from their own, would do things that would cause their hosts a lot of trouble. Their fears were fully realised in 2001, when Al Qaeda carried out its infamous '9/11' attacks on New York.

The USA was angry, and demanded that the Taliban hand over Al Qaeda to them. The Taliban Government, caught between self-interest and their perceived duty to protect fellow Muslims, dithered. The USA did not. It formed a coalition of warlords in the northeast of Afghanistan, called the 'Northern Alliance'. It provided massive air support, which together with US and British special forces supported ground operations (the UK involvement was called Operation VERITAS). The Taliban were quickly crushed as a conventional military force, and those Al Qaeda who were not killed mostly fled across the porous border into Pakistan. A transitional Afghanistan Government was established under Hamid Karzai, a political leader who was prepared to work with NATO.

The period immediately after this was one of optimism, and apparent progress. The Taliban's ruthless methods had certainly delivered a form of security, but it became increasingly obvious that its austere regime did not have the answers to Afghanistan's problems, and its popularity had steadily waned. The majority of the population seemed all too pleased to see the back of them. Influential leaders, who had switched to the Taliban when it seemed to be winning, were happy to desert it when it was not. Schools reopened, western music was heard for the first time for years, Kabul and Kandahar started to buzz, and the promise of massive international reconstruction aid brought a smile to Afghan faces.

INTERNATIONAL SECURITY ASSISTANCE FORCE

Military assistance to the Afghanistan Government was to be provided through the International Security Assistance Force (ISAF), a NATO-led operation authorised by UN Security Council Resolution 1386. Initially, this was a small force (around 2,000 strong) concerned only with training the new Afghan National Army and providing security in and around Kabul. In October 2003, however, the UN Security Council authorised the expansion of the ISAF mission throughout Afghanistan, the start of its growth into a force of over 133,000 by 2011.

OPERATION JACANA (MARCH–JUNE 2002)

In March 2002, the UK deployed a substantial ground force in the form of 45 Commando Group under HQ 3 Commando Brigade. It was based at Bagram Airfield some 35 miles north of Kabul.

REME soldiers on Operation JACANA at Bagram Airfield

Major Dominic Moorhouse REME (then the Staff Officer Grade 2 G4 Operations at Brigade HQ) commented in his article in The Craftsman magazine (September 2002):

> 'Previously occupied by the Soviets before their hurried departure in 1989, the neglect of Bagram Airfield was obvious. It was a mix between a vehicle and an aircraft graveyard, surrounded by a minefield (mostly uncharted) with sand covered lines of tents in various secured camp areas, a whole bunch of old, shot-up Soviet hangars in which various nationalities had set up their headquarters.... Security was the first concern. The area around Bagram was 'relatively' safe in that the Americans were paying the local warlord to keep the peace. However, both the APOD in Kabul and Bagram Airfield were mortared at various stages during the deployment, and attempted night-time infiltration at Bagram was a continuous feature. Whether this was local Afghans scouting for booty from the huge US supply depot, or terrorists 'dicking' the camp was not clear'.

REME, in particular, had a busy time supporting the force's engineer equipment for which there was a high demand. Overall, however, things were fairly straightforward from the REME point of view, as the operation mainly involved infantry forces deploying by CH47 Chinook helicopters, and being resupplied by them. These deployments disappointed those who were hoping for action as 'the birds had flown' and nobody appeared willing to fight the Marines. The Tora Bora area was searched, and a number of arms caches were discovered and spectacularly disposed of, but the force returned to the UK after a three-month deployment without a shot being fired in anger.

OPERATIONS FINGAL, TARROCK AND HERRICK

Operation JACANA was not the only UK involvement in Afghanistan at the time. The Parachute Regiment (2 PARA) had already been sent there on Operation FINGAL. It was based in Kabul, and its role was to train Afghans, contribute to security, and carry out Civil Military Cooperation (CIMIC) tasks. The commitment became an ongoing one, referred to as the Afghanistan Roulement Infantry Battalion (ARIB). It included providing Operational Mentoring and Liaison Teams, in which REME was involved. (**See Plate 14**) In late-2003, the UK-led Provincial Reconstruction Team (PRT) was established in Mazari Sharif in northern Afghanistan, and was commanded in 2004 by Colonel John Henderson and in 2005 by Colonel Jon Brittain, both late REME officers. The mission was to extend the writ of the Afghanistan Government through security assistance and reconstruction, an essentially non-kinetic operation involving persuading warlords to toe the democratic line. This was called Operation TARROCK. In 2004, the UK contribution was centralised under NATO command and renamed Operation HERRICK.

Whilst things were hotting up in Iraq, as invasion was followed by an insurgency, Afghanistan seemed to be becoming something of a military backwater from the UK point of view. The REME component reported itself as being heavily involved in CIMIC projects, such as restoring schools and building playgrounds. In late-2004, a report from the ARIB on Operation FINGAL 7 in The Craftsman magazine (December 2004), the time of Afghanistan's historic first-ever democratic election at which Hamid Karzai's rule was legitimised, stated that:

'… the only gun battle on their tour had been water cannon on their fun day'.

But, things were about to change.

PLANS TO COMMIT A UK BRIGADE-SIZE FORCE

By 2005, time it was clear that the security situation in some parts of Afghanistan was far from satisfactory. One major area of concern was Helmand Province. This was primarily a Pashtun area, and had been a Taliban heartland area. Whilst PRTs could still move fairly safely through the area, it was clear that the Government's grip on the region was tenuous at best. It was assessed that a significant new ISAF force was needed to bolster security. The UK was prepared to provide it.

By early-2006, plans were far advanced to commit a UK brigade-size force to Afghanistan. Given that the Army was heavily committed to operations in Iraq, which were not going smoothly, this may seem a strange course of action to pursue. In fact, from a Whitehall perspective, it seemed a very attractive proposition at the time and it enjoyed Prime Ministerial support.

The war in Iraq, which had always been controversial at home and abroad, was increasingly being seen within the UK as a 'bad' war. The British Army had become embroiled in a very unpleasant counterinsurgency situation that did not play to its strengths, and for which it was inadequately resourced. Whilst the USA decided to 'surge' and build up their force to 20 brigades, the UK was looking for an honourable way to extricate its small brigade-size force that was struggling to contain insurgency in southern Iraq.

Further involvement in Afghanistan seemed to offer the prospect of a 'good' war for the UK, nationally and internationally. The increased UK involvement would be at the request of the internationally recognised Government of Afghanistan (so there were no controversies about invasion or regime change). There were no international objections, and nobody else seemed keen to take on the job of Helmand Province. The UK contribution would come under ISAF, to which its major European allies would also be contributing.

The primary purpose of the intervention was to support economic reconstruction in Helmand Province. This was linked to an anti-narcotics agenda, and one to promote human rights that included rights for women. The Foreign and Commonwealth Office and the Department for International Development saw this as an opportunity to show what they could do, working in cooperation with Non-Government Organisations (NGO). The role of the UK military force was seen as merely to provide the security necessary to allow NGOs and others to pour assistance into the Helmand area, which would have the effect of 'winning hearts and minds' and consolidating support for the legitimate Government of Afghanistan in a peaceful and prosperous Helmand Province. It was hoped that UK forces would be welcomed, and it was felt that, with their experience in such places as Northern Ireland and the Balkans, British soldiers would be adept in this role. The MoD decided it would provide 16 Air Assault Brigade, a relatively new formation, comprising some highly trained and motivated soldiers who were keen to show what they were capable of.

Senior British Army figures made no secret of the fact that the Army had been heavily stretched by its combination of commitments to Iraq and elsewhere. There was an appreciation that taking on a further commitment in Afghanistan involved an element of risk. The Army was in a tricky position, with a Prime Minister clearly keen on intervention, and a Chancellor of the Exchequer keen to rein in military expenditure. It is not hard to imagine the difficulties that would arise for the Army if it were seen to be dragging its feet, or perceived as exaggerating military risks in a way that would undermine what otherwise looked a very promising plan. The politico-military background to the first deployment of 16 Air Assault Brigade and its subsequent operations there is described in a well-researched and well-regarded book 'A Million Bullets: The real story of the British Army in Afghanistan' (James Fergusson, 2008).

Given that many felt the Taliban did not pose a serious military threat, and that a UK brigade had previously deployed to Afghanistan without firing a shot, it was considered that the deployment of a small and fairly lightly equipped formation involved an acceptable degree of military risk in the light of the overall plan for civil/military engagement and its expected benefits. The Secretary of State for Defence, Dr John Reid, reflected this perception when he said:

> '… accomplish our mission and had not fired one shot at the end of it, we would be very happy'.

Although the situation looked very encouraging from a Whitehall perspective, not everyone who had recently been on the ground was so sanguine. A recently retired late REME Colonel working as an employment consultant at the Officers' Association, interviewed a young officer leaving the Army, who had just returned from working with the PRT in Afghanistan. When asked about his experiences, the young officer explained that he felt safe travelling unescorted around the Helmand area (wearing a soft hat) because the locals perceived his team as being entitled to the protection their culture afforded to 'guests'. He felt they enjoyed the status of 'guests' because they were not seen as telling the locals what to do. In discussion, he was asked about the imminent deployment of 16 Air Assault Brigade, and how the locals might react to the arrival of British troops en masse responsible for enforcing security. He said that from the moment the British started to tell locals what to do they would start to be seen as infidel intruders. When asked what that meant, his answer was unequivocal "you will have a war!"

Operation HERRICK 4, which involved the deployment of 16 Air Assault Brigade to Helmand Province was to put the hopes of the Secretary of State for Defence and the fears of the young officer to the acid test.

CHAPTER 11

AFGHANISTAN – THE LONG HAUL (OPERATIONS HERRICK 4–14)

This Chapter covers an eventful period from March 2006 to September 2011 (about as long as World War 2), divided into six-month Operation HERRICK tours. To try and explain in detail what happened on each tour would be both repetitive, and a difficult read. The approach adopted has therefore been to explain in some detail what happened on Operation HERRICK 4 to provide a picture of 'where we started from', which is essential in order to make sense of what happened later. Operation HERRICK 14 is also covered in some detail in order to provide a picture of 'where we had got to'. The intervening period has been covered with an overview, and a number of 'snapshots' at yearly intervals (Operations HERRICK 6, 8, 10 and 12) intended to provide reference information and illustrate the development of the campaign as a whole, especially REME's involvement in it.

OPERATION HERRICK 4 (MARCH–OCTOBER 2006)

Background Factors
In order to appreciate what happened on Operation HERRICK 4 and subsequent British operations in Helmand Province, it is useful to understand some background factors.

Afghans had a tradition of resorting to arms to solve disputes. Following decades of conflict, Afghanistan was awash with modern weaponry. Weapons continued to flow in to the Afghan forces, with a proportion of the weaponry inevitably leaking into the hands of insurgents. Weapons were being fed to the insurgents from a variety of sources, with either an ideological, political or financial interest in supporting them.

Afghan warfare tends to be seasonal. Winter can be bitingly cold and activity tends to die down until summer, which gets brutally hot. Agricultural cycles, such as harvesting, affect levels of insurgent activity.

Many Afghans were not enamoured with the Taliban or their extremist fundamentalism. In particular, many saw education of their children as a path to better things. Memories are long in Afghanistan, however, and taking sides against the Taliban came with a risk of brutal revenge unless one could be sure that they would never regain power locally.

Many, however, approved of the Taliban, because they felt that the stability and justice (albeit harsh) that they brought was an improvement on the rule by corrupt and ruthless warlords, which they had previously endured. The (US-backed) Afghan Government was seen by some as the return of corrupt warlords and their ways. The Afghan National Army (ANA) and Afghan National Police (ANP) were, therefore, not necessarily seen as honest guardians of law and order.

Helmand Province was the major poppy growing area of Afghanistan and around half of the world's heroin came from there. Those making a lot of money out of this had both the cash and incentive to undermine NATO's peacekeeping and economic development agenda in Helmand Province.

Tribal loyalties were important. The Taliban had started as a Pashtun movement, and the majority of the population in Helmand Province was Pashtun. Many of the ANA and ANP there came from tribes that were traditional enemies of the Pashtun.

There was an international dimension to the security problem in Helmand Province. Its borders with Pakistan were porous, and although Pakistan was theoretically 'on side' there is little doubt that shadowy figures in its intelligence and military communities were keen that NATO's operation should not go well.

There was sometimes a religious dimension to the opposition to NATO. It was a key tenet to the faith of many Afghans that they should not be ruled by infidels, and that they had a duty to follow in the steps of their forbears who had made jihad to get rid of the Russians and, earlier, the British.

Deployment

16 Air Assault Brigade initially deployed to Helmand Province some 3,300 strong, with 3 Parachute Regiment Battlegroup (3 PARA BG) (around 650 in all) as its primary combat force. It was responsible for providing security for an area roughly the size of Wales. The original plan was to develop a Main Operating Base (MOB) called Camp Bastion, and to use a single Forward Operating Base (FOB) near Gereshk to secure the Camp Bastion/Lashkar Gah/Gereshk triangle, working with forces already deployed in support of Provincial Reconstruction Teams (PRT).

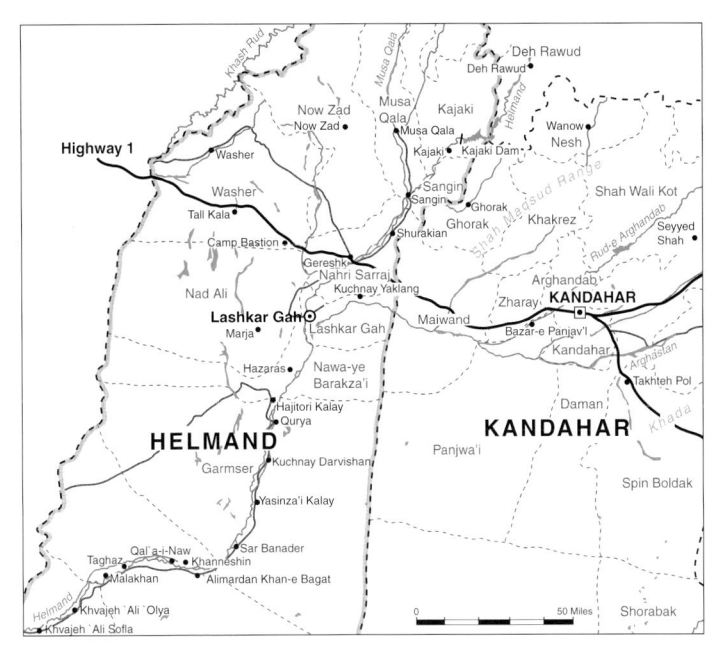

Map showing the Camp Bastion/Lashkar Gah/Gereshk triangle

Highway 1, formally called the Ring Road, is a two-lane road network circulating inside Afghanistan. The River Helmand rises in the Hindu Kush mountains about 80km west of Kabul, flows west and then southwest towards Zabol and the Afghan-Iranian border. A satellite picture shows it running through a swathe of green, which cuts through a huge area of deserts and mountains. This green area comprises mainly fields, trees, farming compounds, hamlets, irrigation ditches, and dirt roads. Gereshk (like many Afghan names, is sometimes spelt differently) is situated adjacent to the point where the River Helmand crosses Highway 1, and is part of an important agricultural and commercial corridor. Further south, Lashkar Gah is the centre of a large agricultural area. It is a more modern town than Gereshk, and is the capital of Helmand Province. Camp Bastion was sited in an unpopulated desert area with easy access to Highway 1.

Outline of Events

With British forces widely dispersed, it was not long before the Taliban mounted a series of concerted attacks. With only about 600 infantry soldiers all told at the beginning, reinforcements were desperately needed.

Some 960 reinforcements arrived in July, including Gurkha and Fusilier companies, which had little time for training and preparation.

The Gurkhas were soon involved in an epic defence of Now Zad. The Fusiliers endured some of the fiercest prolonged fighting of the operation in Musa Qala. The Paras fought tough battles at Sangin and elsewhere. With many of the troops dispersed in isolated locations, much of the fighting was of a defensive nature against Taliban seeking to wear down and then overrun the British positions. That they never did so was, first, a tribute to the courage and professional skills of the defenders and, second, to the use of air power. This included both NATO fixed wing aircraft, and 16 Air Assault Brigade's Apache attack helicopters.

The Brigade carried out manoeuvre operations in order to dominate ground, or to support or relieve defensive forces, but their capability was limited. The armoured element comprised a squadron of the Household Cavalry Regiment (HCR) equipped with CVR(T) (Combat Vehicle Reconnaissance (Tracked)). These were Scimitar (with 30mm cannon) or Spartan (Armoured Personnel Carrier with 7.62mm machine gun) and were essentially designed for reconnaissance rather than close combat. The manoeuvre force would frequently be of no more than combat team (company) size. (**See Plate 15**)

The ANA had its main base in what was to be called Camp Shorabak, which was built for them by the Americans, adjacent to Camp Bastion. They had a British Operational Mentoring and Liaison Team (OMLT) embedded with them. Many of the ANA soldiers were illiterate, poorly trained, and came from tribes that were traditionally hostile to the local Pashtun. Their first attempt at deploying a kandak (battalion) on operations can perhaps fairly be described as ignominious.

The infantry fighting during this period was of a duration and intensity that the British Army had not known since the Korean War. This is probably best illustrated by 3 PARA BG's use of ammunition. This amounted to:
- 480,000 rounds of small arms ammunition (so much for 'not a shot being fired')
- 31,000 cannon rounds
- 8,600 artillery shells and 7,500 mortar rounds
- 1,000 hand grenades and 85 anti-tank missiles.

Although the British had taken a lot of punishment, they had handed out a lot more. By September 2006, the Taliban around Musa Qala had taken a heavy beating and were finding it difficult to get replacements with harvest time coming on. Local leaders, who were desperate for an end to the fighting, approached the British and explained that the local Taliban had agreed to stay away as long as the British withdrew their force from Musa Qala. The British were willing to comply, and withdrew their mixed force of Paras and Fusiliers from Musa Qala.

Operation HERRICK 4 did not achieve what was initially hoped for, and what happened represented a huge shock to those who had planned it, albeit this was tempered in the short term because the full story of what had happened was slow to filter back to the public and some areas of Government. This should not be allowed to obscure the fact that it represented a major feat of arms by a small force whose professional skill and courage avoided what could easily have turned into a bloody debacle.

REME on Operation HERRICK 4

REME personnel played an absolutely critical role in Operation HERRICK 4 and, specifically, in ensuring that ES delivered fit equipment at crucial times. The story of what happened is perhaps best related in the words of those who were there in various roles.

Brigade HQ Perspective. The Brigade Deputy Chief of Staff (DCOS), (then) Major David Eastman REME offered the following recollections, which provide key insights into events from Brigade HQ perspective:

> 'Camp BASTION, when I arrived as DCOS 16 Air Assault Brigade in early April 2006, proved to be nothing more than a few tents, some ISO-containers, a dusty landing strip and some very large sand berms in the middle of a hot and empty desert. … I seem to remember that it took 28 minutes to jog very slowly around the perimeter in 2006 – in 2010 it was more than a marathon to run around the perimeter including SHORABAK and LEATHERNECK.
>
> The initial plan for operations in Helmand, developed by the HQ 16 Air Assault Brigade team in Colchester, revolved around what was known as the 'ink-spot theory' and required us to focus our security and development effort on a few areas, providing exemplars of how development could work, and then using these oases of development to spread the message that British forces combined with aid money were a force for good. The plan was to focus initially on a town called Musa Qala, and then work on a number of other areas using Mobile Outreach Groups (MOGs) –

small mobile teams containing cross-government aid personnel with military security in support. From the ES perspective, delivering this plan needed a concentration of resource in Camp BASTION, with first line detachments deploying in support of the MOGs – easily achievable and controllable within the limited ES resources that were initially deployed.

Unfortunately, the Musa Qala/MOG plan was disrupted very early in the deployment when the Pathfinders became trapped within the District Centre for a period of weeks. This, combined with unexpected threats across Helmand, eventually led to pressure on UK forces from the Governor, Engineer Daud, to protect all of the District Centres across the province and to the subsequent establishment of a deployed static Patrol Base network covering, initially, Musa Qala, Now Zad, Sangin and Garmsir to the south, although this expanded significantly as HERRICK progressed. Once the network had been established, self-sustainment, in all senses of the word, had to become the priority for the force. Given the widespread locations of the deployed operating bases we spent the early part of the operation developing a resupply matrix to make sure that we kept the troops fully sustained; any combat power that was left over once the resupply weekly missions had been completed was then available for combat operations.

Although we had experienced desert operations in Iraq, this set-up and the context that Op HERRICK developed into, especially as a result of the patrol base network, turned out to be a different order of problem altogether. The dispersed dispositions of the patrol bases, and the nature of the threat even at the very early stages of the deployment, reinforced the need for Equipment Support as far forward as possible. This required much of the equipment to be deployed before it was 'up-armoured', which meant when REME tradesmen tried to complete the task in Afghanistan – the equipment often was not correctly configured or did not arrive. This resulted in a huge amount of man-hours spent fitting what we had to whatever vehicle, and then swapping them over as the correctly configured armour arrived. This placed a significant strain on the deployed ES resources and also meant that we had limited control and understanding of ES Mat and the ES Mat picture across the deployed force. With a supply chain running thousands of miles and across tough terrain, trying to develop an understanding of our spares situation and predicting future spares requirements became a priority. Once in theatre, delivering spares forward became a real issue – every combat logistic patrol or helicopter flight added risk to life and needed to be fully justifiable. With this in mind, battlefield damage repair or expedient repair once again became a pre-requisite for our mechanics on the ground in order to keep the fleet of light-wheeled vehicles (Pinzgauer, WMIK and Land Rover Snatch) on the road whilst awaiting spares. One striking memory I have is the engineering ingenuity of our people. I think we had allowed our expedient repair training to lapse, but even without it our people worked wonders producing local solutions to quite complex problems. The Recovery Mechanics were exceptionally busy, in what proved to be a very hostile environment in every sense.

One of my roles prior to deployment was to develop the Force Element Table, which needed to include sufficient combat power to meet the initial plan, Training Teams, Engineers, RMP, dogs and handlers, Aviation and CSS assets able to provide third line support back to the UK, second line support to the deployed force, and enough ES capability to keep the force on the road and in the air throughout. All of this needed to be included within a force that was not to exceed just over 3,000 personnel lest we break the magic number denoting a 'Medium Scale' operation. Needless to say, the pressure to reduce the support element was intense and reduced to a bare minimum. As an example from the ES perspective, one impact was the development of a single 'Bastion LAD' based on personnel from all of the deploying Land forces and under the command of a Captain. This had a significant impact on our ability to resource the changed plan, with a deployed ES capability required at every location rather than just a central location.

The command and control set-up was unusual across the whole UK construct, from the UK one-star (Brigadier Ed Butler who also Commanded 16 Air Assault Brigade) in Kabul, to a Canadian one-star in Kandahar through a full Colonel Provincial Reconstruction Team Commander (Colonel Charlie Knaggs (late Irish Guards)) in Lashkar Gah, separated from the Brigade Headquarters, known as HQ Helmand Task Force, which at the time was run by a few majors. As the DCOS of 16 Air Assault Brigade I was usually responsible for a mix of first and second line capabilities. From the ES perspective, this included the LADs/Wksps from 3 Para,

7 RHA, 23 Engr Regt, 13 Air Asslt Supply Regt, 7 Air Asslt Bn REME and 9 Regt AAC, and second line capability from 7 Air Asslt Bn REME consisting of both aviation and Land ES. The Afghan construct removed the Brigade's second line capability from HQ Helmand Task Force and placed it under initially a National Support Contingent (Afghanistan) (NSC(A)) and then later a Joint Force Support (Afghanistan) organisation ostensibly based on the Joint Force Logistic Component HQ from Northwood. These second line assets became responsible for third line support to the theatre, second line support to the deployed force, and first line reinforcement of 3 Para BG and the Afghan National Army (ANA) Training Team creating an additional cross command and control boundary to overcome and requiring a great deal of liaison between HQ Helmand Task Force and JFSp(A).

As a result of the pressure to remain below 'medium scale', the changes to the initial plan and an unusual command and control construct, it is safe to say that the initial ES laydown proved to be far from ideal. That our soldiers were able to provide such excellent support under these conditions is testament once again to their ingenuity, perseverance and determination to deliver'.

A Second Line Perspective. This Brigade HQ perspective is interestingly complemented by the following recollections provided by the OC 8 Close Support Company (Parachute), (then) Major Andy Teskey REME:

> 'Planning for the deployment of 8 Close Support Company (Para), 16 Air Assault Brigade, began in 2005, the initial Force Element Table (FET) was 'lifted' from a very dated deployment plan that 24 Airmobile Brigade had designed. Our own estimate was constrained significantly by the pressure to remain under the maximum total force size of 3,000 personnel. We eventually were constrained to a deployed force of 4 + 101 for the land-focused REME second line elements. This composite company deployed under command of 13 Air Assault Support Regiment to form a Combat Service Support (CSS) Regiment. The Company would initially be based at Kandahar Airfield, with the intent to deploy forward to the soon to be built Camp Bastion.

After deploying on the recce with Brigadier Ed Butler, and witnessing firsthand the austere conditions we were deploying to and getting some valuable information from the US 174 Airborne Support Battalion, our preparation started to ensure the Company was ready for expeditionary ES and support to combat operations. From an ES perspective, we planned for the worst-case situation and packed to be completely self-sufficient on arrival. This included an additional aircraft (LIBRA) shelter to use as a workshop facility and all the 16/24KVA generators we could muster. Whilst promised a new workshop facility on Kandahar Airfield we were sceptical it would be ready – we were proved right! By the time HERRICK 4 finished in October 2006 the facility had not even been started.

An advanced party deployed to Kandahar Airfield (KAF) in March 2006 in support of 3 PARA Battlegroup with continued reinforcement until mid-May. The initial role of the Company based in the logistic park in the southeastern corner of KAF was to up-armour and fit ECM equipment to all B vehicles as they arrived after their tortuous journey from the UK to Karachi and onward land passage through the Khyber Pass to Afghanistan. The Company proved its core skills, and with the application of LEAN Principles, were fitting these kits quicker than they could be supplied. The Company 2IC (Captain Andy Craig REME) and Company ASM (WO1 Drysdale) recall:

> 'For vehicles such as the Close Support Tanker a bespoke 'core' kit was fitted with relative ease. Significant engineering challenges needed to be overcome on equipment such as DROPS and Bedford whose cabs had never been designed to carry such mass; door hinges quickly bowed at the strain. The irony in the case of the Bedford was that it provided decent blast protection to the radiator and offered no form of protection to the 1970s glass windscreen'.

As 3 PARA's deployment became more kinetic as did the demand for all our tradesmen. The Company provided an almost full-time CVR(T) crew to HCR in support of recce operations in the south of Helmand with Armourers and Vehicle Mechanics deployed forward, often by air, as 'flying-fitters'. The LIBRA shelters proved invaluable respite against the searing 50+°C heat and persistent dust of the desert. Dust storms were not uncommon and could last for a couple of days. All REME tradesmen delivered incredible mission effect but the Metalsmiths proved their absolute worth in the repair of mission-critical equipment and manufacture of spare parts we simply could not get through the convoluted, over-burdened logistic system.

I will remember Op HERRICK 4 as an exciting and successful operation. The Company was fully prepared for the mission and tasks given to it and the highly motivated men of 8 CS ES Coy (Para) shone in both combat and ES operations, all returned from HERRICK 4 safely to their families'.

Soldiers from 7 Air Assault Battalion REME on Operation HERRICK 4

REME Aviation. Air support was critical to what was achieved on Operation HERRICK 4, and the contribution of REME personnel was critical to its success. OC 9 (Attack Helicopter) (AH) Regiment AAC Workshop, (then) Major Dan Scott REME provided the following recollections:

'The Apache entered service at unit level in 2004… Less than two years later the superb attack helicopter would be flying the skies of Afghanistan, alongside American and Dutch Apaches, protecting the international force in southern Afghanistan.

The initial deployment of four Apache aircraft was based, as part of the Joint Helicopter Force (Afghanistan) (JHF(A)), out of Kandahar Airfield. The environment was austere but nothing compared to the forward element (JHF(A) Fwd) when it moved to Camp Bastion later in 2006. The flying contingent was based on 656 AH Sqn (Apache) and 672 Sqn (Lynx) with the maintenance support coming from 9 Regt AAC Workshop and elements of 7 Air Asslt Bn REME. WO2 (AQMS) Steve Parsons, later awarded the MBE for his effort in supporting the fielding and deployment of the Apache, was the lead Artificer, supported by SSgt Richie Twinn and SSgt Chris Brooks.

The principal maintenance location for the Apache remained in Kandahar throughout 2006, supporting HERRICK 4 and 5. The initial limit of 180 flying hours per month, 45 hours per airframe soon proved to be totally inadequate as the rate of combat activity and air support required grew. The aircraft numbers were increased to six Apache plus four Lynx MK9s. The operational situation and endurance time for a pair of Apache was greatly reduced with the transit time from Kandahar into Helmand Province. The operational decision to move Apache forward to Bastion placed great strain on the maintenance crews. SSgt Richie Twinn had the most demanding role establishing a maintenance location on the desert of a growing Camp Bastion. With no protection from the environment (weather and dust), he and his small team delivered exceptional mission-critical support. The two forward-based aircraft were able to deliver rapid and more enduring effect for missions in Helmand and Apaches never left Bastion for the remaining eight years of the conflict.'

(Then) Staff Sergeant Chris Brooks, who deployed as the second artificer to be forward based in Camp Bastion in 2006, recalls:

'Operation HERRICK was undoubtedly the most challenging and rewarding part of my career. For me, the deployment on HERRICK 4 started in earnest with a call to the AQMS's Office for a 'special' assignment a few weeks before deploying. "Plan, organise and manage the regimental move to HERRICK as we don't have a Unit Enplanement Officer anymore!"

Fast forward a couple of weeks and we were at RAF Brize Norton facilitating the air transportation of 14 DROPS vehicles worth of regimental equipment, personnel and aircraft (4 x Lynx Mk 9 and

6 x Apache Mk 1) via a combination of an Antonov 124 and C-17s. On arrival at Kandahar, I spent a week acclimatising and sorting out post-move admin then moved forward to Camp Bastion to take over from my opposite number SSgt Richie Twinn. Camp Bastion was very austere, without hangars or protection for the Apache or repair equipment. When we did move in to the new hangars the facilities were sparse; workbenches had to be made from empty Ammo Cages and flooring liberated from the 3 Para cookhouse. I was responsible for four Apache Mk1s from 656 Sqn and a pair of Lynx Mk 9 from 672 Sqn. The Lynx, which at that time were still fitted with the GEM engine, were only operational when the temperature allowed, with a self-imposed 'no fly' between 1000hrs and 1600hrs. With only a small team based forward at Camp Bastion the remainder of the Fitter Section were based in Kandahar Airfield (KAF) and combined with elements of 7 Air Asslt Bn REME conducted the lion's share of the maintenance, ultimately ensuring that we had the aircraft forward when we needed them. This worked well given the limited facilities (tooling, spares and ground support equipment) forward based in Camp Bastion.

3 Para were heavily engaged in Sangin amongst other locations and as the Apache's capabilities were proven the aircraft became more and more in demand. From that point on, we were pretty much on the go for the whole deployment with 'relief in place' of aircraft becoming the norm. An awesome aircraft, the Apache quickly gained its reputation for being the 'battle winning' capability it undoubtedly is.

The aircraft did receive battle damage on a number of occasions from small arms fire (SAFIRE). The most memorable during my time there was when one of the aircraft was hit by a 12.7mm DShK anti-aircraft round in the front left electronics bay (EFAB). This knocked out a number of key systems. Despite this the aircraft continued on task until the planned sortie was complete only returning to base an hour or so later, a testament to its resilience as well as to the tenacity of its aircrew.

One of the most memorable moments from the Apache's contribution in Afghanistan was the incredible brave and courageous recovery of a Royal Marine (who had been killed in action) from Jugroom Fort using one of the aircraft's stub wings'.

Major Scott summarised the impact of the Apache helicopter:

'The efforts of the technicians from 9 Regt AAC and 7 Air Asslt Bn supported the operational skill of the aircrew and ultimately delivered Apache operational success on its first test. Today, British forces would not consider a deployment without Apache cover. Op HERRICK 4 was the proving ground for that capability'.

REME at First Line. As ever, around two-thirds of REME who were deployed were at first line, doing what they always do *'keeping fit equipment in the hands of troops'*. Operational reports were notable for mention of 'mechanics' getting involved in the fighting at critical times. Thus, REME not only provided a vital reserve of military manpower when it was sorely needed, but was seen by others to have done so. Reports coming back on the REME net triggered an interest at staff level in the adequacy of REME military training (HQ DEME(A) letter of 6 December 2006). Inevitably, this reignited the perennial debate about *'soldier or tradesman first'*. Events in Helmand Province provided a reminder that the argument is academic; history has shown over and over again that REME soldiers must have both trade and military skills, and may have to switch from technical to operational tasks at a moment's notice.

OVERVIEW OF OPERATIONS HERRICK 5–13

Operation HERRICK 5
16 Air Assault Brigade handed over to 3 Commando Brigade for Operation HERRICK 5 (November 2006–April 2007). The agreement with the Taliban did not last long, and the British were forced to recapture the villages they had left. 3 Commando Brigade was better equipped than 16 Air Assault Brigade had originally been. They came equipped with Viking vehicles, armoured articulated tracked vehicles with excellent cross country mobility, which together with its other light armoured vehicles provided a greater capacity for mobile operations that they were keen to exploit. Their scope for doing this was limited, however, as they got involved in heavy static fighting in Sangin, Musa Qala, near the strategic Kajaki Dam and elsewhere, which tied up many of their resources.

Corporal Richard Street – Military Cross

Corporal Street was awarded the Military Cross for his actions in Helmand Province, as described in these extracts from the London Gazette dated 25 July 2008:

> 'Cpl Richard Street was commanding a lightly armoured Foden recovery vehicle in support of The King's Royal Hussars when they were ambushed on the road from Gereshk to Musa Qala in Afghanistan. He braved Taliban RPGs and small arms fire to dismount and hook the Foden to the KRH Squadron Leader's Mastiff, which had been immobilised during the attack'.

Corporal Street's citation praised his leadership of the Foden vehicle, the crew and his personal courage in recovering the vehicle under sustained fire. The patrol fought through the ambush but came up against a bridge that would not take the weight of the 23-tonne Mastiff vehicles. With no alternative but to backtrack into the danger zone, the patrol returned to the ambush site. The Taliban were waiting and launched two more attacks. Small arms fire destroyed the front left wheel of the Foden but Corporal Street pushed forward and fired his pistol from the window while driving one-handed and encouraging his crew. Corporal Street's citation continued:

> 'His decision to continue to drive a partially disabled vehicle with no serious ballistic or mine blast protection through two enemy ambushes kept the route free for the squadron, maintained tempo at a critical time and undoubtedly prevented significant casualties from being taken.
>
> He was an example to all around him, particularly given the paucity of protection he enjoyed and the vicious nature of a contact that saw an armoured squadron post more than 20 grenades and left more than 20 enemy dead. He was a credit to his squadron and Corps and his was a conspicuous display of gallantry'.

A Strategic Stalemate 2006–2009

By the end of Operation HERRICK 5, it was clear that a strategic stalemate had been reached, which was to last the next few years, as outlined here.

The Taliban had realised that attempts to dislodge British troops from fixed bases, or to engage them in major battles was not a good idea. Considering the ferocity of the early fighting, the British casualties had been remarkably low whilst the insurgents had been heavily punished. The Taliban therefore gradually changed to the classic tactics used by the militarily weak against the militarily strong. Major direct assaults became fewer, and greater use was made of Improvised Explosive Devices (IEDs), ambushes on patrols, sniping attacks with small arms and rocket grenades, and even suicide attacks that had previously been a rarity in Afghanistan.

The British steadily built up their forces, in number and capability. 16 Air Assault Brigade initially deployed on Operation HERRICK 4 with a single infantry battalion. When it returned on Operation HERRICK 8 it had five infantry battalions.

This force level allowed deployment to a number of MOBs, FOBs, Patrol Bases (PB) and Check Points (CP) on routes. These could be securely held, and the area immediately around them could be dominated by patrolling.

Force levels were insufficient, however, to inflict an overwhelming strategic defeat on the Taliban, or to win the 'hearts and minds' of the populace to the degree that enough would fully support the Government, and volunteer the intelligence needed to foil and eradicate the Taliban. In the event, the increased use of IEDs started to make movement outside bases, and between bases, increasingly hazardous. Helicopter lift was limited (and expensive), and Combat Logistic Patrols (CLP) became the necessary means of land resupply. These were heavily escorted convoys of vehicles carrying material and personnel. They often had to move very very slowly because of the risk of ambushes and IED strikes, which were an everyday event. They were given the generic title of Operation MUBAREZ. In short, whilst the Taliban showed no signs of defeating the security forces, the security forces themselves seemed to be making little headway in eliminating the Taliban permanently, and the British Army was continuing to take painfully high casualties.

A Combat Logistic Patrol moves through a village in Helmand Province

The Changing Balance 2010–2011

In January 2009, Barack Obama became President of the USA. He was keen to end US (and ISAF) ground force combat involvement by 2014, but accepted that a 'surge' of additional US forces was required to create a situation where the Afghan National Security Forces (ANSF) would be capable of assuming full responsibility for security in Afghanistan. He announced in February 2009 that a further 17,000 US troops would be sent, and in December 2009 that a further 30,000 would follow. The arrival of these troops, in combination with other factors, did not completely break the stalemate throughout the British area of operations, but, specifically, it significantly tipped the balance against the insurgents.

US troops were able to take over some of the most difficult parts of the operational area, including Sangin, Musa Qala and the Kajaki Dam. Initially, they suffered proportionately much heavier casualties than the British had, but were able to swamp the area with sufficient troops to suppress the insurgents.

The British built up their forces, deploying three additional infantry battalions. The overall force ratio had therefore shifted in the right direction. There were now around 30,000 ISAF troops deployed in much the same area that 16 Air Assault Brigade had tried to control with a force of 3,500 on Operation HERRICK 4.

There was more, and better, equipment available. This included heavily armoured wheeled vehicles with a high degree of immunity against IEDs and hand-held anti-tank weapons. These helped to restore mobility to the British forces.

An increasing number of PBs and manned CPs were set up, frequently after operations (some mounted from the air) to clear insurgents from areas that they had previously controlled. Such positions could be rapidly fortified by the Sappers with Hesco barriers (steel mesh and fabric containers that could be filled with material such as sand and rubble). There were also significant developments in Intelligence, Surveillance, Target Acquisition and Reconnaissance (ISTAR) systems, in the form of aerial vehicles and also ground-mounted sensors, including cameras mounted on towers set up in bases.

The ANSF were growing in numbers and competence. Operations were increasingly conducted jointly with them, with responsibility being gradually transferred to them.

The infrastructure was being improved. In particular, dirt roads were being replaced by tarred roads. It is far more difficult to conceal an IED under a 'black top' road than a dirt one. This was an important factor in restoring mobility to the security forces.

Casualties

The figures for fatalities give a useful indication of the way the balance had swung. Between 2001 and 2006, only two British soldiers had been killed by hostile action in Afghanistan. The table at Figure 11.1 (at the end of this Chapter) shows further fatalities up to the end of 2011, excluding those killed in the Nimrod aircraft crash as these would distort the picture. By 2011, the effect of the progress made against the insurgents had led to substantial reduction in casualty figures, which was to be sustained the next year.

The UK Land Commitment to Operations HERRICK 5–13

The UK land forces in Helmand Province were grouped either under a one-star operational HQ, which became known as Task Force Helmand (TFH), or under a one-star logistic HQ. The logistic HQ, which, from early-2008, was called Joint Force Support (Afghanistan) (JFSp(A)) was initially based in Kandahar, but redeployed to Camp Bastion in 2009. TFH was based around a UK operational brigade, which would deploy for a six-month tour with its commander and his HQ team. The logistic HQ and its commander were based on one of the UK logistic brigades, and they similarly did a six-month tour. REME second line support was provided by the Theatre ES Battalion, the core of which was provided by one of the REME battalions. Appropriate elements, from individuals to complete sub-units, were attached or detached to ensure that the Theatre ES Battalion deployed with the right manning, equipment and training for its task. The table at Figure 11.2 (at the end of this Chapter) provides an indication of the size and composition of the UK land commitment for Operations HERRICK 5–14.

In addition to the infantry/Royal Armoured Corps (RAC) units shown in the table, there were contributions (which naturally varied throughout the period) from other arms and services, all of which had equipment supported by REME.

Royal Artillery. The Royal Artillery contribution comprised a regiment equipped with the 105mm Light Gun, a troop of MLRS, a Surveillance and Target Acquisition (STA) battery and an Unmanned Aerial Vehicle (UAV) battery.

Royal Engineers. The Sapper contribution was based on a regiment, but which was heavily reinforced and supported by a variety of specialist sub-units. They played a key role in quickly fortifying bases and checkpoints, in building roads and bridges, and in clearing mines and IEDs.

Army Air Corps. Both Apache and Lynx helicopters were deployed, initially based on Kandahar Airfield, but with Camp Bastion also being used (see also Chapter 15 ('REME Aviation')).

Royal Logistic Corps. A RLC regiment provided the core of a theatre logistic battalion (similar to a theatre ES battalion). Various specialist RLC organisations were also deployed including a Heavy Equipment Transporter (HET – tank transporter in old terminology) squadron, and a substantial element from the RLC Explosive Ordnance Disposal (EOD) Regiment.

Others. There were other contributions including from Royal Signals, a medical unit and a provost organisation.

THE EVOLVING EQUIPMENT DEPENDENCY ON OPERATIONS HERRICK 5–13

It became clear very quickly that UK forces in Afghanistan needed more and better equipment. Urgent Operational Requirement (UOR) programmes were pushed hard, and soon more capable equipment starting reaching the theatre. REME's dependency therefore rapidly increased in numbers and complexity. The UOR process is often a far from perfect way of ensuring that equipment is delivered with a full supporting package of spares, special tools, publications, training courses and the like. As so often in the past, REME's ingenuity and determination was the key to overcoming such deficiencies and keeping UOR equipment operational. Some of the key developments in the equipment dependency are described here, with additional information in Chapter 20 ('Army Equipment and its Management').

Wheeled Armoured Vehicles

Snatch Land Rover was originally deployed to Afghanistan. It is a mobile lightly-armoured vehicle, with useful agility in an urban environment. It provided basic protection against small arms, and a degree of protection against blast, and was satisfactory in the relatively low-threat environment for which it was intended. It proved very vulnerable in the sort of operational environment that developed in Afghanistan, and after attracting considerable adverse publicity it was withdrawn from service and replaced with other vehicles. The Vector vehicle was marginally better protected, but was a fairly basic light-armoured vehicle, vulnerable to buried IEDs, based on the Pinzgauer 6 x 6 chassis. It was retained in service as much more capable equipments were fielded.

Jackal/Coyote. Jackal is an open-topped armoured vehicle based on a 4 x 4 truck chassis, originally developed for UK special forces. It was mobile and agile, and protected the crew from the sides and underneath with heavy slabs of armour (with protection increased in the Jackal 2). It offered excellent visibility and was an excellent weapons platform, albeit that head and shoulders were exposed when firing. It was used for reconnaissance, rapid assault, fire support and convoy protection. Coyote is basically a stretched version of the Jackal (with more carrying capacity) mounted on a 6 x 6 chassis and classed as a Tactical Support Vehicle (TSV).

Jackal vehicle

Mastiff/Ridgeback/Wolfhound Family. Although these vehicles were developed in America, their design drew on the experience of the Rhodesian and South African armies who used mine-protected vehicles in bush wars. Their basic concept was that the vehicle crew would be inside an armoured boat-shaped hull, which would deflect the blast from any mines the vehicles triggered. It was accepted that wheels, axles and other parts of the vehicle could be blown off by the blast, provided that the occupants of the vehicle hull remained safe.

Mastiff 2 Protected Patrol Vehicle (PPV). This is a huge 6 x 6 vehicle especially adapted for British Army use. It was heavily armoured to start with, and had extra armour of various types fitted, including LROD cage armour. Steel cage armour had been around for a very long time as a form of protection against shaped charge weapons, such as RPGs, but had the disadvantage of being very heavy. LROD is an aluminum alternative (produced by BAE Systems), which is as effective, but weighs far less. LROD is now widely used on UK, US and other nations' Protected Mobility (PM) vehicles. Mastiff has a crew of 2 + 8 and mounts a 7.62mm GPMG and a 0.50 (12.7mm) machine gun or 40mm grenade launcher. At the time of drafting this Chapter, nobody had ever been killed by enemy action whilst in a Mastiff vehicle.

Ridgeback PPV. This is essentially a 4 x 4 version of the Mastiff vehicle. Its smaller size made it more manoeuvrable in close country or urban environments.

Wolfhound TSV. This is the 'logistic' version of the Mastiff family, intended for use as a gun limber, logistical load carrier, and a REME support vehicle. (**See Plate 16**)

Buffalo Mine Protected Vehicle (MPV). The Buffalo vehicle represents another variation on the heavy PM vehicle theme. It was originally based on a South African vehicle (the Casspir), and has been fitted with an articulated arm intended to be used for ordnance disposal. (**See Plate 17**)

Panther Command and Liaison Vehicle (CLV). The 7-tonne Panther vehicle is the UK variant of an Iveco armoured vehicle. It has been chosen as the Army's future command and liaison vehicle (FCLV), and is intended to replace Land Rover, Saxon, and some FV430 in these roles.

Husky TSV. The Husky vehicle is a 4 x 4 support vehicle designed especially for the British Army. It is intended to replace Land Rover and

AFGHANISTAN – THE LONG HAUL

other vehicles used for the support of light armour. It is well protected for its size/weight, but does not offer comparable protection to such vehicles as Wolfhound. **(See Plate 18)**

Tracked Armoured Vehicles
CVR(T) was deployed from the beginning, and was soon to be joined by the Royal Marines Viking all-terrain armoured vehicles, as well as various variants of the well-tried Warrior family, and CRARRV. Two new types of armoured vehicle appeared in theatre.

Warhog All-Terrain Protected Mobility Vehicle (ATPMV). This is an adaption of a vehicle developed in Singapore. It is an articulated tracked vehicle which is very similar in appearance to the Viking, but is far better protected. The Warthog, along with Jackal and CVR(T), had an important role to play in the TFH Brigade Mobile Force, whose operations were not restricted to major routes, and which could strike rapidly and unexpectedly by moving through difficult terrain.

Warthog vehicle

Trojan Armoured Vehicle Royal Engineers (AVRE). This 62-tonne vehicle was designed to open routes through complex battlefield obstacles, and to clear a path through minefields. It incorporated a full-width mine plough, dozer blade and excavator arm. Its chassis is based on the

Challenger 2, and its deployment required the deployment of a REME CRARRV to recover it.

Talisman Mine Clearance Vehicle. Talisman was the collective name for a system, which comprised:
- **Mastiff 2 PPV** together with a **Buffalo MPV**
- **JCB** high-mobility engineer excavator – a modified/protected variant of a commercial equipment
- **T-Hawk Micro Air Vehicle** – this extraordinary little craft is not much bigger than a dinner plate and is powered by a horizontal fan, which enables it to hover over its desired target and feed back real-time pictures
- **Talon** – a small tracked remote control vehicle used for dealing with explosive devices – those familiar with the old Wheelbarrow system used in Northern Ireland might call it 'son of Wheelbarrow'.

Wheeled Support Vehicles

A new range of support vehicles (SV) built by MAN was increasingly deployed. This included a recovery version of the heaviest vehicle in the range, the SV(R). This 32-tonne vehicle was deployed to complement the venerable Foden recovery vehicle, which continued to give sterling service. The SV(R) was generally well regarded by its REME crews.

ISTAR and other Electronic/Optronic Systems

This heading covers a hugely important area of development. In essence, the operational challenge was to spot and positively identify an enemy who was not keen to be spotted, who was adept at blending into his surroundings, and who might use mobile phones to communicate or to trigger IEDs. Major efforts went into developing appropriate defensive electronic systems, deploying effective sensors and surveillance systems of many types, and providing the communication/control systems necessary to allow the integration of information from all sources, and its timely dissemination to those in need of it. There were many facets to the work.

Protective Anti-IED ECM Systems. Some of these were man-portable, and some were fitted to vehicles. Their aim was to prevent the enemy from triggering IEDs by electronic means. Fitting, testing and fixing such equipment was a significant task for REME.

AFGHANISTAN – THE LONG HAUL

Royal Artillery Systems. The Gunners operated a variety of specialist systems. These included Mamba, a battlefield radar with 40km range, and a lightweight counter-mortar radar. They flew the Hermes UAV, which was a modified version of an Israeli UAV, and which was to come into full UK service as the Watchkeeper, after some further modification.

Desert Hawk UAV. This is a small UAV, which can be held in one hand and looks like something out of a model aircraft shop. It can be programmed to fly a particular path and feed back live pictures of what it flies over. It is used at company level, and proved very effective in providing pictures of what is 'on the other side of the hill'.

Desert Hawk UAV

REME AND EQUIPMENT SUPPORT FOR OPERATIONS HERRICK 5–13

Operation HERRICK 5 saw the CO of the REME Battalion double-hatted as the Commander ES. He and his successors had to cope with an evolving situation, which was very different from that originally envisaged. Whilst the basic principles on which REME support had traditionally been based proved extremely robust, the way in which they were applied had to be modified to meet the circumstances. Rather than outline what happened on every Operation HERRICK tour, the following REME 'snapshots' of specific tours have been selected, with a view to highlighting the changes and the issues that were important at the time.

A REME 'Snapshot' of Operation HERRICK 6

For Operation HERRICK 6 (March–September 2007), overall ES command and control rested with the Commander ES at HQ National Support Command (Afghanistan) (NSC(A)) based at Kandahar, who was also the CO of 4 Battalion REME. He headed a small ES branch of six personnel, including both RLC and RAF staff. It was responsible for ES for ground vehicles and equipment for UK force elements, and for other embedded nations. Apache and Lynx helicopters were the responsibility of the Joint Helicopter Force (JHF), which was supported by around 90 REME technicians.

First Line. At this stage of the operation, it made sense to 'brigade' many of the LAD resources and, hence, a TFH LAD was created. This was some 160 strong, and was primarily based in Camp Bastion, but with many personnel deployed in outstations around the region. A smaller LAD operated in Kandahar, and an even smaller one in Kabul to provide support for local units.

TFH LAD 'Main' at Camp Bastion on Operation HERRICK 6

Second Line. The second line situation was explained in 'DEME(A)'s Report to the Corps 2007' in the REME Journal (Spring 2008). Around 140 officers and soldiers from 4 Battalion REME provided second line support. Working conditions in Afghanistan were extremely difficult at first, with repairs being undertaken in rapid-erect shelters or in the open, where dust and heat (up to 50°C in the summer) were not conducive to efficient working or engineering hygiene. (**See Plate 19**) By September 2007, a new purpose-built workshop in Camp Bastion was handed over by contractors to REME. This was called Tel el-Kebir Lines (named after REME's largest base workshop in Egypt during World War 2). It was shared by the second line ES Company and TFH LAD, and its two large hangars, overhead crane, lights, power, hard standing and the protection provided against dust all contributed to greater efficiency.

Deployment and Control. The nature of the operation meant that the traditional first/second line structure was pragmatically modified with much collocation and concentration. For example, all Armourers were grouped at first line, and all Metalsmiths at second line. Recovery was concentrated at second line and controlled within the TFH area of responsibility (AOR) by the Brigade EME (BEME). Where technically feasible, and tactically possible, repair took place in the FOBs and MOBs. Recovery was often a dangerous business, and REME personnel frequently had to perform recovery tasks in minefields or under fire.

Equipment Issues. There were 1,700 equipments of at least 120 types deployed, ranging from Warrior to quad bikes. The harsh terrain and environment took a heavy toll of vehicles. It was soon realised that equipment care was a key force multiplier, and that breaking down in the desert or Green Zone was not good news. Equipments were generally inspected at least once every 21 days; also before and after specific operations. Suspension components, brakes and steering took a hammering and required frequent attention. The altitude, heat, dust, harsh terrain, additional weight of armour and payload, coupled with having to run on F63 fuel (AVTUR aviation fuel with added lubricant) meant that many equipments were operating at the extremes of their design limits, and were achieving mean distances between failures (MDBF) that were far lower than their normal planning figures. Spares were often a problem, and various forms of battlefield and expedient repair had to be resorted to. A variety of UOR equipments arrived in theatre, ranging from completely new equipments such as Mastiff and Vector, through to smaller items fitted to existing equipment. These almost invariably came without a complete Integrated Logistic Support (ILS) package of spares, publications, training material and the like. This reduced the capability these equipments provided, and would have done much more so without the ingenuity and technical resourcefulness of REME staff in theatre.

Achievements. Despite all these difficulties an overall theatre equipment availability of 84% was achieved. Around 200 E&MA had been replaced at second line. Recovery tasks varied between 250–550 per month (with 170 tasks in one week in June 2007).

Tribute. The best compliments are those that come from outsiders. The following remarks were extracted from a letter to DEME(A) from the Commander UK NSC(A):

> 'At a recent TFH Planning and Review Meeting, Brigadier Lorimer (Comd TFH) praised REME (both the ES Company and the TFH LAD) as the unsung heroes of the Task Force. The OC of the Brigade Reconnaissance Force also referred to the 'Herculean efforts' of his Fitter Section in keeping his fleet of vehicles available during extended desert patrols.… Throughout their time they have raised the availability of battlewinning equipments. They have also rebuilt vital assets such as WMIK (weapons mount installation kit) from bare chassis using their engineering knowledge and skills to best effect.… Indeed it has become a local 'badge of honour' to be among the elite who have completed a WMIK chassis change.
>
> REME have also been out on the ground supporting patrols, making repair decisions under fire and returning the compliment when they have had the enemy in their sights. The support they have given to the Viking Armoured Support Troop (AST) has been particularly significant.… Such is the close working relationship that … (REME mechanics) … deploy with the AST. All REME tradesmen, from the Aircraft Technician repairing the complex beast that is Apache, to the Metalsmith working in temperatures of over 60°C, can be rightly proud of what they have achieved'.
> **(See Plate 20)**

AFGHANISTAN – THE LONG HAUL

A REME 'Snapshot' of Operation HERRICK 8
A year further down the line, on Operation HERRICK 8 (April–September 2008), saw the growth of IED attacks – up some 700% from previous tours. Movement was becoming increasingly hazardous, and pressure on surface lines of communication (L of C), plus an overworked strategic air bridge meant that minds were turning to the idea of doing more equipment restoration in theatre. Consequently, a Statement of Requirement was submitted to PJHQ for a Level 3+ capability for the regeneration of key equipment fleets, and the integration of UOR equipment. Basically, this was a static workshop capable of doing some of the work that would normally have been done by contractors and base workshops in UK. The aim was to reduce the cost of transporting equipment between theatre and UK, and to reduce the pressure on the L of C.

The ES command ORBAT and system of command and control was continuously being refined. In essence, the REME contribution was being task organised to meet the specific circumstances on the ground, with the laydown being based on capability rather than peacetime ownership. The CO of 7 Air Assault Battalion REME, Lieutenant Colonel Simon Warner REME, assumed the role of Commander ES Group/Commander Equipment Capability. His responsibilities included:

- 7 Armoured Company (from 2 CS Battalion REME), which supported all heavy vehicle assets in Regional Command South (including TFH) – this involved supporting Warrior, Viking and CVR(T) vehicles, and carrying out power pack repair
- 8 Field Company (Parachute) coordinated all recovery support theatre wide and supported DROPS, Foden, Jackal, WMIK variants, Vector and Pinzgauer vehicles
- TFH LAD was 'brigaded' from 22 units under the OC 23 Engineer Regiment Workshop and was responsible for all support forward of Camp Bastion, and had close links with 7 Armoured Company with respect to the provision of FRTs and ISTs
- Kandahar Joint Force Workshop was based on the LADs of 3 PARA and 6 Supply Regiment RLC, and was commanded by a platoon commander from 7 Armoured Company.

A REME Junior Officer's Perspective. The following is an extract from an article about his tour ('A Junior Officer's Perspective') by Lieutenant Gilbey Crilley REME in The Craftsman magazine (October 2008):

'With three months of the tour complete it seems a perfect opportunity to reflect on the REME support in the theatre and consider what the future holds for Equipment Support Group. The entire ES Group continues to work in harmony, deploying tradesmen throughout Helmand, offering technical support and advice to Battlegroups and TFH units. It is clear that ES has improved, operations are joined up and surge operations target expertise and resources in order to optimise effectiveness.

The demands placed on ES Group continue in surges, attempting to predict workload and equipment failures is definitely a betting man's game. For the B vehicle VMs, the greatest workload appears from the Combat Logistic Patrols (CLPs), Interim Safety Inspections (ISI) are completed every 21 days. After hundreds of kilometres of unforgiving terrain in the desert, with frequent skirmishes with the enemy, and indeed the drivers, the vehicles require considerable attention. VM working hours generally spiral as vehicles are regenerated during short periods between each CLP.

The A Mechs are equally stretched, and the aged CVR(T) fleet is beginning to show its age after almost two years continuously operating in Afghanistan. Further UOR additions continue to be a talking point; the Integrated Project Teams have installed new turrets, upgraded the induction system, mounted front and rear security cameras and are currently looking into methods to improve the torsion bar suspension. The WR fleet operates tirelessly for extended periods on the ground. With the focus on forward effect, interim restorations have taken place in FOBs. This has involved considerable planning, reinforced by synchronised spares delivery.

The Metalsmiths continue support vehicle restorations and the CLP restoration work in their usual brutal manner. Their reputation has grown throughout Bastion after completing work for most of the nations operating in Helmand. Finally, the technicians; work is flowing through their un-air-conditioned box bodies in waves'.

A REME Recovery Mechanic's Perspective. This extract came from a report by Craftsman Hughes of his experiences as a Recovery Mechanic:

'I have been at Camp Bastion now for four months and the pace of operations and intensity of the CLPs has been fast and tiring. I have had some great experiences; I've been out with the US Marine Corps for two weeks ... providing recovery support for a bridge crossing. Only 2km from our totally isolated location the firefight and fast air could be heard rumbling in the distance. When on the CLPs in the north, it has become common to be contacted with RPGs small arms and mortars and/or a mine strike! Still, whilst all this is going on you must do the job asked. The CLPs last for anything up to seven days, the preparation for which is exhausting ... Even though I haven't completed a recovery camp and I'm only a Crafty, I've been sent out on several demanding but petrifying jobs, the learning curve had been extremely steep but I have loved every minute of it'. (**See Plate 21**)

A REME First Line Perspective. The majority of REME personnel were embedded at first line, and the following is an extract from a report by Corporal Carl White of a Warrior section:

'On 13 May my Platoon Commander informed me that I was going to deploy forward to support the Warrior Company, 4 SCOTS. That evening we arrived by Chinook at FOB Edinburgh.... Despite the long hours, blazing hot sun and dust, morale in the section was high and the atmosphere was good.... First thing in the morning it was all hands on deck to get 24C (my vehicle) back on the road. After various small arms attacks and a mine strike it needed more than a little TLC. We changed both tracks, sprockets, support wheels, road wheels and reset the rear four torsion bars to compensate for the armoured belly plate fitted.

Current ops with the Warrior Company can be anything from one to four days, however previously they have been as long as six weeks. Each vehicle in the Company is heavily loaded with ammunition, water, rations, personal equipment and spares. This has a noticeable effect on the vehicles' performance, which required more regular servicing and maintenance. On many occasions, we had to have power packs and spares air dropped to our location day and night.

After a number of successful ops, we headed back to Camp Bastion for the vehicle rehab. This was usually an eight to ten hours' journey even with vehicles in tow. One journey took 18 hours! ... It started well with good progress, but it seemed that all was going too well. At just over half way we had half-tracked a vehicle, replaced at least two road wheels for each, with the rest running low. The running gear on the vehicles received a lot of punishment on the demanding journey. With very few spares to fit … Luckily the company made it back to Camp Bastion safe and sound'.

A REME 'Snapshot' of Operation HERRICK 10

Operation HERRICK 10 (April–September 2009) was a period of increasingly intensive operations to deepen the hold in Helmand Province. The British (with the assistance of the ANSF, Danes and other ISAF contributors) led a series of operations called Panther's Claw (July 2009). These involved strikes, by land and helicopter, to dislodge insurgents from areas north and northwest of Lashkar Gah, which had been largely controlled by the Taliban. Having dislodged them, bases and checkpoints were set up to control the local areas. An important 'black top' road (Route Trident) was built by the Sappers, and the ANSF were increasingly involved in taking over security. The Americans were concurrently active in other parts of Helmand Province, increasing the pressure on the insurgents.

Although the infantry, exposed on patrol, bore the brunt of the casualties, REME personnel were frequently involved in dangerous operations, or had to complete their tasks under fire. Sadly, four REME soldiers were killed in action during the preceding year. 558 new UOR platforms were deployed, and the overall strength of the ES Group had risen to 511 (this figure excludes those involved in aviation support).

During this period the support organisation was rationalised:
- the 'brigaded' TFH LAD was broken up into four LADs, each commanded by a Captain able to act as BG EMEs and provide the vital ES interface with the BG CO
- tactical mobility had become an increasing challenge with greater use made of second line to provide ISTs and individuals to enhance support at forward bases (some 20 ISTs being deployed during the tour).

The table at Figure 11.3 (at the end of this Chapter) from 'DEME(A)'s Report to the Corps 2009' in the REME Journal (2010), summarises the work on mechanical equipments carried out by the ES Group during a six-month tour.

It was not only the Vehicle Mechanics who were busy. Around 750 recovery tasks were completed, and both Armourers and Metalsmiths were heavily loaded. The table at Figure 11.4 (at the end of this Chapter) lists the number of electronic/optical equipments repaired.

REME Aviation. REME was well represented within the Joint Aviation Group, as recorded in 'DEME(A)'s Report to the Corps 2008' in the REME Journal (2009). The Senior Engineering Officer with overall engineering and airworthiness responsibility for all UK UAVs and helicopters (including RAF) was a REME major. The Apache Helicopter Squadron was deployed at Camp Bastion along with a detachment (1 + 51) from 3 Regiment AAC LAD (on a 4-month rotation tour). Average availability was 83% despite average usage at 600 hours/month being over the planning figure of 500 hours. Lynx helicopters were deployed to Camp Bastion along with a 21-man detachment from 1 Regiment AAC Workshop. The role of the Lynx helicopters was evolving to include such tasks as airborne mission command, infra-red Nitesun illumination, and escort for support helicopters going to FOBs in lower risk areas (freeing up Apache helicopters). (**See Plate 22**)

CLPs. With the security forces widely dispersed in bases and checkpoints, which the Taliban found increasingly difficult and costly to attack, an obvious response by the Taliban was to try and limit movement between bases by means of IEDs and ambushes. They were thereby successful in limiting the ability of the security forces to manouevre, or resupply their bases (other than by air). The following extracts are from an amusing article in The Craftsman magazine (November 2009), written by Captain Mortimer RLC, titled 'Pulling Squaddies Out of Wadis – Op HERRICK 10':

> 'As the Troop Commander of the HET Troop deployed on Op Herrick 10 you may think it is slightly odd that I should be writing an article for the Craftsman magazine.... I fear that if it were widely known that this article is positive in nature I could be lynched, as it is, I will be writing under my pseudonym Capt A N Loggie to avoid any violent repercussions.
>
> 'Pulling Squaddies out of Wadis' has rather become the job description of both the Rec Mechs from 4 CS Bn REME and the Tank Transporters of 19 Tk Tptr Sqn RLC deployed on Herrick 10. On occasion this crossover of capability has created more than a little tension, but what I have seen on this tour is proof

that miracles really can be achieved when those two bodies of outstanding soldiers pool their resources, and far more, share their resourcefulness. For those not familiar with the Combat Logistic Patrol (CLP) this is the method of moving bulk Container Supplies (CSups) and the like around Helmand (and beyond). The average CLP will comprise around 80 vehicles (up to 130, never less than 40) including intimate force protection, task vehicles and recovery units. The main problem with a CLP is because of its large footprint it is essentially a very large and very slow target, and despite the fact it is well armed, IEDs are a constant and effective threat. The main defence of the CLP lies in the maintenance of momentum, that responsibility lies largely with the recovery assets deployed namely the SV(R), the Foden and HET.

Now to call the HET a recovery asset is a misnomer; HET is purely deployed on the CLP to un-bog bogged in vehicles and occasionally drag vehicles which are broken but able to move. The REME recovery vehicles are there to recover non-moving vehicles and those badly damaged through IEDs. A CLP is a complex beast to plan and to complete takes enormous effort from all involved. At the beginning of the tour there was competition between HET drivers and Rec Mechs, as each had at times to pull the other out of a spot of bother. However, unity does spring from diversity and one operation in particular finally put paid to this unhealthy work ethic.

The Op was a normal CLP to deliver stores to Forward Operating Base (FOB) EDI, but with the additional task of having to recover seven badly damaged Warrior vehicles. For some reason, the operation seems to have had more than the average high level interest and there was a palpable pressure in the air that this operation needed to be a success at almost any cost – I am sure I heard my OC utter in orders 'come back with the Warriors or don't come back at all Capt Mortimer (I mean Capt A N Loggie)'. After all the planning that had gone on for this operation what could possibly go wrong? Well of course just about everything … five IED strikes; two Mastiffs, and EPLS, and SV(R) and HET trailer were taken out of the game in the space of 10–15km, which incidentally took all day to complete. This was combined with the normal bog-ins and breakdowns, which are unavoidable with 100+ vehicles in this environment.

In truth, the task was monumental and unbeknown to us Bn HQ were already CONPLANning options to send out a rescue mission, but they had not bargained how up for it the lads were. All competition was put to one side and I have never seen two separate groups work so hard and so well together for the benefit of all. For around 60km a SV(R) was towing another strike-disabled SV(R), which was in turn towing a strike-damaged Mastiff over terrain that Shackleton would balk at. The HET with the trailer strike (carrying a brace of Warriors) made it back to Bastion, but would have been left burning in the desert if not for the constant support (and winch jobs) from the REME boys. This operation proved to us all how well the two trades and pieces of equipment can complement each other, and it is a relationship I hope to be continued throughout our commitment to Afghanistan and beyond'.

A REME 'Snapshot' of Operation HERRICK 12

The UK force had been increased in size, and a high level of operational activity continued during Operation HERRICK 12 (April–September 2010). The Sangin area was handed over to US forces in September 2010 allowing UK troops to be deployed elsewhere. A combination of additional forces, the cumulative effect of earlier operations and an increasingly effective contribution by the ANSF increasingly took its toll on the Taliban, as new areas (and routes) were firmly secured.

With additional forces deployed to the theatre, there was a need to modify and upgrade the REME/ES organisation. This was now 627 strong (30 + 597). Key changes were made.

A new post for a Colonel Equipment Capability (EC) was set up at HQ JFSp(A). The first post holder was Colonel Mark Gaunt (late REME). His organisation was able to pull together the many strands of managing equipment and its support, including dealing with contractors, and with other staff branches in theatre, UK or elsewhere. This freed up the formerly double-hatted Commander EC/CO REME Battalion to collocate with his Battalion (1 CS Battalion REME – 286 strong – all cap badges), which would enable him to concentrate on operations within TFH, and to give advice to HQ TFH and JFSp(A) when required. A new Joint Force BEME post was created who would report to Commander EC. With the transfer of responsibility for security to the ANA a key long-term goal, it was decided to relocate the ES Battalion LAD to Camp Shorabak (the ANA camp adjacent to Camp Bastion). Some 35 Locally Employed Civilians

(LEC) were taken on as mechanics, partly with a view to breaking down barriers of language and culture. This was seen as a successful example of the 'Afghan First' policy being put into practice.

Second Line. The high level of operational activity on the tour necessitated the continuing and increased deployment of ISTs to forward locations. Soldiers from 1 CS Battalion REME completed 201 IST tasks and deployed to 70 different FOBs and PBs. The support for Base-ISTAR was a commitment that grew exponentially during the tour. Essentially, this involved setting up and maintaining sophisticated surveillance devices (such as cameras and thermal imaging equipment) mounted on tall framework masts set up within bases, and 69 'fly forward teams' were provided to 39 FOBs and PBs, giving REME technicians plenty of experience of climbing up exposed towers within sight of potential enemy.

Recovery. This continued to be a vital function in view of the high level of IED activity. CLPs always included a recovery element, and it was the view of many at the time that recovery vehicles and their crews tended to be particularly targeted during ambushes and the follow up to them. The SV(R) was regarded as an excellent vehicle, but was inevitably vulnerable to a degree to low metal content IEDs that were increasingly used (as they were more difficult to detect). An indication of the scale of the threat is that four of the ES Battalion's Recovery Platoon's nine SV(R) vehicles were damaged by IEDs. The repair of IED-damaged wheeled armoured vehicles became a key REME commitment.

Recovery vehicle 24B recovers the first of 12 Mastiff IED strikes in the shadows of Mount Musa Qala on Operation HERRICK 13

AFGHANISTAN – THE LONG HAUL

First Line Perspective (with the Royal Artillery). As always, much of REME was deployed at first line. The following extracts from a report in The Craftsman magazine (February 2011) by Corporal 'Gaz' Robertson of 4 Regiment RA LAD (equipped with the 105mm Light Gun) gives a feel for life with the Gunners:

> '3/29 Corunna Battery Fitter Section (BFS) deployed to Afghanistan in March 2010. … On arrival at our new home we were greeted by a very happy 1 RHA BFS who took great delight in telling us that we not only had to provide support for our Gun Battery, but also the resident infantry company and their resident fleet of equipment.
>
> Our main task was to support the line of PBs along Route 611 (the road from Gereshk to Sangin and onwards) down to FOB Jackson. One of the secondary tasks was daily sangar duties for all junior ranks.
>
> The start of the tour was very busy as we had good freedom of movement between PBs, so we were able to visit various locations and complete necessary repair and servicing tasks, instructing the Royal Marines how to effectively look after their equipment in such a harsh environment. This all changed once the poppy harvest was complete and the insurgents began to seed 611 with IEDs. As well as the temperature increasing, so did the IED strikes, so our workload went from busy to flat out! …After a couple of months, Route 611 became too dangerous to negotiate so the majority of vehicle movement to the PBs ceased, allowing us to focus on FOB maintenance. … We were informed we would be joined by Kilo Coy from the United States Marine Corps (USMC). We worked with the USMC showing them how we conducted our business, but it was obvious from the beginning that our procedures differed greatly, but we all worked hard to make it work as efficiently as possible.
>
> Looking back, we had a good tour but more importantly we brought everyone back safely. We had the privilege to work with two different nations Marines, and made some good friends from both. We had some laughs; we had some tears, but my God what a tour!'

First Line Perspective (with the Royal Engineers). Support for Royal Engineers' equipment was another important aspect of REME's work. In fact, the TFH Engineer Group LAD had the largest and most diverse fleet of all to look after, some 260 vehicles of around 30 varieties.

This was explained in The Craftsman magazine (April 2011) by OC 21 Engineer Regiment LAD, Captain Phil Noke REME:

'The LAD deployed with 42 tradesmen who were responsible for providing equipment support to five squadrons. A number of the soldiers found themselves in isolated forward locations attached to the troops, as they conducted the various construction and route building tasks. Herrick 12 saw the introduction of the eagerly awaited TALISMAN route proving capability. It was a real challenge for the fitter section to keep the equipment serviceable; this required a lot of patience, initiative and hard work. In addition, the TALISMAN Fitter Section of the LAD supported the TROJAN Troop, another key capability in theatre. The heavy armour deployments required detailed planning, the logistic footprint is immense and the expertise of the armoured vehicle crews and recovery teams was crucial to supporting this heavy armour capability'. (**See Plate 23**)

Staff Sergeant Whittaker of the Talisman Squadron painted this more detailed picture:

'After over 12 months of specialist training TALISMAN set out to do its job. From that moment forward, it was a mission for the fitter section to keep enough equipment fit, especially after 2 Troop had one of each platform in the TALISMAN fleet lost to IEDs during one mission! On only its second mission, the fitter section vehicle was struck by an IED, Cpl Duffy took command of the situation in such a way that it earned him the Squadron Warrior of the Month award from the CRE (Commander Royal Engineers). The Squadron suffered many IED strikes over the next four months; the ES Bn Mastiff Section issued us with our loyalty cards as we became a very good customer. The Fitter Section overcame a huge number of issues associated with the new UOR equipment and all the problems were tackled head on. The Squadron always had what it required for Ops, which is a testament to the boys and girl of the section working tirelessly in all weather and times of day'. (**See Plate 24**)

OPERATION HERRICK 14 (MARCH–SEPTEMBER 2011)

If one compares Operation HERRICK 4 to Operation HERRICK 14, some things had not changed. The climate had not changed. The geography had not changed, the ethnic make-up of Helmand Province had not changed, nor had the basic cultural, religious and political beliefs of most who lived there. The cultivation of poppies remained a significant part of the economy. This had always posed something of a dilemma for ISAF. The narcotics industry corrupted middle men at many levels inside and outside Afghanistan. It was a major cause of instability in Afghanistan, funding terrorism and insurgency. Yet, if ISAF pursued a policy of poppy eradication too aggressively it risked alienating the population by taking away many livelihoods without providing an immediate alternative. There were still many in Helmand Province who either sympathised with the Taliban, or were frightened of opposing them. Nowhere was entirely safe for British Servicemen. The growth of fatal 'green on blue' attacks (ANSF on ISAF), even within base areas, was a worrying trend. There were still areas in the Green Zone and elsewhere, which were far from safe from ambushes or IEDs.

That said, a great deal had changed. Slow but important changes, not always heralded in news headlines, had been taking place in Afghanistan. In 2001, for example, only some 700,000 children, almost all of them boys, had attended school. By 2012, the figure had increased tenfold, with around one-third of the pupils being girls. The security situation in Helmand Province had steadily improved, with the Government gaining tighter control of key urban areas, gradually driving the insurgents from the Green Zone and making travel safe on many main routes. As this happened, more schools could open, more development money could be spent, more jobs could be created, and more businesses start and prosper. More people could also see the Government offering a brighter future than the dark vision offered by the Taliban.

By 2012, the endgame for direct British military involvement in security was in sight, only some two years ahead. All involved realised if the sacrifices made by the British were to bear long-term fruit, they had to leave behind ANSF who were capable of maintaining security on their own. Here again, there were hopeful signs. Whilst the ANSF were far from perfect organisations by western standards, they had made great progress, and were hugely more effective than they had been in 2006. Finally, there had been a step change in British military capability. The force that deployed on Operation HERRICK 4 could not know what it was getting into. It was not resourced, equipped or ideally trained for its task. In contrast, the British force on Operation HERRICK 14 was well equipped, extremely well trained, and knew exactly what it was about.

Training. The soldiers who deployed on Operation HERRICK 4 were highly motivated and well trained in general terms, but had done limited mission-specific training (with those rushed out as reinforcements having done hardly any at all). By the time of Operation HERRICK 14, things were very different and those deploying would generally have done several months of individual and collective training tailored to the current operational situation. A Combat Service Support Training and Advisory Team, which always included a REME representative, would be available to support training in both Germany and UK. The normal progression of training involved Hybrid Foundation Training, Mission-Specific Training, and a Confirmatory Field Exercise. On arrival in theatre, individuals and units would go through a Reception Staging and Onward Integration Package lasting from two to seven days.

Levels of Training. This training package provided three levels of training. Category 1 training was for those personnel whose duties were routinely located within the MOB. All new arrivals had to complete these first two days, which consisted of a series of briefings and personal weapon shoots. Category 2 training (five days) was for personnel whose duties required deployment outside of the MOB. This included counter-IED training through a variety of scenarios, patrol skills, cultural awareness and vehicle drills. Category 3 training (seven days) was for personnel whose duties covered the whole spectrum of operations in Afghanistan and included time on heavy weapons systems, FOB defence, and compound clearance. This training was based on a newly-built facility in Camp Bastion. This included a representative Afghan village, and such facilities as a device to train people to escape from a vehicle, which had rolled over after an IED strike.

Camp Bastion. The most common comment about the Camp Bastion/Leatherneck/Shorabak complex seemed to be along the lines of '*every time I went back there it seemed to have grown*'. By this point, it was home to about 21,000 people of various nationalities. It housed the rear echelons of units deployed forward, as well as a host of supporting organisations, including those provided by contractors, which dealt with medical, technical, logistic, operational and administrative matters. Camp Leatherneck was a 1,600 acre US Marine air and logistic base, built in 2008 adjacent to Camp Bastion. It provided an airbase for fixed wing, as well as for rotary aircraft. A new airstrip capable of taking almost any commercial or military aircraft was completed in early-2011, and around 600 air movements were handled per day.

ES Company heavy repair facility

Strategic Lines of Communication. Afghanistan is a landlocked country and NATO operations there were largely supported via a southern route that involved using sea transport to Karachi, and land transport via Pakistan to Kandahar (around 1,000 miles) or Kabul (significantly shorter). This route was always unreliable and, to a degree, vulnerable to the Taliban; for example, 42 tankers were destroyed in 2008 in a single incident. The route was later to be closed at various times. Specifically, in November 2011, Pakistan was to close its border to NATO convoys for seven months. The alternative land route, the northern route, essentially used the roads and railways the Soviets had used when they had been involved in Afghanistan. These routes were relatively secure, but involved immensely long road/rail journeys (typically well over 3,000 miles). The alternative was to fly men and materiel directly to bases in Afghanistan.

This was hugely expensive (about ten times the cost of transport by road), sometimes prohibitively so.

Organisation for Combined Operations. The underlying intention of UK operations had always been to help the ANSF to develop their own security solutions from which UK forces could extract themselves when the time came. In the early days, however, military operations in Helmand Province tended to be British operations with Afghans in a subsidiary role. This gradually changed to combined operations involving both British and ANA forces. By the time of Operation HERRICK 14, lead responsibility for security was already starting to be passed to the ANA on an area-by-area basis, with a view to handing over responsibility for the entire Province as soon as that was possible.

Outline Organisation for Operations. The international and combined nature of operations was reflected in the outline organisation. TFH had a Danish BG under command. This had been largely supported from MOB Price (near Gereshk), and had been operating in the area of Nahr-e-Saraj (North) (NES(N)). TFH and 3rd Brigade 215 Corps ANA effectively shared responsibility for the same area and locations. The ANA forces were organised in kandaks (battalions) and sub-divided into tolays (companies). 3rd Brigade ANA comprised six kandaks, five in a ground-holding role along the major PB lines, and the sixth based in Camp Shorabak. US forces were deployed in other areas of Helmand Province, including the Sangin area.

TFH Deployment. HQ 3 Commando Brigade provided the nucleus of the TFH HQ. The UK land forces deployed were a mixture of Royal Marines and Army of almost all cap badges. These included some 650 REME, with a further 85 REME supporting Army aircraft. There were a number of Brigade assets, including the Brigade Reconnaissance Force, which included elements of the Royal Scots Dragoon Guards (SCOTS DG), and the TFH Engineer Group. A complete BG was deployed (as it had been for some years) as the Brigade Advisory Group (BAG). It had a mentoring role, with its staff embedded with the ANA to provide appropriate help at all levels – 2 MERCIAN was given this role. Ground-holding responsibilities rested with 'Combined Forces' (CF). These essentially comprised ISAF BGs working closely with ANA kandaks and tolays, and Afghan National Civil Order Police units. These came under

the ANP, but which were something of an elite, being better trained and more deployable than normal ANP forces. TFH CFs comprised:
- CF LKG (Lashkar Gah) – this was home to HQ 3 Commando Brigade/TFH
- CF NES(N) – Danish BG, but with British and other ISAF attached (including 14 REME personnel) – largely supported from MOB Price
- CF NES(S) – 1 RIFLES
- CF Nad-e-Ali (NDA(N)) – 42 Commando Royal Marines
- CF NDA(S) – 45 Commando Royal Marines.

REME soldier on foot patrol in NDA(S) on Operation HERRICK 13

Transitional Changes. The organisation of TFH was to change for Operation HERRICK 15, and a considerable amount of planning and transitional activity was necessary, not least for REME. The key changes were to be:
- the merger of CF NDA(N) and CF NDA(S) into a single CF (CF NDA)
- the takeover of CF NES(N) from the Danes (by February 2012)
- the formation of CF Burma (CF BMA), which would involve some 300 British troops taking over from around 1,200 USMC personnel, and moving back to the Sangin area

- FOB Robinson (originally British, later taken over by the USMC) provided the supporting base for Sangin.

These changes are shown on the deployment map below. The dots on the map represent bases/checkpoints, the shaded area represents the 'brigade battlespace' not owned by any CF.

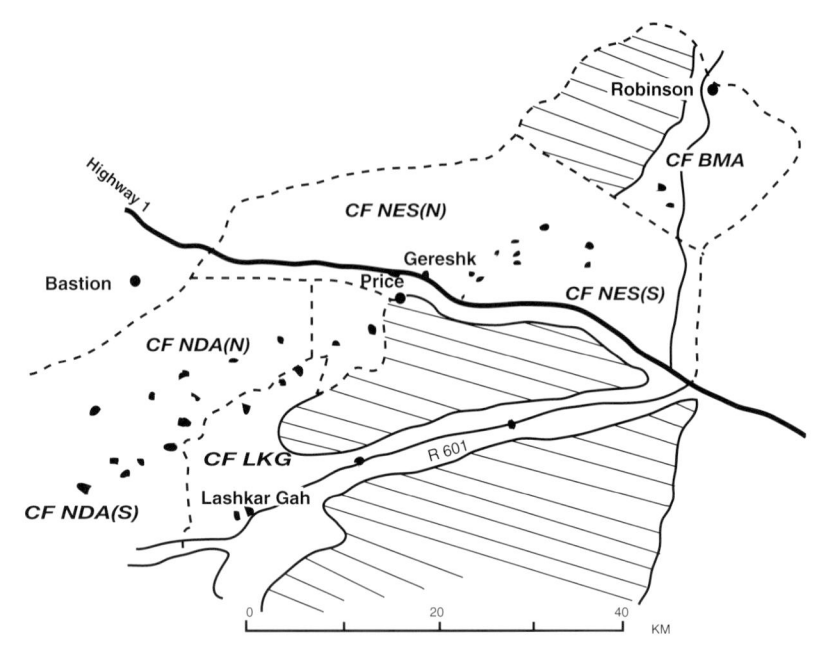

Operational layout for Operation HERRICK 14

Operational Activity. A high level of operational activity continued. Broadly speaking, the security situation in the major urban areas and centres of population continued to be transformed for the better, with responsibility increasingly being taken over by the ANSF, as their grip tightened. There were continuing operations to penetrate into areas in which Taliban influence was still strong with a view to dislodging the insurgents.

EQUIPMENT SUPPORT – GENERAL

ES planners have to think well ahead and thoughts were already turning to drawdown from theatre. Colonel Allan Thomson (late REME), who had taken over from Colonel Gaunt as Commander EC at HQ JFSp(A), made the following general points at the time in The Craftsman magazine (October 2011):

> 'The HERRICK campaign is moving into a transition, and our fitter sections and LADs can expect to move on a more frequent basis. New infrastructure will not be built, so it will be necessary to provide temporary shelter and a working surface, along with lift, power and lighting.
>
> We have a much improved ability to manouevre in theatre with the introduction of a Wolfhound ES variant. It is bringing back the agility lost when our core repair variants were deemed as unsuitable for this Campaign. First line is able to move around the Area of Operations. Add to this the Husky Lightweight Intimate Recovery Capability, due in theatre in early 2012 and we are about to get back into the ES manouevre business. Second line still lacks true agility. For a Battalion to deploy an IST or FRT from Bastion, it is still reliant on aviation or the CLP to move their repair variant or manpower from Bastion through the Brigade Battlespace to the CF location. Once inside the CF Area of Operation these capabilities are much more agile under the force protection of the CFs.
>
> We continue to practice the established REME principle of forward repair, so those at second line should be prepared to deploy forward to some pretty austere locations. The Battalion routinely has 40% of its manpower deployed forward of Bastion, and over 80% have deployed forward at some stage. The spares situation is slowly improving but expedient repair, cross-servicing and cannibalisation remain common occurrences.
>
> Base-ISTAR is a growth area for electronics technicians. For some, the thought of climbing a 30m tower in the middle of a base in the dark does not appeal. However, this is exactly what some Base-ISTAR technicians are required to do. Husky electrics have proved to be a problem area, and better training is required'.

Defence Support Group Facilities in Camp Bastion. By 2009, the need to regenerate assets in theatre was clear. The required capability was named the Equipment Sustainability System (ESS), and the intention was for support to be provided by contractors or the Defence Support Group (DSG). (**See Plate 25**) An Interim Regeneration Capability was in place by early-2010. This involved nine bays in a workshop that was owned by PJHQ, administered by the ES Battalion, and run and manned by KBR (formerly Kellogg Brown & Root – an engineering company) and others in conjunction with the DSG. The basic concept was to take in a 'tired' equipment, carry out an element of Level 3 and/or Level 4 repair, and put it out in prime condition avoiding the time and cost of cycling the equipment back to the UK for Level 4 repair. This got off to a slightly slow start, as a regeneration pool was required, as well as a considerable amount of spares that were not always available. By the time of Operation HERRICK 14 an excellent workshop facility had been built, complete with 29 vehicle bays, as well as optical and electronic repair facilities with clean rooms. This was run by the DSG, with an ex-REME Major in charge, and provided an important complement to the repair work done at first and second line.

REME Second Line Perspective. The Theatre ES Battalion was based on 2 CS Battalion REME, which provided 7 Armoured Company and took under its wing the ES Squadron of the Commando Logistic Regiment Royal Marines. The former was responsible for heavy PM platforms, tracked vehicles, and all Technician, Armourer and Metalsmith operations. The latter (as the Light ES Company) was responsible for all core B Vehicles and the lighter end of the UOR spectrum, namely Jackal and Husky vehicles. The unit now enjoyed excellent repair facilities in Camp Bastion, with the Heavy Repair Facility (HRF) having 14 ventilated and air conditioned bays, two overhead gantry cranes, air compressors and oils and lubricants on tap.

Engineering Operations. These broadly continued their previous pattern and were described in The Craftsman magazine (November 2011). The ES Battalion completed some 20,000 repair missions/tasks on its dependency, which included 2,941 vehicles of 174 variants, 137 ISTAR equipments of 16 variants, and 17,000 weapons of 16 different types. In addition to routine second line work, backfill to first line was a key function for the Battalion, as well as with intimate support to Operation FAHALAWAL (Inspect and Repair Missions), Operation FIX (Hasty Inspect and Repair Missions) and Operation MUBAREZ (CLPs).

Over 250 IST requests were received, which ranged from an individual tradesman for one day, to a first line reinforcement for six months, or a section deployment in support of an Operation FIX. Both support companies had over one-third of their manpower deployed forward at any one time, providing intimate Level 2 and Level 3 support to CFs around Helmand Province. Around 90% of the Battalion deployed forward at some time or another. In stark contrast to the excellent engineering facilities in the HRF, tradesmen working in PBs had to operate under the most austere conditions, and rely on initiative and ingenuity to complete their tasks. Notable highs included the repair of the Brigade Reconnaissance Force's Jackal vehicles and repair of IED-damaged Husky vehicles. All Jackal vehicles were repaired eight days ahead of schedule, and the repair of 12 IED-damaged Husky vehicles required some of the vehicles to have their front ends stripped back to the bare chassis before being rebuilt. Protected Mobility Platoon also became masters of Warthog engine changes, completing 10. In one case, the lack of a replacement engine threatened to prevent a vehicle from deploying. Following agreement from the relevant Project Team, permission was given for a Mastiff engine to be converted for use on a Warthog; the task took four days to complete, but was a triumph of basic engineering.

ES (Materiel) Support. In theory, spares are the responsibility of ES (Materiel) staff who wear a RLC rather than a REME cap badge (or no cap badge at all if they are civilians). In practice, REME's ability to do its job is greatly dependent on getting the spares it needs, and wise REME heads take an intelligent interest in the workings of ES (Materiel). In Afghanistan, spares have been a problem throughout to a greater or lesser degree. Three key factors have undoubtedly played a part in this. The first is that more or less continuous changes to the dependency and the pattern of operations, which do not help provisioning models to work accurately. The second is that a lot of UOR equipment was deployed without a complete and effective support package. Finally, dispersion of forces within theatre, and problems with the supply chain (both within theatre and to/from theatre) exacerbated all the other spares problems. The Battalion's ES (Materiel) organisation had had a very demanding task to perform, having to process around 24,000 transactions per month, and control an inventory with some 21,500 NATO Stock Numbers on it. In fact, through its sterling efforts, the immediate availability of demands was raised from 40% to 60% (and up to 73% for scaled items). Nearly 800 tonnes of stores no longer required were also backloaded through the rear supply chain.

REME in the Mentoring Role. Although little mentioned in this Chapter thus far, REME personnel had been heavily involved in mentoring the ANSF throughout the period covered. This mentoring role was rightly seen as hugely important, as success in the long term would clearly largely depend on enabling Afghans to do things themselves. The following, extracted from reports by REME mentors on Operation HERRICK 14 in The Craftsman magazine (September 2011), bring some of the issues involved to life.

Captain Matt Sutton REME – 2IC 6/3/215 Kandak Advisory Training Team (KATT) (Also OC 9/12 Royal Lancers LAD):

> 'I deployed with B Sqn 9/12L in February 2011 to Nahr-e-Saraj District of Helmand Province as 2IC of a KATT – mentoring and advising an ANA infantry kandak in the heart of the Helmand Green Zone.
>
> Out of the regular 'ES' world and advising the infantry kandak HQ, I have been working with a team of 20 advisers of a variety of cap badges (infantry, RA, RE, REME, RLC and RAC) offering training, advice, support, and at times simply a voice of reason. Development and progress is slow and not always enduring, but each minor step forward (such as the commander actually formulating a plan prior to H Hour) is celebrated as a major victory.
>
> Undoubtedly, there are many frictions caused by cultural differences but regardless of the languages spoken, bonds are easily forged between British and Afghan partners. Particularly encouraging is the way the Afghans have latched on to learning new skills; the kandak's basic workshop (mentored by Cpl Kev Brown and LCpl Pinkney) is full of enthusiastic and capable young Afghan tradesmen and is a good example of ANA progress.
>
> Although often finding myself on the ground as an ECM 'mule' for the Kandak Commander, my main role had been as a staff adviser to the Kandak HQ where previous experience of battlegroup planning, the seven questions and combat support operations do not seem to matter as much as an ability to drink endless cups of 'chai' and eat Afghan food without stomach complaint. G4 is not an area

in which most ANA are comfortable, and the task of mentoring G4 to the ANA has been equated by one of my team as trying to push water uphill with a fork.

The frustration of the role has been tempered by the warm friendship of our Afghan counterparts, evenings spent drinking chai and hearing them relate war stories of days spent fighting for the Russians, against the Russians, for the Mujahedeen, for the Taliban, for the Northern Alliance against ISAF, and now with ISAF. Such conversations bring home that these warriors have known only fighting for much of their lives and our six-month deployment is but one small part of the much longer history of conflict in Afghanistan'.

Captain Sutton returns from a partnered patrol on Operation HERRICK 14

Warrant Officer Class 1 Harry Hazel – OC 3/215 Maintenance Tolay Advisory Training Team (Also ASM 9/12 Royal Lancers LAD):

'The Maintenance Tolay Advisory Team (Maint TATT) comprises 27 REME tradesmen from two Brigades and 11 different regiments, which have been forged together to form call sign ADV52 of the CSS KATT, 3/215 Bde Adv Gp. Trade specific individuals are then detached to seven different locations around Helmand Province. The primary function of the TATT is to mentor and advise the

ANA ES elements within 3/215 on Equipment Support/Capability planning and execution. (**See Plate 26**)

The ANA Maintenance Tolay works to US doctrine. The US have fielded the ANA workshop to be a professional functional working environment and, although far from perfect, the facilities here are more than adequate to ensure success. The Brigade workshop is based within Camp Shorabak which is a stone's throw from Camp Bastion, and is the heart of all maintenance within the Brigade.

The ANA workshop has over 70 tradesmen of differing abilities; most have some form of engineering background. The US has fielded the ANA with a myriad of Ford Rangers, HMMWVs, Crane International trucks and M16 rifles. All of these need to be maintained with no specific equipment courses, no Bde R2, very little literacy and a supply system which is flawed and corrupt. The warriors do not let this dampen their enthusiasm to get the equipment back to the user. Most days the workshop looks like a London 'chop shop' with vehicles being welded together and mechanics rooting through scrap bins to try and find a seal or spring that could be used to get the vehicle mobile. The ANA mechanics are masters of expedient repair, and need to be. We sometimes forget this is a long war for them.

Mentoring the ANA brings with it many frustrations. … is a protracted process which must be done slowly 'evolution not revolution' I am reminded daily. … We were fortunate to see our hard work pay off when during Operation OMID HAFT an ANA vehicle struck an IED within a hostile compound. Although we were present at the time it was rewarding to see the ANA take control of the recovery task, with limited assistance from the Advisory Team. The recovery was a mammoth 13-hour task that saw the ANA and ISAF working together to a common plan'.

Captain Anthony Platt REME – ES Mentoring at Brigade Level (Also OC 3 MERCIAN (STAFFORDS) LAD):

'Having deployed as part of the CSS Operational Mentoring and Advisory Team (OMLT) on Herrick 8, I know this was going to be a very different challenge from being the OC LAD of an Armoured Infantry Battalion. For me, I was tasked with mentoring the ANA Brigade Technical Officer (BTO – think BEME).

After a few weeks of pleasantries and general conversation I could describe the BTO as a very proud man, in his twilight years, technically competent in certain paperwork procedure, but enjoying giving responsibilities to others and was happy to sit back and just let the ANA crack on, aptly described as the 'Afghan Way'. Quite happy to talk about his family (every Afghan will ask about your family within the first conversation), his wife and children, he found it particularly amusing when I told him I was not married and him being in his mid-fifties had a wife younger than me.

When I eventually got the BTO onto the topic of vehicle maintenance, it always led to a heated debate with the BTO describing to me the 'Afghan Way'. … But where I could see an easy fix to an endemic problem the answer was always one of the following: we do not have the trained people; we are not allowed to send parts forward in case they are sold on the market or stolen; the fuel is contaminated so we must add engine oil to thicken it up. All sounds very simple, but that is the crux of the problem with ANA Maintenance, no one in the ES chain is enforced to make decisions, so they don't! Even to the point that a clear failure is about to happen, they will wait until the mentors are in complete panic before casually coming up with a solution as if to say, 'ISAF, stop flapping, we have been fighting for over 30 years, we never ran out of equipment fighting against the Russians'. A bitter pill to swallow when UK CSS Doctrine enforces the principles of foresight and flexibility etc'.

A First Line Perspective (Mobile Operations). REME soldiers at first line naturally continued to do a huge variety of jobs, repairing equipment, carrying out military tasks and mentoring users in equipment care. Having already provided 'snapshots' of REME working at first line with the infantry, RA, RE and RLC, the following report from The Craftsman magazine (April 2012) provides one of REME with the RAC. It is extracted from an account of the fitter section of D (Warthog) Squadron SCOTS DG deployed on Operation HERRICK 14:

'As one of the few truly manouevre assets within TFH, D Sqn and its Fitter Section were some of the most utilised troops in Helmand. Often operating from desert leaguers for weeks at a time, the Squadron was rarely in camp, and earned themselves the nickname 'the Helmand Gypsies' as they tirelessly traversed the TFH AOR supporting anyone from the infantry to the special forces.

In support of the Squadron, the Fitter Section were invariably dispersed; with elements supporting the Sqn Ldr's TAC, two teams supporting the two Fighting Troops, and a base element working from the stability of Camp Bastion.... For those in Camp Bastion, the tradesmen provided the Fitter Section's administrative base, liaised with TFH LAD and carried out the more in-depth repairs, which could only be effected with the correct facilities and STTE. They were the unsung heroes within their ranks.

When on the move 24A and its fellow RRV (repair/recovery vehicles) counterparts performed the same tasks as the other Warthogs; as fighting vehicles. We were equipped with the same weaponry and moved tactically within the fighting troops – gone are the days of the Fitter Sect remaining a tactical bound behind. We were there, in the mix, in contact. The Green Zone offered its own challenges, as did the desert, but our highly mobile vehicles were used to best effect on the urban-rural interface, crossing irrigation ditches, fields and mud berms.

During HERRICK 14 a number of significant acts proved the courage, toil and selfless commitment often required of REME soldiers on operations. Cpl Robertson, a relatively junior commander, and LCpl Anderson were required to recover two Warthogs which had become stranded in the River Helmand. They were very nearly swept away at one point before being engaged by the enemy from a nearby compound, which resulted in a monumental fire fight. Over 36 hours of strenuous activity resulted in the Tech and Rec Mech being airlifted to hospital with dehydration and exhaustion.

Also on 16 June 2011 one of the Rec Mechs, Cfn Andy Found, had dismounted into a cleared area to conduct his assessment of an IED struck vehicle, and effect its recovery. Sadly, he initiated a secondary charge whilst ground commanding his vehicle, and was killed instantly. This giant of a man (all 6ft 6in of him) illustrated courage, dedication and selfless commitment as he made the ultimate sacrifice performing the trade he loved so dearly. He is sorely missed'.

TAKING STOCK

Before moving on to the final Chapter on Afghanistan, Chapter 12 ('Afghanistan – Drawing Down'), and trying to form an overall view based on UK operations in Afghanistan, Iraq and elsewhere, it is useful briefly to review some of the key equipment-related issues that emerge in this Chapter.

As operations in Iraq wound down, Afghanistan became very much the Army's top priority. Excellent new equipment, notably in the form of PM vehicles and protective electronic equipment started to be fielded.

One might have expected that the equipment availability would be a problem for a force operating in a hostile environment at the end of long lines of communication. In fact, REME was generally extremely effective at *'keeping fit equipment in the hands of troops'*. When looking for 'lessons to learn' for REME, the biggest one would seem to be that the old lessons essentially still apply.

The need for REME people to be 'soldier-tradesmen' was proved yet again 'in spades'. They need to be trained as soldiers in order to be able to carry out their repair and recovery role in support of their customers when they most need it and, if necessary, right at the sharp end. Their ability rapidly to switch from technical to military roles if required, provides an important operational bonus; either by REME personnel directly performing operational tasks, or by releasing others from security duties.

The need to deal with battle damage, and cope with a lack of spares meant that REME had to engage in expedient repairs and battle damage repairs. This involved doing things that were never envisaged in the manufacturers' support publications. Such people need an appropriate formal engineering training to give them the necessary depth of technical background.

The basic REME first line support concept yet again proved to be a cornerstone of success. An important role for REME at first line, which is not always appreciated, is that of mentoring users in equipment care. Many soldiers who operate sophisticated equipment are youngsters with little general technical background, and need and welcome advice from their friendly REME fitter or technician.

The basic concept of 'fixing forward', or least as far forward as a sensible balance of technical and operational factors allow, was once more validated.

REME's first and second line organisations proved highly flexible, and proved able to adapt organisationally and technically to a continuously evolving situation. First and second line organisations were pragmatically merged, divided and task organised. The problem of restricted road mobility was countered by making greater use of second line ISTs to repair forward, rather than backloading for repair.

The high regard in which REME was held by its 'customers' was undoubtedly helpful in putting the case for REME in the Strategic Defence and Security Review of 2010.

July–December 2006	2007	2008	2009	2010	2011
24	42	51	109	103	46

Figure 11.1: British fatalities 2006–2011

UK LAND COMMITMENT – OPERATIONS HERRICK 5–14			
Operation/Date	Lead Op/Log Bde	REME Second Line Lead (numbers)	Infantry/ RAC Units
HERRICK 5 Nov 06–Mar 07	3 Cdo Bde	Based on Cdo Log Regt	42 and 45 Cdo, RAC sqn
HERRICK 6 Mar–Sep 07	12 Mech Bde	4 Bn REME (Overall REME: 420 + 90 techs supporting JHF)	3 inf bns, increased to 4 inf bns
HERRICK 7 Oct 07–Mar 08	52 Inf Bde JFLogC	1 CS Bn REME	4 inf bns, RAC sqn. Total UK commitment: 7,800
HERRICK 8 Apr–Sep 08	16 Air Assault Bde 102 Log Bde	7 AA Bn REME	5 inf bns, RAC sqn
HERRICK 9 Oct 08–Mar 09	3 Cdo Bde (5,000 strong, 40% Army) 104 Log Sp Bde	3 CS Bn REME	5 inf bns, RAC sqn
HERRICK 10 Apr–Sep 09	19 Lt Bde RAF-led JFSp(A)	4 CS Bn REME (511 REME in ES Gp + about 90 avn techs)	4 inf bns, LD, RAC sqn
HERRICK 11 Oct 09–Mar 10	HQ 6 (UK) Div 11 Lt Bde 101 Log Bde	104 FS Bn REME	4 inf bns, HCR, RTR sqn then increase of addl 3 inf bns to bring force to 9,000
HERRICK 12 Apr–Sep 10	4 Mech Bde 102 Log Bde	1 Bn REME with 101 Bn REME (627 REME in total)	7 inf bns/RAC regts
HERRICK 13 Oct 10–Mar 11	16 Air Assault Bde 104 Log Bde	7 AA Bn REME (plus 3 Armd Coy)	7 inf bns/RAC regts
HERRICK 14 Apr–Sep 11	3 Cdo Bde RN-Led JFSp	2 CS Bn REME	7 inf bns/RAC regts

Figure 11.2: Size and composition of UK land commitment Operations HERRICK 5–14

Equipment	Number repaired	Number BLR (beyond local repair)	Average time per repair (hours)
WMIK (Land Rover)	80	4	43
Jackal	122	15	18
MAN SV(R)	16	1	134
MAN SV(Other)	33	0	21
Mastiff	61	2	35
Panther	4	0	8
Ridgeback	15	0	4
Warrior	24	4	25
CVR(T)	61	11	12
CV8 (power packs)	40	5	59
Vector	44	0	35
JCB	27	0	35
RTCH (Rough Terrain Container Handler)	3	0	282

Figure 11.3: ES Group mechanical equipments repair tasks on Operation HERRICK 10

Equipment	Number repaired
Bowman PRC	870
Bowman PRR	750
Valon (mine detector)	300
Sights/optics various	1144
ECM equipment	1983
FEPs	52

Figure 11.4: ES Group electronic/optical equipments repair tasks on Operation HERRICK 10

CHAPTER 12

AFGHANISTAN – DRAWING DOWN

OVERVIEW OF OPERATION HERRICK 15 TO THE END OF 2014

In 2009, USA President Obama announced a 'surge' of additional US forces to Afghanistan, but with the caveat that they would start to withdraw from 2011. In June 2011, he announced that 10,000 US troops would withdraw by the end of the year, and a further 23,000 would withdraw by the end of 2012, and that by the end of 2014 responsibility for security would rest entirely with the Afghan Government. The UK plan was consistent with this, and envisaged an end to all combat operations by the end of 2014, leaving a small military presence in Afghanistan with a training and advisory role. This effectively set the agenda for the period covered by this Chapter.

By the start of Operation HERRICK 15, the operational situation was stable and under control, but Afghanistan was still a dangerous place for British troops to be. British fatalities in 2012 were 44, only two less than the year before and against the 103 killed in action in 2010. This year saw the steady handover of responsibilities from British forces to the Afghan National Security Forces (ANSF), which was growing towards 350,000 strong, as well as the transfer of responsibilities between national ISAF contingents as they drew down.

At its peak, in Helmand Province alone, there were 137 UK bases and around 9,500 UK troops. The total number of UK Armed Forces personnel in Afghanistan reduced from 9,000 at the start of 2013, to around 5,200 at the start of 2014, by which time virtually all the UK military forces in Helmand Province were located in Camp Bastion. There were only nine UK fatalities in 2013, and the casualties during the first five months of 2014 were all due to accidents rather than hostile action.

On 9 August 2013, the military headquarters of the UK's Task Force Helmand (TFH) moved from Lashkar Gah to Camp Bastion. On 1 April 2014, it ceased to function as a separate HQ and was subsumed into the wider US-led Regional Command (South West). This was based in Camp Leatherneck (the US base built adjacent to Camp Bastion) with the former

Commander of TFH becoming the Deputy Regional Commander under a one-star US Marine Corps Command General.

For REME, there was a gradual shift of effort from supporting operations to preparing equipment for return to the UK. The withdrawal of UK equipment and materiel from Afghanistan represented a major logistic challenge, which had to be seen in the context of the broader ISAF problem of withdrawing some 130,000 military personnel from 50 different countries. Exact figures are always questionable, but it has been estimated that the UK drawdown alone would involve the withdrawal of around 3,000 armoured vehicles and 11,000 containers, as well as other vehicles and equipment down lines of communication that were far from ideal.

The table at Figure 12.1 (at the end of this Chapter) provides a summary of the UK commitment over the period covered by this Chapter, as a prelude to looking at specific operations and events, and REME's involvement in them.

OPERATION HERRICK 15 (OCTOBER 2011–APRIL 2012)

First Line – HQ TFH ES Branch Perspective

The Brigade EME (BEME) produced an article in The Craftsman magazine (May 2012), which comprised his ES Branch perspective and a consolidated number of short reports from various authors at different levels that collectively painted a picture of what was happening at first line in TFH.

In his introductory section, he commented that they had been through a very busy time, but that each major unit had an EME who would coordinate repair and recovery support, including that provided by units or sub-units, which deployed with only a fitter section. He explained:

> 'The start of the tour was notable for the boundary changes which saw the merger of CF (Combined Force) Nad-e-Ali (NDA) North and South into one and the formation of CF Burma (BMA), which required a great deal of movement of REME personnel and equipment. The first few weeks were a complete whirlwind of ES activity as operators and tradesmen oriented themselves to some very unfamiliar equipment. The electrical system on the Husky Tactical Support Vehicle was to prove a challenge, but one which was conquered by the skill, determination and ingenuity that is the

hallmark of a REME tradesman. By February 2012, the UK took over CF NES(N) (Nahr-e-Saraj North) from the Danes, and a fifth CF LAD was grown from within manning headroom.… Battlefield clearance, increased IED activity against vehicles and the fielding of new capabilities has seen our officers and tradesmen tested to the limit.… with the support of the Theatre ES Bn (3 Bn REME) they have never been found wanting'. (**See Plate 27**)

Supporting contributions to the article were from the CFs (CF BMA, CF NES(N), CF NES(S), CF LKG (Lashkar Gah)), Main Operating Base (MOB) Price, Forward Operating Base (FOB) Shawquat, as well as various Patrol Bases (PB) and Checkpoints (CP). There were also contributions from the Brigade Troops LAD (supporting nine organisations), the Explosive Ordnance Disposal (EOD) and Search Task Force LAD, the Brigade Advisory Group LAD and the Engineer Group LAD. Selected extracts from their reports explain their activities at the time.

CF BMA. The EME reports:

> 'Staff within CF BMA have had to deal with a number of unique and different challenges including setting up an LAD from scratch, combining Protected Mobility and Armoured Infantry priorities and a rather low manning cap of 300, which considering we took over from 1,200 USMC personnel put the job we were aiming to achieve into perspective'.

He invited comments from Lance Corporal Hutchins and Craftsman Johnston who reported:

> 'We deployed to FOB OUELETTE in the upper Gereshk Valley. Arriving in September 2011, we were welcomed by what could only be described as an empty shell as the USMC (expeditionary force) did not bother with the essential amenities for comfort. So our first task was to establish a LAD that was fit for purpose.… It was apparent from day one that this was going to be a demanding tour for all the LAD, which consisted of five personnel from 3 MERCIAN and six from 5 RIFLES.… The fleet that we looked after consisted of Warrior, Mastiff, Husky, Jackal and Quads; and whatever else the AQMS could get his hands on.… It was soon clear to us that

Husky was going to be the problem child due to the complexity of the electrical systems and our lack of experience on this piece of equipment.... Along with staging in our very own sangar and conducting repairs we also crewed the recovery assets. During our first four months, we dealt with 13 IED strikes and 15 breakdowns or accidents involving UK and ISAF vehicles. We also assisted with numerous other ISAF, ANSF and local national incidents'.

CF NES(S) (5 RIFLES). The 22-strong LAD was spread across eight locations. Equipment availability was high, and the dependency included ISTAR equipment for the bases as well as Lightweight Field Generators (LFG) that were not only important for operational reasons, but also to make life more bearable (hot showers getting a specific mention). 5 RIFLES BG had a number of successes and continued to take the fight to the insurgents in order to set up the conditions for transition.

PB 1. Corporal Getty reports:

'I was introduced to Husky electrics and the gremlins therein – all those Husky vets will feel my pain.... the Base has been contacted on numerous occasions and we've swapped spanners for shooters. Cfn Howe our resident TA soldier has been involved in patrolling to Check Points (CP) to carry out servicing on Quads and LFGs.... All in all this is a top job for any REME tradesman, fixing kit, soldiering with a chance to shine as you have enormous responsibility'.

Brigade Troops LAD. The EME explained:

'Bde Tps LAD has evolved over HERRICK 14 and 15 to become an integrated LAD supporting nine units (AI Coy, FR Sqn, WHG Gp, JFTG, TUAS (Tactical Unmanned Air Systems) Bty, PMAG and NES(N)). Whilst each unit has its own Ftr Sect the LAD HQ provides the command and coordination function, taking the pressure off artificers so they can concentrate on their main task of keeping fit equipment in the hands of troops. All in all, the manning sits at 1 + 99, by far the largest LAD in theatre, having it spread across Task Force Helmand AO makes the command task much more difficult. For the majority of the tour, there was roughly a 50/50 split between Camp Bastion and forward locations'.

EOD and Search Task Force LAD. This small LAD supported a Task Force, which was made up of four national contingents and 28 contributing units. It was responsible for supporting search equipment (Vallon, Horn and Goldie), remote controlled vehicles (the venerable Wheelbarrow and the newer Dragon Runner robots), and the vehicles that went with them, which encompassed Protected Mobility (PM) vehicles through to quad bikes that were very popular machines. Clearly, the nature of the IED threat meant the proper calibration, repair, and modification/upgrade of EOD-related equipment was a key function.

CRARRV recovering a Wolfhound vehicle in Nahr-e-Saraj on Operation HERRICK 15

35 Engineer Group LAD. The EME writes:

'The 35 Engineer Group LAD have recovered, repaired and maintained the largest equipment fleet in theatre; supporting over 270 equipments consisting of 47 variants spread across Helmand Province. They have consistently maintained availability in excess of 90% whilst effecting forward repairs ranging from IED rebuilds to recovery and maintenance under contact'.

Talisman Team LAD with a Buffalo vehicle on Operation HERRICK 15

He went on to describe the activities of the Armoured Support Group (ASG), which employed Trojan and CRARRV and was due to return to the UK at the end of the tour with its task completed, and which also provided support for the ongoing Talisman activity.

Second Line – 3 CS Battalion REME perspective
In an article in The Craftsman magazine (June 2012) titled 'Postcard from Helmand' a number of individuals from 3 CS Battalion REME (the Theatre ES Battalion) provided short contributions describing what they had been up to during the first five months of their tour. The broad pattern of their activity was very similar to that of their predecessors. The narrative began:

> 'We have enjoyed highs and lows, torrential thunderstorms and blistering heat. We have spent Christmas on tour and even got away with missing Valentine's Day for another year. Over 80% of the Bn have deployed forward throughout the tour, and the Bn has deployed on over 230 FRTs.… It is true to say that no two soldiers within the unit will have had the same experience thus far. To give a flavour …'

Corporal Martin Pyott, who was attached to 35 Engineer Regiment LAD as a Class 1 'flying fitter', tells his story:

> 'My main role was to set up a mobile workshop and to provide support for a myriad of vehicles such as Medium and Light Wheeled

Tractors, Dumper Trucks, Wolfhound, Husky and Mastiff. On many occasions, I deployed out to where the Engineers were building checkpoints and bridges, not only providing equipment support but also getting involved in force protection. On one occasion, I was contacted at a compound construction site, as the Gunner I quickly reacted, locating and positively identifying the enemy in a nearby wood and then engaging the enemy.... While out with 11 Squadron, we were on a patrol to a compound which had recently been cleared by a 3 SCOTS infantry call-sign, as 11 Squadron progressed along the route they found themselves trapped in by five IEDs. Luckily, a few Engineers and I managed to spot the ground sign left by the insurgents and no one was hurt. It goes to show that the counter-IED training put in before deployment really pays off'.

There were several more accounts of perilous contacts with the enemy, and whilst they make for exciting tales, they should not obscure the fact that 3 CS Battalion REME's significant achievement was in repairing, recovering, modifying or maintaining the equipment needed by TFH to do its job.

3 CS Battalion REME tradesmen change a Mastiff axle in FOB Shawquat on Operation HERRICK 15

This included a lot of rebuilding of vehicles struck by IEDs, as well as the full range of second line repairs normally carried out on equipment being heavily used in an austere environment. Where it was carried out, as always, depended on a balance of operational and technical factors.

Whilst some repairs could be carried out in the relatively benign environment of Camp Bastion, the risks, and time delays associated with backloading casualty equipments meant that many second line repairs had to be carried out in forward locations to give users the level of availability they required. REME second line personnel had to deploy forward exposing themselves to the same risks as the combat troops they were supporting. In broad terms, this had worked as it was supposed to, with many REME personnel clearly relishing the challenge to their skills as a soldier.

Base Intelligence, Surveillance, Target Acquisition, and Reconnaissance
The TFH AO (Area of Operations) become dotted with operating bases (Main, Forward and Patrol) and checkpoints, which represented the protected static nodes that underpinned the overall security plan. The problem with any static base, but particularly small and isolated ones, is that the enemy knows exactly where the occupants are and their routes in and out. The insurgents can contemplate at their leisure the best time, place and manner to carry out their attacks. Intelligence, Surveillance, Target Acquisition, and Reconnaissance (ISTAR) is the means used to counter this.

The term encompasses a wide range of systems from Unmanned Aerial Vehicles (UAV), through weapon locating radars to covert observation posts and a variety of types of sensors. The term Base-ISTAR (B-ISTAR) was coined to cover systems tied to the support of bases. As the importance of B-ISTAR grew in Afghanistan, a number of systems were introduced, several in response to Urgent Operational Requirements (UOR). The underlying technology, having been used extensively in Northern Ireland, was not new and included radar (also weapon locating and movement detecting systems) and increasingly complex electro-optical systems (infrared as well as normal cameras). There were medium systems such as Remover, a trailer-mounted system with a suite of cameras on a mast, and Revivor, another trailer-mounted system, which used an aerostat (balloon) to loft a package of cameras and infra-red sensors.

A key development was the building of tall masts/towers on which heavy systems could be mounted. There were a number of these, which were integrated/updated as the Cortez 'system of systems'. While the systems were operated by a number of different cap badges, the task of deploying the systems, repairing and modifying them fell to REME. A REME technician tells his story in The Craftsman magazine (April 2012):

> 'Since 3 CS Bn REME arrived in theatre, the Optronics Section in the General Platoon has had a busy tour. In particular, one group of tradesmen has spent the past four months working their way around the theatre fixing B-ISTAR. Eighteen soldiers were trained from the Battalion prior to deploying; some on the medium Remover/Revivor systems, some on the heavy Airliner/Livingstone systems (also known as Cortez). From those who were Cortez trained, six then went on a 'rigger's' course allowing them to work at height. This gives the technician the ability to work on the Cortez cameras and mast by climbing up to them rather than by having to lower the equipment which takes away the surveillance asset. … Since arriving in Afghanistan these 'riggers' have been continuously out on the ground, conducting maintenance and repair work as well as completing modifications to the towers. For security, the soldiers 'rig' at night, and climb up to 21m, well above the Hesco perimeter of the base. The work ranges from cleaning camera lenses to conducting complete camera changes, a task which can take four hours. … Then there are the modifications, which are being added to the towers during Op HERRICK 15, a task which requires the 'rigger' to climb for up to four nights in a row, repeatedly exposing themselves to the outside world. … It is not just the 'riggers' who are busy; all the B-ISTAR technicians in theatre are having a daily battle with the technology to ensure it is battle-ready. Since Christmas, work has also begun on implementing a new medium B-ISTAR system called Memphis. This is being put into Check Points (CP), which have never had coverage before'.

It is quite clear from other comments in the article that B-ISTAR suffered from problems. Problems generally associated with hastily introduced systems, a lack of spares and introductory teething problems, which were resolved by the ingenuity and technical knowledge of REME technicians.

OPERATION HERRICK 16 (APRIL–OCTOBER 2012)

First Line

In general, the pattern continued very much as on previous tours but with the process of transition of responsibility to the ANSF starting to gather momentum and, with it, the start of working towards the eventual drawdown of UK forces. Reports from theatre continued to mention that major repairs, such as engine and axle changes on PM vehicles, were being carried out at forward PBs. Movement on roads continued to be hazardous, and the 'repair forward' policy was to be proven, as it had in the North African deserts of 1942, very successful. It had the advantage of REME's 'customers' being able to see what was being done by REME to ensure that their equipment was operational when needed, such as cutting off the wheel station of a damaged PM vehicle prior to fitting a new one in a forward PB. The high level of equipment availability that was achieved, required a good standard of Equipment Care by the users; one of REME's important roles was to provide mentoring as required.

Second Line

The Theatre ES Battalion (4 CS Battalion REME) had a busy and successful tour. It was not surprising it was busy, as it had a dependency of some 3,500 vehicle platforms of over 50 types in Afghanistan. As well as providing immediate support for operations, increasing effort was devoted to deliberate rehabilitation forward (Operation FAHALAWAL). The Battalion also had to cope with new equipments, notably Mastiff 3 and Foxhound. It also made a start on the process of recuperation of equipment, prior to sending it back to UK, and got through the first tranche of Vixen.

REME Support for Aviation

Aviation provided a crucial additional dimension to support for soldiers on the ground with REME playing a key role in delivering it. Aviation was very much joint business, with the Mobile Air Support Unit (MASU) from 1710 Naval Air Squadron (NAS) collocated with the Joint Aviation Group (JAG) at Camp Bastion.

The AAC provided four Lynx helicopters, which were based at Camp Bastion. There were Mk 9A helicopters equipped with the M3 machine gun and MX10 camera. These were primarily used for deliberate operations, overwatch and escort tasks. The MX10 camera provided a real-time downlink enhancing situational awareness and helping enable the positive identification (PID) of the insurgent. This PID allowed engagement with the M3 machine gun, or tasking of Apache helicopters if greater firepower was required. Some 30 Lynx technicians from 9 Regiment AAC Workshop provided an allocated flying capacity of 200 hours across the four aircraft, with a surge capability if required.

Additionally, 10 Apache helicopters from the AAC were also based at Camp Bastion. These were AH 64D armed with four Hellfire missiles, 19 CRV rockets and 1,200 cannon rounds (30mm). These helicopters were at 15 minutes' notice to move, responding to troops in contact or escorting MERT (Medical Emergency Response Team) missions. The Apache Engineering Detachment, staffed by 45 technicians from 4 Regiment AAC Workshop, conducted all maintenance up to and including the 450 hours Forward Servicing Package, providing 650 flying hours per month. Both the Lynx and Apache helicopter support organisations were organised to deploy ground support forward if required.

Hermes 450 UAV

Other aviation assets were unmanned. The Integrated Unmanned Aerial Systems (IUAS) support organisation was staffed by 32 Regiment RA Workshop. They looked after nine Hermes 450 (H450), seven T-Hawk MUAVs (a small UAV), and 100 Desert Hawk 111 MUAVs. The main effort for the 18 REME technicians involved was to provide the five daily task lines of H450 with an allocation of 450 flying hours per week. The H450 provided ISTAR coverage for TFH using its Compass 10 camera giving troops on the ground 'eyes on' for PID, route proving, route search and detailed target analysis. The REME detachment was responsible for all non-flying activities. REME technicians also regularly deployed forward to support Desert Hawk, which was used for rapid and localised ISTAR in support of troops on the ground. T-Hawk was a ducted fan vertical take-off and landing system used primarily as part of the Talisman suite.

Engineering activity was overseen by the Principal Aircraft Engineer (PAE) (Lieutenant Colonel Ian Winthrop REME) holding Level K engineering authorisation, and the Senior Aircraft Engineer (SAE) holding Level J engineering authorisation (Major Simon Hill REME).

Support for the ANSF – the Brigade Advisory Group
The Brigade Advisory Group (BAG), based on 3 RIFLES, had the key role of developing 3/215 Brigade ANA throughout the TFH AO in order that they could achieve operational self-sufficiency by 2014. It included a REME element, which contributed in two ways. First, it had an advisory function headed up by the Brigade ES Advisor (Captain Rob Ashton REME) and also provided an element of real life support (provided by a team of 12 REME personnel). They also had to develop a relationship with the contractors (Alpha Omega Services) who provided a weapons maintenance team and supplied spares. REME personnel clearly had a fascinating time.

On the one hand, there was much challenge linked to a language barrier and clashing ideas, not least about health and safety; also frustration linked to deficiencies in the Afghan supply chain, which functioned poorly even with some 200 vehicles off the road. On the other hand, there was much satisfaction with the progress in helping their Afghan counterparts whom they often found friendly and resourceful. There was much opportunity for REME to show its ingenuity. For example, the story told in The Craftsman magazine (November 2012) about battery charging.

It was realised at some point that a large proportion of the vehicles sitting on the vehicle park could not be used because the batteries did not work. In many cases, the problem was cured by charging the batteries. The battery chargers in the ANA Workshop did not work, and there was no chance of getting any through their stores system. The REME ASM put two REME Vehicle Mechanics on the job and they came up with the solution of a charging system made out of an alternator and the motor from an old washing machine, all of which was designed to be repairable by ANA mechanics. This was duly presented to them, and solved their battery charging problem.

OPERATION HERRICK 17 (OCTOBER 2012–APRIL 2013) – A TIME OF TRANSITION

First Line Perspective

This tour was very much a time of transition. The following comments from an article in The Craftsman magazine (May 2013) by the EME of 1 MERCIAN (Captain Andy Peters REME) paint a very clear picture of what happened:

> 'It is now finally coming to the end of our Op HERRICK tour. After nearly seven months in theatre our replacements are arriving to what is a considerably different Nad-e-Ali (NDA) to when we first came here, late in September last year. For the first few months of the tour, we were still conducting combat operations in the Dasht-e and providing protection to the ANSF on a regular basis. This gave us considerable challenges trying to keep a tired fleet operationally fit in the hands of the user.
>
> To do this, we often deployed tradesmen forward with the fighting troops to carry out repairs as far forward as possible. More recently, our efforts have been focused on base closures as the ANSF take over responsibility for the protection of Afghanistan. Two weeks ago, we ceased all combat operations completely and now only provide a Quick Reaction Force (QRF) to assist the ANSF if things go badly wrong. To be honest, they are coping very well indeed and we are rarely called upon for assistance. I would not advise taking a stroll down to the local bazaar, as parts of the AO are still very kinetic but for the majority of the population within the protected community they have a far better standard of life than they did a few years ago.
>
> The speed of change here has been phenomenal. At the start of HERRICK 17, we took over one FOB, five PBs, and four CPs spread over a wide area. By the time we depart, we will be handing over only FOB Shawquat and PB Folad as we have now closed down all other locations. Closing the locations has seen a huge amount of equipment moved by road and a large number of vehicles returned to Camp Bastion for redeployment.… The works to get these vehicles to an acceptable 'show room' condition has been relentless.
>
> At the start of Op HERRICK 17, we were responsible for a fleet of approximately 210 different equipments including 75 PM vehicles. Our successors … will have a greatly reduced fleet of

around 115 equipments including 51 PM vehicles. In addition to this, the entire Jackal fleet has been withdrawn, which meant that we had to return all of these to Camp Bastion and take over Husky and Foxhound to replace them'.

'Fitter Section in a Box' successfully deployed on Operation HERRICK 17

Second Line Support
The Theatre ES Battalion was provided by 1 CS Battalion REME. The picture at second line was broadly as previous tours had been with many ISTs and FRTs deployed forward, but with an increased emphasis on equipment rehabilitation.

ES in TFH – A General Perspective
Equipment availability remained generally high (80% plus) despite the continuation of IED strikes, with many of the damaged vehicles being repaired forward. Events were being driven by the aggressive Base Realignment and Closure/Transition Plan (BRAC/T). The REME organisation was frequently adjusted to match it. For example, when NES(N) and NES(S) combined, a Transition Support Unit (TSU) was set up based on 1 + 33 from 40 Commando Group LAD and personnel from other local REME first line units. Their workload split between providing ongoing support for operations and preparing equipment for going through the Proof of Good Order (POGO) process (both biological as well as mechanical) at Camp Bastion prior to redeployment. It was clear that REME tradesmen enjoyed a high regard, not only for looking after operational equipment but also for taking on 'extras', such as fixing washing machines and televisions, doing carpentry, and fixing gates, as well as doing their fair share of guards and duties.

HQ UK Joint Force Support (Afghanistan)

There were two UK one-star HQs in Afghanistan at the time. HQ TFH was essentially the headquarters that delivered combat effect; much has already been said about REME repair and recovery activities therein. This combat effect would not have been possible without the enabling action provided by the one-star HQ Joint Force Support (Afghanistan) (JFSp(A)). The good news was that its equipment-related activities were working effectively, as described by the Commander Equipment Capability (EC) (Colonel Martin Court (late REME)) in The Craftsman magazine (April 2013). The bad news is that its structure and function are not easily understandable without familiarity with the MoD's structure for managing equipment and its support at that time. The following paragraphs are therefore intended to make things a little clearer.

The HQ was a joint HQ, and its titles reflected this. Thus, what would have come under the title 'G3' in an Army HQ would be called 'J3'. The one-star commander and the core of the roulement staff came from one of the Army's logistic brigades. The HQ was divided into staff areas J1 to J8 with the EC Branch, which covered J3 EC and J4 ES, being by far the largest Branch. This was headed by a Colonel, whose Branch organisation is shown at Figure 12.2 (at the end of this Chapter).

The staff of HQ JFSp(A) in December 2012

The J3 EC part of the organisation was headed by a Lieutenant Colonel. This was involved with interacting with 'Capability' staff (essentially what was called 'Operational Requirements' in earlier times), and with the Defence Equipment & Support (DE&S) organisation, whose Integrated Project Teams (IPTs) dealt with the procurement of new equipment and support for in-service equipment. This side of the organisation would be very much concerned with the introduction of UOR equipment, and the many and varied problems that they entailed. They would also be involved if any problems arose with in-service equipment that required the involvement of a DE&S IPT, typically to take up a technical or supply issue with the equipment manufacturer.

Given the effort to harness science and technology to improve capability, it made sense to include Scientific Advisors (SCIAD) in the EC Branch.

The J4 ES part of the EC Branch organisation was concerned with the coordination of repair and recovery of equipment other than aviation assets, which came under the Joint Aviation Group. This was not a straightforward business and Colonel Court commented:

> 'Early days in Op HERRICK saw inadequate ES command and control, and crisis after crisis with deployed equipment. Much of this was down to not deploying with LAD commanders or a proper REME command and control structure. We have got it right now and should not forget this lesson or let others do so'.

Whilst the overall strength of the UK force in Afghanistan was relatively low and reducing, its structure was complex as were the various command and functional relationships. ES within TFH was the responsibility of the BEME, who was directly responsible to Commander EC, as was the JFSp(A) BEME, who was responsible for a number of organisations that were not part of TFH, including those in Kabul and Kandahar. The CO of the Theatre ES Battalion also reported directly to the Commander EC. Whilst he commanded his Battalion, he also had the JFSp(A) LAD under his wing, and the Defence Support Group (DSG) regeneration facility in Camp Bastion. More details of the Theatre EC organisation are at Figure 12.3 (at the end of this Chapter).

For this to work efficiently in practice, all ES resources and activities needed to be coordinated so that the right problems were tackled at the right time and with the right resources. This could only happen if the resource and activity were managed by those with the knowledge and experience to understand the diversity of each issue, and had the clout to ensure that sensible solutions to them were found. This idea represents nothing new for REME.

One of the important functions of 'ES Ops' within the HQ EC organisation continued to be that of dealing with teething problems associated with new equipment. Foxhound proved popular with users, but arrived with many teething problems, which 'ES Ops' played a part in sorting out. This illustrates the need for REME to be able to tackle the technical snags, which come with new (and hastily procured) equipment.

OPERATION HERRICK 18 (APRIL–OCTOBER 2013)

General

This was a period during which transition continued. Although the numbers deployed in forward locations were drawing down, and lead responsibility for security increasingly rested with the ANSF, Helmand Province remained a dangerous place for British troops. Those moving outside protected base areas were always liable to IED, RPG or other attack. The pattern of activity at first line continued much as before, albeit with a steady shift from supporting operations to preparing equipment for redeployment.

Second Line Support

6 CS Battalion REME deployed with some 200 all ranks to provide the backbone of the Theatre ES Group. It continued to provide support forward in the form of FRTs and ISTs, and it sent recovery crews to support all Combat Logistic Patrols (CLP). Support for B-ISTAR and other protective electronic systems continued to be an important activity. Preparation of equipment for redeployment absorbed an increasing proportion of the repair effort. After becoming familiar with the Theatre Exit Standard process, the ES Group started by processing the CVR(T) fleet for redeployment. They then went on to Jackal and Coyote vehicles, and by the end of the tour had prepared some 800 vehicles for redeployment. Additional topics were covered in their reports in The Craftsman magazine (December 2013).

Light Company. The Light Company provided support forward as required and, otherwise, concentrated on delivering a Husky modification programme. For the last two months of the tour, it was augmented by Redeployment Platoon whose sole job was to repair vehicles to Theatre Exit Standard. The Recovery Platoon supported some 70 CLPs in addition to general recovery tasks.

The Light PM Hangar during a sandstorm on Operation HERRICK 18

Heavy Company. One of the major tasks for Heavy Company was a substantial modification programme to Warrior vehicles to increase survivability.

Warrior vehicle modified by 6 CS Battalion REME on Operation HERRICK 18

Echelon. Over the previous eight years, large quantities of materiel and spares had accumulated in theatre, which was not required and sometimes not accounted for. The Echelon personnel therefore had a big task on their hands to get their holdings to match their requirements. The RLC Stores Troop, which comprised soldiers from 6 CS Battalion REME, 3 Logistic Support Regiment RLC and 32 Regiment RA, took over the largest single stores account in the British Army. By the end of the tour, they had managed to reduce its stock value from £75m to £60m by withdrawing equipment. The QM's Department, in consultation with the ES Companies, saw the value of the Equipment Table reduced by £3.5m.

End of Tour Reorganisation. At the end of the tour, the Heavy and Light Companies were restructured into a composite ES Company. This was to facilitate the handover to 2 CS Battalion REME, which was to deploy with one company less.

OPERATION HERRICK 19 (OCTOBER 2013–MAY 2014)

General

The process of transition and drawdown continued. At the start of the period, significant force elements were still deployed forward, although the bases were soon to be dismantled or handed over to the Afghan authorities. Lashkar Gah was handed over to the Afghans on 24 February 2014 and PB Lashkar Gah Durai on 8 March 2014. MOB Price was closed down shortly after.

By April 2014, all TFH forces had been withdrawn to Camp Bastion except for those occupying the Observation Post (OP) in Sterga 2. This OP was perched on a hilltop hundreds of feet above the River Helmand. It offered panoramic views of the fields and desert below; an obvious reason for its occupation by the Russians (and quite probably the British during the 19th Century Afghan Wars). Sterga 2 was relinquished in May 2014. Although operations had effectively ceased, there was plenty to keep REME busy with the equipment that was needed for training and operations being kept fully fit and the remainder got into a suitable state for the redeployment to UK.

JFSp(A) EC Branch Perspective

Commander EC (Colonel Adam Fraser-Hitchen (late REME)), who had deployed halfway through Operation HERRICK 18 and had also commanded the Theatre ES Group in 2010, provided a useful theatre update in The Craftsman magazine (March 2014):

> 'REME's first and second line effort had been effectively integrated with the productive effort delivered by the DSG to form three pillars of ES. The need to establish a centralised technical area was clear and was implemented at pace. The former TFH BEME post was merged with that of the BEME JFSp(A) to become the single theatre BEME who oversaw the LAD technical work (Level 2). Whilst, in principle, the Theatre ES Group carried out Level 3 work and the DSG carried out Level 3+ work, there was, in practice, a level of 'best practice' in the mutual support provided between the REME chain of command and the DSG. Two-way mentorship was common between both REME and DSG personnel.

Modifications and Urgent Statements of User Requirement (USUR). Modifications continued either for technical improvements or to fit new systems, which reflected the fruits of earlier USURs. This second category was generally concerned with protection and survivability including more mundane functions, such as snow chains needed for Foxhound on its first winter in Kabul. One of the more innovative developments to protect the PM fleet was a system of protection against RPG attack. Named 'ABEO', this was described as a string vest hung around on the outside of the vehicle. It was an example of the plethora of modification tasks, which continued to be conducted in theatre by REME.

Foxhound vehicle fitted with 'ABEO' protection

Electronic Counter Measures (ECM). ECM for force protection (FP) continued to be an important area of activity with REME and Royal Signals soldiers working closely together. Their work embraced the deployment and fitting of Vehicle Installation Kits (VIK) for vehicle-borne protective systems, as well as man-portable systems.

Forensic REME. The EC Branch included a DSTL Scientific Advisor (SCIAD) and a WO2 AQMS from the Serious Equipment Failure Team (SEFIT). Both added considerable technical depth to the work of the Branch. The AQMS SEFIT, in addition to his routine investigative tasks, delivered a significant amount of work on battlefield forensics. Op HERRICK showed that it was most often REME Recovery Mechanics who arrived first on scene of a vehicle IED casualty and were therefore well placed to collect initial battlefield forensics. The AQMS SEFIT developed and delivered an in-theatre training package for Recovery Mechanics, which taught them how to conduct a 'forensically aware' approach to an IED incident, gathering evidence where possible before recovering the vehicle. Comd EC worked on developing this concept further, with a view to formalising a Land Accident Investigation procedure, similar in principle to the established Air Accident Investigation process'.

A Broader Perspective

Commander EC concluded his article with some 'lessons learned' across the UK's Afghanistan involvement, incorporating the views of previous Commanders EC and focused on the need to reinforce the corporate memory, as the Army looked forward to a new era. They included the following comments:

> 'In the early days of Op HERRICK, the inadequacy of ES C2 was detrimental to the equipment fleet.... LAD commanders must be deployed, within an established REME C2 structure, to deliver equipment advice to unit commanders.
> We need to be able to flow ES capability against a complex and dynamic set of circumstances; the Intimate Support Team (IST) has proved its worth.
> We need to formalise and exploit the use of both civil servants and contractors on operations. The DSG's deployment in the

Regeneration Facility has been a success and has been borne out of high levels of communication.

Although we now have JAMES working in theatre (albeit more painful to use than back in UK), the need to look at Log IT on contingency operations, developing the issue from the hard lessons of HERRICK, is paramount.

As a Corps we need to reflect on the welfare support we have provided to those deployed and those who man the home base – the latter stages of the operation produced a template for future operations'.

OPERATION HERRICK 20 (JUNE–DECEMBER 2014) – THE FINAL ROULEMENT

The final roulement took place in May/June 2014 with fresh troops relieving those who had completed their tour. HQ TFH had ceased to exist, with Commander 20 Armoured Brigade taking over as Deputy Commander of the US-led Regional Command (South West) in Camp Bastion under which the UK forces were grouped. The REME deployment was led by 3 CS Battalion REME, with elements of 20 Armoured Company under command, many other REME personnel from the Battalion and Brigade also deployed in critical G4 accounting and support roles, as the task became clear closer to deployment, with many deploying at short notice due to their training readiness – 100 Battalion personnel deployed.

Key senior staff from 3 CS Battalion REME formed the nucleus of an Equipment Capability Branch, including the SO2 ES/BEME in HQ 102 Logistic Brigade, which had formed the Joint Force Support Headquarters. The CO undertook the dual appointment of the last Commander Equipment Capability and CO of the ES Group, which by that time included the DSG and functional command of first line LADs within the Manoeuvre Battlegroup. Fortuitously, a number of key personalities within HQ Joint Force Support and the Battalion had deployed on Operation BROCKDALE in Iraq. This turned out to be crucial for setting successful conditions for the withdrawal of equipment, including refining the Theatre Equipment Returns System (TERS) process as the withdrawal of civilian air transport towards the end of the redeployment necessitated more risk to be taken with equipment, which had to be prepared and moved safely.

The process of dismantling facilities and redeploying the appropriate equipments back to the UK proceeded at pace. A fine balance was struck between maintaining the military capability to protect Camp Bastion while redeploying sufficient quantities of equipment to meet the political timeline. The opportunity for the insurgent to target a weakening force was a thought paramount in the minds of many.

REME's primary role continued to be to prepare equipment for redeployment against a well-articulated standard, dependent on the method of movement. Quite obviously, the standards for those equipments passing over the air line of communication rated far higher than for those being sent back over ground lines of communication. Again, a tension existed in being able to meet this standard for the final tranche of those departing by air. The brokering of arrangements between the Army's and the RAF's technical personnel eventually led to a way through this conundrum. The necessity to cooperate, particularly with RAF Air Movements staff, was absolutely critical and the fact that the redeployment occurred without major mishap was testament to the level of integration achieved at all levels, right down to REME Vehicle and Recovery Mechanics and RAF Loadmasters forming a joint team at the flight line to ensure loading success.

Crucial to this was the establishment and deployment of an Equipment Reverse Supply Chain Node, based on a Squadron Group from 6 Theatre Logistic Regiment RLC with embedded REME personnel, at the Al Minhad Airbase, just outside Dubai in the United Arab Emirates. This was already in use for logistic freight and personnel moving to and from Afghanistan, and had already processed equipment on an ad-hoc basis depending on shipping availability, but was permanently deployed for the final redeployment. This critical node on the redeployment plan enabled quick turnaround of aircraft and dramatically shortened the flight times in and out of Afghanistan, which was crucial during the final stages. The bulk of equipment went through this staging post onto sea transport back to Marchwood (UK), but some equipment did fly direct to UK. These different end-destination requirements added further complication to the equipment preparation in theatre due to customs regulations, as well as paperwork and political clearances. This required agility in processes and procedures as destinations changed, usually at extremely short notice, depending on aircraft availability and capability. HQ JFSp(A) established a liaison node in Minhad with HQ Joint Force Support (Middle East) (JFSp(ME)) to enable the redeployment and it proved hugely successful.

IED-damaged Wolfhound vehicle outside Camp Bastion on Operation HERRICK 20

The final phase of the redeployment was conducted through Kandahar Airfield and elements of the REME ES Support Group were based there to facilitate this redeployment, which was on a later timeline to Camp Bastion. The final UK force elements, including the final REME

The ES Group facility at Camp Bastion on Operation HERRICK 20

personnel in southern Afghanistan redeployed from Kandahar within a few weeks of the closure of Camp Bastion.

Troops were withdrawn throughout the period with REME's final footprint planned to be the LAD of a manouevre battlegroup plus a recovery platoon from 20 Armoured Company. The departure of these elements would mark both the end of the year and end of the campaign. As it happened, the political timeline sped up and so did the redeployment. Getting home by Christmas, unlike in 1914, became a reality for all on Operation HERRICK.

The other role of HQ JFSp(A) and the REME personnel in Afghanistan was to shape the REME and ES footprint for what would remain in Afghanistan. A small number of British forces remained in Afghanistan, based in Kabul as part of Operation TORAL, supported through HQ JFSp(ME). A large number of personnel from the ES Group deployed to Kabul to cover critical absences, particularly during R&R phases throughout the campaign and more so at the end as resources became scarcer. Up to the redeployment, most of the support for British forces in Kabul was provided through Kandahar and Camp Bastion, which presented a challenge to be overcome before redeployment was complete.

A number of personnel deployed up to Kabul, including Commander Equipment Capability (Lieutenant Colonel Paul Loader REME, also CO 3 CS Battalion REME), on numerous occasions to assist the nascent HQ BRITFOR with their planning for Operation TORAL. It must be recognised that a considerable amount of REME and equipment resource and expertise was redeployed to Kabul in advance of the closure of Camp Bastion. A small number of British forces remained in Afghanistan, based in Kabul as part of Operation TORAL. These are not considered in this Chapter given their advisory/training role rather than an operational one.

AN OVERVIEW OF OPERATIONS FROM 1993 TO 2015 AND A LOOK AHEAD

This is the last of a series of chapters about operations. What is notable, is the variety of operational activities REME has been involved in during a period of little more than two decades, and the differences between the situations at the beginning and end of it. It is, therefore, perhaps worth briefly reviewing the period as a whole and picking out some points to ponder.

AFGHANISTAN – DRAWING DOWN

The public mood at the start of the period covered by this book was one of confidence in the military. The Soviet threat had evaporated and with it the need to keep forces at high readiness in Germany. The Gulf War had demonstrated the overwhelming nature of US/UK military power and their willingness to wield such power if provoked. This went with the idea that once any repressive regimes and international renegades had been brought into line, and their people had enjoyed a taste of capitalism and liberal democracy, they would aspire to nothing else.

The first decade of this book covers a period of unbroken British military success. Operations in the Balkans involved the successful combination of powerful deterrent land forces, and the use of air power, combined with peacekeeping operations at which the British forces were particularly adept, being able to draw on experience in Northern Ireland, and were widely recognised as such. Following '9/11', UK played a minor role in the rapid overthrow of the Taliban regime in Afghanistan, which was virtually bloodless from the US/UK point of view. UK then took a major role in the invasion of Iraq contributing around 46,000 people to what was seen as very much a US/UK affair. It is easy to forget, in the light of later events, that this was a very successful operation, which proved that UK was still well capable of engaging in expeditionary and high-intensity warfare. It was not hard to argue at this point in time that UK's investment in a small but capable Army had helped it 'punch above its weight' in the international arena.

Following initial success in Afghanistan and elsewhere, the USA Secretary of Defense Rumsfeld was sure that success in the future would be based on 'shock and awe' and that his military advisers' views on the need for 'boots on the ground' tended to be outdated and overstated. He was proved spectacularly wrong.

The decade that followed the invasion of Iraq was in many ways a very difficult one for the Army. The situation in Iraq deteriorated and the UK contingent found itself involved in counterinsurgency operations, which it was not properly resourced or equipped to deal with. UK did not match the resulting 'surge' in US commitment (from 15 to 20 combat brigades) intended to bring the situation under control. In contrast, the UK force reduced to some 5,000 strong, which was concentrated in a Contingency Operation Base (COB) on the outskirts of Basra before withdrawing entirely.

Meanwhile, what had been intended as a straightforward peacekeeping operation in Afghanistan had found the UK involved in a very tough counterinsurgency operation. The personal gallantry and professionalism of British soldiers in both Iraq and Afghanistan had been truly remarkable and inspiring, and has been generally recognised as such by the UK public. Less easy to recognise was the clear cut and obviously successful outcomes that UK had become used to. This went with the growing general realisation that the removal of a repressive and undemocratic regime would not necessarily pave the way to a more stable, just and reasonable regime.

The end of the period covered in this book sees an unsettled UK public sometimes wondering whether intervention in Iraq and Afghanistan was actually a good idea. It is less confident in the judgment of military leaders, and less willing to take it on trust that money spent on defence is always wisely used by the MoD. This is not a happy position to be in, given that the world seems to be more dangerously unstable than it has been for a long time in the light of turmoil in the Middle East, a resurgent Russia, and the rise of religious and sectarian extremism, often linked to terrorism, in several parts of the world. It is beyond the scope of this book to explore these issues, but three points are perhaps worth considering.

First, the UK public has arguably got used to the assumption that there are a lot of terrible things happening in the world, but they are going on 'over there', and they do not seem to cause any real problem 'over here', provided we ignore them. History has shown the assumption that UK will never be forced to protect its security and vital interests is a dangerous one. Second, there is no way of forecasting what the UK's next operational commitment will be. Quite possibly, it will be nothing like its recent operation in Afghanistan, and it may be important to understand the lessons from very different types of operations. Third, whatever capability UK decides it needs, it will not work properly unless its ES component works properly. The following paragraphs elaborate on this point.

By and large, the REME/ES system has worked remarkably effectively during the operations covered in this book. This should not induce complacency. The need to keep essential lessons alive to enable ES to be successfully delivered in some very different operational scenarios is key to future UK military success.

The most demanding ES scenario is the deployment of a large expeditionary force at short notice. In order to identify key problems and solve them in a timely manner when under pressure in this scenario, it is necessary to exchange and integrate information, feedback and decisions from multiple sources. These sources include the ES organisation of the deploying/deployed force, operational planners at JHQ and elsewhere, industrial suppliers, support or procurement project teams, and many others. The issues involved may be highly technical, and may require an understanding of the interplay of technical and operational issues, as well as the situation on the ground and in the industrial base.

For example, feedback on actual failure rates will impact on assessment of operational sustainability, and give an early indication of which assemblies or components are likely to become critical to supportability. The equipment dependency must also be kept under review, despite the invariable modification programmes to be implemented. Operation GRANBY offers a classic example of this type of situation, and the invasion of Iraq a broadly similar one on a somewhat smaller scale. In such situations, it is crucial to have strong REME representation in the planning and procurement arena, and at the right level in the support structure. REME personnel are often the only individuals able to combine professional engineering knowledge with front-line experience of operational issues and an understanding of how the complete support system works. Problem solving is also often easily facilitated if those involved know each other, trust each other, and are able to 'talk the same language'. The ability to exchange ideas informally on 'the REME net' has often proved hugely helpful.

Before and after the formation of DGES(A)'s organisation, the space between 'procurement' (a Defence responsibility, overseen for the Army by the Master General of the Ordnance (MGO)) and 'support' (an Army responsibility, overseen by the Quartermaster General (QMG)) was seen as problematic. The interface issue was a common subject for discussion and lectures ('mind the gap') with regular joint QMG/MGO project reviews intended to promote understanding across the interface.

Chapter 18 of this book ('Support for Army Equipment – An Overview') describes how Army ES had become very well integrated under DGES(A), with an unbroken functional chain from his level down to junior tradesmen at the front line. Detailed Integrated Logistic Support (ILS) procedures were developed at the time to close the gap between procurement (Defence) and ES (Army) at a technical level.

Chapter 18 further explains how the higher management of ES was taken away from the Army and put into a Defence Logistic Organisation, which then merged with the Defence Procurement Agency to form the DE&S organisation with a large civilian component.

Whilst this improved the interface between 'procurement' and high-level 'ES' (both within a large and complex DE&S), it also created a new ES fault line between the DE&S facing elements and the Army facing elements. In principle, a combination of ILS and the capability management organisations, which were set up and intended to manage efficiently across this interface. In practice, the management of this interface (and the application of ILS processes) is far from straightforward, evidenced by the fact that it took such a long time to get the right ES/EC structure into Afghanistan.

During the first part of the period covered by this book, the procurement effort focused largely on major projects that would be brought into service in a measured way, applying formal ILS procedures in the process. Things did not always run smoothly and it was frequently REME people who played a key role in addressing issues by dealing with other REME people and/or directly with contractors on technical issues. REME personnel embedded in the procurement system provided a vital contribution to all levels.

During the final decade, the emphasis shifted to the procurement of UOR equipment in support of operations in Iraq and Afghanistan. There was no time for the process of ILS, and equipment often had to be delivered without the package of spares, tools, training and technical information that should ideally have gone with them. REME personnel again played a critical role in providing pragmatic and workable solutions to such issues at every level from involvement with industry to implementation at the front line.

Clearly, the one lesson from this history is the benefit borne from having REME representation in both ES and procurement roles at all levels. The combination of professional engineering and military skills often providing the key to solving problems.

The employment of REME staff in the DE&S also offers a potential 'win-win' in terms of both the skills that REME staff can usefully apply in the DE&S and the commercial understanding (and knowledge of the DE&S), which they take with them when they return to the Army side of the Army/DE&S interface. At the start of the period covered by this book, REME effectively still 'owned' substantial base repair and technical support organisations. Looking ahead, particularly in the light of the sale of the DSG, it seems that first and second line repair will still largely be carried out by REME organisations and that, generally, everything else will be done by contractors. Military officers (and civil servants) at times lack insight into the mindset of commercial organisations and the way contractors operate; having REME staff in the Army system who have had substantial commercial exposure can only be helpful.

Whilst concluding this Chapter, the author noted that the House of Commons Public Accounts Committee had stated on 20 March 2015:

> 'Ironically Defence Procurement and Support is planning to spend £250m over the next three and a half years on contractors to advise on how it can reduce its over-reliance on contractors'.

It is to be hoped that the contractors will fully understand the value of talking to REME staff when preparing their advice.

Operation	Op Bde HQ	Log Bde HQ	REME (lead Bn)
Herrick 15 Oct 11–Mar 12	20 Armd Bde	HQ 101 Log Bde	3 CS Bn REME
Herrick 16 Apr–Oct 12	12 Mech Bde	HQ 102 Log Bde	4 CS Bn REME
Herrick 17 Oct 12–Apr 13	4 Mech Bde	HQ 104 Log Bde	1 CS Bn REME
Herrick 18 Apr–Oct 13	TFH 1 Mech Bde Around 7,900 UK forces by Jul 13	Air Comd Individual Augmentees HQ	6 CS Bn REME
Herrick 19 Oct 13–May 14	7 Armd Bde Around 5,200 UK forces by Jan 14	101 Log Bde	2 CS Bn REME With one less coy than previous bn (around 200)
Final Roulement Jun–Dec 14	20 Armd Bde	102 Log Bde	3 CS Bn REME

Figure 12.1: Summary of the UK commitment over the period covered by this Chapter

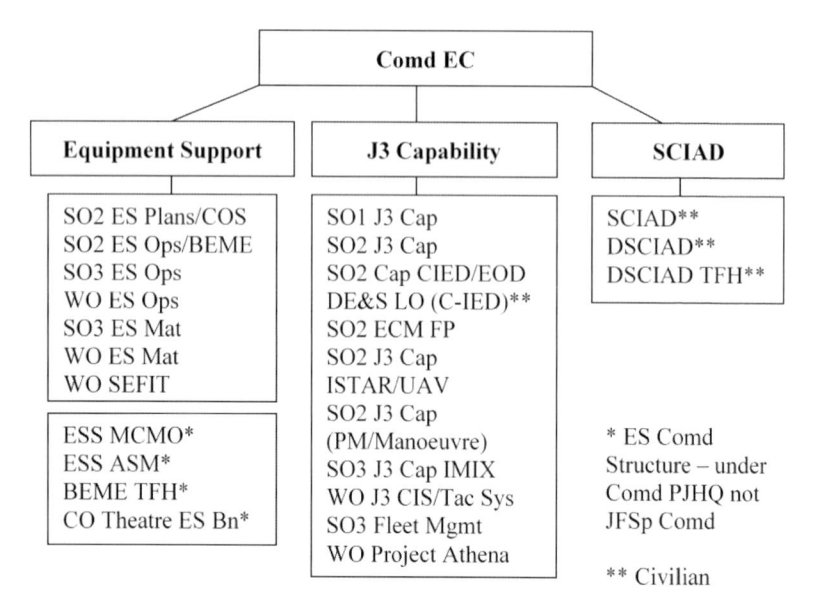

Comd EC

Equipment Support
SO2 ES Plans/COS
SO2 ES Ops/BEME
SO3 ES Ops
WO ES Ops
SO3 ES Mat
WO ES Mat
WO SEFIT

ESS MCMO*
ESS ASM*
BEME TFH*
CO Theatre ES Bn*

J3 Capability
SO1 J3 Cap
SO2 J3 Cap
SO2 Cap CIED/EOD
DE&S LO (C-IED)**
SO2 ECM FP
SO2 J3 Cap ISTAR/UAV
SO2 J3 Cap (PM/Manoeuvre)
SO3 J3 Cap IMIX
WO J3 CIS/Tac Sys
SO3 Fleet Mgmt
WO Project Athena

SCIAD
SCIAD**
DSCIAD**
DSCIAD TFH**

* ES Comd Structure – under Comd PJHQ not JFSp Comd

** Civilian

Figure 12.2: HQ JFSp(A) EC Branch

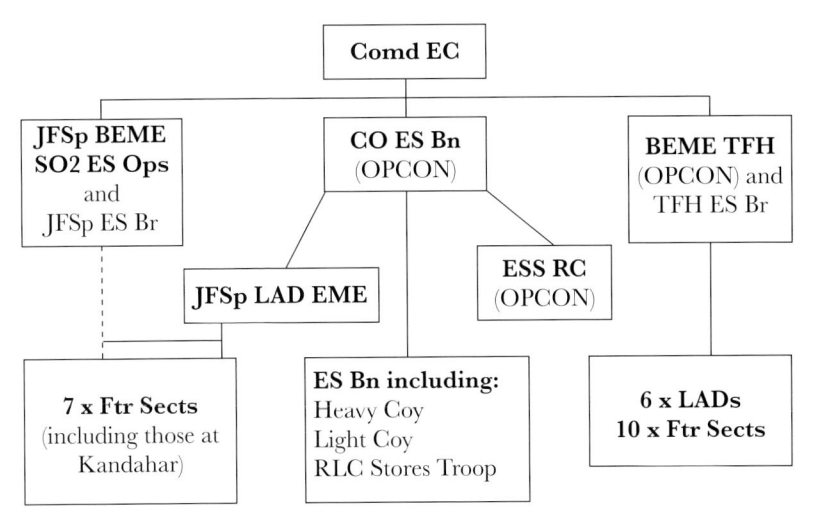

```
                        ┌──────────┐
                        │ Comd EC  │
                        └────┬─────┘
         ┌───────────────────┼───────────────────┐
┌────────────────┐   ┌──────────────┐   ┌──────────────────┐
│ JFSp BEME      │   │  CO ES Bn    │   │ BEME TFH         │
│ SO2 ES Ops     │   │  (OPCON)     │   │ (OPCON) and      │
│ and            │   └──────┬───────┘   │ TFH ES Br        │
│ JFSp ES Br     │          │           └──────────────────┘
└────────┬───────┘    ┌─────┴──────┐
         │            │   ESS RC   │
         │     ┌──────────────┐ (OPCON) │
         │     │ JFSp LAD EME │    │
         │     └──────┬───────┘    │
┌────────┴────────┐   │            │
│ 7 x Ftr Sects   │  ┌┴──────────────────┐  ┌──────────────────┐
│ (including those│  │ ES Bn including:  │  │ 6 x LADs         │
│ at Kandahar)    │  │ Heavy Coy         │  │ 10 x Ftr Sects   │
└─────────────────┘  │ Light Coy         │  └──────────────────┘
                     │ RLC Stores Troop  │
                     └───────────────────┘
```

Figure 12.3: Theatre EC organisation

CHAPTER 13

REME IN THE UK – STRUCTURE AND ORGANISATION

Although a proportion of the Army was stationed abroad (as described in Chapter 14 ('REME Overseas')), or was involved in operations or exercises overseas, the majority of the Army was based in UK throughout the period covered by this book.

Given that so much of REME is deployed at first line, it is broadly the case that REME is based where the Army is based. Changes to lifestyle in REME units also reflect changes in the Army as a whole. Changes in technology and social practices in the civilian world (such as getting tattooed!) have inevitably had an effect, and certain aspects have changed at unit level. For example, much Single Living Accommodation has been improved (with more soldiers having their own rooms) and the Pay-As-You-Dine Scheme has been introduced, which means soldiers pay for what they eat rather than paying a standard charge for food, whether they eat it or not. Change has tended to be incremental, and the ethos and pattern of activity of REME personnel has remained broadly unchanged because the factors that drive it have remained essentially the same, not least the need to *'keep fit equipment in the hands of troops'*.

In order to understand how REME has been structured and managed in UK, it is necessary to understand how the Army has been structured and managed. The purpose of this Chapter is to explain these two linked topics, as well as looking ahead to the basing plan for Army 2020.

THE EVOLVING ARMY STRUCTURE AND MANAGEMENT OF ARMY ES

During the Cold War, Army units in the UK came under HQ UK Land Forces (HQ UKLF) based in Wilton (near Salisbury Plain). Army units in Germany came under HQ British Army of the Rhine (HQ BAOR) based in Rheindahlen, which was responsible for the administration of support of up to four divisions that were formed as a Corps under the operational command of HQ 1st British Corps (1 (BR) Corps) in Bielefeld. There was no equivalent Corps level of command in UK. HQ BAOR controlled large workshop facilities, and had significant delegated responsibility for managing equipment and its support.

The 'Options' exercise brought the size of the force in Germany down to a single division, 1 (UK) Armoured Division, which was put under the operational command of the HQ at Wilton, whose considerably expanded role went with a change of title to HQ Land Command (HQ LAND). HQ BAOR was closed down, and the rump of its responsibilities that could not be satisfactorily exercised from the UK, and did not comfortably rest within an operational division, were taken over by the newly formed UK Support Command (Germany) (UKSC(G)) headed at two-star level.

A new Corps HQ was set up in Bielefeld (Germany), which was called the Allied Command Europe Rapid Reaction Corps (HQ ARRC). As its name suggests, this was a NATO organisation, but it was one that the UK authorities were keen to support, partly because the British played a significant role in setting up and supporting the HQ, and also because it provided useful links to its US and other NATO allies. Many Army units and formations were earmarked to support the ARRC.

At the start of the period covered by this book, ES was still very much a single-Service responsibility. At this time, global management of Army ES was exercised by a two-star Director General Equipment Support (Army) (DGES(A)), based in Andover, accountable to the Army's Quartermaster General (QMG). On its formation, DGES(A)'s organisation absorbed most of the high-level support management functions previously carried out in BAOR. Back in UK, the relationship between DGES(A)'s staff and the ES staff at HQ LAND tended to be close, as most of the key players involved were REME officers who both knew each other well, and had a good understanding of the practicalities of ES on the ground. This was broadly the position in the early-1990s (around the start of the period covered by this book), and might be seen as the culmination of 'post-Options' reorganisation.

Since then, there has been almost continuous organisational change, much of which has had an effect on REME, ranging from trivial to important. Some of the change can only be fully understood in the context of high-level issues, which affected the management of Army equipment and its support that Chapter 18 ('Support for Army Equipment – An Overview') seeks to outline.

To track every change in organisation would require an indigestible narrative with numerous charts and wiring diagrams. However, not to explain any of the organisational changes in UK would mean that events described in other chapters of this book would lack context. A compromise solution is therefore adopted in the narrative that follows, which seeks to explain the Army's structure at the start point in 1995, and to outline the subsequent main changes to its organisation and management structure with particular reference to their impact on REME's business.

THE START POINT – 1 APRIL 1995

The Land Command organisation was split into deployable formations, which comprised two deployable divisions with their allocated Combat Support (CS) and Combat Service Support (CSS) units, as shown in Figure 13.1 (at the end of this Chapter).

The remainder of Land Command's organisation comprised 'regenerative formations', districts, and overseas detachments. It worked through a two-star structure, as shown in Figure 13.2 (at the end of this Chapter).

The ES function across Land Command was controlled by a one-star Commander ES whose Directorate worked 'rearwards' to DGES(A)'s two-star HQ and 'forwards' to Commanders ES, or other ES staff at subordinate HQs. The ES Directorate sat within HQ LAND, and naturally worked closely with other directorates therein.

By no means all of REME's activities in UK came under HQ LAND. REME people were active in a variety of other HQs, training organisations, procurement organisations and the like, the most significant of which are described elsewhere. Overseas operations did not come under HQ LAND, they were the responsibility of a Joint HQ (JHQ) set up for the purpose at Northwood.

STRATEGIC DEFENCE REVIEW 1998 AND THE SCENE IN 2000

As at the year 2000, the ES function at HQ LAND was still headed by a one-star REME officer (Brigadier Mike Huntley (late REME)). By this point, the JHQ at Northwood had become established as a permanent organisation, was renamed Permanent Joint Headquarters (PJHQ) and had a small ES cell embedded in it. It came under a three-star Chief of Joint Operations whose role was:

'…to exercise operational command of UK forces assigned to overseas joint and combined operations; and to provide politically aware military advice to the MoD in order to achieve MoD UK's strategic objectives on operations'.

By this point, the Defence Logistics Organisation (DLO) was starting to form up. The fragmentation of responsibilities to Integrated Project Teams (IPT) under the new Defence structure had started, but in practice many of the same people were still doing the same thing in the same place, so personal links between REME people still played an important part in the identification of equipment-related problems and their rapid resolution.

In essence, the one-star Commander ES at HQ LAND issued ES functional direction to the Army through Commanders ES at subordinate formations, whilst working closely with the relevant IPTs in the DLO (and Defence Procurement Agency (DPA) when necessary), DEME(A) and ES staff in PJHQ. This helped ensure that the Army's ES plans were coherent from the procurement, support planning and operational points of view.

A number of organisational changes had also taken place. These included the move of 2 Division from York to Edinburgh where it absorbed HQ Scotland. A study had also been launched to look at the future structure of Land Command. This was called Landmark.

SITUATION IN 2001 AFTER LANDMARK

The overall structure of HQ LAND after Landmark is described in the following paragraph [from Appendix A to LAND/G3 ORG 30165 dated 23 August 2001].

It was headed by a four-star Commander in Chief with a number of two-star officers reporting directly to him. These included his Chief of Staff (COS), his Deputy COS (DCOS), and the heads of the Joint Helicopter Command, 2, 4 and 5 Divisions, London District and UK Support Command (Germany) (UKSC(G)). A three-star Commander Field Army/Inspector General of the Territorial Army also reported directly to the four-star Commander in Chief. He had a one-star COS, and had four two-star officers reporting to him, who headed 1 Division, 3 Division, Theatre Troops and Theatre Support Command (Land).

The Theatre Troops organisation came into being on 31 August 2001 and lasted until September 2013 when it became Force Troops. Its role, as described in an article in The Craftsman magazine (September 2009) by the GOC Theatre Troops, was:

> '… to provide essential 'capabilities' – such as Intelligence, Surveillance, Target Acquisition, and Reconnaissance, deep strike, specialist engineers, communications, medical support, air defence and logistic resupply…. In essence, when a formation … is deployed it will come up with a 'shopping list' of assets that are required…. Theatre Troops will provide the force elements …'.

HQ Theatre Troops required an ES organisation. This was set up under the former Commander HQ REME TA, who had also been double-hatted as the Deputy Commander Combat Service Support Group UK (CSSG(UK)). His REME TA responsibilities ceased with the change.

Landmark also resulted in the loss of the one-star Commander ES post. The ES function was to be headed by a Deputy Assistant Chief of Staff (DACOS) ES at Colonel level who reported to a one-star head of 'Logistics', who reported to COS HQ LAND. The role of 'availability management' was transferred to Arms and Services Directors including DEME(A).

HQ LAND ES AS AT 2005

By 2005, it had been realised that organisational changes had created a situation where the MoD felt it was no longer an 'intelligent customer' for equipment and ES. In a review of ES Branch, the DACOS ES at the time, Colonel Clive Ward (late REME), explained (his article in The Craftsman magazine (April 2005)) the need to develop an Intelligent Customer Capability. It was realised that DEME(A) simply could not do some of the things that had been expected of him, so responsibility for availability was transferred back to HQ LAND, and the DACOS ES became the Land Environment Equipment Availability Manager. He was responsible for delivering inter alia:
- the HQ LAND focal point for Land Environment equipment (safety, Equipment Failure Reports, Equipment Care)
- the fleet management of Land Command assets and the asset liability match to meet HQ LAND's priorities
- equipment sustainability advice

- fleet sustainability (spares and resources other than spares)
- information to the DLO on equipment usage
- the provision of ES advice on new equipment
- the monitoring of performance of equipment Private Finance Initiative/Contractor Logistic Support arrangements on behalf of HQ LAND.

To deliver this new role, ES Branch reorganised into three cells, each headed at Staff Officer Grade 1 level, and gained 14 additional staff. The cells were Policy Plans, Combat Service Support and Manoeuvre. They contained Availability Managers who were aligned to the IPTs linked to their equipments.

AVAILABILITY MANAGEMENT AND ES BRANCHES IN HQ LAND AS AT 2006

As part of HQ LAND's plan to develop its Intelligent Customer Capability, a new ES Branch was formed. Effectively, this represented a split of the previous organisation and a reshaping of it into two branches that worked closely together, as explained by Colonel Alistair Duncan (late REME) in The Craftsman magazine (February 2006).

The 'new' ES Branch under Colonel Duncan (DACOS ES) was to be the focus for ES policy and plans including ES materiel issues. It would also lead on equipment safety, Equipment Care and associate inspections. It incorporated the Inspectorate of Engineer Resources, which was responsible for the world-wide examination of equipment that was repaired by the Royal Engineers. One of its major tasks was the development and implementation of an effective Equipment Care Inspection (ECI, broadly the same idea as the old Periodic REME Examination (PRE)).

The Availability Management Branch, which continued under Colonel Ward, tended to focus on providing links with the DLO, Arms and Services Directors, and others to promote equipment availability.

HQ LAND AND HQ LAND FORCES – ES AS AT 2008

The merging of the DLO and DPA into the Defence Equipment and Support organisation (DE&S) in April 2007 (see Chapter 18 ('Support for Army Equipment – An Overview')), was one of the further drivers for organisational change at HQ LAND. By this time, arguments were increasingly couched in terms of 'Capability'. This was understandable in a MoD increasingly dominated by large, complex, ever-changing Defence structures suffering from lack of finance and run by a mixture of civilians (civil servants and contractors) and staff from all three Services. It made sense to justify requirements in terms of *'this money is needed to provide this capability, because …'*.

In 2007–2008, the Equipment Division within HQ LAND therefore underwent radical changes. The former Availability Management Branch and the Capability Development Branch reorganised and formed the Support Equipment Branch. Within these branches, Capability Integration Managers worked to bring into service new equipment, and also provide support to existing equipment. The changes reflected those within DE&S and were consistent with the approach promoted by the Defence Acquisition Change Programme (from The Craftsman magazine (February 2008)).

Meanwhile, ES Branch under DACOS ES had as its top priority the support to current operations. Other main concerns included the management of Contractor Field Support, much provided by the Army Base Repair Organisation later the Defence Support Group (see Chapter 19 ('Technical Support and Base Repair Agencies')), and further work on ECIs, which was linked to work carried out by DEME(A) and others on Engineering Standards.

Project Hyperion involved the creation of HQ Land Forces (HQLF) by merging HQ LAND (based at Wilton) with HQ Adjutant General (AG) (based at Upavon). The new HQ was to be based at Andover to take advantage of real estate no longer required by DE&S. While the organisational merger took effect from 1 April 2008, the building and preparation of the real estate was not going to allow physical collocation before 2010. A top-level organisational review was under way, and it was expected that Arms and Services Directors would come under HQLF.

HIGHER STRUCTURE OF THE ARMY AFTER THE STRATEGIC DEFENCE AND SECURITY REVIEW 2010

The HQLF site was formally opened in July 2010, and has been named Marlborough Lines. The Army continued to be headed by a four-star Chief of the General Staff (CGS) who represented the Army at the highest levels in the MoD. His role (in 2014) was described thus on the MoD website in May 2014:

'CGS commands a single Army Staff which works out of Army HQ in Andover. CGS exercises command of the Army through three 3-star subordinate commanders: Commander Land Forces (CLF), Commander Force Development and Training (FDT) and the Adjutant General (AG).

Commander Land Forces is the primus inter pares at 3-star. He acts as the Chief of the General Staff's deputy and he is the commander responsible for delivering the Army's principal outputs. The Field Army, the Reserves, the Firm Base and the Joint Helicopter Command are integrated through the establishment of a Land Force Command'.

In essence, the four-star Commander in Chief Land Forces post had gone. The 'regenerative' Divisional HQs (2, 4 and 5 Divisions) were closed down in mid-2012, and brigades that came under them transferred to a new single two-star HQ Support Command based in Aldershot.

Force Troops Command (FTC), based in Upavon, was due to become the largest two-star command in the British Army. All the Army's units providing Combat Support, Command Support, certain Combat Service Support and specialist support to the Reaction and Adaptable Forces will be commanded by FTC.

The ES organisation to support these changes will doubtless evolve as the complex process of reorganisation and rebasing takes place.

REME REBASING UNDER ARMY 2020

The Army's 'Rebasing Plan' has always been an important part of the plan for Army 2020. The plan for REME Reserve units is set out in Chapter 16 ('REME and the Reserve Army'), and some of the key unit moves of second line Regular units have already been covered in Chapter 3 ('Strategic Defence and Security Review 2010 and Army 2020'). Much of REME is, however, at first line, so it is useful to get a broader picture of the Army's rebasing plans. This information from an article in The Craftsman magazine (May 2014) reflects the picture at that time:

'The Army of the future will be concentrated in seven areas – Tidworth, Catterick, Aldershot, Edinburgh/Leuchars, Colchester, Donnington and Cottesmore/North Luffenham. Consolidating around the seven centres will significantly reduce the need for moves, giving Army and Corps personnel and their families real benefits in terms of increased stability, access to long-term spousal employment opportunities, continuity in schooling for children and the chance to set down roots and access the benefits of home ownership.

The Army Basing Plan will affect most areas of the Army as more than 100 units will either relocate, re-role, convert or disband over the next six years. This is a huge project lead by the Army Basing Team and HQ Support Command. They are working jointly with the Defence Infrastructure Organisation (DIO) and liaising with the chain of command to refine unit locations within the new locations.

A budget of £1.6bn has been set aside to implement the Regular Army Basing Plan of which £800m will be invested in Army living accommodation, providing nearly 1,900 new Service Families Accommodation and 4,800 Single Living Accommodation bed spaces. The Corps has attracted funding in excess of £50m for 'new build' technical accommodation in both Cottesmore and Tidworth that will house 5 FS Bn and 3 Armd CS Bn respectively ...'

(Author comment: the plan was later changed with 5 FS Battalion REME due to go to Hullavington instead). The article continues:

'However in the majority of cases the infrastructure will consist of a mix of 'new build' and 'improved' existing facilities which have been funded.

Army Concept. The Basing Plan is designed to allow the Army to generate its military capability in the optimal manner. There are two key principles:
- the armoured infantry brigades of the Reaction Force should be collocated around the Salisbury Plain Training Area (SPTA) as it is the only place in the country that can accommodate the complex and demanding exercises that they require
- the Army must retain a UK-wide footprint, maintaining the vital link to civil society, fostering close links between Reserve units and their partner Regular units and supporting nationwide engagement.

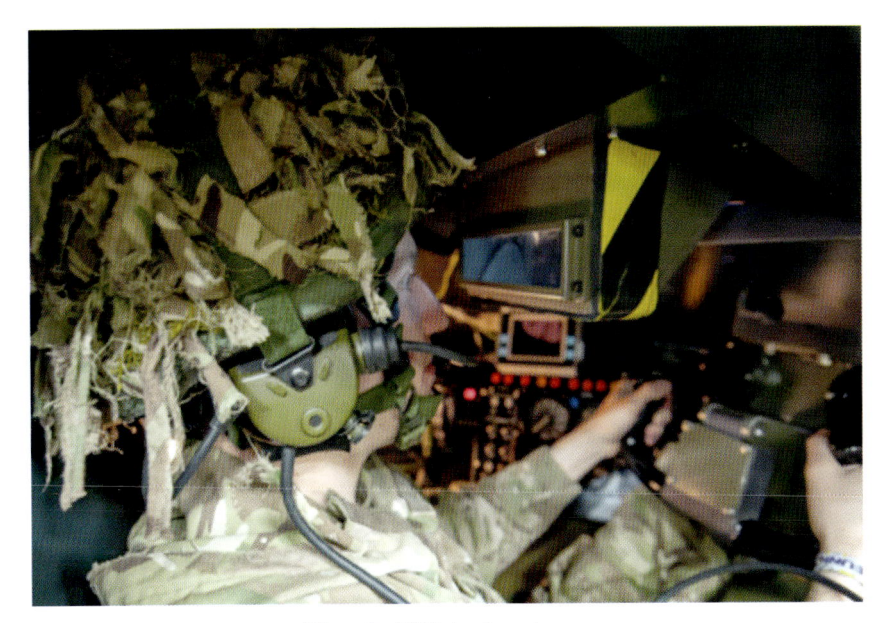

Plate 1: AFV simulator in use

Plate 2: REME Foden vehicle recovering UN Warrior vehicle in Bosnia 1994

Plate 3: Supporting training on the Krivolak Training Area

Plate 4: Aerial view of Vitruvius Lines

Plate 5: Vehicles of 2 Battalion REME on the move

Plate 6: Engineer Regiment CVR(T) needs attention

Plate 7: 'Thrown Tracks'

Plate 8: Deployment after the invasion – several key posts were held by REME personnel Picture (January 2004) left to right: Lieutenant Colonel Jones (COS HQ UK NSE), Lieutenant Colonel Birrell (DCOS HQ UK NSE), Major General Figgures (DCG(PH) CJTF 7), Major Mulholland (OC SLB), Major Bell (OC ES Company in Shaibah)

Plate 9: PWRR LAD at work in Camp Abu Naji on Operation TELIC 4

Plate 10: Grounds of Basra Palace after the invasion

Plate 11: 1 Highlanders LAD Basra April 2006

Plate 12: 4 ES Company outside the CESTA in the COB on Operation TELIC 11

Plate 13: Convoy of transporters laden with Warrior vehicles ready to leave for the boats

Plate 14: REME personnel on Operation FINGAL 7 admire the scenery 2004

Plate 15: HCR (Formation Reconnaissance) D Squadron Fitter Section on Operation HERRICK 4

Plate 16: REME Wolfhound vehicle in the Forward Repair Team role

Plate 17: Buffalo Mine Protected Vehicle

Plate 18: Husky vehicle

Plate 19: 10 CS Company facilities before workshop build on Operation HERRICK 6

Plate 20: 1 Battalion REME Group at Camp Bastion on Operation HERRICK 7

Plate 21: Recovery of a Viking vehicle following a mine strike on Operation HERRICK 8

Plate 22: REME personnel in JHF(A) at Camp Bastion on Operation HERRICK 10

Plate 23: REME CRARRVs support Trojan vehicles on Operation HERRICK 12

Plate 24: Light Wheeled Tractor engine change in a FOB on Operation HERRICK 12

Plate 25: Shop floor of Equipment Sustainability System on Operation HERRICK 14

Plate 26: Call Sign 52 of 3/215 Brigade Advisory Group on Operation HERRICK 14

Plate 27: Armistice Day Service for members of the Corps on Operation HERRICK 15 at the REME Memorial in Camp Bastion

Plate 28: REME TA personnel on Exercise KUKRI SPANNER in Brunei enjoy a journey by boat 2013

Plate 29: REME Reservists at the Force Workshop Cyprus on Exercise LION SPANNER 2012

Plate 30: Members of the Falkland Islands MTW on parade 2003

Plate 31: 71 CS Company completing Gazelle helicopter head change on Operation TELIC 1

Plate 32: Apache helicopter DSU Pulse 1 and 2 finished 2007

Plate 33: REME TA Recruit Course outside HQ REME TA Bordon circa 1994

Plate 34: Volunteers from 102 Battalion REME (V) who served in the Balkans in 2000

Plate 35: 103 Battalion REME (V) on SOUTHERN BLUEBELL 2006

Plate 36: REME TA soldiers on SOUTHERN BLUEBELL 2013

Plate 37: REME TA soldiers on a production task on SOUTHERN BLUEBELL 2014

Plate 38: Her Majesty The Queen visits 101 Battalion REME (V) on 4 June 2003

REME Concept. The first principle … dictates the location of the REME Armd CS Bns. They must be in a position to train alongside their respective brigades; therefore 3, 4 and 6 Armd CS Bns will be located within Tidworth Garrison. Fortunately, 4 and 6 Armd CS Bns are already in place and housed within purpose-built technical accommodation. 3 Armd CS Bn is not scheduled to return from Germany before 2017, and has been allocated funds for a new build technical facility. Tidworth Garrison is full to capacity, and it is for this reason that 5 FS Bn is due to relocate. The second principle… has also had a significant effect on the basing of the Corps. The CS Bns maintain a presence in the North with 1 CS Bn remaining in Catterick and 2 CS Bn relocating from Fallingbostel to Leuchars in 2015. 7 Air Assault Bn will remain in the East at Wattisham…'

The original REME Second Line Rebasing Plan as at 2014 is shown on the map below. As explained in Chapter 3 ('Strategic Defence and Security Review 2010 and Army 2020'), plans for Army 2020 would inevitably be subject to change, and by the time of final editing the map below was out of date in that 2 CS Battalion REME is already in Leuchars and it had been decided to move 5 FS Battalion REME to Hullavington instead of Cottesmore (as noted earlier).

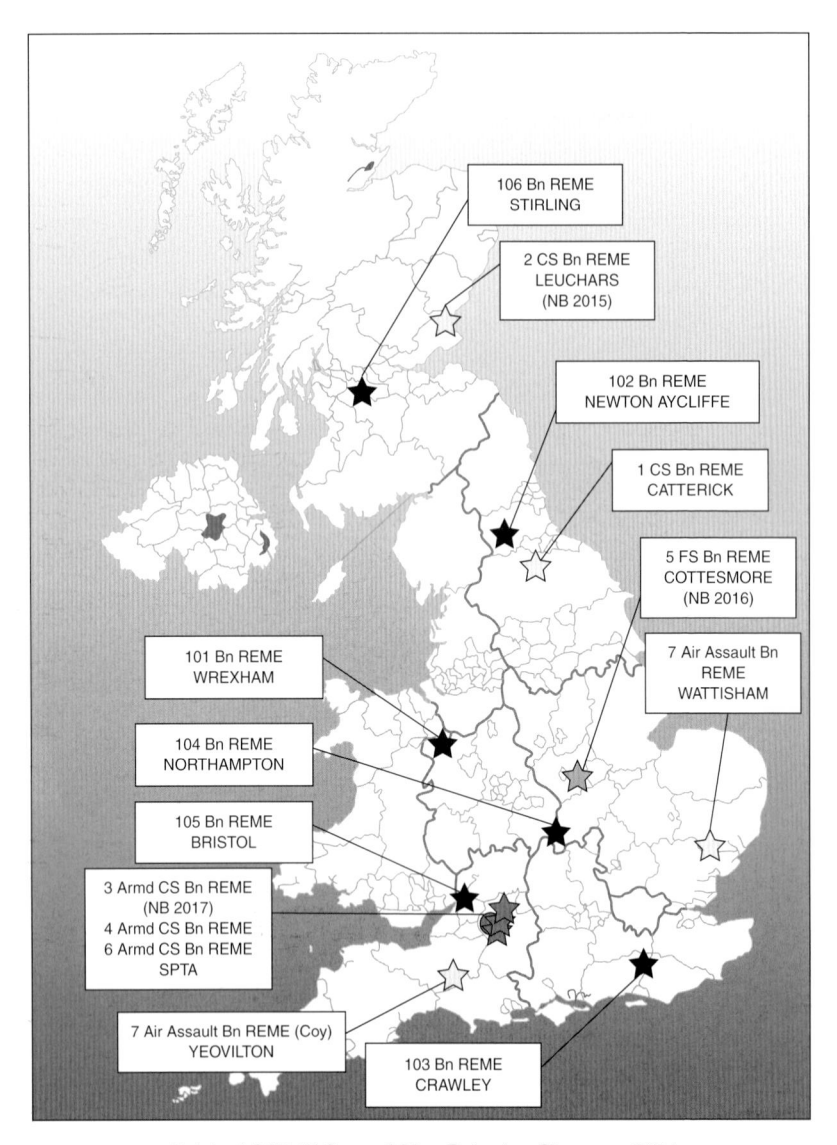

Original REME Second Line Rebasing Plan as at 2014

REME IN THE UK – STRUCTURE AND ORGANISATION

DEPLOYABLE FORMATIONS (COMBAT FORMATIONS)	
1 (UK) Div – Herford	**3 (UK) Div – Bulford**
4 Armd Bde – Osnabruck	1 Mech Bde – Tidworth
7 Armd Bde – Hohne	5 AB Bde – Aldershot
20 Armd Bde – Paderborn	24 Airmob Bde – Colchester
DEPLOYABLE FORMATIONS (SUPPORT)	
CSSG(UK) (Tidworth) for which 102 Bn REME (V) was the only second line REME unit	
CSSG(G) (Gutersloh) for which 105 Bn REME (V) was the only second line REME unit	
Note: 'ARRC Troops' was shown as a grouping of support units (including 7 Bn REME) under the OPCON (Operational Control) of various divisional HQs, but there was no separate UK ARRC HQ	

Figure 13.1: Organisation of Land Command in 1995

REGENERATIVE FORMATIONS AND OVERSEAS DETACHMENTS	
HQ	**Location/Comments**
2 Div	York – 15 (NE) Bde, 49 (EM) Bde, plus Div Tps
4 Div	Aldershot – 2 (SE) Bde, 145 (HC) Bde, plus Div Tps
5 Div	Shrewsbury – 42 (NW) Bde, 143 (WMid) Bde, 160 (W) Bde, plus Div Tps
London District	London
SCOTLAND	Edinburgh – 51 (H) Bde, 52 (L) Bde, Div/Dist Tps
UKSC(G)	UK Support Command (Germany) based in Rheindahlen
Overseas Detachments	Wilton – BATUS, BATSU, Belize, Brunei Gar etc
Note: A more detailed diagram going down to unit level would show a substantial grouping of units shown as Theatre Troops (including 104 Bn REME(V)) but, as with ARRC Troops, all were normally OPCON of one of the various divisional HQs, and there was no Theatre Troops HQ at this time	

Figure 13.2: Regenerative Formations and Overseas Detachments in 1995

CHAPTER 14

REME OVERSEAS

Many of REME's activities overseas could be classified simply as 'operations', 'collective training' or 'adventurous training' and, as such, appear in the relevant chapters of this book. This Chapter describes the various aspects of REME involvement overseas, which have not been covered therein.

REME IN GERMANY

By far the biggest REME involvement overseas has been in Germany. During the Cold War, 1 (BR) Corps was based there under HQ British Army of the Rhine (HQ BAOR) in Rheindahlen. The armoured divisions based in Germany were at a state of high readiness, with a technical and logistic infrastructure in place to support combat operations if required. This is described in some detail in Volume 2 of Craftsmen of the Army.

1 (BR) Corps disbanded in 1992 and BAOR formerly disbanded in 1994. The drawing down of forces resulted in a single division, 1 (UK) Armoured Division, being formed out of the Army elements that remained in Germany. Its HQ was in Herford, and it comprised divisional assets and three strong armoured brigades. These were 4 Armoured Brigade based in Osnabruck, 7 Armoured Brigade based in Hohne, and 20 Armoured Brigade based in Paderborn. A Combat Service Support Group (Germany) (CSSG(G)) was based in Gutersloh. This was to be renamed 102 Logistic Brigade in due course.

This force in Germany came under the direct command of HQ LAND in UK, as with the divisions based in UK. The fact that the formation was based in Germany meant, however, that there were various administrative, technical and diplomatic functions that were best exercised in Germany rather than UK, and which represented tasks not appropriate for an operational division such as 1 (UK) Armoured Division to take on. A new organisation, UK Support Command (Germany) (UKSC(G)), was therefore formed to take these on. This was headed at two-star level. Its HQ was based in Rheindahlen, and it included an ES Branch.

By this point, the British forces stationed in Germany were no longer there to defend Germany. In reality, they were largely there because the German Government was prepared to let them stay, and because it was the most suitable place for them to be based, given the availability of well-established facilities, and the lack of suitable alternatives in UK. In short, Germany was no longer considered a potential theatre of operations, but a place where British troops could be based, train, and from whence they could deploy to engage in operations in the Balkans, Iraq, Afghanistan and elsewhere.

REME Organisation

In principle, the REME first line organisation was unchanged and consistent with that in UK. The second line battalions were based on existing sites. The process of forming the battalions required some reshuffling of people and equipment (and alterations to the infrastructure), but the exercise was fairly straightforward, and went smoothly. The way the battalions worked was based on familiar and proven principles, and the only difference in principle between battalions in UK and Germany was that the latter had under command Garrison Workshops, essentially manned by locally employed civilians (LECs). These were created from former Station Workshops, or the large Civilian Detachments that had been attached to Armoured Workshops.

REME units that were part of 1 (UK) Armoured Division came under the technical direction of the Commander ES (a REME Colonel). The small ES Branch set up at HQ UKSC(G) picked up many of the supporting technical tasks that had formerly been done by REME Technical Services BAOR. The substantial REME base organisation in Germany was dismantled as described in Chapter 19 ('Technical Support and Base Repair Agencies') and technical support not available in theatre generally came directly from the UK. Divisional ES Staff would arrange this through HQ LAND, or, where appropriate, directly with HQ DGES(A) staff in Andover or contractors. Broadly, the same pattern was followed when HQ DGES(A) was subsumed within the Defence Logistic Organisation (DLO), which was in turn subsumed within the Defence Equipment and Support (DE&S) organisation.

Training

Training was driven by mandated Army requirements, notably the Force Readiness Cycle explained in Chapter 4 ('Collective Training for

Operations'). Certain aspects of training were familiar to old BAOR hands, not least because much of it used excellent training facilities, such as those at Sennelager and Bergen-Hohne, which had been used by the Army for decades. After the Cold War, the German Authorities were much less willing to countenance training activities outside designated military training areas. The training areas themselves became subject to much tighter environmental constraints. Such restrictions led to increasing reliance on overseas training in Canada, Kenya and the Drawsko Pomorskie Training Area in western Poland as described in Chapter 4 ('Collective Training for Operations'). As the Army became stretched by its operational commitments in Iraq and Afghanistan, training naturally became more oriented towards preparation for the type of operations that were going on there.

Lifestyle
Whether people enjoyed serving in Germany or not was generally a matter of 'lifestyle choice' influenced by issues such as proximity to family, links with local communities and the like. For many people, a tour in Germany was a very attractive option. Commander ES, Colonel Steve Williamson (late REME), explained some of these advantages in his article in The Craftsman magazine (November 2007).

The Local Overseas Allowance (LOA), meant to compensate for the cost of living abroad, could often more than compensate for it if wisely used. It was still possible to buy tax-free goods (cars, cigarettes and drinks). Married Quarters were generally within a short drive of barracks. Schools were good, and generally got better results than equivalent schools in UK. The military community, including those supporting it such as teachers and administrators, tended to be quite close knit, but also enjoyed a comfortable relationship with the local people. Many people enjoyed this, as well as the opportunity to get out and about and see parts of Europe they would probably never otherwise visit. Many of the facilities were excellent, and there were plenty of opportunities to engage in sport, particularly skiing.

Changes during the period 2005–2009
In 2007, it was decided that 4 Armoured Brigade would be re-roled, and would return to UK. This largely happened in 2008 when 4 Armoured Brigade became 4 Mechanised Brigade and moved to Catterick. This resulted in the closure of Osnabruck Garrison and the handover of the

facilities and real estate there to the German Authorities. The formation was not replaced in Germany, so 1 (UK) Armoured Division was reduced to two combat brigades.

In 2005, the former ES Branch of UKSC(G) moved from Rheindahlen to Bielefeld (Rochdale Barracks), and reformed itself as Equipment Support Services (Germany) (ESS(G)), which was described in an article in The Craftsman magazine (March 2007). It was headed by a REME Lieutenant Colonel and comprised a mixture of serving personnel and civilians (many ex-REME). It included the Contract Repair Branch (Germany), the Army Calibration Laboratory (Germany) and the Medical and Dental Servicing Section. It supported, inter alia, the civilian workshop elements remaining in Germany (1, 2 and 3 Civilian Workshop, and Rhine Area Workshop). Its other main area of responsibility related to Equipment Care. In particular, it dealt with German regulations that applied to British equipment, such as those which concerned the inspection of goods vehicles.

Army 2020 and the Army Basing Plan

This is outlined in Chapter 3 ('Strategic Defence and Security Review 2010 and Army 2020'). The plan for Germany saw all 20,000 troops stationed there leaving, around half by the end of 2015. It was to be a very complex exercise that needed to be conducted in close coordination with the Defence Infrastructure Organisation (to ensure the availability of facilities for units when they moved to UK). By 2020, it was expected that the Army will have returned to the Federal Authorities: 28 barracks, 22 Service Children's Education Schools, 14 medical centres, 7,000 single bed spaces, 7,000 Federal Services Accommodation (FSA) Homes, and 5,000 leased FSA Homes.

Various units closed or moved in 2014, including 28 Engineer Regiment, whose disbandment would allow the closure of Hameln Garrison. Major rebasing moves from Germany were planned to occur in 2015 with 7 Armoured Brigade units moving from Bergen-Hohne and Fallingbostel, HQ 1 (UK) Armoured Division moving from Herford, and 16 Signal Regiment and 1 Armoured Division Signal Regiment rebasing from Elmpt and Herford to Stafford, enabling the closure and release to the German Federal Authorities of Bergen-Hohne Garrison as well as Elmpt and Herford Stations. Some 3,300 German nationals were scheduled to lose their jobs, including many who had served loyally in REME workshops for many years.

REME IN BRUNEI

The British Army has had a continuous presence in Brunei at the invitation of the Sultan (subject to a five-yearly renewable agreement) since 1962. At the time of writing, there was a permanent garrison of about 900 all ranks, based on a resident infantry battalion and a flight of AAC Bell Helicopters (212 Helicopter Flight AAC). In addition, Brunei served as one of the British Army's major training areas, specialising in jungle warfare, with the Jungle Warfare Training School (also known as Training Team Brunei) running the Jungle Warfare Advisor's Course and the Military Tracking Instructors Course in conjunction with the infantry battalion (normally Gurkha).

The British Garrison was based on four sites with a small Garrison Workshop sited in Medecina Lines in the Belait District of Brunei. This provided second line REME support, which complemented the unit first line REME support. Brunei has also been visited by REME TA personnel, in the form of Exercise KUKRI SPANNER. They were hosted by the Garrison Workshop and unit LAD, and combined useful productive work with a chance to enjoy some recreation and see the country, as described in an article in The Craftsman magazine (February 2014). (**See Plate 28**)

REME IN CANADA

The British Army Training Unit Suffield (BATUS), has already been mentioned in the context of 'collective training'. BATUS is located in the vast training area near Suffield in Alberta, which is on an indefinite lease from the Canadian Authorities. The Salisbury Plain Training Area would fit into it some seven times over.

Since the Cold War era, it has been used for the collective training of armoured units. Because of the weather, training only takes place during the summer months. Normally four to six battlegroups are exercised, each exercise being called Exercise MEDICINE MAN (MM) and given a number (such as MM1, 2, 3). Each exercise lasts around 30 days. The duration of the exercises, and size of the training area, allow all elements of a combined arms battlegroup (infantry, armour, artillery, engineers, air defence, logistics and ES) to conduct realistic tactical effect simulation exercises, and live firing training at all levels, and to practise sustaining this activity over a long period of time.

REME OVERSEAS

20 CS Company supporting training in BATUS 2008

Visiting units take over their equipment from the BATUS training fleet, and hand it over to the unit that follows them. Units bring their own first line REME support, and a slice of second line REME support. This has the bonus of being great training value for REME, but REME's priority is to ensure that the complete range of vehicles, weapons and other equipment is safe and serviceable when required. The handover/takeover period is a busy one for REME, as equipments have to be inspected and brought up to an acceptable condition. Many of the younger equipment users are on a steep learning curve and, in their enthusiasm to practise their primary military skills, are prone to damage their equipment. The REME dependency includes not only the battlegroup being exercised, but the OPFOR (Opposing Force – the 'live enemy') that normally deploys for a full BATUS season, and the 'Red Top' fleet, so called because they have tops painted red to show that they are safety vehicles, and not part of the tactical exercises.

In addition to visiting first line REME with its slice of deployable second line, there is a large workshop complex, the BATUS Workshop REME. This sits in a large hangar complex, and has extensive repair facilities. It cannot carry out all types of base repair, so assemblies that cannot be repaired to base level have to move through a repair loop back to the UK. During the training season, the primary purpose of the Workshop is to support training.

BATUS 2013 Winter Repair Programme – REME soldiers on the CVR(T) Line

During the winter period, a Winter Repair Programme (WRP) is carried out. The purpose of this is to bring equipments that have suffered from being heavily used during the exercise season back to a fully fit and presentable condition. The WRP is normally assisted by staff from a REME battalion. The gist of what they do is explained in this extract from an article in The Craftsman magazine (November 2013) on the Winter Repair Programme 2013:

> 'In early January 2013, having shaken off the festive season, soldiers from 3 CS Bn REME left Paderborn in Germany to make the annual pilgrimage to BATUS, to conduct the BATUS Winter Repair Programme. Under the command of Lt Col Paul Loader, they formed the 3 CS Bn Winter Repair Group, a 450 strong workforce which includes BATUS Wksp, and covers all the REME ground trades, an Air Trooper, RLC Suppliers, and many Level 1 maintainers from various cap badges. A total of 74 units are represented.
>
> Their task is to repair over 1,200 equipments. The repair effort is not confined to vehicles – all sighting equipments, and turret systems, Bowman and weapons must also be rehabilitated. This task is made all the harder by temperatures which have plunged as low as −35°C with wind chill. The soldiers have set about the work with

gusto, working repeated 12-hour days. The soldiers are driven by weekly output targets which, if achieved, mean that some of their weekends are free'.

In addition to lots of hard graft, some soldiers have had the opportunity to go to Trails End Camp and experience some extreme adventurous training in the form of ice climbing and dog sledding as well as numerous ski courses. The BATUS ice hockey bug has also bitten several of them.

Members of 6 CS Battalion in BATUS on adventurous training

REME IN CYPRUS

The British Army has continued to have a presence in Cyprus throughout the period covered by this book. REME soldiers who go to Cyprus do so for a number of reasons.

First, many have been there wearing light blue berets as part of the British contingent of the United Nations Force in Cyprus (UNFICYP). The primary purpose of this Force is to maintain the integrity of the Buffer Zone that runs between the Greek and Turkish Cypriot Zones. UK provides lightly-equipped battalions who do six-month unaccompanied tours taking REME soldiers with them to provide repair and recovery support. Also, as explained in Chapter 5 ('Operations General'), in 2012, a REME unit, 101 Battalion REME Group, did a tour in the role of a roulement battalion.

Alternatively, they may go to a Sovereign Base Area (SBA) wearing their normal berets. In 1960, a treaty of establishment allowed Cyprus to become an independent Republic, free from British control. Within the agreement, two SBAs at Akrotiri (WSBA) and Dhekelia (ESBA), were identified as real estate that would remain as British sovereign territory, and therefore remain under British jurisdiction indefinitely. The SBAs, which cover 98 square miles, enable UK to maintain a permanent military presence at a strategic point in the eastern Mediterranean. RAF Akrotiri is an important staging post for military aircraft and the communication facilities are an important element of UK's world-wide links. REME soldiers wearing their own berets may go there to provide technical support, either with visiting units or on full-tour postings, or to undergo non-technical training that may be of the military or adventurous variety. They frequently do a mixture of both of these.

The Army contribution to Cyprus has been a significant one. It has varied over time, but, as of 2014, it included, two resident infantry battalions, an element within the Joint Services Signals Unit at Ayios Nikolaos, 62 Cyprus Support Squadron RE and a flight of AAC Gazelle helicopters based at Dhekelia.

7 Air Assault Battalion on Exercise LION SUN in Cyprus 2002

Resident Army units, and those visiting to exercise, have their normal first line REME support. Second line support is provided by a REME workshop company, which operates very much within a Joint environment. A snapshot of life is Cyprus in 2005 is given in an article in The Craftsman magazine (December 2004), which explains how hard everyone works, but somehow does not quite dispel the prevailing impression that a sunshine tour in Cyprus was no bad way to spend a couple of years.

Main vehicle repair section Force Workshop Cyprus 2005

The Force Workshop Company, a Joint unit, sat within the Cyprus Service Support Unit, which included a logistics company. The Workshop Company was commanded by a REME Major. Its military element consisted largely of REME soldiers, although it incorporated some RAF technical staff, and these were complemented by LECs. The Company comprised a HQ, Recovery Section, Vehicle Platoon, General Platoon, and Calibration Centre and Electronic Repair Workshop. The main element of the Company was based at RAF Akrotiri, but it also comprised a Force Workshop (East) based in Dhekelia (in the ESBA), which provided essentially the same services but on a smaller scale. The Company provided recovery and general electro-mechanical and electronic repair for British units based in Cyprus, or visiting for training. Cyprus is a popular training destination for REME reservists as it provides an opportunity (as in BATUS), to combine technical work and training with adventurous training in an interesting environment. (**See Plate 29**)

REME IN THE FALKLAND ISLANDS

UK has retained a small garrison in the Falkland Islands throughout the period covered by this book. Their protection depended primarily on a naval deterrent and a RAF airbase at Mount Pleasant. The Army commitment was for a resident infantry company (to supplement around 200 local reservists). REME contributed to the Motor Transport Workshop (MTW) at Mount Pleasant. An article in The Craftsman magazine (August 2005) gives its strength as 1 + 32 Army (on six-month tours), 10 x RAF (on four-month tours), and 13 civilian tradesmen. **(See Plate 30)**

The workload includes recovery, vehicle repair (a light line, and a heavy line for BV206 and other 'heavy' vehicles), an armament and general section, a snow and ice maintenance section (to keep snow/ice clearance equipment fully operational) and a 'Spec' line run by RAF MT Technicians and civilians, which looks after specialist aircraft support equipment such as fire tenders, tugs, fuel tankers and the like. On Friday nights, staff retire to the 'World Famous Crab and Sprocket' – a watering hole, which as its name implies, serves both Army and RAF members of the workshop. It was clearly a lively place as it attracted a number of celebrities, and was used to raise a lot of money for charity. Service in the Falkland Islands clearly had its lighter moments.

The 'World Famous Crab and Sprocket' 2003

REME IN KENYA

The British Army Training Unit Kenya (BATUK) is a permanent training support unit based mainly in Nanyuki, 200km north of Nairobi in Kenya. Kenya has been used for British Army training for many years. By 2011, it was being used to complement BATUS as an overseas training area for battlegroup-level training. The exercise package was called Exercise ASKARI THUNDER, and ran six or seven times annually for around six weeks. In terms of training jargon, it was a 'Collective Training Level 3 Exercise, part of Hybrid Foundation Training, based on an austere expeditionary environment'. In layman's language, whilst the 'heavy metal' battlegroups worked up at BATUS, the more lightly-equipped battlegroups did their training in Kenya, where they had the opportunity to replicate some of the situations they might encounter in places such as Afghanistan.

BATUK Workshop Summer Repair Programme 2013 at night

First line REME elements that deployed with their units were supported by the BATUK Workshop. This comprised 1 + 19 military staff, and 46 LECs. It was split between the Workshop Main in Nanyuki and smaller Workshop Rear some 170km away on the outskirts of Nairobi. The Workshop provided a full range of repairs (Levels 1–4) as well as recovery for some 700 platforms, essentially wheeled vehicles.

During gaps in the training programme, the Workshop undertook equipment rehabilitation programmes. Typically, 70 Land Rover vehicles and 120 Bedford trucks would go through a 'Lean Line', prior to issue to an incoming battlegroup, as explained in The Craftsman magazine (February 2011).

As with BATUS, REME units send additional manpower to assist with repair programmes. For example, 101 FS Battalion REME organised a team of 65 personnel from a variety of units to help out with the Summer Repair Programme in 2013 (The Craftsman magazine (February 2014)). Whilst those going on such programmes are expected to work hard, there are compensations in the form of opportunities to enjoy safaris and adventurous training.

Refurbished vehicles from BATUK Workshop Summer Repair Programme 2012

REME staff have additionally done a significant amount of CIMIC (Civil Military Cooperation) work, specifically in support of an orphanage outside Nanyuki, and a 'special needs' school there. These short assistance programmes are well suited to the TA, and a number of REME TA personnel have taken part in them.

Refurbished tractor and trailer for the Olphec Orphanage in Kenya 2013

Training looks set to continue in Kenya in the long term, and the country provides an opportunity for those posted there to enjoy a varied and interesting lifestyle.

REME ON LOAN SERVICE

REME personnel have filled a variety of loan service posts, largely in the Middle East. The largest ongoing REME commitment has been to the Royal Army of Oman (RAO). The RAO operates some fairly sophisticated equipment, including a regiment of Challenger 2 tanks, and welcomes the depth of technical expertise REME loan service personnel are able to provide, particularly as there is no formed Omani equivalent to the DE&S.

REME loan service personnel advising on tank repair Oman 2004

The composition of the REME team has varied over time but, as at 2004, it comprised the CO (Lieutenant Colonel), assisted by a Major and around 16 senior artificers, as described in The Craftsman magazine (December 2004). The team was more useful and influential than its numbers suggested. The CO worked closely with the Colonel in charge of the RAO EME organisation, the team members worked in inspection teams, in the EME school as advisers/trainers/course planners and as trade advisers with 1 Main Battle Tank Regiment (equipped with Challenger 2). Loan service required not only technical expertise, but the ability to work harmoniously and constructively with Omanis and others (including Pakistanis) involved in supporting their equipment. In general, the REME loan service staff have enjoyed a mutually respectful and very happy relationship with the Omanis. They also appreciate the chance to experience an exciting and different environment, and one in which work often involved less hustle and bustle than would be normal in a British field force environment.

Oman loan service personnel 'team building day' spent diving 2010

REME IN NEPAL

There are areas of Nepal where large communities of Gurkha ex-Servicemen and their families live. Every year since 1982, a small REME team has gone there to improve the standard of their medical and dental support. Exercise **HIMALAYAN BLUEBELL** 13 (in 2013), described in The Craftsman magazine (July 2013), was typical. The team described moving through stunning and varied territory on its way to work at 22 hospital sites. They worked on a variety of equipment including generators and x-ray machines at least three decades old. In general, they were very successful at getting equipment to work, by one means or other. Their reward was the obvious gratitude and friendliness of those whom they had come to help.

REME personnel on Exercise HIMALAYAN BLUEBELL 11
with the children and staff of the Amar Singh Blind School

REME AND OTHER OVERSEAS COMMITMENTS

The list of other overseas commitments for REME is not exhaustive; groups of REME personnel have been active in other parts of the world for a variety of reasons including training (notably aviation training in America), humanitarian relief activities and Defence Engagement in a number of countries including Uganda. Some REME overseas commitments have ceased or diminished during the period covered by this book, notably these two:

- Hong Kong – REME involvement ended when the British withdrew in 1997
- Belize – for decades, Belize had provided a major base for jungle warfare training; use of the facilities declined, and in 2011 they were mothballed (exercises have since been carried out there, and its use has appeared to be on the increase).

CHAPTER 15

REME AVIATION

In 1957, it was decided that the Army Air Corps (AAC) would be responsible for manning and operating single-engine, unarmed light aircraft (not exceeding 4,000lbs) used in air observation post and light liaison roles. In 1958, REME took over responsibility from the RAF for servicing these at first and second lines. Details of the background to this and changes up to 1992 are covered in Volumes 1 and 2 of Craftsmen of the Army.

Since then, there have been significant changes in Army Aviation. The AAC's key equipment is now the Apache helicopter in the attack helicopter (AH) role. This has a two-man crew, with a loaded mass of over 8,000kg (17,637lbs), is packed with advanced electronic sensors and carries devastating weaponry. It has proved to be one of the Army's key battle-winning weapon systems, and is maintained by REME at first and second line. REME support for aviation has been a considerable success story, and its 'light blue beret' organisation has had influence out of proportion to its numbers in areas such as engineering flight safety and airworthiness standards, which reflect the disciplines required in the Joint military aviation environment.

THE SITUATION IN 1992

At the start of the period covered by this book, REME Aviation provided support to a range of flying platforms. This included a small number of fixed wing Islander aircraft used for manned surveillance, which they continued to do at the time of writing. It also supported a few small-population specialist fleets, such as the Scout helicopters used in Brunei, replaced by the Bell helicopter in 1994. However, by far its most important task was to support the two types of helicopter that were the mainstay of the AAC – the Gazelle helicopter and the Lynx helicopter.

SA342 Gazelle Helicopter

This is a light single-engine helicopter of Anglo-French origin, which came into service in 1973. It was used for observation/liaison and was generally unarmed, although it had been fitted with SNEB (unguided) rocket pods during the campaign in the Falkland Islands. A small fleet remained in service at the time of writing, primarily supporting special forces in the ISTAR (Intelligence, Surveillance, Target Acquisition and Reconnaissance) role. (**See Plate 31**)

Gazelle helicopters on Operation TELIC 1 Iraq 2003

WG-13 Lynx Helicopter

This was a larger twin-engine helicopter, designed and manufactured in UK by Westland. It was basically a utility helicopter, which was modified for a number of roles, including shipboard use. The Fleet Air Arm operated Mark 3 and Mark 8 Lynx helicopters in maritime roles. The Army's Lynx AH Marks 1 and 7, were equipped to carry two outboard booms each carrying four TOW anti-tank missiles, and a machine gun, operated by the Air Gunner from the door. This aircraft was modified for desert operations and was used in the first Gulf War in the anti-tank role. It is probably fair to say that, at this point, the AAC had started to get into the armour-hunting business, although the 2km range of the TOW missile limited its effectiveness.

Indeed, the Army as a whole had not fully adjusted to the idea of integrating its helicopters as key offensive weapons within the framework of its all-arms tactical planning. At this time, the Gem engine had been uprated (the Gem 42 or 'GTI' – the sobriquet 'GTI' was applied to Mark 1 Lynx helicopters that were fitted with Gem 200 Series engines and used in Northern Ireland), but was already struggling in hot and high conditions, limiting the payload, range or time-on-task markedly. Additionally, three squadrons' worth of airframes were modified to the light utility role as the Mark 9 Light Utility Helicopter (LUH), for troop lift or C2 (Command and Control) roles in 24 Airmobile Brigade.

Aircraft Basing

At this time, most operational Army helicopters were based in Germany (1 Regiment AAC in Hildesheim, 3 Regiment AAC in Soest and 4 Regiment AAC in Detmold), and a large single second line REME workshop, 71 Aircraft Workshop, was based in Detmold. This was to close, and in due course only 1 Regiment AAC would be left in Germany (moving to Gütersloh from Hildesheim (Tofrek Barracks) in 1993). Middle Wallop provided the major centre of helicopter activity in UK, although 9 Regiment AAC had formed up in Dishforth (North Yorkshire) in 1991. Wattisham Airfield was activated as an AAC-led flying station in 1993–1994 following the final withdrawal of the RAF (less B Flight 22 (Search and Rescue) Squadron) on 1 July 1993.

Operational flying continued in Northern Ireland (based at Aldergrove and Ballykelly) with soldiers still detached on Operation BANNER tours from other units. Aldergrove became the Main Operating Base for Northern Ireland when 655 Squadron moved from Ballykelly to form the Northern Ireland Regiment. All support to Northern Ireland has since been provided from Aldergrove (the Northern Ireland Regiment having been renamed 5 Regiment AAC). There was also 660 Squadron in Hong Kong (operating Scout helicopters) plus a number of independent flights based abroad (for example, BATUS, Brunei, Belize and Cyprus – operating Gazelle, Allouette and Lynx helicopters) and in support of the Territorial Army around mainland UK.

EARLY JOINT SERVICE RATIONALISATION – THE DEFENCE HELICOPTER SUPPORT AGENCY

The management and support of helicopters had become seen as an area that was ripe for tri-Service rationalisation. In 1993, Brigadier Mike Carey (late REME) explained in an article in The Craftsman magazine (June 1993) how in 1992, as Director of Equipment Support 3 (DES 3), he had taken on the lead for REME support for aircraft when he took over the old EME 9 (transformed into ES 33). This included responsibility for the direction of Aircraft Branch REME (based at Middle Wallop), which became part of the Army Technical Support Agency (ATSA) in 1995.

In the event, he was soon to oversee the transfer of these responsibilities to a new Defence Helicopter Support Agency (DHSA) that was to form up in April 1994 at Yeovilton under the stewardship of the Royal Navy. The DHSA would have responsibilities for engineering, procurement, supply, quality, third and fourth line repair, overhaul and logistical support, plus the various other aspects of high-level equipment support management. Implementation, incidentally, was headed by Brigadier Rob Jones (late REME). In theory, that left REME responsible for just delivering first and second line support. In practice, REME individuals were to play key roles in helicopter procurement and support, particularly when there was a need to resolve issues that crossed inter-Service boundaries.

APACHE HELICOPTER – THE 'GAME CHANGER'

The Apache AH had been developed in the USA by Hughes (then McDonnell-Douglas), and the 'A Model' came into service there in 1986. It was used in the Gulf War to devastating effect. Apache helicopters from the US Army's 6th Cavalry Regiment firing the opening shots of the war by destroying Iraqi air defence radars. During the 100-hour ground war a total of 277 US Apache helicopters destroyed 278 tanks, as well as numerous other armoured and light Iraqi vehicles at the cost of one Apache helicopter downed, from which the crew survived. The UK decided this was what it needed to provide an effective AH capability and a procurement assessment was made against the Bell AH-1W Cobra, Eurocopter Tiger and South African Rooivalk helicopters. A heavily-modified version of the (now) Boeing Apache Longbow helicopter was selected, to be completed in UK under licence by Westland Helicopters (now AgustaWestland), and was called the WAH-64D (the 'D Model'). An order was placed in 1996.

It was a twin-engine craft, which retained the armour and robustness/redundancy of its US parent, as well as the nose-mounted Hughes 30mm chain gun. All 67 aircraft boasted a millimetric mast-mounted Longbow Fire Control Radar above its main rotor that could acquire and prioritise 256 targets and the TADS/PNVS (Target Acquisition and Designation System/Pilot Night Vision Sensor) sight system (uprated to M-TADS in 2009). UK-specific modifications included Rolls-Royce Turbomeca RTM-322 engines, which improved performance by nearly 30% to the envy of the US Army, the enhanced Selex Helicopter Integrated Defensive Aids Suite (HIDAS) chaff and flare system and a tailored UK communications fit. The four hard-points on the stub wings facilitated the fitment of up to 16 Hellfire 2 missiles and 76 CRV7 rockets, giving it the potency of a World War 2 Divisional Artillery Group. REME personnel in the Apache Project Team were involved in the development of further modifications after deployment to Afghanistan in May 2006, which included crashworthy external fuel tanks and lightweight armour for the CRV7 launcher system.

FORMATION OF 16 AIR ASSAULT BRIGADE

The Army had realised that it needed to think in terms of a new capability, not just better/extra helicopters, and its plan for this was set out in the Strategic Defence Review of 1998 (SDR 98). 24 Airmobile Brigade and elements of 5 Airborne Brigade were merged to form a highly mobile force of parachute troops and light units. The new Brigade had three regiments of helicopters, which could be used in the air manoeuvre/assault role, and, in due course, would take command of the Apache helicopter force. 16 Air Assault Brigade formed up on 1 September 1999, with its HQ in Colchester. Its aircraft were based at Wattisham Airfield in Suffolk and Dishforth in Yorkshire. REME first line support was provided by integrated regimental workshops of three officers plus 127 other ranks.

REME second line support was provided by 7 Air Assault Battalion REME, which formed up in 1994 in the newly-built Building 700 in Wattisham. It was created from the former 71 Aircraft Workshop, and its aircraft companies took the historical numbers 71, 72 and 73. Additionally, it incorporated the former 8 Field Workshop, which became 8 (Parachute) Field Company, to support the ground elements of the Brigade, and become the REME focal point for airborne training.

In due course, 7 Air Assault Battalion REME would provide a highly flexible capability of depth repair for the Apache helicopter, as well as second line support for its dependent helicopters (and augmentation of first line when required). Of note is that 70 Aircraft Workshop REME in Middle Wallop finally closed in 2006 becoming the Multi-Platform Support Unit, conducting depth servicing of Gazelle helicopters.

633 Squadron AAC CS Section in Afghanistan 2012

FORMATION OF THE JOINT HELICOPTER COMMAND

One of the major outcomes of SDR 98, was the formation of the Joint Helicopter Command (JHC). Standing up in 1999 to bring together under one command the battlefield helicopters and air assault force elements of the Royal Navy, Army and Royal Air Force in UK and overseas. It was a unique organisation (with its HQ in Andover at the time of writing), and although it was very 'purple' (Joint Service) in character, its two-star commander reported through the Army.

In 2012, it was responsible for over 250 aircraft and employed some 15,000 personnel, around 8,000 of whom were in 16 Air Assault Brigade, with a number of REME personnel serving in the HQ including a rotational OF5 (Colonel level) Chief Air Engineer JHC appointment. Since 1999, REME first and second line aviation support elements have therefore generally operated under the aegis of a Joint Helicopter Force (JHF), including those set up to support operations, such as JHF(I) for Operation TELIC in Iraq and JHF(A) for Operation HERRICK in Afghanistan. This latter deployment had the JHF(A) retitled as the Joint Aviation Group (JAG), which came under the operational command of 3 MAW (Marine Aviation Wing) of the US Marine Corps. Although REME aircraft engineers had held engineering responsibility for aircraft from the other Services before, notably in Northern Ireland, the JHF organisations provided many more opportunities for REME officers, mainly at Major and Lieutenant Colonel levels. They successfully filled the appointments of Senior Aircraft Engineer and Principal Aircraft Engineer for these deployments.

The main elements of the JHC comprised:
- 16 Air Assault Brigade, the principal formation under its command and a key Army rapidly-deployable, versatile intervention capability
- all AAC front-line aircraft, including fixed wing not in 16 Air Assault Brigade
- the Commando Helicopter Force, based at the Royal Naval Air Station Yeovilton and equipped with Lynx Mark 3 and Mark 8 helicopters and Sea King Mark 6 helicopters
- the RAF Support Helicopter Force, based at RAF Odiham and RAF Benson, including Chinook CH47 helicopters, Merlin HC3/3A helicopters and ageing Puma HC1 helicopters.

THE APACHE HELICOPTER INTRODUCTION INTO SERVICE – FIRST LINE PERSPECTIVE

Lynx and Gazelle helicopters were firmly the bedrock of the Army rotary wing capability, but the exciting introduction of the Apache helicopter into the Army was a step change for all concerned. Despite the application of Integrated Logistic Support, the introduction of the Apache helicopter into service was not without its problems, which had to be solved by REME staff working with the contractors, the Apache Integrated Project Team (IPT) and the various other agencies and staff branches involved.

A useful account of this from a first line unit perspective was written for the REME Journal (Winter 2004) by Major Richard Aspray REME who commanded 9 Regiment AAC Workshop from August 2001 to July 2004. This was based in Dishforth in North Yorkshire, and was the first Field Army unit to receive the Apache helicopter. The Apache helicopter had originally been planned to arrive in Dishforth mid-2001, but the Regiment did not receive its first aircraft until June 2003 – the sixteenth (and last) arrived in May 2004. A lot happened even before the arrival of the first equipment.

Technicians had to be trained at the new Aviation Training International Limited (ATIL) facility in Arborfield, where technicians completed a 7-week aircraft or a 10-week avionics equipment conversion course. The Workshop was also able to benefit from the work done by a small, especially-established Attack Helicopter Fielding Squadron (651 (AHF) Squadron AAC), which was based at Middle Wallop. It developed tactics and procedures, and included a REME element, who worked with contractor staff and others to identify and resolve numerous technical and support issues. The posting of key artificers across to 9 Regiment AAC prior to the arrival of the first Apache helicopter proved of immeasurable benefit.

9 Regiment AAC Workshop REME had a complex transitional process from supporting a Regiment equipped with Lynx and Gazelle helicopters, with continuous commitments to operations and training, to a new structure that comprised two squadrons of Apache helicopters and one of Lynx helicopters. The arrival of the first Apache helicopters was not without its teething problems. Major Aspray wrote:

> 'Each aircraft which arrived had to undergo a JHC Acceptance Inspection … Despite most of the aircraft being a few hours old, and having undergone internal and MoD quality assurance testing at the manufacturers, the number of faults found often gave cause for concern … These inspections and the associated rectification work often took several weeks to complete. Some took much longer'.

Support was plagued by a gamut of problems: training issues, inadequate technical publications (fault-finding was difficult with electronic publications that could be viewed only one page at a time), insufficient support equipment, infrastructure and facilities. Despite the Workshop being fully manned, in early 2004 it was struggling to achieve 50% aircraft availability and the average ratio of maintenance man-hours per flying hours (MM/FH) was 30:1 (planned figure 15:1). Things improved over the next few months as availability rose to around 60% and the MM/FH ratio had fallen to around 20:1. In broad terms, things continued to improve thereafter and fall into place, as the Army gained experience of using and supporting the Apache helicopter, but it would be unfair to say this, without the rider that it could not have happened without the effort and skill of REME personnel.

APACHE HELICOPTER SUPPORT – FURTHER DEVELOPMENTS

Reorganisation of Support – as at 2007

The Apache helicopter was being procured and brought into service at a time of organisational turmoil in the world of Defence acquisition and support. The initial support arrangements for the Apache helicopter were complex and initially problematic, so they were substantially revised – the new arrangements perhaps offering ideas for the ways in which other complex systems would be supported. The Defence Logistic Transformation Programme (2004–2006), which evolved from the End-to-End Logistics Review, had revised the well-established first to fourth line support process. It was simplified to 'Forward' and 'Depth', the former being mainly the military domain and the latter becoming industry's bailiwick.

The changes were explained in an article in The Craftsman magazine (May 2007) by the Attack Helicopter Team Leader, Brigadier Nick Knudsen (late REME), who happened to be a former CO of 71 Aircraft Workshop REME and double-hatted as the Army's Principal Aircraft Engineer.

Support arrangements suffered from being complex and 'linear' with information on such things as spares, technical publications and technical support flowing down lines that went from the industrial supplier to the front line organisation, and back again, through IPTs and various interfaces. A decision had to be made at each interface, and each decision might either create delay or be based on an incomplete understanding of all relevant facts.

The answer was to be an integrated support solution involving Defence manufacturers. This model was commonly referred to as the 'Decider – Provider' relationship; the concept had already been applied to the Royal Navy and Royal Air Force but this was a 'first' for the Army. The broad idea was that the industrial 'Provider' (of goods and services) would become much closer to the user, and the IPT would act as the 'Decider'. The idea sounds simple but, in practice, it is not always easy to contract for. In the case of the Apache helicopter, the arrangements took the form of an industrial alliance of Boeing, Lockheed Martin and Longbow International, led by AgustaWestland. Support for the Apache helicopter was to be concentrated at a single Main Operating Base at Wattisham. The IPT organisation was changed, with many of its staff being embedded in the 'alliance'. REME was closely involved in support, and a REME company was actually to be under the operational control of industry for routine daily tasking, in supporting service delivery.

Establishment of the Apache Helicopter Depth Support Unit in Wattisham

The implementation of some of these ideas was explained in an article in The Craftsman magazine (May 2007):

> '… as each Apache completes 300 flying hours it will be sent to Wattisham airfield. There, a new centre to service all the Army's Apaches has been established, the Depth Support Unit, manned for the first time in partnership by both military technicians and civilian industry, the only such Hub in the Army, making it the centre of excellence for the maintenance of all Apaches'. (**See Plate 32**)

Lieutenant Colonel Phil Davies REME, the Depth Support Unit (DSU) Manager explained:

> 'Previously Apaches had their major servicing conducted at airfields across the country … in the past, each aircraft was fully serviced by a crew of Army technicians. Now each aircraft will go along a Pulse Line, with six stages, where technician and civilian staff will specialise in a particular stage of the process. Each Pulse Line service takes 42 days from start to finish… There has been close cooperation between the Integrated Project Team, civilian contractors and the military. 7 Air Assault Battalion and the Apache Depth Support Unit have fully embraced Lean principles, and are seeing benefits extending far beyond saving money. … A close partnership with the outside agencies was initially difficult, however, it is now working well'.

The DSU incorporated:
- 72 CS Company, part of 7 Air Assault Battalion REME
- representatives and technical staff from AgustaWestland, and around 50 engineering fitters and supervisors provided by Serco Defence and Aerospace.

In 2009, further improvements were made to the support contract, which was the latest evolution of an output-based availability contract, called Apache Integrated Operational Support. The multi-million pound 5-year support contract was based on 'output' and the contractor was incentivised by payments being linked to the achievement of five Key Performance Indicators such as hours flown, operational availability and fleet size, availability of Deployable Spares Pack, and support to other platforms (that is, commodity spares availability). The Pulse Line was subjected to sustained continuous improvement review, and the 'Depth' 'plot' remained the key driver behind the fleet maintenance programme. Due to operational commitments, 72 CS Company was 'pushed' into a larger 'Forward' maintenance organisation, supporting both UK flying and training in the USA, and JHC contracted for more civilian manpower to augment the Main Operating Base and DSU.

Apache Helicopter Support – Excitement and Challenge
Whilst depth support work at Wattisham was an important commitment, it was only one facet of REME's support to the Apache helicopter. An article by Captain Jacques Steyn REME in The Craftsman magazine (May 2009) about REME on Operation HERRICK 9 (2008–2009) provides a useful counterbalance. It explains:

> 'The Apache Engineering Detachment on Op HERRICK 9 comprised a mix of technicians from 7 Air Assault Bn REME and 4 Regt AAC Wksp REME. The workshop members arrived with a joyful prospect of sun, sand and serviceable aircraft which was quickly shattered by an unfortunate accident involving ZJ177.
> This early challenge set the tone for what was to be a very busy tour with several 'firsts' in which skilled technicians worked hours which would make civilians collapse under the mental strain … Problems were plenty, and the pilots did their best to test the dogged determination of REME technicians by throwing over-speeds, over-torques and all kinds of complaints of switch 'stiction' and 'ghosts' in the machines. REME responded admirably, demonstrating professionalism and composure in the face of obvious adversity. This was all orchestrated by WO2 (AQMS) Byng whose determined approach and uncompromising attitude motivated the troops to work harder, faster and better than before 'because that's what we do".

The Apache helicopter has been deployed on all the usual training areas used by the Army, although most ranges prohibit the use of its weapons systems. Additionally, it has been deployed for pre-deployment training and aircrew conversion-to-role training with its US counterparts on training areas and ranges in the USA. 3 and 4 Regiments AAC regularly deployed, with elements of 7 Air Assault Battalion REME, on Exercise CRIMSON EAGLE to train in Arizona and California at El Centro Naval Air Facility, and USAF Gila Bend for periods of eight weeks (and longer) with JHF(USA). This training was described by Major Matt Arnold REME, 3 Regiment AAC Workshop REME, in an article in The Craftsman magazine (December 2011). Given the sustained demands of UK flying training, technicians gained little respite, due to the operational cycle imposed by the training and deployment to Afghanistan, which was a challenging variety.

In 2011, this was compounded by the requirement to embark a squadron of five Apache helicopters for Operation ELLAMY (Libya) on HMS Ocean, supported by a REME CS Section. The Apache helicopter was a 'dry-built' airframe and required considerable modification for ship-borne operations, including a modification programme in depth and a burdensome regime of preventive maintenance checks and application of greases and oils to prevent corrosion in the salt-laden atmosphere. With preparation for, and recovery from flight, including blade-folding and other 'hangar gymnastics', MM/FH peaked at 99:1, but the team recovered this to 60:1 by the end of this first-of-type embarked operation.

Despite these demands, the Apache helicopter performed well, firing nearly 200 Hellfire missiles and destroying a number of key high-value targets. Its value was in precision attack and flexibility of tasking, where a Royal Air Force fast jet with a 500lb J-DAM bomb was a much 'blunter' means of prosecuting a target. The REME section, commanded by Captain Charlotte Joyce REME, had integrated fully with the ship's crew, earning praise from both the ship's CO and the Royal Navy Air Group Commander. For her exceptional performance on Operations HERRICK and ELLAMY, Captain Joyce went on to win the Institution of Engineering and Technology Young Woman Engineer of the Year Award 2011.

HADDON-CAVE AND THE CHIEF AIRCRAFT ENGINEER ROLE

In September 2006, RAF Nimrod MR2 XV230 crashed with the loss of 14 lives, the biggest single loss since the war in the Falkland Islands. Mr Charles Haddon-Cave QC led an independent review, which proved to contain some devastating criticism. In his report, Mr Haddon-Cave condemned the change of organisational culture within the MoD between

REME technicians viewing an Apache helicopter accident Operation HERRICK 9

1998 and 2006, when financial targets came to distract from safety, quoting a former senior Royal Air Force officer who told the inquiry:

> 'There was no doubt that the culture of the time had switched. In the days of the RAF Chief Engineer in the 1990s, you had to be on top of airworthiness. By 2004, you had to be on top of your budget if you wanted to get ahead'.

The report was specifically about airworthiness, criticising the institutional failings of the MoD. It had left the single Services operating equipment, and providing much of the front-line maintenance manpower, whereas overall responsibility for support rested with a Defence structure comprising numerous agencies and organisations interacting with industrial suppliers through complex contracts. This effectively meant that liability for safety was so widely smeared that no single person or organisation could be called to account. This argument applied in principle as much to an armoured vehicle, which could plough into a crowd of schoolchildren if a track failed, as an aircraft, and as much to the Army and Royal Navy.

This issue was addressed by making changes, introducing the 'Duty Holder Construct', which placed responsibility squarely with the single

Services. The Chief of the General Staff (CGS) became the Army's Senior Duty Holder and DEME(A) became his Responsible Authority for Army Equipment. In line with the Haddon-Cave Review, the Army was to re-establish the post of Chief Aircraft Engineer (Army) (CAE(A)) in July 2010. CAE(A)'s organisation was set up in HQ DEME(A) to provide aviation engineering assurance and to ensure the airworthiness of Army aircraft platforms. Colonel Rod Williams (late REME) headed this organisation and additionally took on the role of Commander ES Aviation, a role formerly held by the Staff Officer Grade 1 J4 Attack/Utility in HQ JHC. He had a direct Letter of Delegation from CGS, as his Army Competent Authority and Inspector for Aviation Engineering.

Colonel Williams provided an update on REME Aviation in an article in The Craftsman magazine (November 2011). He explained that his role might be summarised as 'ensure, assure and enable'. He had a new Staff Officer Grade 1 Aviation Engineering Operations assisted by a Staff Officer Grade 2 Aviation Plans whose responsibilities included the coordination of TECHEVAL (taken over from JHC).

A further effect of the Haddon-Cave Report was to move the Accident Investigation and Engineering Flight Safety Officer's accident investigation role into the newly-formed Military Aviation Authority Military Air Accident Investigation Branch, located alongside the Civil Aviation Authority's Air Accident Investigation Branch at Farnborough. This had left a Staff Officer Grade 2 and senior artificer providing engineering flight safety advice and conducting flight safety audits and training. CAE(A) had the benefit of a civilian section head, Mr Charles Davison, whose dedication, knowledge and experience provided valuable continuity, having been in EME 9, ES 33 and HQ DEME(A) since 1999. In turn, he took on the 4-man team left from the Rotary Wing Support Group in Middle Wallop, when the DE&S rationalised further. CAE(A)'s organisational structure is shown at Figure 15.1 (at the end of this Chapter).

TYPES OF AIRCRAFT IN SERVICE

It was not only the Apache helicopter that was being heavily used on operations and elsewhere.

Lynx Helicopter

Although no longer an anti-tank platform, as the TOW system was taken out of service in 2004, the Lynx helicopter was in constant demand. The Gem engine lacked the power to operate in Afghanistan in the summer months and so an Urgent Operational Requirement (UOR) was developed in 2008 to upgrade 22 wheeled Lynx Mark 9 helicopters with more powerful engines. The resultant Lynx Mark 9A helicopter incorporated the LHTEC CTS-T800 4N engine (developed for the cancelled US Comanche Programme), giving a 37% improvement, and a digital 'glass cockpit'. A squadron from 9 Regiment AAC deployed in 2010, and its improved ISTAR capabilities and the M3M 0.50 calibre door-mounted heavy machine gun quickly proved extremely effective.

Gazelle Helicopter
This continued to provide useful service in Manned Airborne Surveillance (MAS) UK wide, CASEVAC and exercise support in Canada (BATUS), and specialist support to special forces. Its compact, 'relatively simple' yet versatile design, provided an excellent platform for specialist fits.

Islander/Defender Aircraft
These MAS aircraft continued to be used in Afghanistan and in UK (including Northern Ireland). Defender was a UOR project for Iraq, with three aircraft procured by the Helicopter and Islander Combined Integrated Project Team. The success of the aircraft in Iraq led to it being taken into core and more were purchased.

Specialist Aircraft
REME technicians provided valuable support to the Shadow UOR (a modified light aircraft used for surveillance in Afghanistan) and provided continuing support for special forces rotary wing aircraft under exclusive MRCOA (Military Registered Civilian Owned Aircraft) arrangements for air safety.

Unmanned Aerial Systems
The role of unmanned aerial systems (UAS) had become an area of growing importance, evolving rapidly from the limited capability offered by Phoenix in Iraq on Operation TELIC 1. The critical safety issues became no less important for UAS than for manned aircraft. In outline, Commander 1 Artillery Brigade had become the Delivery Duty Holder with specific responsibility for 'risk to life'. To support this role, a Brigade Aviation Role Office (BARO) was set up under a REME Staff Officer Grade 1 (Lieutenant Colonel James Crawford REME). This

was established in 2010 to manage the operational fleet and to optimise capability and sustain airworthiness.

This involved taking responsibility from JHC and placing it under one Aircraft Operating Authority, Commander 1 Artillery Brigade, although in 2013, this responsibility was transferred to Commander JHC as the Operating Duty Holder. The Royal Artillery was already flying Hermes 450, lightweight Desert Hawk and counter-IED Tarantula Hawk on Operation HERRICK, based in Camp Bastion. 'Green eyes' live imagery was exploited and proved increasingly effective in operational planning and conduct. The introduction of Thales Watchkeeper UAS was eagerly anticipated, but the programme suffered delays and an interim 'Release to Service' was not achieved until early 2014, prior to its deployment for the last months of Operation HERRICK in August that year.

Lynx Wildcat

With the potent Apache helicopter tending to get into the headlines, it is easy for the valuable role played by the Lynx helicopter to be overlooked. It had been a mainstay of helicopter support for Army formations since 1979, and there was a continuing need to complement AH capability with a capable battlefield utility helicopter. At the time of writing, the Lynx helicopter was being replaced by the AW159 Wildcat, built by AgustaWestland at Yeovil, for use with both the Royal Navy and the Army. It is a development of the upgraded Lynx Mark 9A helicopter (occasionally referred to as 'Mildcat', as it has many similarities and uses, and much of the same defensive aid suite).

The airframe has, however, been radically redesigned to accept the additional power of the T-800 engines. Much of the avionics suite is modern, including the ability to integrate with Bowman, and a suite of four integrated display units, which display everything from primary flight data to visual/thermal images and tactical battlefield information. The Wildcat Fielding Team (Army) was set up at Yeovilton, which included a REME contingent headed by Major Mark Nolan REME, who described their role in an article in The Craftsman magazine (January 2012). Their implementation plan saw 1 and 9 Regiments AAC being equipped with Wildcat, then later combining and moving to Yeovilton in due course from their bases at Gütersloh and Dishforth respectively.

Wildcat Production Aircraft No 1 (ZZ398) 2011

STRATEGIC DEFENCE AND SECURITY REVIEW 2010 AND THE DEMISE OF DEME(A)

The Strategic Defence and Security Review 2010 led to the demise of DEME(A), but not the need for someone to retain the responsibilities of his Chief Aircraft Engineer. In his article in The Craftsman magazine (August 2012), Colonel Williams explained the situation as at mid-2012. In essence, his organisation had been lifted with HQ DEME(A) and fitted into the Capability Directorate Combat Service Support (CD CSS) within Army HQ, and adapted to his new role. In outline, he:

- continued to be CAE(A) to CGS, the Army Senior Duty Holder, and continued to develop assurance mechanisms and single-Service Army Aviation Engineering Policy
- acted as Assistant Director Aviation Engineering within CD CSS, undertaking the Capability Development role for ES(Aviation) and acting as the Training Requirements Authority for Aeronautical Engineering
- was the Professional Head for Army Aircraft Engineering, and had responsibilities for providing sufficient competent, Suitably Qualified and Experienced Personnel (SQEP) across REME Aviation.

AFTER OPERATION HERRICK

With the completion of Operation HERRICK at the end of 2014, the focus for the forces has firmly switched to contingent operations. The reductions of the Army down to the 2020 structures and increased emphasis on the Army Reserves, required the Army to seek more innovation in support solutions. At the time of writing, JHC was leading a 'Whole Force Approach' to look at how the potential of industry could be harnessed and combined in a Regular and Reserve force mix, with REME Aviation considering how Reserves could be introduced and used effectively in the technical support area.

SUMMARY

Army Aviation, and arguably Defence Aviation, had proved a capability growth area, reflecting outstanding success on operations, with REME officers and soldiers having played an essential part in enabling it. The aircraft maintained by REME at the end of the period covered by this book had become far more complex and capable than those that went before, and the regulatory frameworks far more demanding.

Structures for procuring and supporting equipment underwent almost continuous change, but these three factors remained constant:

- the ability to deploy the capability in support of operations or training depends on the deployment of adequate REME support forward, augmented by an element of second line and depth support
- the successful fielding and exploitation of complex new equipments requires direct engagement between industrial suppliers and REME technical staff; never more so than at the time of writing, with the continuing drive to reduce logistic footprints and increase operational effect
- the quality, skills and competencies of REME Aviation technicians and engineering officers remained absolutely essential to the success of Army Aviation.

Wattisham had become the primary home base for the Apache helicopter, and the location of its DSU. This offered a new model for Army technical staff to be integrated with contractors under a 'Whole Force Approach'. Wildcat was to be based in Yeovilton and UAS were being operated from Larkhill, Boscombe Down, BATUS, BATUK and Aldergrove, whilst REME continued to provide support to permanent aviation detachments around the world, and the special forces.

ISTAR had become a much more important capability, and REME had proved key to the support of fixed wing aircraft, and increasingly the evolving world of UAS.

Many key posts related to Army Aviation support no longer sat within a REME organisation, but were filled by REME engineers whose professional skills were essential to ensuring that Army aircraft are fully operational when required, as well as safe to use. Sustaining this intellectual capability is essential for Army Aviation. The specialist role of the Aircraft Engineering Officer (AEO) has been increasingly recognised by the Army as vital, particularly their role in the Joint Military Air Environment of the Military Aviation Authority and the DE&S organisation. As Colonel Andy Allen (late REME) wrote in an article in The Craftsman magazine (March 2010), this has opened up a wide range of career opportunities to those who maintain their 'competence' as aircraft engineers.

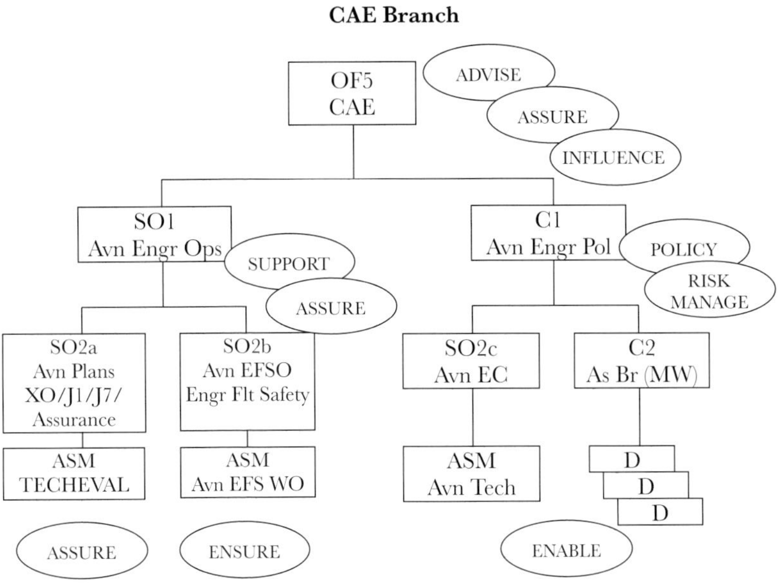

REME AVIATION

CAE Branch

Figure 15.1: Organisation structure of CAE(A)

CHAPTER 16

REME AND THE RESERVE ARMY

The Territorial Army (TA) was established in 1908 to provide volunteers raised locally on a county basis as a trained reserve for the Regular Army. It was embodied in the Regular Army during both World Wars and was formed again after World War 2 when, in 1947, REME TA units became part of the Order of Battle. This is dealt with in Volume 2 of *Craftsmen of the Army*.

National Service continued after World War 2, with the last conscripted soldiers leaving the Army in 1963. This had provided a pool of trained reservists for the Army Emergency Reserve (AER). With the end of conscription and the flow of reservists it generated, the AER was amalgamated with the TA in 1967 to form the Territorial Army and Volunteer Reserve (T&AVR), redesignated the TAVR in 1971.

REME TA units at that time provided first line support, which broadly mirrored the pattern for the Regular Army. For example, individual tradesmen were attached to infantry battalions, whilst the likes of armoured reconnaissance regiments or transport regiments had integral REME sub-units in the form of LADs or regimental workshops to provide support. There were also second line REME units, which provided repair and recovery support at this level.

The TAVR comprised two types of unit – Independent (subsequently to be called Regional) and Sponsored (later referred to as Specialist and, subsequently, National) units. Whilst the terminology has changed, the underlying characteristics of these units, if not the arrangements for training and recruiting, have remained broadly unchanged as have the minimum annual commitments.

Independent units worked from their own local TA centres, held their own equipment tables and trained at weekends and on drill nights. They recruited their own soldiers, who did their initial recruit and trade training at Bordon, but carried out much of their special-to-role training at unit level. Their minimum annual commitment was 27 days; a 15-day camp and 12 training days.

Sponsored units were recruited on a national basis by what became HQ REME TA at Bordon. The idea was that only those who already had the required technical skills would be recruited for these units. Recruit training was carried out at Bordon, which provided the administrative base for all the units, and a pool of resources on which they could draw. Because it was assumed that the necessary technical skills were already present, the minimum annual training requirement was only 19 days; a 15-day camp and two training weekends.

By 1984, REME's Regular Army strength was 13,000 and that of REME TA was 5,000, of which 3,250 were in Independent units and 1,750 in Sponsored units. At this point, the Cold War was still very much ongoing, and combat arm TA units were being re-armed with weaponry that brought them more closely into line with scales and types of equipment held by the Regular Army. This provided a considerable first line technical support challenge for the 50 or so first line REME TA organisations that were of varying sizes. At second line, REME TA comprised an assortment of workshop and recovery companies, generally with specialised roles, such as port support, lines of communication cover, reclamation and the like. As with first line, second line comprised both Independent and Sponsored units.

By the mid-1980s, the primary role of the TA was to complete the Army Order of Battle for NATO assigned forces. It had the secondary roles of providing additional security for the UK base, as well as a framework for future expansion if the situation demanded it. In essence, the concept was that signs of imminent aggression by the Warsaw Pact forces would trigger complete mobilisation of the Army, a key objective being the rapid reinforcement of the British Army of the Rhine (BAOR). The TA would play a key role in this by providing additional combat arm units, and, crucially, would also thicken up the lines of communication and support logistic/technical infrastructure that would otherwise have been dangerously limited in capability. REME TA collective training naturally tended to reflect units' envisaged roles on mobilisation with units deploying to, and linking up with, their Regular Army counterparts or practising for their specialised roles.

At this time, REME TA would have been seen by many as comprising stalwart men (and, increasingly, women) who were prepared to rally to the flag at a time of national peril, as their forefathers had during two World Wars, but did not expect to be asked to contribute to the Regular Army's ongoing operational commitments. The MoD website (at the time of writing) referred to them as having then been a *'force of last resort'*.

'OPTIONS FOR CHANGE' AND ORGANISATION IN THE MID-1990s

The late-1980s saw the rapid winding down of the Cold War, with the public and politicians looking for a 'peace dividend'. The demise of the Warsaw Pact, and with it the 'short warning scenario' for an attack on Germany, meant that Defence planners needed a fundamental overhaul of their operational ideas. The cast iron justification for permanently stationing large armoured forces at high readiness in Germany evaporated, and the nature of the threat the UK armed forces were expected to counter became very difficult to define. The name of the MoD's main study of the way ahead in 1990, 'Options for Change', itself reflected this uncertainty. In the event, the 'Options' work was interrupted by the Iraqi invasion of Kuwait, which led to the UK's response to this in the form of Operation GRANBY (1990–1991). This provided a timely reminder of the unpredictability of military threats, but the rapid and overwhelming success of this operation, however, led to 'Options' thinking resuming along much the same lines as before it.

The 'Options' work resulted in a large reduction in the size of the Regular Army from about 150,000 in the mid-1980s to around 110,000 after 'Options'. REME escaped amalgamation with any other Corps and, broadly speaking, took a pro rata cut. Its first line units were cut when the parent units were cut, but the first line support concept remained essentially unchanged. In contrast, the second line Regular Army organisation was to be substantially restructured. All elements, bar a few specialised sub-units, were formed into REME battalions instead of a mixture of independent sub-units and major units all with the title of 'Workshop' – a nomenclature that had thoroughly confused the rest of the Army. All this is covered in more detail in Chapter 2 ('The Fundamentals and Organisation to 2010').

A broadly similar approach was adopted with the reorganisation of REME TA. First line REME TA units were cut along with their parent units. All second line assets were restructured into REME battalions whose roles were linked to the Army's new 'Options' structure.

This structure saw most of the Army's deployable assets being formed into two large divisions (each of three multipurpose combat brigades). 1 (UK) Armoured Division was based in Germany, and 3 (UK) Division was based in UK. Both of these divisions were earmarked to support the Allied Command Europe (ACE) Rapid Reaction Corps (ARRC), which had its HQ in Bielefeld (Germany). Units that were not part of these divisions, including most of the TA, generally came under the command of regional brigade HQs, which were grouped under divisional HQs, some deployable and some regional.

The deployable divisions, which had to be capable of operating worldwide, required fundamentally different Combat Service Support (CSS) arrangements from those designed to support BAOR during the Cold War. Each division therefore had its CSS Group (CSSG), commanded at one-star level, which comprised a substantial TA element along with its Regular Army units.

In Germany, CSSG(G), based in Gutersloh, supported 1 (UK) Armoured Division and which changed its name in 1999 to 101 Logistic Brigade; a less clumsy and more readily understandable title. In UK, CSSG(UK), based in Aldershot, supported 3 (UK) Division and was renamed 102 Logistic Brigade in 1999.

The role of second line REME TA on mobilisation was both to provide units for these logistic organisations, and to 'thicken up' REME within the deployable divisions by providing both individual reinforcements (IR), increments (as a group), or formed organisations as required.

The initial 'Options' plans for REME at second line envisioned the formation of four battalions by 31 March 1995, later changed to five as shown in Figure 16.1 (at the end of this Chapter).

The outline structure for managing and commanding REME TA was based on several factors. HQ REME TA with some 60 permanent staff was based at Bordon. This was commanded by a Regular Army Colonel, the Commander HQ REME TA, generally referred to as Commander REME TA. His organisation delivered functional direction across REME TA on relevant technical, administrative and Corps matters. The HQ also provided a single point of contact with the chain of command and REME/ES, on policy, organisation, operational planning and other issues that had a general impact on REME TA. The organisation at Bordon provided basic training for all REME TA recruits, as well as administrative, training and mobilisation support for Sponsored/Specialist units. (**See Plate 33**)

At his right hand, he had Colonel REME TA, the senior serving REME TA officer. His role was, broadly, to work hand in glove with Commander REME TA to provide advice and the insights into REME TA matters that a Regular Army officer might lack. First line and Independent second line REME TA units generally came under the command of their local regional HQs – the regional two-star HQs (2, 4, and 5 Divisions, London District, Scotland). These generally had a REME TA Lieutenant Colonel acting as SO1 Equipment Support (Volunteer) responsible for monitoring and managing REME TA issues as necessary.

THE MID-1990s AND EVOLVING IDEAS ON THE TA

By 1992, the first phase of the reorganisation after the Cold War had happened, and the first British forces had deployed to Bosnia. Over the next few years, it seemed that a new stable ongoing pattern of operations had emerged with the UK continuously deploying the equivalent of a brigade, with supporting elements, on peacekeeping operations at any one time. There was a significant REME TA involvement in these, which is covered later.

During this period, there was continued downward pressure on the Defence budget as the Government sought to squeeze out an ever larger 'peace dividend'. Budgets had increasingly been delegated to commanders and managers, and there seemed to be endless 'initiatives' and 'efficiency measures' linked to the need to meet budgetary cuts or targets. Before too long, REME TA needed to fight its corner in the run-up to what was to become the Strategic Defence Review 1998 (SDR 98). The Commander REME TA at the time commented:

> 'Recently rereading a paper we wrote in 1997 reminded me of some of the issues we encountered at that time. I had arrived in post with little knowledge of REME TA (which did not matter, as Col George Illingworth, then Col REME TA, was around to put me right), but an all too clear understanding of the way in which the MoD's corporate planners worked. Some essentially saw the TA as a way of balancing their books by replacing expensive Regular soldiers with cheap Reservists. By emphasising the 'One Army' concept they could run together the total number of Regulars and Reserves as a way of camouflaging the full extent of the capability being cut. They also realised that TA soldiers could be substituted for Regulars on operational tours, which helped an already nascent overstretch problem.
>
> The concept of soldiers who only got paid when they were on operations (and could use existing equipment when they did so) was also one likely to make those struggling to balance the MoD budget salivate. The idea of making more effective use of the TA, whose true value lay in the quality, enthusiasm and adaptability of its members, seemed to me a great idea in principle. In practice, it risked being undermined by officials who did not understand that the TA was a 'lifestyle choice' for many of its members, and that it needed an adequately resourced package to attract and retain the

right sort of volunteers. There was a temptation within the MoD at the time to see the TA as a 'soft target' for relatively minor short-term savings, such as reductions in man training days, which were counterproductive against the strategic aim'.

THE STRATEGIC DEFENCE REVIEW 1998

SDR 98 was launched in 1997 by the incoming Labour Government. It represented not so much a new look at Defence, as the culmination of work that had been carried out over the previous few years (often with an element of tacit cross-party support) to refine ideas of what the Army was needed for in the era after the Cold War, and therefore how it should be organised and funded.

The usability of the TA on routine operations was one of the issues that was under ongoing review. Prior to 1996, individual TA soldiers could only be compulsorily mobilised by Royal Prerogative. This was expected to be applied in a time of national danger or emergency, not for the sort of 'operations of choice', which were being conducted in the Balkans and elsewhere at the time. At that time, the Army could only use TA soldiers who had specifically volunteered for such operations. The number responding to any call to arms depended on a number of factors, and was therefore inherently unpredictable from a planning point of view. One general pattern that emerged was that the first call to a new operation generally got a better response than subsequent 'trips to the well'. Clearly, operational planning that depended on a guess as to how popular an operation might be, or how many people might decide to turn up on the day, was not a good way of doing business.

The Reserve Forces Act of 1996 (RFA 1996) sought to address such issues. It allowed for the compulsory mobilisation of Reserves without resorting to the Royal Prerogative. It also sought to protect volunteers from financial loss caused by mobilisation, both through direct financial support to the individuals involved, and by encouraging their employers to provide financial support. The concept of Sponsored Reserves was also initiated, which should not be confused with the Sponsored units previously mentioned. The scheme was intended to overcome one of the fundamental problems associated with contracting out support tasks, which had previously been done by the military, namely that contractors who provided support to troops in their peacetime situation could not generally deploy with them on operations (when the support was likely to be most critically needed). The concept was for contractors to get relevant staff who provided peacetime support enrolled and qualified as reservists so that they could deploy on operations if necessary. This principle was adopted as an element of a tank transporter private finance contract, but was not otherwise much taken up.

Although RFA 1996 was helpful to the TA, it by no means provided complete answers to the many inherently tricky problems associated with mobilisation. In practice, loopholes in the legislation meant that employers could not always be forced to protect mobilised reservists from a direct or indirect financial penalty. Both individuals and employers could also lodge appeals against being called up. There were also a number of limitations on the powers of compulsory mobilisation. For example, soldiers could not be compulsorily called up for more than 12 months in any three-year period. Soldiers were generally mobilised for six-month tours, but these normally involved pre-mobilisation training of some three months and post-tour decompression and leave of around two months, so in reality the commitment amounted to about 11 months. RFA 1996 certainly made the TA more usable, but in practice its powers needed to be exercised circumspectly if they were not adversely to impact on recruiting and retention.

SDR 98 was very much about readiness, which had been identified as a major cost driver. It envisaged a three-year readiness cycle for Regular Army units (high readiness year, other tasks year, training year) to meet ongoing operational commitments, and to provide a baseline from which mobilisation for larger scale deployments (concurrently or otherwise) could start. A fuller explanation of these ideas is given in Chapter 4 ('Collective Training for Operations'). 'Large Scale' operations involved a framework division being deployed, and came with the assumption that compulsory mobilisation of the TA would be necessary; also that there would be a preparation time of up to 90 days. A 'Very Large Scale' (VLS) operation involved the deployment of a full division (with the TA deploying as formed units) and went with the assumption of a preparation time of 24 months.

The subject of Reserves was one of the most controversial parts of SDR 98. It resulted in significant cuts to TA numbers overall, from around 57,000 to around 40,000 (from an established strength of 91,000 in 1991), which was the fourth round of cuts since the end of the Cold War. The infantry was particularly hard hit with 87 companies in 33 battalions reduced to 67 companies in 15 battalions. The readiness of most of the

TA was reduced to R8 (180 days) in the Long Term Costing for 1997. An assumption was also made that, in general, formed TA units would not be deployed with less than two years' notice, which provided a convenient justification for limiting TA equipment holdings, or expenditure on anything for the TA that was not essential for their peacetime training.

REME TA came out of SDR 98 fairly well. It inevitably lost some first line posts when the parent units were cut but, in practice, the individuals concerned could often transfer to a nearby first or second line REME unit. REME's footprint also meant that it could sometimes gather in useful trained TA soldiers from other capbadge units that were disbanded.

The existing second line REME TA structure fitted the required model well, as it both offered battalions that would be needed for VLS deployments, and could provide the reinforcement needed for smaller scale operations, either as trained individuals or formed bodies. Sadly, 105 Battalion REME (V) was disbanded. This was an interesting hybrid with two Independent companies and two companies of Specialists. Its role was the support of CSSG(G) in which it was exercised in Germany in 1998 on Exercise RHINO REPLEN under its CO, Lieutenant Colonel John Harvey REME (V). It was disbanded in 1999 after a thoroughly enjoyable training camp in Gibraltar on Exercise MARBLE TOR. Although the unit disappeared, almost all the individuals stayed on and its companies were reassigned to other REME battalions. Lieutenant Colonel Harvey, went on to become Colonel REME TA.

It had also been recognised by this time that a centralised system was needed for ensuring that TA soldiers deploying on operations were appropriately trained, and that the mobilisation/demobilisation process worked efficiently. A Reserves Training and Mobilisation Centre (RTMC) was therefore set up in 1999 at Chilwell to take on this role. The word 'Reserves' was later changed in its title to 'Reinforcements' as the role of the RTMC was expanded to take on the pre-deployment training of Contractors Deployed on Operations (CONDO) and other civilians. A Reserves Manning and Career Management Division in the Army Personnel Centre (Glasgow) was also set up to centralise all personnel management for the TA, bringing it into line with the Regular Army.

Basic training for REME TA soldiers was taken away from Bordon after SDR 98, and was to be done at centralised training units. Although HQ REME TA had lost some of its responsibilities for basic training and individual mobilisation, SDR 98 left the system for managing REME TA essentially unchanged.

105 Battalion REME (V) on Exercise MARBLE TOR in Gibraltar 1999

REME TA IN THE DECADE PRIOR TO 2001 AND '9/11'

Having looked at the high-level structure and policy in this era, it is useful to get a picture of the realities of life at the time. The following paragraphs seek to provide a picture of the type of people who were in REME TA, what they got up to, and to provide a few snapshots of their activities.

The People
A few Regulars were posted to the TA. For example, Independent battalions would sometimes have a Regular Army CO as the role was time consuming and it was not always possible to find a TA officer both willing and able to take on such a commitment. Units would also have a small number of permanent staff with various titles. The Permanent Staff Admin Officer (PSAO) was usually an ex-Regular with an administrative background, who dealt with budgets, Man Training Days, accounts, administration of civilians, and such matters. Other Non-Regular Permanent Staff (NRPS) with appropriate skills were often, but by no means invariably, ex-Regulars who were contracted to provide specialist

support (generally of a quartermaster, training or technical nature) to a particular unit.

Some TA personnel were employed on Full Time Reserve Service (FTRS). These posts required specialist skills, and were generally filled by ex-Regulars or long-serving TA personnel with appropriate backgrounds or specialist expertise that the Regulars were short of. Some worked in TA units, but many others were employed in roles that had nothing at all to do with the TA, and were essentially full-time posts within the mainstream Services, which happened to be filled by TA personnel who were contracted to do specific jobs alongside Regular Army staff.

On leaving the Army, Regular Army soldiers automatically went onto the Regular Reserve, and were liable for call up. They therefore formed part of the Army Reserve, but in practice they were unlikely to be called up unless they had decided to join the TA, which provided the most likely route through which they would deploy on operations after leaving the Regular Army.

Those who did not fall into any of the above categories, the majority of those in REME TA, could come from any walk of life. The Specialists (19 days annual training liability) had invariably started with a relevant specialist skill. Many of the remainder had come in with some sort of technical background, but this was not an essential pre-condition for joining. Despite their varied backgrounds, REME TA people tended to have certain things in common. First, they tended to be enterprising, enthusiastic and energetic people, or they would not have contemplated taking on the physical and personal challenges associated with military service. Second, they tended to be people who enjoy working as part of a team. Undoubtedly, what attracted many to the TA was the camaraderie, and the satisfaction that comes from taking on difficult challenges in the company of kindred spirits.

Linked with this, there was often a strong territorial affiliation, particularly as many TA soldiers served only in one locally-based unit where they worked with people whom they had known for many years. The Specialists did not have quite the same territorial linkage, but they all met up at Bordon, and tended to be long serving and close knit. REME's national footprint has proved helpful during the many organisational changes that have affected the TA. A former CO of 102 Battalion REME (V) (Lieutenant Colonel John Saville REME, CO 1999–2001) reflected on this situation in 2006:

'102 Bn was mercifully spared the cuts which affected many other units in the North East. It was an opportunity to 'mop up' some dedicated, skilful TA soldiers looking for a new home. This we did, bringing all the Companies up to full strength in 2000. We also found a home for the Tyne Pipes and Drums, which were to disband with the demise of 72 Engr Regt RE (Newcastle). But the Pipes and Drums soon settled into 102 Bn, and have become a real asset to the Bn to this day'.

Training

Individuals joining REME TA started with a two-week period of basic military training, unless they were already adequately trained. Their technical training requirement depended on their existing qualifications and experience, but for many a two-week technical training course at Bordon was required to give them the basic skills they needed to start doing useful work at unit level. They would gain more technical experience 'on the job' and could go on further residential courses at Bordon to upgrade their skills and qualifications.

Members of the TA would attempt, if possible, to go on their own unit's annual two-week training camp. These provided an opportunity for REME battalions to deploy to training areas in UK or Germany. Their training package would be crafted to the needs of the unit. It frequently included involvement with other exercising units or formations, or linkage with a Regular Army unit. The training might be focused on military skills, often with an element of adventurous training, or involve a production exercise that developed technical skills, frequently completing useful 'real' repairs in the process, or any combination of these.

REME soldiers at first line were constrained by their parent unit's plans for annual camp, and the need to provide support for it. They were, however, able to get an element of REME special-to-arm input by taking part in specialised collective or regional REME training. Recovery Mechanics were a case in point, as they needed to attend specialist recovery camps to develop their skills and improve their qualifications. These were frequently organised by the recovery companies of REME TA battalions on training areas in UK, such as Exercise HARD PULL, or in conjunction with Regular Army REME units in Germany, such as Exercise ROCK STEADY.

Normal weekend or mid-week evening training at unit level was complemented by annual regional weekend training exercises such as

SOUTHERN CRAFTSMEN for units based in the south of UK, and NORTHERN BLUEBELL for those in the north of UK. They were organised as competitions that allowed both first and second line REME units to compete, and were valuable both from the point of view of 'Corps bonding' as well as actual training. REME TA participated in the annual CORPSAAM (Corps Skill at Arms Meeting) and organised their own SPECSAAM, in which about 60 REME Specialists took part.

Winning team and trophies on Exercise NORTHERN BLUEBELL 2002

Overall, the battalion structure worked very well, and facilitated the administration of such things as adventurous training and overseas training. The extent of the overseas training opportunities at this time is illustrated by an advertisement in The Craftsman magazine (March 2002), which sought volunteers for Exercises LION SPANNER (Cyprus), RIBSTONE CREEK (Canada), AFRICAN STORM (Kenya), CARIBBEAN STORM (Belize), CASCADE STORM (Canada) and AFRICAN SUNSET (Kenya). REME TA units also took part in a wide variety of adventurous training activities, including skiing and sailing. Overall, therefore, REME TA could offer a wide variety of activities to tempt and challenge its volunteers.

Operations

At the beginning of this period, the idea of TA personnel deploying on peacekeeping operations was something of a novelty, but by a few years down the line it was not seen as particularly surprising that a deployed force could comprise around 10% reservists. The use of the TA was not without its complications, however, and an account, written in 2006, by Colonel John Saville (late REME), a former CO of 102 Battalion REME (V) highlights some of the issues associated with a deployment to Kosovo in March 1999:

> 'Soon after SDR, Kosovo provided the first test of whether the TA could and should be used in large numbers. An opposed entry to Kosovo would have required several TA units in the force, but as events unfolded, wide-scale mobilisation of the TA was no longer required. … an opportunity to test mobilisation, even a limited compulsory call-out was not to be. This was because a compulsory call-out would have had to be demonstrably necessary for the National Interest, if not only the public, but also particularly employers of the TA were to accept it. This was a disappointment to many in the TA, who wanted their chance to take their place alongside Regulars on an operation, so long as they were given the protective cover of a compulsory call-out. Although Territorials can volunteer to be mobilised if they wish, those who do so risk being thought of as disloyal by their employer – not to mention their families.
>
> The length of tour was considered carefully. Market research within the Battalion showed that many would have liked a three-month tour, which would have been quite easy to justify to employers, with a swap over of volunteers halfway through the six-month tour. However, this would have set a precedent for which there was no support at high level, where the prevailing view was that a three-month tour was not 'good value for money'.

The Battalion was keen to deploy a complete platoon to Kosovo to help the overstretched Regulars, but there were a number of obstacles, which had to be dealt with. Colonel Saville continued:

> 'Sixty-three originally came forward as volunteers, but when it became clear that the voluntary nature of the Op Tour would have to be declared to employers, twenty-one dropped out of the running. … The

CO sent personal letters to thirty-one senior employers, explaining that mobilisation of a platoon of volunteers from the northeast was an important contribution to the Army's efforts in the Balkans. The personal approach helped considerably, and only thirteen of the thirty-one were refused permission to volunteer.

The serious business started when the volunteers reported to the Reserves Training and Mobilisation Centre (RTMC) at Chilwell, for two weeks' mobilisation training. This relatively new system for mobilising TA and Reservists is a vast improvement on past ad hoc mobilisation centres. Those volunteers who remembered the old system were impressed by the service at the RTMC. It also acted as an informal audit of the Battalion's military training skills.

So began a thoroughly successful tour for the twenty-one volunteers with 3 Bn REME, who quickly realised what assets had joined them. The volunteers were a mixture of trades including VM, Rec Mech, Veh Elec, RS, Chef, Sup Spec and Dvr/Rad Op. Because 102 Battalion spends a good proportion of its training time on 'Production Exercises' fixing a Regular unit's kit, our volunteers were able to slot rapidly into their jobs in 3 Battalion. Our Territorials were also able to bring other skills to the party – some of them were skilled electricians, carpenters and decorators'. (**See Plate 34**)

This account gives a good feel for the issues associated with the use of REME volunteers on operations at this time, many of which are of continuing relevance. It explains why, without a compulsory mobilisation order, it took a major effort to produce a deployable platoon from a REME battalion, and why it would be difficult to raise the same number of people for tour after tour. Clearly TA soldiers may need to go up a steeper learning curve than their Regular Army counterparts when they arrive in theatre. The consistent pattern, which emerges from this and other accounts, was that they generally settled in quickly and soon became regarded as indistinguishable from their Regular Army equivalents.

The View of Colonel REME TA

The overall state of play at the end of this era was summarised by Colonel REME TA, Colonel John Harvey (late REME (V)), in an article in The Craftsman magazine (December 2002) about the future of REME TA. The following extracts highlight some of the points he made:

'Who We Are. There are about 3,000 REME TA weekend warriors, every one of whom is keen, enthusiastic and itching to play his or her part in whatever military conflict our Government wishes to launch us into. Some 1,600 of these work in the second line REME Battalions … the remaining 1,400 provide first line support to other Arms and Services TA units … Virtually all units supported by REME TA come under the operational command of GOC Theatre Troops.

Recent Achievements. REME TA officers and soldiers have been volunteering to undertake six-month operational tours for at least the past 10 years. Unfortunately, accurate records have only been kept since the formation of the RTMC. … In the last three years, 200 REME TA personnel have volunteered for either six-month operational tours or Full Time Reserve Service (FTRS) contracts'.

A graph shows that around 23% of the total deployed were on FTRS. Colonel Harvey continued:

'… In addition, as part of their technical training TA units frequently deploy to Regular units where we carry out what we affectionately call 'Prodexs' – helping units to reduce or clear their backlog.

The Future of REME TA. To ensure that REME TA policy is developed in parallel with the rest of the Corps a TA Policy Cell is to be set up in DEME(A)'s HQ from January 2003. It will be headed by Col REME TA and will comprise a Regular SO1, a TA SO2 (Maj) and a Regular Staff Warrant Officer (WO2). In parallel with this, there will be significant changes to HQ REME TA. The Commander HQ REME TA, Col Phil Gray, is currently double-hatted as Comd ES Theatre Troops. He will move to devote 100% of his time to Theatre Troops ES and HQ REME TA will revert to a Central Volunteer Headquarters (CVHQ) and will be headed by an OC (Maj). CVHQ will remain at Bordon in Louisburg Barracks and the TA Policy Cell will be at Arborfield. In summary, REME TA of today is a professional, committed and coherent organisation delivering real output and making a tangible contribution to military operations – the future looks rosy'.

REME TA FROM 2003 TO THE STRATEGIC
DEFENCE AND SECURITY REVIEW 2010

The Invasion of Iraq and Immediate Aftermath (Operations TELIC 1 and 2)

The attack on New York on 11 September 2001 did not have an immediate effect on REME TA, but was to have profound long-term effects. By November 2002, contingency planning for participation in an invasion of Iraq was well under way. Colonel Phil Gray (late REME), who was still double-hatted as both Commander HQ REME TA and Commander ES Theatre Troops at the time, provided an account in The Craftsman magazine (September 2003) of the planning and subsequent deployment process.

He explained that the initial theoretical requirement was for the deployment in a couple of months of a 550-strong formed REME TA battalion (so much for previous readiness assumptions). This set in train a process of planning for 'intelligent mobilisation' with Colonel Gray as the 'capbadge champion'. The first task was to identify those who were Fit-for-Role (FFR); that is, they met age and skills criteria and had no known inhibiting domestic or employment factors. The four Independent TA battalions could produce around 1,000 FFR personnel. A mobilisation ratio was also applied to take account of the likely dropout rates for medical reasons, personal or employer appeals or the like. The ratios used were 1.5:1 for formed bodies, 2:1 for Individual Reservists (IR), and 4:1 for Regular Reservists.

In the event, the original plan to invade through Turkey had to be aborted, and the southern approach option had to be adopted. This resulted in changes to the force structure. REME TA was not required to provide any formed units, but only 240 IRs to top up all types of REME unit once Regular-to-Regular backfill had been completed (the availability of Regulars being restricted because of Operation FRESCO commitments – the firemen's strike). When various additional requirements were added, the total REME TA deployment on Operation TELIC 1 (the initial invasion of Iraq) was to be a total of 308 personnel – a significant part of one of the largest TA mobilisations since World War 2.

Once the details of the required slots were known, Colonel Gray's team had only 24 hours to put names to slots. He tried to make maximum use of ex-Regulars for slots at battlegroup level, as these were most likely to have the specialised knowledge of armoured operations and equipment. He also maximised the use of Specialists, as, first, he had a better handle on their trade skills, and, second, they were accustomed to being scattered to a variety of units. He felt soldiers in Independent units were more used to working in formed TA units, and would be in at the deep end if they were away from their usual TA environment. He was also keen to preserve the cohesion of the Independent battalions against the future requirements, which he rightly guessed would materialise.

He commented that the tight timescale, and the use of the TA as individuals rather than formed units, made aspects of mobilisation ragged, despite the huge efforts by RTMC in Chilwell and elsewhere. In the event, the TA personnel were effectively absorbed in their units in good time and played an important part in the Operation, including one Corporal Marven, some of whose exciting and amusing adventures are recounted in Chapter 8 ('The Invasion of Iraq (Operation TELIC 1)').

The replacement for the original invasion force (Operation TELIC 2) involved the deployment of 5 Battalion REME to Iraq when REME at second line was still heavily stretched (with Operation FRESCO still causing complications). The CO of 5 Battalion REME described how REME TA came to the rescue in an article in The Craftsman magazine (November 2003). He explained how, after much negotiation, it was agreed that his Battalion would receive three formed TA platoons – one recovery, and two workshop platoons. He said that this did not cause him a problem and that in the light of his experience he would have been prepared to accept a formed company. He explained:

> 'It was about this time that Comd Theatre Troops, Col Phil Gray, called me to provide some advice. Chief amongst this was to retain the TA in formed bodies and not split them up across the battalion unless absolutely avoidable. I have to say that this proved sound advice. Looking across the theatre of operations there are one or two examples where units did split up formed bodies, and according to anecdotal evidence they paid a heavy price in morale and efficiency terms. Sadly, some of these units tried to lay the blame on the TA soldiers involved rather than looking at how their own decisions and leadership might have affected the integration.
>
> … as for equipment, the TA platoons came complete with their own vehicles, all of which were in a good state and entirely fit for purpose. They did, however, lack some special tools and test equipments, which are not routinely held by TA battalions. Throughout this period and since, I was always careful to treat

the Regulars and Reserves in exactly the same way. I also issued instructions that all were to use the TA chain of command and not go through the Permanent Staff Instructors (PSIs). This was a deliberate way of demonstrating confidence in both TA officers and NCOs and it paid dividends. I further directed that once we had settled into theatre I wanted the PSIs to recover back to their parent battalions. ... It was during this initial period that some of the TA first realised the breadth of skills required of a deployed soldier. Whereas their TA training had probably concentrated on ITDs (Individual Training Directives) and trade, time available had not permitted them to undertake many other tasks ... escorting convoys ... wiring parties ... camp hygiene and initial set up ... security patrols and Ops with the infantry'.

The tour was a demanding one in searing heat and the CO commented further:

'Again the TA did not let me down and I quickly came to trust them and rely on them. So much so that I came to realise that my earlier decision to treat the TA the same as Regulars may not have been required after all; after a couple of weeks I could not at my level tell the difference'.

He concluded:

'Overall I would say that the Battalion could not have achieved its mission without TA reinforcements. Despite the compulsory nature of the call-up they kept their chins up and produced the goods whilst maintaining an excellent disciplinary record. They endured harsh conditions and danger without flinching, and proved excellent ambassadors for the TA'.

Continuing Operations in Iraq and Afghanistan

After a brief honeymoon period following the invasion, the British forces in Iraq encountered an increasingly difficult security situation. The size of the deployed British force was reduced fairly soon after the invasion to some 6,500 and, subsequently to some 5,000 before withdrawal as described in Chapter 9 ('Iraq – Aftermath of the Invasion (Operations

TELIC 2–13)'). Compulsory mobilisation of the TA was no longer required, but TA volunteers continued to be sought.

With operations still at a difficult stage in Iraq, 16 Air Assault Brigade was deployed to Afghanistan on what was hoped would be a relatively benign peacekeeping operation. Chapter 11 ('Afghanistan – The Long Haul') describes how it turned into anything but that, and reinforcements had to be rushed in. During the next few years, the Regular Army, including REME, was heavily stretched. The contribution made by REME TA around this time is well described from the point of view of the Regular CO of 102 Battalion REME (V), Lieutenant Colonel Paul Wise REME, in his article in The Craftsman magazine (September 2009), along with some general views on the TA from a Regular Army perspective, as follows:

> 'Working alongside a Craftsman VM who is also a qualified and practising barrister is not something we come across during out normal regular service. Neither are we necessarily used to the idea of having to make our training interesting enough to entice our soldiers to turn up. ... Planning a Battalion training event, but being unsure how many (if any) soldiers will attend takes some getting used to ... certainly leads to some imaginative training plans. ... But the sheer enthusiasm, dedication and upbeat positivity of our TA soldiers is truly remarkable. The thought of working Monday to Friday, 8 to 6 during the week, whilst juggling all the usual family pressures, and then spending evenings and weekends working for the Army as well is almost beyond comprehension for many Regulars, I suspect.
>
> And many are serial deployers. Shortly after my arrival, I interviewed SSgt Friend (now a WO2 (CSM)) who had not long since returned from Op HERRICK where he had been attached to the R IRISH BG. They had made him CSM in a very active Forward Operating Base where he had excelled. ... WO2 Monkhouse also has some very interesting stories of his time spent with 1 PWRR BG in CIMIC house in Al Amarah during a famously intense period – they certainly kept DEME(A) enthralled during his recent visit!
>
> In the last nine months, seven members of the Battalion have deployed on Ops TELIC, HERRICK and TOSCA, with an additional 10 members filling key FTRS posts in direct support of operations – most delivering Urgent Operational Requirement

instruction at DST Leconfield. Currently, 14 members of the Battalion have volunteered to deploy on Op HERRICK 12 with our sister Battalion – 1 CS Battalion REME. … REME TA offers a slightly different perspective on things: the opportunity to test our leadership in a slightly different way, a chance to work with soldiers who must enjoy what they are doing or they simply would not have turned up. … one night a week attending 'drill night' and support to the TA training every second weekend. … The possibility of deploying overseas to support the TA's 'annual camps' adds an exotic flavour (members of 102 Bn will have deployed to Germany, BATUS, Cyprus and Kenya this year alone). … There is still the requirement to prepare for and undergo TECHEVAL, ECI, LSI, AAU, SPS inspections etc. So life is never dull!!!'.

In due course, operations in Iraq wound down with the operational commitment to Afghanistan ramped up. A TA perspective on the TA contribution to Operation HERRICK 15 (late 2011) is given by Captain Warwick Izzard REME (V) in the Broxhead Bulletin (February 2012). He explains that a force generation process run by 101 Battalion REME (V) resulted in him and some 35 soldiers being mobilised through the RTMC at Chilwell. He explained that the TA augmentees were warmly and professionally welcomed by 3 Battalion REME, but added:

'But my time spent with 3 Bn had a clear emphasis on personal fitness and it was evident to me that, with some notable exceptions, a significant number of TA soldiers struggled to meet the standards of their (mostly younger) Regular counterparts. We must recognise that the annual MATTs fitness tests represent the minimum standard for those aspiring to mobilise on operations … it is also noteworthy that a high proportion of 3 Bn soldiers deploy forward at some stage as ISTs, or backfilling slots created by R&R, so TA mobilisation to a second line REME Bn on HERRICK is not a deployment to a rear area'.

Captain Izzard was deployed with HQ Joint Force Support so did not have personal involvement with the technical work done by TA tradesmen, but commented as follows:

'I have heard nothing but positive comment from my contact with 3 Bn both prior to and during the op to date. My feeling is that this reflects a combination of being keen and eager to turn spanners and the added value of knowledge brought by those TA tradesmen with current civilian experience some of whom may be a step ahead of their Regular counterparts in some aspects of the automotive technology'.

The overall 'numbers game' for REME TA by this time was summarised in the following extract from DEME(A)'s Report to the Corps 2011 (with accompanying table showing the number of volunteers on Operation HERRICK):

'The number of personnel deploying on operations has over the past number of rotations increased, but we are still short of our target of 43 personnel (10% of the deployed REME force) … REME TA manning liability is 184 officers and 2,354 other ranks. Our actual strength is 123 officers and 1,681 other ranks. It remains a challenge to recruit suitable individuals; the manning of 2Lts/Lts and Cfn, with 20% Subalterns and 50% Cfn'.

Number of Volunteers	7	5	10	7	17	19	21	38	17	32	27	36
Operation HERRICK	H4	H5	H6	H7	H8	H9	H10	H11	H12	H13	H14	H15

Non-Operational Activities
Much of this Chapter is about REME TA on operations, and associated issues related to organisation and mobilisation. The REME TA of 2010 was somewhat different from REME TA shortly after 'Options'. It was significantly smaller, around half the size. Compulsory mobilisation was not seen as a remote possibility and the idea of TA soldiers serving on operations did not seem at all novel or extraordinary. The Regular Army and TA had a much better understanding of each other, REME TA having a hard core of those who had gained serious operational experience working alongside the Regular Army.

All this should not obscure the fact that at any time most REME TA people are not involved in operations. The basic pattern of non-operational activity had also remained broadly the same. There were still training weekends, drill nights, and the annual two-week camp. The organisation of second line units into battalions had proved a very sound idea, which had facilitated the planning and management of non-operational activities. REME remained fortunate in being able to offer a wide variety of activities.

Annual Regional Competitions. Annual regional competitions such as NORTHERN BLUEBELL, SCOTTISH BLUEBELL and SOUTHERN BLUEBELL continued. These were linked with prestigious awards such as the Blackford and Gardiner Trophies (for first and second line units respectively). Unit training was frequently overseas, particularly in the case of units linked with Regular Army units based in Germany. **(See Plates 35 and 36)**

Colonel Mifsud (Colonel REME TA) presenting the Blackford Trophy 2009 to Captain Callaway REME (V) (151 (London) Transport Regiment RLC (V) LAD)

Overseas Exercises. Many small (and not so small) detachments continued to deploy on a number of overseas exercises, which REME TA personnel particularly welcomed because of the productive work they carry out. This technical work is normally linked with a non-technical package that allows them to see something of the country they are visiting and to enjoy charitable, adventurous or simply relaxing activities. In 2011, for example, REME Overseas Training Exercises included visits to Belize, Kenya and Cyprus. A total of 3,096 Man Training Days were used for this, and around 10,000 hours of productive work was delivered that year. (**See Plate 37**)

Other Activities. REME TA Battalions also engage in many of the sort of activities that any TA unit might undertake, such as parades, open days, VIP visits, charitable work and the like. (**See Plate 38**)

The Broxhead Club. The Broxhead Club derives its name from Broxhead House in Bordon, which used to be home to REME TA Specialists until it was sold off for development. Its members comprise serving and retired REME TA officers, and Regular Army officers who served with REME TA. It holds an annual dinner linked to a briefing/study day, which provides a wonderful opportunity for the 'old and bold' ('Senibus Audacibusque') to meet those currently serving and to renew friendships and generally network.

The Worshipful Company of Turners. The Worshipful Company of Turners is one of the oldest Livery Companies in the City of London, and has had beneficial links with REME, both Regular Army and TA. Each year, the Turners Shield is presented to the winners of Exercise SOUTHERN CRAFTSMAN. (**See Plate 39**)

Organisation and Deployment

Events after '9/11' accelerated thinking within the MoD on how UK Defence should be organised and managed to provide the best possible balance of capability in the light of perceived threats, and within the limits of the finance likely to be available. During this period, there was a perception among many that the Prime Minister, Tony Blair, was generally favourable to the idea of military intervention as a means of solving international problems, whilst his Chancellor, Gordon Brown, intended to keep a very tight grip on the military purse strings.

Events in Iraq provided a reminder that if powerful force had to be rapidly projected, it was likely that the logistic/equipment issues would be the limiting factor. This led to a number of strands of thinking that became interlinked. These influenced what was to be called 'Future Army Structure' (FAS) work. They included looking at how logistics was delivered, the Defence Logistics Transformation Plan, which in turn was linked to an 'end-to-end' study. It was realised that some rebalancing of the Army was required if it was to be able to deliver 'rapid effect'.

This was based on the idea that a rapid intervention with overwhelming force could avoid, or reduce, protracted problems down the line. One of the ideas that went with this was to reduce the initial deployment footprint by holding back second line REME assets involved in repairing assemblies replaced at first line, such as AFV power packs or electronic 'black boxes'. A new term, 'Off Platform Repair' (OPR), was coined to describe such repairs. Clearly, OPR assets do not need to be near equipments when they break down, provided there are adequate reserves of assemblies and a secure rearward repair loop. OPR assets might therefore be deployed in a rear area in a force support role. This topic is covered in a broader context in Chapter 2 ('The Fundamentals and Organisation to 2010').

It was also clear that both 101 and 102 Logistic Brigades needed a REME battalion that could provide support at short notice, which meant that a substantial element of it needed to be from the Regular Army. Colonel REME TA and his team were intimately involved in this force development work, which was focused on this problem as he explained in his 'State of the Nation' Report to the Broxhead Club on 26 May 2006.

One of the outcomes of the 'FAS' work was the decision to produce two hybrid Regular Army/TA Force Support Battalions to support 101 and 102 Logistic Brigades. The idea was to have a Regular Battalion HQ, a Regular OPR Company, a Regular Workshop Company, plus two TA Workshop Companies and a TA Recovery Company. This new organisation became effective in 2008 – with the TA second line outline structure as shown in Figure 16.2 (at the end of this Chapter).

This organisation reflected the mutual understanding that had grown between the Regular Army and TA within REME during the past 15 years or so of working and fighting together.

How well this was to work in practice was described by Major Nick Sharples REME in an article in the REME Journal 2010 titled 'Are Hybrid REME Battalions a Success?' Not everything was plain sailing and he commented:

> 'The majority of the Regular element of the battalion had little exposure to the TA, and there was a degree of mutual scepticism. …

It is fair to say that many of the TA soldiers who were mobilised for operations had a lot of catching up to do across trade and military skills and levels of fitness'.

He goes on to say that, as they worked with the Regular Army, the TA soldiers were quick to overcome their shortcomings (a familiar tale). The TA element was put to the test when the Battalion deployed as the lead of the 583-strong ES Group on Operation HERRICK 11. The Battalion deployed with 33 TA soldiers of its own (and four from other units). He commented:

> 'Having been in theatre now for 3 months it is impossible to determine the TA soldier from his regular counterpart. There is no doubt that the TA soldiers have brought much to the party from their civilian careers, including a VOSA inspector, health and safety inspectors and vehicle fleet managers to name but three'.

He concludes unambiguously:

> 'So, yes, hybrid REME Battalions are very much a success'.

These very positive messages had to be seen in the light of concern about manning and recruiting. The 2006 'State of the Nation' talk (mentioned earlier) came with concern about manning and recruiting. Colonel REME TA advised that overall manning stood at around 73% of an established strength of about 3,000, and explained that a positive overall trend in recruiting masked a severe shortage of officers. Only some 102 out of 182 tied officer posts (56%) were filled, and he believed that recruiting the next generation of REME TA officers was of great importance. He believed that the requirement for officers in REME TA to have an engineering background should be waived in some cases in order to recruit the right people.

One of the final tasks of the post-SDR 98 restructuring of REME TA was the closure of the CVHQ at Bordon and the transfer of responsibilities elsewhere on 8 April 2010. Administration and training of National (formerly Specialist) TA largely transferred to 102 and 103 Battalions REME (V); the REME Arms School took over delivery of Senior Command Leadership and Management (V) training. The remaining functions, Military Secretary matters and TA Training, along with four staff were transferred to the REME TA Policy Branch, HQ DEME(A), but with the staff physically remaining at Bordon, as described in an article in The Craftsman magazine (June 2010).

STRATEGIC DEFENCE AND SECURITY REVIEW 2010, ARMY 2020, AND THE CHALLENGE OF TRANSFORMING REME RESERVES

The background and an outline of the Strategic Defence and Security Review 2010 (SDSR 2010) is given in Chapter 2 ('The Fundamentals and Organisation to 2010'). A major plank of SDSR 2010 was to cut the Regular Army to 82,000, and to increase reliance on the TA, which was renamed the Army Reserve (AR). The AR was established at 30,000 strong with the assumption that there would be another 8,000 in the training pipeline, giving a headline 'One Army' strength of 120,000 (82,000 + 38,000) – around the same as the post-'Options' strength of the Regular Army. This was somewhat disingenuous as the TA actual strength at the time of SDSR 2010 was around 20,000, but its established strength was 40,500. The new establishment figures for the new AR therefore represented an increase against the actual strength of the old TA, but a reduction against its establishment.

The follow-on work resulted in a formulation of a plan for the Army called Army 2020. By this stage, it had been realised that ideas for a 38,000-strong AR were unrealistic, and the planning total was reduced to 30,000. The 'One Army' concept had not, however, changed. It involved a heavy reliance on the AR deploying in the form of operational units and sub-units from the start, rather than filling gaps within Regular Army organisations, or providing formed units/sub-units months or years down the line. Army 2020 was still being refined at the time of writing, and the overall REME and Army plan is covered in Chapter 3 ('Strategic Defence and Security Review 2010 and Army 2020'). This Chapter seeks to elaborate on issues relevant to REME TA, which was retitled REME Reserves.

The Army 2020 plan represented a huge 'ask' for a TA that had been steadily declining in numbers, with each capbadge having its own set of issues to contend with.

At first sight, the challenge for REME Reserves did not seem too difficult. Its liability actually dropped by 20% to 2,010 personnel (210 officers + 1,800 other ranks) while its strength in 2013 was 1,744 (846 at first line, 898 at second line – 69% manned). These overall figures, however, masked two underlying problems.

The first was related to age profile. Few young soldiers and officers had joined in recent years to replace those who had left, leaving a high proportion of older officers and soldiers, including a fair number over 50 who would clearly not remain active for many more years. The second was that competence at trade was very variable. There were many (including ex-Regulars) who had joined with excellent trade skills, or had acquired them. A significant proportion, however, had joined without any real technical skills, and had undergone limited formal training since doing so. This tended to apply particularly at first line, where routine equipment maintenance was normally done by civilians (or contractors) rather than REME TA soldiers whose activities had often been driven more by the priorities of the parent unit than the need to get REME staff technically proficient. This did not rest easily with the operational requirement, which was for technically competent staff.

From the occasional bad experience in Afghanistan and elsewhere, it was clear that the idea of sending TA soldiers who did not have comparable technical competence to their Regular Army counterparts on operations was not a good idea. The numbers that went with the operational requirement also represented a stiff target. For instance, it was assumed that in the case of an Enduring Medium Scale Operation, REME Reserves would deploy 94 personnel on Roulements 1–3, and 299 personnel (including two sub-units) thereafter. This represented a significantly greater commitment than REME TA had delivered during the previous two decades on an enduring operation.

Clearly, training was going to be a key issue. Solutions were in place for non-technical training, with REME complying with the national model for basic military training. This saw two phases of training for REME, known as Trained Soldiers Course (TSC) (A) and (B). TSC(A) could be delivered to Regional units over six weekends, or as a single two-week course. REME TA had also put in place recently updated Command Leadership and Management Courses for Volunteers, for JNCOs and SNCOs. Both were eight-day residential courses.

The main problem area centred on technical training. DEME(A) had done much work in preceding years on Engineering Standards, for which he had formal responsibility. The 'One Army' concept meant that TA soldiers had increasingly been carrying out the same sort of repairs on military equipment as Regular Army soldiers. SDSR 2010 implied a continuation of this trend. The difficult question was how, in an increasingly litigious world, DEME(A) could ensure that the Regular Army soldiers and REME Reservists worked to the same acceptable standards, given that the TA's Man Training Day ration would generally not allow anything near the same amount of formal technical training as the Regular Army received.

In 2012, the REME Reservist who was in the hot seat on this issue was Colonel Mandie Cran (late REME (V)), Colonel REME TA. In her article 'Forward Together' in The Craftsman magazine (December 2012), she outlined both the problem and the solution as she saw it:

> 'For years, REME has struggled to attract tradesmen whose civilian trade matches their TA one. Many mechanics work on vehicles in small businesses, sometimes their own business; others work in shifts; not all want to spend their free time doing the same thing as they do at work. If you combine this with no accreditation, and no opportunity to do or learn something different, the result is low manning (50% Craftsmen, 20% Young Officers and only 15% are from an equivalent civilian trade).
>
> The second problem is the perception that a TA soldier can never be as good as a Regular Army soldier, either in military skills or as a tradesman (after all, they only train for 27 days a year, don't they?).
>
> Army 2020 requires that the TA deploy in formed units at up to company level, not just fill individual gaps in Regular Army units. So officers and SNCOs will command and lead the teams they built up on operations. To achieve this, we are forming six TA battalions across the UK, based in the engineering areas, making REME TA more accessible. To fill these Battalions recruitment needs to increase, and our training needs to be much more effective, so that a TA career is more attractive to engineers at all levels'.

The article went on to explain how formal accreditation was beginning to be introduced. The first step was for new TA officers to gain the Engineering Officer (EngO) qualifications (exactly the same as for the Regular Army), which could provide a path to Chartered Engineer (CEng). It stated:

> 'TA training at all levels will be modularised and flexible. TA trainees will achieve the same standards as Regulars, and the same

accreditation for the training they complete. However, they will do so in a different timescale.... We have been trialling a TA Education and Qualification Scheme (TEQS) – a TA apprenticeship in all but name.... We have been building links with industry ... we now have a partnership with the AA who recognise that their people benefit from being with REME TA, and we recognise that our soldiers benefit from working in the AA'.

An understanding of this thinking is useful background to the update on REME Reserves given by Colonel Ian Adkins (late REME (V)), Colonel Cran's successor (whose former job title of Colonel REME TA had changed to Colonel REME Reserves).

In an article published in The Craftsman magazine (April 2014), he outlined the way ahead. He explained that first line would no longer continue in its present form and:

> '... 800 or so Reservists will move from LADs to the three existing REME Reserve Battalions and the three new ones'.

He continued:

> 'Enhancing and ensuring universally high trade standards is an important part of our design for the future, therefore we will be organising ourselves into six Reserve Battalions where we will have the expertise and facilities to consistently deliver good trade training as well as military training and enhanced career development. Nearly three-quarters of our existing LADs (60 out of 84) have five or fewer tradesmen, which makes it impossible to deliver this'.

Although first line support for AR equipment maintenance in barracks would be done by contractors or civilian staff, who had been doing much of the work anyway, there was no intention to give up providing first line REME support in the field. The change was that it would come from REME battalions who would '*continue to provide FRTs, fitter sections and even complete LADs to the units we support when and where they need it*'.

THE TRANSFORMATION STRATEGY

Colonel Adkins updated and elaborated on some of these points in a presentation to the Broxhead Club on 10 May 2014. He stressed that if REME Reserves was to meet the challenge ahead it was necessary to review fundamentals with a view to putting in place a transformation plan, rather than just a reorganisation. He described the overall mission as:

> 'Creating a part-time, professional engineering force, an integral part of the Army ES capability within the REME family, integrated with UK engineering'.

Some of the issues he covered are summarised below.

The Closure of First Line Units
There had been a few well-founded first line units, but the majority comprised less than five members and the standard of expertise in them was highly variable. Most were incapable of organising the sort of technical training that would be required in the future. They also offered very limited scope for career development opportunities (with a rank ceiling of Captain for LADs). The REME battalion structure has proved a success, and offered the only realistic transformational route. It was hoped that many of the best individuals at first line would not be lost as they would transfer to second line units. The requirement for second line REME Reserves units to deliver support to first line units provides an important new challenge and opportunity.

Technical Training
It was hoped that the move of REME training from Bordon and Arborfield to Lyneham would open up new opportunities. The move was going to be linked with an active review of training both in terms of duration and content. For example, it was believed that the residential element of the REME Vehicle Mechanic Class 3 Course could reduce from perhaps 70 to 50 days. The methods of delivery were likely to make increasing use of online modules, and other forms of graduated distance learning. Colonel Adkins believed this could lead to a situation where a recruit would plan his technical training from the start, looking at various options such as two years to completion of a Class 3 Course, or alternatively completion over four years. Although the minimum annual commitment for a soldier was 27 days, it was hoped that the average commitment would

be around 40+ days per year. This would make the idea of a 'two-year Class 3 Vehicle Mechanic' soldier viable, and a 'four-year Class 3 Vehicle Mechanic' soldier comfortable. This would be a great advance on the existing system whereby REME Reserves soldiers might serve for eight years or longer without getting a formal trade qualification. The overall aim was to transform REME Reserves into an organisation in which all of its members (rather than just a proportion) have vocational engineering training and experience.

Recruiting
Recruiting represented a great challenge. In broad terms, it involved getting around 1,000 more soldiers or officers into REME Reserves, ideally mainly younger ones, who would be prepared to buy into the new training concept. The recruiting strategy reflected an analysis of stakeholders and potentially interested parties, and of ways to engage them and get their support.

Potential Volunteers. Potential volunteers must be attracted by the 'brand' of REME Reserves. The idea of getting a proper technical education, with formal qualifications that may open up new employment possibilities, is an idea that may clearly be sold to some. The Regular Army is a key potential source of volunteers and the only way in the short term to get significant numbers of volunteers who already have the essential technical, leadership and military skills. More needed to be done to attract them into REME Reserves. Colleges and universities represented another source of recruits. Many young people join UOTCs, some go on to join the Regular Army, the rest have generally left education without being much aware of what REME Reserves offers.

Employers. Employers may be a help or a hindrance. On the face of it, the idea that they may suddenly lose key staff for up to a year on an operational tour is not likely to please them, particularly if they run small firms. On the other hand, experience has shown that REME reservists make excellent employees. They enjoy additional training, they tend to be fitter (enjoying lower sickness rates), more committed, offer lower recruitment costs, and may bring transferable leadership and management skills. The REME Reserves 'offer' therefore must be sold to employers.

Engineering Organisations. These include the professional engineering institutions such as IMechE, SOE and IET. Also, trade bodies, the likes of IMI, EEF, BEMA, Oil & Gas UK and SEMTA.

REME and the ES Organisation. 'Pairing' between Regular Army and REME Reserves units is an obvious and important element of this, but it is necessary to exploit all the formal and informal links that exist within the REME 'family', serving and retired, Regular and Reserve.

Rebasing. The new organisation for REME Reserves would involve the creation of two new battalions, and the provision of a new Battalion HQ for 104 Battalion REME (V). The intention had been to expand the REME footprint into new areas, particularly those which are seen as being promising from the recruiting point of view. The plan, as shown in Figure 16.3 (at the end of this Chapter), represents the best pragmatic solution that could be achieved given the constraints of available real estate, and allowed resources. It sought also to make best use of former first line REME reservists and TA soldiers from other capbadge units that have been disbanded. The new battalions were still at the embryonic stage, but their formation and development had started.

CONCLUSIONS

During the previous two decades, REME TA has come a long way from being part of a 'force of last resort' to being much more integrated with the Regular Army in its new guise as REME Reserves. It had become a smaller organisation, but it has a proud record of operational achievement, and has become in many ways a potentially more operationally usable force. An exciting challenge lay ahead.

Its achievements reflect the willingness of many talented and busy people to give their time and attention to REME in parallel with busy jobs. A full list of those who deserve an honourable mention would be impossible to compile but Appendix A lists the two REME TA officers who reached one-star rank, and those who have served as Colonel REME TA (or Colonel REME Reserves).

Bn and HQ Location	Role	Sub-units/Locations
101 Bn (V) Chorley	Independent support of 1 (UK) Div	126 Reclamation Coy (V) Coventry 119 Recovery Coy (V) Prestatyn 127 Workshop Coy (V) Manchester
102 Bn (V) Newton Aycliffe	Independent L of C support and support of CSSG(UK))	124 Recovery Coy (V) Newton Aycliffe 146 Workshop Coy (V) Rotherham 186 Workshop Coy (V) Newcastle 218, 219 Port Workshop Coy (V)
103 Bn (V) Redhill then Crawley	Independent support of 3 (UK) Div	128 Reclamation Coy (V) Portsmouth 150 Recovery Coy (V) Redhill 133 Workshop Coy (V) Ashford.
104 Bn (V) Bordon	Sponsored support of UKLF	201 Workshop Coy (V) 209 Workshop Coy (V) 210 Port Workshop Coy (V) 216, 217, 220 Port Workshop Pl (V)
105 Bn (V) Bordon	Hybrid Independent and Sponsored support of CSSG(G)	118 Recovery Coy (V) Northampton 153 Workshop Coy (V) Grangemouth (to go to 101 Bn (V) post SDR) 207 Port and Reclamation Coy (Specialist, to merge with 211 Coy (V) and move to 104 Bn (V) post SDR) 211 Port and Reclamation Coy (V)

Figure 16.1: Initial 'Options' plan (later amended as above) for REME at second line

Integrated (mixed Regular Army and TA) Force Support Battalions			
Battalion	Supporting	Bn HQ	Coy Designations
101 FS Bn REME	102 Log Bde	Wrexham	50 OPR, 20 Fd, 126 & 127 Fd (V), 119 Rec (V)
104 FS Bn REME	101 Log Bde	Bordon	55 OPR, 146 &147 Fd Coy (V), 118 Rec (V)
Territorial Army			
102 Bn REME (V)	Regional Forces	Newton Aycliffe	186 Fd, 153 Fd, 124 Rec
103 Bn REME (V)	Regional Forces	Crawley	201/207/210 Incr, 128 Fd, 133 Fd, 150 Rec

Figure 16.2: Roles of REME TA Battalions in 2008

REME AND THE RESERVE ARMY

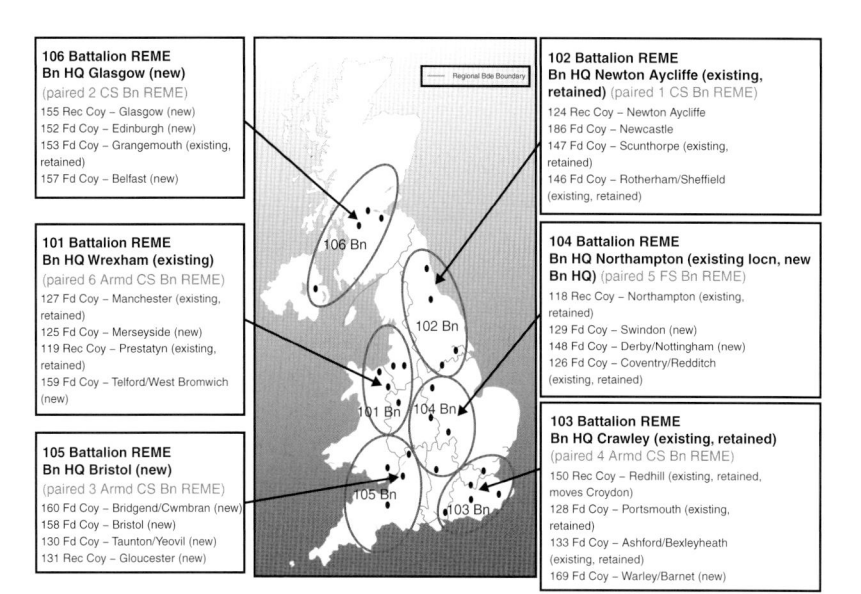

106 Battalion REME
Bn HQ Glasgow (new)
(paired 2 CS Bn REME)
155 Rec Coy – Glasgow (new)
152 Fd Coy – Edinburgh (new)
153 Fd Coy – Grangemouth (existing, retained)
157 Fd Coy – Belfast (new)

101 Battalion REME
Bn HQ Wrexham (existing)
(paired 6 Armd CS Bn REME)
127 Fd Coy – Manchester (existing, retained)
125 Fd Coy – Merseyside (new)
119 Rec Coy – Prestatyn (existing, retained)
159 Fd Coy – Telford/West Bromwich (new)

105 Battalion REME
Bn HQ Bristol (new)
(paired 3 Armd CS Bn REME)
160 Fd Coy – Bridgend/Cwmbran (new)
158 Fd Coy – Bristol (new)
130 Fd Coy – Taunton/Yeovil (new)
131 Rec Coy – Gloucester (new)

102 Battalion REME
Bn HQ Newton Aycliffe (existing, retained) (paired 1 CS Bn REME)
124 Rec Coy – Newton Aycliffe
186 Fd Coy – Newcastle
147 Fd Coy – Scunthorpe (existing, retained)
146 Fd Coy – Rotherham/Sheffield (existing, retained)

104 Battalion REME
Bn HQ Northampton (existing locn, new Bn HQ) (paired 5 FS Bn REME)
118 Rec Coy – Northampton (existing, retained)
129 Fd Coy – Swindon (new)
148 Fd Coy – Derby/Nottingham (new)
126 Fd Coy – Coventry/Redditch (existing, retained)

103 Battalion REME
Bn HQ Crawley (existing, retained)
(paired 4 Armd CS Bn REME)
150 Rec Coy – Redhill (existing, retained, moves Croydon)
128 Fd Coy – Portsmouth (existing, retained)
133 Fd Coy – Ashford/Bexleyheath (existing, retained)
169 Fd Coy – Warley/Barnet (new)

Figure 16.3: Army 2020 – REME Reserves Rebasing Plan (as at 2014)

CHAPTER 17

REME EQUIPMENT AND TECHNOLOGY

The purpose of this Chapter is to describe some of the specialist equipment REME has used during the period covered by this book, and to give an insight into some of the technical issues that affected its design and use.

RECOVERY AND REPAIR VEHICLES

One of the reasons for REME's early success was that it coordinated repair with recovery and backloading at all levels. This remains very much a feature of the way REME operates. REME Recovery Mechanics are a hardy lot and your author is certainly not alone in having found them a very refreshing and entertaining group of people to work with. They are skilled, and have to be able to deal with the most complex recovery tasks, including those involving heavy vehicles that have come to grief in situations, which make their extrication extremely difficult. In such situations, the formulation of a recovery plan is often of itself a technical challenge as it may well involve more than one recovery vehicle, and require the use of any combination of cranes, winches, earth anchors and recovery techniques. On operations, such a plan may have to be executed whilst under enemy fire.

The Army continued to place great importance on the key ES principle of 'repair forward', as close to the point of failure as tactically and technically possible. Operations in Iraq and Afghanistan amply demonstrated the need for REME's repair assets to have adequate protection and mobility matched to the supported units' equipment. This is reflected in the plans for Army 2020 and in the REME Battlefield Equipment Support Doctrine:

> 'tasks are often conducted close to the contact battle hence repair asset protection and mobility must be matched to the force element they are supporting'.

In future, first and second line REME units will therefore continue to see an allocation of armoured and protected mobility (PM) vehicles, as well as dismounted close combat equipment that is matched to the supported units' equipment.

Tracked Recovery and Repair Vehicles
As a rule of thumb, satisfactory towing/recovery of one vehicle by another requires the towing/recovery vehicle to be of at least the same weight as the vehicle being towed. From World War 2 onward, the need was therefore appreciated for heavy armoured vehicles to come into service with a variant designed for front-line towing and recovery. The Chieftain Armoured Recovery Vehicle (CHARV) was an example. It came with a 30-ton direct pull winch, and had what appeared to be a dozer blade on its front. This blade was actually an earth anchor, which was designed to be pushed into the ground to hold the vehicle whilst it winched out a casualty (with a 3:1 rope layout the pull on the vehicle could be up to 90 tons).

The primary vehicle for repairing armoured fighting vehicles (AFVs) by major assembly exchange at the time was the FV434, the repair variant of the FV430 family. This had a crane suitable for this role, and the rear part of the vehicle incorporated a 'well' into which AFV power packs

CRARRV repairing a Challenger tank in Iraq

(PPs) or other assemblies could be placed. With the advent of armoured vehicle PPs that were easy to lift or replace, it became clear in due course that the CHARV would be a much more useful vehicle if it incorporated a crane. This was duly done and CHARV was converted to Chieftain Armoured Repair and Recovery Vehicle (CHARRV), which was used until well into the 1990s.

Exactly the same concept was applied to the REME variant of Challenger (CR), which was called the CRARRV. This incorporated a powerful winch (with a 50-tonne straight pull), a 6.5-tonne crane, and is capable of carrying a Challenger PP (or alternatively towing PPs on a trailer). In practice, due to the demand for CRARRV as a recovery vehicle, the second line forward repair capability for changing PPs was rarely used.

The Warrior family came with two REME Variants. The FV512 is the Mechanised Combat Repair Vehicle. It is equipped with a 6.5-tonne crane and a trailer capable of carrying two Warrior PPs or a single Challenger PP.

Warrior FV512 on operations in Iraq

The FV513 is the Mechanised Recovery Vehicle (Repair). It has the same crane and repair capability as the FV512, is equipped with a 20-tonne winch and has two spades at the rear that have a similar function to the earth anchor blade on the front of CRARRV. The Warrior Repair and

Recovery variants were undergoing a capability sustainment upgrade at the time of writing as part of the Warrior Capability Sustainment Programme. The new Warrior Repair (FV522) and Recovery (FV523) variants will then remain in service until at least 2040.

Warrior FV513 on operations in Iraq

A recovery (but not repair) variant of the Combat Vehicle Reconnaissance (Tracked) (CVR(T)) range was produced. It was called the Samson, and provided recovery support across the formation reconnaissance regiments. It was judged that CVR(T) needed a dedicated recovery vehicle with the same characteristics as the supported vehicle. Since the supported regiments operated forward of the front line, recovery variants were therefore required with matched mobility, protection and stealth. There was, however, no recovery version in the FV430 family, and such vehicles were light enough generally to be recoverable by a heavy wheeled recovery vehicle. During the early-2000s, a large number of FV430 series vehicles were upgraded with a new diesel engine, transmission and running gear, and renamed Bulldog. The REME variant, FV434, also received the upgrade and continued to be the workhorse for fitter sections supporting medium armoured units.

The new Ajax Specialist Vehicle fleet (see Chapter 20 ('Army Equipment and its Management')) is planned to include recovery and repair variants, which have been named Atlas and Apollo respectively.

Apollo and Atlas

Wheeled Recovery Vehicles

The Foden 6 x 6 recovery vehicle (12.5-tonne crane, 22.5-tonne winch), which came into service in 1986 has proved to have an excellent capability, and remains in service.

Foden 6 x 6 recovery vehicle in Iraq

It is steadily being supplanted by the 8 x 8 recovery variant of the new Support Vehicle fleet (see Chapter 20 ('Army Equipment and its Management')). Called the Support Vehicle (Recovery) (SV(R)), it weighs 32 tonnes, and can be fitted with an appliqué armour cab. It has a winch and a 15-tonne crane, and is capable of towing vehicles up to 44 tonnes. It was introduced into service in 2009 and was quick to earn its spurs in Afghanistan, where it was well received by REME Recovery Mechanics. **(See Plate 40)**

For the recovery of lighter vehicles, the Bedford MJ light recovery vehicle was introduced in 1981 and based on the Bedford 4-ton truck. It came equipped with a 6-ton winch and a 6-ton crane. With limited cross country capability and a limited towing capability, this vehicle was mainly used with light forces. Latterly, it was used by 3 Commando Brigade and 16 Air Assault Brigade, before being taken out of service in 2013; there remained a capability gap for a light PM recovery vehicle to support these two brigades.

The introduction of the PM fleets into the British Army during Operations TELIC and HERRICK brought a capability gap due to the absence of a recovery capability matched in protection and mobility. On Operation HERRICK specifically, the only option was to employ the SV(R) which, on many occasions, was simply too big for the job with a large turning radius that could not reach the casualty in confined areas. An Urgent Operational Requirement (UOR) generated the Husky recovery vehicle (RV); these were normal Husky vehicle variants modified to be a recovery vehicle by the addition of a winch and earth anchors. Small numbers of Husky RV saw service in Afghanistan but the vehicle was a severe compromise and was not well received; an abject lesson on the difficulties of modifying an in-service vehicle for the recovery role.

Other Vehicles

It is intended that REME will get its fair share of PM vehicles although there was some uncertainty about the form this would take, and whether or not it would be a variant of an in-service PM vehicle. It will, in addition, get an appropriate allocation of SVs, manufactured by the German company MAN, to meet its repair and logistic needs. This is shown in the illustrative Army 2020 allocation of heavy vehicles for REME battalions at Figure 17.1 (at the end of this Chapter), which is taken from an article in The Craftsman magazine (July 2013).

ELECTRO-MECHANICAL REPAIR

REME's electro-mechanical tradesmen ideally do their business in large climate-controlled workshops complete with overhead cranes, power, compressed air, lathes and the like. On deployment, they would look for facilities that came as close as possible to meeting this requirement. This would be subject to the overriding principle of 'repair forward', which could leave them without any facilities at all other than those they are able to bring with them. The following paragraphs outline what these are.

Power Pack Repair Facility

The Power Pack Repair Facility (PPRF) supports the classic REME Off Platform Repair (OPR) function. The basic requirements are fairly simple. They need a lift capacity of at least 6.5 tonnes for large PPs, but lesser capacity will suffice to lift large modules such as cooling groups. Modern PPs generally include a heavy engine and gearbox, and frequently one or other needs to be changed; a special splitter frame is required to separate them and mate new assemblies as required. The PP needs to be run up for testing after and possibly before repair, so a package is required that includes all the ancillaries such as umbilical connections, instrumentation, power, and fuel, to allow the specific type of pack to be run up. Last, but not least, there must be a mechanism for muffling the noise of the exhaust.

During much of the Cold War, PP repair capacity was provided by 10-ton 'barns'. These were 10-ton AEC trucks with large foldable sides that could be linked up to provide an enclosed working space, which was intended to look like a German farm barn. The demise of the 10-ton truck was followed by the arrival of the Demountable Rack Offload and Pickup System (DROPS), which was capable of carrying easily demountable 20-foot ISO containers and flat racks. It therefore made sense for a new PPRF to be based in such containers, which was exactly what happened and a Containerised PPRF (CPPRF) resulted. This should

Deployed CPPRF

be seen as a complete system comprising cranes, and a number of flat racks and specialist containers, some of which can be opened up so their sides provide flat working surfaces, which together provide a complete deployable PP repair capability. The system has been used operationally, and remains in service. (**See Plate 41**)

Deployable Machine Shop

The idea of putting repair facilities into DROPS portable containers was also applied to general mechanical repair. REME's venerable 'machy wagon' was therefore replaced by the Deployable Machine Shop (DMS) mounted in a 20-foot container, the first of which came into service in 2009.

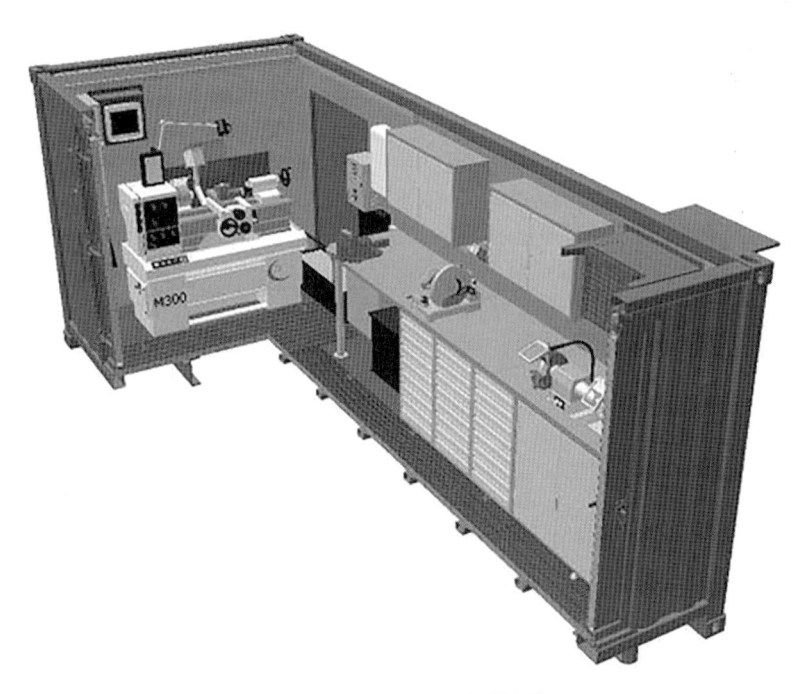

Cutaway illustration of a DMS

'Fitter Section in a Box'

In operational situations where no suitable hangar space was available, considerable use was made of inflatable shelters of various makes and sizes. This led to the idea of building the facilities a fitter section would be most likely to require into a 20-foot ISO container, and linking it to two inflatable working bays, one either side. The resulting 'Fitter Section in a Box' (FSIAB) was developed as a UOR using modified PPRF containers. It was deployed in Afghanistan, where it was very well received, not least because it provided warm and comfortable working conditions when the temperature outside was freezing. Its main limitation, from the user point of view, was that it was not possible to get lift (in the form of a SV(R) crane) into the working bay.

OPTRONIC REPAIR

If one analysed an armoured vehicle from the 1950s, it would be possible to break it down into electro-mechanical systems (or purely mechanical systems), which would be repaired by a Vehicle Mechanic, possibly assisted by a Vehicle Electrician; electronic systems, the radios, repaired by a Telecommunications Technician; optical systems in the form of sights or viewing devices, repaired by an Instrument Technician; armaments, repaired by a Gun Fitter or Armourer; and if the movement of the turret was electronically controlled one would call on a Control Equipment Technician (oddly, always referred to as an 'ECE') to repair it.

In a modern armoured vehicle (or 'platform'), things are very different. First of all, the sight is likely to be a combination day/night sight incorporating thermal imaging/image intensification technology, linked to a laser range finder and possibly a ballistic computer, which electronically injects an aiming mark. The sighting system is therefore a combination of electronic and optical equipment, hence the phrase 'optronic'. Many other systems within the vehicle may have an electronic component, which is likely to be integrated with another system. This leads to the notion that one is dealing not so much with a 'vehicle' as a 'platform' incorporating a 'system of systems'. This had driven the rationalisation of REME's trade structure, reflecting a requirement for a deep understanding of a specific trade discipline to be overlaid with the ability to deal with a multi-technology system.

Optronic systems, or others driven by electronics, should be designed so that the major electronic parts are packaged into units, which are easily removable, and are therefore called Line Replaceable Units (LRUs). These may be conceptually thought of as electronic 'black boxes'; some LRUs actually look like black boxes, others not at all. They all involve an input and an output normally through one or two connecters, which link with interconnecting cable(s), but sometimes a human interface is involved in the form of a switch or keypad.

Platform Repair
In principle, platform repair involves, first, identifying that there is a fault, second, diagnosing which LRU or interconnecting cable is causing the fault, and then, finally, either fixing the fault in situ or replacing the LRU. In practice, this is not always as simple as it sounds, and the process of diagnosis is not always straightforward. This may be done in the following ways.

Guesswork/Elimination. In theory, if one changes half the LRUs in a faulty system and that does not fix the problem, changing the other half should do the trick. In practice, an experienced technician is unlikely to go that far, as he will often be able to make a well-educated guess at where the problem lies, with a good chance of success.

Built-in Test Equipment. Electronic Built-in Test Equipment (BITE) (either 'press to test' or continuously running) offers something better. In addition to helping a technician with diagnosis, BITE may warn the user of a problem and possibly help him resolve it without calling for REME help. The quality of BITE is important. Developing good BITE may not be easy, and, in the case of complex systems, the task may actually be more technically demanding than developing the system itself. In the case of AS90 self-propelled artillery gun and Challenger 2 tank, REME technical staff spent a lot of time and effort helping the contractors to develop good BITE, and avoid the temptation to cut their costs by fudging results or not doing a complete Failure Mode Effects and Criticality Analysis (FMECA). BITE for such complex systems will never be 100% correct but the difference between good and poor BITE can have serious knock-on effects down the support chain. Many car owners will have found spurious or incorrect fault indications – a surprising number of car owners would also have been horrified if they knew how often they paid for an expensive replacement 'black box' to be unnecessarily replaced, either because their garage got its diagnosis wrong, or saw an easy and profitable way to effect a repair.

Plug-in Test. Owners taking modern cars to a garage will often find the mechanic plugging a laptop or handheld electronic test device into a diagnostic socket in their car. This is very much the way things are moving in the Army as well. New vehicles and platforms generally come into service with special-to-system test sets, or test sets with special-to-system software on them to complement any BITE and help REME technicians to diagnose faults. In many cases, the function of these is to interrogate built-in commercial software.

Electronic Off Platform Repair
The fate of LRUs once they have been removed depends on the relevant repair policy. They may be returned directly to the manufacturer for repair, or may go to second line for what now tends to be called Off Platform Repair (OPR). This may be done by the OPR Company of a REME battalion deployed in a 'force support' role. Alternatively, a REME Electronic Repair Vehicle (ERV) may deploy in any suitable forward location, sometimes collocated with their supported units acting as a Forward Repair Team or Intimate Support Team.

One important function that may be carried out at second line is a screening test. A proportion of LRUs may prove to be No Fault Found (NFF) and be reusable. This figure may be significant; for example, at one point around 40% of a key Multiple Launch Rocket System (MLRS) LRU were deemed faulty, as they were being found to be NFF. If these had all been sent back for Level 4 repair in Luxembourg through NAMSA (NATO Maintenance and Supply Agency (now NATO Support Agency)), the repair pool of spare assemblies would have been inadequate to support MLRS on operations during Operation GRANBY (the first Gulf War). LRUs may be repaired as well as screened. The classic second line repair concept sees the LRU as comprising a 'box' containing a 'motherboard' and a number of Printed Circuit Boards (PCBs). Second line diagnostics identifies which of the PCBs is faulty, and replaces it from a stock, which is replenished from manufacturers or Level 4 repairers. In practice, things are not quite like that as technicians often use their knowledge and experience to decide the optimum repair approach in any particular case. If the operational system warrants it, this could include cannibalisation; making one good LRU out of two that did not work.

General Purpose Automatic Test Equipment
By the end of the 1970s, the Army was seeing a lot of new equipment arriving with a significant electronic element. Each came with its own set of second line special-to-type Special Tools and Test Equipment (STTE).

REME trucks groaned under the weight of all these adapters, test sets and rigs. In many cases, common elements such as signal generators and other elements of automatic test equipment (ATE) were more or less replicated in several sets of second line STTE. REME's solution, accepted in 1980, was to develop a vehicle-borne General Purpose Automatic Test Equipment (GPATE). This was to be a combined Digital and Analogue Test Equipment called DIANA, which incorporated many of the common elements found in ATE, and was fitted into a container body that could be carried on a 4 x 4 truck. The intention was that future equipment suppliers would not provide standalone test systems, but interfaces that would allow their 'black boxes' to be tested on DIANA to the level required for second line (Level 3) screening and repair. These interfaces were called Application Test Packages (ATP).

A similar philosophy was applied to thermal imaging equipment, and the General Purpose Thermal Imaging Repair Facility (GPTIRF) was similarly fitted into a vehicle-borne container body. The complex sighting systems in Challenger 2, however, required a new specialist repair container, the Sight Repair Facility (SRF), another piece of mobile ATE.

DIANA in use

This general approach was well suited to its time, and worked well at the time. Such equipments as MLRS, AS90 and Challenger 2 all came with ATPs, which enabled effective second line repair to meet the operational needs of the time and the decade that followed. The GS companies of REME battalions were equipped with DIANA, GPTIRF and SRF. The systems worked well when they were static but one criticism, especially of DIANA, was that it was fairly 'brittle' and it took a technician a long time to get the system functioning after a road move.

Move on a few years, and the future of Army GPATE was starting to look questionable. In 2009, a review of the requirement for a new Digital Diagnostic Repair Facility concluded, and reported in the REME Journal 2009, that the most effective way ahead was for DIANA and GPTIRF to soldier on until 2025, albeit with modifications including re-containerisation into a DROPS-portable 20-foot ISO container. These would be used along with a new Combined Instrument Repair Facility (CIRF), also based on an ISO container, 13 of which were procured, the first coming into service in 2008. (**See Plate 42**)

Army GPATE – A Cloudy Future
The uncertainties about the future of Army GPATE were driven by a combination of technical, operational and organisational factors. Manufacturers have always needed ATE in their factories to test and subsequently repair the electronic equipment they produce. In the days when DIANA was conceived, such ATE would be quite possibly of mainframe size, and entirely unsuitable for militarisation and deployment in the field. By a couple of decades later, such ATE had shrunk in size, and the sort of functionality that DIANA provides could often be easily and cheaply built into a micro-electronic system. The idea of developing ATPs to interface with an increasingly antiquated Army ATE therefore became steadily less financially and technically sensible.

DIANA was developed in an era when the Army was contemplating deploying a whole Corps, complete with a large number of tanks, in mobile high-intensity combat. After the invasion of Iraq, attention tended to be focused on the subsequent counterinsurgency operations there, and later in Afghanistan. Much of the new equipment was acquired in response to UORs and, in many cases, involved equipment that was in use with other armies. The UK would therefore have a tendency to take what the suppliers could provide in the way of Level 1, 2 and 3 STTE.

The Army no longer controlled the maintenance policy (through its own ES organisation) for the equipment it procured. Procurement was in the hands of a largely civilianised DE&S headed by a civilian, who contemplated outsourcing the running of his organisation. It would be surprising if industry did not push for Level 1 – 4 maintenance policies, which involve the least repair by REME/the user, and the greatest continuing involvement for themselves. They would have an interest in entering contracts with Intellectual Property Rights (IPR) clauses that underpin this. The idea of being the monopoly supplier of a critical service, which would generate a revenue stream throughout the complete life cycle of an equipment is indeed a commercially attractive one. BGTI, E-SPIRE and TNTLS (see Chapter 20 ('Army Equipment and its Management')) are all repaired at Level 3 and 4 by the manufacturer. REME technicians do a 2-week Level 2 repair training course; on a turret trainer in the case of BGTI, and on hot rigs for E-SPIRE and TNTLS.

Counterinsurgency operations in Afghanistan featured a secure Main Operating Base (Camp Bastion) and a secure air link back to the industrial base. In this secure environment, after a time the Defence Support Group (DSG) and contractors were able to set up in-theatre repair operations. These and other issues were tackled in an insightful article by Major Ellen Bruce REME on optronic repair and the future of the REME technician, which was published in the REME Journal 2011. There was also concern that Whole Fleet Management would result in less equipment being normally held by units in peacetime, with much peacetime repair being done by contractors who would not be around in the event of an operational employment.

DIANA was 're-containered' but is now essentially out of service, GFTIRF and SRF are largely mothballed, and generally used for screening purposes only. This does not mean that REME is incapable of screening and sometimes repairing optronic equipment at first and second line. It has returned to the situation where there are a lot of special-to-system STTE and test/repair packages for such equipments as Bowman, Rapier (FSB2), Starstreak, various classified ECM equipments and many others.

The future of Army GPATE is therefore in doubt, and there are difficult questions to which there are no simple answers in a changing world. On the one hand, sticking with concepts because they worked in the past, and keep REME technicians employed, may be a very bad idea if it gets in the way of more efficient and pragmatic ways of working in partnership with industry. On the other hand, signing up to arrangements that are comfortable and profitable for industry, but only work in peacetime (and would fail a serious operational test) could also prove a very bad idea.

Vehicle Type	Unit Establishment (after transition)				
	Reactive Force			Adaptive Force	
	Armd CS Bn	AA Bn	FS Bn	CS Bn	Reserve Bn
CRAARV	6				
Warrior Variants	16				
Atlas Variants	4				
Bulldog Variants	13				
PM Variants	41	2	35	32	
MAN SV Variants	116	141	179	104	58

Figure 17.1: Illustrative Army 2020 allocation of heavy vehicles for REME battalions

CHAPTER 18

SUPPORT FOR ARMY EQUIPMENT – AN OVERVIEW

During the Cold War, any student of this topic would have learned by way of introduction that 'logistics is a single-Service responsibility'. Also, that in the Army three main Corps were involved in logistics. They were the RCT (Royal Corps of Transport), which moved things about; the RAOC (Royal Army Ordnance Corps) stored them, procured replacement items (including spare parts), and managed commodities and B Vehicles (essentially unarmoured wheeled vehicles); and REME, which repaired Army equipment at all levels. This included doing complete overhauls of major equipments (such as tanks) and assemblies (such as engines and 'black boxes') in largely civilianised base workshops, or by contract.

In broad terms, industry built new equipment, and REME fixed it and upgraded it as necessary. Each Corps was headed by a two-star Director General (DG) who might be regarded as having a dual (but closely intertwined) set of responsibilities. The first was concerned with managing the functions carried out by his Corps. The second concerned management of his Corps itself (its recruitment, training, manning, equipment, and regimental business). The DGs were responsible to the Army's Quartermaster General (QMG) who had overall responsibility for the Army's logistics.

This 'three pillar' structure had been arrived at for historical reasons, and was successful in delivering operational availability. This was because good men and true, who fully understood their own organisation and had the best interests of the Army at heart, cooperated to make the system work. That system itself, however, had some inherent drawbacks and disadvantages for a modern army.

Responsibility for equipment availability was uncomfortably split. RAOC provided spares; REME did repairs but could do little without spares. This provided inherent scope for things to go wrong at a technical level, as well as offering the temptation to engage in a blame apportionment contest if things went wrong. Post Design Services and modifications to equipment, which might improve availability and reduce spares and repair costs, were controlled and funded outside the Army by the Ministry of Defence Procurement Executive (MoD PE).

Costs were aggregated at a high level, and funding tended to be aligned to organisations and 'inputs'; for example, separate votes for REME manpower costs and Army spares. This concept certainly made finance simple, and kept down the number of staff involved. It also meant that nobody had a clear idea of the actual cost of many of the 'outputs'; for example, the cost of operating particular equipments, and the cost of supporting particular formations and their activities. Managers and decision-makers therefore lacked a holistic view of the cost of supporting equipment. Many, even at very senior level, did not actually hold budgets themselves, and thus had little incentive to look for trade-offs or better ways of doing things that would reduce their overall cost to the public purse.

The split of responsibilities made it difficult to manage complete processes such as assembly 'repair loops', which involved removal of defective items by REME, transport by RCT, base overhaul by REME, storage by RAOC, and refitting by REME.

Many other armies had successfully adopted a 'two pillar' structure to perform the same roles as the British Army's 'three pillar' arrangement. A Logistic Support Review (LSR) headed by the Army's QMG concluded that a 'two pillar' structure for the Army would allow a more rational re-alignment of responsibilities, and would have the additional advantage of allowing a two-star headquarters to be cut at a time when there was pressure to reduce staff. A new 'two pillar' top-level organisation took effect from April 1992 with different responsibilities.

REME provided the framework for an 'Equipment Support' (ES) 'pillar'. This was headed by Major General Mike Heath, as Director General Equipment Support (Army) (DGES(A)). He was a late REME officer, who had played a key role in the LSR in his capacity as the Director of Support Planning (Army). It took over staff responsibility for the supply management of equipment spare parts from RAOC, along with responsibility for the management of B Vehicles. REME retained its name and essentially those who had been capbadged REME continued largely to do what they had been doing before, albeit with 'ES' in their title instead of 'EME'.

A new Corps, the Royal Logistic Corps (RLC), was formed from those formerly capbadged RCT and RAOC, as well as a number of smaller Corps. The two-star RCT DG became head of a new 'Logistic Support'

(Log Sp) 'pillar', which took over most of the rest of the old RAOC's organisation, thereby effectively taking control of the Army supply chain and depot organisation. Nomenclature could be a bit confusing as both 'ES' and 'Log Sp' were still seen as elements of 'logistics' (and part of QMG's 'logistics' empire).

THE ORGANISATION OF THE DIRECTOR GENERAL EQUIPMENT SUPPORT (ARMY)

The New Organisation
From 6 April 1992, DGES(A)'s HQ comprised five directorates headed by Directors of Equipment Support (DES) numbered 1–5 (all brigadiers). It also included a Finance and Secretariat (F&S) organisation headed by a Grade 6 civil servant. Here is an outline of their responsibilities and the links to the previous organisation.

DES 1 was the lineal descendent of the DEME (Org and Trg) function, whose role is explained in Volume 2 of Craftsmen of the Army. His organisation included ES 11 (organisation, deployment, planning and resources) as well as ES 12 (corporate planning, secretariat, training policy and civilian management). His primary job was to manage the Corps of REME.

DES 2 was the lineal descendent of DEngPol(A) and now included an element of QMG's London Staff (QMG 4). His organisation included ES 21 (ES Information Systems policy, reliability and availability), ES 22 (ES plans, Integrated Logistic Support projects, development and management) and ES 23 (ES services, Total Quality Management, ES publications, projects' procedures cell, standards). In essence, he was responsible for technical policy and support issues, which were not equipment specific.

DES 3 was the lineal descendent of DEE 1 and was the support manager for electronics, guided weapons and aircraft. His organisation included ES 31 (communications and CIS), ES 32 (guided weapons, radar and general electronics including test equipment) and ES 33 (engineering authority for Army and Royal Marines aircraft).

DES 4 was the lineal descendent of DEE 2 and was responsible for armoured vehicles and weapons. His organisation included ES 41 (armoured vehicles and workshop equipment) and ES 42 (weapons, plant, marine and railways). He gained responsibility for Royal Engineers specialist equipment, but relinquished that for Army aircraft (mentioned under DES 3).

DES 5 had effectively moved across from the old RAOC organisation. He brought in senior-level expertise on the supply management of spares, and the management of the B Vehicle fleet. His organisation included ES 51 (planning and budgets), ES 52 (B Vehicles and general mechanical equipments) and ES 53 (technical spares procurement).

Head of ES (F&S) was responsible for general finance and secretariat support, and specifically for managing DGES(A)'s Higher Level Budget (HLB) and the REME Intermediate Higher Level Budget (IHLB) within the Army's Individual Training Organisation (ITO).

DGES(A)'s Evolving Responsibilities and Organisation

DGES(A) had a very wide range of responsibilities. He had functional responsibility for ES across the Army. The ES function reached all the way from its HQ at Andover to the most junior REME tradesmen at unit level. At divisional level, the ES function was headed up by a Colonel (who took over the tasks previously carried out jointly by REME and RAOC Lieutenant Colonels). DGES(A) was answerable to the Army Board (through the QMG) for the operational availability of its equipment. DGES(A) directly or indirectly controlled all the key organisations critical to the delivery of ES. These included:

- a spares procurement organisation (and its budget for spares), which was inherited from RAOC and subsequently turned into an agency to become the Equipment Support Spares Procurement Agency (ESSPA)
- REME's base repair organisation, which was slimmed down and also became an agency to become the Army Base Repair Organisation (ABRO) – see Chapter 19 ('Technical Support and Base Repair Agencies')
- REME's technical support organisations (organisations such as the former Vehicles and Weapons Branch, and Electronics Branch), which were brought together in the form of a single agency, the Army Technical Support Agency (ATSA) – see Chapter 19 ('Technical Support and Base Repair Agencies')
- activities at training organisations, including a new School of Equipment Support (Army) that was a development of the former REME Officers' School – whilst the large REME training organisations at Bordon and Arborfield were 'owned' by the Army's

Individual Training Organisation (subsequently to develop into the Army Training and Recruitment Agency (ATRA)), DGES(A) could exert significant control because of his budgetary responsibilities (explained in more detail in Chapter 23 ('Individual Training Organisations')).

The nature of DGES(A)'s role was such that he had broad influence on policies and plans related to equipment, both during the procurement and in-service phases, and for providing technical direction to users, as well as to REME maintainers. DGES(A) was the 'Head of the Corps of REME' and had responsibility for all Corps and regimental matters.

REME AND THE PROCUREMENT OF NEW EQUIPMENT

From its inception, part of REME's role has been to influence the design of new equipment to ensure that it was operationally supportable, and fit for use when the user required it. Its contribution evolved over the years, and to get things in perspective it is useful to describe the start of the story in the early-1970s.

Equipment was procured in a tri-Service MoD PE. Project teams working on Army equipment reported to the senior Army representative, the Master General of the Ordnance (MGO). Procurement was largely from UK companies, and the MoD usually paid for development, and production on a 'cost plus' basis. Separate contracts were let for an initial stock of spares, special tools, technical publications and other items necessary to launch the equipment into service.

There was no doubt that the Army was the 'customer'. The Chief of the General Staff was both responsible for carrying out Army operations, and for stating what equipment he needed to do so (through his Operational Requirements (OR) staff). When new equipment was procured, lead responsibility for operating the equipment passed from MoD PE to the Army from the In-Service Date (ISD), normally the date when the first complete unit was equipped with usable equipment. Lead responsibility for supporting the equipment passed from MoD PE to the Army (QMG and REME) at the so called Quartermaster Readiness Date (QRD). Ideally, ISD and QRD would be the same date.

The system was elegant in theory, but there were many pitfalls in practice. There was an obvious potential 'pass the parcel' problem between MoD PE (MGO) and the Army (QMG). OR staff were also often keen to get the latest operational 'bells and whistles' incorporated into equipment, and to deploy it as quickly as possible. They, with procurement teams and contractors, had an incentive to cut corners (and costs) on matters to do with reliability and support issues. Much research and development work was done 'in-house' at this stage, so pinning responsibility on contractors (or anyone else) was not always easy. Contractors certainly had no commercial incentive to supply reliable equipment.

By the 1980s, the consequences of this approach were all too apparent. The Chieftain tank was a very good example of how all this could evolve. It was described as being 'the best tank in the world provided it breaks down in a good fire position'. It was hugely expensive to maintain (the life of its major assemblies was typically one-tenth of its German equivalent), and it was not unknown for armoured battlegroups training in Canada to find they had but a single working tank at the end of their battlegroup exercise.

Through the 1980s, realisation grew that better logistic support planning had to be built into the procurement process; also that REME had the technical expertise to provide leadership in this field. REME officers played key roles within the Army's logistic support planning organisation set up under QMG in London. Technical branches provided input on reliability and maintainability to the procurement process. HQ DGEME took the lead on ideas for 'contracting for reliability'. Most important, however, was that a REME Lieutenant Colonel, the Engineering Support Planning Officer (ESPO), was allocated to key projects from an early stage to make sure that all aspects of engineering support were effectively planned and coordinated to ensure a seamless transfer of responsibility for engineering support from MoD PE (the relevant MGO team) to the relevant REME equipment branch. ESPOs went on to play a key role in the successful fielding of the Warrior vehicle and the Challenger tank.

Challenger, however, posed some difficult problems for support planners, including the then Lieutenant Colonel Philip Corp REME working as the MGO Deputy Project Manager in London (and who later succeeded Major General Heath as DGES(A)), who came with a formidable personal understanding of technical and planning issues. Challenger was a development of a cancelled tank developed for Iran (the Shir). A high-level decision was taken to cancel the ambitious national MBT80 (Main Battle Tank for the 1980s) project and rescue Shir by accepting the tank for the British Army 'warts and all'. This limited the leverage it was possible for REME to apply to designers and manufacturers.

In the late-1980s, a novel procurement approach was tried for the new 155mm self-propelled artillery gun. The exercise was run as a competition, with contractors being asked to offer a fixed price contract. This was to include not only delivery of the main equipments, but a concurrent logistic support package that would ensure the guns could be fully supported from the time they were delivered. This allowed the procurement process to be greatly speeded up, and transferred much risk to the contractor.

It was clearly crucial to get the contract right, with the support package being the longest and most complex part of the contract. The ESPO, with the support and advice from REME colleagues, had a key role to play in doing this. Based on REME advice, an In-Service Reliability Demonstration (ISRD) programme was built into the contract. It was appreciated that maintenance policy should be the core around which the support plan needed to be integrated, and it was accepted that REME (as the Maintenance Authority) owned it. Maintenance policy drove the requirement for spare parts and repairable assemblies, the tools and technical training required by operators and repairers at every level, the contents of support publications, the contractual rights to allow the ABRO to overhaul equipments and assemblies, and much else.

As the senior logistician seconded to the procurement team, the ESPO took the lead in coordinating and integrating the support package, and actually called the resulting plan the 'Integrated Logistic Support' plan. Payment milestones were linked to progress with the support package, and to satisfactory reports by REME artificers embedded within the contractor's organisation. It was accepted that REME, as the Maintenance Authority, 'owned' maintenance policy, and after a tussle with the project contract staff it was agreed that the ESPO should vet the wording of the support package items in the final contract. The winner of the competition was AS90 (Artillery System for the 1990s) manufactured by Vickers Shipbuilding and Engineering Ltd (VSEL). The AS90 project proved swift and successful, and by the early-1990s the Army had a reliable and highly capable new self-propelled artillery gun in service.

This expanded role for the ESPO worked well at the time as it had clear advantages. The ESPO was a senior REME officer who was both a professional engineer, and had in-depth practical knowledge of how the Army operated and supported its equipment. As a Grade 1 'Weapons' Staff Officer, he had experience of the MoD's procurement system, and had been involved with (or exposed) to commercial and contractual environments.

Although seconded to a project team, he did not work exclusively for it. He was also responsible for the support of in-service artillery equipment, and was also the ESPO for MLRS (Multiple Launch Rocket System). He was based in the Equipment Branch (EME 7) responsible for the support of all Army vehicles and he could turn for advice to its head (then Colonel Alan Sharman (late REME)). Colonel Sharman later became Colonel Project Manager Logistic Vehicles, then the one-star Director of Tank Programmes and, finally, the two-star Director General Land Systems in MoD PE – the latter two posts had never previously been held by a non-combat arms officer. The ESPO's job was made somewhat easier because AS90 had started as a Private Venture (PV) project, with a sound basic design intended for overseas sales and came without earlier MoD 'baggage'.

He therefore had a network of colleagues and contacts (not all REME) through his work, who could alert him to (and advise on) such topics as Intellectual Property Rights, issues linked with base repair, or problems associated with the repair of obsolescent electronic equipment (and how to avoid them). As a bonus, through MLRS, he became familiar with the practicalities of US Integrated Logistic Support (ILS) procedures (further explained later in this Chapter). Crucially, he represented the 'customer', and he was ultimately answerable to an Army organisation, which would inherit the problem of supporting the equipment that was being procured (not the MoD PE Project Manager). This was a crucial factor in applying leverage to ensure that the final contract was the one the Army needed, not the one the MoD contracts staff were nearly persuaded to agree to by the Prime Contractor.

The next major armoured vehicle project was Challenger 2, which resulted in Challenger being renamed Challenger 1 for obvious reasons. Colonel Corp played an important role in the support aspect of this project, initially when on QMG's planning staff (as Colonel QMG 4), and subsequently when he became DES 4 when HQ DGES(A) formed in 1992. By this stage, the plan to implement ILS meant that the REME officer responsible for coordinating support aspects was called the ILS Manager (ILSM) rather than the ESPO. He now also came under the direct line management of the Challenger 2 Procurement Project Manager, but took his technical direction from the head of the relevant ES branch (Colonel ES 41). These changes were perhaps less significant than they seemed.

Detailed direction on ILS methodology was not available, and in practice the project followed very much the same pattern as AS90 (Colonel ES 41 also happened to be the former ESPO AS90). Like AS90, Challenger 2 had started as a PV project, and broadly speaking the procurement programme ran very successfully, often for much the same reasons as AS90. The tank entered service in June 1998, several months later than planned. The contract included a requirement for an ISRD, which was done on an early production tank chosen at random, before deliveries, and payment, could commence. The number of turret system failures exceeded the maximum permitted, so all the tanks coming off the production line were placed in controlled humidity storage at the factory until fixes had been developed, the ISRD passed, and the fixes had been retrofitted. No 'warts and all' this time. Challenger 2 subsequently proved its reliability and supportability during the invasion of Iraq, and in its aftermath. A post operational report by 2 Battalion REME on Operation TELIC 2, following a visit by Force Development Staff, stated:

> 'Challenger 2 was the star of the show in Basra. The up-armoured Challenger 2 was a significant capability against a mixed non-traditional enemy'.

The Advantages of ILS

UK support planners had long been aware of the need properly to integrate the various aspects of support planning and managing support for new equipment. Whilst they achieved that very effectively for AS90 (and MLRS), there was an element of 'making it up as they went along', which meant the need to justify, explore and explain issues as the projects moved forward. Decisions were based on experience backed up by relatively crude analytical processes. Something more structured and formal was clearly required. Meanwhile, the US forces had already come to similar conclusions some time before and put a vast amount of money and academic effort into producing a comprehensive, structured methodology for dealing with support issues. This was called Integrated Logistic Support (ILS) and the procedures for applying it were set out in US MILSTD 1388. This offered a lot of advantages as a potential 'oven ready' answer to the UK requirement.

The UK would be using the same processes as its major ally (as a spin-off, UK defence contractors would be well placed to bid for US contract work). The ILS methodology was intended to minimise whole life equipment costs. It could therefore be presented as a cost-saving exercise. It was possible to ride on the back of the work done by the Americans. ILS was effectively a new discipline, which came with a comprehensive 'how to do it' guide.

Once the methodology had been validated and accepted by the Treasury and UK military officialdom it would no longer be necessary to argue specific support issues on a case-by-case basis with financial scrutineers, or with operational staff who had little interest in support issues and wanted to rush equipment into service. In theory, if the ILS process had followed the book it must have come up with the most cost-effective support solution; end of argument unless anyone could prove that the ILS exercise had not been done properly. This was something few officials had the technical competence to do.

UK Adopts ILS
The RAF was initially ahead of the Army with ILS, due to the experience gained when the US Marine Corps acquired the AV-8B Harrier aircraft. Nevertheless, REME officers played a key role in getting ILS adopted as UK tri-Service policy in 1989. One of these was the Director of Support Planning (Army), Brigadier Heath, assisted by Colonel QMG 4, Colonel Corp. Later, as DGES(A), Major General Heath tasked DES 2 with developing ILS policy, and contributing to the production of an 'anglicised' version of ILS, which was to become DEFSTAN 0060. ILS Managers (ILSM) were to be embedded in procurement teams, and although these were under the line management of procurement project teams, they received functional direction from DES 2 on policy matters, and guidance from the relevant equipment branches on technical matters. In principle, it seemed at last that:
- support issues would be properly and rigorously addressed throughout the procurement project phase
- the 'pass the parcel' problem between MoD PE (Centre) and QMG (Army) would be eliminated; as when DGES(A) took over responsibility for new equipments he would be taking over support arrangements that he was completely familiar with, and to which his staff had contributed.

ILS in Practice
In practice, life was never going to prove that easy. Once formal UK ILS guidance had been set out, it provided a complex and comprehensive set of

procedures, that could be applied to the procurement of everything from a mousetrap to a moon rocket. To apply it effectively and economically, the procedures had to be tailored to the particular circumstances of the project to which it was applied. A REME officer with the qualifications of an old-style ESPO was ideally placed to do this, and his professional and military experience (and a wide set of useful contacts) should enable him to make the sound judgement necessary to make ILS work well. The need for this was not always clearly understood, and ILS started to be seen by some as offering a defined set of mandatory procedures a generalist manager could follow.

Based on this reasoning, the ILSM did not need to be a military officer (let alone a REME officer), or have any specific support management or engineering expertise. This could lead to a situation where a civilian ILSM, who did not really understand his business, could be working under the direct line management of a civilian project manager who had only a rudimentary understanding of support issues. This increased the potential for things to go wrong (with REME personnel often being the ones called in to get things back on track). Because ILS processes could be complex and were not always well understood, ILS-related tasks (such as Logistic Support Analysis) were often outsourced. Some contractors undoubtedly saw ILS as licence to make money by doing expensive analytical work, which was not really useful because it rested on highly questionable assumptions (that they understood, but their customer did not). It was also not unknown for them subtly to build in study assumptions that would produce outcomes in their commercial interests. To summarise, ILS, properly tailored by those who fully understood how to apply it had great merits; in the hands of those who did not, and approached it with a 'tick-box' mentality, it was likely to prove anything but a panacea.

THE EQUIPMENT SUPPORT ORGANISATION 1992–1999

When the Equipment Support Organisation (ESO) formed, many saw it as the old REME organisation with a spares supply management organisation and some additional functions bolted onto it. There may have been an element of truth in this at the time but, in reality, the change was much more fundamental. In principle, 'ES' was a function, and it no longer mapped accurately across to 'REME' (an organisation – a Corps of Army engineers) and the divergence would grow. From the point of view of the REME historian, from 1992 to 1999 the 'Head of the ESO' was also the 'Head of REME'. So many REME personnel worked at HQ DGES(A) that it would be remiss not to provide an overview of what happened there during that time.

The period was characterised by much change and intellectual activity. The new QMG, General Sir John Learmont, a late RA officer of great energy and force of character, had moved his headquarters from London with the formation of the ESO. He told DGES(A) how impressed he was by the 'powerhouse' of ideas and initiatives coming from the ES directorates and their hand-picked one-star directors. REME was led by numerate people, many professional engineers with significant exposure to commercial management practices. They were well aware that the Services had to downsize and make savings following the end of the Cold War (and the first Gulf War). A good many ideas for change came from within REME and fed into the new ESO, which now had in its hands the means to deliver better equipment reliability and availability (at lower cost). It was commonly said (in REME circles at least) that many of the best ideas for improving the support of equipment originated in the bar of the Corps Officers' Mess (West Court), and this most probably had an element of truth at the time.

Devolution of Budgetary Responsibility

The process of devolving budgetary responsibility was driven by Michael Heseltine (then Secretary of State for Defence) and his New Management Strategy (NMS) of the mid-1980s. He understood the way in which military finance was linked to 'parliamentary votes' for specific purposes; for example, 'Vote 2K1' covered all Army spare parts. He appreciated that the way in which these votes were managed meant that many senior managers had little idea of the true cost of their organisations, and often little direct budgetary accountability for the costs their organisations generated.

The broad idea of NMS was to align budgetary authority with operational responsibility, and to bring in management ideas from the private sector. The concept offered great benefits, but was far from easy to implement. The private sector is driven by different forces from the public sector, and has different constraints and freedoms. Practices do not, therefore, always read across easily from one sector to another. For example, the 'just-in-time' concept that is sound in commercial or manufacturing practice where demand is steady, is not easy to apply in the case of military items that are not in production, and for which there may be surge demands. The military also pose a particular problem in that many of their activities are highly specialised, and appropriate expertise often cannot simply be bought in from the market.

Very different specialised activities also tend to be highly interdependent on each other. For example, equipment, training, logistics, and engineering must all mesh together to deliver operational capability, which is vulnerable to a failure in any of these areas. The delegation of financial and operational responsibility required by NMS therefore required new means of coordination, notably by using formal 'Customer-Supplier Agreements' (CSA) as a means of managing relationships between budget holders. Within the ESO, DGES(A) devolved budgetary responsibilities to directorates and branches, which necessarily became much more involved in financial issues, and therefore needed financial staff to help them manage these responsibilities.

Early Achievements of the ESO

The combination of budgetary delegation and the new organisation, which helped engineers, supply experts and financiers to get their heads together, did not take long to deliver both significant financial savings and better ways of doing things. Given his involvement with industry and equipment procurement, Major General Heath was well aware of the major efficiency gains made in the commercial world in the 1970s-1980s through the introduction of modern quality systems. He was determined that the ESO should match up to the best commercial standards, and drove the introduction of a system called 'Total Quality' (TQ).

This involved critically examining processes in conjunction with those involved with a view to improving them. Guidance was produced for the whole Corps and the REME Officers' School (renamed the School of Equipment Support (Army)) provided instruction. Inevitably, such a positive and structured approach to change led to many specific successes and improvements in effectiveness and efficiency. The ideas behind TQ have continued to live on in the form of REME's commitment to 'lean' management.

Setting Up Agencies

One of the ideas that stemmed from NMS was the forming of public sector organisations into semi-autonomous agencies. They would be headed by Chief Executives, who would be given targets and budgets, and were expected to run their agencies on a quasi-commercial basis.

Two important parts of the old REME organisation were set up as agencies – the base repair organisations (which became the ABRO) and the Technical Branches and Authorities (which were brought together as the ATSA). Their stories are told in Chapter 19 ('Technical Support and Base Repair Agencies').

DGES(A) was the 'owner' of these two agencies. Additionally, he 'owned' what became the Equipment Support Spares Procurement Agency (ESSPA), which was much more an 'ex-RAOC' rather than 'ex-REME' organisation. He did not directly control REME training as it had been decided that training should go into the newly-formed Army Training and Recruitment Agency (ATRA); however, he had responsibility for that part of their budget that was devoted to REME training. The in-depth repair of helicopters was not in his direct control, as it had gone into a 'purple' agency, the Defence Helicopter Support Authority (DHSA), with Brigadier Rob Jones (late REME) as its first head, but funding for the support of Army Aviation flowed through his budget. Apart from these limitations, DGES(A) had financial responsibility for all the levers that controlled the support of Army in-service equipment.

Post Design Services and Modifications

Post Design Services were services provided by equipment manufacturers and/or design authorities after equipment had entered service. They might involve anything from a significant upgrade programme to a minor modification, or replacement of an item with a better/more readily available one. Traditionally, they were the responsibility of the MoD PE and their contract staff. Around 1995, the responsibility (and financial cover for it) was transferred to the relevant equipment branches in HQ DGES(A), which used QMG's contract staff to deal with contractual aspects.

This change made a lot of sense as the equipment branches were perfectly placed to decide what was really useful. Also, for ensuring that effective plans were made for introducing modifications either during base-level overhauls, or at first or second line. Poorly planned implementation of modifications had been a weakness in the past. In the case of the armoured vehicle fleet, the transfer resulted in a hard-headed review of the programme, with proper plans being made for implementing genuinely useful modifications, but many of the others being scrapped. Many of those scrapped were considered to be a 'nice little earner' for the contractor, and not genuinely useful to the user. Significant savings resulted from this exercise.

The Multidisciplinary Approach

Clearly by this point, the equipment branches at Andover had moved on a long way from being purely engineering organisations. Engineering remained a major core function, but branches included specialists involved in asset management (which was not an original REME function), supply management, finance and budgets, and contract management. ES branches at Andover had therefore become very much multidisciplinary organisations, well placed to coordinate support and explore trade-offs.

Hierarchical and Functional Organisations, and Multidisciplinary Teams

The UK economy was still struggling in the mid-1990s and, faced with increasing competitive pressures, civilian firms were looking for ways to cut their cost bases. Two ideas for making organisations 'leaner' were very much in vogue. One was 'delayering' by taking out layers of management. The other was to do away with hierarchical functional organisations by hiring functional experts, who did not need functional direction, and embedding them in multidisciplinary teams. DGES(A)'s HQ was essentially a multidisciplinary functional organisation with a largely hierarchical structure based on sections//branches/directorates.

Thoughts for organisational change at Andover therefore moved in the direction of 'delayering' and working in multidisciplinary teams with more autonomy, headed by a manager whose main role was to coordinate the work of the team's various functional experts. Civilian human resources theory was moving in the direction of recruiting against the 'competencies' required for a job rather than promoting on the basis of successful specialist experience. This could open the door to organisations being run by those with appropriate management competencies, not necessarily linked to any specific military cap badge experience, or indeed any military or professional engineering experience.

Civilianisation and Contractorisation

Against this background, one obvious way to make savings was to replace military staff by civilians with appropriate competencies where possible, given that civilian staff were generally significantly cheaper to employ. 'Outsourcing' was another avenue for cutting costs, which was also enjoying a wave of popularity at that time in many sectors of the economy. The MoD had actually already been looking in this direction since the mid-1980s. This had led to significant gains early on, as managers were quick to realise that it was much cheaper, for example, to get a contractor to cut the grass in barracks than to own capital equipment and employ a civil servant to do it. Once the 'low fruit' had been plucked, however, the process of further contracting out became more difficult or risky.

In the commercial world, enthusiasm for outsourcing was to become tempered over time with the realisation that contracting out 'core functions' could be a bad idea, and previously outsourced functions started sometimes being brought back 'in house'; for example, the maintenance of rail track. Politicians and senior MoD officials under continuous pressure to make further savings were naturally keen to see if they could pull the proverbial rabbit out of a hat by embracing contractorisation. Those who were not commercially or technically savvy could naturally be vulnerable to commercial lobbying, which sometimes came with the heady whiff of possible lucrative future employment. It was easy to be persuaded that the Army's technical experts were parochial meddlers and not to spot that convincing consultants or salesmen could have a hidden commercial agenda, and were not always as capable or knowledgeable as they made out. In truth, contractors tend not to have their own unlimited pool of expertise and the best results are often obtained when they work closely with military experts.

The successful Challenger 2 project was a case in point. The Procurement Project Manager (privately) pointed out that although the project was supposed to be a 'hands-off, eyes-on' (with the contractor doing everything and MoD merely looking on from the side), in fact by the mid-1990s there were 39 Army personnel (many of them REME) directly involved in developing the tank and its support package. There was a fair amount of arm-wrestling between the contractor and REME's technical experts, but their input was greatly respected and the outcome was a very successful project. The Project Manager in question felt he had received his reward in 2003 when he learned how delighted the soldiers and officers of his regiment had been with the performance of Challenger 2 during the invasion of Iraq.

Top-down Management, Efficiencies and the Role of the 'Central Pillar'

The public sector, in general, had moved into an era when efficiencies were frequently sought through 'top-down' initiatives instigated in Whitehall, and linked with budgetary and performance targets. The MoD was by no means exempt from these. Some were steered at ministerial level, such as the Defence Costs Study of 1994, also called 'Front Line First'. This sought to do away with 18,700 posts across the Services, and was based on the wearily familiar idea that it was a good idea to 'cut the tail without cutting the teeth'.

There were also further ongoing year-on-year requirements to find efficiency savings, either in absolute terms or in terms of a percentage of a budget, which were cascaded downwards. Initiatives could also be instigated at QMG level. Traditionally, the QMG had been a senior officer who did not come from a logistic corps. Obviously, personalities and circumstances varied, but broadly he was seen as someone who came without logistic 'baggage', who could test ideas, bang heads together within the world of logistics when necessary, ensure that logistic plans met the Army's needs, and represent logistics issues at Army Board level. This was a concept that often worked very well.

Following the Logistic Support Review, QMG moved from London to Andover where he was collocated with his two-star DGs of ES and Logistic Support, the two support 'pillars'. He also set up a 'central pillar' under his two-star Chief of Staff. Its role was to oversee and coordinate the other two 'pillars', and deal with other QMG matters that did not clearly fall into either area. In the brave new world of budgets, targets and action plans, it would be surprising if in due course the QMG would not want to take a more proactive and direct role in managing the organisations responsible to him than had been the case hitherto. With the arrival of Lieutenant General Sam Cowan (late Royal Signals) in 1996, the Army got a QMG who clearly relished this challenge. He was to be assisted by Major General Kevin O'Donoghue (late Royal Engineers) as his Chief of Staff.

Initiative Overload
Initially, the concept of setting top-down budgetary targets was very fruitful. Savings targets were generally hit, although not always for the reasons initially envisaged. This was done without much real pain as there was still 'fat' in the system and those who headed up large functional organisations knew where to find it. Once the requirement to find further efficiency savings became recurrent, it became progressively more difficult to make painless savings, particularly as ever more functions were devolved to agencies, or contracted out. Operationally risky assumptions began increasingly to be made to allow targets to be met. Sometimes cost-saving initiatives either did not achieve the targets they were set, or were actually

counterproductive in financial terms. There were two broad reasons for this – unintended consequences and business process sub-optimisation.

Unintended Consequences. The law of unintended consequences seems to operate powerfully in the public sector and the greater the pace of change the more likely it is to take effect. For example, in the late-1990s, HQ QMG's 'central pillar' was much taken with the idea that savings could be made by disposing of slow-moving stock. A stock reduction exercise was launched. Targets were quickly met, efficiency savings were declared, and formal commendations made with significant publicity. Shortly after, it emerged that the repair pool of electronic assemblies for AS90 had disappeared. This was a stock of 'black boxes' unique to AS90, which had been procured cheaply as part of the support package. They were essential to the long-term support of the equipment and were extremely difficult and expensive to procure after the production line ceased. They had been scrapped, and had to be replaced at great expense, because they had not moved. They had not moved for good reason, because this aspect of support was still being provided by the contractor (but not for much longer).

Business Process Sub-Optimisation. A study by consultants commissioned by QMG's staff concluded that efficiency savings measures were often not achieving the desired effect because they were creating 'business process sub-optimisation'. This concept is perhaps best explained with an illustration. In the late-1990s, the regional Army HQ in York, pressed to make civilian savings, removed the civilian mechanics attached to TA units who provided essential vehicle maintenance. The local Commander ES's solution to the problem of keeping their vehicles fit for legal use was to get them transported by the Defence Transport and Movement Executive on low-loaders from the northeast of England to the Army Base Storage and Distribution Agency Vehicle Depot on the other side of the country. They were held there until they could be removed to an ABRO workshop for inspection/repair prior to going back to units the way they had come. The regional HQ had made its 'savings', the agencies involved had all increased their 'outputs', but clearly the cost to the public purse of achieving the same goal had hugely increased. Put simply, organisations under pressure to make savings they cannot sensibly achieve, look for ways to play 'beggar my neighbour' and either pass on costs to other budgetary areas or create additional deferred costs. The problem is by no means limited to the MoD, and perhaps helps explain why the cost of the public sector increased, and its productivity dropped, during a decade when seemingly endless top-down initiatives were launched.

Tri-Service Rationalisation
The Services evolved as large separate organisations with their own depots, supply chains, IT systems, and training organisations; for example, to train helicopter pilots and mechanics. With the Services getting smaller and relentless pressure for economies, the scope for making savings through rationalisation needed to be explored. Savings may be achieved in two broad ways – reorganisation and rationalisation.

Reorganisation. Reorganisation on a tri-Service basis (as 'purple' or 'Defence' organisations) seems at first sight the most obvious solution, and in some instances has clearly proved the best way to go. This approach is not without its pitfalls, however, as the Canadian forces, who took tri-Service rationalisation to its extreme in the 1970s, discovered. Management theory suggests that the most efficient organisations are often small, lean, focused on their customer needs, and staffed by people who are highly expert specialists at what they do. REME, for example, provided a highly specialised service. It had been kept 'lean' by the Army because its manpower comes out of the overall Army headcount and it had to compete for its resources against those who are well represented at the top level. It remained highly 'customer focused', not least because most of its manpower continued to be embedded within customer units, and the annual performance appraisals of many officers are written by their 'customer' commanders. At first sight, the option of rationalising three smaller (single-Service) organisations into one much larger Defence (tri-Service) organisation may offer the prospect of savings through cutting overheads. It can also carry the risk of any such benefits being outweighed by creating a larger organisation with additional layers of coordinating bureaucracy and more driven by internal dynamics. In short, a less expert, less 'customer focused' and less efficient organisation.

Rationalisation of Processes and Services. A less radical alternative is to rationalise processes, services and IT systems without radical reorganisation. The merits of the three Services using a completely integrated and interoperable supply chain are obvious. Provided the processes and IT systems are properly integrated, it may not necessarily matter greatly which Service 'owns' a particular resource, such as a depot or workshop. The Army, for example, happily uses the postal service without owning it in any way. A great deal of work was done at Andover during this period to lay the groundwork for rationalising procedures, both between the ES and Logistic Support organisations, and between the Services. In general, the 'central pillar' took a lead role in this work, but REME personnel, mainly in the ES organisation, made a major contribution.

Management Information Systems
The first DGES(A) recognised at the outset that the ES organisation lacked adequate Management Information Systems (MIS). He set up an Equipment Support Information System Strategy (ESISS), which was run by DES 2. A considerable amount of work was done over several years. An underlying problem was that the various attempts over the years to provide comprehensive/integrated MIS for the QMG area had met with limited success. A graphic representation of the various IT systems (single and tri-Service) being developed or actually in use at the time resulted in a diagram of almost nightmarish complexity, with overlaps/gaps/interoperability problems all too evident. In the late-1990s, QMG commissioned a consultancy study into ESISS. It concluded as a result that ESISS should be largely dropped, and solutions sought in the context of the wider logistic MIS requirements in the Services.

Coherence
It is not possible to explain in a few paragraphs all that happened at HQ DGES(A) during the time of the three REME DGES(A)s – Major General Heath, Major General Corp and Major General Peter Besgrove respectively. The overall picture, however, is of a very dynamic organisation, open to ideas and focused on supporting the Army's equipment. It delivered what it was supposed to deliver – effective and efficient support for Army equipment – through a difficult time when change was endemic, and it was subject to many pressures.

'ES' did not exactly equal 'REME' but the new ESO stood on the shoulders of the old REME organisation, and was largely manned by REME personnel. Underlying everything was an intellectual drive towards coherence, and a joined-up management structure. A single officer, DGES(A), had responsibility for the support of Army equipment, and had the authority and organisation necessary to meet that responsibility. The ESO had become just about as coherent as it could be in an imperfect world in terms of linking procurement processes to in-service support; linking the management of in-service support to front line user requirements; and to the management of the Corps primarily responsible for providing front line technical support. This coherence, however, was predicated on the key assumptions that 'logistics is a single-Service responsibility'.

THE STRATEGIC DEFENCE REVIEW 1998

The Labour Government that came into power in 1997 instigated a Strategic Defence Review (SDR). The report that emerged contained a simple statement to the effect that logistics were to be reorganised on a tri-Service basis. This came as a bolt out of the blue to most REME personnel.

The background to it was that the Army's QMG (Lieutenant General Cowan) had taken the view that single-Service logistic organisations had been squeezed to the extent that they could not possibly make the large additional savings the SDR was looking for in the support area. He considered the only possible way of achieving them was to consolidate single-Service logistic organisations into a single Defence Logistics Organisation (DLO), which he was duly given the task of setting up, thereby becoming the first Chief of Defence Logistics. This new assumption 'logistics is a Defence responsibility' undermined the whole rationale for the existing ES organisation, and a new way ahead was required.

The management of the Corps of REME would be disconnected from the management of ES. DES 1 was the director with most responsibility for running the Corps. He was to become the Director of Electrical and Mechanical Engineering (Army), DEME(A), and his organisation would provide the core for a new HQ DEME(A) that was to move to Arborfield, and incorporate the existing Regimental Colonel's organisation. This would put him in the same position as other one-star heads of Arms and Services. Along with them, he would report to the Assistant Chief of the General Staff. REME, the Corps, would therefore remain firmly within the Army fold. The story is told in more detail in Chapter 21 ('HQ DEME(A) and RHQ REME').

The rest of HQ DGES(A), along with the agencies it 'owned', would in due course be incorporated within the new 'purple' DLO, and were no longer part of the Army. Whereas REME and 'ES' had not been quite synonymous before, they were now distinctly different. In principle, REME (an Army organisation) was to implement ES policy decided by a 'purple' logistics organisation that would resource, support and guide its activities as required.

THE DEFENCE LOGISTICS ORGANISATION AND DEFENCE PROCUREMENT AGENCY 2000–2007

This book is essentially a history of the Corps of REME. An obvious question for the author is how much, if anything, it should say about the DLO, which was not a REME organisation. It has been decided that, since many REME officers played key roles within the DLO, and that much of REME's business was linked to the DLO or the Defence Procurement Agency (DPA), it would be useful to outline what these organisations did, and how they interacted with REME.

The changes that took place over the next few years were hugely complex and the following list highlights just some of the key events that affected REME:

- Brigadier Rod Croucher (late REME) moved to Arborfield in September 1999 as DEME(A) to set up HQ DEME(A)
- Lieutenant General Cowan became the Chief of Defence Logistics and left Andover in 1998 to start setting up the new DLO; he handed over to Lieutenant General Scott Grant (late Royal Engineers) as QMG
- DGES(A) had meanwhile changed his title to DGES(Land), with Major General David Judd (late REME) taking over from Major General Besgrove in due course; he and his agencies joined the DLO, and their evolution continued as part of the DLO
- Major General Mike Huntley (late REME) took over as DGES(Land) at Andover in 2002, with his title being subsequently changed to DG Land Forces Logistics.

The DLO was a hugely complex organisation. It knitted together the former single-Service ES organisations together with a 'purple' supply chain and a variety of 'enabling' organisations, which provided specialist support. A lot of work went into ensuring that all support processes were looked at 'end to end' ('factory to foxhole'), and that these were integrated efficiently with procurement processes in the DPA to ensure seamless through-life support for equipment. The new organisation continued the movement towards multidisciplinary working. The basic operational building block within the DLO was to become the Integrated Project Team (IPT). The organisation of an IPT was tailored to its role. It would comprise a team leader and whatever it needed in the way of engineering, finance, contracts or other specialist staff that it might require to carry out its role.

MoD PE was also greatly changed by the SDR. An in-house study on Smart Procurement was taken over by the consultants McKinsey. Their report recommended the adoption of through-life IPTs and major changes to the procurement process. MoD PE was also transformed into the DPA as part of these reforms. DPA IPTs continued to have ILSMs with responsibility for addressing through-life support issues throughout the procurement phase. The US forces dropped MILSTD 1388 in 1997 in favour of a more pragmatic and tailored approach to ILS, and the UK has broadly followed them. The inherently flexible structure of IPTs meant that an IPT could support an equipment throughout its complete life from procurement to disposal. An IPT could therefore start life procuring equipment in the DPA, and then transfer itself across to the DLO to manage its support once it entered service, thus providing continuity of management.

Staff Savings and the Demise of ATSA
In order to man IPTs in the DLO and to meet required manpower savings in parallel, the ATSA was sacrificed. The story is told in more detail in Chapter 19 ('Technical Support and Base Repair Agencies').

The Equipment Capability Customer
Operational Requirements (OR) became a 'purple' function in the mid-1980s when the General Staff OR branches became Land Systems OR (LSOR) and moved into the Defence Staff. Their role was further refined by the SDR and the organisation took on the new title of Equipment Capability Customer (ECC), under Directors of Equipment Capability. The purpose of the new organisation was to provide a much stronger customer focus for DPA IPTs, with its other roles broadly unchanged from those of the old OR, that is to evaluate threats, monitor technical developments, define consequent capability requirements and translate them into a funded programme that the ECC would manage.

Evolving Procurement Ideas and 'Hunt the Customer'
In the mid-1990s, the MoD's procurement organisation migrated from its miscellany of offices (many of them in drab London buildings) into a superb purpose built site at Abbey Wood near Bristol. It sought around that time to brush up its business processes, as well as its accommodation. Consultants were employed who pointed out that suppliers found the MoD difficult to deal with, as they met many people from different organisations and were often unsure who to listen to. Their ongoing work led to the advice that the MoD should adopt a 'single customer' approach to procurement. This idea duly ran into difficulties when no consensus emerged as to who the 'single customer' might be, as it could hardly be the largely civilianised IPTs at Abbey Wood.

Further consultancy was clearly required, and this resulted in the conclusion that since no 'single customer' had been found, there must be two customers, who were to be imaginatively called 'Customer 1' and 'Customer 2'. This did not immediately resolve the problem, as there were numerous claimants for 'Customer 2' (such as CGS, HQ Land, the ECC, Arms and Services directors, and equipment maintainers/trainers). Eventually, the problem was solved by accepting that almost all of these had a legitimate 'customer' interest, and 'Customer 2' became effectively a matrix of interested parties. This approach was in due course embodied into Smart Procurement processes.

Industrial and Commercial Developments
During the 1980s, the Government moved away from ideas of 'national champions', 'cost plus' contracts and paying for development. It sought an 'open market', 'competitive tendering' and 'fixed price' contracts. At that point, there were still a fair number of potential UK suppliers, such as VDS, VSEL, Alvis and GKN, who all supplied armoured vehicles to the UK. With the decline in the size of the UK defence organisation, such suppliers suffered from individually lacking the critical mass to survive and compete in the global market.

In the event, British Aerospace (which became BAE Systems), acquired many UK defence suppliers of sea, land and air systems and some foreign ones. It thereby gained the critical mass needed to become a global player (employing 100,000 staff by 2010), and became the predominant UK top-level defence equipment supplier. There was a steady move away from the 'open market' concept, as it was considered that it could put strategic UK defence industrial capability at risk. This was recognised in Lord Drayson's Industrial Strategy of 2005, which sought to deliver a better partnership between UK industry and the Services. Many training, support, administrative, and technical functions continued to be provided by companies such as Serco, Babcock and VT, with the Government having a keen eye for reducing defence expenditure through using them further, and where possible making use of public/private partnerships, private finance initiatives and the like.

Organisational Relationships
The diagram at Figure 18.1 (extracted from DLO and DPA information publications, at the end of this Chapter) shows the situation as it was in around 2005. SDR had created two large and very complex 'silo' organisations in the form of the DLO and DPA, which had undergone continuous change over a number of years. Those who ultimately used and maintained the equipment in the field were in different organisations. Despite the theoretical simplicity of the IPT concept, the practical difficulties of ensuring that everyone involved fully understood everything they needed to understand were immense.

The Invasion of Iraq
The invasion of Iraq in 2003 put these organisations under huge pressure. Most things went well, but inevitably there were problems and shortages, and no less inevitably these were seized upon by the media. Air Marshal Malcolm Pledger, who had taken over as Chief of Defence Logistics in 2002, understandably had a difficult time in front of the Public Accounts Committee. It operated against the background of a lot of anger about loved ones who died for the lack of such items as combat body armour. The simple truth was that the root of most problems lay in decisions taken in the past with the laudable aim of containing the cost of supporting Defence. Given that there was no rush by such people to accept responsibility, Air Marshal Pledger had a difficult case to argue, and he relinquished the post of CDL earlier than expected, and was replaced in 2005 by General O'Donoghue (formerly Chief of Staff of HQ QMG). He pointed out that one of the main problems the DLO faced was that it had been unable to realise the savings that were supposed to be achieved by merging the Services' logistic organisations.

Operations in Afghanistan

By this stage, operations in Afghanistan were starting to build up, and there was much media criticism at the lack of helicopters, suitable vehicles, and individual equipment. Support for operations became the top priority for the DLO and DPA, and great progress was made in many areas if not always to the satisfaction of the media.

REME Contributions

Although REME as an organisation did not contribute to the DLO or DPA, REME (and late REME) staff made a huge personal contribution. At two-star level, Major General Huntley held the post of DG Logistics (Land) within the DLO from 2002–2006. He was replaced by Major General Tim Tyler (late REME), who went on to be the DG Land Equipment within the newly formed DE&S (covered later), and additionally filled the role of QMG. He was replaced by Major General Ian Dale (late REME) in 2008. Both the DLO and DPA lacked internal technical support, so an organisation called the Technical Enabling Services (TES) was set up in 2005 under Major General Andrew Figgures (late REME) as Technical Director (and MGO), which drew on existing staff from Andover, Whyton, Bath and elsewhere and reported to both the DLO and DPA Boards. He retained his connection with the world of equipment when he moved on promotion to be Deputy Chief of the Defence Staff (Equipment Capability) from 2006 to 2009 and, in due course, the first Master General REME. It was, of course, not just at senior level that REME staff made an important contribution. They did so at every level, and the DLO and DPA could not have achieved what they did without the huge contribution of REME staff who had first learned their business under the old REME system.

MERGER OF THE DLO AND DPA – THE NEW DEFENCE EQUIPMENT AND SUPPORT ORGANISATION

The disadvantages of having two large 'silo' organisations concerned with equipment and logistics sitting beside each other are very obvious. The formation of the TES had already demonstrated the benefit of consolidating resources. A decision was eventually made to merge the DLO and DPA to form the new Defence Equipment and Support Organisation (DE&S). The new organisation became live on 2 April 2007 under General O'Donoghue who took the title of Chief of Defence

Materiel. Its organisational concept is shown in the diagram at Figure 18.2 (extracted from DE&S information publications, at the end of this Chapter).

DE&S, ES and REME
The newly-formed DE&S was a huge and very complex organisation. In broad terms, it procured new equipment and oversaw the support of equipment in service, with REME providing the manpower and organisation to carry out most of the first and second line repair of Army equipment. The complete system came to involve some very complex interactions between Defence elements ('purple' organisations such as PJHQ, Defence Training, and IPTs in the DE&S) and single-Service organisations (such as Army HQ, and single-Service elements of the ES system – including REME). For the complete system to work, it was clearly essential that those who worked in it fully understood the interactions involved and communicated with all the right people. The personal links and shared experience of REME staff played a crucial part in this.

Politics and Finance in the Years up to 2010
The complex Defence structures that had been set up inevitably provided plenty of scope for internal politics, with inter-Service differences in the background. National politics was naturally also an important driver of events. Tony Blair, Prime Minister from 1997–2007, was enthusiastic about deploying British forces abroad to make the world a better and safer place. His Chancellor of the Exchequer, Gordon Brown, whilst accepting the ends, appeared less than enthusiastic about providing the means. It became steadily clearer that the Defence budget would not stretch to both the proper support of current operations, as well as providing the Services with the equipment they would require in the long term if they were to sustain their position in the 'premier league' of armed forces.

Desperate attempts were made to keep projects alive and to balance the budget by delaying or extending. Industry was in a difficult position, despite having considerable lobbying power. Rescheduling projects would increase their costs, but if projects were seen to be unaffordable they risked being cut completely. The financial crash of 2008 and the ballooning national deficit meant that such problems obviously could not be solved by large injections of money into the Defence budget as some had once hoped. With an election on the way it was not in the interests of the incumbent Government to advertise the full extent of the Defence funding problem. Meanwhile, there was a steady stream of media criticism of the MoD and its procurement system, sometimes clearly more motivated by the desire to excite readers or audiences than provide a balanced account of the underlying problems.

General Election of 2010 – a new Government
In May 2010, the Labour Government was ousted and a Coalition Government was formed. This was committed to cutting the national deficit as quickly as it reasonably could. It had an interest in laying bare the full extent of the shortfall in the Defence budget it had inherited, to which it sought to make significant cuts. Bernard Gray, a former journalist and special adviser to the MoD who had written a scathing report on the MoD's equipment programme, was selected to take over the role of Chief of Defence Materiel and to lead DE&S forward. Inevitably, changes and ideas for change continued, and in 2015 a proposal largely to outsource much of the work of the DE&S to defence contractors was turned down.

SUMMARY

The business of procuring and supporting equipment for modern armed forces is a complex and difficult business, and always has been. There never has been a 'golden age' when officials were infallible and equipment procurement and support arrangements all worked with perfect efficiency and economy. Retracing one's steps is normally not a viable option, so the real benefit of studying the past comes from learning lessons from both success and failure. One common lesson to emerge is that it is often relatively easy to spot what is going wrong, and to offer superficially plausible solutions. It is much more difficult to find plausible solutions that do not have unfortunate unintended consequences.

Those with long memories know that all too often today's problems have been caused, or exacerbated, by what seemed to be the solution to yesterday's problems. Another key lesson is that it is usually the quality of the people involved that makes the difference between success and failure. An imperfect system run by people with the right motivation, skills and experience may trump a theoretically better system run by less able people.

REME personnel working outside the Corps within the wider world of ES and procurement, both before and after logistics ceased to be a single-Service responsibility, have collectively by their skills, experience and energy made a huge personal contribution to the success of the organisations they worked for. Some of the issues involved have been covered from a slightly different perspective at the end of Chapter 12 ('Afghanistan – Drawing Down').

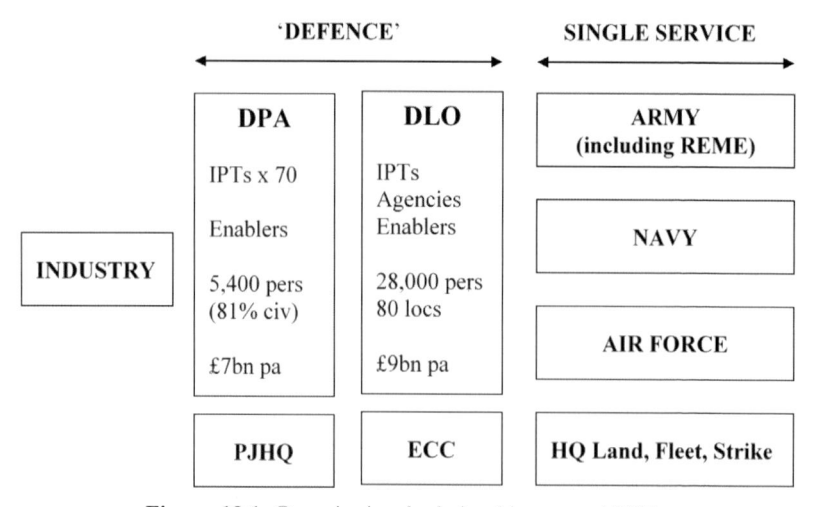

```
          'DEFENCE'              SINGLE SERVICE
       ←——————————→            ←——————————→

       ┌─────────┬─────────┐   ┌──────────────────┐
       │  DPA    │  DLO    │   │      ARMY        │
       │         │         │   │ (including REME) │
       │ IPTs x 70│ IPTs   │   └──────────────────┘
       │         │ Agencies│
       │ Enablers│ Enablers│   ┌──────────────────┐
┌────────┐      │         │   │       NAVY       │
│INDUSTRY│ 5,400 pers│ 28,000 pers │         │
│        │ (81% civ) │ 80 locs│   └──────────────────┘
└────────┘      │         │
       │ £7bn pa │ £9bn pa │   ┌──────────────────┐
       │         │         │   │    AIR FORCE     │
       └─────────┴─────────┘   └──────────────────┘

       ┌─────────┬─────────┐   ┌──────────────────────┐
       │  PJHQ   │   ECC   │   │ HQ Land, Fleet, Strike│
       └─────────┴─────────┘   └──────────────────────┘
```

Figure 18.1: Organisational relationships around 2005

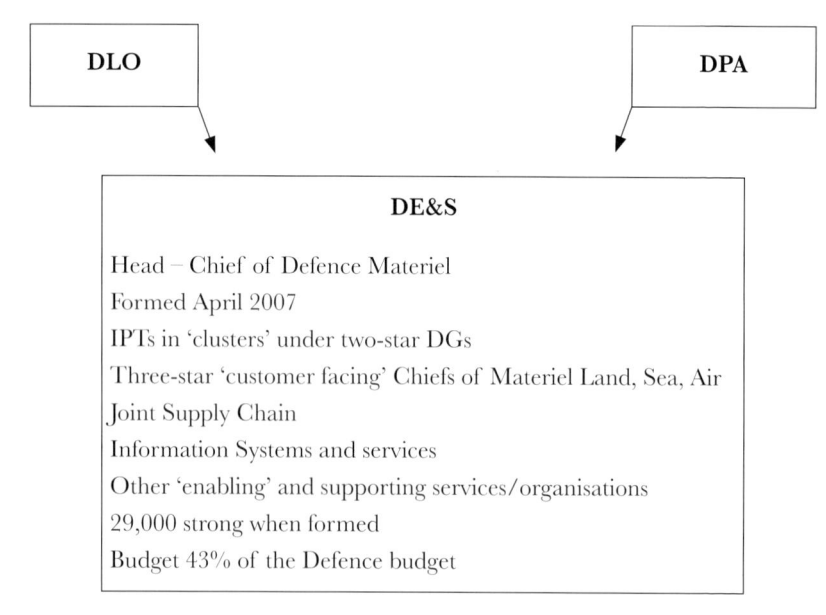

┌────────┐   ┌────────┐
│ DLO   │   │ DPA   │
└────────┘   └────────┘

┌──┐
│   DE&S   │
│ Head – Chief of Defence Materiel   │
│ Formed April 2007   │
│ IPTs in 'clusters' under two-star DGs   │
│ Three-star 'customer facing' Chiefs of Materiel Land, Sea, Air│
│ Joint Supply Chain   │
│ Information Systems and services   │
│ Other 'enabling' and supporting services/organisations   │
│ 29,000 strong when formed   │
│ Budget 43% of the Defence budget   │
└──┘

Figure 18.2: Organisational concept of the new DE&S organisation

CHAPTER 19

TECHNICAL SUPPORT AND BASE REPAIR AGENCIES

When REME was formed, it was intended to provide the Army with a complete engineering support service. This included providing, or contracting for, base-level repair and required the setting up of a variety of organisations that provided specialist technical support to REME's activities. When the new Equipment Support Organisation (ESO) came into being in April 1992, the Director General Electrical and Mechanical Engineering (DGEME) became the Director General Equipment Support (Army) (DGES(A)). Whilst his base repair and technical support organisations continued to be controlled by him, they actually ceased to be part of REME as they came under him wearing his ES 'cap' rather than his REME one (as explained in Volume 2 of Craftsmen of the Army).

A purist might argue that there is therefore no reason to mention them further in this book. The counter-argument is that when they transferred to the ESO they were still very much 'semi-REME', with many key roles being filled by serving REME personnel. In due course, they were selected to become part of the Government's agency programme. Although the agencies were still 'owned' by DGES(A), until the formation of the DLO in 2000, each had its own Chief Executive who was given much wider delegated powers, a separate budget and personal financial and performance accountability. Much has changed further since then but REME, and REME personnel in staff posts, were to have many dealings with their successor organisations. It therefore seems worth telling the tale of what happened to REME technical support and base repair organisations, and explaining how things ended up the way they have.

THE ARMY TECHNICAL SUPPORT AGENCY

In general, REME's technical support organisations have always had to be prepared to face two ways. On the one hand, they had to look inwards to REME units to help to identify and solve their problems, in modern parlance, acting as 'subject matter experts' (SMEs). On the other hand, they had to look outwards to provide important REME input, which reflected REME's practical experience, to organisations outside REME. These included Government research and development (R&D) organisations, manufacturers, planners, procurers, policymakers and the like. By the early-1970s, the technical support organisations were grouped under a two-star REME HQ based at Woolwich (HQ REME Support Group). With the demise of this HQ in Woolwich in 1977, the technical organisations came under direct control of the new two-star DGEME at Andover as his Technical Branches and Authorities (TBAs).

Until the 1970s, much development of military equipment took place in Government R&D facilities, such as the Fighting Vehicle Research and Development Establishment (FVRDE) at Chertsey. REME's technical branches were therefore generally collocated with the R&D establishment most relevant to their work. As time moved on, development was increasingly outsourced, with the former Government R&D establishments moving much more into a test, evaluation and technical advisory role. Their associated REME units therefore rebalanced their efforts towards providing small Maintenance Advisory Groups (MAGs), which often worked closely with contractors, sometimes providing embedded advisers who played an immensely useful role in explaining the realities of using and repairing Army equipment in the field. Specifically, their input could be of enormous value during the process of procurement or contracting out. They could be important both in helping to define requirements related to reliability, maintainability and the like; and, then, in ensuring that they were actually being met. In particular, they were of great value to Engineering Support Planning Officers (ESPOs) (later to become Integrated Logistic Support Managers) both as SME advisers, and 'eyes on the ground'.

An internal MoD study in 1993 concluded that the Army's TBAs should be combined in the form of a Defence Agency. This resulted in the following statement to Parliament on 23 November 1995:

> 'On 16 October 1995, I agreed to the formation of the Army Technical Support Agency as a defence agency from the former technical branches and authorities. ATSA will remain part of MoD but the chief executive will have delegated executive powers to discharge his responsibilities. ... ATSA comprises a headquarters in Andover and currently occupies six main sites at Middle Wallop, Malvern, Chertsey, Woolwich – two sites, and Chilwell. It employs some 1,250 staff, 900 of which are civil servants, with the balance

being military. A major strategy within the ATSA initiative is to reduce the number of main sites and a study is now examining the options for collocation'.

The new organisation, which was vested on 19 October 1995, took over responsibility for the following: Aircraft Branch (HQ in Middle Wallop with a detachment at Brize Norton); the Army Scaling and Cataloguing Authority (HQ in Woolwich with a group at Chilwell); Electronics Branch (HQ in Malvern, Area Communications and CIS (Command and Information Systems) at Blandford, Special Projects at Fort Halstead, Royal Artillery CIS at Larkhill); the Medical and Dental Section at Ludgershall; the Publications Branch at Woolwich; REME Technical Services at Dusseldorf; Vehicles and Weapons Branch (HQ in Chertsey, Maritime Branch at Marchwood, embedded staff with several contractors).

After vesting, most of the organisations remained in their existing locations, with ATSA's HQ being formed in the former Andover Officers' Mess on the North Site at HQ QMG Andover. REME Technical Services was disbanded and became Maintenance Support Group (Germany) (MSG(G)) based in Mossbank Barracks, Bielefeld. A new group, Maintenance Support Group (UK) (MSG(UK)), was set up in Chertsey.

The first Chief Executive was John Prince. Colonel Mike Capper (late REME), the ATSA Director Engineering, explained in an article ('ATSA – My Part in its Downfall') that the civilian HQ initially had a difficult time establishing relationships with some of the military staff it had to deal with. Brigadier Tony Ball (late REME) took over as Chief Executive early in 1997 and, having been a Director of Equipment Support, he brought a wealth of understanding of all aspects of ES, which helped things move ahead more smoothly after that.

The collocation strategy looked at various options including Chertsey and Malvern, but eventually opted for a new building at Andover, which would be funded as a Private Finance Initiative (PFI). Meanwhile, a new structure was worked out that included the formation of Technical Support Teams (TSTs), the work being driven forward under the energetic leadership of Lieutenant Colonel Barry Williams REME. The organisation was 'customer focused' and the key idea was to align the structure as far as possible with 'customer' branches in HQ DGES(A) and the Defence Procurement Agency (DPA). An advanced IT structure was created, which was allegedly the envy of the rest of the MoD, and which operated very effectively across the many sites and outstations. The outline organisational structure was as shown in Figure 19.1 and Figure 19.2 (both at the end of this Chapter).

Within each group, there were one or more TSTs providing the engineering, ranging and scaling, and publications support. Each TST had one point of contact for 'customers'. 'Customers' could include HQ DGES(A), the DPA, Land Command or the other Services. Staff were also deployed to Bosnia, Kosovo and BATUS to ensure good links to operational theatres. Although some migration of personnel occurred, by and large existing sites continued to be used. The excellent IT intranet system (the brainchild of Mike Stockbridge, ATSA Director PFI) was, however, of great value in minimising the difficulties caused by this.

Regular programme meetings were held, but with the chairmanship transferred to the 'customer'. This resulted in the number of projects being greatly reduced as the 'customers' tidied up their tasking and priorities. The establishment of standard procedures across the organisation allowed ATSA to achieve ISO 9001 accreditation; it also achieved Investors in People status, no mean feat given the dispersed locations.

The links with its 'customers' were further developed by creating helplines at the MSGs for all technical queries from throughout the MoD and all the Services. The helpline gave a central point of contact from which queries would be passed to the relevant group. The success of these helplines, and a spares helpline to Chilwell, gave ATSA a significant role in supporting the Field Army. This was expanded by the detachment of Warrant Officers as Technical Advisers to all operational theatres to provide a link back to ATSA for technical support, and to carry out technical and accident investigations in theatre.

The scale of ATSA's business is shown in Figure 19.3 (at the end of this Chapter), with details extracted from the published Agency Reports for the years 1996–1997 to 1999–2000.

To summarise, by the time the Millennium approached, ATSA was a forward-thinking, 'customer'-oriented organisation providing technical support that was of immense value not only to those supporting existing equipment, but those procuring new equipment. Typically, it was handling some 70,000 'customer' enquiries, completing some 1,300 'customer' projects and evaluating some 24,000 equipment failure reports annually.

Sadly, by that time the DLO was struggling to achieve its promised savings targets. One of the options for balancing the books was to disband the ATSA. This decision was duly taken, and on 31 March 2000 the ATSA ceased to exist. The 'ATSA building' was finally finished as Building 400 at

Andover, but as a MoD-funded project and not a PFI, as had been intended at one stage. The staff were slowly dispersed and former ATSA sites sold off.

Colonel Capper made the following comments in 2006 on ATSA's legacy in his article referred to earlier:

> 'Thus ended formed technical support for the MoD. Many of the staff were absorbed either into Integrated Project Teams (IPT) or the Director Technical as part of DLO(Land). This new organisation did not have centres of excellence for its major policy functions. It too died, and IPTs now suffer from little or no experience in ranging or scaling or clearly defined process, which they refused to absorb from ATSA as being 'not invented here'. As a recent example, a contractor had to provide an IPT with an old ATSA SOP (Standing Operating Procedure) so an Ease of Maintenance Assessment (EMA) could be carried out. ILS contractors are now strongly manned with former ATSA personnel selling their services back to the MoD. A tri-Service technical support organisation is being established to replace the likes of ATSA. What a pity the transition could not have been a seamless one, to prevent so many wheels being reinvented whilst the IPTs suffered'.

Colonel Capper's comments are obviously heartfelt, and to a degree partisan. Savings had to be made somewhere, and if the ATSA had not been disbanded somebody else would doubtless have had to take the financial bullet. The Director Technical in the DLO, Brigadier Richard Rickard (late REME), was certainly disadvantaged by the loss of centralised centres of excellence, but was able to deal with many issues satisfactorily, not least because many key REME artificers were transferred from the ATSA to IPTs.

At the end of the day, however, it is hard not to agree that Colonel Capper had a point. By the time he wrote his article, the MoD had already privately admitted at a senior level that it was 'no longer an intelligent customer' and was calling on the services of a late REME officer, Major General Andrew Figgures, to set up a tri-Service technical support organisation. It is easy to assess the money saved by disbanding the ATSA. It is impossible accurately to assess the cost of not being an 'intelligent customer', but common sense suggests it was far greater than the cost of the ATSA. On balance, the decision precipitately to disband it does not seem obviously to be one of the MoD's wiser ones.

BASE REPAIR AND THE ARMY BASE REPAIR ORGANISATION

REME's task *'to keep fit equipment in the hands of troops'* has always involved striking a balance between the requirement to repair as far forward as possible for operational reasons, and the technical requirement to carry out repairs as efficiently (and economically) as possible.

From the technical point of view, the best place in which to carry out repairs is a static workshop with a comfortable working environment and all necessary tools, facilities and expertise on tap. There may also be technical and economic benefits to concentrating specialised types of repair at particular specialised facilities.

On its formation in 1942, REME took over almost all existing static workshops. These comprised not only Royal Army Ordnance Corps Base Workshops but those of the Royal Engineers (specialist equipment), Royal Tank Corps (tanks and armoured cars) and Royal Army Service Corps. The workshops' organisation expanded during World War 2, with many of those working in them being uniformed; either by people who came to the Army with a technical skill, or by soldiers who were entirely trained by REME. By 1944, there were some 145 static workshops in the UK alone, and many more in operational theatres abroad.

After the war, the base organisation slimmed down, and with the end of National Service the workshops became largely civilian manned, although they continued to be commanded and managed at higher level by military staff. Static workshops fulfilled a number of roles.

Base facilities in operational theatres could repair battle-damaged equipments, cannibalising them as necessary and returning them for combat. Volume 1 of Craftsmen of the Army explains how this was done to huge effect before and after the battle of El Alamein. During the Cold War, part of the justification for having the huge 23 Base Workshop facility in Wetter (Germany) and 37 Rhine Workshop in Monchengladbach (Germany), was that these units would have a crucial operational role to play in returning battle-damaged vehicles quickly to the fray in the event of an attack on West Germany by Warsaw Pact forces.

Base workshops also carried out programmed refurbishment of equipment based on such factors as age or mileage. Early armoured vehicles did not have easily replaceable major assemblies such as engines or gearboxes. These, and other mechanical assemblies, tended to have a finite wear life, and after a certain amount of usage they started to become increasingly unreliable, which was bad news for their users, and also for REME at first and second line. The answer was a complete vehicle rebuild in a base workshop, which returned them 'good as new'. In some cases, they returned them 'better than new' as, increasingly, programmed overhauls became the point at which major upgrades and improvements were made. Programmed repair was not confined to armoured vehicles, and could apply to wheeled vehicles or other equipment as a way of extending their life indefinitely.

Static workshops also carried out the repair and overhaul of major mechanical assemblies such as engines, gearboxes, as well as smaller items when this made economic or operational sense. This would usually involve a complete strip down and rebuild, Level 4 repair in current terminology. They similarly repaired both 'black boxes' (electronic Line Replaceable Units) and the sub-assemblies within them (such as printed circuit boards). Such work was highly specialised and it usually made economic and technical sense to centralise the repair work in one or two locations. The correct functioning of Level 4 repair was, and continues to be, essential to REME's ability to provide operational support to the Field Army. In essence, if REME does not have spare assemblies such as engines or 'black boxes' when it needs them, it cannot repair equipments that fail at unit level. Effective planning of the complete repair loop is essential, because if things go wrong it is not possible to buy in extra assemblies 'off the shelf' and it may take months or years to sort out a major problem, during which time a cumulative number of equipments become non-operational.

In addition to the centralised and specialist base workshops, there were workshops that were responsible for supporting particular formations or geographical areas (called Station, District and Command Workshops). These could provide Level 2 and Level 3 support to units, reducing the load on REME at first and second line.

In the early-Cold War era, the majority of the Army's base repair was done in REME Workshops, which were substantial organisations. For example, in the mid-1970s, the strengths were: Donnington – 1,081, Chilwell – 1,052, Old Dalby – 576, and around 1,800 German civilians were employed at 23 Base Workshop, as described in Volume 2 of Craftsmen of the Army. The continuous pressure for financial savings in the 1960s and 1970s resulted in a number of studies. These sought to cut headcount, rationalise sites, transfer work to UK from Germany when operationally possible, as well as to increase the amount of work contracted out. By the mid-1980s, around 18% of repair was contracted out. A target of increasing this to 36% was set in 1984, which had been met by the time the Army Base Repair Organisation (ABRO) was formed.

The end of the Cold War and the Logistic Support Review ushered in a period of change and contraction, which was interrupted by the first Gulf War (Operation GRANBY 1990–1991). By then, the threat of a 'short warning scenario' attack on Germany had evaporated, which meant that there was no longer an operational imperative to retain major base facilities in Germany. 37 Rhine Workshop was closed in 1992, and 23 Base Workshop in March 1994. Meanwhile, control of the remaining regional workshops had been taken away from Districts and centralised under REME's Director of Production Engineering, Brigadier Jim Drew (late REME).

In deciding what was going to happen to Level 4 repair for the Army, there were clearly arguments for keeping an in-house capability. These were around the fact that much of the Army's equipment was highly specialised, and that without an in-house provider the Army risked being dependent on a monopoly supplier, either from technical necessity, or for contractual reasons related to Intellectual Property Rights (IPR). This had to be balanced against the fact that the MoD was operating in an austere budgetary environment where a 'peace dividend' was expected to follow the end of the Cold War. Nationalised industries had been successfully privatised, and ideas for making savings by contractorisation and outsourcing were very much in vogue.

The decision was therefore taken to 'market test' the base repair organisation. The outcome was a decision to turn REME's base organisation into an agency. Implicit in the deal was the idea that the agency would have a Chief Executive who would sharpen up the whole organisation and run it in a quasi-commercial manner. This was a fair challenge, as workshops had traditionally been 'demand driven' and lacked costing systems of a commercial standard. Although their work was technically of a high standard, there was suspicion that, at times, more was done than could be operationally justified.

The task of turning REME's base organisation into a commercially competitive agency was given to Brigadier Drew, who became the Chief Executive of the ABRO, which came into being on 31 March 1993. He remained a Brigadier until he reached retirement age in 1996. An open competition was held for his job, for which he successfully applied (leaving his office as a Brigadier on Friday and returning as a civilian the following Monday).

ABRO consisted of its HQ at Andover, and Base and District Workshops in UK (excluding 46 Northern Ireland Workshop). It was established for only 11 military posts. Along with a change of status came a conscious effort to create a new corporate image and approach. District Contract Repair Support Agencies ... (Arborfield, Bristol ...) were retitled ABRO Contract Repair ... (Arborfield, Bristol ...). On 1 July 1994, the workshops were retitled, as shown in Figure 19.4 (at the end of this Chapter, from The Craftsman magazine (September 1994)).

Jim Drew set about his task with a will, gathering a very effective team around him. By the mid-1990s, the ABRO had a very different feel to it from the old base repair organisation.

Colonel (Retd) Richard Peregrine (late REME) offers the following 'customer' perspective (recalled in 2013) on the way things had changed:

'In the late-1980s, as SO1 Arty Systems, I was effectively double-hatted as the manager of support for in-service artillery and as the ESPO (doing what an ILS Manager now does) for the project to procure a new self-propelled artillery equipment (which was eventually to be the AS90). The project was very innovative and with the MoD not paying for development, I could see a big potential problem down the line if the MoD did not have access to the Intellectual Property Rights (IPR) and technical information to allow it to base repair the main equipment and key assemblies. I had seen the way in which the MoD could be shamelessly ripped off when it was contractually bound to go to a monopoly supplier for base repair. By forcing the IPR issue at the beginning of the competitive tendering process we came up with an acceptable solution.

I was not, however, an uncritical fan of the base organisation at the time. They did a good technical job, but still tended to be 'old public sector' (pre-Thatcherite) in their thinking. I recall attending a production meeting, chaired by one of their civilian staff, where I caused much upset by insisting the programme to base overhaul the guns, which were due to be replaced by AS90, should be cut on the grounds that it would not yield any operational benefits and would cost a lot of public money that could be better spent on other things. The Chairman made no bones about the fact he considered me a misguided upstart who would not make such silly decisions once I had been around long enough to 'know the score'.

I returned to Andover as Col ES 41 shortly after the formation of ABRO. ES 41 was the branch responsible for ES for the armoured vehicle fleet – which made it ABRO's biggest customer in terms of cost and volume of work placed. I found ABRO an excellent organisation to deal with, with a very different ethos from five years before. It was very aware of cost, and was full of forward thinking ideas about 'value engineering' and 'total quality'. It was also 'customer focused'. Working with a flexible organisation which was 'on the same side' ('owned' by the same master, with no hidden commercial agendas) had operational benefits.

For example, during the mid-1990s, I got wind that the operational staff were thinking of sending a Challenger tank regiment to the Balkans in about nine months' time. I knew that would be around the time at which our stocks of spare tank engines and gearboxes would hit zero because of BATUS and other commitments. I (rightly) guessed that we would get minimal formal notice of the deployment, and that I would have no chance of getting extra funding (or letting any extra contracts) until it was publicly given. That would be far too late, and the deployment would either have to be curtailed, or some other unpalatable option (such as cannibalisation) pursued. In the event, I explained my problem to Jim Drew, who understood the situation exactly. After some horse trading on non-urgent programmes to square away the budget, he put into place a crash tank assembly repair programme which did the trick (with the deployment going smoothly and, unsurprisingly, no bouquet for Jim Drew for making it possible!)'.

This transformation was discussed with Jim Drew many years later in June 2013. He pointed out that the formation of the ABRO was at the trailblazing stage of the MoD's agency programme. He believed he would be unable to do what was required if he was to be second-guessed by the MoD's finance, human resources and contracts staff, so he sought full delegated powers in those areas. He had a bruising battle before he got them, not so much with Whitehall that tended to be sympathetic, but with his local masters who pointed out that in some respects he would have greater delegated powers than QMG. He believed that his delegated contractual powers represented a key weapon, because it allowed him to play contractors off against his own organisation. This forced both his own workshops to sharpen up, and put the squeeze on contractors. The medicine clearly worked, and ABRO's workforce was reduced by almost a half, to around where it would be 15 years later.

This anecdotal evidence that ABRO had become an efficient and cost-effective supplier to the Army was supported by hard evidence. The idea that it might be possible to make savings by somehow outsourcing or contractorising what ABRO did never really went away during the 1990s. 'Market testing' or 'competing for quality' exercises always seemed to be under way, or being discussed. One resulted in three 'market test' tenders being submitted in August 1996. These were the in-house bid plus bids from Ryder Defence (which included RACAL) and TLS (which involved SERCO, VDS, GKN and others). The in-house bid won.

When the DLO was set up in 2000, the ABRO became part of it, thus further distancing it organisationally from REME. It was continuing to move in the direction of becoming a quasi-commercial organisation, and was to be headed by civilian Chief Executives (who were not ex-REME) who would lead it that way. In 2002, it took a formal step down the commercial path when it became a Trading Fund.

The DLO's Director Technical, Brigadier Rickard, provided some insights of the issues around that time and later:

'... arguments ... (about the need for in-house capability) ... were a perennial topic, often driven more by the prevailing ideology of the day than by hard facts. During my time as Director Technical, it even attracted an NAO study. Perhaps the key counter to staying in-house is the industrial strategy argument (although it was virtually impossible to get anyone to define a meaningful industrial strategy) that, with at least 10 years between major equipment renewal programmes (25 years plus being more likely for armoured vehicles) UK defence manufacturing companies needed constant ongoing work if they were to remain in business until the next new-buy order – and base refurbishment could provide this.

My view was that a significant part of Level 4 work could be contracted out, but that at least 10 – 20% should remain in-house in order to provide comparative costs, competition and a viable way around any IPR issues (no company was going to allow a commercial rival access to its IPR and, try as we might, no procurement IPT Leader was prepared to include the costs of IPR in his programme). The risk with this approach was that it might reduce ABRO to a size that became non-cost effective, below critical mass. Once ABRO became a Trading Fund and started acting like a fully commercial company, it became even more difficult to champion it, unfortunately. Without being able to persuade anyone in authority to endorse a base repair strategy (and …the dearth of engineering and logistic understanding in HQ DLO at that time) ABRO was left to float in a sea of uncertainty'.

Nevertheless, REME continued to rely on and work closely with the ABRO. This is illustrated in the article in The Craftsman magazine (October 2005) by the ABRO Chief Executive, Peter Moore. He advised it had a turnover in 2004–2005 of £151m of which 90% was MoD work. It employed 2,500 civilians at 11 sites working on over 900 product lines of military vehicles and equipments, as well as completing over 131,000 specific calls on repair assets. As well as its traditional base repair role, he was keen for ABRO increasingly to provide in-barracks support for units to allow them to train.

By 2008, ABRO was in the throes of a merger with the rump of DARA (Defence Aviation Repair Agency) to form a new agency, the Defence Support Group (DSG). DARA had itself been formed out of a large RAF repair organisation and the Naval Aircraft Repair Organisation (NARO), which provided base repair for rotary wing aircraft, including the Army's. DARA had fared less well than ABRO as an organisation, as much of what it had done was contracted out, with its rotary wing repair business sold to Vector Aviation.

The rationale was outlined by the Defence Minister in 2007:

'Commitment from the MoD to sustain essential levels of capability and capacity will provide the new Defence Support Group with greater clarity, and allow it to implement a programme of continuous improvement. At the same time, the new organisation will look to consolidate and build on ABRO's and DARA's existing defence industry relationships and partnerships, by entering into agreements on future equipment programmes. These will ensure the MoD retains the Intellectual Property and design skills required to maintain operational sovereignty in key areas, as set out in the Defence Industrial and Technology Strategies'.

The new DSG organisation was to have around 3,500 employees, with an annual turnover of some £200m, as described in the Defence Management Journal (Issue 41). ABRO's survival had been clearly due in part to the 'can do' attitude it showed in meeting surge requirements, and urgent problems created by unforeseen operational developments. The DSG stated its intention to build on this, and as a significant Defence-owned technical organisation to develop positive relationships with its customers in the Services, with commercial organisations, and with Defence organisations involved in the procurement and support of equipment.

The DSG appears elsewhere in this book, notably in the context of operations in Afghanistan where the DSG set up an in-theatre regeneration facility at Camp Bastion. Although the DSG was no longer part of REME, it is hard not to conclude that the success of this exercise was due, in part at least, to the fact that the DSG has roots in REME, a long history of working with REME, and, not least, that a significant percentage of its staff in Afghanistan were ex-REME.

The sale of the DSG was announced by the Parliamentary Under-Secretary of State for Defence (Philip Dunne) on 6 January 2015 as follows:

> 'I am pleased to announce the successful sale of the Defence Support Group (DSG) land business to Babcock for £140 million. As part of the transaction, a 10-year contract (with options to extend to 15 years) worth some £900 million has been agreed for the delivery of DSG services and the transformation of the Army's vehicle maintenance, repair and storage. The contract covers the DSG's fleet management and engineering support services and will generate savings to the Army of around £500 million over the 10-year period – a saving of over a third. This contract has the potential to grow to around £2 billion as a broader scope of services under the DSG sale contract are optimised, subject to value for money, as part of the planned programme'.

Looking ahead to Army 2020 and beyond, it is clear that REME's operations will have to be based on integrating what it does closely with the DSG (in whatever form it takes) and other contractors.

ATSA Executive Management Board

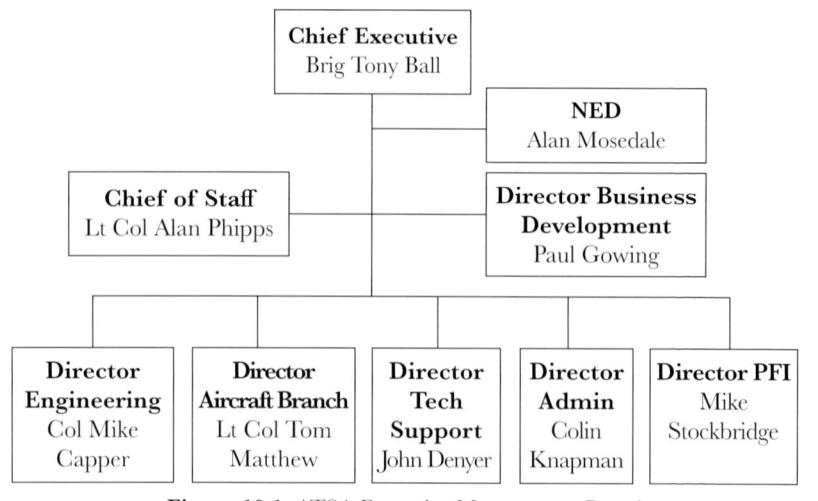

- **Chief Executive** — Brig Tony Ball
  - **Chief of Staff** — Lt Col Alan Phipps
  - **NED** — Alan Mosedale
    - **Director Business Development** — Paul Gowing
    - **Director Engineering** — Col Mike Capper
    - **Director Aircraft Branch** — Lt Col Tom Matthew
    - **Director Tech Support** — John Denyer
    - **Director Admin** — Colin Knapman
    - **Director PFI** — Mike Stockbridge

Figure 19.1: ATSA Executive Management Board

ATSA ENGINEERING STRUCTURE

- **Director Engineering** — Col Mike Capper
- **Tech Report Processing Section** — Lt Col Barry Williams

Combat Eqpt Division Lt Col Andy Topp	Log Eqpt Division Lt Col Ray Gatward	Electronic Eqpt Division Lt Col Alistair Booth	Spec Tech Support Division Dick Holder	Tech Supply Sp Division Colin Longford
Hy/Med/Lt Combat Vehs, Ord/Wpns and Instruments	Log Vehs, Engr Sp, Fd Eqpt and Rec, Maritime and Railways	C3I Eqpt Sp, Fd Comms, Med & Dent, Rapier, Spec Projects, Surv and GW	MSG(UK) MSG(G) Reliability Tech, Maint	TSS 1 TSS2

Figure 19.2: ATSA Engineering Structure

Business Summary	95–96	96–97	97–98	98–99	99–00
Operating Costs (£M)	N/A	49.5	49.9	52.9	50.1
Capital Expenditure (£M)	5.4	1.4	0.5	2.1	0.4
Total Fixed Assets (£M)	24.9	24.3	22.9	25.3	23.7
Staff in Post at 1 April	1,209	1,137	1,123	1,098	1,040

Figure 19.3: Scale of ATSA's business

Old Title	New Title
18 Base Workshop	ABRO Bovington
34 Base Workshop	ABRO Donnington
35 Base Workshop	ABRO Old Dalby
27 District Workshop	ABRO Warminster
31 District Workshop	ABRO Catterick
36 District Workshop	ABRO Colchester
43 District Workshop	ABRO Aldershot
44 District Workshop	ABRO Ashford

Figure 19.4: Retitling of ABRO Workshops in 1994

CHAPTER 20

ARMY EQUIPMENT AND ITS MANAGEMENT

The Army is dependent on REME to support all its equipment, less a few exceptions such as trunk communications equipment (looked after by Royal Signals Technicians), some specialist engineer equipment (looked after by Royal Engineer Plant Fitters), and equipment repaired directly by contractors. This overall 'equipment dependency' has changed significantly over the period covered by this book, and many specific changes are covered in other chapters. This Chapter aims to consolidate the equipment picture, less matters related to aircraft that are covered in Chapter 15 ('REME Aviation'). It seeks to fill in the gaps on some of the changes, at the same time mentioning some of the technological drivers of change, and REME's involvement in dealing with them. The management of support on operations has already been covered, as well as general issues relating to the procurement and support of equipment. The matter of the overall management of equipment fleets, and how they are stored and deployed to support training and operations, which has not been touched on elsewhere, is dealt with in the later part of this Chapter.

ARMOURED FIGHTING VEHICLES – TRACKED

During the Cold War, the Army's greatest threat was deemed to be the armoured forces of the Warsaw Pact. The UK deployed its own armoured forces to Germany to counter the threat. These predominantly comprised tracked vehicles, which gave the off-road mobility required in the terrain they were expected to be used in. The Army's relatively small fleet of wheeled armoured vehicles was primarily intended for low-intensity operations elsewhere. The inherent problem with tracked vehicles is that they have a high rolling resistance, and the grinding of metal tracks on sprockets means that they require a lot of maintenance, even when they are inherently fairly reliable. The rate at which tracks and mechanical assemblies wear out translates into very high operating costs per kilometre.

Tanks

Armoured warfare came of age in World War 2. The main battle tank (MBT) was to emerge as 'the queen of the battlefield'. It was designed to provide the best possible combination of firepower, protection and mobility. The more armour a tank carried, the fewer weapons it was vulnerable to, and the shorter the range at which it was vulnerable to kinetic projectiles.

The Army's principal MBT during the Cold War era was the Chieftain, which was finally phased out of service in 1995. Its poor reliability and durability are touched on in Chapter 18 ('Support for Army Equipment – An Overview'). In 1983, Challenger, which was to become Challenger 1 when Challenger 2 appeared, was introduced into service. These vehicles had originally been intended for the Shah of Iran, but when he was deposed the contract was cancelled, and the tanks were modified for UK use and bought by the MoD. The automotives were a big improvement on Chieftain, but the turret systems were effectively a rehash of those in Chieftain, which by then were something of a 'mix and match' of old and new, following various modification programmes. Challenger nevertheless performed very effectively during the Gulf War of 1991.

Chapter 18 outlines REME involvement in the procurement of the Army's next tank, Challenger 2, right from the start. The 65-tonne tank was a highly complex beast. Its 20-tonne turret and 120mm gun were stabilised, as was its sighting system. This incorporated laser range finding, thermal imaging and an independently stabilised commander's sight. It was a modern system, which was controlled by over 50 'black boxes'. Because test and diagnostic features had been built in, and maintainability had been considered from the outset, the tank achieved excellent operational availability. It entered service in 1998, and gave the UK a first class MBT. It acquitted itself with honours during operations in Iraq. Challenger 2 was not ideal for the sort of counterinsurgency operations of the type embarked on in Afghanistan where there was no threat from hostile tanks or large-calibre high-velocity weapons, and it was not deployed there. Although it perhaps dropped out of the limelight as a result, it remains a formidable weapon system and has a capability to engage in high-intensity armoured operations for which the wheeled armoured vehicles deployed to Afghanistan would not be well suited. Three Challenger 2 regiments were included in the plans for Army 2020 and a Challenger 2 Life Extension Programme was planned. (**See Plate 43**)

Other Families of Tracked Armoured Fighting Vehicles and Types

Tanks do not normally operate on their own but as part of all-arms battlegroups. The infantry and other supporting arms clearly have to be able to stay with the tanks, which reinforced the need for most UK armoured vehicles to be tracked in the Cold War scenario.

Combat Vehicle Reconnaissance (Tracked) Family. Combat Vehicle Reconnaissance (Tracked) (CVR(T)) was a family of small, lightweight armoured vehicles intended primarily for reconnaissance.

CVR(T) Scimitar of 9/12 Lancers in Afghanistan 2012

A combination of lightweight aluminium armour and a Jaguar petrol engine made them the 'sports cars' of the armoured vehicle world when they were introduced in the 1970s. They were great fun and it was not uncommon to see them doing 60mph. They were lightly armed (the most common variant had a 30mm cannon) and relied as much on stealth and agility as armour for protection. They came in several variants including a command version, and REME recovery version (Samson). They were to be considerably modified over the years. Various improvements were made to their sighting and communications system, as well as the automotive side (the Jaguar engine being replaced by a sensible diesel). Their level of protection was considerably enhanced following experience in Iraq and Afghanistan, but ultimately they are light-armoured vehicles and there is a limit to the protection they can provide. At the time of writing, there was no plan to take them out of service entirely but many will be replaced by the Ajax family of vehicles covered later.

FV430 Family. These vehicles were next up in size and weight, and the first versions came out in the 1960s. The most numerous version was the FV432. This was a very simple vehicle. It was essentially an armoured box on tracks designed to carry an eight-man infantry section.

FV432 in its early infantry 'battle taxi' form

It was fitted with a pintle-mounted machine gun but the vehicle commander had to expose the upper part of his body to fire it. The robustness and simplicity of the basic design meant that it was easily adaptable for a number of purposes, and numerous variants materialised. It was commonly used as a command vehicle; there was a REME variant, and several others. This family of vehicles, which has seen many modifications over the years, largely remains in service. In general, the family should be seen as being more protected carriers, or utility armoured vehicles adapted for various purposes, than as combat vehicles. The FV432, however, evolved into the Bulldog, which has been heavily uparmoured to give it a comparable level of protection to the Warrior vehicle.

Bulldog vehicle

It was fitted with the Enforcer Remote Weapons Station (RWS), which could be operated from under armour using either day or night sights (thermal imaging). Fitted with a heavy machine gun, it had become more a combat vehicle than a simple armoured personnel carrier. The Enforcer RWS, which can be fitted with different types of weapon, was fitted (or retrofitted) to a number of types of armoured vehicles.

Enforcer RWS fitted with 7.62mm machine gun

Warrior Family. Warrior was initially primarily intended as an Infantry Fighting Vehicle (IFV). It offered much better protection than FV432, and at 25 tonnes it weighed around twice as much. The IFV had a two-man turret, which mounted a machine gun and a 30mm cannon. It was of a simple and robust design, and proved excellent at what it was designed for. There were several variants, including a command version and REME repair and recovery variants. As with FV432, it was much modified and uparmoured over the years. At the time of writing, it was due to continue in UK service indefinitely, and a contract had been let for a part-fleet modification to the Warrior Capability Sustainment Programme Standard, which included fitting a fully stabilised 40mm gun turret. (**See Plate 44**)

Engineer Equipments. The Royal Engineers used Chieftain variants as the Armoured Vehicle Bridge Layer (AVLB) and as the Armoured Vehicle Royal Engineers (AVRE), both of which were used in a mobility support role. These were replaced by equipments based on the Challenger hull, which are called Titan (a bridge layer) and Trojan Combat Engineer Vehicle (fitted with an excavator arm and full-width mine plough). They also used a much lighter vehicle (around 17 tonnes), the Combat Engineer Tractor (CET or FV180). This carried aluminium armour, is amphibious, and is fitted with a large bucket in the front. This came into service in the 1970s and was being replaced at the time of writing by the Terrier, a heavier steel armoured vehicle, which will similarly be used for towing, digging, or in a mobility support role.

Trojan combat engineer vehicle

Viking and Warthog. Viking is a lightly-armoured articulated vehicle, which has its crew in a front compartment, and carries personnel (or other loads) in a separate tracked 'box' linked to it. The vehicle is unusual in that it has rubber tracks. It offers excellent cross country mobility, and can swim. It was successfully used by the Royal Marines in Afghanistan, but the protection it offered was considered inadequate in the face of the developing IED (Improvised Explosive Device) threat. (**See Plate 45**) A fundamentally similar, but better protected vehicle, the UK variant of a vehicle developed in Singapore, was therefore procured under an Urgent Operational Requirement (UOR) to replace it. This was called the Warthog and gave good service, but it lacks the ability to swim and was to go out of service in 2015. Both are pictured in Chapter 11 ('Afghanistan – The Long Haul (Operations HERRICK 4–14)').

Artillery Systems
The end of the Cold War saw the Army with a 105mm self-propelled gun, Abbott, which was a member of the FV430 family. Its shell was considered to be too light to be suitable for use against armoured forces, so it was complemented by a number of regiments of M109 guns. These were US-produced, and had an effective 155mm (6-inch) gun in a turret. Depth fire was provided by two types of guns, which used a similar chassis, but were not turreted, and therefore offered less crew protection. These were the M107 (with a long-barrelled 175mm gun) and the M110 (with a shorter 210mm gun), which had been procured to fire nuclear shells, but had a useful conventional capability as well.

Multiple Launch Rocket System. These depth fire systems (M107 and M110) were to be replaced by a US-designed Multiple Launch Rocket System (MLRS) built under licence by a European industrial consortium. It comprised a 'launcher loader module', which sat on a tracked armoured chassis. It was 'black box' controlled, and the advice to the UK technical authorities was to treat it as 'a low flying aircraft with tracks on' from the maintenance point of view. The system was brought into service and successfully used in the first Gulf War of 1991, ahead of its planned in-service date. This was possible because REME staff had been involved in the development of the UK support package, and were able to overcome the support problems associated with a premature deployment. This version fired a pod of 12 unguided rockets containing dual-purpose anti-armour/personnel sub-munitions. MLRS was upgraded to fire guided

MLRS firing

AS90 firing a calibration shoot in Basra 2008

rockets employing GPS technology. These have a range of around 70km (around twice the original rockets) and deliver a 200lb warhead with great accuracy. The new system became Guided MLRS (GMLRS) and remains in service.

AS90. Abbott, FH70 (a towed 155mm howitzer) and M109 were replaced by the AS90 155mm self-propelled gun manufactured by Vickers Shipbuilding and Engineering Limited. It had originally been produced as a private venture, but it proved the winner of a competition that began in 1987 to provide a fleet of guns with a concurrent support package. REME was deeply involved in the procurement process, especially the support package, as described in Chapter 18. The programme was very successful and meant that the Army had a reliable and capable modern self-propelled gun system in service by the mid-1990s.

WHEELED ARMOURED VEHICLES AND PROTECTED MOBILITY VEHICLES

The Army had traditionally used lightly-armoured four-wheeled vehicles for reconnaissance and liaison. During the 1950s, it developed a range of six-wheeled vehicles. These were the Saracen armoured personnel carrier (APC), the Saladin armoured car, which mounted a 76mm gun, and the Stalwart unarmoured high-mobility load carrier. These were intended for 'colonial' or low-intensity operations, and were very good vehicles for their time. Saracen was successfully used in Northern Ireland along with the very basic lightly-armoured Humber 1-ton carrier (the 'Pig'). These were all 'UK-only military specials', which were not cheap or easy to maintain. They were therefore phased out, as the Army increasingly focused on tracked vehicles suitable for use in Germany.

To complement them, the Army procured a basic wheeled 'battle taxi', the Saxon, in the early 1980s. It was essentially a steel plated 4 x 4 truck capable of carrying ten infantrymen, or an equivalent load. It was used in the Balkans and thereafter, but has since been phased out. Another lightly-protected vehicle, the Vector, was procured and was based on a 6 x 6 Pinzgauer chassis. This was used in Iraq and Afghanistan and was taken out of service in 2015. A lightly-armoured version of the Land Rover, the Snatch, was developed for use in Northern Ireland where its combination of agility and protection made it a useful vehicle in urban environments. All these vehicles were developed with the idea of providing protection against hand-held small arms, and a degree of protection against blast weapons including hand grenades, or modest IEDs.

During operations in the Balkans, and those following the invasion of Iraq, it became clear that the Army needed vehicles with a much greater degree of protection than existing wheeled armoured vehicles had to offer. It therefore relied heavily on tracked vehicles, as it had nothing else, and these did sterling service. Tracked vehicles, however, have a number of inherent drawbacks in such operational environments. One is the cost of maintenance effort per track mile, another is that they are inherently vulnerable to attack from below. If any track link (or its track pin) on either side of a tracked vehicle is fractured, the vehicle is immobilised, and if it is moving fast at the time it can throw off its track in a dangerous manner. It can then do no more than pivot around a point driven by its one working track, a disabled track can also complicate recovery. Tracked vehicles also tend to be noisier and therefore less stealthy than wheeled vehicles. Unlike tracked vehicles, wheeled vehicles may have a degree of mobility even if a wheel station is blown off. The South African Army was involved in bush wars in the 1970s, which led to the development of a range of wheeled vehicles specifically designed to provide protection against mines and ambushes.

When the US forces found themselves involved in counterinsurgency operations in Iraq, they therefore drew on South African ideas and technical knowledge very quickly to produce a range of similar vehicles for themselves. They called this the Cougar range of vehicles. The British became involved in the programme and produced UK versions of the family. These were: the Mastiff, a 6 x 6 Infantry Mobility Vehicle (IMV); a smaller 4 x 4 IFV (more suited to urban/close country situations) called the Ridgeback; the Wolfhound, a 6 x 6 Tactical Support Vehicle (TSV), which was essentially a load carrying version of Mastiff; and the Buffalo, a 6 x 6 Mine Resistant Ambush Protected (MRAP) vehicle, primarily intended for route clearance and dealing with mines/IEDs. There is more detail about these and other vehicles that became classed as Protected Mobility (PM) vehicles, including REME's involvement in supporting them, in Chapters 9 to 12 (covering operations in Iraq and Afghanistan).

Protection technology to improve the survivability of these and other vehicles did not stand still. Wheeled vehicles could not carry the same weight of solid armour as MBTs, but a good degree of protection against Rocket Propelled Grenades (RPGs) could be achieved by fitting a relatively light grid of bars or wire mesh outside the armour of a vehicle, which would disrupt their warheads. This explains why many of the wheeled armoured vehicles used in Iraq and Afghanistan appeared to be festooned with wire bars or meshes. Such upgrades often went with the fitting of various types of appliqué armour, including special armour panels. The relatively thin basic armour of PM vehicles in Afghanistan was acceptable because there was no threat from tanks or large-calibre high-velocity anti-tank weapons.

Ridgeback IFV

As basic versions of PM vehicles would generally easily survive the strike of a normal military mine, the insurgents set about developing ever larger and more ingenious types of IED. It therefore became important to start looking at the effect of a large explosion on those inside a vehicle, even if the blast did not penetrate the vehicle. For example, it was realised that soldiers with their feet on the floor of a vehicle when there was a major explosion underneath could suffer splinter fractures of the shin or ankle that tended not to heal properly, were difficult to treat, and often resulted in amputation. It was therefore necessary to look at improving such things as shock-resistant mountings for seats, restraining straps and shock-absorbent surfaces. Anti-spall liners also offered a degree of behind-armour protection against flying fragments in the event of armour being penetrated. A combination of such measures meant that, by the later stages of operations in Afghanistan, soldiers travelling in heavy PM vehicles such as the Mastiff had an excellent chance of surviving attack by even a very large IED.

Electronic systems represented another form of protection. Insurgents must decide how to detonate their explosive devices. If they are triggered by a vehicle passing over them, they risk being detonated by a friendly vehicle. A command wire represents another option, but it tends to put the operator at the end of it at risk. It was soon realised that remotely activated electronic devices (including suitably modified mobile phones) could offer an attractive way of activating IEDs without putting the firer at risk. Electronic Counter Measure (ECM) systems (of a classified type) were therefore developed and widely fitted to vehicles to protect against this threat.

As well as the lightly-armoured Snatch Land Rover, the Army had a version of the Land Rover that was fitted with thick armour panels, and which mounted considerable firepower in the form of a light machine gun, a heavy machine gun, or grenade launcher (in any combinations). It was called the WMIK (Weapons Mounted Installation Kit). It was agile, stealthy, and packed a punch that made it suitable for reconnaissance and fire support for convoys or troops on the ground.

The limited protection offered by both WMIK and Snatch made them increasingly vulnerable as the IED threat grew, attracting unfavourable press comment. The MoD therefore turned to a UK supplier they had used before (Supacat) to provide a sturdy 4 x 4 vehicle, which was open topped, but provided very much better protection particularly against IEDs. This was to become the Jackal WMIK, intended for similar roles to its Land Rover counterpart. It came with a 6 x 6 version called the

Land Rover WMIK

Coyote, which had a load carrying area at the rear and was classed as a TSV (Tactical Support Vehicle). (**See Plate 46**)

The composition of the UK wheeled armoured fleet by the end of operations in Afghanistan had come about through the need to meet UORs with what was readily available rather than equipment that required a lengthy development or procurement process. Further types of vehicle were procured.

Foxhound met the need for a vehicle that was much better protected than the Snatch Land Rover, but smaller and more agile than Ridgeback, and therefore better suited to urban environments. This was procured from Force Protection Europe, a subsidiary of the US firm General Dynamics, and was largely designed and built in the UK. Husky was a well protected 4 x 4 support vehicle, which could be used for such roles as delivering rations and supplies. It was procured from the USA.

The approximate composition of the UK PM fleet in 2014 is summarised in Figure 20.1 (at the end of this Chapter).

UPGRADES OF VEHICLE SIGHTING AND NAVIGATIONAL SYSTEMS

Battlegroup Thermal Imaging System. During the 1990s, it was realised that the night sighting equipment used on Scimitar and Warrior vehicles was not satisfactory for the long term, so the Battlegroup Thermal Imaging System (BGTI) was developed with Thales Optronics as the lead contractor. The BGTI system fitted to the Scimitar and Warrior vehicles (excluding repair and recovery variants, which have a different system) is modular in design and comprises an integrated gunner's sighting system providing a 24-hour capability, a commander's sighting and observation system, and an inertial navigation facility that can operate independently or in conjunction with the Global Positioning System (GPS) provided by Bowman communications equipment. The sight comprises visual and thermal band sighting channels. It is capable of elevation and depression, which is equal to the range of movement of the host vehicle's 30mm RARDEN Cannon. The first system was installed in 2005, with the intention of the system being used until, possibly, 2035.

Enhanced Sight Periscopic Infrared Equipment. The Enhanced Sight Periscopic Infrared Equipment (E-SPIRE) is an integrated system with three principal electronic sub-systems: thermal imager, laser rangefinder, and aiming mark controller. It replaced the Sight Periscopic AV No 52 Mk 4 and Image Intensifier (II) L2A1 (or L1A2 depending on the variant fitted). The original II cowl is fitted to the gun mantlet, with a counterbalance weight to compensate for the removed II sight. The aiming mark control in E-SPIRE provides an improved fire control capability.

Tactical Navigation and Target Location System. When installed in a vehicle, the Tactical Navigation and Target Location System (TNTLS) provides a highly accurate means of navigation using the TACNAV Fibre Optic Gyro and GPS. The system also provides relative turret traverse position and, when interfaced with the vehicle laser range finder, can compute the target grid location.

ARMOURED VEHICLES – THE FUTURE

From the mid-1990s, the Army began thinking about replacing its existing fleet of medium armoured vehicles with two new fleets of armoured vehicle, one wheeled and one tracked. This was to result in a formal requirement for some 3,700 armoured vehicles, collectively referred to as the Future Rapid Effects System (FRES). These were to be 'network enabled' and well protected, and to meet many requirements. At one point, it was envisaged that it would comprise five families of vehicle with 16 variants.

The FRES programme had a chequered history, and it is beyond the scope of this Chapter to follow its twists and turns, but it is perhaps worth mentioning a few salient points. At one time, it was being billed as the UK's largest procurement programme at some £13bn procurement cost, and around £60bn whole life cost. Early on in the programme, it seemed as if a joint UK/German/Dutch vehicle called the Boxer would meet much of the wheeled vehicle requirement.

The MoD, which was struggling with the complexity of the project, announced in 2006 that an alliance arrangement would be put in place for FRES, similar to the UK Future Aircraft Carrier Alliance. The FRES Alliance was led by the MoD with the support of an industrial system of systems integrator (SOSI) and a group of three industrial teams for each of the FRES vehicle families. The industrial teams for each vehicle family included a vehicle integrator, vehicle designer and vehicle manufacturer. The SOSI was General Dynamics, and the preferred vehicle to meet the major wheeled vehicle requirement was their Piranha vehicle, originally developed in Switzerland. Various technology demonstrator and trials programmes were carried out, but by the time of the Strategic Defence and Security Review 2010 (SDSR 2010) these had not resulted in any firm and properly funded programme. By that time, there was no money for FRES and insider sources were talking of FRES being 'dead in the water'. There was talk of existing equipments being upgraded and kept in service for the long term, and many of the UOR equipments (notably the PM vehicles) being 'taken into core'. At one time, it seemed there might be no new types of armoured vehicle for the Army for the foreseeable future.

More recently, a contract was signed for a new family of armoured vehicles, the tracked Scout Specialist Vehicle (SV) family. A public release advised that:

> 'General Dynamics UK was awarded £3.5 billion to deliver 589 SCOUT SV platforms to the British Army on 3 September 2014'.

These vehicles are intended to replace CVR(T) and other armoured vehicles in due course, and may be seen as the resurrection of part of the FRES concept. Scout, which was still very much in the development phase, was described thus in the release:

> 'The SCOUT SV programme includes six variants: Scout Reconnaissance, Protected Mobility Reconnaissance Support (PMRS), Command and Control, Engineering Reconnaissance, Repair, and Recovery. Each SCOUT SV platform variant will be a highly-agile, tracked, medium-weight armoured fighting vehicle, providing British troops with state-of-the-art best-in-class protection.… Each SCOUT SV platform variant has extensive capabilities, including acoustic detectors, a laser warning system, a local situational awareness system, an electronic countermeasure system, a route marking system, an advanced electronic architecture and a high performance power pack'.

Shortly thereafter it was decided to rename the Scout family of vehicles the Ajax family, and their variants were given the imaginative names shown in Figure 20.2 (at the end of this Chapter).

OTHER WHEELED VEHICLES

Traditionally, armoured vehicles were called A Vehicles, unarmoured vehicles were called B Vehicles, and engineer plant was called C Vehicles.

Prior to the invasion of Iraq, most of the Army's transport fleet offered little or no special protection. Events in Iraq and Afghanistan, and the concept of 'non-linear' warfare, led to this changing. Initially, all that could be done was to retrofit fairly basic protection kits in the form of protective grilles and panels for cabs. Much improved systems came later, either in the form of protection that was built in, and/or retrofitted in theatre (work in which REME was often involved). Bullet proof glass, slatted metal armour and added armour panels became very much the norm along with protective electronic systems. This accounted for the distinctive appearance of vehicles deployed in Afghanistan compared with those of the same type that had been deployed initially in Iraq, or were being used unmodified for training in UK or elsewhere.

The repair of B Vehicles had always been a major part of REME's workload because the Army has always had a lot of them. For example, in 1998, the Army inventory included 54,840 B Vehicles of which 38,062 were prime movers. These came under 197 liability codes, each reflecting a different functional requirement. A liability may be met by assets of different makes/versions of vehicle, which required different parts and therefore a different asset code. In a 1998 working document, it states that 541 asset codes met the 197 liability codes. A detailed analysis of the fleet and, changes to it, is well beyond the scope of this Chapter, but this overview of some of the main families of vehicle may be useful.

Heavy Equipment Transporter and Wheeled Tanker. At the heavy end of the spectrum, the Scammell Commander Tank Transporter was successfully replaced by the Oshkosh Heavy Equipment Transporter (HET), which is the UK version of the US Army HET. Oshkosh also supplied a new wheeled tanker, which has become the backbone of the bulk water and fuel carrying fleet.

Demountable Rack Offload and Pickup System. Demountable Rack Offload and Pickup System (DROPS) vehicles are large 8 x 8 wheeled vehicles equipped with load handling systems designed to load and offload standard 20-foot ISO containers with the aid of simply attached X-frames and rollers, or to carry loads of up to 15 tonnes secured on 'flat racks' of the same platform. They were designed, developed and manufactured in the UK, and came into service in the late-1980s. There are two versions, the Medium Mobility (most of them) and Improved Medium Mobility, and, overall, have proved very successful vehicles. Some had been replaced at the time of writing by the Enhanced Palletised Load System (EPLS) but many remained in service and will do so until the Threshold Palletised Load System comes.

DROPS Medium Mobility Load Carrier

Enhanced Palletised Load System deployed in Afghanistan

The MAN Support Vehicle Family. This family of wheeled vehicles is based on a design by the German Company MAN. It was intended to replace the existing 8 and 14-tonne fleet and other vehicles. The Support Vehicle (SV) family comes in numerous variants from 8 x 8 down to 4 x 4, and includes a REME recovery variant (see Chapter 17 ('REME Equipment and Technology')). A 15-tonne variant was converted to the EPLS in response to a UOR reflecting the demands of operations in Afghanistan. The family of vehicles is obviously of more modern design than those replaced, with a distinctive look of the cab, and there is a good degree of commonality between variants. In April 2010, 7,285 vehicles were ordered and at the time of writing they were in the process of replacing existing service vehicles.

MAN SV 4 x 4 vehicle

Land Rover. Technically, Land Rovers are not really Land Rovers at all, they are 'Trucks Utility' (with various suffixes such as Heavy, Medium, or FFR (fitted for radio)). The Army has had various small fleets of 'green' utility vehicles that were not made by Land Rover, such as the Pinzgauer 4 x 4 used by 16 Air Assault Brigade and 3 Commando Brigade, but most of them have been. This has continued with the Wolf and Defender having taken over from the 110 model. Land Rovers come in a number of variants, and these are fitted with a great variety of weapons, sensors, communications fits and forms of added protection.

Quad Bikes. At the bottom end of the size spectrum, quad bikes have proved very useful vehicles in Afghanistan.

Quad bike in Afghanistan

WEAPONS AND TOWED ARTILLERY

Weapons. There have been a number of specific changes to the small arms, mortars, heavy machine guns and other weapons used by the Army, but the overall picture has not changed greatly throughout the period covered by this book. The weapons themselves did not raise any serious supportability difficulties for REME. The significant changes tended to be related to the sighting and surveillance systems used with them, covered elsewhere.

Towed Artillery. The venerable 105mm Light Gun was used successfully in both Iraq and Afghanistan. Its calibre meant that is was not well suited to high-intensity armoured operations, but was ideal for some of the close support tasks encountered in Afghanistan. New associated electronic systems, such as velocity analyser, positioning and surveillance systems, enhanced its effectiveness.

ARMY EQUIPMENT AND ITS MANAGEMENT

105mm Light Gun firing at BATUS

BOWMAN COMMUNICATIONS EQUIPMENT

Bowman had been a very important communications equipment project for the Army. REME was heavily involved in the 'Bowmanisation' of vehicles, and the support of Bowman became one of the major tasks for REME Electronic Technicians.

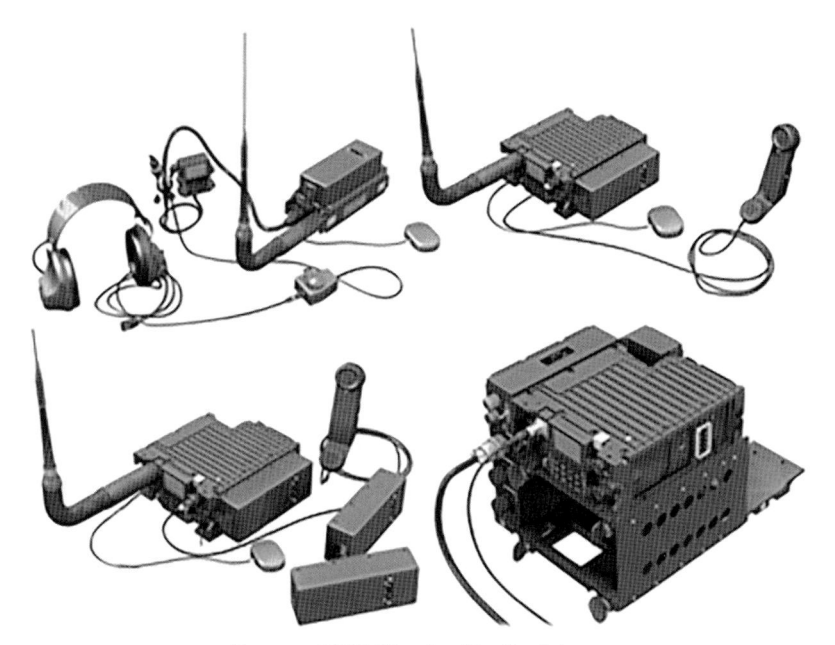

Bowman CNR (Combat Net Radio) sets

Bowman tended initially to be regarded as essentially a family of secure digital radios to replace the ageing Clansman system. In the event, it turned out to be much more than that, and provided the basis for the Army's plans for a 'network enabled capability'. The concept was ambitious and very complex, and the following paragraphs give a very simplistic explanation of it.

At the bottom level, it offers a family of HF (High Frequency) and VHF (Very High Frequency) Combat Net Radios (CNR). Broadly, they do the same thing as their Clansman equivalent, but are secure and use frequency-hopping technology. They include a small personal radio set carried by individual infantrymen (reducing the need for them to communicate by shouting or hand gestures). Communication is not always directly between one radio and another, an area relay system (think mobile phone) may be involved.

At the top level, Bowman has high-capacity digital systems that interface with other Services' top-level systems, effectively ensuring that all the Services are linked by high-speed data systems.

Bowman uses GPS technology, which not only tells a platform where it is, it automatically tells a HQ or other platforms fitted with appropriate Bowman equipment where it is by using a High Capacity Data Radio. Linking all the Bowman elements in a vehicle, there is the Vehicle Internal Distribution System (VIDS) that can be fairly complex. (**See Plate 47**)

Tactical data and location information (from GPS) can be presented on a system situational awareness system called COMBAT. This is essentially a screen that a vehicle commander, pilot or staff officer can view, which displays a map with overlays and locations. (**See Plate 48**)

The Bowman project was triggered by a requirement started in 1999. Its procurement had a long and chequered history, with a number of consortia involved in the development and bidding process. This process culminated in the failure in 2000 of the preferred bidder, Archer, to deliver the requirement within budget and on time, and the resultant cessation of the contract by the MoD. The subsequent rebidding process for the contract was won by CDC Systems UK Ltd, now General Dynamics United Kingdom Ltd, as prime contractor.

There were plenty of technical teething problems, and the National Audit Office and Public Accounts Committee were very critical of the way procurement had been carried out. By 2004, many of the problems had been ironed out and the process of 'Bowmanisation', which was to last several years was under way. This was to involve the conversion of around

15,700 land vehicles, 141 naval vessels, and 60 helicopters (mainly Chinook and Merlin), with training for some 75,000 service personnel. Around 45,000 personal role radios, 47,000 manpack and vehicle radios, and 26,000 computer terminals were acquired through the initial main contracts.

INTELLIGENCE, SURVEILLANCE, TARGET ACQUISITION AND RECONNAISSANCE

Intelligence, Surveillance, Target Acquisition and Reconnaissance (ISTAR) became an area of technology growth in which REME was heavily involved. Aspects relating to Unmanned Aerial Systems (UAS) are outlined in Chapters 11 and 12 (covering operations in Afghanistan) and Chapter 15 ('REME Aviation'). Its support for Base-ISTAR was also a major commitment in Afghanistan, as explained in Chapters 11 and 12.

REME continued to support numerous types of sights and surveillance devices including such complex new equipments as the MAMBA (Mobile Artillery Monitoring Battlefield) locating equipment.

SUPPORT FOR OTHER ELECTRONIC OR GUIDED WEAPON SYSTEMS

Anti-aircraft systems have not made many headlines, as the Army has not faced a significant air threat. REME nevertheless remains responsible for supporting the Rapier anti-aircraft system, which had been upgraded over the years with Field Standard C being introduced in 1992. This was effectively a new system, although Blindfire radar was little changed. It could fire both Mark 1 and Mark 2 missiles and its surveillance radar was removed from the launcher and became a separate element. REME also supported the smaller Starstreak missile, both in its shoulder-mounted and vehicle-mounted forms.

Electronic Counter Measures. Chapters 11 and 12 make it clear that the support of ECM capability, both fitting equipment to vehicles and maintaining it, became a major technical commitment for REME. Much of the UK ECM capability was first developed during the conflict in Northern Ireland, as an element of the complex counter-IED technology that was needed to protect both military and civilian lives. As the equipment was classified, there is not much that can be said about it other than that the commitment is likely to continue.

FLEET MANAGEMENT

Looking back some decades the Army had an Equipment Management (EMan) staff, which managed equipment. In due course, it was realised that the fleet management of complex equipments was best carried out by the organisation responsible for maintaining them. The EMan organisation was dismantled with many of its former functions being absorbed by REME staff branches. These involved 'asset management' to meet 'liabilities'. The principles at the time were basically simple. Most of the Army was at reasonably high readiness, and the maintenance system rested on the principle that it should be 'designed for war, adapted for peace'.

Units held most of their equipment all the time, but received a War Fighting Increment (WFI) of men and materiel to bring them up to full strength for operations. Units could train on training fleet equipment, notably at BATUS in Canada, but this was not seen as affecting their need to hold peacetime equipment, nor to affect their usual maintenance structure. This was very much the picture at the time of the formation of the Equipment Support Organisation in 1992, and its equipment branches had embedded 'fleet managers'. As the Army moved over the next few years to a state of graduated readiness, the possibility emerged of managing equipment in a very different way, with much peacetime training done using training fleets, and greatly reduced peacetime unit equipment holdings. Clearly, such ideas have important implications for REME, not least the operational risks associated with going too far down the route of outsourcing the peacetime support of training.

Army 2020 Equipment Allocation Concept

SDSR 2010, and the work that followed it, required a radical look at how the Army would work after its withdrawal from Afghanistan, at a time when it was assumed its operational commitments would have been drastically reduced. A new concept for allocating equipment was therefore developed concurrently with the force structures. This was explained in an article in The Craftsman magazine (July 2013), from which the following has been extracted:

> 'Unsurprisingly some of the ideas reflected earlier thinking on Whole Fleet Management (WFM), although the terminology had changed. The ideas were still being refined at the time of writing, but the following explains some of the thought processes involved, and the acronyms which go with them.

The Land Fleet Requirement (LFR) methodology seeks to determine the most efficient generation of Land capability to deliver mandated defence outputs. The LFR is defined as: 'The LFR is the minimum equipment fleet size required to equip the Force Driving Defence Operational Liability' the latter having the magnificent acronym FDDOL. This is in turn '… defined by Defence Planning Assumptions (DPA) scales of effort, readiness and concurrency. It must also equip Permanently Committed Forces (PCF); enable sustainability and essential requirements for the generation of FE and/or FE@R to meet DPAs'. Essentially the exercise involves the familiar staff exercise of justifying an equipment requirement and a concept for deploying it with new acronyms. In the future, it is intended that equipment will be deployed into three fleets'.

Equipment deployment into three fleets is shown in Figure 20.3 (at the end of this Chapter).

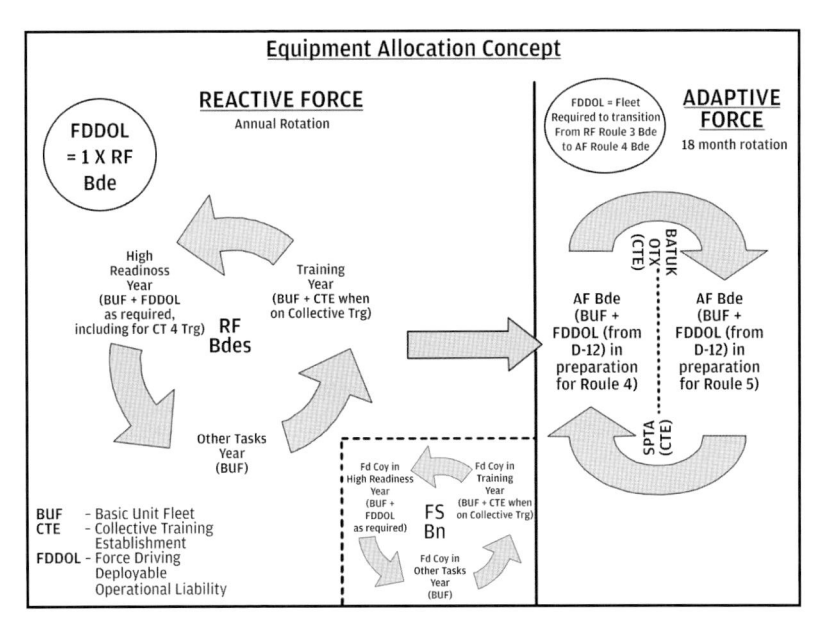

Equipment allocation concept diagram

As the concept of equipment allocation reflects some of the ideas that lay behind WFM, a brief account of the background and early history of WFM may be helpful as some of the issues are of continuing relevance to REME.

Whole Fleet Management – Background and Early Ideas

Chapter 4 ('Collective Training for Operations') explains how the realisation by the mid-1990s that not all the Army need to be on high readiness paved the way for the concept of the Force Readiness Cycle (FRC, later to be known as the Force Operational Readiness Mechanism (FORM)), which offered a route to less training and thereby a reduction in training costs.

It also started to be appreciated that if troops were to spend less time training, they would need to make less use of equipment, and that this might be translated into significant savings both to the cost of equipment procurement and its support.

There were a number of strands of thinking, which came to be loosely connected under the umbrella title of WFM. One was that since units were not all going to need their equipment for training at the same time, it would be possible to buy less in the first place provided the equipment was cleverly managed. This could be linked to the assumption that there would be two years warning of a major conflict, and that it might not be necessary for equipment to be held, which could be procured during the warning period. Other ideas related to the reduction of maintenance costs. For example, by optimising base repair intervals, or by storing vehicles in a Controlled Humidity Environment (CHE) where they would need virtually no maintenance at all.

It was felt that the use of CHE, combined with the greater use of training fleets, could both save money and improve life at unit level by reducing the burden of maintaining equipment that was not being used. Finally, it was considered that there were opportunities for making significant savings by contracting out the supply and support of equipment, quite possibly including private finance initiative (PFI) arrangements.

Supply and support of the 'white fleet' (administrative vehicles of a standard commercial type, so called because they were not painted green) had already been contracted out with significant savings. HQ QMG was keen to press ahead with a PFI deal for Land Rovers, which they felt could potentially deliver even greater savings. This happened at a time when there was great pressure to identify further efficiency savings. QMG was keen on forming 'tiger teams' to implement change, with 'Land Rover PFI' being seen as something that needed to be pushed forward as a 'Central Pillar' initiative to be carried forward within the DLO as it formed up.

WFM was frequently mentioned in equipment circles and widely assumed to be a 'good thing' that would be a key enabler of significant savings. QMG's two-star Chief of Staff (COS), in particular, was very much behind the idea. The snag at this early stage was that nobody was quite sure what WFM was, least of all existing equipment fleet managers. They knew that they already managed their whole fleet, and already had the concept of a peacetime Unit Entitlement (UE) to which a WFI would be added for operations. They already supported training fleets, and managed maintenance and base repair programmes, and were unclear about what WFM would, or would not, change.

A team was therefore set up to work out a way ahead for WFM. It was headed by an infantry Brigadier who was assisted by a REME Colonel (Colonel WFM) who was to act as his technical adviser. The team fairly swiftly produced a report. It suggested a pragmatic and progressive approach to implementing WFM. It believed that vehicles, which sat long term in unit hangars or on vehicle parks, should be stored in CHE. It envisaged greater use of training fleets, but made a distinction between simpler common-user equipments (such as basic Land Rovers and trucks) and complex military equipments. It believed that the former could increasingly go into training fleets, which should grow as suitable management information systems (MIS) were developed to support this. It considered that some of the more complex equipment could be pooled or stored, but much could be held in unit storage in CHE when not required (fitting CHE to unit hangars was a relatively cheap and simple process). It did not envisage fundamental change to the maintenance system. Equipment reductions predicated on WFM had already been pencilled in to procurement plans, so there was no obvious room for further savings in that respect.

Everyone agreed that the proposals would be workable, and would result in something better than the existing system. COS HQ QMG was, however, clearly very disappointed. WFM had been much talked up within the MoD, and the General Staff had taken it on board as one of its important 'efficiency measures', and at one time had pencilled in savings of £400m. COS HQ QMG (who was to move to the General Staff as the two-star Assistant Chief) believed that the WFM Team had failed to take a radical enough approach to their task and the result had been a 'damp squib'. He told them to go back to the drawing board and to look for a far more radical solution, which was based on much greater use of training fleets. To put some drive behind this, a Brigadier with an equipment background (but not in practical support or fleet management roles) was given temporary two-star rank and put in charge of the WFM Team to drive things forward.

This resulted in a superbly crafted report, which jumped all the MoD staffing hurdles and was to be accepted as policy by the Army Programmes and Resources Committee. It advocated an 'extreme' form of radical WFM with the UE being as close as possible to zero, with most equipment being provided from training fleets. These would be centralised adjacent to training areas, and much of their maintenance and management would be contracted out. This arrangement seemed to offer something for everyone. It would give the user equipment in full working order when he wanted it, and would take it off his hands when he did not. It was even good for REME personnel, as they would have much less work to do, although it was accepted that they would have to do a certain amount of technical work to keep their hand in. The timetable for putting this regime in place was aggressive, it was all due to happen in the next few years. In the event, things did not work out as then envisaged. The former Colonel WFM (Colonel (Retd) Richard Peregrine (late REME), Colonel WFM from June 1998 to August 2000) recalls the following personal perspective on what transpired at that time:

> 'I think I was picked for the WFM job because I was an experienced equipment manager, and was seen as someone with a 'can do' approach to novel ideas. After our first WFM report, however, COS HQ QMG clearly changed his views and decided I was really a reactionary REME foot-dragger in disguise. Although he disagreed with much in our report, he agreed that better MIS was required, and decided to take action. Presumably, to show me how things should be done. I was invited to an initial high-level meeting with some of his 'Central Pillar' staff to tackle the problem. The meeting resulted in an agreed plan to produce an asset management system MIS called DRUMM, which would meet the needs of WFM, and would start to go live and be useful within about five months. I had a considerable knowledge of the problems which go with equipment-related MIS and I rightly guessed exactly where the DRUMM project (now long forgotten) would be in five months – I was not invited to comment at the meeting and felt it would be wisest not to offer any. It does not surprise me that we are still having problems with the JAMES MIS some sixteen years later.
>
> I was also invited to sit in on the Land Rover PFI bidders conference. The bidders were well aware that the 'white fleet' PFI had been essentially a straightforward lease-hire agreement.

Such deals involve contractors buying vehicles in bulk from manufacturers willing to sell at rock bottom (undisclosed) prices to meet their volume targets, with the vehicles being sold on at the optimum resale point. Any make of vehicle could be supplied, and maintenance could be contracted out to any garage or supplier. They fully appreciated that the Land Rover PFI would be something in a completely different league. The Land Rover fleet itself was a large and complex one, of over 12,000 vehicles, with the numerous liability codes each reflecting different vehicle functional requirements. Vehicles needed to be fitted with different harnesses (wiring looms built in), so that required communication kits, sensors, weapons and so on could be installed and plugged in. They also needed installation kits (IK), which needed to be fitted to allow the installation of the communication kits, weapons, classified ECM equipment and so on. Pictures of Land Rovers being used on operations give an idea of the range of items which may be fixed on them.

The vehicles were used by many units for numerous tasks including operations and training world-wide. The bidders understood the implications of this, and asked many pertinent questions about where their responsibility for such things as maintenance, fleet/configuration management, spares, support on deployed operations and so on, would start and finish. Also, whether the 'Land Rover PFI' had to be for Land Rovers only or whether other makes were eligible. The Chairman (a military project leader, but not REME) answered along the lines "… um, yes, we know how astute you contractors are, and we were hoping you would tell us what you thought you should do – and, by the way, if your offer is good enough you can have our existing fleet for nothing".

I did not speak during the meeting, but I had some interesting chats after the meeting as several of the bidders' representatives were old chums from my days as a desk officer in B Vehicle Operational Requirements. These conversations involved a fair amount of 'eye rolling' and 'head shaking' by my contractor friends. Following the meeting, all the bidders replied 'thanks but no thanks' and the Land Rover PFI was effectively dead. I felt sorry for the Chairman who was a decent person, but who lacked the commercial insight and technical understanding of the realities of fleet/support management (including the limitations of MIS), which would have enabled him to realise that the concept he was trying to formulate would hit a brick wall as soon as it met commercial reality.

My reservations about 'radical' WFM did not arise from any innate conservatism, but because I had actually done my sums. I had carried out a 'quick and dirty' analysis of the training fleets' sizes that would be required (and their activity rates) to support the FRC scenario. I was glad to discover some years later that the figures I arrived at were validated almost exactly by a full-scale study by consultants. The training fleets would be huge, and all our experience of training fleets suggested that they would be extremely expensive to run. The 'radical WFM' idea also flew in the face of the well-proved principle that 'ownership' is a key promotional factor for effective equipment care (or equipment husbandry as it used to be called). Soldiers may at first sight seem to be spending more time than necessary on the vehicle park 'first parading' their vehicles, but often in the process young soldiers gradually absorb an understanding of (and respect for), the complex equipments on which their lives might depend (especially if there is a REME soldier around to mentor them).

My analysis also suggested that these ideas were very operationally risky. We had moved well past the former guiding principle during the Cold War of 'organise for war, adapt for peace', and I felt we had gone much too far in the direction of 'organising for peace, and hoping we can adapt for war'. We had used training fleets for years, but these had been 'as well as' substantial unit holdings, rather than 'instead of'. I could see it might be possible to organise 'radical WFM' so that it worked like clockwork – provided that the FRC also worked like clockwork. In the event of the need to react rapidly to an unforeseen crisis (which most are), it was possible to foresee huge problems associated with units being unable to train until other units had handed over training fleet vehicles, also the need fully to activate LADs and take on unit spares holdings, whilst simultaneously needing to activate equipment from long-term storage, which has generally involved modification work.

In my view, however, the huge 'poison pill' that came with the concept was a financial one, which could have potentially toxic operational consequences. The savings that would stem from reduced equipment numbers had already been taken, and yet more savings were pencilled in. I could not see where they would come from (and nor could some officers senior to me, whom I had invited to look at the issue). I could not believe that any savings through reduced unit maintenance would outweigh the huge additional costs generated by inexperienced testosterone-fuelled young soldiers thrashing training fleet equipments. Although I could not see where savings would come from, I had no problem seeing where additional costs would come from. Contractors would also need to be paid for supporting and managing equipment, and experience with the sort of PFI deals that were being contemplated had shown that they often prove extremely expensive in the long term. I believed that once these financial penalties started to become apparent, there would be a hunt for a financial 'get out of jail card'.

An obvious one would be to suggest that since units do not have their equipment much of the time, they do not need expensive REME technical staff twiddling their thumbs in the unit when it does not hold anything for them to work on. WFM came with a big disclaimer 'this is not about REME cuts', but it was not hard to imagine how that might change as when 'the financial chickens came home to roost', or what operationally impractical schemes would be cooked up for using contractors or sponsored reserves in lieu of Regular Army engineers. Having studied the way various armies maintained their equipment, when working in REME's Combat Development Cell, I felt we were at risk of throwing away a system that had evolved in war, and had been proved over and over again to work on operations, in favour of an untried concept that carried great operational risk, was likely neither to be adequately funded to work well, nor to deliver the savings expected of it.

This period was an uncomfortable time for me personally because, for the first and only time in my career, I felt it my duty to tell people senior to me things that I knew they did not want to hear, and did not agree with. A consolation was that I knew a number of senior REME officers privately shared my concerns and were grateful that I had alerted them to some of the issues involved.

In the event, 'radical WFM' as originally planned did not happen. Over the next few years, against a background of harsh operational realities, the more extreme ideas on WFM were to be moderated into something close to the original WFM Team suggestions.

I hope that this account will not be seen as ancient history, but a heartfelt cautionary tale of what can happen when a superficially attractive idea for cutting costs that has not been properly examined from the technical and operational points of view, gains traction at high level. It will certainly continue to be important to be proactive and innovative in seeking to improve the way in which the Army manages its equipment business. It will be no less important to spot innovative ideas that are going to be counterproductive and damaging, and to be prepared to explain the reasons for this to the senior officials who manage the Army's equipment and its support. These are increasingly likely to be civilians with no personal experience of the realities of mounting or supporting major operations who are likely to be offered ideas from those with a commercial axe to grind'.

Name	Role (estimated total number in 2014)	Notes
Foxhound	4 x 4 IMV (400)	Smaller and lighter than Mastiff and Ridgeback (7.2 tonnes), but well protected for its weight, and better suited than them to urban environments
Mastiff	6 x 6 IMV	Estimate total number of Mastiff, Ridgeback and Wolfhound was approximately 855 in 2014, weight approx 22 tonnes
Ridgeback	4 x 4 IMV	Smaller than Mastiff, but from the same (formerly US) family
Wolfhound	6 x 6 TSV	TSV version of the Mastiff
Panther	4 x 4 Command and Liaison Vehicle (400)	Italian origin (7 tonnes – air transportable)
Vector	6 x 6 IMV (343)	Lightly armoured IMV/light gun tractor, based on Pinzgauer 6 x 6 chassis
Husky	4 x 4 TSV (338)	US origin, fairly well protected, but controversial
Coyote	6 x 6 TSV (76)	6 x 6 version of the Jackal
Jackal	4 x 4 IMV (502)	Open top, suitable for reconnaissance, fire support
Buffalo	6 x 6 MRAP (19)	

Figure 20.1: Approximate composition of the UK PM Fleet in 2014

Variant	Name	Greek Character
Reconnaissance/Strike	Ajax	Hero notable for strength and courage
APC	Ares	God of war
Command and Control	Athena	Goddess of intelligence, battle strategy and wisdom
ES Recovery	Atlas	God who carried the world
ES Repair	Apollo	God of healing
Engineer Reconnaissance	Argus	All seeing giant

Figure 20.2: Names of the Ajax Family variants

Fleet	Components	Comment
Operational Fleet	Force Driving Deployable Operational Liability (FDDOL)	Total vehicle platforms and equipment required to meet DPAs (would change if these change)
	Permanently Committed Forces (PCF)	Committed to MACA and Permanent Joint Operating Bases
Training Fleet	Basic Unit Fleet (BUF)	Formerly Unit Holdings – equipment held at unit level to deliver effective individual training and meet other essential ongoing requirements
	Reinforcing Fleets	To enable collective training
	Overseas Training Area Fleets	Such as BATUS
	Reserves Fleet	Enables training of the Reserves
Sustainment Fleet (to cater for essential repair and upgrades)	Operational Stocks	To support anticipated deployments/operations
	Repair Pool	Required to enable the repair loop to function
	Attrition Reserve	To make good equipment damaged or lost when not on operations

Figure 20.3: Equipment deployment into three fleets

CHAPTER 21

HQ DEME(A) AND RHQ REME

THE FORMATION OF HQ DEME(A) IN 1999

The origins of the formation of Headquarters Director Electrical and Mechanical Engineering (Army) (HQ DEME(A)) lay in the fundamental examination of all aspects of ES initiated by the Quartermaster General (QMG) in 1997, called the 'Next Steps Review of ES', which was explained in The Craftsman magazine (May 1999). This envisaged restructuring QMG's equipment directorates into groups of Integrated Project Teams, as well as the formation of a new organisation, HQ DEME(A). Complementary background and detail is given in Chapter 18 ('Support for Army Equipment – An Overview'). This review was swept into the Strategic Defence Review (SDR), and once it was decided to form a tri-Service Defence Logistic Organisation (DLO) it became clear that HQ DEME(A), which was at first primarily about managing an Army organisation, might sit more comfortably within the Army. It was therefore decided to put DEME(A) under the Assistant Chief of the General Staff along with other Arms and Services Directors.

The new organisation was set up in Hazebrouck Barracks in Arborfield, under Brigadier Rod Croucher (late REME), who migrated from Andover with most of the staff of ES 11, and some elements of ES 21/23/33. These combined with Regimental Headquarters (RHQ) REME and the REME Training and Development Team (already in Arborfield) to form the new organisation. On 1 April 1999, Brigadier Croucher ceased to be Director of Equipment Support 1 (DES 1) and became DEME(A). When that happened, he took over as 'Head of the Corps' from the Director General Equipment Support (Army) (DGES(A)), Major General Peter Besgrove (late REME).

This was of huge significance. First, the 'Head of the Corps' was now a one-star officer. Second, the management of the Corps of REME was now clearly separate from the management of ES for the Army. The former was an Army responsibility; the latter had become a DLO responsibility. Previously, there had been some ambiguity about what was REME and what was ES, because the 'Head of REME' was also the 'Head of Army

ES'. Despite this formal organisational separation, in practice, many people continued doing much as they had done before. And personal links between the many REME people involved were an important contributor to the relatively smooth change to the new structure.

Brigadier Croucher's organisation comprised a small secretariat, and three main 'pillars'. Colonel Clive Ward (late REME) acted as the Chief of Staff (COS) and headed the Force Development and Policy Branch. This was responsible for doctrine, operational requirements, unit and career employment group structures, establishments, equipment tables and workshop procedures. Colonel Andy Philp (late REME) headed the Recruiting, Training and Aircraft Engineering Branch. This was responsible for recruiting, policy for Phase 2 and 3 Training, and REME training development. He was also the Army Chief Aircraft Engineer with responsibility for aircraft engineering policy, and accident investigation and engineering flight safety. Colonel Robin Joy (late REME), as Regimental Colonel, was responsible for the control and management of 'regimental' matters, as well as recruiting, selection and training advice for REME soldiers and officers, the Corps Band, the REME Museum of Technology plus archives, and the REME Headquarters Officers' Mess and Corps Sergeants' Mess.

OVERVIEW OF THE PERIOD FROM 1999 TO 2012

During the period from 1992 to 2012, the DEME(A) post was filled by five (late REME) officers: Brigadier Rod Croucher (April 1999–February 2002), Brigadier Stephen Tetlow (February 2002–December 2004), Brigadier Nigel Williams (January 2005–December 2007), Brigadier Brian McCall (January 2008–December 2010) and Brigadier Martin Boswell from January 2011 until further reorganisation of Army structures and the demise of HQ DEME(A) in April 2012.

The rank of the 'Head of the Corps' may have dropped from Major General to Brigadier with the formation of DEME(A), but the new arrangement had the advantage that the Brigadier could focus on the Corps, without being distracted by the multitude of other equipment-related issues to which DGES(A) had needed to attend. An important part of DEME(A)'s role was to get out and visit units and HQs. When he did so, REME personnel could get to know him as their 'tribal head', and he was able to consider their interests from the REME perspective, without any potentially conflicting or distracting, broader responsibilities.

A significant change took place on 1 May 2002, which was described in The Craftsman magazine (August 2002). The Landmark Study (see Chapter 13 ('REME in the UK – Structure and Organisation')) resulted in the loss of the one-star Commander ES post at HQ LAND. This left HQ LAND without a Brigadier-level adviser on REME matters. This resulted in additional responsibilities falling to DEME(A), whose revised mission was:

> 'To provide policy, advice and guidance to the General Staff and HQ LAND on REME matters, and to ensure that the Corps of REME is manned, trained, structured and motivated to fulfil its roles in peace, crisis and war, and to manage REME regimental activities'.

With the additional responsibilities came changes to the organisation of HQ DEME(A). The structure of three 'pillars' was retained, but with a significant reshuffle of responsibilities and staff. The COS headed up a renamed and reorganised Force Development and Doctrine Branch and became the COS/Colonel Force Development. The head of the second pillar was renamed Chief Engineer REME. The Regimental Colonel and RHQ REME retained their titles (certain responsibilities for recruiting and training having already been transferred to him).

Chapter 16 ('REME and the Reserve Army') explains how DEME(A) also became more involved with REME TA matters when the post of Commander HQ REME TA was dispensed with, and his HQ acquired a TA Policy Cell comprising the Colonel REME TA, a Regular Lieutenant Colonel and Warrant Officer, and a TA Major. This was enlarged when four additional staff were transferred in, following the closure of the Central Volunteer HQ in Bordon in 2010.

The role of DEME(A) was not directly comparable to that of any of the other Arms and Services Directors. The role of managing the Corps of REME could not be isolated from what was happening to Army equipment, or what the rest of the Army was doing. Almost all Army units relied critically on having the right embedded REME first line resources. Overall, DEME(A) had about 350 'posting points' to support (including the REME battalions). The problem of keeping the right number of people, with the right skills (and specialist equipment knowledge) in the right units at the right time, working to common engineering standards, would be a difficult and complex job. Successive holders of the DEME(A) post had also to cope with a host of problems, including resource shortfalls, rapidly-changing operational demands, and the almost continuous fielding of new equipment, procured to meet Urgent Operational Requirements (UOR). In order to do his job, DEME(A) therefore needed to have a broad understanding of what was going on across the Army, and to engage positively with what was going on in the world of operations, engineering, training and equipment (both the procurement of new equipment and support for existing equipment). Whilst doing this, he needed to maintain a strategic view of REME's future, and to be proactive in identifying necessary changes and driving them ahead.

When Brigadier Tetlow arrived in post, the arrangements for the invasion of Iraq were getting into gear and, early in his tour, he had to deal with many issues that arose from this and subsequent operations in Iraq. The pressure of operations in Iraq revealed that the MoD's system for managing equipment procurement and support was far from perfect. By 2005, concern was being aired at top levels in MoD that it was no longer an 'intelligent customer'. Chapter 19 ('Technical Support and Base Repair Agencies') explains how the complex arrangements for managing Army equipment and its support went through deep organisational change, adding to the difficulty of ensuring that Army equipment was properly supported on operations and elsewhere.

As problems were identified, much work went into overcoming them and developing more coherent overall approaches. This included numerous studies and exercises, such as the Defence Logistics Transformation Programme (incorporating the 'End-to-End Study').

Against this background of the need to produce a more effective structure for REME within tight resource constraints, Brigadier Tetlow and his successor, Brigadier Williams, drove through several significant lines of work to improve REME's efficiency and effectiveness. One was called 'rebalancing', which sought to optimise the balance of resources between repair organisations at first and second line. This delivered some manpower savings but its principal effect was to deliver greater flexibility. This exercise allowed essential savings to be made, and paved the way for much greater use of second line Intimate Support Teams in the years ahead. The various lines of work led to a number of other significant changes including:

- a major trade structure review (described in Chapter 22 ('REME People')), which was aimed at providing a trade structure that would meet the future needs of the Army, gave trade groups equitable

career opportunities, and came with a training requirement that was economical and affordable
- REME officers taking on greater responsibility for the scaling of spares in REME second line units
- the implementation of improved planning of major repair activities
- a review of trade training, which sought more closely to align the time at which training was delivered with the time at which it might be used, spreading trade training more evenly through a soldier's career and reducing repetition
- the implementation of 'lean' tools and techniques.

Meanwhile MoD 'head office' in Whitehall was looking to transform itself, in the light of events in Iraq and the 'intelligent customer' debate. New posts such as Director of Capability Integration and Director of Capability Improvement came into being as a result. DEME(A) headed a Corps responsible for delivering capability at the sharp end, and was able to call on a deep pool of expertise on broader equipment issues. He was therefore able to make an important contribution to the work on equipment capability issues. The broader contribution of the Corps was reflected in its new strapline in 2008 – 'Supporting Equipment Capability in the Army', which was explained in The Craftsman magazine (November 2008).

In particular, DEME(A) regularly provided constructive support or advice on operational support issues, particularly those related to UOR equipment projects. This focus on operations was linked to doctrinal work and, in April 2008, DEME(A) produced his pamphlet on 'Battlefield Equipment Support Doctrine'. This is an example of proactive work, which produced an important and coherent guide to ES matters that was assessed as 'fit for purpose' in the context of later developments.

DEME(A)'s work on engineering standards, and compliance with them, became of increasing importance in an ever more litigious world. The protection afforded by Crown Immunity was lost, when the courts deemed it inconsistent with human rights. This meant that the Army had to come to terms with such legislation as the Corporate Manslaughter and Corporate Homicide Act (2007).

This issue was highlighted by the crash of the RAF Nimrod MR2 aircraft, XV230, in September 2006 over Afghanistan. It was followed by a hard-hitting report by Mr Charles Haddon-Cave QC, as outlined in Chapter 15 ('REME Aviation'). Although focused on the Nimrod crash, it covered broader failings of the MoD's airworthiness regulation and processes. Consequently, the Chief of the General Staff (CGS) was given new and clarified responsibilities, with DEME(A) (and his engineering staff) supporting him in the role of Competent Army Authority and Inspectorate for relevant Army engineering matters. Haddon-Cave had recommended that each Service should have a senior aircraft engineer who was clearly responsible to the Head of the Service. As a result, DEME(A) gained a fourth part of his organisation in the form of the Army's Chief Aircraft Engineer (CAE) – whose role is further explained in Chapter 15.

In the years leading up to 2008, many of the issues with which DEME(A) had to deal were directly, or indirectly, related to the Defence budget. It was clear that Prime Minister Tony Blair's enthusiasm for projecting British military force abroad was not matched by an equal enthusiasm on the part of his Chancellor of the Exchequer, Gordon Brown, for funding Defence generously. There was a continuous struggle to match ends to means by one expedient or another – often fuelled by the hope that at some point 'new money' would be found that would enable workable solutions. In 2008, a global financial crisis arose, which caught Britain with a substantial budget deficit. In these circumstances, it was abundantly clear that there was no prospect of 'new money' for Defence, and that the Defence budget was going to be significantly cut as part of a strategy to reduce the deficit (whichever party was in power). Clearly, the very considerable amount of work that had been undertaken by DEME(A) and many others, on such topics as the Future Structure of the Army, had put the Corps in a good position to weather the storm.

In May 2010, the Coalition Government came to power and carried out a short, sharp review, the Strategic Defence and Security Review (SDSR), which reported later that year. The outcome of this is described in Chapter 3 ('Strategic Defence and Security Review 2010 and Army 2020'), and involved a reduction in 'starred' officer posts and the significant downsizing of the Army as a whole. To reduce the one-star count in the Army, CGS decided to cut the one-star posts of the Arms and Services Directors, including that of DEME(A). This also served to appease the Heads of the other Services who had long protested that the Army's Arms and Services Directors were an unaffordable luxury. Early in 2012, therefore, Brigadier Boswell, who was mid-stream in re-organising the size and shape of REME to match the requirements of an Army rationalising from 101,000 to 82,400 Regular personnel, ceased to be DEME(A). He moved on to HQ Land Forces to take up a post as the Capability Director

Combat Service Support (CSS) (a competed post with responsibilities embracing REME and RLC Capability Development and Integration). Two Assistant Directors (AD) looked after ES at Colonel level, namely the AD ES (Land), and AD ES (Aviation). The changes had been made swiftly, and further information is given in Chapter 13 ('REME in the UK – Structure and Organisation').

A key feature of these changes was that the Equipment Capability Customer branches in MoD Main Building were dismantled in the process and placed back into the front line Command Headquarters (in effect going from MoD 'Centre' to the Navy, Army and RAF). As Director CSS, Brigadier Boswell assumed responsibility for all the Land equipments previously sponsored by Director Equipment Capability Expeditionary Logistics Support. Army governance was by a two-star Director General Capability, who controlled four key directorates – Combat, Combat Support, Combat Service Support and Information. These organisations, led at one-star, were formed out of merged Arms and Services Directorates and MoD Main Building staff and immediately focused on closing out the structures and equipments for Army 2020.

As a generalisation, it is clear that DEME(A) proved to be a very effective organisation under able Directors, who safeguarded the interests of the Corps and maintained its ethos and strength as an engineering organisation, during a period of huge operational and financial pressure. The detailed outcome for REME of SDSR 2010 is explained in Chapters 3 and 13, but in broad terms, given the circumstances, REME came out of it very well. This undoubtedly reflected the enviable reputation that REME officers and soldiers had earned for supporting their Army 'customers', when the chips were down – on operations, or elsewhere.

THE HQ DEME(A) THREE 'PILLARS' AFTER THE REORGANISATION OF 2002

The diagram at Figure 21.1 (at the end of this Chapter) provides a snapshot of HQ DEME(A) organisation in mid-2002 with each of its three 'pillars' headed by a Colonel. The paragraphs that follow outline what went on in each 'pillar' at the time, and how things moved on thereafter.

The COS/Force Development 'Pillar'
The COS/Force Development Branch was initially responsible for doctrine, operational requirements, unit and career employment group

structures, establishments, training needs and development, equipment tables and workshop procedures. The Branch therefore had a heavy baseload of work, concerned with the time-honoured business of sorting out organisations and structures, justifying them, reconciling manpower totals and producing policies intended to ensure that units had the right combination of numbers and skills to enable them to meet their training and operational commitments. The Head of the Branch, in his role as COS, would also coordinate business across the HQ, and be the normal first point of contact when issues arose that were not part of the routine work of any other branch. These might be internally initiated, for example as a result of DEME(A) visits, or externally driven by almost anything, including the seemingly endless stream of initiatives, savings measures and other ideas coming from above.

By May 2002, the COS had a small section titled 'Ops & Plans' working directly to him, responsible for coordination, budgets, IT and administration. The main part of his Force Development Branch comprised a Force Development Section (under a Lieutenant Colonel) and a Structures, Organisation and Deployments Section (also under a Lieutenant Colonel). The former Equipment and Logistics Section had been disbanded, with the operational requirements staff moving to the Force Development Section, with the Equipment Table and Sponsor and Writer posts moving into the Organisation and Deployments Section.

At this time, the Force Readiness Cycle was a major driver of planning; this concept is explained in some detail in Chapter 5 ('Operations General'). There was a major revision of planning assumptions in 2003 and further change in 2005. A National Audit Office Report from June 2005 indicated the degree to which readiness was seen as an important and complex subject, which needed to be managed top-down by the MoD. The Services and the organisations that supported them were, by this time, very focused on budgets and customer-supplier relationships. Readiness levels were the subject of periodically-updated Public Service Agreements, and needed to be properly defined, measured and reported. They were predicated on Defence Planning Assumptions, which were in turn related to budgets. This was because readiness costs money, and a change of readiness could impact on the budget of numerous agencies and other organisations, which were themselves linked by customer-supplier agreements. For example, an increase in readiness would require additional training – this would not only impact on the training organisation that had to support it, but on the ES organisation, including the DLO, which would have to adjust stock levels. DEME(A)'s staff were inevitably involved in some of the issues that arose.

Despite all the planning and study of readiness issues, when 16 Air Assault Brigade deployed to Afghanistan on Operation HERRICK 4 in 2006 it found itself under-resourced in a very difficult and dangerous situation (see Chapter 11 ('Afghanistan – The Long Haul (Operations HERRICK 4–14)'). The reinforcements that had to be rushed out had little preparation for the desperate defensive battles they were soon to engage in. As the operational situation in Afghanistan and Iraq became more difficult, the provision of support for current operations naturally moved up the list of priorities for the Branch and others slid downwards. There were, nevertheless, many hot topics that could not be ignored. A review of live topics in 2008 would, for example, include the Defence Training Review (see Chapter 23 ('Individual Training Organisations')), the Defence Logistics Transformation Programme (an important change programme, which was led by the DLO but had implications for ES/REME), the 'Future Structure of the Army' work and much else. In short, COS DEME(A) was always busy.

The Engineering 'Pillar'
From 2002, the Head of the Engineering 'Pillar' was titled Chief Engineer REME. He was double-hatted as the Army Chief Aircraft Engineer (CAE) and therefore had to hold aircraft engineering qualifications. A study into Defence Airworthiness in 2004–2005 led to a MoD decision to remove all reference to maintenance or engineering airworthiness and to disestablish the Services' Chief Aircraft Engineer posts. Notwithstanding this, an aviation engineering group remained within HQ DEME(A) answering to the Chief Engineer REME, who could thereby maintain a vital grip on aircraft engineering matters. The organisation of the Chief Engineer REME comprised two sections.

Land and Training Standards. The role of this section was to monitor the equipment engineering and training standards required throughout REME. The Land Standards element provided specialist REME advice on health and safety, quality management, engineering policy and associated matters. A primary responsibility for this new Branch was to author DEME(A) Engineering Standards, which for the first time brought the competence and development of both Regular and Reserve REME to a common standard. The Training Standards element conducted external validation on all REME/ES courses and advised on all civilian technical qualification issues. Initially, the REME Training and Development Team was under the command and control of the Regimental Colonel but eventually transferred to the Chief Engineer REME.

Air Standards. This section had responsibility for the maintenance and airworthiness policy for Army aircraft, which included advising Joint Helicopter Command and Director Army Aviation. It was required to investigate Army aircraft accidents or serious incidents and provide expert advice to related enquiries. It carried out Unit Flight Safety Inspections, monitored Services-sponsored engineering modifications and liaised with the Civil Aviation Authority, as necessary. Following the merging of single-Service policies into Joint Air Publications, and subsequently the creation of the Joint Military Aviation Authority, the Branch contributed increasingly to best practice in the 'Joint' environment.

The RHQ REME 'Pillar'
The background to the formation of RHQ REME at Arborfield in 1991 is given in Chapter 24 ('Corps ('Regimental') Matters'). Its evolving role led to the post of Regimental Colonel becoming a full-time Colonel appointment in 1993.

The role of RHQ REME evolved further soon after the formation of HQ DEME(A). It continued to be responsible for 'regimental' matters in much the same way as before, including such areas as the Museum, Band and Headquarters Messes (all covered in the chapters on Corps and 'regimental' activities), but increasingly began to act as a more conventional staff branch, supporting DEME(A) on what might be called 'people' issues (as opposed to technical, organisational or operational issues on which the other 'pillars' would provide a lead).

By the nature of things, such issues are interactive and cannot be looked at in isolation. In very broad terms, the COS/Force Development 'Pillar' studied and argued the case for REME's structure, and the number of people required to fill it (the 'liability'). The Army Personnel Centre managed the 'available assets' in terms of numbers, ranks and skills, in the light of advice given by DEME(A) on operational priorities. Individual training courses were mostly provided by the Army Training and Recruitment Agency (ATRA).

The recruitment requirement could be worked out by considering all these factors in conjunction with overall constraints on numbers and

Plate 39: Presentation of the Turners Shield 1999
Picture left to right: Colonel (Retd) Lucas, Lieutenant Colonel O'Leary (CO 103 Battalion REME (V)), Major General (Retd) Tyler (Master of the Turners), Major Cooper (150 Recovery Company), Captain Lawson (150 Recovery Company)

Plate 40: Support Vehicle (Recovery)

Plate 41: CPPRF repair container

Plate 42: CIRF mounted on a DROPS vehicle

Plate 43: Challenger 2 tank of the Queen's Royal Hussars at Bergen-Hohne January 2014

Plate 44: Warrior vehicle in Afghanistan (uparmoured, with protective electronic fit)

Plate 45: A Viking vehicle towing a DROPS vehicle carrying a Vector vehicle on Operation HERRICK 7

Plate 46: Coyote Tactical Support Vehicle

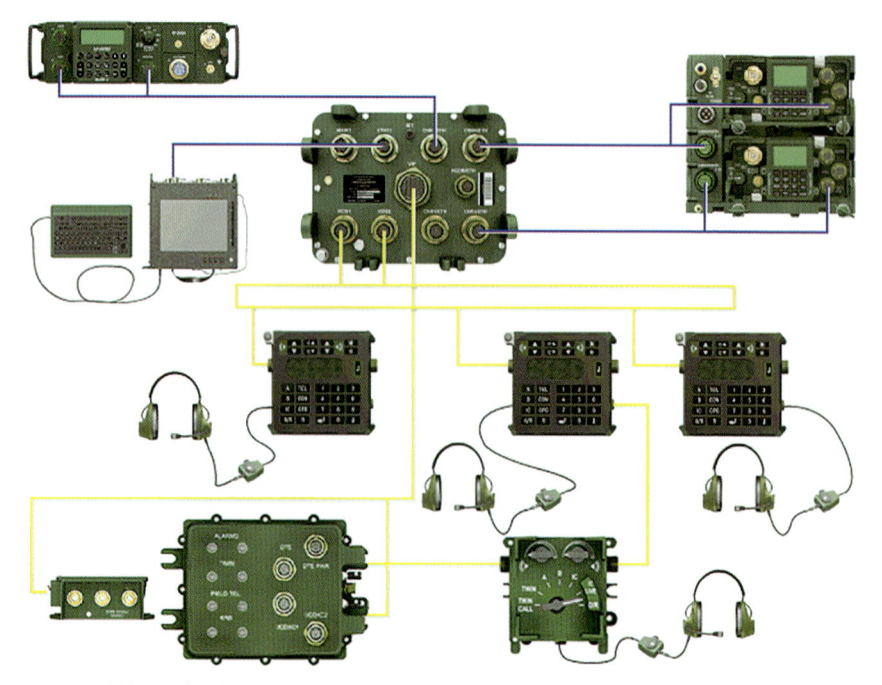

Plate 47: Illustration of Bowman Vehicle Internal Distribution System

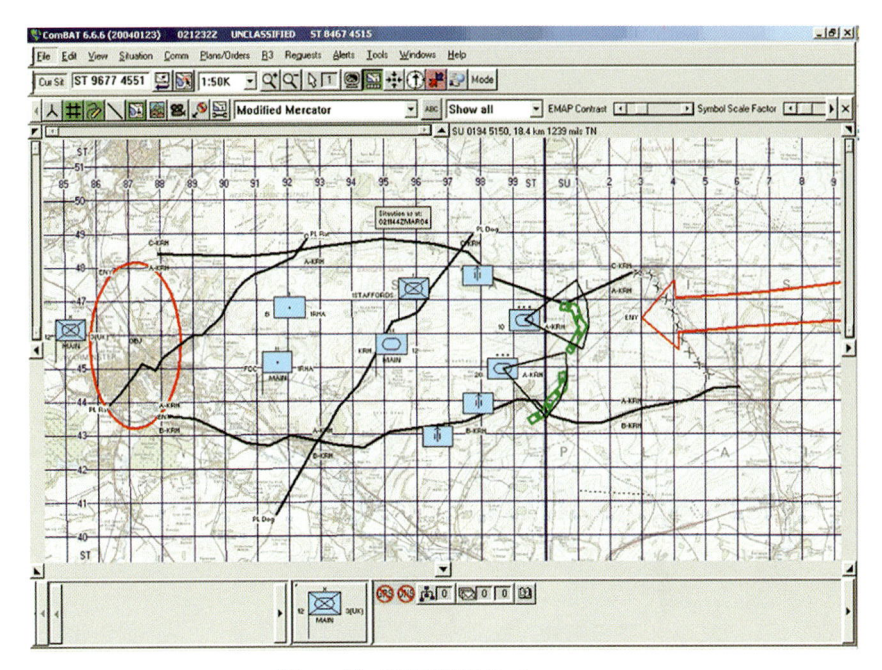

Plate 48: COMBAT display screen

Plate 49: REME Association members at the REME Memorial at the NMA

Plate 50: The Colonel in Chief unveiling a plaque at the REME Memorial on 9 July 2009

Plate 51: The Colonel in Chief meets REME Association members and serving REME personnel at lunch following the opening of the REME Memorial at the NMA

Plate 52: The Colonel in Chief views the Historic Vehicle Display on 31 July 1997
Left to right: Brian Baxter, Roger Jones, Lieutenant Colonel (Retd) Le Var, the Colonel in Chief, Brigadier Palmer, Colonel Millington

Plate 53: Display in the Prince Philip Vehicle Hall

Plate 54: WestFest – the end of an era

Plate 55: 'Mr Green' at West Court

Plate 56: The first six Corps ASMs (Swan, Lamont, Jones, Walker, Howell, Murley) dine out Angela Evans (PA to DEME(A) from the formation of his HQ to its closure in 2012)

Plate 57: Personnel serving in Germany make use of the REME Hotel for a triathlon camp

Plate 58: Mr Andrew Haines, the Colonel in Chief and the Representative Colonel Commandant (Major General Tyler)

Plate 59: RHQ REME Lyneham

Plate 60: Brunel Building Lyneham

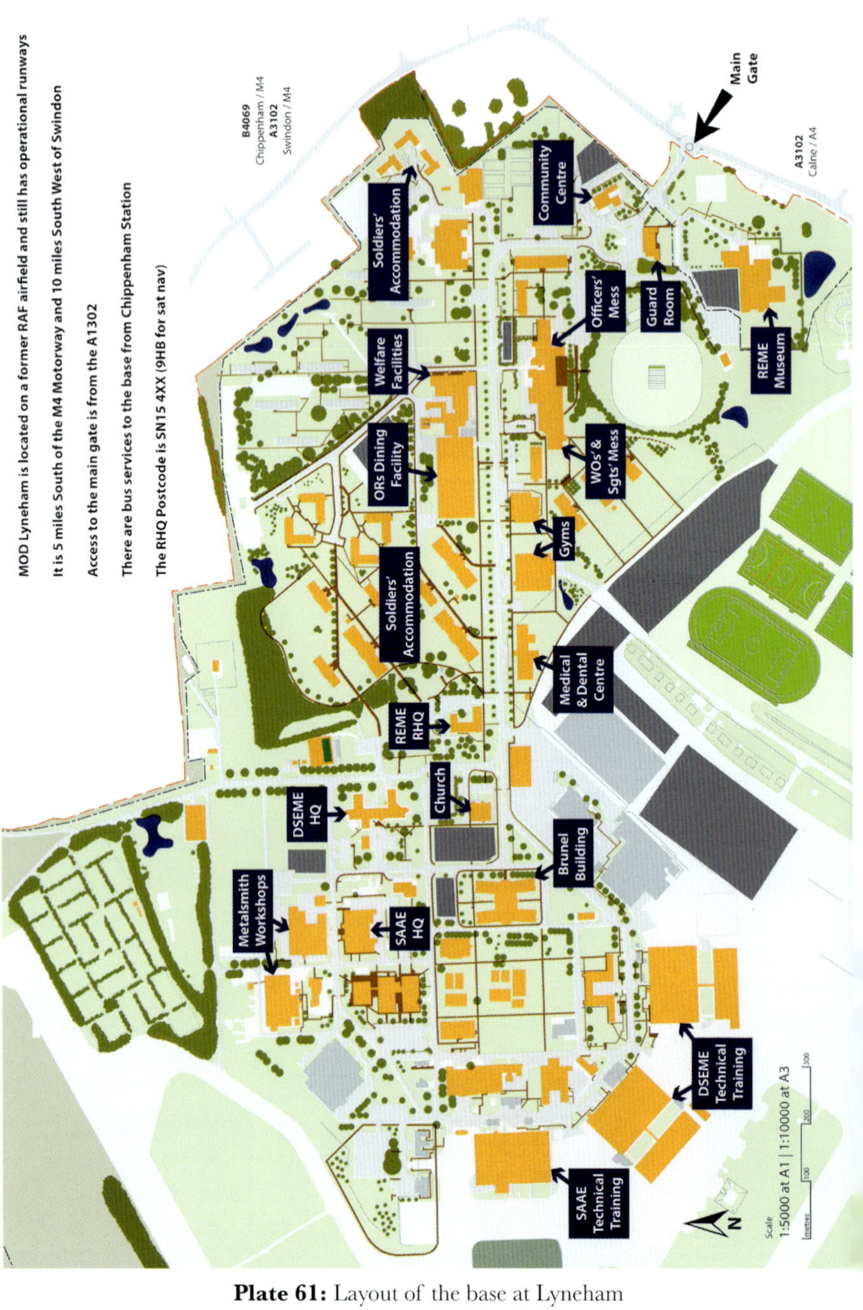

Plate 61: Layout of the base at Lyneham

Plate 62: 3 Battalion REME 1998
Winners Germany Army Cup and Army Challenge Cup

Plate 63: REME Inter-Corps Badminton Champions 2015

Plate 64: REME Stallions at the Canadian EME Championships 2012

Plate 65: REME Display Team in formation 2009

Plate 66: REME crew of 'Endeavour' for the Rolex Fastnet Race 2007 at Plymouth Winners of Inter-Regimental Cup and Culdrose Trophy

Plate 67: HRH The Princess Royal presents Major Barham with a RYA Outstanding Commitment Award November 2008

Plate 68: Major Lethbridge Army and Combined Services Champion

Plate 69: Berghaus Lieb

funding (which were subject to an annual MoD negotiating cycle). Clearly, such matters would affect the overall training requirement, which had to be matched to the requirement both to train new recruits, and provide career and technical training to support the career progression of existing REME personnel. The latter was linked to promotion quotas, and the need for every trade or skill group to have the right structure in terms of rank and experience, as well as a fair prospect of promotion.

Training. The Regimental Colonel's increasing involvement led to the establishment of a training element under a Lieutenant Colonel (initially called the Staff Officer Grade 1 Training and Recruiting). One of its key outputs was the Statement of Training Requirement, which represented the 'customer' requirement that the ATRA was asked to deliver, in terms of types of course and number of people who needed to be trained on them. The lead on matters related to the technical content of the courses, especially those for new equipments, still generally lay with the relevant training staff in the Engineering 'Pillar' at this stage.

Recruiting. When the new Regimental Colonel took over from Colonel Joy in 2000, DEME(A) explained that one of his main concerns was that the Corps was '*bleeding to death*' because the inflow of recruits was not matching the outflow and he wanted the issue to be given a high priority. An informal look at what ATRA was doing to recruit on behalf of REME left the RHQ REME team unimpressed, not least by some of the very expensive advertising provided by its commercial advisers. In time-honoured REME fashion, it decided that they would attack the problem themselves. Their work started with an analysis of their target population, the product which REME had to offer and how to market it and how to present it to key youth 'gatekeepers' who would advise young people on careers. They realised that the quality of the product they had to offer (the young REME soldier and officer) was fantastic and the best way to sell it was to show it off. Recruiting teams were set up, and were generously loaned vehicles free of charge by Volkswagen, which had enjoyed a long and happy relationship with REME, since Major Ivan Hirst REME helped regenerate their factory in the aftermath of World War 2 (see Volume 2 of Craftsmen of the Army). This, and other measures, did the trick, and soon REME's problem with ATRA was not a lack of recruits for training but so many of them, which created an ongoing training backlog (covered in some detail in Chapter 23).

Personal Development. When it joined DEME(A), RHQ REME brought with it responsibilities for the selection and career development of REME Regular Young Officers (RYOs), which it had in turn inherited from the former REME Officers' School, along with the relevant staff. It soon became clear that the subject of career and personal development was one of growing importance in a world where formal qualifications were increasingly necessary to demonstrate that technical personnel met the required competence standards for Suitably Qualified and Experienced Personnel. Work on personal development therefore became a growth area, which expanded from dealing primarily with REME RYO matters to those relevant to officers and other ranks at all levels. Chapter 22 provides additional relevant information. As the workload increased it became clear that there was a need for an additional post at Lieutenant Colonel level. This was duly established, with duties split between one post covering Training (which had increasingly become a tri-Service issue) and the other Recruiting and Personal Development.

Corps Secretariat. If the Corps Secretary was a retired senior officer with appropriate experience, he could do much more than just his primary job of running the Corps Secretariat. He could bring continuity of experience, the ability to spot problems and to resolve them without fuss by drawing on his personal experience at senior level and his contacts. He could also be a person with whom the Regimental Colonel or DEME(A) could discreetly discuss issues, which were not necessarily related to Corps Secretariat business. When DEME(A) was formed, the Corps was fortunate to have Colonel (Retd) David Axson (late REME) in post as a Corps Secretary who fitted this mould, was deeply committed to serving the best interests of the Corps and had an encyclopaedic knowledge of it. The considerable concern about who would replace him was allayed when Brigadier (Retd) Tony Ball (late REME) took up the post in 2002 and stayed in it until the period when the post of DEME(A) was being dissolved in 2012. He came as a former Chief Executive of the Army Technical Support Agency and prior to that had twice been a Director of Equipment Support at Andover. He therefore combined an in-depth knowledge of the Corps with a deep understanding of ES issues generally, and had a very useful list of personal contacts. He was another excellent servant to the Corps and in addition to his many proactive contributions his presence meant that the Regimental Colonel could rest assured that routine Corps Secretariat business was being efficiently overseen. The Corps Secretariat's business included:

- matters related to the various Corps Committees and their charitable governance work
- publications – including the excellent monthly magazine The Craftsman, the REME Journal and the annual REME Officers' List (known colloquially as the 'Blue Book', listing posts held by serving REME officers, and listing serving and retired officers, who are members of the REME Institution)
- welfare issues and matters related to the REME Institution and the REME Association (and its Job Agency)
- financial matters, including the allocation of funds for sport and adventurous training.

FURTHER DEVELOPMENTS AND FINAL ORGANISATION OF HQ DEME(A)

Territorial Army. As outlined in Chapter 16 ('REME and the Reserve Army'), the demise of the Regular post of Commander HQ REME TA led to Colonel REME TA heading a TA Policy Branch in HQ DEME(A), which included both a Regular and a Reserve Lieutenant Colonel post, and had an outpost at Bordon headed by a retired Major.

Aircraft Engineering. As explained in Chapter 15, the findings of the Haddon-Cave Review into the crash of a RAF Nimrod aircraft led to the decision to remove engineering and maintenance airworthiness responsibilities from the single Services being rescinded. The post of CAE was reinstated in HQ DEME(A) and an aircraft engineering branch was set up. Colonel Rod Williams (late REME), ably assisted by Mr Charles Davison, assumed this role. In short order, they delivered the necessary aviation engineering standards, training requirements, and engineering requirements as part of the aviation Release to Service authorisation process; and seized the opportunity to develop the aircraft engineering career structures, in conjunction with the REME Division in the Army Personnel Centre, to support Army 2020. When HQ DEME(A) closed, he continued this work as an Assistant Director Aircraft Engineering and CAE in the new Capability Directorate Combat Service Support.

Training, Recruiting, Force Development, Personnel and Welfare Responsibilities. There was a realignment of responsibilities that saw RHQ REME hand over responsibility for training to a reconfigured

Training Branch, which pulled together training and training development work under the COS. The Chief Engineer REME lost his responsibility for aircraft matters and took on responsibility for force development, with a Lieutenant Colonel responsible for force development and another for training standards. The remaining Lieutenant Colonel in RHQ REME was retitled Staff Officer Grade 1 Recruiting and Personnel. As the effects of operations in Iraq and Afghanistan were increasingly felt by returning Servicemen and women and their families, the need for more work to be done for their welfare was evident. A new Regular Warrant Officer Class 2 post was created within the Recruiting and Personnel Section to deal with the casework involved. The cumulative changes outlined above meant that, as at September 2011, HQ DEME(A) had the organisation shown in Figure 21.2 (at the end of this Chapter).

TRANSITION AND THE FUTURE ROLE OF RHQ REME

As DEME(A)'s organisation was broken up in 2012, most of it was absorbed into the Army Headquarters and Capability Directorate Combat Service Support. The Regimental Colonel was renamed the Corps Colonel REME ('Colonel REME') and his organisation was restructured to match his changed responsibilities. He lost the Lieutenant Colonel post responsible for recruiting and personnel, but gained one responsible for the Defence Technical Training Change Programme with special reference to planning the transfer of technical training from Bordon and Arborfield to Lyneham. The need to tie together the various aspects of dealing with manpower issues (the 'liability', managing available manpower, recruiting, training, career development training, and so on) had by no means gone away, and the need to deliver the right people to populate the new structures for the Army 2020 and Future Reserves 2020 programmes added an extra dimension. The new 'Manning Brick' in Army HQ and the 'Four Balls' model described in Chapter 3, represented the basis of the new method for achieving this. Colonel REME, as nominally the most senior serving officer appointment formally representing the interests of REME, was to have a key role in this arrangement.

His new organisation included a COS (Major), the Corps Adjutant (Captain) and the Corps Artificer Sergeant Major, as well as a recruiting organisation and administrative staff. The Corps Adjutant was also appointed Assistant Equerry to His Royal Highness The Prince Philip the REME Colonel in Chief. The changes gave Colonel REME an enhanced role as a member of various Boards at the Army Personnel Centre in Glasgow. He also assumed the role of ADC to Her Majesty The Queen, and gained responsibility for providing direct support to the new appointment of Master General REME, whose role is titular 'Head of the Corps' – Regular, Reserve and retired. In short, he had gained a role as key guardian of REME's heritage, ethos and the interests of all its members.

The Corps Secretariat was to continue to manage much Corps and 'regimental' business under his direction on broadly the same lines as before. Some changes did take place in early 2013; responsibility for liaison with the Colonel in Chief's Office was taken on by the Corps Adjutant, and a separate Corps Communications Manager, reporting directly to the Corps Colonel, removed responsibility for REME Publications from the Corps Secretary. The Corps Secretaries during the period covered by this book were:

- 1995   Colonel (Retd) David Axson (late REME)
- 2002   Brigadier (Retd) Tony Ball (late REME)
- 2013   Colonel (Retd) Sam Jarvis (late REME)
         Lieutenant Colonel Mike Tizard REME (August)
         Lieutenant Colonel (Retd) Bill Barclay REME (November onwards).

Some explanation for three Corps Secretaries in 2013 may be called for. Brigadier (Retd) Ball, who had been the mainstay of the Headquarters and Secretariat for some 11 years, and the architect of the governance changes leading to the establishment of the Corps Council and the Master General REME post, decided to retire finally in late 2012. His replacement, Colonel (Retd) Sam Jarvis (late REME), came to the Secretariat from industry in early 2013 but found the lure of working in industry too attractive, finally returning to it at the end of July. Lieutenant Colonel Mike Tizard REME, who was still serving and already covering an extremely busy post in the move of technical training to Lyneham, stood in as Corps Secretary until the tortuous Civil Service recruitment process could produce a more permanent replacement, Lieutenant Colonel (Retd) Bill Barclay REME. Lieutenant Colonel Tizard's short tenure proved, once again, the truth in Benjamin Franklin's quote, "if you want something done, ask a busy person."

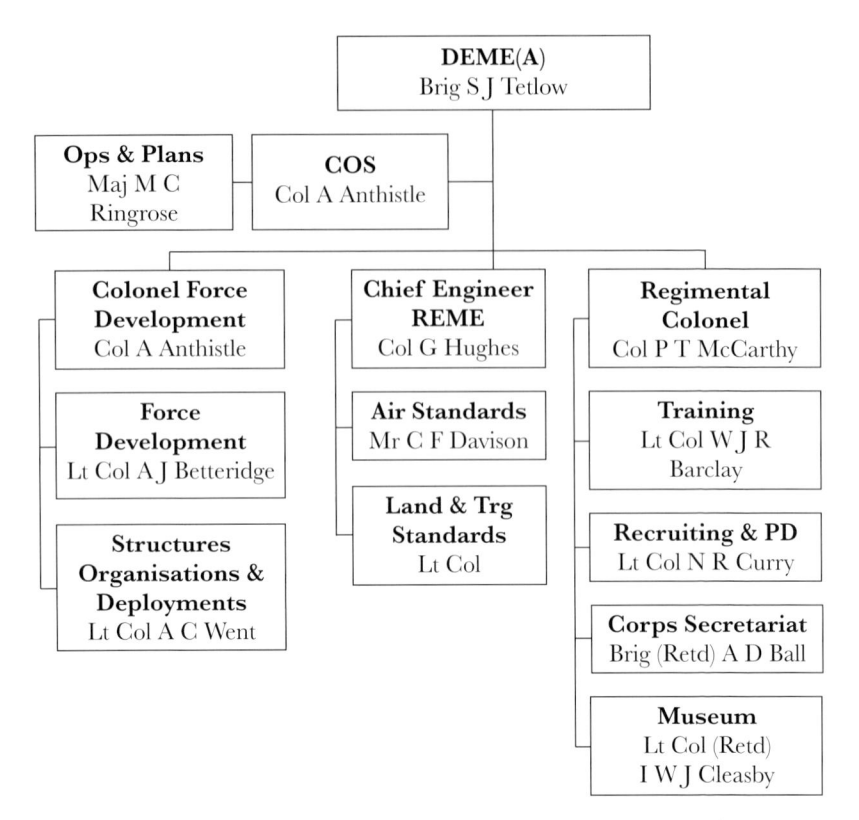

```
                    ┌─────────────────────┐
                    │      DEME(A)        │
                    │   Brig S J Tetlow   │
                    └─────────────────────┘
┌──────────────┐    ┌──────────────┐
│ Ops & Plans  │    │     COS      │
│   Maj M C    │    │ Col A Anthistle│
│   Ringrose   │    │              │
└──────────────┘    └──────────────┘
```

Colonel Force Development Col A Anthistle	Chief Engineer REME Col G Hughes	Regimental Colonel Col P T McCarthy
Force Development Lt Col A J Betteridge	Air Standards Mr C F Davison	Training Lt Col W J R Barclay
Structures Organisations & Deployments Lt Col A C Went	Land & Trg Standards Lt Col	Recruiting & PD Lt Col N R Curry
		Corps Secretariat Brig (Retd) A D Ball
		Museum Lt Col (Retd) I W J Cleasby

Figure 21.1: HQ DEME(A) three 'pillars' after the reorganisation of 2002

HQ DEME(A) AND RHQ REME

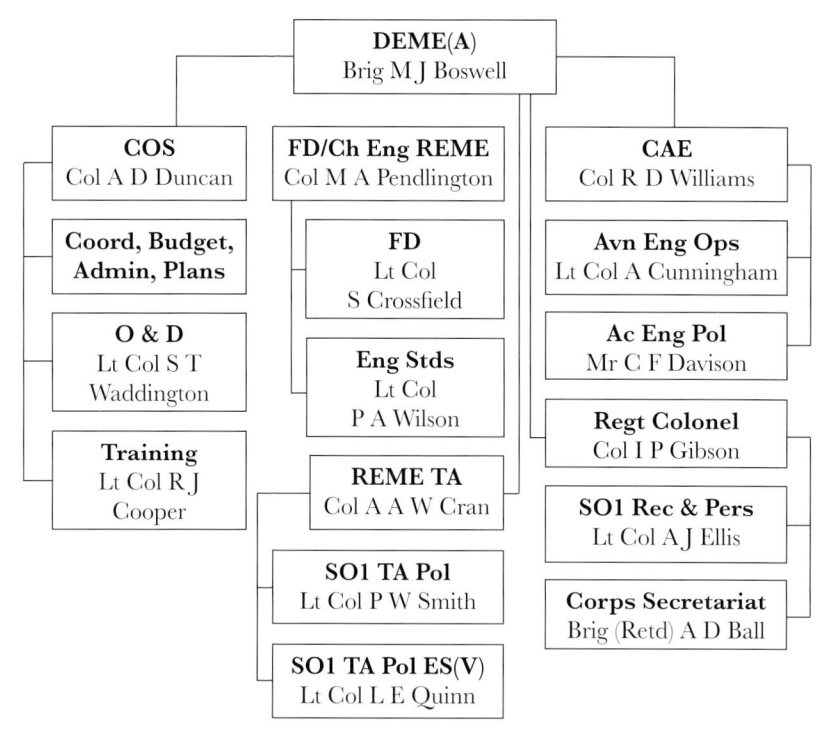

```
                        DEME(A)
                     Brig M J Boswell
                           │
   ┌───────────────────────┼───────────────────────┐
   │                       │                       │
  COS              FD/Ch Eng REME                 CAE
Col A D Duncan   Col M A Pendlington         Col R D Williams
   │                       │                       │
Coord, Budget,            FD                  Avn Eng Ops
 Admin, Plans           Lt Col              Lt Col A Cunningham
                      S Crossfield
   │                       │                       │
   O & D               Eng Stds                Ac Eng Pol
Lt Col S T              Lt Col               Mr C F Davison
Waddington            P A Wilson
   │                       │                       │
 Training              REME TA              Regt Colonel
Lt Col R J           Col A A W Cran         Col I P Gibson
 Cooper
                           │                       │
                      SO1 TA Pol            SO1 Rec & Pers
                    Lt Col P W Smith         Lt Col A J Ellis
                           │                       │
                    SO1 TA Pol ES(V)      Corps Secretariat
                    Lt Col L E Quinn       Brig (Retd) A D Ball
```

Figure 21.2: Organisation of HQ DEME(A) as at September 2011

CHAPTER 22

REME PEOPLE

MANAGEMENT OF REME PERSONNEL

The REME manpower requirement is rightly driven by the needs of the Army. This reflects the number of units that have to be supported, their role, the equipment they hold, as well as the repair policy for that equipment. Recruiting, training and retaining the right number of 'REME people' with the right skills at the right levels, and filling vacancies across the Army (and elsewhere in Defence) is a hugely complicated business, which this Chapter seeks to explain.

With the formation of HQ DGES(A) in 1992, the former DEME (Org & Trg) became the Director of Equipment Support 1 (DES 1) but in essence his task was little changed. His task included negotiating the manpower allocation to REME through the various Army and Defence committees. This involved agreeing establishments for independent REME units, and for REME organisations embedded in other units (Light Aid Detachments (LADs), Regimental Workshops and attached tradesmen). This led to a total 'liability' based on these establishments, which, in theory, defined the intended size and shape of REME. It was then necessary to go on and negotiate manpower cover (the number of military and civilian staff actually available/affordable) and then to define the policy for manning units.

For officers, the subsequent planning and management of individual careers was then the responsibility of the Colonel Personnel Branch 21 (Col PB 21) and his staff at Stanmore. Other ranks were managed by the REME Manning and Records Office (RMRO) at Leicester. In essence, these organisations had to manage a multi-dimensional jigsaw, the complexity of which involved several hundred establishments. Their first priority in all of this was to meet the needs of the Army. A second and related priority was to provide a career structure within each career employment group (CEG), which would attract and retain the right people, give them a fair chance of progression and ensure that the Army has the right mix of ranks and expertise within each CEG. In essence, these priorities have never changed.

The organisation for managing REME personnel was overhauled radically in 1997. Against a background of the rationalisation of personnel matters across the Services, it was decided that all Army manning and records offices would be collocated in Kentigern House, Glasgow, as part of a new Army Personnel Centre. The RMRO was therefore to be re-engineered and called the REME Manning and Career Management (MCM) Division and became responsible for all REME career management on 17 March 1997. This made sense from an Army perspective, particularly as officer management branches were collocated as well, and the old PB 21 was to become the REME Officer Wing.

The change was not without its drawbacks from the REME point of view. The organisation in Leicester had been staffed by many long-serving and loyal civilians who not only had a deep understanding of their work but had come to know many of the people they dealt with, and were highly regarded for the service they provided. It was simply not possible for them to move to Glasgow. The closure of the RMRO therefore involved many sad farewells, at a time of great upheaval as the data and systems that had developed over the years in Leicester had to be transferred to Glasgow. Inevitably, there were teething problems, such as when a question from a unit received an answer from someone who was clearly new to the job. With a core of military personnel to provide continuity, however, new systems and new civilian staff gradually bedded in and the REME MCM Division quickly became as effective as Leicester and Stanmore had been.

The structure of the planning system changed radically when the DLO was created in 2000, although the processes themselves remained essentially the same. As described in the previous Chapter, HQ DEME(A) took over responsibility for the 'people' side of the Corps (including DES 1's manpower planning role) on its formation in Arborfield in 1999. The demise of the DEME(A) post in 2012 led to a REME 'manning brick' being set up in the Army HQ in Andover. Its 'four balls' approach to managing REME manpower is explained in Chapter 3 ('Strategic Defence and Security Review 2010 and Army 2020').

AN OVERVIEW OF REME SOLDIER SELECTION AND TRAINING

The complex task of organising REME's manpower is inextricably linked with that of training them. In essence, REME cannot recruit fully trained soldiers and must ensure that those who join, who have often just left school, are transformed into the highly-skilled technical workforce it requires to fulfil its role.

For the training to work, the right people must be selected in the first place. Those wishing to join the Army undergo a series of tests and assessments. The outcome of this is an evaluation of the suitability of the candidates for the various roles the Army has to offer. REME entry standards (which differ for various trades) are high, and REME therefore takes a good percentage of the higher-calibre candidates. The following paragraphs describe the selection and training process for Junior Entry and Standard Entry Soldiers at the time of writing.

Junior Entry Soldiers
Those who have passed a selection test and have good GCSEs (or equivalent) in English language, mathematics and a science may join the Army aged between 16 years and 17 years five months as Junior Entry Soldiers. REME's Junior Entry Soldiers then go on a 42-week course at the Army Technical Foundation College (ATFC) in Winchester, Hampshire. This includes a period of basic military training, as well as leadership training and the opportunity to go on adventurous training activities. As part of the 'Technical Stream', REME soldiers will complete a Common Foundation Module of training, which leads to a Foundation Modern Apprenticeship in Engineering. This enables them to link up with Standard Entry Soldiers on training as the latter go into their Phase 2 (Technical) Training. After completion of this, both Junior Entry and Standard Entry Soldiers follow the same career pattern.

Standard Entry Soldiers
The training of Standard Entry Soldiers is progressive and provides the individual with the military, technical and other skills needed in the posts he, or she, is to fill. A broad description of this process is set out below.

Selection. Those aged between 17 and 33 years may join as a Standard Entry Soldier provided they meet specified academic requirements and pass the Army selection system.

Phase 1 (Basic Military) Training. This comprises 14 weeks of basic military training. It is common across the Army and is delivered by Army Training Regiments, with REME soldiers normally attending those at either Pirbright or Winchester.

Phase 2 (Technical) Training. This should follow immediately after Phase 1 Training. Electro-mechanical trades have done their training at Bordon, and electronic and aviation trades have been trained at Arborfield. The next Chapter outlines the history of the training establishments there, and the process of collocating them at Lyneham that was under way at the time of writing.

On-the-Job Training. On completion of Phase 2 Training, soldiers are classified as Class 3 tradesmen and go to units where they gain experience at their trade under the supervision of a Class 1 tradesman. After a period of consolidation, their competencies at trade are assessed and, if satisfactory, they are awarded Class 2 trade status.

2 – 1 (Technical) Upgrader Course. After a few years' service at unit level, soldiers will undergo a further period of technical training (once done at Arborfield and Bordon, now being delivered at Lyneham) that will bring them to Class 1 status in their trade. Those in artificer feeder trades will have a first assessment made of their suitability for artificer training.

Qualifying Courses. Command, leadership and management (CLM) training is necessary to qualify soldiers for the majority of promotions through the ranks, and is provided at four levels: Potential Non-Commissioned Officer, Junior Command Leadership and Management, Senior Command Leadership and Management, and Warrant Officer Command Leadership and Management. Each CLM Course is split into three parts. Successful completion of Part 1 is a key element of qualifying the individual for immediate promotion, while completion of Part 2 and Part 3 qualifies the individual for subsequent further promotion.

Equipment Courses. These relate to specific equipments, and are attended by those who need to be qualified to inspect and repair these specific equipments.

Other Training and Qualifications. REME soldiers undergo training in many non-technical areas too, from health and safety to adventurous training. There is also a conscious effort to map training in REME across to recognised civilian qualifications. For example, technical training may count as a BTEC (Business and Technology Education Council) qualification, artificer training could result in a HND (Higher National Diploma), HNC (Higher National Certificate) or a degree. This tends to give REME soldiers a head start when they leave the Army and move on to new careers.

PRINCIPLES OF THE REME TRADE STRUCTURE

REME's trade structure and its related detailed training requirement is kept under continuous review and has been the subject of a number of major studies. These have been driven by many factors, one of the most important being the advance of technology. When REME was formed, tradesmen and technicians dealt with the sort of technology now found in classic cars, and in electronic equipment in museums. In those days, it was usually easy for someone with a sound engineering background to identify faults by eye or by ear. Faults could often be fixed by welding, turning, soldering and by replacing or mending mechanical or electrical components.

As technology has moved on, there has been a move towards equipment that incorporates sealed-for-life modules (replaceable but not repairable) and 'black boxes', which can only be monitored by digital test equipment. Clearly training and trade structure has had to evolve in line with these changes. This should not be taken to mean that REME tradesmen and technicians have become mere changers of assemblies and boxes. There is still a requirement for traditional trade skills and knowledge. In particular, basic engineering knowledge and skill tends to be at a premium in difficult operational situations. Battle damage and operational wear and tear take their toll, and it is often not possible to get spare parts for complex military equipment when and where they are needed. Vehicles, weapons and other systems need to be made operational very quickly. This can often only be done by stripping good parts from unserviceable equipments, or carrying out 'expedient repairs' (or 'battle damage repairs'), which would not be undertaken under normal peacetime circumstances. This requires robust and versatile technical staff with an appropriate general engineering background.

OVERVIEW OF THE REME TRADE STRUCTURE

In general, there has been a trend towards consolidating CEGs. This means that some specialised skills are spread more widely, although this may go with the requirement for more supplementary specialist training, but in general it provides greater flexibility and broader career opportunities for individuals. This is illustrated in the table at Figure 22.1 (at the end of this Chapter), which gives snapshots of the trade structure in 1998 and the Army 2020 trade structure that the Corps will move to by early 2016 (numbers and liability are shown in brackets). It also indicates the entry requirements and civilian qualifications that may be gained in each CEG (as at 2015).

SPECIFIC CAREER EMPLOYMENT GROUPS

Control Equipment/Telecommunications Technician
Traditionally, Control Equipment Technicians (for some reason, unknown to the author, commonly called 'ECEs' – pronounced 'eck-ees') dealt with such things as tank fire control systems, whilst Telecommunications Technicians tended to deal with radios and communications equipment. With equipment being increasingly driven by 'black boxes', the technological overlap between the disciplines meant that it made sense to merge them into the new trade of Electronics Technician.

Instrument Technician
In its early days, REME needed Instrument Technicians to repair the Army's many binoculars, weapon sights and the like. As sighting systems became increasingly integrated with electronics and, with more complex repair work being done by contract, the Instrument Technician CEG became less viable. Instrument repair work was therefore to be absorbed by Electronics Technicians who underwent specific supplementary training depending on their unit's equipment type.

Gun Fitter
Gun Fitters specialised in large calibre weapon systems, above the 30mm RARDEN cannon and 81mm mortar. They were therefore assigned to Armoured Regiments equipped with the main battle tank and its 120mm gun or with the RA regiments on a range on weapons, including 155mm howitzers and the 105mm Light Gun. Their role was absorbed within the Armourer CEG, with specialised training given as necessary.

Vehicle Mechanic
Vehicle Mechanics have always been the largest trade group within REME. During the Cold War era, the trade was split between Vehicle

Mechanics A (VMA, who worked on heavy tracked vehicles) and Vehicle Mechanics B (VMB, who worked on other vehicles). This provided a desirable pool of specialist heavy armoured vehicle expertise, but meant that VMAs were likely to spend most of their time in Germany. The VMA and VMB CEGs were combined in the form of a 'universal' VM trade, with specialist training given to those who were going to work with heavy armour.

Technical Storeman/Regimental Specialist/Technical Support Specialist

In most arms and services in the Army, the roles of military trainer, company/regimental quartermaster storeman (CQMS, RQMS), and company/regimental sergeant major (CSM/RSM) are all very much part of the mainstream career path for those of that capbadge. In REME, whilst technical tradesmen clearly have the potential to fill such posts, this is arguably not the best use of the Army's investment in expensive technical training. The non-technical Regimental Specialist CEG was therefore created to take on such roles. There are certain inherent problems with this approach, the most obvious being that the CEG required a top-heavy rank pyramid.

To overcome this, REME took in transferees from other capbadges who have most of the skillset required and were already some way up the rank ladder when they joined. This provided a pragmatic but not problem-free solution. Those transferring in have a lot to learn about how the technical and military aspects of REME interact, this problem being exacerbated because Military Training Instructors generally had to go directly into training organisations, where they learned little about REME in the field force. REME technical tradesmen could also transfer into the Regimental Specialist role, in some cases giving them the opportunity to progress further in rank than if they had stayed in their technical role. Such factors, along with issues related to REME's overall manpower ceiling, have meant there had always been a degree of controversy about this area.

A variety of options were looked at, including the abolition of the Regimental Specialist role. The upshot has been the formation of a re-engineered CEG in 2008, the Technical Support Specialist, which provided an all-round solution. This would continue to draw on both internal and external transferees, and provide a better managed career structure. This would include three professional career pathways, which would come with accredited civilian qualifications. These are:

- teaching, training coaching (based around the Military Training Instructor role)
- logistics (technical storekeeping and all-arms CQMS/RQMS qualifications)
- management – various leadership and management training courses leading to accredited diplomas in leadership and management.

ARTIFICERS

REME's technical Warrant Officers fill very demanding roles. They need a combination of technical and managerial skills, which they often have to exercise with a high degree of autonomy, often in difficult operational circumstances, working for demanding 'customers' who do not wear the same capbadge as they do, or understand all they need to about their equipment. REME's artificer system, which is unique in the Army, evolved with a view to selecting those suitable for such roles fairly early on (normally in their mid to late-20s) and providing them with around 18 months of additional formal training and education. They emerged from this as Staff Sergeant artificers, and entered the pool from which technical Warrant Officers would be selected.

Potential artificers must come from a relevant feeder trade. As with the feeder trades, the artificer structure has been rationalised in recent years as shown in Figure 22.2 (at the end of this Chapter).

Selection was carried out for many years by the Artificer Selection Board (ASB) (poorly named as it didn't make selections), which later became the Potential Artificer Assessment Board (PAAB) – both lasted for four days. It was interesting to note the difference in perception between those who were assessed by the PAAB, and those who were doing the assessment (PAAB members). The former would generally comment along the lines that the system generally seemed to be good, but that physical ability to get over obstacles, perform difficult team tasks when hanging from ropes for example, perhaps played too important a part. In reality, the members of the PAAB were hardly interested in whether candidates could cross obstacles or do tasks hanging from ropes. What really interested them was how the candidates reacted when they, or members of their group, could not perform the tasks, which was often highly revealing. This PAAB system had many advantages:
- the PAAB looked at all the evidence available about the candidates (including appraisals, reports from their units and all their courses),

which was looked at in conjunction with their performance on the PAAB itself (interviews, group tasks/discussions, individual tasks and written work)
- the approach was scientific and transparent, and offered a level playing field
- the assessments were made by military officers (each group would be observed/led by a Captain, a Major and a Lieutenant Colonel) who were able to apply judgement and common sense, but were expected to be able to offer evidence to support their view
- the length of the selection process offered certain advantages; in most cases, the PAAB members had a pretty good idea after the first day on the definite 'passes' and definite 'fails' in the group being assessed but
   - there were always some who managed to 'talk the talk' at the beginning of the PAAB, but were thoroughly discredited by the end of it
   - and those who did not project themselves at the start of the PAAB (despite being told they must do so), but who had proved themselves 'solid gold' by the end of it.

No form of 'yes/no' staff selection system can be 100% foolproof and fair to everyone. Inevitably, the bar will be slightly higher or lower at different times depending on the needs of the Army and the competition. There will also inevitably be those who, for whatever reason, do not do themselves justice during the selection process. Overall, the REME system has been very effective at screening out those who were not suitable, and in providing a pool of trained and talented people from which the first-rate senior technical leaders have emerged. The REME Corps Instruction on this subject makes it clear that artificers should represent the 'gold standard' of Senior Non-Commissioned Officers across the Corps and, arguably, across the Army. Once a candidate had passed the four-day PAAB, selection for artificer training by the Artificer Selection Board was more or less a given.

In 2005, the four-day PAAB was replaced by a new system at the direction of DEME(A). The new system involved a one-day PAAB at the end of an individual's 2 – 1 Upgrader Course. This was a greatly streamlined version of the four-day PAAB. Candidates who passed this had to become fully qualified and, provided they had unreserved recommendations in their Soldier's Joint Appraisal Report (SJAR), they would be considered by an Artificer Selection Course Loading Board (ASCLB) at the Army

Personnel Centre. The ASCLB would make selections on the basis of 'first past the post' considering all the written evidence available, a process used by all boards.

There were essentially two reasons to change the system at the time. The first was that the old system was not pulling through enough candidates. The second was that the four-day PAAB was very much a 'Rolls Royce selection system' and took a lot of Directing Staff away from other duties. The essential difference between the two systems is that the four-day PAAB represented almost the culmination of the selection process and was the key 'yes/no' decider. The current one-day PAAB happens earlier in the selection process and filters the candidate in for selection, which may happen much later, with the ASCLB having the benefit of several subsequent SJARs to guide its decisions. Inevitably, there will be an element of controversy about the two systems, but the intention in the case of both has been the same, that is to select for the 'gold standard'.

Once candidates have commenced artificer training they have a long haul ahead both physically and mentally. There are three phases to the Artificer Command and Field Course (ACFC). ACFC Phases 1 and 3 are held at the REME Arms School. ACFC Phase 1 is a short introductory course providing management training. ACFC Phase 3 covers CLM training, and is a physically demanding 10-week course. ACFC Phase 2 is the technical phase of the ACFC and is run at the relevant technical school.

ARTISAN WARRANT OFFICERS

Although the REME artificer system has been extremely successful overall, it historically went with the drawback that it created a 'glass ceiling' at Staff Sergeant level for those not selected for artificer training. This inevitably meant that some hugely-talented soldiers, who did not get through the system, were unable to fulfil their potential despite having amply demonstrated their ability, albeit later on in their careers. This was a potential loss to the Army and so a revised system allowed artisan Staff Sergeants from artificer feeder trades to compete, on a level playing field, for Warrant Officer appointments outside of their CEG. Company Sergeant Major and Assistant Regimental Career Management Officer typify the appointments they can be selected for.

OFFICERS

Essentially there are two routes to becoming an officer in REME – Direct Entry (DE) and Late Entry (LE). The DE route is open to those aged under 26 years (29 years for serving soldiers) who either have a relevant technical degree or the prospect of getting one. LE Officers, selected for commissioned service in REME from Warrant Officer rank, make up 30% of the Army 2020 liability.

DE Officers

Potential DE Officers have to pass the Army Officer Selection Board and then successfully complete the Commissioning Course at the Royal Military Academy Sandhurst, alongside their peers being commissioned into other Corps and Regiments. On commissioning from Sandhurst, they are awarded a Short Service Commission, initially for 12 years, which can be converted to an Intermediate Regular Commission allowing them to serve for up to 20 years. They can then apply to convert to a Regular Commission, which allows them to serve a full career for 34 years or until the age of 60 (whichever comes first).

After Sandhurst, REME Young Officers complete the Military Systems Engineering Course (Land), after which they are assigned to a REME battalion to fill a platoon commander post followed by a spell as a platoon commander in either a Phase 1 or 2 Training Establishment. Most will then return to a REME Battalion in a junior Captain appointment and should attain their Land Systems Engineering Officer (EngO) competency during this appointment, but those wishing to be employed in Army Aviation will be required to do the Officers' Long Aeronautical Engineering (OLAE) Course, which lasts for seven months. Once selected for LAD command, or as a Company or Workshop Second-in-Command, or as a REME Battalion Operations Officer or Technical Officer, they will attend the REME Captains' Course.

Historically, the Army picked out its potential 'high flyers' by selecting around 100 senior Captains/junior Majors (including a proportion from REME) and sent them to the Army Staff College at Camberley aged around 30 years. The one-year course qualified them for 'Straight Staff' appointments at Grade 2 (Major equivalent) level. Those with science qualifications at A Level or above, which included all the REME officers, also did a one-year course at Shrivenham doing what was to become a MSc course on military equipment and related topics. This qualified them for 'Weapons Staff' posts at Grade 2.

The system originated prior to World War 1 when most Regular Officers were not graduates, and were at regimental duty aged about 20 years. It had some obvious pros and cons as a way of sorting out the best from the rest at an early stage of their careers. Things changed radically in the 1990s. The single-Service staff colleges were closed and merged in 1998 in the form of a new Joint Services Command and Staff College, which moved to Shrivenham. This was to be incorporated into the Defence Academy of the United Kingdom (also based at Shrivenham) in April 2002, which took in the Royal College of Defence Studies (in London) and, later (in 2004), the Defence College of Management and Technology (DCMT, also based in Shrivenham but with links to many academic institutions).

This led to a change in the pattern of selection and training, which became more tri-Service in outlook. On promotion to Major, DE Officers were to attend the Intermediate Command and Staff Course (Land) at the Defence Academy (Shrivenham) prior to their initial Grade 2 staff appointment. On selection for Lieutenant Colonel, not all eligible officers were to attend the 46-week Advanced Command and Staff Course at the Defence Academy, which meant effectively that the process of sorting out the potential 'high flyers' had gone up a rank compared with the old system. Selected officers at Colonel level also attended a 14-week Higher Command and Staff Course.

LE Officers

REME is fortunate in having a large pool of highly trained and talented Warrant Officers from which to select its LE Officers. Selection remains competitive and applicants undergo several interviews at various levels (up to one-star) within their chain of command before being filtered for attendance at the Late Entry Assessment Panel for final selection. In other parts of the Army, LE Officers tend to be associated with certain types of appointments, such as Quartermaster and Training Officer. REME LE Officers are also employed in similar posts, but are also afforded the opportunity to work in other areas too.

Whilst providing the technical strength in depth of the Corps, a healthy proportion have successfully competed with their DE peers for the same command and staff appointments. LE Officers have been successfully employed in all varieties of LAD and sub-unit command and an ex-LE Officer, who had converted to DE terms of service, has been selected for unit command as a Lieutenant Colonel recently. LE Officers bring enormous practical engineering experience to the body of officers in REME, and they enjoy a full and rewarding commissioned career. REME is truly blessed by the calibre of its LE Officers.

Structure in 1998	Army 2020 Structure	Entry Requirement 2015
Telecommunications Technician Radar Technician Control Equipment Technician Instrument Technician	Electronics Technician (680)	GCSE: Grade C or better in English language, mathematics and a science BTEC: Electrical/Electronic Engineering City & Guilds: Level 2 Training may lead to: BTEC National Certificate in Electrical and Electronic Engineering Four Professional Development Units for Incorporated Engineer NVQ Level 3 in Engineering Maintenance HND in Electrical and Electronic Engineering
Aircraft Technician	Aircraft Technician (525)	GCSE: Grade C or better in English language, mathematics and a science BTEC: Electrical/Electronic Engineering City & Guilds: Level 1 or partial completion of Level 2 in appropriate modules Training may lead to: BTEC National Certificate in Aeronautical Engineering NVQ Level 3 in Engineering Maintenance
Avionics Technician	Avionics Technician (339)	GCSE: Grade C or better in English language, mathematics and a science BTEC: First Certificate or National Certificate in Electrical/Electronic Engineering or completion of City & Guilds Level 2 Training may lead to: BTEC National Certificate in Electrical and Electronic Engineering and four Professional Development Units for Incorporated Engineer NVQ Level 3 in Engineering Maintenance HND in Electrical and Electronic Engineering

Structure in 1998	Army 2020 Structure	Entry Requirement 2015
Armourer	Armourer (539)	GCSE: Grade D in English language, mathematics and a science First or National Certificate in Engineering, City & Guilds Level 1 in Basic Engineering Competence or partial completion of Level 2 modules Training may lead to: City & Guilds Part 3 in Engineering Systems Maintenance Competencies NVQ Level 3 in Engineering Maintenance BTEC HNC in Engineering
Gun Fitter		
Vehicle Mechanic	Vehicle Mechanic (3187) Special modules for those who do Vehicle Mechanic A (heavy track vehicles) and Vehicle Mechanic B (other vehicles) work	GCSE: Grade D in English language, mathematics and a science, or National Certificate in Engineering BTEC: National Diploma in Motor Vehicle Studies City & Guilds: Level 2 qualifications. Training may lead to: Full driving licence (all types) NVQ Level 3 in Engineering Maintenance City & Guilds Part 3 in Motor Vehicle Craft Studies
Vehicle Electrician	CEG removed, the responsibilities being covered by the Vehicle Mechanic trade	NA
Metalsmith	Metalsmith (149)	GCSE: Grade D or better in English language, mathematics and a science City & Guilds: Level 1 in Basic Engineering Competence (Fabrication) and appropriate modules completed at Level 2 Training may lead to: City & Guilds Parts 2 and 3 in Welding Craft Studies City & Guilds Part 2 in Sheet Metal and Thin Plate Craft Studies

Structure in 1998	Army 2020 Structure	Entry Requirement 2015
Shipwright	Shipwright (32)	In 2015, REME removed Shipwright as a CEG; it will be managed as a Career Employment Qualification within the Metalsmith CEG
Recovery Mechanic	Recovery Mechanic (559)	GCSE: Grades A–D in mathematics, science and English language Training may lead to: LGV and HGV licences and a City & Guilds qualification (Part 2) in Light and Heavy Vehicle Recovery
Technical Storeman	Technical Support Specialist (463)	GCSE: Grade D or better in English language and mathematics City & Guilds: Levels 1 or 2 in Vehicle Parts Personnel or Vehicle Parts Distribution and Supply Training may lead to: City & Guilds Certificate Part 1 after initial trade training and Part 2 later Eventual membership of – the Institute of Purchasing Supply and/ or the Institute of Logistics and Distribution Managers
Regimental Specialist		

Figure 22.1: REME trade structure in 1998 and the Army 2020 structure

Structure in 1998	Army 2020 Structure (numbers)
Artificer Weapons	Artificer Weapons (88)
Artificer Aircraft	Artificer Aircraft (96)
Artificer Avionics	Artificer Avionics (67)
Artificer Vehicles	Artificer Vehicles (527)
Artificer Instruments*	Artificer Electronics (136) (* absorbed into Artificer Electronics)
Artificer Electrical Control*	
Artificer Radar*	
Artificer Telecommunications*	

Figure 22.2: REME artificer structure in 1998 and the Army 2020 structure

CHAPTER 23

INDIVIDUAL TRAINING ORGANISATIONS

INDIVIDUAL TRAINING – ORGANISATION AND RESPONSIBILITY

This book covers a period during which there were numerous reviews of individual training, with many changes of titles and responsibilities. Underlying this, there was nevertheless a strong element of continuity. In practice, the numerous changes left largely the same sort of students continuing to be taught much the same things in the same places. Before looking at individual organisations, it is useful to understand how overall responsibility for training changed throughout the period, and to appreciate some of the key drivers of change. The best way to do that is perhaps to pick a start point just before the drawdown after the Cold War got fully into its stride.

The Start Point
Around 1990, responsibility for REME individual training was seen as resting primarily with REME, with REME organisations delivering it. Training requirements, plans and policies were overseen by a Brigadier on DGEME's staff (DEME(Org & Trg)), who provided an interface with the Army and the MoD staff on matters related to training. The two main training centres were at Arborfield and Bordon. These were seen as essentially REME garrisons, and each was commanded by a REME Brigadier. There was an additional REME training outpost at Middle Wallop, in the form of the School of Aircraft Engineering (SAE), which sat in a REME enclave within the AAC base at Middle Wallop. A summary of the types of training provided is described in the paragraphs that follow.

Arborfield. This might be regarded as the 'Home of the Corps' as Arborfield Garrison embraced the HQ Officers' and Sergeants' Messes, the Corps Museum and these units:

- **REME Training Battalion and Depot** – provided military training, notably basic training for all REME soldiers, as well as administrative 'depot' functions
- **Princess Marina College (PMC)** – formerly the Army Apprentices College, provided training for REME junior soldiers
- **School of Electronic Engineering (SEE)** – provided training in electronics and related disciplines (up to artificer level)
- **REME Officers' School** – had always provided special-to-arm training for officers and it increasingly provided management courses as well, including some aimed at Senior Non-Commissioned Officers, other capbadge personnel and civilians.

Bordon. Unlike Arborfield, Bordon had an adjacent heathland training area that was suitable for recovery and tracked vehicle training. It tended to be regarded as the home of 'the black hand gang'. Bordon Garrison included these elements:
- **School of Electrical and Mechanical Engineering (SEME)** – provided or oversaw technical training in the electro-mechanical trades (Vehicle Mechanic/Vehicle Electrician, Armourer, Gun Fitter, Metalsmith, and Recovery Mechanic) up to artificer level for REME personnel as well as for Royal Marines, civilians from REME workshops and foreign and commonwealth officers and soldiers; it also provided driver training, including training on tracked vehicles for non-REME soldiers, acting in this capacity as an outpost for the Army School of Mechanical Transport; it delivered training for the remaining non-technical REME trades of Technical Storeman, Regimental Specialist and, after the amalgamation of these two trades, for Technical Support Specialists; and, in broad terms, the courses were generally shorter than their equivalent technician courses at Arborfield, but with more students to be trained
- **HQ REME TA** – based in Louisburg Barracks, its functions included REME TA training
- **REME Workshop Company** – this was an operational unit, not involved in technical training, but part of the Garrison; initially, this was 14 Field Workshop, previously the Berlin Garrison Workshop, later joined by 9 Field Workshop and these two sub-unit sized workshops were part of 6 Battalion REME, before the formation of 4 Battalion REME and 5 Battalion REME in 1999.

The Technical Training Area Bordon 2010

Middle Wallop. A technical training wing was established at the AAC base at Middle Wallop in 1958. It became the Aircraft Engineering Training Wing (AETW) in 1964 and the School of Aircraft Engineering (SAE) in 1988. It was collocated with 70 Aircraft Workshop (a second line aircraft workshop) and provided training for REME aviation trades, as well as for artificers and officers.

Drivers of Change
The factors that drove change in the training organisation were broadly the same as those that affected the Equipment Support (ES) organisation as a whole, and are explained in some detail in Chapter 18 ('Support for Army Equipment – An Overview'). Some of the issues are worth reviewing in the context of the training organisations.

Finance and Budgets. Chapter 18 explains how the introduction of the New Management Strategy (NMS) from the late-1980s led to a shift from managing Defence spending on the basis of Parliamentary votes for specific purposes to one based on the delegation of budgets to the commanders or managers of large organisations. NMS was implemented over a number of years, with a view to providing better visibility of costs and to injecting commercial management practices into the military. Organisations were given budgets, and their managers were given budgetary responsibility, and targets to meet. There was a new emphasis on costing 'outputs' rather than 'inputs', and at setting up quasi-commercial 'customer-supplier' relationships between military organisations, which interacted with each other. The new system facilitated 'top-down' management by setting budgetary and other targets.

The Search for Savings. The purpose of NMS was to minimise the cost of Defence by defining essential Defence outputs, and finding increasingly cost-effective ways of delivering them. Individual military training represented a significant element of overall Defence expenditure, and obvious avenues to explore in the search for reduced costs included: replacing military staff with (cheaper) civilians, contracting-out services, Private Finance Initiative (PFI) schemes, asset release (selling off non-essential land and facilities), reducing training (and looking for more efficient ways to deliver it), and rationalisation both within the Army (for example by centralising basic training) and between the Services.

Successes and Snags. NMS was initially very successful. In its early days, targets could be met with little pain by contracting-out a range of services, which did not really need to be done by public servants, by removing military staff from jobs that could be adequately done by civilians, and by generally shining a budgetary light on activities that had been comfortably inefficient for a long time. NMS was never, however, envisioned as a one-time efficiency squeeze, but an ongoing process with new 'efficiency savings' being demanded each year. It is not surprising that each time the financial lemon was squeezed anew, it became more difficult to meet the target by finding measures that had no hidden long-term drawbacks. All the avenues for making savings came with potential pitfalls. The MoD was not always an 'intelligent customer' and those negotiating contracts did not always have a clear understanding of how contractors' minds worked, or how they intended to make money out of the MoD. Rationalisation carried the risk that smaller highly expert and 'customer-focused' organisations would be brought together to form a much larger organisation in which expertise was diluted and internal dynamics would make it less attuned to its customers' requirements. The concept of management by top-down budget setting in large and complex organisations also carries the risk of creating 'perverse incentives', which force the budget holder to do things that are not to the benefit of the organisation as a whole. For example, as explained later, in the late-1990s the success of DEME(A)'s recruiting strategy resulted in a surge in recruit numbers, which meant that the Agency responsible for providing initial technical training did not have enough instructors to meet demand. This led to a backlog of trainees in the training organisation, with many soldiers waiting for one year or more for their course to start. This was potentially demoralising, as the soldiers were being paid to do nothing whilst their career development was effectively on hold. REME was keen to solve the problem by posting in suitably qualified instructors from the Field Army to help out until the backlog was cleared. It was generally agreed that this was the best possible practical solution, and could be delivered with zero additional cost to Defence. The scheme encountered high-level insistence that the cost of any military instructors lent to the Agency would have to be included in their budget, which would have put them over target. This killed off the scheme, leaving the backlog problem to continue for several years.

OUTLINE OF CHANGES IN STRUCTURE AND RESPONSIBILITY IN THE 1990s

As explained in Chapter 18, REME came through 'Options for Change' and the Logistic Support Review without having to merge with any other organisations. Its former head (DGEME) took on additional responsibilities for ES and became DGES(A). Trained manpower was a key enabler of ES, and a case could be made for putting the REME training organisation under DGES(A), making him both their primary 'customer' and their budgetary 'owner'. In fact, the ball bounced the other way, and it was decided that the 'product' of the REME Training Organisation was 'individual training' and should be owned by the Army's Individual Training Organisation (ITO). REME lost the one-star post at Bordon, and SEE, SEME, SAE and Princess Marina College were packaged as the REME Training Group under a single Brigadier. This was moved across to the Army ITO, representing one of the largest groups within it. The Army ITO was at that time being prepared to become an agency in the form of the Army Training and Recruitment Agency (ATRA), which it became on 1 April 1996. It was 'owned', in budgetary terms, by the Director General of Army Training and Recruiting (DGATR). This was linked with a number of changes in the early or mid-1990s. For convenience, these are summarised below, before looking at specific organisations in more detail.

Basic military training was to be done to the Common Military Syllabus for all capbadges, which allowed its rationalisation across the Army. This resulted in REME basic training being transferred to the Army Training Regiment (ATR) at Pirbright. This undermined the justification for REME's Training Battalion and Depot, which was closed in 1992 and so space was freed up in Rowcroft Barracks within Arborfield Garrison.

A review of junior training led to a decision to reduce the two-year apprentice course to a one-year course for REME junior soldiers. This, in turn, led to the closure of Princess Marina College in 1995, and the formation of the Army Apprentices College, renamed the Army Technical Foundation College (ATFC) in 2000, which ran the shorter course for Royal Engineers and Royal Signals as well as for junior REME soldiers. The unit was set up in Rowcroft Barracks, Arborfield, with the closure of Princess Marina College releasing space within Hazebrouck Barracks, the main compound in Arborfield.

The REME Officers' School changed its title to the School of Equipment Support (Army) (SES(A)) in 1992, to reflect the increased responsibilities of DGES(A) and to provide appropriate training to support them. It was able to move into space vacated in Hazebrouck Barracks. The former REME Officers' School complex was converted into a community centre as part of an arrangement with developers who, by that stage, were building houses on the former Bailleul Barracks area, which had already been sold by the MoD.

SAE moved from Middle Wallop to Arborfield in November 1995 into space freed up in Hazebrouck Barracks, merging with SEE to form the School of Electronic and Aeronautical Engineering (SEAE).

In April 1999, DEME(A) set up his organisation in Hazebrouck Barracks and took over the role of 'customer' for REME technical training, with **RHQ REME** as part of his organisation. This is covered in more detail in Chapter 21 ('HQ DEME(A) and **RHQ REME**').

OVERVIEW OF SPECIFIC TRAINING ORGANISATIONS AND TYPES OF TRAINING

This section looks at specific units and types of training, excluding the Defence Training Review and its impact, which is covered later.

Recruit Training and the Closure of the Depot. Recruit training, common across the Army, was designated Phase 1 Training. This was followed by Phase 2 Training, which gives soldiers the special-to-capbadge skills required before joining their first unit. Phase 3 Training embraces career courses, which happen later in a soldier's career (see Chapter 22 ('REME People')). With the closure of the REME Training Battalion and Depot, all future Phase 1 Training of REME soldiers was to happen in ATRs. REME recruit training was consolidated in 1992 into a new Rowcroft Company prior to the move to Pirbright. An account of what followed was provided, several years later in 2006, by Colonel John Saville (late REME):

> 'Integrating Rowcroft Company was a challenge. The task fell to the OC, initially Major Mike Hughes and from 1993 Major John Saville, and to the Company Sergeant Major, WO2 George Skivington. Much of the challenge lay in the Guards Depot Sgts' Mess where the arrival of REME outsiders was not entirely welcome. In spite of some difficulties, including on the hallowed Pirbright Square where no prisoners were taken, the professionalism of the REME Permanent Staff won the day. By the time that the Other Arms Companies arrived at Pirbright to form ATR Pirbright, Rowcroft Company was regarded as the model for how the ATR should work. For his part in this success, WO2 Skivington received the MBE'.

Junior Training. Over the years, REME has been hugely blessed by the services of 'Ex Boys' who had in the early days completed a three-year apprenticeship. One suspects the process that recruited them in the first place must have been fairly canny; they also certainly picked up fitness, self-confidence, self-discipline and teamwork as well as a sound military and technical grounding during their 'boy service'. Many went on to do great things, both in the Army and afterwards, remaining proud and appreciative of the start that apprentice training gave them in their careers. Historically, the much increased retention rate for ex-apprentices, plus the disproportionately high number of those selected for artificer training and LE commissions, more than compensated for the increased costs involved in maintaining an apprentice entry. The increase of the school leaving age from 15 to 16 years in 1972 meant that the apprentice course was reduced to two years, inevitably somewhat diluting its effect. The much shorter course offered in 1995 at Arborfield represented an even bigger step change. It lasted less than one year and was to be called a 'foundation modern apprenticeship'. It was valuable in terms of drawing in talented youngsters who had left school and wanted to join the Army, and who might otherwise have opted for another career if they could not join it for another year. It had, however, only time for the Common Military Syllabus and a junior leadership package; it offered very limited technical input apart from classroom academic work. The Army Apprentices College (later ATFC) at Arborfield was never, however, a REME unit, although it had a REME trainee company within it, and many of the staff (including three of the Commanding Officers) were REME. The College was closed in 2004. Junior soldier training for REME was to move to the Army Foundation College (AFC) in Harrogate. At the AFC, REME junior soldiers would do a 23-week 'Phase 1 Course' (military training, adventurous training, leadership training) after which as part of the 'Technical Stream' they would go to SEAE/SEME for 'Phase 2 Junior Technical Training' much as before.

SEE/SEAE

In 1991, a three-year contract was negotiated with Serco for the provision of instructional services at SEE, which was seen as something of a groundbreaking exercise at the time. In essence, the directly employed 'Burnham Scale' instructional staff (and almost all of the serving REME instructors) were replaced by contract staff. The arrangement worked well, perhaps partly because Serco had the wisdom to employ an ex-REME contract manager. In essence, whilst the overall framework remained controlled by the military, contractors provided almost all the technical instruction, as well as many support functions, such as catering, maintenance and administration.

There remained the problem of what to do with soldiers when they were not actually undergoing technical training. The combination of those on initial Phase 2 Courses, but not actually engaged in technical training, and the growing number of Soldiers Not Under Training (SNUT) in the late-1990s meant that there were a lot of young soldiers around who were not undergoing any technical training at all. They were typically in their late-teens, and had started their military life with around 12 weeks of basic training in an environment unrepresentative of that which they would encounter during their career. They were at a formative stage in their career and their motivation and attitudes, including their military and capbadge ethos, needed to be positively nurtured. In addition, there were many older and more experienced soldiers doing a variety of long courses, such as Class 1 Upgrader Courses, equipment/specialist courses and artificer courses, who needed to be administered (they were more likely to be married and have families), and kept up to the mark on fitness as well as such things as their annual training tests. The situation in Arborfield in 1996, shortly after the merger of SEE and SEAE, was covered in an article in The Craftsman magazine (August 1996) by the then Commandant, Colonel Mike Dorward (late REME), from which the following is extracted:

> '… the lack of funding and the spare capacity in the adult training establishment generated by drawdown led to a review of apprentice training. After much heartache, it was decided to reduce the time spent in Princess Marina College to two terms, (8 months) on a foundation course whilst all trade training would be conducted at SEAE and SEME. This resulted in the expansion of the Basic Electronics Section to cater for the additional courses. To accommodate this, the maths and Phase A electronics training moved to a building vacated by Princess Marina College, and a contract amendment was raised. … To cope with the increased number of personnel, courses and trades, SEAE restructured to meet the revised situation.
>
> The formation of SEAE Regiment under a CO has been advantageous from a number of points:
> - it has enabled the technical branches to concentrate on technical training and associated problems
> - it has enhanced our ability to deal with students as individuals
> - the company structure allows the School to undertake military training and adventurous training using A and B Companies respectively as a focus'.

The organisation of SEAE in Arborfield in 1996 is at Figure 23.1 (at the end of this Chapter). Colonel Dorward also outlined the process by which SAE had been integrated with SEE:

> 'Once the decision was made to move SAE to Arborfield the planning and preparation began in earnest. This required the construction of a brand new hangar and the refurbishment of existing classrooms and laboratories … The actual move from Middle Wallop to Arborfield was achieved on target with very little fuss and Air Systems Branch (formerly SAE) was ready to begin training on 5 Dec 1995'.

There have been many changes to the organisation and contracts at Arborfield since the time of that article, but the broad concept remained the same until the closure of Arborfield Garrison. In essence, technical training, the raison d'être for SEAE, was a contractor responsibility not a REME one, albeit provided in response to REME 'customer' requirements. It was overseen by military officers, many of whom were REME, but all of whom were 'owned' by a Defence agency. SEAE Regiment, whatever the formal budgetary arrangements, was to all intents and purposes a REME unit. In due course, it was to change its name in 2009 to 11 Training Battalion REME. It allowed REME soldiers in Arborfield to feel proper members of REME and to participate fully, and often brilliantly, in sporting, adventurous and other activities described elsewhere in this book. As at 2012, 11 Training Battalion REME comprised three student companies – A Company (Foundation), B Company (Combat Systems), and C Company (Aviation).

The changes in the late-1990s included the start of the construction of a new aircraft maintenance training facility provided by Aircraft Training International Limited (ATIL) at Arborfield under a PFI scheme arranged by the Defence Procurement Agency linked to the support package for the new Apache attack helicopter.

As at 2012, SEAE dealt with approximately 1,130 students per year on a range of 53 different courses including an artificer course, which resulted in the award of a foundation degree. In outline, the Phase 2 Training it provided was structured in this way:

- six months Foundation, the first part being a three-month Common Foundation (basic mathematics, science, drawing/materials, workshop) followed by a three-month Technical Foundation (advanced maths and science)
- training thereafter was tailored to different disciplines/equipments; for example, Aircraft Technicians did a 12-month Aircraft Technicians Course; Electronics Technicians split into Combat/Land and Avionics specialisations and they did a combination of common electronics training, specialised training and equipment training (the Challenger 2 equipment training course being about the longest at around four months); and, all technicians left Phase 2 Training as Lance Corporals, and so it was necessary to fit a Potential Non-Commissioned Officer Course in with other training.

SEME

Events at SEME followed a broadly similar pattern to those at SEAE except that it catered for different disciplines. It provided training up to artificer level, and delivered specialist equipment courses as well as Phase 2 and 3 Training Courses. In general, these were shorter than the equivalent courses provided for electronics and aircraft technicians at Arborfield, and had less academic content.

As with Arborfield, numbers of students at Bordon dropped following drawdown, and non-REME tracked driver training on behalf of the Army School of Mechanical Transport ceased. Contractorisation also arrived, albeit rather later at Bordon than Arborfield. The chosen main contractor was Vosper Thorneycroft, which was later to pick up some of the contracts at Arborfield, and was to be taken over by Babcock in due course. SEME Regiment was formed around the same time as SEAE Regiment. It performed a very similar function and was retitled 10 Training Battalion REME in 2009.

SEME, like SEAE, trained Royal Marines as well as REME soldiers. Around 2009, it was running about 450 courses of some 150 types, in order to train: Armourers, Vehicle Mechanics, Recovery Mechanics, Technical Support Specialists, Metalsmiths, and Artificers Vehicles and Artificers Weapons.

A useful summary of the important issues as at 2009 was provided by the Commandant, Colonel David Egan (late REME), in an article in The Craftsman magazine (May 2009):

> '… having not seen much of Bordon since completing my RYOs' Equipment Course in 1981. Initial impressions, from a distance, were that not much had changed. How wrong I was, SEME is buzzing. We are training more soldiers than ever before, with average Phase 2 and 3 populations of well over 1,500. This says much for the success of our recruiters, and the attraction of a REME career that offers real operational challenge, transferable technical qualifications and some fun.… SEME must be alive to changing requirements and agile enough to deal with them. Specifically, providing maintainer training for a growing number of Urgent Operational Requirements (UORs), often at short notice, has been a real test'.

The deaths of soldiers undergoing training at the Royal Logistic Corps training base at Deepcut (two in 1995, two in 2001 and 2002 respectively) caused much public disquiet and provided a stark reminder that, notwithstanding the need to take advantage of the savings achievable by contractorisation, young soldiers (particularly with access to weapons) are very vulnerable, and the presence of officers and experienced Non-Commissioned Officers is essential to care for them and to educate them. Colonel Egan continues by alluding to this aspect of his role:

> 'Training the requisite number of soldiers and marines for the front line commands is my priority, but in parallel, and equally important, is my duty of care to our trainees, which I see as an integral part of command. The Corps has an excellent record in this regard, largely due to the high quality, dedicated officers and soldiers who fill the supervisory care and training appointments. These are demanding but rewarding jobs, which can open up new career opportunities, unavailable to those without a training organisation track record … Today at SEME, only a small percentage of the instructional staff are military, with over 90% of training being delivered by Vosper Thorneycroft contract staff. The professional relationship with Vosper Thorneycroft is excellent, and their dedicated staff, many of whom are ex-military, take a genuine interest in the success of our young soldiers. My performance and that of SEME in discharging its duty of care and training responsibilities is subject to scrutiny by a number of independent organisations, the highest profile of which is Ofsted.
>
> DEME(A)'s Training Vision (D/DEME/7000/01/05 dated 31 January 20017) recognised the need for our training to meet the operational requirement. DTR (Defence Training Review) promises much in terms of training transformation but we cannot afford to wait. Indeed, our training is evolving constantly and a notable example has been the in-house development of a limited e-learning capability. Originally called 'SEME Net', this is now planned to migrate to be a more widely available 'REME Net'. Whilst currently restricted to Phase 2 soldiers on the Common Foundation Module, the aspiration is for continuation training, and even some equipment training, to be available via the internet. The capability is still some years off, but will be part of any future 'blended learning solution'. What is 'blended learning' you might well ask? Traditionally, we have brought soldiers back to schools for career and equipment courses, but this will change. In addition to residential courses, more use will be made of 'work-

based learning' using work books and computer-based techniques to deliver the right training at the right time. The Vehicle Mechanic Basic Course is currently the focus for transformation, and a pilot course may be run later this year. Whilst meeting the operational need has primacy, we will not neglect the importance of training accreditation in terms of recruiting and retention.

Running SEME at or near capacity brings with it a range of challenges, but my top priority is dealing with the long standing problem of SNUT (Soldiers Not Under Training). A small 'header tank' of soldiers awaiting training is important to ensure that courses start with a full complement but over many years the total has grown steadily'.

Colonel Egan described various measures to reduce SNUT, including the simple expedient of getting a driver training contract to enable soldiers waiting at Bordon to be trained there, whilst they had nothing to do, instead of going on to Leconfield, which normally resulted in them staying there, largely unproductively, for 10–12 weeks. He concluded on a domestic note:

> 'Casual observers may think that some of SEME's infrastructure looks a little 'tired', but real improvements have been made recently, particularly to the SLA (Single Living Accommodation), and the welfare facilities here are second to none. Add to this the opportunities for sport and adventurous training and temporary respite from op tours, and a posting to Bordon in an instructional or supervisory role, or as a student, is an attractive proposition'.

School of Equipment Support (Army) and the REME Arms School
The formation of the Defence Logistics Organisation and the establishment of HQ DEME(A) meant that SES(A), which was essentially an Army/REME organisation, was no longer well placed to deliver broad ES training to a Defence organisation. It therefore focused more sharply on providing specific-to-REME training, and in fact was the only training establishment with a special-to-REME role. It therefore changed its name to the REME Arms School on 1 August 2003. It was responsible for the delivery of all REME officer, artificer and command, leadership and management (CLM) training across REME Training Group. SES(A) continued to have an ongoing remit to provide instruction for the wider

ES community, but this fell naturally out of its primary role to support REME in the Field Force, described by the Commandant, Colonel Sam Jarvis (late REME), in an article in The Craftsman magazine (January 2004). As at 2004, the training it delivered included:

- **soldier training** – it developed the Junior CLM Course for those selected for promotion to Corporal; this could be delivered at Bordon, or on a distributed basis to the Field Army under the supervision of Commanders ES and the Senior Military Certificate Course was reduced to six weeks
- **artificer training** – it provided an Artificer Command and Field Course (ACFC) in two phases; the first lasted three weeks and the final phase, just before graduation as artificers, ran for five and one half weeks
- **DEME(A)'s Engineering Standards** – a course on DEME(A)'s Engineering Standards was incorporated into career courses for officers and artificers; the Assessors' Course was an important one for those involved in technical inspections
- **officer courses** – SES(A) ran all REME career courses for officers, and provided coaching for senior officers selected as Army runners for Acquisition Stream posts.

DEFENCE TRAINING REVIEW AND THE 'HOME OF REME'

In 2001, REME's Regimental Colonel presented an overview of REME individual training to the Assistant Chief of the General Staff at HQ DEME(A). There was a good story to tell. REME had applied intelligence and thought to its training. From the late-1980s, it had successfully implemented the 'Systems Approach to Training', which involved a structured Training Needs Analysis, as well as an assessment and feedback loop (the 'Mellor Loop', named after the late REME Brigadier who developed it). This meant that training had continuously adapted to evolving requirements. The ATRA had therefore received the legacy of a very good REME training system.

It was further concluded that REME training was broadly comparable with that of 'quality' engineering firms (or franchised garages) in terms of the training standard required. REME soldiers could only be regarded as over-trained in comparison with 'second eleven' fitters who needed to be competent in only a very limited technical field. Under-training usually created hidden costs for the customer because poorly trained staff took longer to effect repairs, and the customer often paid for unnecessary component or assembly changes. Given that the cost of REME Phase 2 Training represented 2.3% of the annual Land equipment maintenance bill, clearly small savings to REME training had the potential to create much larger costs elsewhere.

The system of REME training, and the accreditation that went with it, clearly had an influence on retention. On average, REME soldiers served for twice as long as their infantry counterparts. This meant that the average annual capbadge training cost for a REME soldier was less than that for a Royal Logistic Corps soldier; the comparable cost for a Royal Engineers' soldier was 68% higher. It was pointed out that a 'competing for quality' exercise had been carried out in the late-1990s, which was supposed to achieve savings of around £1.5m per annum over five years. It was suggested that the exercise had proved counterproductive, as these relatively minor savings had not all materialised, and had probably ended up by costing more overall as well as producing a less flexible system 'with inadequate military nurturing and ethos'. To summarise, from a single-Service perspective, REME training had been rationalised about as far as it could be under ATRA. A good system was in place, and whilst it needed continuously to evolve, budget-driven tinkering with the system carried the risk of being counterproductive.

If one was to look at training from a Defence rather than a Services perspective, however, other considerations came into play. The Services had shrunk, and not all their training real estate was fully utilised. Processes and procedures were also tending to be rationalised across the Services, driven by such things as the move to a single Defence supply chain. Members of the different Services often do similar things; such as repair diesel engines or work as electricians. Common sense suggested that there must be scope for savings through tri-Service rationalisation. Such ideas were very much in tune with the thinking of politicians and senior officials struggling with the perennial problem of balancing the Defence budget. This resulted in the launch of the Defence Training Review (DTR) in 1999 under the control of Vice Admiral Jonathon Band. It reported in 2001 and advised:

- future Defence training needed to be more integrated, and managed on a Defence basis
- rationalisation of training organisations and real estate would deliver savings
- it envisaged most of the Defence rationalisation being achieved in the form of two major packages; Package 1 (of concern to REME)

embraced engineering and communications, and Package 2 related to logistics, security and policing (not considered further in this Chapter)
- it was envisaged that much of this training could be delivered through a complex Public-Private Partnership (PPP) or PFI deal.

These recommendations were broadly accepted, and the DTR transformed itself into the Defence Training Rationalisation (DTR) Programme. REME did not fight the basic conclusions. Control of its technical training organisations had already been taken from it and put under a Defence agency largely run by those who were not themselves technical, and had had to cope with underfunding and sub-standard facilities. Being the largest 'customer' within a new Defence grouping, which delivered technical training, could clearly have some advantages for REME. REME's major caveat to the DTR proposals was that if it was to lose the structures and organisations at Arborfield and Bordon, which helped promote the ethos of the Corps, it needed (and deserved) to have them replicated by equivalents when these garrisons closed. This was very successfully presented as the 'Home of REME' argument. The 'Home' embraced such things as the REME Museum, and the Corps Officers' and Sergeants' Messes. In broad terms, this argument was accepted, and the 'Home of REME' requirement became incorporated with the technical training package. It therefore seemed that all that needed to be done was to devise a workable plan, and to get on and implement it.

This did not happen as quickly as was hoped. Put simplistically, Plan A was superseded by Plan B, which collapsed and was followed by Plan C that is close to completion at the time of writing.

Plan A

Plan A was quite a long way down the line by mid-2002. It envisaged a move of most of what was being taught at Bordon, plus some training in electronics, to a new Defence Engineering Training Establishment (DETE) based on HMS Sultan, a Royal Navy shore-based training establishment in Gosport on the south coast. The balance between the Services there was expected to be Army/RN/RAF 6:4:1 (measured in man training days). HMS Sultan had a lot of free technical accommodation, and it was believed that the 'Home of REME', including the REME Arms School, could be fitted in or near it. That left aircraft technician training, as well as much of the electronic training then being done at Arborfield, still needing a new home. This was expected to go to RAF Cosford where appropriate extra facilities would be put in place.

As is so often the case, detailed study of the plan revealed that not everything would be as simple as first hoped. For example, an in-depth study of electrician training showed that students were best taught by combining theoretical work with practical work. REME students did their practical work on trucks and Land Rovers, which meant that they were already competent on the vehicles they were most likely to have to work on when they went to their first units. RN students did their practical work on heavy current equipment, such as the powered capstans that they were likely to encounter on ships and quaysides, which gave them useful competences when they joined their first unit. This meant that a rationalised training course for REME and RN electricians would either have to be longer and more expensive or at least one of the Services would get a less immediately useful electrician out of the training system. The electrician problem was not significant on its own, but illustrated the sort of difficulties that may cumulatively make it difficult to achieve both rationalisation and efficiency. Plan A had a significant drawback in that HMS Sultan is in a relatively congested part of the south coast with no heathland training area to allow the sort of tracked vehicle and recovery training that was carried out at Bordon. It was never finally firmed up as a plan, and never got an unequivocal 'tick in the box' against various commercial bids with which it had to be compared. As at 2002, however, it was still intended that the new organisations would be up and running by 2007.

The Demise of REME Training Group
By late-2003, work was still going on to engage with industry and refine and define the DTR concept. A decision was taken to change command and control in advance of full DTR by forming federated colleges from 1 April 2004, with a view to clarifying responsibilities and providing single points of contact for bidders. It was intended to put together a Defence College of Aeronautical Engineering (DCAE, with its HQ at RAF Cosford), which would subsume air systems training at SEAE, as well as a Defence College of Electro-Mechanical Engineering (DCEME, with its HQ at Gosport). This was accompanied by no physical moves of training and, apart from these higher structural changes, things went on much as before at Arborfield, with the last Commander REME Training Group, Brigadier Richard Rickard (late REME), commenting in an article in The Craftsman magazine (October 2003):

'The only people out of a job are me, and my heads of Finance and HR'.

Plan B

By 2008, the initial plan was greatly changed. It envisaged a complex PFI deal with a consortium called Metrix, which had achieved 'preferred bidder' status in January 2007. Its two principal sub-contractors were Land Securities Trilium (a property company that would deliver and manage the estate) and QinetiQ (that would deliver the training). At the heart of the scheme, there would be a huge new Defence Technical Academy built on the site of RAF St Athan in South Wales (west of Cardiff) to deliver technical training to all three Services, and to embrace both 'Packages 1 and 2'. The plan was not just about providing real estate; it was very much about 'training transformation'.

This aspect was led by QinetiQ, which was linked with Raytheon who had experience of transforming training for General Motors, and of working for the US Department of Defense. It aimed to reduce course length by around 20%, and to change the way in which training was delivered. It involved 'blended learning' solutions that made use of state of the art technology, including such things as computer-based training and video conferencing, as well as traditional classroom instruction. A significant proportion of the training would be delivered at Metrix Learning Centres that would be located adjacent to existing Education Centres, which were generally within easy commuting distance for soldiers based in UK. A 'Home of REME' element would be incorporated into the St Athan complex. Although military manpower overall would be reduced, there would be a proportional increase in REME military staff carrying out a 'duty of care' role, which was explained by Colonel Paul Mitchell (late REME) in The Craftsman magazine (July 2008).

By mid-2008, there were many details that still needed to be resolved, but it was hoped that the new arrangements would be in place by around 2014. It was helpful that the Chancellor of the Exchequer of the day (Gordon Brown) was comfortable with the idea of PPP/PFI deals. The rationale, which went with them, was that the private sector was generally more efficient at providing goods and services than the public sector. If the private sector was given a long-term contract it was hoped that they would invest their own money in resources, which would make them even more efficient, so that they would be able to recoup their capital outlay, and provide the public sector with better value for money whilst still enjoying a reasonable return on their investment.

Analysing the Metrix project with hindsight, one might comment that it included some very good ideas for improving training; REME could undoubtedly benefit from evolving training methods and technologies, and they needed to be pursued whether they were provided by Metrix or someone else. By 2010, a new Government was in power and the economy was in trouble. Experience had also led many to be sceptical of the PFI concept. Their argument was that PFI deals were generally born of a lack of public funds to refurbish, or replace important facilities that were expensive to run, and that PFI deals had many inherent potential snags. These included the higher cost of capital to the private sector, and the problems that went with the public side being locked into using a monopoly supplier who would typically be able to spend some twenty years exploring ways to milk its PFI contract. Negotiating contracts was a difficult business and the public officials involved did not always have the commercial, financial, or subject matter expertise required; they also used consultants who could have their own axes to grind. Senior officials who were contemplating a second career would also be less than human if their attitudes were not sometimes influenced by the realisation that they could be negotiating with their next employer. Sceptics argued that for such reasons PFI deals had generally proved a very successful way of removing liabilities from the public sector balance sheet in the short term (because public accounting rules allowed this) but they generally provided extraordinarily poor value for money over the longer term, particularly if assets that were important to the public side had been disposed of for less than their true worth.

The End of Plan B

Whatever the reasoning, the end of Plan B was announced to Parliament as follows:

> 'The termination of the Defence Training Rationalisation (DTR) project and the Metrix Consortium's appointment as preferred bidder has been announced by Defence Secretary Dr Liam Fox today, 19 October 2010. The Metrix Consortium was appointed as preferred bidder in January 2007 subject to it developing an affordable and value for money contract proposal. Given the significance of this project and the opportunity to provide a world-class training facility, the Ministry of Defence has worked tirelessly to deliver this project. However, it is now clear that Metrix cannot deliver an affordable, commercially-robust proposal within the prescribed period and it has therefore been necessary to terminate the DTR procurement and Metrix's appointment as preferred bidder'.

Plan C – The Defence Technical Training Change Programme
Plan C was to be a 'change programme' not a PFI deal. It was more pragmatic and less prescriptive than Plan B, and was less grandiose, but its long-term objectives were essentially unchanged. One of the major immediate problems was to get REME out of Arborfield and Bordon. The sites were attractive to developers, the facilities there were not fully used, and some were in need of expensive refurbishment. The Strategic Defence and Security Review 2010 had led to the closure of RAF Lyneham, which released a large site with a lot of existing technical and administrative facilities. In 2012, the Secretary of State for Defence stated:

> 'RAF Lyneham is the preferred location for future Defence technical training. This confirms that the department will withdraw from Arborfield in Berkshire and Bordon in Hampshire, releasing the sites for sale by 2014–15 at the latest'.

The movement of REME into Lyneham was the first priority, and was called Tranche 1. Essentially, this involved transferring the training done at Arborfield and Bordon to the new site, and putting in place there the new 'Home of REME', including RHQ and the REME Arms School. By January 2013, a 'Home of the Corps' Customer Group was looking at estate solutions to the housing of RHQ, Corps Messes, Museum, Band, Church and Corps sport. The planning of the real estate was called Project Rowcroft. Given the state of public finances there was concern about funding but, in December 2013, the MoD announced a £121m contract for the first stage of work on a Defence College of Technical Training (DCTT) at Lyneham in Wiltshire.

The need to release the Arborfield and Bordon sites for sale implied a tight timetable for the move to Lyneham, with work there starting in 2013 and the actual move scheduled to happen from 2015. The only training resource due to stay in Arborfield indefinitely would be the ATIL facility used for equipment-specific training for the Apache attack helicopter, which was contractor owned, and was expected to continue to operate in an enclave there.

The site at Lyneham had much to commend it for REME. For the first time, all REME individual technical training would be collocated. The site was reasonably close to the Salisbury Plain Training Area, and the Army HQ at Andover. The case for the 'Home of REME' had been essentially accepted. The site was a large one, and offered a combination of a 'domestic area' (soldiers' accommodation), a technical training area, a support area, sports facilities and an outdoor training area, all of which would be improved and developed in the course of preparation for Tranche 1. REME would be first into the site, and could expect always to be the largest overall 'customer'.

OUTLINE ORGANISATION AND RESPONSIBILITIES AS AT MAY 2014

Given all the various changes of name and organisation, it is useful to take a snapshot of overall Defence responsibilities for technical training as at May 2014. By this point, all Defence technical training was deemed to be provided by a federated DCTT, headed up by Commodore David Elford RN with his headquarters based at HMS Sultan. He came under the aegis of 22 Group RAF commanded by Air Vice Marshal Lloyd until 2014 and, at the time of writing, by Air Vice Marshal Turner (as did the Defence Technical Training Change Programme). The DCTT comprised four schools, two of which were relevant to REME. They were:

- **Defence School of Maritime Engineering (DSMarE)** – this sat 'one-on-one' over the existing RN DSMarE
- **Defence School of Aeronautical Engineering (DSAE)** – this sat over three organisations – the RN Aeronautical Engineering School (RNAESS); the Army organisation (formerly part of SEAE), which had been retitled School of Army Aeronautical Engineering (SAAE), commanded at the time of writing by Lieutenant Colonel Gary Crichard REME; and, the RAF's Number 1 School of Technical Training (1 SoTT)
- **Defence School of Electronic and Mechanical Engineering (DSEME)** – this sat over two Army organisations of the same name at Arborfield and Bordon respectively (former SEAE and SEME), as well as the RAF's Number 4 SoTT; DSEME was commanded by Colonel Mike Pendlington (late REME) throughout the closure of Arborfield and Bordon and for the move to Lyneham
- **Defence School of Communications and Information Systems (DSCIS)** – this is mentioned for completeness, although it has no direct relevance to REME; it sat over the Army's Royal School of Signals, the RN CIS Training Unit and the RAF 1 Radio School.

The organisation of DCTT is shown in the diagram at Figure 23.2 (at the end of this Chapter).

The DCTT already operated very much on a tri-Service basis. Course design started with a Training Needs Analysis (TNA). In the case of REME, this was carried out by its Training Development Team (TDT) based at Arborfield. Following on from the TNA an Operational Performance Statement was produced, which outlined what training was to be delivered. This went to a Joint TDT (Electro-mechanical) at HMS Sultan or Joint TDT (Aeronautical Engineering) at RAF Cosford. The relevant Joint TDT completed the formal training statement that went, in due course, to the designated school for course design. Courses would be continuously improved over time by applying a process of internal validation (inval) and external validation (exval), as described in The Craftsman magazine (May 2014).

LOOKING AHEAD – THE LONGER TERM

The RAF No 22 Group website painted the picture thus in May 2014:

'Technical training is currently provided on behalf of the three Services by the Defence College of Technical Training (DCTT). Training is delivered across several sites including: Arborfield, Blandford, Bordon, Cosford, Gosport and St Athan. A number of improvements can be made to the efficiency of delivering the training by co-locating these activities, for example, in some cases common elements of training are currently carried out at separate locations. Under the proposals a number of technical training activities will be brought together at Lyneham. The MoD will make these changes incrementally, and each 'tranche' will be judged on its own merits. The proposed first tranche is the move of the Army's Royal Electrical and Mechanical Engineers (REME) training currently delivered at Arborfield and Bordon'.

Clearly, the long-term intention remained to move all Defence technical training to Lyneham. Studies have suggested that this would result in an increase of its population from around 2,000 for Tranche 1 to some 5,000 at the 'end state'. The real estate is available to support this, but further major building and infrastructure programmes would be required to proceed past Tranche 1. Tranche 1 was securely funded, and Chapter 28 ('The Plan for Lyneham') explains how the plan for Lyneham moved forward from 2014.

INDIVIDUAL TRAINING ORGANISATIONS

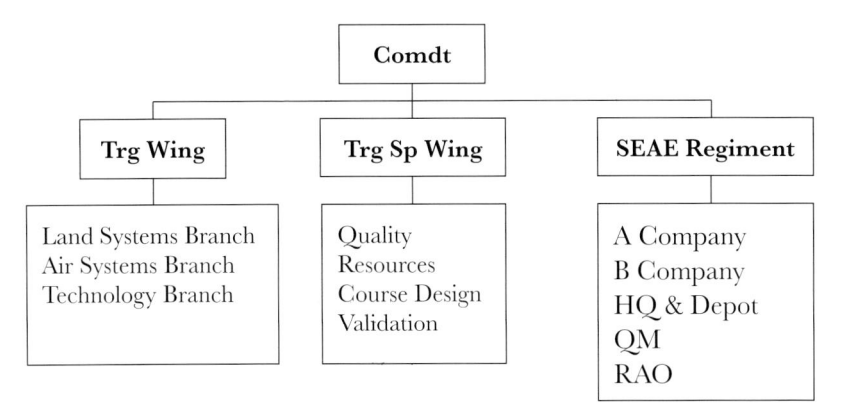

```
                    Comdt
        ┌─────────────┼─────────────┐
    Trg Wing      Trg Sp Wing   SEAE Regiment
```

Trg Wing	Trg Sp Wing	SEAE Regiment
Land Systems Branch Air Systems Branch Technology Branch	Quality Resources Course Design Validation	A Company B Company HQ & Depot QM RAO

Figure 23.1: Organisation of SEAE in Arborfield in 1996

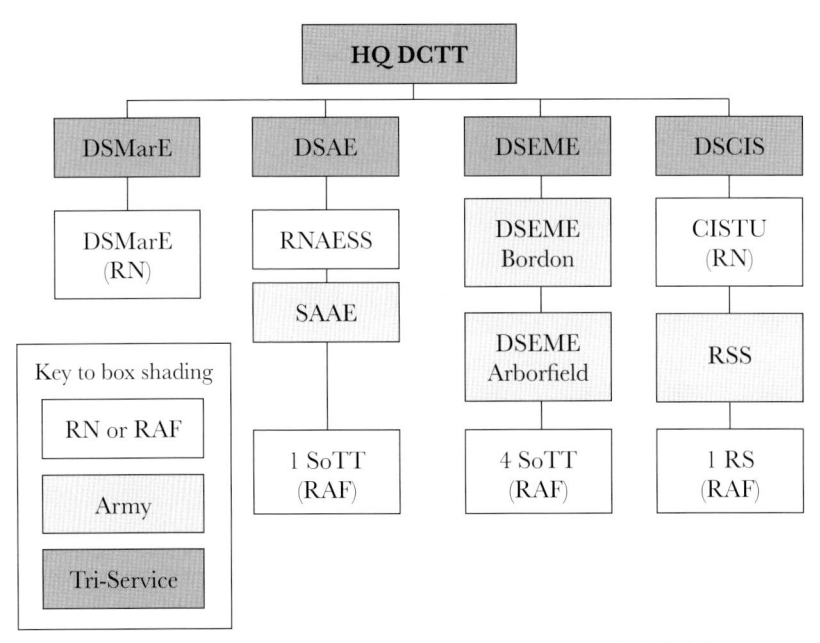

```
                    HQ DCTT
        ┌───────┬────────┬────────┐
     DSMarE   DSAE    DSEME    DSCIS
```

DSMarE	DSAE	DSEME	DSCIS
DSMarE (RN)	RNAESS	DSEME Bordon	CISTU (RN)
	SAAE	DSEME Arborfield	RSS
	1 SoTT (RAF)	4 SoTT (RAF)	1 RS (RAF)

Key to box shading:
- RN or RAF
- Army
- Tri-Service

Figure 23.2: Organisation of Defence College of Technical Training

CHAPTER 24

CORPS ('REGIMENTAL') MATTERS

Corps matters (also known as 'regimental' matters) cover those elements of military life that are not directly part of its operational purpose. The aim of this Chapter is to introduce this subject and to explain the governance arrangements, by way of background for these Chapters that follow:
- 'The REME Association and Veterans' (Chapter 25)
- 'REME Charities and the REME Museum' (Chapter 26)
- 'Other Corps Institutions, Facilities and Activities' (Chapter 27), including the REME Institution, Messes, the Band, Church and involvement with the Bloodhound project
- The plan to move the 'Home of REME' to Lyneham (partly implemented at the time of writing) is covered in Chapter 28 ('The Plan for Lyneham')
- 'REME Sporting and Adventurous Activities' (Chapter 29).

Throughout the period covered by this book, the Corps was honoured to have Field Marshal His Royal Highness The Prince Philip, Duke of Edinburgh as its Colonel in Chief. He has been very generous with his time, as evidenced by all the pictures in The Craftsman magazine of his attendance at a great variety of Corps events over many years. This support has been greatly valued by the Corps.

Corps matters are not directed entirely by the normal MoD chain of command, and further essential direction is provided by committees in which Colonels Commandant play an important role. The name refers not to a rank, but a title and Royal appointment. The Colonels Commandant are senior officers who may be serving or retired. In the case of REME, one of the five (later six) Colonels Commandant has always been non-REME. At the start of the period covered by this book, it was the practice for one Colonel Commandant to take on the role of Representative Colonel Commandant for a year, during which he shouldered the main burden of representational work, that included chairing (amongst other committees) the Corps Committee.

This was the key Committee that oversaw Corps business, to which various sub-committees reported. The Vice-Chairman was the serving

'Head of the Corps', initially the Director General Equipment Support (Army) (DGES(A)), later the Director Electrical and Mechanical Engineering (Army) (DEME(A)) as explained in Chapter 21 ('HQ DEME(A) and RHQ REME'). The other members of the Committee were officers serving in roles crucial to the management of REME's business (such as the Commanders ES of the deployable divisions in UK and Germany). Much of the work was done in such subsidiary committees, with the Corps Secretariat managing day-to-day business.

Some aspects of Corps business are technically 'charitable'. For example, all ranks are invited to donate one day's pay, which goes into a Central Charitable Trust. To handle such matters, the members of the Corps Committee effectively had to put on a separate 'Trustee' hat, and act in accordance with the governance requirements that go with charitable status. This system worked satisfactorily until the Strategic Defence and Security Review of 2010, which resulted in the end of the post of DEME(A), as explained in Chapter 3 ('Strategic Defence and Security Review 2010 and Army 2020') and Chapter 21. A new structure was devised that involved the creation of the new post of Master General REME (MGREME). And the following two new Committees were formed, which replaced the old Corps Committee:

- the Corps Council of Colonels Commandant headed by MGREME
- the Corps Trustees Committee, chaired by one of the Colonels Commandant, which would take on charitable governance roles.

The following more detailed explanation of these events, and the rationale behind them, was provided in 2015 by Brigadier (Retd) Tony Ball (late REME) who, as Corps Secretary between April 2002 and December 2012, played a significant role in many of the events outlined.

'At the start of the period covered by this book, the Corps had three registered charities: the REME Central Charitable Trust; the REME Benevolent Fund; and the REME Museum of Technology. The Central Charitable Trust had been formed in 1986 and had taken ownership of all assets of the other charities. The quid quo pro was that it would provide the funding support for the other charities. Full details of the genesis of these charities is contained in Craftsmen of the Army, Volume 2, Chapter 13. Corps charity matters were directed by the Boards of Trustees with all other non-charity aspects directed by the Corps Committee. All were supported by a small

Corps Secretariat headed by the Corps Secretary (a recently retired senior REME officer).

The Trustee Boards and the Corps Committee were chaired by the Representative Colonel Commandant and the Vice-Chairman was the DGES(A), who was also the serving 'Head of the Corps'. The Trustees and Committee Members were senior officers drawn from across the Corps. The Trustees and the Corps Committee routinely met twice yearly. Specific aspects such as investments, benevolence, publications, sport and adventure training were managed by sub-committees of the Corps Committee and also met twice yearly. This meant that day-to-day activities were managed by the Corps Secretariat, based in Arborfield, while direction was provided mostly from DGES(A) in Andover. In order to improve the 'remote control', it was decided in 1991 to establish the post of Regimental Colonel in Arborfield. Initially, the Commandant of the REME Officers' School was 'double-hatted' as the Regimental Colonel and the first incumbent was Colonel Andrew Platt (late REME). Subsequently, in December 1993, the post was properly established as a full-time appointment, and the Corps Secretariat became an integral part of a newly-formed Regimental Headquarters (RHQ).

There were five Colonels Commandant, an honorary post appointed by Her Majesty The Queen, each serving a five-year term of office and taking it in turns to act as the Representative Colonel Commandant for a one-year term. Four of the Colonels Commandant were late REME and the fifth was from another Corps or Regiment. The system of having one 'external Colonel Commandant' remains to this day. Apart from the Representative Colonel Commandant, the remainder played little part in the governance of Corps matters although they did meet infrequently as the Colonel Commandants Committee. Responsibility was largely devolved to the DGES(A).

In 2000, the two-star (Major General) DGES(A) and his staff became part of the Defence Logistic Organisation and the responsibility as 'Head of the Corps' transferred to a new one-star (Brigadier) post – the Director Electrical and Mechanical Engineering (Army) or DEME(A) – see Chapter 1. DEME(A) and his staff were based in Arborfield and the RHQ became part of his organisation. In order to maintain a two-star perspective, the Colonels Commandant became more engaged in Corps business and were briefed by DEME(A) on activity at their meetings. However, these tended to focus more on military and operational matters rather than the 'regimental' issues. So apart from DEME(A) replacing DGES(A) as the Vice-Chairman of the committees, the governance of Corps matters was largely unchanged with one exception. To simplify administration and because membership of the Corps Committee and the Boards of Trustees was identical (the membership adjustments had happened in the late 1990s), it was decided to hold their meetings concurrently. To ensure coherence and a clear chain of responsibility, each of the sub-committees (such as benevolence, sport, finance, investment) was chaired by one of the Trustees. It was also decided that, once a DEME(A) had completed his term of office, he would become the sixth Colonel Commandant until eventually being replaced by his successor. This system remained in place until 2012.

In 2011, it became clear that the Army had decided to create a new Army Headquarters based at Andover and intended to relocate and re-role the Arms and Services Directors (of which DEME(A) was one) into its new structure. The Regimental Colonel would become the Corps Colonel and replace DEME(A) as the serving 'Head of the Corps' with a slightly strengthened RHQ. Thus in the space of just over 10 years the serving 'Head of the Corps' had been downgraded from two-star to Colonel. (See also Chapter 3). The Colonels Commandant and the outgoing DEME(A) expressed concern that the new Corps Colonel would be overburdened by the additional responsibilities and that there was a need somehow to retain a two-star perspective. The Corps Secretary (Brigadier (Retd) Tony Ball) proposed the creation of a Master General REME and a revised governance structure. He suggested that the Corps should follow the example of others such as the Royal Artillery (with a Master Gunner), the Royal Engineers (with a Chief Royal Engineer) and the Royal Signals (with a Master of Signals). He was duly tasked by the Colonels Commandant to draft a paper proposal and after gaining support from the Military Secretary and Adjutant General, and informal approval by the Colonel in Chief, the appointment of Lieutenant General Andrew Figgures as Master General REME on 1 April 2012 was approved by Her Majesty The Queen. The Master General was in addition to the six Colonels Commandant.

In parallel, a study of the Corps governance structure was commissioned. The findings of the study by Brigadier (Retd) Ian Simpson (late REME) were largely accepted but with some amendment. In essence, the Colonels Commandant Committee would become the Corps Council, chaired by the Master General. Four of the Colonels Commandant would each take on a specific area of responsibility (trustees/investments, engineering, personnel, and regimental matters including sports) and chair an appropriate committee. The existing sub-committees would report through one of these intermediate committees to the Corps Council. The Master General would be President of the REME Institution (supporting serving and retired officers) and the REME Association (supporting all veterans). After a year's experience, a fifth Colonel Commandant portfolio was added – Corps strategy – and the Regimental Committee was transformed into the Corps Colonel's Committee chaired by the Corps Colonel, although a Colonel Commandant remained as President of the Sports Association. The Corps retained its three registered charities, as well as the arrangement whereby the Central Charitable Trust provided the funding streams to support the other two charities together with other Corps activities.

Over the period of 25 years, the responsibility for Corps matters evolved from being mostly vested in the 'Head of the Corps' to a more collegiate approach with greater involvement of the Colonels Commandant led by the Master General. The reason for the changes was not because of any perceived weakness in the governance system but because of externally imposed change to the Army structure. The principle of officers gaining experience of Corps governance through membership of the sub-committees prior to assuming more senior appointments such as trusteeship (in due course) was retained throughout'.

CHAPTER 25

THE REME ASSOCIATION AND VETERANS

The REME Association was formed in 1945, with the intention of retaining comradeship and providing a service to its members. Its aims are given in its rules, which are to:
- foster the 'esprit de corps' of the Corps of Royal Electrical and Mechanical Engineers both serving and retired
- keep those who have served in or with the Corps in touch with one another, with a view of keeping alive a spirit of comradeship
- help, in conjunction with the REME Benevolent Fund and other welfare agencies, both serving and ex-serving members of the Corps and their dependants who find themselves in difficult circumstances
- assist serving and ex-members of the Corps with resettlement in civilian life.

It operates under a set of 'Jubilee Rules' developed by Major General Vincent Metcalfe (late REME) in the early-1990s. These Rules set out a new governance structure, as well as defining the way in which REME Association Branches should operate and how the REME Association should be financed. Shortly after they join the Corps, its Regular members are invited to subscribe one day's pay per year (two days in the case of officers) to support the Corps through its Central Charitable Fund. The first time they do so, a small one-time levy is passed to the REME Association. Subscribers thereby become Life Members of the REME Association. This means that the vast majority of those who have served with REME as Regulars are Life Members of the REME Association, along with a smaller proportion of those who have served with the Reserve Army.

The REME Association Headquarters is based at RHQ REME (at Arborfield until 2015, then to move to Lyneham). The Executive Committee consists of former and serving members of the Corps. They meet twice a year to discuss matters arising within the REME Association and new ways to develop further the organisation. It was chaired for 10 years by Brigadier (Retd) Jim Drew (late REME). He took over the role from Brigadier (Retd) Sam Webber (late REME), who had also held the post for well over 10 years. Brigadier Drew stepped down in 2013 and handed over to Brigadier (Retd) Nigel Williams (late REME).

The collocation with RHQ REME, and the Corps Secretary's organisation, is beneficial in terms of linking the REME Association with other Corps activities, and facilitating the financial and administrative tasks, including running the Annual Reunion, which need to be done centrally. The REME Association Job Agency (RAJA) is also based there. It is run by a senior Warrant Officer who has links to the Services' resettlement organisation, as well as his own contacts (there is a national shortage of people with the kind of managerial/technical skills that the more senior serving REME personnel can offer). The sale of REME branded goods from the REME Shop also provides a useful stream of income, with a wide range of gifts, trophies and clothing always on offer.

REME ASSOCIATION BRANCHES

Its Branches are the 'heart' of the REME Association. It is in the Branches that fellowship is developed; hugely enjoyable social functions are often held and mutual support given. Many Branches organise fascinating and successful trips, and short holidays. Each Branch holds regular meetings and has its own Chairman, Secretary and Treasurer. Every Regular REME unit should have an appointed REME Association representative, and most Branches have close contacts with Regular or Reserve Army REME units in their local area.

Each REME Association Branch has its own story to tell, which inevitably reflects the personalities and interests of those who take the lead. An inherent challenge that affects the REME Association is related to the continuing reduction in the size of the Services since World War 2, through the period of conscription to the major reductions in recent decades. This tends to leave REME Association Branches (like other Services' membership organisations) with an ageing membership profile, which can make it more difficult to attract the diminishing pool of serving and recently retired members of the Corps. Some REME Association Branches have, however, proved able to buck this trend.

The paragraphs that follow provide some snapshots of what members of the REME Association have been up to, and paint a picture of some lively people putting in a lot of work to support the aims of their organisation.

Over time, REME Association Branches have closed down, or been formed (or reformed or renamed) so the number of Branches has varied. The table at Figure 25.1 (at the end of this Chapter) shows the REME Association Branches at the time of writing. Up-to-date information can be found on the REME Association website (www.reme-association.org.uk), which includes contact details and information complementing that in this Chapter.

REGULAR ACTIVITIES – THE ANNUAL REUNION AND DELEGATES' CONFERENCE

The REME Association holds its Annual Reunion each year on a weekend in April from Friday to Monday. It is a very popular and hugely enjoyable event. All members and their families are welcome to attend. It gives former REME members a chance to catch up with one another, in one location, and gives new members the opportunity to meet other members. Attendance is usually between 250 and 300 members and wives. There is a parade of Branch Standards on Saturday afternoon with a military band in attendance, followed by the Gala Dinner and Dance in the evening. On Sunday, there is a church service celebrated by the Corps Padre, which allows a Corps-orientated Act of Remembrance to be made. The event tends to be held in a location in central England to give as many members as possible the chance to attend. Additionally, the Delegates' Conference is held in July every year. Two members from every REME Association Branch are invited to attend, as it gives them an opportunity to discuss any concerns or ideas they may have about the REME Association.

OTHER ACTIVITIES AND ACHIEVEMENTS

Regimental Sunday at the Royal Hospital Chelsea
In 2006, Brigadier Drew thought that it would be a good idea to get all the ex-REME In-Pensioners at the Royal Hospital Chelsea together for a photograph. He then extended it to include Yeoman Warders of Her Majesty's Royal Palace and Fortress the Tower of London and Members of the Sovereign's Body Guard of the Yeomen Guard Extraordinary (known as the 'Beefeaters'). Accordingly, plans were put in place and the Colonel in Chief kindly agreed to attend.

The occasion was a church service in the chapel, followed by a photograph of those attending and lunch. Whilst at the Royal Hospital Chelsea, Brigadier Drew chatted with some of the officials present and found that many Corps and Regiments hold a Regimental Sunday there every year. Armed with this knowledge, Brigadier Drew raised it with the Corps Committee and it is now a firm annual event for the Corps and Royal Hospital. It is held on the third Sunday in July, and, whilst it started with the REME Association and remains supported by them in a major sense, it is now a Corps event.

Naming a Train from First Great Western in Honour of the Corps
The Corps has had two locomotives named in the past, which is recorded in Volumes 1 and 2 of Craftsmen of the Army. In 1958, London, Midland and Scottish Railway named a rebuilt Patriot Locomotive (Number 45528) 'REME'. In 1987, a British Rail Class 47 Inter-City Locomotive was named 'Craftsman'. But, by 2006, there was no locomotive operating that carried a REME name. With several railways' enthusiasts on the REME Association Executive Committee, it was agreed that this situation should not continue. After much writing, persuading and help from a myriad of sources, the Chief Executive of First Great Western agreed that one of the company's Inter-City Locomotives could be named 'The Royal Electrical and Mechanical Engineers'. The REME Association was honoured that the Colonel in Chief agreed to unveil the nameplate on the locomotive, which took place on 16 October 2007. It was a splendid day at Paddington, with the platform reserved for the locomotive, the REME Band playing on the concourse and areas roped off for spectators.

Christmas Parcels to Afghanistan
During operations in Afghanistan, many REME Association Branches and Members sent parcels at Christmas to soldiers in Afghanistan. The process was somewhat random with some REME soldiers not receiving any. The Executive Committee felt that the REME Association might be able to harness its collective efforts and make the addressees more REME specific. This worked well for a couple of years but very understandably, the chain of command became concerned at the strain on logistic resources.

The REME Association mulled over this difficulty and arranged for its Branches to pack their parcels by early summer and bring them to the REME Association Delegates' Conference. They were collected in Arborfield and transported to the REME battalion due to deploy to Afghanistan in the autumn. By prior arrangement, the REME battalion had agreed to provide a small proportion of their container freight allowance for the parcels. Once in theatre, the parcels were then distributed to all REME soldiers in theatre using the REME repair transport chain. It was a huge success and extremely well received. It was all achieved at no cost to the public, with no operational penalty or security risk, and is a wonderful example of how the REME family works together to provide successful solutions to tricky problems.

Special Interest Groups
The REME Association recognises that, whilst its Branches provide the focal points for members in a local area to get together, there are also groups of members who wish to meet to pursue (or renew) a common interest but who are scattered more widely. These groups are known as Special Interest Groups. In some cases, affiliation is formal and others are informal. Some of the groups with which the REME Association has links are:
- Caravan and Camping Club
- The REME Yacht Club
- Arborfield Old Boys
- Chepstow Old Boys
- Association of Artificers RA
- The Armourers Association
- Hadrian's Old Boys.

THE NATIONAL MEMORIAL ARBORETUM

The National Memorial Arboretum (NMA) was set up to provide a tribute to those who died in conflicts of the 20th Century and beyond, with its inspiration drawn from the National Arboretum and Arlington Cemetery in Washington. Following the launch of an appeal in 1994, 150 acres of land within the National Forest in Staffordshire was leased to the Arboretum on a peppercorn rent. Planting of the site began in 1997 and, by the end of 2007, over 50,000 trees had been planted and over 100 plots, dedicated to various organisations, had been created. Entrance to the NMA is free, and it welcomes many thousands of visitors throughout the year. There is a chapel, in which a short poignant service called 'The Homage' is held every day at

10.50 am. This service includes the 'Two-Minute Silence' and reflects the whole ethos of the NMA. Visitors to the Arboretum are welcome every day between 9.00 am and 5.00 pm except on Christmas Day.

The Corps did not respond to the initial invitation in 1994 to establish a memorial plot, there being some uncertainly about how significant the site would be. Others, however, did respond and, in 2003, the Royal British Legion, as principal custodian of national remembrance, assumed responsibility for the NMA. In late 2007, Her Majesty The Queen opened the Armed Forces Memorial, which commemorates the 16,000 lives that have been lost since 1945. It has now become the nation's principal alternative memorial to the Cenotaph.

On a visit to the NMA, Brigadier Drew was embarrassed to discover that there was no REME Memorial. There were several isolated memorials but, unlike most Regiments and Corps, there was nothing for the whole Corps family. He was determined to put that right and held detailed discussions with the REME Association Executive Committee, which was unanimous in its strong approval. On reflection, though, he felt that it should not be led by the REME Association for it needed to be a memorial for the whole Corps, past, present and future. He therefore outlined the REME Association proposal to the Corps Committee. After due preparatory work, a paper was presented to the Corps Committee recommending the creation of a REME plot within the NMA to commemorate those who have served in the Corps. This was agreed, as was Corps funding to complement that provided by the REME Association.

The design of the REME Memorial Plot, which the Corps Committee agreed to fund in February 2008, was an imaginative and attractive one that comprised:

- a woodland area of some 50 metres by 50 metres to be planted with English oak, and a carpet of bluebells in due course, to reflect REME's appointment title of 'Bluebell' on insecure radio nets
- a mound near the centre of the plot on which the Memorial sat
- the Memorial of Portland stone, carved and constructed by Mr Alan Micklethwaite (a sculptor who had worked on the restoration of Lincoln Cathedral and other projects), in the form of a circular seat with a buttress at either end sculpted with the past and present REME badges, and the inscription around the inside surface 'Dedicated to the Past and Present Members of the Corps'
- a gravelled approach road flanked by pedestals, coming from the direction of the Armed Forces Memorial to the north; the nature

of the ground meant that a bridge had to be built to allow the necessary drainage to take place.

There was much do in order to implement this concept, and a REME Memorial Development Committee was formed to pursue the project. It comprised the Regimental Colonel (Colonel Richard Bennett (late REME), who was to play a key role in managing the project), the Corps Secretary, the Chairman of the REME Association Executive Committee, the Commander ES 5 Division and the Secretary of the REME Association. In due course, the Royal Engineers agreed to take on the task of constructing the mound, and building the approach road and its bridge. Commitments associated with operations in Afghanistan delayed work until early 2009, but the excellent job done by 24 Commando Regiment RE made the delay well worth it.

On 9 July 2009, His Royal Highness The Prince Philip was present at the dedication of the REME Memorial at the NMA. The Colonel in Chief was joined by veterans and serving members of the Corps for the event hosted by the Representative Colonel Commandant, Major General Mike Huntley (late REME). The dedication service was conducted by Padre Stephen Thatcher, Senior Chaplain of the Corps Church of St Eligius. Immediately after the service, the Colonel in Chief was invited to unveil a plaque commemorating the day followed by the laying of a wreath at the Armed Forces Memorial below the list of those killed in 2008 including Corporal Gardiner and Corporal Barnes, killed on operations in Afghanistan. The Colonel in Chief then met serving members of the Corps and members of the REME Association over lunch.

In 2014, some further work was commissioned as the location of the REME Memorial, in the damp conditions close to the river, had resulted in some weathering of the stone and deterioration in the gilding of the lettering. The embossed badges were replaced by carved granite, which was also used to replace the inlaid brass inserts on the pedestals. The path was resurfaced and edged with granite curb stones; the bank and mound were reprofiled and relaid with turf; and the lettering deepened and repainted. At the time of writing, the planned carpet of bluebells on the site will be planted in the Autumn of 2015. (**See Plates 49–51**)

Andover & District	Doncaster & District	Scarborough & District
Arborfield & District	Eastbourne & District	Shropshire
Ashford (Kent)	Humberside	South London
Birmingham	Kettering, Corby & District	South West Durham
Bordon & District	Lancashire	Surrey
Bournemouth	Lincolnshire	Swansea & District
Brighton, Hove & District	Manchester	Scotland
Bristol	Mid Anglia	Teesside
Cromer	North and East London	Thetford & District
Coventry	Northern Ireland	West Yorkshire
Derby/Nottingham	Potteries & District	Widnes
Overseas Branches are in South Australia, New Zealand		

Figure 25.1: REME Association Branches (at the time of writing)

CHAPTER 26

REME CHARITIES AND THE REME MUSEUM

THE CENTRAL CHARITABLE TRUST

Volume 2 of Craftsmen of the Army recounts the early history of the Central Charitable Trust (CCT), which was set up in 1986 to act as the all-embracing amalgam of Corps funds. This replaced the REME Benevolent Fund as the main source of funding for Corps activities. This arrangement worked well and gave the Trustees the flexibility to apply resources efficiently to further the Trust's stated objectives and support the Corps charities. An article in The Craftsman magazine (November 2013) provides a useful illustration of the work of the CCT by providing a snapshot of its activities in 2012. Although this is a little dated, it shows the spread of resource allocation.

Income
Most of the CCT's income came from subscriptions through the Regular Army's Day's Pay Scheme to which all REME officers and some 94% of soldiers were committed, the highest take up of the Regular Army's Day's Pay Scheme across the Army. Soldiers paid 100% of one day's gross pay into the CCT. Officers paid 200% of one day's gross pay, with 60% of one day's pay notionally allocated to the Headquarters Officers' Mess, and 40% of one day's pay to the REME Institution. Investments provided additional income, as did contributions from officers and soldiers of the Territorial Army, legacies, donations and grants from other charities. The total gross income was £1,201,414.

Expenditure
A variety of grants were made, but key specific areas of expenditure were:
- **The REME Benevolent Fund** – some £338K was disbursed largely in the form of grants-in-aid; individual grants were made regularly to members and ex-members of the Corps who had particular needs, a number resulting from injuries sustained on

operations; ex-REME residents of the Royal Star and Garter Homes and the REME In-Pensioners at the Royal Hospital Chelsea were supported; and a substantial annual grant was made to the Army Benevolent Fund

- **The REME Sports Association** – £221K was spent in support of 27 official REME sports
- **Adventurous Training** – £73K went to 163 adventurous training exercises in which 1,711 members of the Corps participated
- **The Craftsman magazine** – £75K was granted, which enabled the continued free distribution of the magazine to unit level
- **The REME Museum of Technology** – £15K was granted, which supplemented the income the REME Museum gained from admission fees and other sources
- **Others** – these included the REME Association, the REME Institution, the Corps Headquarters Officers' Mess the Corps Sergeants' Mess, the REME Band and a number of unit grants to provide improvements to welfare facilities; also, it was possible to put some £450K into investments in order to build up financial reserves to support the move to Lyneham of the 'Home of REME'.

Organisation

Until 2012, the members of the Corps Committee were also, ex-officio, the Trustees of the CCT and the other REME charities. The demise of the Corps Committee in 2012, following its replacement by the formation of the Corps Council and the establishment of the post of Master General REME (MGREME) (see Chapter 24 ('Corps ('Regimental') Matters')), led to the separation from the Corps Council of the Trustees Committee overseeing the management of the Corps Charities but with one of the Colonels Commandant from the Corps Council appointed as Chairman of Trustees. Major General Ian Dale (late REME) held this post until December 2013, when he was succeeded by Major General Stephen Andrews (late REME). The other Trustees were, ex-officio, the holders of the following appointments:

- Colonel REME (also Vice-Chairman of Trustees)
- Colonel REME Reserves
- Commander ES 1 (UK) Division (retitled DCOMD ES 102 Logistic Brigade in 2015)
- Commander ES 3 (UK) Division (retitled DCOMD ES 101 Logistic Brigade in 2015)

- Commander ES Force Troops Command
- Commandant Defence School of Electronic and Mechanical Engineering
- Assistant Director Project Rowcroft.

FROM TRUST TO CHARITABLE COMPANY

By early 2014, it was becoming clear that changes to the way in which charities were regulated meant that REME's model for managing its finances as a trust was becoming increasingly outdated. The rules meant that a trust was unable itself to own property or employ staff directly; such things had to be done on behalf of a trust by one or more trustees personally. Trustees had an unlimited liability for the performance of the charity and, in extremis, could find themselves personally financially liable for any mishaps or losses. The increasing focus on regulation by the Charity Commission, and the need to demonstrate that the governance of the charities was independent of the chain of command and MoD, led to a desire to broaden REME's Trustees' body by bringing in external trustees with a proven record in finance, investment management and charity law. However, such trustees were unlikely to join a charitable trust, which left them with a potentially unlimited personal liability. Most modern charities, including Services' charities that owned property and employed staff, had got round such difficulties by adopting an incorporated structure. It was therefore decided that REME should go the same way and form a charitable company.

The new company, called 'The REME Charity' was due to be formed in early 2016 (shortly after the time of writing) as a company limited by guarantee. The Trustees were to be the directors of the new company, which was then registered with the Charity Commission as a charity. This was to take over the assets of the CCT and the REME Benevolent Fund, which were to become dormant but retain their separate identities and be formally linked to The REME Charity. The REME Museum was to retain its separate charitable status and identity, but its Board of Trustees was to be replaced by The REME Charity as a single corporate trustee. The REME Museum's affairs are covered later in this Chapter, and those of the REME Association are covered in Chapter 25 ('The REME Association and Veterans'). The short update on the REME Institution that follows is intended to help complete the picture on REME's charities.

THE REME INSTITUTION

The genesis of the REME Institution was described in Volume 1 of Craftsmen of the Army and its role, which largely remained unchanged, is well covered in Volume 2 of Craftsmen of the Army, although by 2015 its membership had reduced to 1,850. This was in line with the reduction in the size of the Corps. The REME Institution continued to run the very successful Beating Retreat and Cocktail Party, and the equally successful Retired Officers' Dinner on an annual basis. The Officers' Summer Ball also continued to be run at West Court until 2011. In 2013, the Committee decided to make a break from West Court, which was struggling to cope with the numbers at a reasonable cost, and an external venue was booked (Wokefield Park Hotel, near Reading), which proved a great success. There was no Summer Ball in 2015, with the very successful WestFest (see Chapter 27 ('Other Corps Institutions, Facilities and Activities')) replacing the Ball in that year.

The popular Quinquennial London Reception continued, also to be sponsored by the REME Institution, with each event being oversubscribed but also attracting back to the UK members of the REME Institution who had retired overseas. Finally, the REME Institution is more than just a social club for officers and it continues to produce the REME Journal annually, as well as sponsoring the award of prizes to young officers including the MGREME's Sword to the best REME officer cadet on each Commissioning Course from the Royal Military Academy Sandhurst. It continues to contribute to 'esprit de corps' by providing a mechanism through which the serving, retired and Reserve Army officer communities remain in touch with each other and what is happening in the Corps.

THE REME MUSEUM OF TECHNOLOGY

The background to the REME Museum is described in Volume 2 of Craftsmen of the Army. In outline, a small Regimental Museum was first set up in the late-1950s in rooms in Moat House in Arborfield. This housed some useful archived documents, but the limited space available meant that displays were very limited. Much other material of historical interest was located elsewhere. A comprehensive collection of small arms was built up and housed at Bordon in the School of Electrical and Mechanical Engineering (SEME). A number of historic vehicles were also housed there, where they were mostly kept in full working order by Mr Roger Jones, so they could be deployed on displays elsewhere if required.

Meanwhile, a collection of electronic equipment and material had been gathered at the School of Electronic Engineering (SEE) at Arborfield, and aeronautical exhibits at the Aircraft Engineering Training Wing (AETW) at Middle Wallop. These displays in training units were often intended not only to preserve the artefacts, but also to support teaching by showing progress in design and repair techniques.

The REME Museum was moved from Moat House to newly-built premises in Isaac Newton Road, Arborfield, in 1985. Initially, this was not a great step forward as the new arrangement essentially comprised an office occupied by Brian Baxter and a display spread along a corridor, along with a number of unpacked boxes in an adjacent room. Mr Brian Baxter had been appointed Deputy Curator in 1983 to support the Corps Secretary, who was then the Curator. He was to continue to make a great contribution to the REME Museum in various posts over the next 32 years, until it moved in 2015, and thereafter on a consultancy basis. Fortunately, the Deputy Corps Secretary, Lieutenant Colonel (Retd) Larry Le Var REME had the interests of the REME Museum very much at heart, and after lobbying various senior officers was able to obtain considerable extra accommodation in the form of an adjacent building, which was not much used and could be freed up for the REME Museum.

Lieutenant Colonel (Retd) Le Var was to become the REME Museum Director in 1988, and was to fill this post until June 1999. During this period, the REME Museum flourished, as a team of enthusiastic staff (both paid and volunteer) moved the organisation forward. In 1989, Major (Retd) Derek Gilliam REME was appointed part-time Corps Archivist, and with the assistance of volunteers transformed a loose collection into a properly housed and documented archive. In 1990, it was inspected and recognised by the Public Record Office as an authorised location for holding State Papers. The Pictorial Archive was set up in parallel and was opened in 1992. In the latter half of the 1990s, a website was designed for the REME Museum by Mr Peter Eldred. This facilitated world-wide access to the historic vehicle collection and, subsequently, to other parts of the collection. This proved very popular and in a short space of time the site had received 5,000 'hits'.

As displays were improved, the REME Museum increasingly became a place worth visiting, and open days as well as activity days for families started to become common occurrences. A new dimension opened up when a pilot education session for schoolchildren was held in November 1997. This was the brainchild of Mrs Christine Keymer, a volunteer and trained teacher whose husband Lieutenant Colonel (Retd) David Keymer REME was to be employed as a very energetic and effective REME Museum Development and Fundraising Officer from 1997 to 2011. The success of this exercise led to the appointment in 1998 of a full-time Education Officer who, working with local schools, developed a number of education workshops that delivered specified National Curriculum outcomes. Between the launch of the first session in 1997 until January 2014, over 22,000 schoolchildren attended formal education workshops at the REME Museum. The 'family friendly' nature of the REME Museum was enhanced in 2009 with the purchase of an extremely popular children's assault course.

On 31 July 1997, the Colonel in Chief visited the refurbished REME Museum of Technology. He was guided on a tour by the REME Museum Director (Lieutenant Colonel (Retd) Le Var), accompanied by Brigadier John Palmer (late REME) (the Arborfield Garrison Commander), Colonel Tony Millington (late REME) (the Regimental Colonel), Brian Baxter and Roger Jones. (**See Plate 52**)

In 1995, a 'Gold Card Scheme' (payment for a lifetime membership/ entrance card) was successfully launched to raise further funds for the REME Museum Development Fund. When Major General Peter Besgrove (late REME) was appointed Director General Equipment Support (Army) in 1997, he was a strong supporter of the need for REME to have a museum that would do the Corps justice. A considerable amount of money was raised or provisionally allocated from Corps funds and, after various iterations, a plan was made, which included building two large halls that would be adjacent to the existing REME Museum facilities.

The building of the first of these halls, which was to be called the Prince Philip Vehicle Hall duly went ahead and was opened by the Colonel in Chief on the 22 October 1999. The Prince Philip Vehicle Hall was large enough to house a collection of both wheeled and tracked repair and recovery vehicles, as well as a Scout helicopter and a variety of other items of interest. (**See Plate 53**) The bulk of the vehicle collection, though, remained at Bordon. It put the REME Museum into a different league, with lots of things for visitors to see and lots of space in which to hold and organise activities. Shortly before the opening of the Prince Philip Vehicle Hall, Lieutenant Colonel (Retd) Le Var handed over the reins of REME Museum Director to Lieutenant Colonel (Retd) Bill Cleasby REME who held the post with distinction until 2012.

By around 2000, the REME Corps Museum Committee had to decide whether or not to go ahead with the building of the other large hall. By that point, progress with the Defence Training Review suggested that REME was not likely to remain in Arborfield for the long term, and there was a risk that the Corps would gain little benefit from a major investment in a new building. Around that time, a new opportunity presented itself. Poperinghe Barracks in Arborfield closed in 1997 and Taylor Woodrow, the contractor that was developing the site, generously offered to dismantle the old guardroom and rebuild it at the REME Museum. It was a wooden building of World War 1 vintage, which would have to be knocked down anyway, and perhaps the task of reassembling it did not at first seem a particularly daunting or expensive commitment. The original idea was that it would be very much an 'added extra', which would simply be next to the REME Museum and might house some sort of a display or be an exhibit in its own right.

The REME Museum Committee drew on its considerable collective commercial and technical experience, and could see the opportunity to do much more. This involved looking at the REME Museum as a business, and analysing such things as the likely footfall pattern in the same way as a shop would. The outcome was a plan to integrate the guardroom to the existing facilities, not only to house new displays but also to use it as public entrance/exit point that incorporated a tea room and the relocated REME Shop. In the light of this, the earlier plan to build a new hall was dropped.

The rebuilt guardroom had to be properly wired and plumbed in, in order to comply with current building regulations. This meant that much of the structure was a modern well-built replica of the original, and must have cost Taylor Woodrow more than they originally expected. They generously stuck to the spirit of their original offer, and it was fitting that the new facility was opened in November 2004 by Mr Malcolm Pink of Taylor Woodrow.

The concept proved a great success. The tea room was easily accessible to those working in Arborfield Garrison, and was a convenient drop-in or meeting point for families. It was also 'outside the wire', which meant that it was accessible to the public without any special security requirements.

Poperinghe Barracks Guardroom rebuilt at the REME Museum site

New displays were added within the REME Museum complex over the years. The rebuilt guardroom was home to innovative displays, including a 1950s guardroom complete with an 'animatronic' guard commander, whose voice was activated by people passing by. Two further notable displays were added elsewhere in the complex.

The Armourers Hall display opened in 2006, and showed a range of weapons from arrows and spears through to the most modern firearms. The collection had been started prior to World War 2, as part of a technical training programme in Hilsea (near Portsmouth) before finally being transferred from SEME Bordon to the REME Museum.

The Johnson Room was named after Major General James Johnston (late REME), who had been a keen and generous supporter of the REME Museum for many years. The display incorporated a selection of electronic items including radios, valves, computers and medical equipment, and a 'listening cage'. It was opened in June 2007.

By this stage, it was widely felt that REME had a Museum of which it could feel justly proud. Interestingly, it had been singled out on a number of occasions by various senior officials in the field of military museums as an example of how a military museum should be developed and managed.

The 'listening cage' in the Johnson Room

As well as its permanent displays, the REME Museum had hosted a number of temporary exhibitions. Some focused on particular parts of the collection, others on key figures in the history of REME, such as the Fox's Gold Exhibition, which featured as part of the 2012 London Olympics celebrations and focused on Captain Jim Fox REME winning a gold medal in modern pentathlon at the 1976 Munich Olympics. A number of exhibitions have been tied into key anniversaries. For example, in 1994, the D-Day Exhibition was held and, one year later, an exhibition was mounted to celebrate the 50th Anniversary of VE Day.

The great progress made during these years reflected the enthusiasm and ability of many volunteers as well as employed staff. They include Ms Judy Booth who retired as REME Museum Curator in 2014 after over 22 years' service, taking with her a MGREME Commendation. Later the same year, Colonel (Retd) Mike Sibbons (late REME), the Corps Archivist, retired. He had not only enhanced the REME Museum's research service but also produced the regular 'From the Archives' articles for The Craftsman magazine.

In October 2011, Lieutenant Colonel (Retd) John Edwards REME took over as REME Museum Development and Fundraising Manager and he continued to market the 'Gold Card Scheme' to new members of the Corps, ensuring a steady take-up until his retirement due in the Spring of 2016. In 2012, Lieutenant Colonel (Retd) Bill Cleasby retired as Director after a very fruitful time in the post, and passed the baton into the capable hands of Major (Retd) Rick Henderson REME. By that time, it was clear that the major challenge over the next few years would be to manage the move of the REME Museum from Arborfield to the new 'Home of REME' at Lyneham. Meanwhile, the REME Museum had not lost its innovative mindset and, in 2014, Miss Jennifer Allison, who had taken over as REME Museum Curator, secured a £15K grant to allow the REME Museum to host the 'New Grounds' contemporary art exhibition.

In 2013, it was confirmed that the former Officers' Mess at Lyneham would become the new site of the REME Museum. The move to Lyneham afforded the REME Museum the opportunity to look afresh at its collections, displays and public programmes. A series of focus groups, which included serving officers and soldiers as well as families and non-military personnel, were consulted to understand better what individuals expected from the REME Museum. Professional internal exhibition designers were selected to help create a modern museum of which the Corps can be proud.

The REME Museum in Arborfield closed in April 2015 and was planned to reopen in Lyneham in Autumn 2016, but this has been delayed because of building problems. The new REME Museum at Lyneham will draw on the success of its predecessor at Arborfield and will include a REME Museum shop and café, an education suite for user groups of all ages, and a dedicated temporary exhibition space. It will also offer a combined archives area with an attached reading room for use by external researchers and members of the Corps.

CHAPTER 27

OTHER CORPS INSTITUTIONS, FACILITIES AND ACTIVITIES

REME HEADQUARTERS OFFICERS' MESS WEST COURT

The history of West Court is covered at some length in Volume 2 of *Craftsmen of the Army*. The Corps continued to enjoy this wonderful facility until it was closed prior to the move to Lyneham. It was decided that REME's time in West Court should end with a bang not a whimper, and a superb final party was organised for it, which was called WestFest. It took place on Wednesday 18 July 2015, and was attended by about 650 people. A hugely varied music programme started at midday, and festivities went on late into the evening, with the formal celebration concluding with a firework display and a stirring rendition of 'Land of Hope and Glory'. But the REME Band agreed to stay on and continue to entertain into the early hours. (**See Plate 54**)

The music included contributions from the Wokingham Rock Choir, the Arborfield Military Wives Choir, the Band of the Royal Logistic Corps, a stunning operatic recital by Erin Hughes, a contribution by Tim Russell, jazz from Tipitana, rock music by Firing Blanks, as well as a performance by the three very glamorous members of the Electric String Trio. There was food and drink aplenty and there were fairground entertainments, such as dodgem cars. The weather was beautiful and WestFest offered a chance to eat, drink, and talk of 'old times' on the lawn in the afternoon, with things livening up later. All in all, there was a wonderful atmosphere and a general agreement that the programme provided a fitting end to REME's 62 years at West Court.

The structure of West Court remained essentially unchanged through the period covered by this book. It was enhanced by the purchase of further pictures, continuing to build on what is regarded by experts as an exceptionally fine collection of modern art. As such, the pictures were not only enjoyable in their own right, but represented a sound financial investment. The Corps also commissioned portraits of its two Lieutenant Generals, Lieutenant Colonel Bob Fram MC and Mr David Green.

Change tended to be incremental. The contracting out of catering and other services inevitably changed the atmosphere and the way things were done to a degree. Such changes were, however, softened by the continued presence of Mr David Green who had been the Mess Manager since 1980, and who retained some of his management responsibilities under the new contractual arrangements. He was known to all REME officers as 'Mr Green'. He had a wonderful sense of humour and a 'twinkle in his eye'. He was well known and well liked by officers of the Corps from the highest to the lowest. He had a wonderful fund of stories. When Mr Green was around, one had a comforting sense of continuity and assurance that he would deal with anything that needed sorting out and come up with a solution, which would at least leave one smiling even if it was not what one originally envisaged. Mr Green undoubtedly helped generations of REME officers feel that West Court was a very special place, and one in which they could enjoy the company of friends, feel happy and 'at home'. Sadly, Mr Green passed away in mid-2015 after a relatively short final illness. (**See Plate 55**)

THE CORPS SERGEANTS' MESS

There never was a separate Corps Sergeants' Mess building. The concept was that the most appropriate Sergeants' Mess would be designated as:

> '… a central mess to which all warrant officers and sergeants of the Corps belong, and at which they may hold social functions and offer hospitality'.

Over time, a number of messes in Arborfield and Bordon were used in this way, driven by such changes as the closure of Poperinghe Barracks and the REME Training Battalion & Depot. By 1994, the Bailleul Mess in Arborfield had been designated as the Corps Sergeants' Mess, and was to continue as such until the move to Lyneham in 2015 when the Mess of the newly-formed 8 Battalion REME took on this role as described in Chapter 28 ('The Plan for Lyneham').

The Corps Sergeants' Mess was presided over by the Corps Regimental Sergeant Major (RSM), and, in due course, by the Corps Artificer Sergeant Major (ASM), as explained later in this Chapter. The Mess held many formal and informal functions, but the main routine Corps events were to become the Spring Dinner Night and the Autumn Ladies Dinner Night.

To enhance the Mess and recognise their achievements, paintings were commissioned of current and former members who had received awards for gallantry. These were of: Corporal Adam Miller CGC (Conspicuous Gallantry Cross), Sergeant Michael Dowling MM (Military Medal), Corporal Craig Comber MC (Military Cross), Corporal Richard Street MC, Corporal Jason Garrett and Corporal Justin Simons (both MID (Mentioned in Despatches), in the picture 'Thrown Tracks').

THE ROLE OF THE CORPS RSM AND CORPS ASM

At the start of the period covered by this book, REME had a Corps RSM but no Corps ASM. The Corps RSM was also RSM of the School of Electronic Engineering in Arborfield, reflecting REME's traditional practice of double-hatting the Corps RSM role with that of RSM of a major training establishment. This meant that, by definition, all those who held the post of Corps RSM would be a Regimental Specialist. As such, they had the advantage of expertise in matters related to drill, ceremonial, discipline, quartermaster-related issues and general management, including mess management. It also meant they had the drawback of coming from a fairly narrow and essentially non-technical sector of REME manpower.

They were therefore not well placed to give advice on matters, which had a technical dimension. Initially, this did not matter, and this was not something they were normally expected to do. Following organisational turmoil of the late-1990s and after, it became clear that the Director Electrical and Mechanical Engineering (Army) (DEME(A)) and the Regimental Colonel would benefit from the input of a very senior Warrant Officer who could understand Corps technical matters, as well as regimental aspects of Corps business. The post of Corps ASM therefore came into being in 2004 alongside that of the Corps RSM. In 2007, the role of Corps RSM was discontinued, with the Corps ASM taking over most of his functions.

The Evolving Role of the Corps ASM
The Corps ASM initially worked primarily to DEME(A)'s Policy Board. The demise of the Corps RSM post in 2007 saw the Corps ASM take on the role of senior soldier in the Corps. An underlying purpose of this role was the enhancement of morale and moral cohesion within a large Corps, with the benefit, amongst others, of aiding the recruitment and

retention of high quality personnel. The status of the Corps ASM was also enhanced in 2014 when the Chief of the General Staff decreed that all Corps and Divisional RSMs/ASMs should be appointed as Command Sergeant Majors. By this point, the Corps ASM had a vital role to play in Corps regimental and ceremonial affairs. These included regular events such as parading the Standards at the REME Association weekend, organising the Service of Remembrance at the National Memorial Arboretum, the Regimental Sunday at the Royal Hospital Chelsea and the Corps Birthday Parade. Another key aspect of his role was to represent the soldiers of the Corps and deliver their concerns, opinions and ideas at a number of boards and conferences. At the time of writing, these included:

- promotion and assignment boards at the Army Personnel Centre, Glasgow
- The Army Engineering Committee
- The Senior Warrant Officers' Committee (for the Chief of the General Staff)
- The REME Adventurous Training and Enterprising Activities Committee
- The Corps Sports Committee
- The Corps Sergeants' Mess
- The Corps Benevolence Committee.

A full list of the Corps ASMs is at Appendix A ('Key Corps Post-Holders and Awards'). (**See Plate 56**)

THE REME HOTEL IN BAVARIA 1993–2014

REME has been involved with two properties in Germany. One was the REME Adventure Training Centre (ATC), also referred to as the 'REME (Ski) Lodge', which is described in Chapter 29 ('REME Sporting and Adventurous Activities'). The other was the REME Hotel ('Haus Urban') in Wertach, Bavaria. (**See Plate 57**)

The background to the REME Hotel concept is covered in detail in Volume 2 of Craftsmen of the Army. In essence, a hotel was purchased for some £263K by the Corps and opened in 1982. The concept was to provide holiday, recreation, recuperation, training and other facilities for serving and retired members of the Corps and their families. At that time, many members of the Corps were based in Germany so the REME Hotel was accessible by car. As it was comfortable, very affordable and located in a stunningly beautiful part of Germany, it soon proved a great success.

During the years from 1993, the REME Hotel went from strength to strength. It underwent a major refurbishment programme, converting many of the rooms into en-suite facilities. The REME Hotel was utilised by a variety of entitled groups over the years, such as REME Association Branches, family skiing trips, even a wedding reception. Many family members of the Corps had their first exposure to winter activities from the REME Hotel. The REME Hotel served the Corps well for over 30 years, but, as a result of changes linked to the Strategic Defence and Security Review of 2010 and the withdrawal of the Army from Germany, the Corps had to make the hard decision to close the REME Hotel in 2014. To that end, the REME Corps Council, headed by the Master General REME directed that the REME Hotel was to be sold by the Corps Trustees for the best possible price and the funds returned to the REME Central Charitable Trust.

SAINT ELIGIUS CHURCH AND THE ARBORFIELD GARRISON CHURCH

Volume 2 of Craftsmen of the Army explains how Saint Eligius was selected as the Patron Saint of the Corps in 1959. REME is a widely-spread Corps, and its members therefore tend to be in a minority when they contribute to worship in their local garrison or civilian churches. In the predominantly REME Garrisons in Bordon and Arborfield, however, the Corps has taken the lead in running and supporting active churches. St Eligius Church in Arborfield was to have a special significance as through the efforts of some very dedicated people it was to become the Corps Church (as well as a local centre of music in Arborfield). Its story is outlined below.

St Eligius Church was dedicated on Sunday 3 December 1989 by the Chaplain General, the Reverend James Harkness. It became the first multi-denominational Garrison Church in Arborfield since the Remount Depot opened in 1904. The building was based on the former Garrison Theatre, which had originally been a reception stable for horses arriving at the Remount Depot. The idea of doing this arose in the late-1980s, and as the project attracted no official funding a significant fundraising effort was organised. Lieutenant Colonel Larry Le Var REME was appointed Project Officer by the Garrison Commander. This was to prove an

St Eligius Church in Arborfield July 2011

inspired decision, as Lieutenant Colonel Le Var and his wife Dr Rita Le Var were to play important roles in the life of the Church for the rest of REME's time in Arborfield.

St Eligius Church at Christmas 2007

Lieutenant Colonel Le Var was successful in raising funds from a variety of sources with the help of a number of people, including Major Dennis Knight REME and Major Frank Reynolds REME. This allowed the former theatre to be turned into a very attractive church, which reflected the great deal of thought and work that had gone into its design.

The new St Eligius Church soon became the focus for inter-denominational worship in the Garrison. A new dimension was added with the addition of a Corps Memorial Chapel and four beautiful stained glass windows in the main church: St Eligius, The Garden of Eden, Jesus in the Carpenter's Shop, and The Creation.

The Church was used by the Ministers of the Church of England and other reformed churches who acted as Garrison

Stained glass window – Jesus in the Carpenter's Shop

REME Memorial Chapel 2011

Padres with overall responsibility for the spiritual welfare of the soldiers and their families in the Garrison. There were close and constructive relationships with the Roman Catholic Church, and Catholic Masses were held in the Church since its dedication. Chaplaincy to the Roman Catholic members of the Garrison was provided by the Roman Catholic Chaplains based at the Royal Military Academy, Sandhurst.

Although St Eligius Church started with essentially two congregations (Roman Catholic Masses being held on Sundays at 9.00 am and Anglican/Reformed Services at 10.30 am), many ecumenical (multi-denominational) activities developed over the years, including fellowship and study activities, and services such as Stations of the Cross on Good Friday. The Church also began to be used regularly for funerals, baptisms and weddings, including the wedding of two young people whose fathers had both served as DEME(A). The Church was naturally involved with Garrison and Corps events, which had a religious dimension, such as the Remembrance Sunday Service and annual St Eligius Day Service.

The Church was a place where both sacred and secular music came to be played and sung. The Arborfield Garrison Singers (led by Nicholas Ballard in later years), practised weekly in the Church building since its inception. The Church Choir was established in 2012 for the major Christian Festivals in the Church Year by Rita Le Var, (who was also the organist from 2009–2015). The Choir contributed to special services, such as Carols by Candlelight and the Royal School of Church Music Sunday Services.

Monthly lunch-time concerts, organised by Rita Le Var, were held in the Church from October 2011 to September 2015. The concerts covered a wide range from band concerts to piano, organ, violin, viola, cello, harp and song recitals. The REME Band supported the concert on six occasions and gave its last public concert in the Church. Other performers included the opera singer David Durham (baritone), and Carla Rees (alto and bass flute specialist). During holiday periods, school children and students from the Farnborough Sixth Form College gave delightful concerts and recitals.

All the concerts were memorable in their own way and greatly appreciated by the audience. Everyone visiting the Church commented on the beautiful surroundings and the warm reception they received. One performer described the audience as "a large, enthusiastic and appreciative music society". The Choir of the Royal Memorial Chapel, Sandhurst, with Peter Beaven, Director of Music, and Simon Dinsdale, Sub-Organist, gave the final concert in September 2015 to a full Church.

A bi-annual concerts' newsletter was produced, which contained details of the disbursement of the charitable donations to the REME Benevolent Fund from the military church communities. In all, the concerts raised £14,568.

The structure for managing the Church evolved over time, with a Church Council being established in 2006, with the Garrison Chaplain as Chairman, and Rita Le Var as Secretary until the closure of the Church. The first Corps Chaplain, the Reverend Stephen Thatcher, was appointed in 2009 with Lieutenant Colonel (Retd) Le Var having taken on the role of Corps Church Warden from 2003, and Viscount Alanbrooke the role of Garrison Church Warden.

It is not possible to list all that went on at St Eligius Church, but the following description of it seems to offer a very fair summary:

'In the 26 years of its existence, St Eligius Church has been the centre for Christian worship and fellowship in Arborfield Garrison and within the Corps of REME. Within its walls, soldiers and their families received a warm welcome as did other people living nearby with connections to REME. The ministry provided support that took account of the particular pressures and hardships of military life. Over the years, the Church has undertaken the mission for which it was dedicated to the Glory of God, in praise and prayer'.

During the final year of St Eligius Church as a military church, discussions led by Padre Stephen Thatcher, took place with the developers, Crest Nicholson, and a local Anglican parish about the possibility of St Eligius Church continuing as a civilian church once the military garrison closed. They achieved a successful outcome.

Looking Ahead to Lyneham

The new church building in Lyneham was converted from the Royal Air Force in-flight catering facility. After considerable interior redesign, it consists of the main church, a chapel, sacristy, vestry, church office, verger's office and kitchen facilities. Padre Stephen Thatcher was involved with the planning for the new church and ensured that the building was converted according to the agreed plans.

In the sanctuary of the main church behind the altar is the painting Christ in the Battlefield by David Shepherd, the baptismal font, the eagle lectern and candelabras from the Bordon Church. The main church also contains the St Eligius window, the 120-year old altar and the organ from Arborfield, amongst other artefacts from both churches.

The chapel is named St Eligius Memorial Chapel of the Corps of Royal Electrical and Mechanical Engineers. It contains the three stained glass windows from Arborfield: The Garden of Eden, Jesus in the Carpenter's Shop, and The Creation. The Book of Remembrance is kept in the Memorial Chapel and the REME Overseas Operations lists are replicated on the wall in the same fashion as before.

Thus, the artefacts from the Bordon and Arborfield churches make a significant historical and spiritual connection with the new church and form part of the surroundings for continuing worship by the REME family.

THE REME BAND

Volumes 1 and 2 of Craftsmen of the Army explain that the REME Band was formed in 1947 and covered its history up until 1993. Although it had been reduced in numbers from 54 to 34 in 1981, it remained an excellent band and achieved a grading of 'outstanding' in external inspections.

In centuries past, regiments each had their band of musicians that accompanied them when they were on the march or in battle, and whose trumpets and bugles provided a means of communication and of regulating daily life. In the post-Cold War era, Army bands no longer had any direct operational role, and quantifying the value of such things as heritage and contribution to 'esprit de corps' in a harsh financial climate was inevitably going to be difficult and emotive to a degree. A number of studies were carried out and, perhaps inevitably, the general direction of travel has been towards reduced numbers and consolidation or specialisation of bands to maintain standards.

The 'Options for Change' Defence Review triggered a study of bands, which led to the formation of the Corps of Army Music (CAMUS) in 1994. This resulted in all Army musicians transferring on 1 September 1994 from their parent regiments or corps into the newest and most junior Corps in the Army. At the same time, the number of Army bands was reduced from 69 to 30, with the number of bandsmen being reduced to 1,129 (some 43% of their previously established strength). Whilst the loss of regimental bands was painful to those affected, the reality was that not all were in good shape, with some functioning with less than 20 members. The REME Band was highly regarded and emerged intact from this exercise. It also survived a CAMUS reorganisation and restructuring exercise in 2004, which saw a reduction of 283 posts and a reduction in the number of bands from 29 to 23. It continued to function broadly as it had before until a further major review of Army bands in 2012.

During the years leading up to this, the REME Band continued to earn plaudits as a first rate military band. Some of the highlights during this period are described in the following paragraphs.

In 1995, which was a very busy year for the REME Band, it toured in Hong Kong for six weeks representing the Corps during a series of concerts, beating retreats and mess functions in the New Territories, Kowloon Peninsula and Hong Kong Island.

The REME Band celebrated its 50th Anniversary in October 1997, with a spectacular concert to a capacity audience. In addition to a host of VIPs, including eight former Band Presidents and three past Colonels Commandant, four former Directors of Music took to the rostrum as guest conductors. The concert provided a performance of a wide range of music encompassing all aspects of the REME Band's musical output; the concert received the warmest of accolades from those who attended.

In 2008, the REME Band embarked on a long tour of Canada. Army bands had long supported BATUS, and also engaged with the local community. This year, Quebec City celebrated its 400th Anniversary and the 10th Anniversary of the Quebec Festival of International Military Music and Tattoo. Twenty-five bands from 15 countries supported this momentous occasion over a period of 10 days with audience numbers of 20,000 at the Tattoo and a street march with an estimated attendance of around 150,000.

The REME Band was tasked with two prestigious tours during 2009. The first was a one-week tour to Jordan to celebrate the Anniversary of the Ascension to the Throne of King Abdullah II. Throughout the week, the REME Band remained in the spotlight; performing at a beating retreat before the King of Jordan and at an air show featuring the Red Arrows and the Jordanian Royal Falcons. The beating retreat, performed alongside the massed band of the Jordanian Corps of Army Music, featured a piece specifically composed for the occasion by the Director of Music, Captain Darren Wolfendale. 'Unity' was very well received and to mark the occasion further, a printed copy of the music was presented to the King by the youngest member of the band. The second major event in 2009, was the REME Band's participation in the two-week international military music festival in Moscow in September called 'Spasskaya Tower'.

In combination with the Pipes and Drums of 102 Battalion REME, the performances took place in the stunning arena of Red Square and the sight of the various bands in their immaculate colourful uniforms added to the surrounding architecture and truly presented a visual feast. Whilst the REME Band had taken part in many international musical tattoos over the years, they felt hugely honoured to have performed at such a spectacular event.

At the start of 2010, the REME Band had the privilege to host Her Royal Highness, The Countess of Wessex, Colonel in Chief of the Corps of Army Music. During her visit, she listened to the REME Band perform two pieces of music and spent some time meeting key personalities, families and children at a local school.

The study on Army music in 2012 was called 'The Future of Army Music in the 2020 Era'. The Chief of the General Staff was keen to maintain regimental affiliations but looked for a structured review, which took into account such realities as the harsh financial environment, the failure of CAMUS to recruit enough musicians and the need to protect Household Division Bands that were very much in the public eye. In order to make the figures add up, a scheme was devised that saw five existing Corps bands transformed into Reduced Capability Bands (RCB), which

The REME Band in Moscow

would be 'twinned' with full-sized bands that could be called upon when needed. The REME Band was one of those selected to be a RCB and was to become one of three new Specialist Contemporary Bands and relocate to Catterick Garrison. On the 14 February 2014, the REME Band formally departed and closed down the band block at Arborfield before starting its next phase as an eight-strong band based at Catterick.

On a positive note, the REME Band comprises highly skilled musicians, specially selected from across CAMUS for their ability to perform rock and pop music. It has the capability to perform contemporary music to a higher standard than a normal marching band. This appeals to many, and the REME Band was quick to build its reputation at a variety of events including a carol concert in Afghanistan. It continued to nurture its relationship with the Corps and its contribution to such events as dinner nights has been well received. It was 'twinned' with the Royal Logistic Corps Band, which could be called upon if the capability of a full marching band was required.

At the same time, there is no disguising the fact that there was sadness that the Corps lost a full marching band, which had earned an enviable reputation over the years and saw it replaced by a much smaller band, albeit one with something new and interesting to offer.

THE BLOODHOUND SUPERSONIC CAR PROJECT

The Bloodhound Supersonic Car (SSC) Project was headed up by Mr Richard Noble, who set the world land speed record of 633 mph in 1983 in a jet-powered car called Thrust 2. He drew in Wing Commander Andy Green RAF, who set the current land speed record of 763 mph in the Thrust SSC in 1997.

One of the aims of the Bloodhound SSC Project was to follow this success by building a car, which intended to achieve a speed of 1050 mph to break the world land speed record again, this time in South Africa. There were, however, broader aims that went with the Project, which were described in The Craftsman magazine in January 2013. These were to create:
- a national surge in the popularity of science, technology, engineering, and mathematics subjects
- an iconic project requiring extreme research and technology, whilst simultaneously providing the means to enable the student population to join in the adventure.

The First REME Bloodhound SSC Team (Gallagher, Sergeant, Fenn, Edwin, Morgan) with Phillip Dunne MP, Wing Commander Andy Green RAF and Richard Noble

The Project was not Government funded and relied on the support of sponsors. The Bloodhound Team approached REME for support in the form of technical manpower. A plan was agreed at MoD level, and a team of five REME personnel met up on 3 September 2012 before moving to the Bloodhound Technical Centre in Bristol. The REME Team was headed by Major Oli Morgan REME and comprised an Artificer Avionics (Warrant Officer Class 2 Mark Edwin), an Artificer Vehicles (Staff Sergeant Neil Gallagher), a Vehicle Mechanic (Craftsman Rob Fenn) and a Metalsmith (Lance Corporal Graham Sergeant).

The Project was an innovative and technically exciting one, as it involved using hybrid rocket and jet engine power (basically the same engine as in the Tornado aircraft), and was still in development at the time of writing. It was a great success from the REME point of view. The Bloodhound Team was delighted with the skills that the REME Team brought with them.

The Project attracted considerable media and public interest, particularly amongst those interested in science and technology, and therefore provided an excellent showcase for REME's technical skills. It was also a fascinating and technically exciting challenge for the REME Team. Team members were generally attached for nine months and

OTHER INSTITUTIONS, FACILITIES AND ACTIVITIES 519

enjoyed the mentoring of high-calibre engineers from the world of aerospace and Formula 1 racing. The Team had increased to seven at the time of writing, with Colonel (Retd) Rod Williams (late REME) also acting as a risk consultant to the Project.

NAMING THE TRAIN

In 1958, a Patriot Class steam locomotive was named 'REME' as a result of a staff suggestion from a British Rail Fireman. In October 1987, a Class 47 Inter-City Locomotive (47501) was named 'Craftsman'. The tracking down and recovery of the 'Craftsman' nameplates several years after the engine had gone out of service by some diligent enthusiasts of the REME Association provided the inspiration for the naming of another train (see Chapter 25 ('The REME Association and Veterans')). **(See Plate 58)**

On Tuesday 16 October 2007, First Great Western High Speed Train Power Car Number 43070 was named 'The Corps of Royal Electrical and Mechanical Engineers'. The ceremony took place at Paddington Station in London and the Colonel in Chief formally unveiled the nameplate. The Colonel in Chief was received at Paddington Station by the Representative Colonel Commandant, Major General Tim Tyler (late REME), who then introduced the Managing Director of First Group, Mr Andrew Haines.

The naming and unveiling ceremony was followed by the train pulling out of the station to the strains of 'Lillibulero' played by the REME Band, as described in The Craftsman magazine (December 2007). The High Speed Train 'The Corps of Royal Electrical and Mechanical Engineers' was planned to run on the Bristol/South Wales line for many years to come.

CORPS PUBLICATIONS AND COMMUNICATIONS

The Craftsman Magazine

The Craftsman magazine continued to flourish throughout the period covered by this book, with free copies being provided to units. At the time of writing, it was one of only three regimental magazines published monthly with around 6,000 copies being produced. Around two-thirds of these went to serving members of REME, with the remainder largely going to retired members of the Corps. It therefore provided an excellent mechanism for keeping the entire REME family, both Regular and

Reserve, up to date on matters affecting the Corps. Its content included guest editorials, routine reports and notices on such matters as obituaries and awards, along with a wide variety of articles submitted on operations, training, sports, adventurous training, and many other topics likely to be of interest to its readers.

The technology used to produce the magazine changed with the times and was to move on to desktop publishing. From 1992, all covers were in colour, and the magazine became full colour in 2006. The Craftsman magazine's offices were collocated with RHQ REME from 1994. Those who contributed to the success of the magazine included Major Peter Beeken REME who retired from the Army in 1993 but continued as Editor until 2003. Zoë Skivington then took over as Editor, with Major (Retd) John Holman REME taking on the role of Managing Editor amongst other duties. Zoë Skivington had joined The Craftsman magazine as Assistant Editor in 1989, and became Deputy Editor in 1992. She retired in 2013 having earned a Master General REME's Commendation for her contribution over 24 years. In 1992, she was joined by Mr John Worrall who became the Assistant Editor. They formed a highly effective team and when John Worrall retired in 2014, he also received a Master General REME's Commendation for his 22 years' service to The Craftsman magazine.

The REME Journal

The REME Journal complements The Craftsman magazine. Since 1951, it has generally appeared annually, with around 3,000 copies being dispatched in 2014. The REME Journal was intended to be pitched at a professional engineering level, with the idea that it should be read by REME officers and some Warrant Officers, and could also be sent to a wider readership in the Army, the MoD and the Professional Engineering Institutions, as a means of presenting information about REME.

Articles come from a variety of sources, but mostly from serving officers and Warrant Officers. Typical content related to Corps engineering, equipment support, engineering management, history, sport and regimental matters. It was also used by DEME(A) to keep REME personnel aware of developments in the Corps. By 2009, a comprehensive 'Report to the Corps' was being produced embracing such matters as the sustainment of operations, people, equipment, the REME Association, the REME Benevolent Fund, welfare, prizes, honours and awards. This was superseded by a 'Colonels' Commandant Report' from 2012, intended to serve broadly the same purpose.

The Officers' List
The Officers' List (affectionately known as 'The Blue Book') has changed little in appearance and format. It provides a seniority list of serving REME officers, Reserve and retired officers, listing REME Institution members and recently deceased officers, and the members of key Corps Committees. The frequent posting and promotion of REME personnel make its upkeep a complex and time-consuming task, but it is an invaluable reference document for both those serving, and for retired members of the Corps. Around 3,000 copies were dispatched in 2015, of which just under one-third went to serving officers.

The REME Calendar
The attractive REME Calendar publication was first produced in 2010, under the direction of Major (Retd) Mike Brown REME. It is issued free to units, and may be bought from the REME Shop or online. A competition is run to select the colour photographs that are used, with entries largely coming from REME units and individuals. In addition to its practical use, the REME Calendar therefore provides a 'shop window' for the many and varied activities undertaken in the Corps.

Corporate Communications
By 2013, it was clear that the Corps hard-copy publications had served it very well and would continue to be important, but that they needed to be seen in the broader context of a world in which social media and other means of digital communication were of growing importance. This resulted in the decision to set up the Corporate Communications Department based at RHQ REME under a corporate communications professional. Mr Ed Paice (a Civil Service Higher Executive Officer) was appointed in August 2013 to head this new Department. This was to take over responsibility for existing publications, and to develop two new areas, 'digital' and 'brand', with a view to developing communications both within the overall REME family, and those with whom the Corps needs to communicate.

For the digital environment, The Craftsman magazine was put onto the Defence Intranet, and work was done to improve digital in-house capability, including that for desktop publishing. Additionally, in 2014, the first 'official' social media platforms/presences were established, REME Facebook and REME Twitter. These were followed by YouTube and

Google+ in 2015. In October 2015, the annual Corps Conference had 'live' social media coverage for those who could not attend in person.

The REME 'brand' became better established, utilising the Tactical Recognition Flash blue, as its defined 'brand' colour. The Corps Engagement Team clearly benefited the most from the new corporate images, trade videos (including input from the BBC and ITN), marketing literature, display boards, gazebos and merchandise.

CHAPTER 28

THE PLAN FOR LYNEHAM

Chapter 23 ('Individual Training Organisations') explains the background to the move of REME training to Lyneham. In essence, after some dozen years of looking at other solutions for rationalising Defence technical training, the idea of developing the former RAF base at Lyneham came onto the scene as a late runner. It had been vacated by the RAF in 2010, and became MoD Lyneham. In 2012, the Secretary of State for Defence announced that Lyneham was the preferred location to develop technical training facilities as part of the Defence Technical Training Change Programme (DTTCP). At that time, the move of REME training to Lyneham was seen as the first priority. This would involve closing down and moving the School of Army Aeronautical Engineering (SAAE) at Arborfield, as well as the Defence School of Electronic and Mechanical Engineering (DSEME), which encompassed the rest of the technical training organisation at Bordon and Arborfield.

The move of REME training was referred to as 'Tranche 1' and came with £121m of firm funding to set up facilities, essentially for REME, with a total population of around 2,000. Further 'tranches' were envisaged, which would involve the move of RN and RAF technical training to Lyneham, with an end-state population of around 5,000. The timetable for 'Tranche 1' was tight, driven by the need for REME to be clear of Arborfield and Bordon by around the end of 2015. This Chapter outlines what happened from late 2013 to the end of 2015, by which time the relocation of training had been successfully achieved.

During this time, the Defence Board reviewed the plan for subsequent 'tranches' of the DTTCP. In autumn 2015, it ratified an estate plan that would see the three Services consolidate their technical training on HMS Sultan, MoD Lyneham, and RAF Cosford. This meant that the plans to move RN and RAF training to Lyneham were shelved, and Lyneham would effectively be a REME enclave for the foreseeable future. This rested comfortably with the decision to locate the 'Home of REME' in Lyneham. 'Home of REME' was the original term used when the plan to move from Arborfield and Bordon was first proposed. Within the planning for Lyneham, this component became known as the 'Home of the Corps' and will be called that hereafter.

An investment appraisal exercise was followed by the award of a contract to Hercules Joint Venture (Hercules JV) (a collaboration between Balfour Beatty and Kier Construction) in December 2013. This was for the prime design, and the building of the new facilities. REME was represented on a day-to-day basis within DTTCP by a team called Project Rowcroft, headed by Colonel Ian Gibson (late REME). He described what followed thus:

> 'The site at MoD Lyneham is 450+ hectares in size and straddles the Wootton Basset to Calne main road, the A3102. The main site, clearly dominated by the runways, was set out in a typical air station layout with a technical area at the centre of the site with living and 'life support' towards the main entrance. The opposite side of the road from the main site contained the married quarters and the former site of 47 Air Dispatch Squadron RLC, which at the time of occupation by the Corps was being used as part of the refurbishment of vehicles returning from Afghanistan. The regeneration of MoD Lyneham also saw approval given by the Government for the installation of a solar farm on the area to the north of the main runway; consisting of 170,000 panels covering 80 hectares it was the largest single site in Europe when it started generating power in the spring of 2014. Although the vast site of MoD Lyneham was included in the Defence Footprint Strategy and the ongoing Army Basing Review, there was no firm decision as to which other units or organisations might join the Corps on the site downstream as the relocation of DSEME and SAAE began.
>
> In the first few months of 2014, all of the stakeholders worked frantically with the architects from Hercules JV to mature the plans that had been developed as part of the tender process before the award of the contract. Time was particularly tight as ever and this time a much greater level of detailed planning was required in order to develop the mechanical and electrical drawings down to every plug socket type and voltage, and air-line point with operating pressure. Lt Col Mike Tizard led the 'Home of the Corps' involvement while Maj Mick Patey and Mr Tom Cambridge (formally of the Corps) rolled up their sleeves for the electro-mechanical and aviation training requirements respectively. At the same time, Hercules JV staff were swarming all

over the site conducting their detailed site surveys and preparing for the onset of their operation. Dr Andrew Murrison MP, the Minister for International Security Strategy, fired the starting gun for the build on 13 February 2014 with a commemorative sod-turning ceremony.

On the 23 March 2014, the MoD handed over the site in its entirety to Hercules JV in order that they could maximise building efficiency. Regular visits to the site from DTTCP and the Corps would continue daily but would now require six points of personal protective equipment; the Corps was immersed in the business of civil engineering for a change. The preparation of the site was to involve the development of around 100 assets (from technical training spaces, accommodation, medical centre, gymnasiums, messes, church and museum etc) around two-thirds of which would be completely new builds with the remainder being refurbished former RAF facilities. The Hercules JV workforce, under the direction of their leader Mr Roger Frost, soon ramped up to meet the challenge and for much of the build period had well in excess of 1,000+ tradesmen on site every day.

The most challenging build schedule was arguably the main training building (now known as the Brunel Building), three stories, 30+ classrooms, 30+ laboratories, a 200+ seater auditorium and many other facilities; the foundations were laid by late May 2014 and it was planned to be finished the day before it was due to be occupied. There were some entertaining moments across the rest of the site when the architects and builders attempted to understand the requirement for 'metal' trees to replicate the recovery training heath at Bordon and the military training fire and manoeuvre lanes were initially thought to have something to do with driving fire engines around. As the build progressed, designs were refined in parallel and over £60m+ changes were incorporated before it would be complete'.

The plan to hand back the site from Hercules JV to the MoD was effectively in two phases; one at the end of May 2015 and the other at the end of September 2015. Project Rowcroft would act as the interim head of establishment until the new Garrison Commander, Colonel Mike Pendlington (late REME), took up station at the end of the year. In between, the MoD portion of the site would be grown incrementally to allow it to become a living barracks once again. The relocation plan was linked with the letting of a ground-breaking support contract through

the Defence Infrastructure Organisation and an innovative CIS teaching network that was at the forefront of Defence information management. The move from Arborfield and Bordon was in two phases, aligned to the site handover plan. The main components were the move of:
- SAAE and its 'life support' starting in August 2015
- DSEME and 'Home of the Corps' starting in October 2015.

The moves were planned to take no more than six weeks from the cessation of training to it restarting in Lyneham. They represented a major achievement in their own right and saw the move of some 2,500 personnel, 360+ articulated trucks of training aids, 190+ prime vehicles (including museum vehicles), and in excess of 70+ ISO containers. There was also the delivery to site of 1,500+ beds, 2,500+ desks and chairs, and thousands of miscellaneous sundry items. Staff at DSEME and SAAE were helped by contract support from Babcock International and their logistic transport contractors Swains and Sons. This contract was managed by Mr Peter Longmore (a retired Colonel (late REME) and a previous Commandant of SAAE). Initial Operating Capability for training commencement was declared for Phase 1 movers on 5 October 2015, and Full Operating Capability was declared for all movers on 1 February 2016.

'HOME OF THE CORPS' ASPECTS

Lieutenant Colonel Mike Tizard REME arrived at RHQ REME in October 2011, taking up the position of Staff Officer Grade 1 DTTCP. Working initially with the then DEME(A), Brigadier Martin Boswell (late REME), he was responsible for ensuring that all technical training and 'Home of the Corps' requirements were accurately captured and included in the various requirement documents. After the programme had passed MoD scrutiny and was given formal approval, Lieutenant Colonel Andy Teare REME and Major Mick Patey REME took the DSEME lead, leaving Lieutenant Colonel Tizard to continue with the 'Home of the Corps' aspects of the move.

With the disbandment of DEME(A), Colonel Gibson changed title from Regimental Colonel to Colonel REME, and, as such, became the serving 'Head of the Corps'. When replaced, he moved to Project Rowcroft to lead the move.

RHQ REME

After looking at various options, Building 245 was selected as the new home for RHQ REME. (**See Plate 59**)

It required major refurbishment, but its central location made it an attractive long-term option. Unfortunately, in late 2015, just prior to completion of the refurbishment work, the building suffered a major failure of the roof and as a result required major repairs. RHQ REME had temporarily to operate from within split locations in Lyneham, but the 42 members of RHQ REME staff were able to move into the new building on 7 March 2016. By then, it had been fitted out with REME memorabilia and stood out as a prominent 'REME branded' building near the centre of the site.

The Corps Messes

The Corps messes represented a much more complex challenge, as this part of the programme involved combining messes from both Arborfield and Bordon. During the design stage of the programme, locations for the messes were quickly identified and a plan produced. Following Defence Infrastructure Organisation guidelines, the messes were to be combined into a single building with a single centrally positioned kitchen catering for messes at either end. The chosen building was the old RAF Warrant Officers' and Sergeants' Mess, Building 326, which would require substantial modification and refurbishment.

The first and second floors and adjoining accommodation were demolished and a new-build modern mess added. The Officers' Mess would occupy the refurbished part of the building and the Warrant Officers' and Sergeants' Mess the new build. The Presidents of the Mess Committee (PMC) of both messes were fully involved in the design of the floor plans. There was much to do including reducing the mountain of property down to a manageable level. After a short period settling in, where minor interior works were completed, paintings hung, chandeliers installed and other such tasks completed, the mess PMCs agreed they were at an appropriate standard and opening ceremonies were arranged.

The Officers' Mess was officially opened on 11 February 2016 by His Royal Highness Prince Michael of Kent and given the official title of 'HRH Princess Marina, The Duchess of Kent Officers' Mess'. For the Warrant Officers' and Sergeants' Mess, the first PMC, Warrant Officer Class 1 (Regimental Sergeant Major) Stuart Kitchen invited the senior Army Warrant Officer, Warrant Officer Class 1 (Army Sergeant Major)

Glen Haughton, to Lyneham on 3 February 2016 to open formally the Gallantry Bar and the Corps Colonel authorised the mess to be named 'Harris MM Warrant Officers' and Sergeants' Mess'.

The REME Museum
The REME Museum had moved with a view to reopening in the autumn of 2016. As described in Chapter 26 ('The REME Charities and the REME Museum') this was to be based on the former RAF Lyneham Officers' Mess building and was to build on the success of the REME Museum at Arborfield. An additional benefit of the move was that it allowed the collection of historic vehicles, formerly kept at Bordon, to be stored in an aircraft hangar on the northern outskirts of the MoD Lyneham site with easy access to both the main site and the main road. The REME Museum retained the benefit it had enjoyed at Arborfield of being 'outside the wire', which allowed unchecked access to the public.

The Corps Church
The Corps Church was located in the building adjacent to RHQ REME, which complemented the 'Home of the Corps' theme. Located next to the marching route, REME soldiers could not fail to notice the REME Soldier Memorial Statue and the Corps Church on the way to their classes. The building, which was formerly the RAF in-flight catering facility, was tastefully refurbished and provided a fitting home for the artefacts from Arborfield and Bordon as described in Chapter 27 ('Other Corps Institutions, Facilities and Activities').

THE END STATE AT LYNEHAM

The overall organisation at Lyneham, as at March 2016, is shown in Figure 28.1 (at the end of this Chapter).

8 Training Battalion REME
This was formed in August 2015 from an amalgamation of 10 Battalion REME and 11 Battalion REME based at Bordon and Arborfield respectively, with training restarted at Lyneham in October 2015. The move to Lyneham provided an opportunity to implement a training modernisation programme supported by a bespoke virtual learning environment. Each student had been issued with their own laptop to access wirelessly their learning programme, additional course materials and shared learning forums. This created a student-centred, blended-

learning approach incorporating traditional training techniques, as well as current working practices of the Field Army. The unit was the largest unit in the British Army. Its strength would fluctuate according to the number of students under training, but it would normally expect to have around 1,500 trainees on its strength. In addition to its administrative functions, it provided military and other training (including sporting and adventurous training) in the context of the regimental environment needed to promote military ethos and values, particularly in the more junior trainees.

DSEME
DSEME provided the bulk of the technical training for the electro-mechanical trades, recovery mechanics, technical specialists and artificers.

SAAE
SAAE provided training up to artificer level in aircraft and avionics disciplines. It was part of the Defence School of Aeronautical Engineering (DSAE), which had its headquarters in Cosford, but from the administrative and regimental point of view it was integrated with the REME structure at Lyneham in much the same way as it had been in Arborfield.

The REME Arms School
The purpose of the REME Arms School was to provide special-to-arm training, in order to:

> '… deliver sufficient professional, competent and highly motivated technical leaders and engineering managers in order to support equipment capability …'

Its headquarters was based in the rather fine new Brunel Building, and it had five areas of activity:
- **officer training** was provided at various levels from the Military Systems Engineering Course for junior officers through to courses for REME Lieutenant Colonels
- **artificer selection and training** – it provided facilities for assessing potential artificers, as well as training input on Artificer Command and Field Courses
- **Command Leadership and Management Courses** – training for junior soldiers was remotely delivered; courses were provided for REME senior soldiers and REME Warrant Officers

- **engineering management training** – this embraced training on health and safety management, Land Equipment Engineering Standards, Technical Evaluation (TECHEVAL) assessment, Equipment Care management and engineering systems auditing and management
- **trainer training and development** – a variety of courses were run, linked to providing trainers with the skills and qualifications necessary for their roles. (**See Plate 60**)

LOOKING FORWARD

For the first time, the bulk of REME technical training had been collocated at a single site, along with RHQ REME and 'Home of the Corps' elements. Essentially, Lyneham had become a REME base, and seemed likely to remain as such for the foreseeable future. The layout of the base is shown at Figure 28.2 (at the end of this Chapter).

At the time of final editing in March 2016, there remained much still to do at Lyneham, not least to uplift a number of the sports facilities to a standard that the Corps had become accustomed to after years of investment on the previous sites. The Corps Trustees were working hard with a number of external agencies such as the Army Sports Control Board to ensure that Lyneham will be able to deliver facilities of the highest standard across all areas. (**See Plate 61**)

THE PLAN FOR LYNEHAM

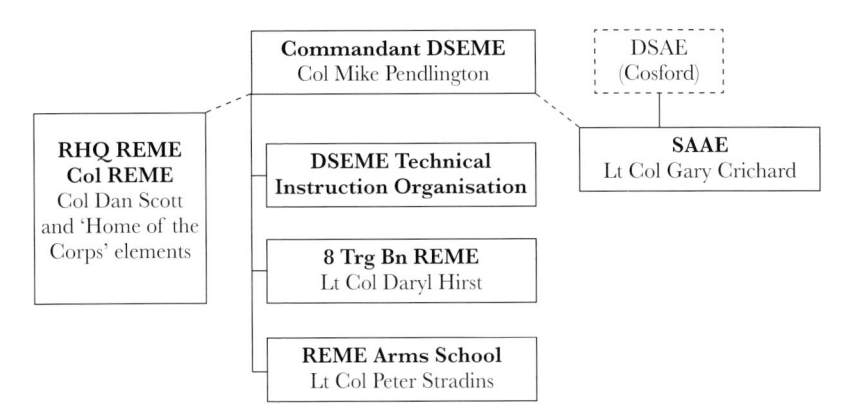

```
                    ┌─────────────────────────┐     ┌─────────────┐
                    │   Commandant DSEME      │     │    DSAE     │
                    │   Col Mike Pendlington  │     │  (Cosford)  │
                    └─────────────────────────┘     └─────────────┘
                                │                          │
┌──────────────┐   ┌─────────────────────────┐     ┌─────────────────┐
│  RHQ REME    │   │    DSEME Technical      │     │      SAAE       │
│  Col REME    │   │  Instruction Organisation│    │ Lt Col Gary Crichard│
│ Col Dan Scott│   └─────────────────────────┘     └─────────────────┘
│ and 'Home of │
│ the Corps'   │   ┌─────────────────────────┐
│ elements     │   │      8 Trg Bn REME      │
└──────────────┘   │    Lt Col Daryl Hirst   │
                   └─────────────────────────┘

                   ┌─────────────────────────┐
                   │    REME Arms School     │
                   │  Lt Col Peter Stradins  │
                   └─────────────────────────┘
```

Figure 28.1: The overall organisation at Lyneham as at March 2016

CHAPTER 29

CORPS SPORTING AND ADVENTUROUS ACTIVITIES

The Corps recruits people who are bright and well-motivated enough to deal with the technical and military tasks that REME performs on operations, during training and in barracks. REME also gives them wonderful opportunities to engage in sporting and adventurous activities, and it is not surprising that so many have excelled in these areas.

It is perhaps also worth mentioning that around two-thirds of REME people are deployed at first line, and often play sport in their unit or sub-unit teams, frequently being leading competitors. They have therefore made a significant collective contribution to Army sporting and adventurous activities beyond that recorded below.

SPORTING ACTIVITIES

Much of the period covered by this book was a time of organisational upheaval and heavy operational commitments. This tended to take its toll in terms of the numbers available for competitive team events in the major traditional sports, although not necessarily in the standards achieved. At the same time, a number of new and specialised sports have come onto the scene and prospered, with members of REME often making an important contribution at Army and Combined Services levels. It is impossible in this single Chapter to do full justice to the complete picture of REME's involvement in all sports. The recognised sports, which have been given financial support by the Corps are listed in the table below. Thumbnail sketches of activities in each sport are provided in this Chapter, except those marked with an asterisk.

Archery*	Angling	Association Football
Athletics and Cross Country	Badminton	Basketball*
Boxing*	Canoeing*	Climbing*
Cricket	Cycling	Duathlon/Biathlon*
Equitation	Golf	Hang Gliding and Paragliding
Hockey*	Ice Hockey	Kart Racing*
Martial Arts	Modern Pentathlon	Motorcycling
Netball	Orienteering	Parachuting
Rowing	Rugby	Sailing
Squash	Strength Sports	Swimming and Water Polo
Target Shooting	Tennis*	Winter Sports

ANGLING (COARSE)

Angling has a small but enthusiastic group of followers. This is not least because Warrant Officer Class 2 Jason Nicholls (Corps Secretary since 2010, Captain since 2011, selected to represent the Army Angling Team in tri-Service and inter-Services events) has harnessed the power of Facebook and the internet to keep the REME angling community in touch. REME last won the Inter-Corps Championships in 2012, and hopes to again. The Corps Championships is now a very enjoyable two-day event. In short, REME angling is very much alive and fishing.

ASSOCIATION FOOTBALL

Overview
Football has continued to be a hugely popular sport within REME at all levels, with many Corps players representing the Army and Combined Services (and one, Lance Corporal Maik Taylor, making the leap to a professional career through to international level, where he captained Northern Ireland in 2011). A brief outline of the main competitions

in which REME is involved may be useful. The Craftsman's Cup, as its name implies, is a competition for REME units. There is a cup for major units and a cup for minor units. There was hot competition both in UK and in Germany; in 1994, REME BAOR (British Army of the Rhine) became REME(G). The winning team in UK would then meet the winning team from Germany to compete for the Trussler Trophy, which was first presented in 1983 in memory of Sergeant Alan Trussler who was sadly killed after returning to the School of Electrical and Mechanical Engineering (SEME) after the Army Cup Final. Unfortunately, the return of the Army from Germany has also meant the end of the Trussler Trophy and with it the keen rivalry between teams from across the channel.

REME also enters teams into the Army Football Association Challenge Cup, which was started in 1888, and is one of the world's oldest football cup competitions. Success at this level has enabled REME teams to go on to compete at inter-Services level for the Jubilee Cup. The Corps also competes in the Army Inter-Corps League (which became the Massey Trophy in 1994, named after Brigadier Massey, a former Chairman of Army Football), as well as the 'Quads' a quadrangular tournament dating back to 1969. This is contested by REME, the Royal Artillery, Royal Engineers and Royal Signals. The great operational pressure on units during much of the period covered by this book led to a significant decline in unit participation in competitions. On a more positive note, the REME Women's Football Team was set up in 2002, and the Corps has also embarked on a number of very successful and enjoyable football tours during the period covered.

REME Football Successes at Army and Inter-Services Level 1998–1999
A full list of Army Cup winners can be found on the Army Football Association website. With Major Danny McCreesh REME as Manager, 3 Battalion REME dominated Army Football for two seasons in 1998 and 1999 when they won the Germany Army Cup, Army Challenge Cup and Jubilee Cup. They became the first REME field force team to win the Army Challenge Cup and the first Germany-based unit to win the Jubilee Cup. The latter being a result of a rule change that allowed the winners of the Army Challenge Cup to represent the Army against the RAF and RN champions regardless of being a UK or Germany-based unit. (**See Plate 62**)

In 1998, the team was led to victories by Sergeant Taff Edwards RLC (Royal Logistic Corps) who was an elegant footballer and great leader.

A 2–1 victory over 7 Signal Regiment in the Germany final was tense throughout. This led to a Challenge Cup semi-final against 3 Division Signal Regiment at Blandford, which was no less tense right through to the end of extra time and a penalty shoot-out. Penalties were even until the Royal Signals team missed their fifth and Staff Sergeant Dennis Nunn slotted home for 3 Battalion REME. This tight game led to a comfortable 2–0 victory over 3 Royal School of Military Engineering Regiment in the Army Challenge Cup final. The Jubilee Cup was sealed by a convincing win over the RN in Paderborn and RAF in Arborfield. The latter win is infamous for Craftsman Hanks snapping his cruciate ligament whilst scoring and indicating to Major McCreesh that he needed to come off. His reply to which was "you've just scored; you're playing well – run it off!" Ten minutes later, he was taken off and sent to hospital.

In 1999, 3 Battalion REME again won the same collection of trophies, led this time by Staff Sergeant Ian Dawson, with a comfortable victory over 26 Regiment RA (6–0) in the Germany final, which included two goals from Craftsman 'Digger' Downes who proved to be a prolific goal scorer over the years. This was followed by a 2–1 semi-final victory over 28 Engineer Regiment in a fierce game. The 1st Battalion the Cheshire Regiment were to be Army Challenge Cup final opponents, a physical game with both Corporal 'Tommo' Thomson the goalkeeper, and Staff Sergeant Henry Heard both suffering head injuries from the Cheshire's centre forward, who was lucky to remain on the pitch. A tight 2–1 victory at the Aldershot Military Stadium was sealed by a goal from Craftsman Downes and a 79th minute strike by Craftsman 'Ashy' Ashurst, with Man of the Match going to Staff Sergeant Heard, who played on despite his earlier head injury. A nervy victory in Catterick against the RAF and a comfortable win against the RN at HMS Culdrose sealed the Jubilee Cup. The Jubilee Cup Man of the Match in both years was dominated by Sergeant Shane Smith, maybe the best player the Corps ever had not to make it as a professional.

REME Football Successes at Army and Inter-Services Level 2003–2005

The REME football successes in 2003 – 2005 were achieved by 6 Battalion REME based in Tidworth. Their team included a number of former 3 Battalion REME players, blended in with some great new players by Captain Paul Denton REME, the Team Manager. The 2003 final against 11 Signal Regiment proved to be 'a walk in the park', two goals from Warrant Officer Class 2 Bob Corner, and one each from Lance Corporal

'Bri' Combellack and Lance Corporal Craig Wall sealed a comfortable 4–0 win. However, they had earned this easy final by beating 7 Signal Regiment in the semi-final in a very tense 1–0 victory. That year, the 6 Battalion REME team was captained by Warrant Officer Class 2 Heard who, after two previous Army Challenge Cup wins, finally got to lift the trophy on behalf of REME.

The 2005 victory was a much tougher affair against 4 Regiment RLC with the game being tied at 2–2 after extra time and going to penalties. The team from 6 Battalion REME held its nerve and came out winners 4–2 in what was a memorable and nervy game. These victories were separated by another 6 Battalion REME appearance in the 2004 final which they lost 1–0 to 1 Royal Irish. The Jubilee Cup success of 2003 by 6 Battalion REME saw them beat the RAF 2–1 with goals from Lance Corporal Craig Wall and Craftsman Micky Longfellow who went on a solo run and hit a bullet from outside of the box giving the keeper no chance. Craftsman Longfellow went on to be the NAAFI sponsored Man of the Match. The victory over the RN proved to be more comfortable with a 7–3 victory. Goals from Corporal Terry Lynch, Warrant Officer Class 2 Bob Corner and Lance Corporal 'Bri' Wood PWRR (son of the REME legend Gavin Wood and later awarded the Military Cross in Iraq) got them on their way to half-time. The RN team was to have its period of the game and scored two goals, but 6 Battalion REME, now under pressure, hit back with goals from Minett, Atherton and Corner again. Warrant Officer Class 2 Corner lifted the Jubilee Cup and was named Man of the Match for his robust leadership and two goals.

The Craftsman's Cup

The Craftsman's Cup competitions have been the staple diet of REME unit football over the years, but have been affected by a shrinking Army and operational commitments. The entry numbers for these competitions have fallen markedly, particularly in Germany, which would regularly attract 50 to 60 entries but dwindled to a handful of units in 2014. In UK, the competitions have been similarly affected but continue to draw a good representation from across the Army and remain keenly contested. Over the years, the Major Units Cup has been dominated by UK and in particular the trade schools at Arborfield and Bordon. This dominance was interspersed by periods when REME units such as 3 Battalion REME and 6 Battalion REME were strong and winning the Army and inter-Services competitions. The school at Arborfield (variously called

SEE, SEAE and 11 Battalion REME) won the Major Units Cup on 12 occasions during this period. The loyalty to the schools, in particular Arborfield, is still strong from their former players with annual reunions and football games. The Minor Units Cup is a different story and hotly contested between minor units in Germany and UK. In fact, there has been no dominance from either side as UK has won 11 and Germany 10.

The Quadrangular Tournament
The Corps team continued to achieve success in the Quadrangular Tournament, known as the 'Quads', during the 1990s with four victories in Seasons 1992/1993, 1993/1994, 1994/1995 and 1996/1997 under such notable coaches as Mr Chris Eade and Staff Sergeant Gavin Wood. The 1996/1997 victory was particularly notable as, going into the last match on the Friday, any of three was in a position to win. The Royal Engineers and Royal Artillery drew their match and a 25-yard 'screamer' from Staff Sergeant Trevor Done put REME 2–1 ahead against the Royal Signals and sealed the win for REME. The new century started promisingly with a victory in Season 2000/2001 with Captain Campbell Moffat REME coaching the side, however, that was to be REME's only victory in that decade and it would not be until Season 2011/2012 when REME lifted the trophy again.

The 2011/2012 Massey League was tight going into the final three fixtures, with the Royal Engineers being hot favourite with a five-point lead. The first game was a nervous affair against the Royal Artillery and, after going behind, REME fought back to earn a draw. The second game was the head-to-head fixture against the Royal Engineers who selected a strong side to bully a very young REME team, which nevertheless managed to win. With REME one point behind the Royal Engineers, they faced the Royal Signals needing to win. This turned out to be a feisty game with eight yellow cards early in the game followed by two red cards reducing both teams to 10 men. The Royal Signals went one up but REME equalled through Lance Corporal McKenzie before half-time. Staff Sergeant Lynch, on again as a substitute, floated a free kick to the back post which Lance Corporal Phil Lucas put past the keeper. The 2–1 win made REME the champions.

Inter-Corps Football
REME has had some success in inter-Corps football in Germany and UK over the period, although less than might be expected given REME's

Army Cup victories. After winning the inaugural Massey Trophy in 1994, the Corps had to wait 18 years until they won the trophy again in 2012; the best season the Corps had seen for many years, as they also won the Quadrangular Tournament. This 2012 success was largely down to the REME support staff. Team Coach Captain 'Daz' Willshire REME and Secretary of the time Major Del Rogers REME, worked tirelessly to improve player availability with units, a constant battle for all secretaries over the years. The Team Manager, Captain Danny Proctor REME, a Corps and Army stalwart, who was in the previous winning teams as a player, and was thought to be the first to win the 'Quads' as a player and manager.

REME Germany and the Trussler Trophy
REME(G) competed well (but with no victories) in the inter-Corps competitions through the 1990s and 2000s. Lack of success in the Inter-Corps League through the 1990s was eased somewhat by four Trussler Trophy victories over its great rivals from the UK. These memorable victories and teams were led by the likes of John Shaw and Paddy Swan and underpinned by the rampaging Sergeant 'Nico' Nicholson, who tore through the midfield of many a Corps team. Regardless of current form, this trophy is always hotly contested and huge 'bragging rights' go to the winners. Over the period of this book, the UK team has dominated with Germany having only seven victories with the majority of those in the 1990s.

Supporting Contributions
Corps footballers have been served extremely well by many keen and committed REME and late REME officers acting as committee members, including as Corps Chairman: Brigadiers 'Mitch' Mitchell and Mike Selby, Colonels Maurice Bulmer and Max Joy, Lieutenant Colonels John Edwards and Tony Workman. Also as Corps Secretary: Majors Andy Anderson, Iain Fountain, Campbell Moffat, Del Rogers Ian Dawson, Danny McCreesh and Captain Ivor Gallagher.

REME Women's Football
The REME Women's Football Team was founded in 2002 by Lieutenant Colonel John Edwards REME, at the time Commanding Officer of 10 Training Battalion REME. Later that same year, they played their first competitive match in the Women's Inter-Corps League against the Royal Signals. Due in part to the relatively small number of women who were serving with the Corps, the initial years proved a struggle for the REME Women's Team and despite a huge effort from those involved at the time,

they were at one point very close to folding as a competitive entity. In Season 2005/2006 the organisation was given a complete overhaul, which, combined with a steady inflow of talented new recruits, saw the Corps team flourish.

In 2009, the team lifted the first of their three Inter-Corps League titles and soon followed this triumph with an Inter-Corps Cup victory. The Corps Women's Team has now won five of the last six Inter-Corps Cup competitions, including the inaugural Edwards Trophy at the Army Stadium. In all, since Season 2008/2009, the REME Women's Team has claimed eight of the 13 major trophies on offer and have never been outside the top two, a truly magnificent achievement. The Corps has also provided numerous players to the Army Squad and five players have gone on to represent the Combined Services: Craftsman Jules Jefferis, Craftsman Maxine McIvor, Craftsman Rachel Gwilliam, Craftsman Jess Moran and Lance Corporal Bianca Ross.

The committee and management team in the latter years has seen extraordinary stability with Lieutenant Colonel Edwards, Captain Scotty Lamont REME, Captain Gino Hinson REME and Warrant Officer Class 1 Al Woolley providing the conditions for the team to be successful on the pitch. Sergeant Sophy Frapwell and Lance Corporal Yvette Kemp also deserve special mentions in their roles as Corps Captains, and have been pivotal to the team's progress and success. The REME Women's Squad has also successfully toured Cape Town (South Africa) in 2010, and North America in 2014 when they played in Las Vegas, Los Angeles and San Francisco. These tours have done a great deal to cement both the long and short-term cohesion and winning spirit within the Squad.

REME Women's Team with the Edwards Cup

REME Football Tours
Tours at both unit and Corps level have become a regular activity over the last two decades. REME teams have toured to many locations, such as South Africa, Australia, USA and Cyprus. The tours to Australia and South Africa in the 1990s, organised by Major McCreesh, were great successes, particularly the tour to South Africa, which was conducted soon after the end of the apartheid era. The USA tours have seen REME players and staff such as Lieutenant Colonel Edwards, Staff Sergeant Jimmy Isbister and Captain Willshire unashamedly 'schmoozing' with the superstar inhabitants of Los Angeles, of whom the greatest of all was football and movie legend Vinnie Jones. The 2000 tour to Cyprus saw the REME team unbeaten and giving a football lesson to the then Army champions, 1st Battalion Cheshire Regiment through a 5–0 victory. The REME team, run and coached by Iain Fountain and Campbell Moffat, played some excellent possession football in which Sergeant Shane Smith and Lance Corporal Craig Wall were, from all accounts, simply outstanding.

ATHLETICS AND CROSS COUNTRY

The Corps has a proud tradition in athletics, with Captain Harry Whittle REME and Captain Jeremy ('Jim') Fox REME being successful at Olympic level (in London 1948 and in Montreal 1976 respectively). REME athletics continued to thrive during a period of increased sporting competitiveness, although the high operational tempo during the latter part of the period covered by this book has had the effect of reducing the numbers of those involved in competitions.

1992–1998
In 1992, the Corps Championships were held in the Palmer Park Sports Stadium in Reading, with women being welcomed into the competition for the first time. This meant that there was not only a Victor Ludorum (Corporal Beaumont, a Recovery Mechanic who was one of the most successful and well know of REME athletes over a number of years), but a Victrix Ludorum (Craftsman Christie) the female equivalent.

Around this time, there was an increase in participation in marathons (generally for charity). In 1992 in Germany, for example, over 80 REME personnel took part in the Moenchengladbach REME City Marathon, which was won by Corporal James Cargill. Meanwhile in UK, Sergeant Anthony Leibrick from SEME was making his mark as a marathon runner, and achieved a time of 2 hours and 37 minutes, which would qualify him for the competitive category of the London Marathon and selection for the Army Squad. He was to go on to win four consecutive REME marathon titles (a feat only equalled by Captain Jonathon Creak, who transferred from REME to the Adjutant General's Corps (AGC)).

The Inter-Unit Championships represented an annual opportunity for REME athletes to meet and compete. During this period, SEME was seen as the predominant team, but victory was not to be taken for granted. In 1996, 7 Battalion REME only just lost to them and, in 1998, in another exciting finish, 7 Battalion REME emerged the winner. The Corps also entered teams in the Army Inter-Corps Championships. It never defeated the RLC, which was the predominant team, but it put in many creditable performances, managing to come second to the RLC in 1996.

Craftsman Christie (Victrix Ludorum) and Corporal Beaumont (Victor Ludorum) in 1992

1999–2015

From 1999 to 2000, the REME Championships were held at the Aldershot Military Stadium. Participation in the event was now decreasing due to external commitments, but it was at this stage that Corporal Beaumont, then of the School of Electronic and Aeronautical Engineering (SEAE), showed that he still had what it takes to be the winner of the Victor Ludorum trophy. It would be his final time as the trophy holder, having won it six times over a period of nine years, which was a remarkable achievement.

In 2000, SEME once more took back the title of REME Inter-Unit Champions. In 2001, SEME had repeated their winning formula with the Victor Ludorum being awarded to Staff Sergeant Walker from 7 Battalion REME. This was also the first year Potential Officers from the Royal Military College of Science, Shrivenham, were allowed to compete in the competition, as they were sponsored for later commissioning into the Corps. This would be the only year the event was to be held at HMS Temeraire Military Stadium in Portsmouth.

The Inter-Unit Championships were held for the last time at the Aldershot Military Stadium in 2002. The trend for athlete participation continued to decline due to operational commitments. Seven teams entered the competition, but many athletes were required to take part in five events each to ensure maximum points were scored. For the first time in the history of the Corps, the Inter-Unit Championships resulted in a tie between 7 Battalion REME and SEME. For the next two years, the event would be hosted at SEME Bordon, the perceived home of the inter-unit title.

With a win for 7 Battalion REME in 2003, attention now turned to the Inter-Corps Athletics Championships held at the Royal School of Signals. REME was now feeling the true effect of operational tempo, but the Corps fielded the best possible team it could, based on the results of the REME Championships held only the previous month. On a windswept and somewhat undulating course, the team produced a sixth position out of the eight teams taking part.

From 2004, the REME Championships would be held at the Tidworth Oval. Against tradition, the event was held on a hot summer's day with some 14 teams taking part in what was the best turnout for over a decade. The competition went right down to the wire and was relying on the result of an unusual final event, the triple jump. Led by Staff Sergeant Jonathon Creak, 13 Air Assault Regiment RLC Workshop triumphed. This would pave the way for success for REME units serving within 16 Air Assault Brigade for the following two years until 2007, when SEME decided to return the trophy to where they felt it truly belonged.

From 2001 onwards, with the exception of 2004, the participation in athletics was in slow decline and the number of teams competing reduced year on year. The lack of reporting of REME athletics in The Craftsman magazine and other publications would prove a difficulty for such vital archiving of Corps history. During this period, however, it has been encouraging to see REME personnel with a distinct passion for athletics who would continue to strive to compete at the top level, whilst touring across the world taking on other nations. Whilst the following list is not exhaustive, the accounts have been made accessible after being published as articles from The Craftsman magazine, the REME Journal, the public domain and personal accounts made by REME athletes.

Notable REME Athletes

Major Rob Shenton REME. In 2008, Major Shenton had started his quest to run ultra-marathons to raise money for the charities that were helping his father in his battle with lung cancer. In 2011, he took part in the Marathon des Sables (MdS), which is a gruelling multi-stage adventure through a formidable landscape in one of the world's most inhospitable climates – the Sahara Desert. The rules required him to carry everything he needed to survive (less water and a tent) on his back and to cover a total distance of 155 miles in six stages over six days. Major Shenton's article in the 2011 REME Journal told the dramatic tale of how he completed the MdS despite sandstorms, rationed water, and seeing other competitors surviving on drips. He has since successfully completed the much acclaimed Everest Marathon and, at the time of writing, is planning to take part in the North Pole Marathon for his chosen charities.

Major Shenton at the 2011 Marathon des Sables

Captain Jonathon Creak AGC. A young Craftsman Creak found his love for running in 1993 at his first unit. He started by competing in the 800 metres both in the REME Germany Championships and Corps Championships in Reading, but later that year moved across to cross country and marathon and, in his first year, won the junior cross country title in Germany. Continuing to compete in several cross country and athletics events, he decided to add the 3,000 metres steeplechase to his repertoire of events. The demands of his career meant that running had to remain essentially a hobby until he was posted to 13 Air Assault Support Regiment Workshop RLC in 1999. He then finished second in the Corps Half-Marathon Championships and won the REME Marathon Championships finishing eighth in the Army. Over the next few years, he would compete with distinction in a number of cross country and steeplechase competitions. In 2002, he deployed to Iraq, but by delaying his anthrax vaccinations to the day of his flight, he was able compete at the Corps Cross Country Championships finishing second. Three days after returning from Iraq, he saw fit to make the most of his post-operational tour leave by competing in the Inter-Corps Championships winning the 3,000 metres steeplechase. His efforts for 2003 didn't stop there when he also later won the REME and Army Marathon Championships with a personal best of 2 hours 37 minutes. It was of note that from the 2003 to 2004 season, Staff Sergeant Creak was the first, and is still the only, holder of all running titles from the 3,000 metres steeplechase to marathon on all surfaces (cross country, road and track). From 2004 to 2006, he would go on to win the REME Cross Country Championships twice more, one REME Marathon Championships and other track golds, along with winning the Army orienteering title in 2005. Now commissioned into the AGC, Captain Creak continues to run regularly representing the Army and his new Corps at orienteering.

Captain Frazer Alexander REME. Captain Alexander achieved a notable success in 2005, when he beat the record for the 3,000 metres steeplechase at the Royal Military Academy Sandhurst. After commissioning in December 2005, he deployed in April 2006 on Operation TELIC 8 with the Queen's Dragoon Guards and, whilst in Shaibah Logistic Base, won the half-marathon. His next posting to SEME at Bordon allowed him to develop his love for running. He achieved success at the Army Unit Cross Country Championships, and gained an Army place at the Inter-Services Cross Country Championships. He also won the Corps Championships that year and represented the Corps in the Inter-Corps Championships. In 2008, he ran the Marathon des Sables and came a respectable 171st, improving on that by running again in 2009 and finishing 108th. In that year, Captain Alexander won the British Army (Germany) Cross Country Championships, 2011 was his fastest year. He became the Army Half-Marathon

Captain Alexander and James Cracknell at the 2009 Marathon des Sables

Champion, and performed very creditably in three other marathons; the London Virgin Marathon, the ING Europe Marathon in his native Luxembourg, as well as the US Marine Corps Marathon Forward, which he ran when he deployed with his unit to Afghanistan.

Staff Sergeant Patrick McGeever MBE. Staff Sergeant McGeever has been the long-serving, influential driving force behind REME Cross Country. For 15 years, he has been a dedicated second-in-command of Corps Cross Country, all the while competing as an athlete. He has been the key organiser of the annual REME Cross Country Championships, which have been held at Bordon since 2000. Before joining the Army, he had competed in the National Cross Country Leagues as a youngster in the 1970s. Joining REME in 1995, he brought his passion for the sport with him. He played an important role in the mentoring and development of REME athletes, and many of them attribute their success to him.

Staff Sergeant McGeever at the London Virgin Marathon

In the 2006 to 2007 season, he was the Army Veteran Half-Marathon Champion and, in 2010, was the REME Champion over the same distance. At the marathon distance in 2009, he posted a time of 2 hours 42 minutes at the London Virgin Marathon, qualifying him as the second fastest Army veteran. A seasoned endurance athlete for 30 years, he has represented at Regimental, Corps and Army level both at cross country and marathon. Wanting to do something longer than a marathon, he decided to compete in the ultra-marathon distance as well. In 1995, as part of a four-man team, he won the arduous Special Forces Royal Marines Lympstone to Poole event, taking away the title away from the Royal Marines for the first time in 25 years. At the time of writing, he manages the Army Veteran Team and continues to organise the annual REME Cross Country Championships.

Sergeant Craig Williams. In 2006, during initial technical training, Craftsman Williams was spotted as a likely long distance prospect by Staff Sergeant McGeever and Mike Lovell. Under their influential guidance, he began training at the Aldershot Athletics Club with Captain Keith Donkin RAPTC (Royal Army Physical Training Corps). He went on win the REME Cross Country Championships in 2007 and was selected for the Army team as a junior. Operational commitments had limited his ability to compete, but he was able to impress in the civilian circuit where he ran for the South of England in the Manchester 10km posting a time of 30 minutes 27 seconds. Feeling confident, he decided to move up to the half-marathon distance and completed his first in a time of 69 minutes 30 seconds at Bristol, a time that was later recognised as the fastest in the UK for his age group. His dedication to running continued and he won the REME Cross Country Championships a further five times and became the Army Cross Country Champion. He transferred to the RAPTC in 2013.

BADMINTON

The Corps Team has performed well in the Inter-Corps Championships since 1992, winning the competition in 1993, 1994, 1997 and 2004. A long period of achieving several second and third placings followed, before winning the competition again in 2014, beating the RLC in a hard fought final before retaining the title in 2015 after beating the Royal Signals. (**See Plate 63**) The Corps team has been fortunate enough to compete in two overseas tours, one to Denmark in 1998 and, more recently, to Sydney (Australia) in 2012. The most recent tour saw the Corps team win three of its five matches against tough civilian and Royal Australian Navy teams. Key administrative appointments have been held by Lieutenant Colonel Paul Fletcher REME in the role of Chairman from 2004 to 2015 and Captain Stu Bass REME as the Secretary from 2006 to 2015.

Notable REME Players
Warrant Officers Class 1 Dixon, Cyrans, and Chidgey all dominated REME badminton from 1990 to 1996 before stepping aside to make way to Staff Sergeants Harrow and Mills, both of whom have won a considerable number of titles between them.

Staff Sergeant Danny Mills was arguably the most successful REME player the Corps has seen, representing the Combined Services, Army,

Corps and various units, winning eight Army titles and 14 runner-up medals, as well as over 100 Corps and Divisional-level trophies.

Staff Sergeant John Harrow was a player with a natural gift to play the sport. His effortless ability to move around the court and put the shuttle onto a part of the court that seemed impossible, frustrated even the most experienced players. His titles included winning the men's doubles from 1998 to 2006 with various partners as well as several singles, mixed and veteran's titles.

Staff Sergeant Daley first represented the Corps in 1997 and the Army in 1999. His first representation at Combined Services level was in 2006 and, since then, he has competed in sports tours of Canada, Hong Kong, South Africa and Thailand. His successes include two Inter-Services wins, five Army-level titles, two Inter-Corps titles and 12 REME titles.

CRICKET

REME cricket is a sport that was significantly affected by the many structural changes the Army went through during the period covered by this book. By the end of the period, the Corps squad was only 35 strong, including a small contingent of players based in Germany. Sadly, the pace of Army life and commitments in later years made it difficult to get more than the bare eleven to any one match.

Facilities
The Corps enjoyed a picturesque ground in front of the Hazebrouck Warrant Officers' and Sergeants' Mess in Arborfield, which was regarded as one of the best in Army cricket. The Corps allocated funds to pay the local Finchampstead Cricket Club groundsman to maintain the grass wicket. This decision reaped rewards as the pitches became progressively better with each season. It is hoped that it will be possible to build a similar relationship with a local club after the move to Lyneham.

The Fixture List
The REME Corps Cricket fixture list is a busy one with three main competitions consisting of the 50-over Inter-Corps Power Cup, the Inter-Corps T20 Competition and the annual two-day Parnaby Cup against the RLC. The Inter-Corps T20 Competition was introduced in 2007, with players wearing coloured clothing.

Outstanding Performances

On the 12 May 2009, several Corps cricket records were set in a match against the Royal Armoured Corps, starting with an incredible opening partnership of 254 between Warrant Officer Class 2 Clive Bate (128 runs off 120 balls, with 14 fours) and Warrant Officer Class 2 Ian Dixon (128 runs off 108 balls, with 13 fours and one six). REME closed with an incredible 453 for 7 on the scoreboard. A day of records indeed, with the highest total score (453 for 7), highest partnership for any wicket (254), highest opening partnership (254) and biggest winning margin (378 runs, which is more than the previous highest score). Also, this was only the second occasion when two Corps batsmen have scored a century in the same innings.

Three players have topped the season's batting averages on four separate occasions in the last 25 years: Staff Sergeant Dean Woodhouse, Warrant Officer Class 1 Stephen Hole and Warrant Officer Class 2 Ian Dixon. Whilst Staff Sergeant Woodhouse had retired from the Army at the time of writing, both Warrant Officer Class 1 Hole and Warrant Officer Class 2 Dixon were still playing and have an eye on beating the all-time record of Major Martin Beer REME of topping the batting averages in five different seasons.

Lieutenant J Houghton REME set the highest individual score of 157 on 2 July 1955 against the Royal Army Pay Corps. This score stood as the best for 50 years until it was finally surpassed by Warrant Officer Class 2 Dixon when he scored 161 against the Defence Academy. He pushed the bar higher on two other occasions with a new high of 177 in 1990, which gave him the five highest individual scores since 1985. He has proved to be truly phenomenal in Corps cricket; his first hundred came against the Royal Military College of Science in 2003 and, at the time of writing, had scored 30 centuries, which was spectacular as the next highest number is four. Warrant Officer Class 2 Dixon's five highest scores since 1985 are:

- 177 versus Army Medical Services, 10 July 2009
- 163 versus Intelligence Corps, 8 June 2006
- 161 versus Defence Academy, 10 May 2005
- 152 versus Royal Artillery, 5 June 2006
- 145 versus REME (Germany), 7 July 2007.

REME UK enjoyed many a success, winning its first competition in 1991. It then went on to win the Inter-Corps League 10 times and the Inter-Corps T20 once, making the semi-finals (at least) in every season.

Lifetime Achievement

In 2014, Warrant Officer Class 1 Hole received a lifetime achievement award for his contribution to Corps, Army and Combined Services cricket. For 20 years, his commitment to REME cricket has been exceptional. He is the most capped player at Army and Combined Services levels, playing at this level for 19 seasons. At the time of the award, he had scored over 2,000 runs in 68 matches with a batting average of almost 50 runs per match and a bowling average of one wicket for every 21 runs he concedes. Since becoming Corps Captain in 2010 until the time of writing, the team reached the Inter-Corps 50-over final four times, winning it three times and being runner-up once. In the same period, the team has won the Inter-Corps T20 once, been runner-up twice and reached the semi-final. He has also been awarded the Inter-Services Man of the Match and Inter-Services T20 Man of the Series.

CYCLING

History

Cycle racing in the Army only started in 1942, with the Egypt-based 'Buckshee Wheelers' riding time trials on desert roads. The Corps was some way behind, with REME cycling starting in 1953. The most notable REME representative from this era was Craftsman Ray 'The Boot' Booty, the first man to break 4 hours for a 100-mile individual time trial with a record time that was to stand for six years. In 1958, Booty became the Commonwealth Games road race champion at Cardiff, his winning-time was three minutes ahead of the Australian Frank Brazier, who took silver.

After a period of decline, there was a resurgence in the 1980s with the team from Princess Marina College enjoying many successes in Junior Army competitions against the other apprentice colleges. Staff Sergeant 'Davie' Campbell was a notable performer in this era, winning both BAOR and full Army titles, as well as the Army 50-mile time trial in 1991. The end of the 1990s saw Staff Sergeant Gary Kristensen (road racing) and Warrant Officer Class 1 Paul Haggerty (time trialling) in the driving seat at both REME and Army Championships. Warrant Officer Class 1 Kristensen then ran the Army team for some five years, which included taking a full team to the Isle of Man International Week winning the week-long competition on no less than three consecutive years and supported by REME cyclists Geoff Weir and the former Junior National Champion Mark Dolan. Warrant Officer Class 1 Haggerty was a legend of time trialling, a regular winner of local competitions who also put in sterling performances at national events. He was famed for his use of the indoor 'turbo' trainer and his five-hour indoor sessions were known throughout the country. The early-1990s saw the decline of REME cycling as a standalone sport, as it came under the banner of triathlon and duathlon.

Recent History
More recently, cycling in REME has been resurrected under the watchful eye of Colonel Jon Mulroy and later Colonel Adam Fraser-Hitchen (both late REME). REME has had notable success at all disciplines, leading the other Army Corps in terms of professionalism, clothing, race strategy and results. In the Mountain Bike (MTB) Inter-Unit Competition during 2013 – 2014 both 2 Battalion REME and 3 Battalion REME dominated events with a strong team ethic. In road racing, REME won the 2013 season Inter-Corps Cycling Competition. On the road, the influence of REME is enormous with the 2015 Army Team comprising no less than three riders and two support staff: Captain Ryan Perry REME, Captain Matt Cryer REME and Sergeant Mark Robertson, and Colonel Simon Holford (late REME) and Warrant Officer Class 2 Rob Jones respectively.

Notable REME Cyclist
Captain Ryan Perry REME was one of the most talented cyclists in the country at MTB, road racing and time trialling, and so deserves individual mention. He is the current Inter-Services Champion at both MTB and road racing. He also holds the British Cycling Time Trial third place, previously won by Alex Dowsett, a continental professional and former world one-hour record holder until Bradley Wiggins beat him. Captain Perry is also the reigning National Champion at the Blue Riband 25-mile time trial event. He would have added the 10-mile event to this, already five seconds up on second place, had he not suffered a mechanical failure halfway round. The irony of this happening to a REME officer will not escape many. Captain Perry is making history and is highly likely to continue to do so.

EQUITATION

REME has a fine heritage of equestrians, most notably Captain Jim Fox REME, who represented Great Britain in several Olympic Games, winning a gold medal in the Modern Pentathlon Team Event at the 1976 Montreal Olympics. He was a leading figure in the rise of modern pentathlon in Great Britain. The stables at Arborfield were used for many years to train REME athletes until its eventual closure.

The REME Equestrian Association (REA) was formed in 2012 to provide equestrian support to all members of the Corps. The team quickly organised itself and entered the Royal Windsor Horse Show where the team of Warrant Officer Class 2 Matthews, Craftsman Holmes and Craftsman Kennedy were placed a creditable 14th from 46 teams.

Later in 2012, the team went to compete at the Royal Tournament held at the Defence Animal Centre, Melton Mowbray. Again, the REME Team represented by Captain Hannah Adams REME and Warrant Officer Class 2 Matthews recorded great results, firmly putting REME on the military equestrian map. Further successes were enjoyed at the Forces Equine Games, Scope Festival of Jumping and at the Jersey Horse of the Year Show, at which the REA was selected to represent the Army. The team consisting of Warrant Officer Class 2 Matthews and Lance Corporal Farish recorded a second place in the prestigious team event, which was the best result ever for a military team at the show.

Warrant Officer Class 1 Matthews at the Royal Windsor Horse Show 2013

The REA had a great year in 2013. The team focused on the Royal Windsor Horse Show and a team comprising Captain Adams, Warrant Officer Class 1 Matthews and Craftsman Holmes met at Sandhurst for a pre-competition training camp. On show day, Warrant Officer Class 1 Matthews jumped first recording a fast clear round. Unluckily, Captain Adams had a fence down and was followed by Craftsman Kennedy jumping extremely well and clear. The REA was sitting in fourth place going into the jump-off. Craftsman Kennedy was selected to represent REME in the jump-off and recorded the fastest clear round promoting the team into third place. This result was truly remarkable and was further enhanced when Craftsman Kennedy was awarded the Best Young Rider Award and was presented with a bridle by Her Majesty The Queen.

The future is bright for the REA with new members joining and the team increasing its influence on military riding.

GOLF

The REME Golf Association (RGA) has undergone significant change since 1993. The Central Committee of REME agreed, in 1950, to the awarding of colours for Corps sport but, at that time, a decision was taken not to award colours for golf, as the sport was open only to officers. As it stands in early 2015, with well over 100 personnel playing Corps golf, none are serving officers. For many years, the RGA consisted of societies, REME Officers Golf Society (ROGS) and the REME Soldiers Golf Society (RSGS), which would run separate society meetings and fixtures throughout the season. The two societies would come together for the major fixtures in the calendar, such as the Corps Championships, and for matches against other Corps or golf clubs. In 2009, however, due to the reductions in numbers over the years the RGA Committee decided to amalgamate ROGS and RSGS so that all meetings and fixtures are now attended by all association members. This has ensured that all meetings remain well attended and competitive.

The RGA has embraced the digital age and, in 2012, developed and launched the RGA website – www.remegolf.co.uk. This has helped to improve the flow of information to members and reduce the administration burden on the committee.

Members of the RGA have provided invaluable support to major professional golf competitions, such as The Open and the Ryder Cup for a number of years. The RGA provides people to fill vital roles, such as marshals and even on-course 'spotters' providing valuable feedback to the TV companies that cover the events. The professionalism of the REME personnel at these events raises the corporate image of the Corps and REME golf, as they are regularly name checked on TV by the commentators.

The 2012 RGA Captain's Trophy Competition at the Belfry

HANG GLIDING AND PARAGLIDING

Hang gliding and paragliding had thrived in UK under the control of the British Hang Gliding and Paragliding Association (BHPA). They are closely related, and both provide the same exhilarating sense of freedom. In essence, paragliders are more portable than hang gliders and a little easier to learn to fly, but they are more hampered by strong winds. Both paragliders and hang gliders have been flown for over 250km in UK, and those who wish to fly unsupervised need to be trained as pilots to meet BHPA standards.

REME individuals had been involved in these sports for many years, but the formation of the REME Hang Gliding and Paragliding (HG&PG) Association in 2010 helped the sport take off in the Corps. Activities included those with a training or instructional dimension, which led to an increase in the number of active pilots. REME personnel increasingly became involved in competitive flying; as individuals entering non-Service competitions, as members of the Army team in inter-Services competitions, and as members of a very successful Combined Services team. They also took part in adventurous and recreational flying, often in interesting or exotic locations. The REME HG&PG Association has contributed to the wider arena of this competitive and challenging Services sport. Its aim is to continue this progress in the future, developing Association members, in order to promote the Corps on the UK and international scene.

The paragraphs that follow pick out some of the highlights that give a flavour of what happened in the five years after the formation of the REME HG&PG Association.

Pilots lining up at the launch point

2010 Season

This year was an active year starting with Exercise FAMARA GLIDE in Lanzarote, followed by Exercise GRANADA GLIDE in Spain. Both were well attended and a great opportunity for pilots to enjoy the air currents again following the UK winter. The Association then laid on Exercise SHROPSHIRE WINGS in May and a scattering of entries into the British Clubs Challenge, mainly in southeast Wales, including a couple of individual entries into the Ozone Open in France.

The sports tour to Lanzarote was over a 10-day period in spring with the flying being extremely challenging but also rewarding. Respectable distances of up to 40km were achieved in testing conditions, and gave pilots an opportunity to test their limits and improve their personal bests in a delightful island setting. In the Inter-Services Paragliding Championships, the Army Team once again secured victory against the RAF and RN in a close fought battle, with the REME team making a very successful contribution, including some personal bests of over 60km.

2011 and 2012 Seasons
The 2011 Season had been a quiet one because of operational commitments, so one of the key aims for the year was to run cross country workshops. The first was under the guidance of Pat Dower (a national competition-level pilot), which was directed at all levels of pilots and aimed to enhance skills. It was structured to cover all the important aspects of flying to give the strongest possible foundation for a competition career. Some of the strategies, tricks and techniques used by the top pilots were truly eye-opening and he wove them all into a two-day event.

The second coaching opportunity was a meet at 'Wessex Wings' on the 8 April 2011. This was held over a two-week window and ran on the principle of pilots attending around their work commitments. The intention was to build on their cross country knowledge through a syllabus of theory and practical coaching. This was quickly followed by another session undertaken at the Joint Services Hang Gliding and Paragliding Centre (JSHPC) at Crickhowell on the 26 April 2011 under the direction of Major Colclough RAPTC.

This training led members of the REME HG&PG Association to enter the 2012 Ozone Chabre Open in the French Alps, as part of a tri-Service team. The Ozone Open is an international friendly paragliding cross country competition held in June at sites in and around the Laragne and Sederon areas of southeast France. Sponsored by the paraglider and kite manufacturer, Ozone, the event is organised by the Laragne-based club, Chabre Vol Libre, with further support from Les Loups Volants at Sederon. The Ozone Chabre Open is, first and foremost, designed to be a friendly, fun competition.

There was a tri-Service team for what was to be a memorable trip. During the first week, the pilots were guided in and around the sites in Laragne to get some free flying done, prior to the competition. This week pushed everybody to their limits, as the conditions in southeast France can be tricky due to the strong thermic/wind combination, but there were plenty of opportunities to destress in local pubs. The second week was the start of the competition and the team, against fierce competition, took a very respectable second place.

2013 Season

The year was notable because the Combined Services Team, in which REME was represented, won the British Clubs Challenge paragliding competition. The event was made up of six rounds (only four were able to be flown due to weather constraints), mainly in southeast Wales, but the Combined Services Team managed to beat the competition in every venue. The beauty of the event was that it was spread over the entire season enabling team members to compete and fly in and around busy diaries. Flights from 9km to 90km ensured that the team held off the competition until the very end. Victory was sweet, with strong club teams, such as Avon, being displaced from the top spot.

The next event was a Jockey Sanderson (British national pilot) Cross Country Weekend in and around the flying sites at the Crickhowell Centre. Bad weather on the Saturday meant that flying was limited, which gave the opportunity for additional theory training by 'the master'. The second day gave the opportunity for some exciting cross country flying.

The Inter-Services Competition was then hosted by the JSHPC. The weather was generally kind, and although the RN won a hard-fought contest, the combined Army/REME Team, which included plenty of new talent, could take much satisfaction from its performance, which included several personal bests and flights of over 60km.

The Association then embarked on a tri-Service paragliding expedition to Spain on its annual sports tour to refine cross country skills in preparation for the 2014 competition season. This year, the sports tour was an organised trip to the Piedraheta Mountain Range in Spain. Sixteen tri-Service personal attended, all with mixed flying ability. The week was hosted by GB team member, Steve Ham. He provided a purpose-built six-day package catering for the development of pilots within the relative safety of a group. This incorporated a 'live-track' system, which monitors the progress of each individual pilot whilst on-route and offers a panic button that gives the pilot's location in the event of an incident.

Conditions in the Piedraheta Mountains can be extremely challenging. Early in the morning, light winds and gentle thermals brush up the face of the mountain making it almost impossible for the pilots to stay up. From midday onwards, the thermals build and could make launching a paraglider an extremely hazardous activity. In early evening, the winds and thermal strength subside and made the air a buoyant smooth playground for all to enjoy. It wasn't uncommon for those on the package to be flying for three hours before making their way to the landing area for a final sunset glide. As a rule, tasks were set in the region of some 60 – 70km and, generally, saw at least two of the team achieve that goal.

2014 Season
This was the twelfth year in succession in which this expedition, Exercise GRANADA GLIDE, was held, and saw a record attendance, with a hotel full of Army pilots, and their instructors from the Adventurous Training Group (ATG) at Oberstdorf. The flying was from sites at Cenes, Otivar and Herradura.

Cenes is an excellent flying site, which faces west/northwest, but is also great in a light easterly as it is protected by the Sierra Nevada Range. The take-off and landing areas are huge. Otivar is a spectacular site and has a real Andalucía feel to it. The surrounding countryside is preserved just as one would have found it centuries ago. From take-off, the Mediterranean can be seen about 15km away, and there were many successful flights that ended with a beach landing, which was the main objective of flying there. Many of the team had successful flights landing at the beach and others will be back to try again the following year. Herradura is on the coast, and a successful flight from Otivar to Herradura entitles the pilot to the award of a spectacular 'O2H' badge.

ICE HOCKEY

In January 2000, following a winter deployment to BATUS, Sergeant (as he then was) Graham Harrold, decided that he would establish a REME UK ice hockey team based at SEME. He enlisted the help of Major Bob Eddy, the Canadian Exchange Officer at Bordon at that time. Warrant Officer Class 1 Chris Thompson had already started a rink hockey team in 1999 with members of SEAE, so the two groups got together, secured funding, negotiated ice-time at Guildford and thus the REME Stallions ice hockey team was born. Lieutenant Colonel John Edwards REME, who had previously taken up ice hockey as the British military exchange officer in Base Borden, Canada, stepped forward as Chairman of the REME Stallions.

He was Chairman of REME Ice Hockey from 2000 through to 2011. On retirement from the Army, he handed over to Lieutenant Colonel

Tim Gillies REME, who was one of the original novice players to take up ice hockey in 2000. Following the formation of the REME Stallions, the Corps has been at the forefront of Army and Services ice hockey. Over the years, personal commitment from the numerous Corps Team Managers has enabled REME ice hockey to flourish. The Corps Team Managers over this period include: Captain Garry Patey REME (the initial Team Manager), Major Ben Durand (Canadian Exchange Officer, Bordon), Staff Sergeant Jonny Gracianio, Warrant Officer Class 2 Del Davies and Warrant Officer Class 2 Mark Carter (the Corps Team Manager at the time of writing). Throughout this period, and at the helm, the team has benefitted from the wisdom, support and guidance of Corporal Rob Taylor, an ex-professional player and REME Vehicle Mechanic reservist, who has acted as Corps Team Coach throughout.

The REME Stallions team has competed in the Canadian EME 'The John Muise Memorial' Championship annually since 2001. Over the 13 years (to date) of competition, the REME Stallions team has won the B Division of the Canadian Championships on numerous occasions and has competed in the A Division. With REME providing strong representation on an annual basis in the Army team, as well as support to the Army team in management appointments, such as the Chairman of the Army Ice Hockey Association since inception, REME remains a dominant force in Army and military ice hockey.

Ice hockey is now a recognised Army sport thanks to the consolidated efforts of the early REME pioneers. With the transition and consolidation of Arborfield and Bordon to Lyneham, it is anticipated that Corps-level and grass roots ice hockey will continue to prosper over the coming years. **(See Plate 64)**

MARTIAL ARTS

The term 'martial arts' covers a wide variety of disciplines that require years of dedication and practice to achieve competency. Martial arts have only relatively recently been recognised and regulated at Army level. The Army Martial Arts Association (MAA) was officially formed in 1995, to cater for practising martial artists and to provide a single body to regulate competition and insurance requirements across the recognised martial disciplines. The five main competitive disciplines currently recognised by the Combined Services Sports Board are: Karate, Taekwondo (International Taekwondo Federation (ITF)), Taekwondo (World Taekwondo Federation/Olympic Taekwondo), Kendo and Weapons

(Kata only). Judo also has recognised sports status, but at Army level is catered for by a separate association.

Martial arts, as the name implies, have benefits in a military environment, as they can promote physical and mental toughness, self-discipline, leadership, confidence, composure under pressure and respect for one's opponent. REME's involvement in Army and Combined Services martial arts has been significant. The Army MAA's Executive Committee had an evident REME influence through its President at the time of writing, Colonel David Ansell (late REME, and also President of REME Martial Arts) and Chairman, Captain Paul Reynolds REME. Also, the following were discipline team captains: Karate – Staff Sergeant Brian Hall, ITF Taekwondo – Warrant Officer Class 2 Colin Sayer, and Kendo – Captain Reynolds. Until a short time before writing, the Secretary had been Warrant Officer Class 2 Andy O'Neill. The Army Karate and Kendo Team Captains were also performing these duties at Combined Services level.

Turning to Judo, at the time of writing, the Corps had provided a number of key players within the Army Judo Association (AJA), including Major Martin Leach REME (AJA Secretary) and Warrant Officer Class 2 'Bomber' Brown (AJA Team Manager). There were significant REME numbers throughout the grading levels and a large number of qualified coaches. REME personnel had also done particularly well in the most recent Army Judo Championships with silver and bronze medals in the senior team category, and in the individual category taking three gold, three silver and five bronze medals. Over the years before that, a large number of REME players successfully represented the Army at Combined Services level.

Within REME, martial arts achieved associate status under the REME Sports Association. At the time of writing, REME Martial Arts under its President not only looks after Judo alongside Karate, Taekwondo, Kendo and Weapons disciplines (all the recognised disciplines with the Combined Services Sports Board), but also provides direction and advice for REME personnel pursuing other disciplines.

The Army Judo, Karate and ITF Taekwondo Squads, in particular, have enjoyed a strong REME contingent and recruited well from both Arborfield and Bordon-based soldiers on Phase 2 Training. This has been largely due to REME Senior Non-Commissioned Officers, such as Warrant Officer Class 2 Sayer, and Staff Sergeants Andy McKenzie and Neil MacDonald. They have freely given their time, including a significant number of weekends, to the encouragement, training and development of young soldiers, having offered them an avenue into a sporting activity that provides robust physical and mental benefits.

REME recipients of awards at the 2014 Martial Arts Open Competition

REME soldiers have competed all over the country in civilian events either as individual entrants or as part of the Army or Combined Services Teams. At Army Squad level, REME soldiers' training and instruction benefitted from the passion and experience of seasoned veterans such as Major Leach and Warrant Officer Class 2 Brown for Judo, Warrant Officer Class 2 O'Neill and Staff Sergeant Hall for Karate, Warrant Officer Class 2 Sayer for ITF Taekwondo and Captain Reynolds for Kendo. The citation submitted for Staff Sergeant Hall as a contender for the 2013 REME Sportsperson of the Year included so much evidence from over two decades of teaching and competition that it led to the initiation of the Lifetime Achievement Award.

The first Corps trophy presentations for Karate, Taekwondo, Kendo and Brazilian Jiu-Jitsu were awarded to discipline winners from REME participants at the Army Open Competition in October 2014. REME martial arts also presented trophies to category winners at the 2014 Inter-Services Judo Competition. This marked the first step in the initiative towards a true inter-Corps martial arts competition, on which REME is leading the way. REME personnel currently represent and are involved in the training of national martial arts teams. REME personnel also continue to play a significant part in the leadership, management and training, as well as participation in the fighting for Army and for Combined Services martial arts teams. REME martial arts has been a remarkable success story, with much optimism for the future of this arduous and demanding family of sports.

Notable REME Players
Many individuals helped the continuous growth in popularity of REME martial arts, including the following who were awarded full REME colours.

Captain Paul Reynolds REME – Kendo. Captain Reynolds has been involved in the Army MAA since 2005, and held a position on the Executive Committee as the Kendo representative since 2008. He has represented the Army at Kendo for some nine years and has fought for the Combined Services since 2011. He was made Captain of the Combined Services Kendo Team in 2014. In 2012, he was selected as the Chairman of the Army MAA for a three-year tenure. Later that year, he also assumed the duties of Chairman of the Combined Services MAA, as a two-year rotational post between the three single-Service leads. He won the 2010 Inter-Services Individual Competition and has reached the final in several other years. He holds a Third Dan grading with the British Kendo Association and a Second Dan grading with the British Bushido Association.

Warrant Officer Class 2 Colin Sayer – Taekwondo. Warrant Officer Class 2 Sayer is an individual whose evident drive, passion and sound management have assured continued momentum behind ITF Taekwondo within the Army and in REME. As an individual, he continues to compete successfully in Army MAA and Combined Services MAA events and has recent National Squad involvement in his discipline. Warrant Officer Class 2 Sayer's organisational, coaching and motivational contributions have, however, had a much wider impact across martial arts in the Services. As the Head of Army ITF Taekwondo, he has successfully organised and run squad training, team selection and coaching, produced calling notices and joining instructions for various training events and competitions in both the military and civilian arena. He has continued his presence in the ring as a senior grade and is an outstanding example to junior Servicemen and Servicewomen through his participation with both the Army and the Combined Services ITF Taekwondo Squads.

Warrant Officer Class 2 Andy O'Neill – Karate. Warrant Officer Class 2 O'Neill has been involved with Army Karate for over 10 years and has represented both the Army and the Combined Services at a multitude of Services and civilian competitions. He is also a vital member of the Army Karate coaching staff and is dedicated to the development of the discipline and of practitioners in the Services. In addition to his continued practice and competition, Warrant Officer Class 2 O'Neill has been relentless in his efforts to progress martial arts in the Services. Embracing new disciplines and developing relationships with external sporting bodies, he has introduced new opportunities for countless soldiers, many of whom are REME.

Staff Sergeant Brian Hall – Karate. Staff Sergeant Hall started his martial arts career in 1994 and obtained his First Dan Black Belt in Shotokan Karate in 1997. Due to the lack of instructors in Germany at the time, he was asked to instruct his first club at an early stage and went from strength to strength running 10 different clubs in nine different locations. Over the last 17 years, he has taught in excess of 1,000 students (many of them serving REME soldiers and their dependants). He currently holds a Fifth Dan Black Belt and continues to run two civilian clubs in the northeast of England. Not only does he compete at an extremely high level, as part of the England National Squad, he is committed to the development of tri-Service Karate, devoting a significant amount of his time to teaching and coaching.

Warrant Officer Class 2 O'Neill, Lance Corporal Gladding and Staff Sergeant Hall competing in Karate October 2014

Sergeant Scott Caswell – Taekwondo. Although relatively new to Army-level sport, Sergeant Caswell has practised Taekwondo for many years and his progression is seen by younger soldiers as a good example of what can be achieved by determination and training. This man has demonstrated real courage and tenacity. He suffered a knock-out against a national champion in the 2012 English Open Competition, whilst representing the Army, and then, following recovery, came back to win individual gold in the Army Open Competition against a strong field of Senior Dan grades (Black Belt practitioners). His next challenge was the 2013 ITF Taekwondo World Championships in Coventry, where he managed to get through to the semi-final against an Argentinean competitor. Again, it was a hard fight and Sergeant Caswell showed gritty determination and, in the end, he managed to come away with a bronze medal. Following this performance, he was then selected for the Army Team to compete in the Inter-Services Competition in July 2013, where he won an impressive silver medal.

Corporal Stuart Owen – Karate. Corporal Owen has been a valuable member of the Army Karate Team since 2009, and the Combined Services Karate Team since 2010. In this time, he has competed in many national and international competitions, his best result was in the Welsh National Championships in 2011 where he won two bronze medals. He also won the Army Championships in 2011. He has represented REME next to Staff Sergeant Hall and Corporal Hall in the three-man Kumite (Fighting) Team in the Army Championships winning a gold medal.

Corporal Kevin Hall – Karate. Corporal Hall has been a member of the Army and Combined Services Karate Teams since leaving Phase 1 Training in 2007. After settling into the team, he first became Army Champion in 2008 and Inter-Services Champion in 2009. He has gone on to win the Army and Inter-Services Championships three times. He was selected to go onto the Army's Elite Sportsman List in 2010 so that he could concentrate on training with the English National Karate Squad, but he has subsequently decided to concentrate on his Army career as a REME Technical Support Specialist. He remains competitive at the highest levels in the Services and is a proud representative of the Corps at Army events, and of the Army at inter-Services events.

MODERN PENTATHLON

The 1990s was a crucial period for the survival of modern pentathlon. Its place in the Olympic movement was placed under scrutiny as never before. The new face of the International Olympic Committee was modernism and, in 1993, the sport changed to become a one-day event. To enable this to happen, air pistol replaced the '.22' live pistols, the swimming events were seeded so that the fastest swimmers swam last, and the run course was reduced to 3km.

REME modern pentathlon was still being led by the charismatic Major Terry Bunyard REME. In 1992, the Army and REME Squads were forced to move out of their Moat House headquarters and back into Rowcroft Barracks within what was the newly-formed Apprentice College. Coaching staff included Staff Sergeant Bernie Moss, Staff Sergeant Peter Whiteside and a new fitness coach was employed, Sergeant Jim Dancy. The most accomplished athlete was Corporal Frank Quinn, who was now embedded in the Army Squad, having been seconded to the Centre of Excellence by his parent unit. By 1993, Corporal Quinn had already competed at international level and had secured four consecutive REME Championships.

The 1992 Barcelona Olympics, was the first and last occasion since Captain Jim Fox REME claimed a gold medal in the 1976 Montreal Olympics that a REME athlete or coach had not represented Great Britain at the Olympic Games. Military organisations were experiencing a wind of change that was threatening the use of the facilities including the Centre of Excellence at Arborfield. Cutbacks in military spending meant that personnel were rarely free to pursue sport in the way they had in the past. Despite REME having enjoyed the publicity of its highly successful modern pentathletes for many years, modern pentathlon was in danger of being side-lined. The REME Chairman Colonel Mike Selby (late REME), Captain Fox and Major Bunyard identified Sandhurst as the future for REME modern pentathlon, because as a key training unit it represented the essential values of the origins of the sport. So, in 1997, the REME and Army Modern Pentathlon Centre of Excellence was established in Mons Hall, at the Royal Military Academy Sandhurst.

The new millennium brought immediate and unexpected success, and media interest in the REME Centre of Excellence. At the 2000 Sydney Olympics, in the inaugural Olympic women's individual event, Steph Cook won a gold medal in a sprint finish, whilst Kate Allenby finished with a bronze medal. Significantly, both medallists had spent many hours utilising the facilities available at the time at the home of REME modern pentathlon.

Operational commitments both in Afghanistan from 2001 and then Iraq in 2003, meant competitor attendance reduced during this period. But REME modern pentathlon formed a proactive alliance with REME triathlon to ensure that the opportunity to compete at biathlon up to and including tetrathlon was actively encouraged. From 2000 to 2008, Captain Mark Wilson REME assumed the duties of the Secretary. Women's individual and team competitions were introduced to REME modern pentathlon. Notable Corps champions included Craftsman Natalie and the team from SEAE Arborfield. The men's event during this period was dominated by Corporal Zoran Maric and Captain Wilson. In 2009, Captain Frank Quinn took over secretarial duties for modern pentathlon and his first appointment was to persuade General Sir Peter Wall (a Colonel Commandant of the Corps) to become President of REME Modern Pentathlon. General Wall had trained as a 15-year old athlete at the Arborfield Centre of Excellence with Captain Fox. He retained this appointment even when, in 2011, he became Chief of the General Staff. Team Army was founded in 2011, and significant investment was to follow with REME modern pentathlon benefitting from this and increased attendance at events.

In the 2012 London Olympics, where several REME athletes helped in delivering the event at the Olympic Stadium and Greenwich Park, modern pentathlon was a tremendous success for the sport. Captain Quinn was seconded to the Games in the role of International Federation Manager, and other REME athletes including Warrant Officer Class 1 Graeme Matthews assisted in the riding competition.

The REME Modern Pentathlon Championships was combined with the Army Modern Pentathlon Championships and took place after the Olympic Games. Competition was fierce, with the overall winner a current Great Britain international. Corporal Maric's third place in the Army Individual Championships was therefore an exceptional achievement. Captain Wilson, Corporal Dean and Lance Corporal Hood also formed the REME Team that was victorious in the Army Unit Team Championships and the REME Team Competition.

General Wall, Chairman of Army Modern Pentathlon, again presented the prizes. He made particular reference to the REME revival and the work that the Corps had done to raise the profile of the sport. The unprecedented success during the preceding 12 months had taken even the most optimistic by surprise. The focus at the time of writing, was to build on these tremendous foundations and take modern pentathlon within the Corps to another level, with new training centres planned to support some extremely promising talent with potential international status, which had been discovered.

The promotion of the sport, and highlighting the opportunities available, has again delivered a positive outcome during the period running up to the time of writing. The exposure of the sport in both The Craftsman magazine and at road shows to the training schools, culminated in over 50 REME personnel and at least 10 Corps teams participating in the three major Army-level events that were held throughout the sporting season. The road shows were based around the Army Modern Pentathlon portable display stand and a laser pistol range, combined with some epée blades and equipment.

Continuing the theme, there was also an exhibition in the REME Museum based around the history and origins of the sport and how Captain Fox and his achievements at the 1976 Montreal Olympics will forever link the Corps to modern pentathlon, and represent a sporting achievement of the highest order for the Corps. The encouraging response led to the remainder of the winter season being centred on establishing a training and development programme, based at the Army Centre of Excellence at Sandhurst.

MOTORCYCLING

Army motorcycle sport underwent huge changes through the 1990s and 2000s. Replacement General Service (GS) motorcycles were purchased in fewer numbers, the Can-Am 250 motorcycles were replaced with fewer Armstrong 500 motorcycles, and they were replaced with even fewer Harley Davidson 350 motorcycles. Eventually, as a result of ever improving secure battlefield communication systems, an increase in operational tempo and tight budgetary measures, the Army GS motorcycle was phased out of service in 2010. The sport also moved from being part of Army training to being recognised as an Army sport funded by the Army Sports Control Board. A mix of military and civilian events changed to an all-civilian format with one sponsored military event per year – the Army Motorcycle Championships. Road race was also added as a sporting discipline.

Throughout this period, REME motorcycling remained ahead of its competitors and led the field in both trials and enduro disciplines, helped in part by strength in depth across the rank range and the boundless energy and commitment of all those involved. The Corps teams were called upon to perform at the various open days at Arborfield and Bordon, and always put on a memorable show.

As one would expect, REME riders have always been particularly interested in the quality and reliability of the motorcycles they ride. The Enduro Team Manager's mantra was always 'to finish first, you first need to finish', and so prior to any event a great deal of attention was paid to machine preparation. The team continued to ride the ever popular Kawasaki KDX 200 motorcycle, but in the late 1990s moved to KTM and, eventually, under the management of Warrant Officer Class 1 Graham Gorse to Honda. Things did not, however, always run to plan.

In 1998, a deal was struck for new KTM motorcycles for £17,000. The invoice was paid, but the KTM motorcycles were never delivered. After arrests and a lengthy court case, the Corps eventually got its money back and the perpetrator was imprisoned. Thankfully, the Corps loaned the motorcycle team the funds, new machines were purchased and competition continued. A new enduro motorcycle from Yamaha prompted another change and, in 2000, the Corps Team Manager (Warrant Officer Class 1 Steve Eggleton) and Major Mike Tizard REME negotiated a commercial deal. The Corps stayed with Yamaha for the next 10 years and scored many notable victories with the brand. In 2010, the tide changed again and KTM became the market leader, and Staff Sergeant Tommy Graham along with Major Tizard negotiated the KTM deal for six new bikes.

Events

Exercise NATTERJACK. Exercise NATTERJACK was initially organised by Mr Ted Johns, an ex-Recovery Mechanic working as an instructor in SEME, as a means of generating additional funds to offset the annual running costs of the team. The event started in the late-1970s and, today, over 30 years later, the event is of national status and remains a firm favourite on the national enduro calendar. REME riders turn out in large numbers to support the event and, later in their careers, they find themselves as the lead organisers.

Exercise ENDURING HELP. Exercise ENDURING HELP was a charity fund-raising event based around a 24-hour non-stop off-road military motorcycle competition. The concept was thought up by Major

Jason Butler REME, assisted by Captain Helen Currie REME and Warrant Officer Class 1 Marc Bartolini, who were serving with SEME at the time. It involved a unit team of four riders riding one Army GS motorcycle for as many laps as possible in the 24-hour period. It was a resounding success and regularly attracted over 100 teams generating thousands of pounds.

The Scottish Six-Day Trial. The Scottish Six-Day Trial, based in the Scottish Highlands, is the flagship event of the trials calendar. REME was well represented with Captain Sandy Mack REME taking a leading role for over 20 years. Corporal Mack (as he then was) first rode the event in 1993, when he showed great determination to finish after the drive sprocket bolts on his machine failed. After an ingenious repair, he limped home and finished just within his time allowance. He went on to ride for a further 15 years, moving to become Corps Team Manager in 2008. REME always featured strongly in the Army team, either as riders or support crew. Major Tizard (1998 to 2000), Staff Sergeant Billy Rhodes (2001 to 2003), Lance Corporal Neil Hawker (2001 to 2006) and Sergeant Daz Hestleton (2002 to 2015) all justified their selection by putting in determined rides and ultimately finishing the event on multiple occasions.

The International Six-Day Enduro. The International Six-Day Enduro, often referred to as the Olympics of off-road motorcycling, in which over 30 nations compete, is one of the toughest events in the world. The Army Team always has a strong REME presence with the support crew being an entirely REME affair. Riders Corporal Steve Hunt, Corporal Kevin Murray, and Lance Corporal Neil Hawker dominated the Army Team over a number of years, finishing well up the field in their various classes. In 1998, Corporal Murray and Corporal Hunt were selected to ride for the Great Britain Under 23 Squad and competed for Great Britain in the World Championships in Spain and Wales. Over a number of years, the trio achieved the following medal tallies: Corporal Hunt – two gold and five silver; Corporal Murray – four gold, two silver and two bronze; Lance Corporal Hawker – one silver and two bronze. In 2008, during a tough event held in the high desert plains of Chile, Corporal Murray was selected as the Great Britain reserve rider. Although not called upon, he rode as part of the Army Team, which finished eighth in the world.

The Army Championships

The Army Championships are held annually with the aim of determining the Army Champion. The event is seen as the pinnacle of Army motorcycling competition, with fierce rivalry between the top Corps riders. Although for the most part, the best traditions of gentlemanly sporting traditions were maintained, there was the occasional bout of skulduggery. On one such occasion in 1993, the leader's bike was sabotaged with sugar in the fuel and he was forced to retire. Some years later, and after an Army-level enquiry, it was discovered to be an all RCT (later RLC) affair.

The 1990s saw the dominance of the RCT riders fall into decline and the rise of a strong young REME cohort of riders. Between 2000 and 2015, REME was the Corps to beat winning 13 from the 15 Championships with Corporal Bob Braithwaite (one), Corporal Hunt (four), Corporal Murray (four) and Lance Corporal Hawker (four) taking the coveted Army Champion title. In 1996, after being dismayed by the lack of imagination and organisation, the then Captain Tizard volunteered to organise the next event. Trials and enduro dominated, but also included were an acceleration and brake test, and a graded hill. One year, the riders even made a visit to the rifle range, with points added for missing the target. Keeping the format fresh every year, Captain Tizard went on to organise the event for 17 years.

Notable REME Riders

REME personnel have always been heavily involved with motorcycling at both Corps and Army level. Individuals would pass through the ranks riding for the Corps, starting as young riders and honing their skills, before being promoted into junior management positions and passing on their knowledge to develop the younger riders. Riders such as Tony and Craig Altass, Bale, Cotty, Case, Eggleton, Gordon, Gorse, Green, Graham, Neil and Daz Hestleton, Johns, Langmead, Mack, May-Miller, Martin, Summerfield, Taylor and Tizard all went on to mentor REME riders and to manage the REME Team.

Upon their retirement, Warrant Officer Class 1 May-Miller and Warrant Officer Class 2 Martin went on to support and manage the Great Britain national teams for the International Six-Day Enduro for well over 10 years. Calling upon their REME peers they made a huge contribution to the Great Britain team.

Lieutenant Colonel Tizard started riding Army motorcycles in 1986 and, after successes as a rider, manager and organiser he took the role of

Head of Army Motorcycling. In 2015, for his longstanding contribution to Corps and Army motorcycling, he was presented with a Lifetime Achievement Award by the Corps. Upon his retirement, he handed over his duties to Lieutenant Colonel Bob Case REME, another long-standing REME motorcyclist and so the baton was passed on.

The Future
In 2015, REME closed its well-established Corps motorcycle club in Bordon and moved to the new 'Home of the Corps' in Lyneham. The location may have changed, but the Corps will continue to excel in motorcycle sport through its people, their boundless enthusiasm, drive, skill and determination, which will ensure success for a long time to come.

NETBALL

Overview
Interest in REME netball has steadily grown over the years and peaked in 2014 with the team winning Division 2 of the Inter-Corps Championships. The calendar for netball starts in October each year with this competition, although some of the large Corps hold their own inter-unit competitions. During the Inter-Corps Championships, there are two divisions and, in 2014, there was the largest ever entry of 16 teams, with the AGC and RLC entering three teams each. It is at this competition that the Army Coach identifies talent and invites players to attend Army trials.

Again in 2014, a record number of players attended trials and, after two days of selection, a squad of 40 players was chosen to represent the Army throughout the season. These were split into two squads, Open Squad and Development Squad, and they train and play against civilian teams. After each training weekend, the squad is reduced to 24 so that prior to the Inter-Services Competition in March there are only the two squads of 12 remaining. Each squad plays against the other Services over a three-day period and this year both squads were undefeated and were crowned Inter-Services Champions. During this competition, the Combined Services Coach and two civilian guest selectors select the Combined Services Squad who train and compete against the civilian Service teams (Fire, Police, Prison, Civil Service), as well as other civilian events throughout the summer, before the whole process starts again in October with the Inter-Corps Championships.

2014/2015 Season

Historically, REME has entered at least one squad into the Inter-Corps Championships, although in 2010 there were sufficient numbers to enter two teams. With a few days training prior to the event, the 2014 REME Squad was confident that it could do well. After winning all pool stages, the REME Team found itself against the RE in the final, who were the Division 2 Winners the previous year. With a number of new players in the squad, nerves played their part in the first half and REME found itself four goals down at half-time. With just one positional change at half-time, Warrant Officer Class 2 Caswell coming on in defence, and a team talk that simply said "we have nothing to lose so go for every ball", REME came out strongly.

Craftsman Stanley took the team talk to heart and came out with a number of outstanding interceptions early in the second-half. This gave the centre court players of Warrant Officer Class 1 Rudge and Warrant Officer Class 2 Stones the chance to move the ball down to our shooting end, where our shooters, Major White and Lieutenant Martin had the opportunity to score. With one minute remaining on the clock and the scores level, the RE Team had the advantage of the centre pass, which was swiftly passed into their shooting circle, but their shooters couldn't perform under pressure, the shot was missed, the rebound was secured and the ball was swiftly moved up the court into the hands of Lieutenant Martin who scored the winning goal with less than 10 seconds on the clock. REME then just had to hold onto the ball on their centre pass to win 12–11 and be crowned Division 2 Winner 2014, which is the best result for the Corps in its history.

Notable REME Players

There have been a number of REME players who have represented the Army over the years: Major White, Lieutenant Field, Warrant Officer Class 1 Rudge, Lance Corporals Farish and O'Brien, Craftsman Ramsden, Stanley and Tester. This season, only Craftsman Stanley and Major White were selected to attend Army trials but, unfortunately, Craftsman Stanley then deployed to BATUS as temporary staff for the winter and so was unable to take part in any training session.

Major White was initially selected for the Army Squad in 2007 and the Combined Services Squad just two years later. Since then, she has not only been a player, but she has coached, captained and been the general glue that has kept both squads together. As a goal shooter, she is one of only two people out of a team of seven on court who can score a goal, so the pressure to score within three seconds of receiving a pass is something that she puts in a great deal of practice in order for her to remain as accurate as she is (82% shooting average for the 2014/2015 Season). But the game can't be won without the whole squad working together, and it is under her direction as captain, that the Army Open Squad has been undefeated for the past four seasons and the Combined Services won the World Corporate Games title in 2013. She was also named Player of the Tournament at the 2013 Inter-Services Competition. Major White is a significant driving force of netball in the Hampshire area; she coaches, umpires and plays for an Andover-based team that plays in a number of leagues including the Hampshire Regional League.

ORIENTEERING

The history of orienteering begins in the late 19th Century in Sweden, where it originated as military training. The actual term 'orienteering' was first used in 1886 at the Swedish Military Academy Karlberg and meant the crossing of unknown land with the aid of a map and a compass. The British Army has followed suit and still, as of 2015, considers orienteering to be military training.

Orienteering is a distinct form of navigation, a challenging outdoor adventure sport that exercises both the mind and the body. The aim is to navigate in sequence between control points marked on a unique orienteering map and to decide the best route to complete the course in the quickest time. Orienteering can take place anywhere from remote forest and countryside, to urban parks and cities. Most soldiers have had a bad experience with a map and compass on a military training area during a long, cold and wet night. It's therefore quite understandable why the appetite for orienteering has not always been huge amongst soldiers.

There remains a regular group of dedicated orienteers within the Corps that continue to keep REME on the map, literally, and they are always looking for new participants. Orienteering takes place every Wednesday with almost all cap badges leaning on the British Army Orienteering Club for regular events. The Corps holds the REME Orienteering Championships annually, and regularly provides runners for the Army and Combined Services Orienteering Teams. Orienteering is an activity that anyone can take part in and prior experience is not required. Those wanting more information should contact the REME Orienteering Secretary, whose updated details are available from the REME Corps Sports Secretary.

PARACHUTING

The Corps Team has maintained a strong tradition of competitive and display parachuting over the last 20 years, while evolving along with the sport. The core of the parachute team is made up of dedicated individuals who have, in many cases, stayed with the sport from joining as a Craftsman through to Warrant Officer level and then commissioning. The team 'grows' its own instructors, who have gone on to inspire junior members of the Corps. This, coupled with a targeted recruitment programme at the Phase 2 Training Schools, has kept a steady stream of talent coming into the sport.

Competitive Parachuting

It is not possible to list all those who have competed for the Corps during the period covered, but the individual and team successes that follow deserve mention.

Captain Sarah Laughton REME was a young Lieutenant in 1993, when she was taken on her first student skydive by Lieutenant Colonel Mike Smith REME. She progressed rapidly in the sport, joining the Army 8-Way Formation Skydiving (FS) Team in 1994 and winning a bronze medal at the National Championships in 1995, followed by a gold medal in 1996. After this, she went on start the Vmax Team in 1998, the hugely successful Woman's 4-Way FS Team that won the World Championships in 1999, 2000 and 2003 in Australia, Spain and France respectively.

The Army 8-Way FS Team through the 1990s had a strong contingent of REME skydivers. Along with Captain Laughton, Lieutenant Colonel Smith, Major John Horne REME, Warrant Officer Class 1 Brian Dyas and Sergeant Rob Ames all represented the Army in various years. Warrant Officer Class 1 Dyas and Captain Laughton were part of the 1996 Army Team, which won the National Championships and went on to became the British 8-Way Team that represented UK at the World Championships in Turkey in 1997.

Lieutenant Colonel Smith, who retired from the Army in 2007 at the age of 63, was one of the longest serving members of the team. He has championed the sport throughout his career. In 1992, he convinced the

Nuffield Trust to provide a super grant of approximately £180,000 to purchase a Britten-Norman Islander Aircraft for the British Forces Cyprus Parachute Club, which is still active today. In 1997, he staffed a paper to obtain funding to procure a pool of parachute equipment to be used for military adventurous training expeditions. The pool of equipment was used extensively year on year and expanded to some 30 sets from the original 15 that were bought. Competitively, he has won innumerable medals at 4-way and 8-way formation skydiving, representing REME and the Army. He was a member of the Army 8-Way Team from 1993 to 1997, Army 4-Way Champion in 1998, Army Individual Accuracy Champion in 2003, along with overall Armed Forces Champion. On top of this, he is a prolific instructor, training students on expeditions since 1991. Although retired from the Army at the time of writing, he was still an active instructor on Army expeditions.

Corporal Darryl 'Daz' Gardiner started parachuting with the Corps Team in 2001. He was a most enthusiastic and capable student parachutist who in a very short space of time developed into an outstanding parachute instructor. His love of the sport knew no bounds. He won his first two Armed Forces gold medals in 2003 and, by 2007, he had added a further seven medals to his collection. He made a huge contribution to the Army Parachute Association and to REME as an accelerated free fall instructor, organising three expeditions to the USA, and as a static-line instructor where he trained over 200 'first jump' students. As a display parachutist, he acted as the second-in-command of the team, carried out over 30 displays for the Corps and 20 attached to other teams. In all, he made a phenomenal contribution to the team in only six years. Corporal Gardiner sadly died in Afghanistan in January 2008 whilst on operations with the Brigade Reconnaissance Force, but his memory lives on in the form of the 'Daz Gardiner Sword'. This is presented to the best intermediate 4-way formation skydiving team at each year's Armed Forces Parachute Championships. The REME Team last won the Daz Gardiner Sword in 2013.

Four members of the Senior REME FS Team entered the UK National Championships in 2001. The team trained and evolved over the years that followed, going on to win the Best Corps Team Trophy at the Armed Forces Parachute Championships four years running in the period 2004 – 2007.

Outside of the more traditional disciplines of formation skydiving and accuracy, the relatively new discipline of competitive wingsuit flying grew in popularly within the REME Team. The Armed Forces Championships in 2014 saw REME enter a team and win a silver medal. The growth in popularity of wingsuit flying has been led by Warrant Officer Class 2 Steve Murfin, who has competed in national and international competitions.

Display Parachuting
Alongside the competitive aspect of the sport, the REME Display Team has carried out many displays each year, parachuting into parades, shows and events around the country and internationally. (**See Plate 65**)

Since the Army Display Team Review in 2009, all display teams within the Army have been under increased pressure due to the element of high risk, deemed to be outside of Army core business. The challenge of retaining the REME Display Team was taken on by Colonel Martin Oakes (late REME), who took over as Chairman in 2007. Colonel Oakes had come to the sport from military parachuting, via a posting as Commander of the Joint Air Delivery Test and Evaluation Unit and was the driving force behind the adaptation of the REME Display Team to ensure its continued existence. He campaigned tirelessly to keep the REME Display Team authorised as all other official Army parachute teams folded, other than the Red Devils, the full-time team.

This effort has borne fruit with the REME Display Team going from strength to strength thereafter. Led by Warrant Officer Class 1 Shane Cook as the REME Display Team Leader from 2004 to the time of writing, the Team has gained an excellent reputation. Particular highlights included performing at Tank Fest at the Bovington Tank Museum every year from 2009 to 2013 and enduring support to the Army versus Navy Polo Match. Warrant Officer Class 1 Cook was selected to lead the display into the National Armed Forces Day events in 2013 in Nottingham.

In 2014, the REME Display Team was chosen to take part in the Commonwealth Games Queen's Baton Relay. This involved a huge amount of media coverage as the team jumped with the baton, flags and smoke into Gleneagles on live TV. Warrant Officer Class 1 Cook has said "carrying the Commonwealth Games Queen's Baton into Gleneagles is the highlight of my display career."

ROWING

REME at the Henley Royal Regatta
For the 10 years prior to the time of writing, REME soldiers and officers have regularly contributed to both Army and Combined Services elite-level

crews. The pinnacle and finale of the rowing season is the Henley Royal Regatta, where crews ranging from club to international level compete over five days in and amongst the pageantry of this great British summer occasion. REME rowers represented the Army in the Regatta every year since 2005, with many notable successes, including winning the Britannia Challenge Cup (Coxed Four) in 2006, qualifying for the elite-level Silver Goblets (Pairs), only being beaten by the Olympic Bronze Medallists in 2008. REME also made up half the Army crew that qualified for the Prince of Wales Challenge Cup (Quadruple Sculls) in 2012.

The 4 Battalion REME Successes in 2006
Fresh from a year that saw deployment to both Afghanistan and Iraq, 4 Battalion REME released 20 novices to attend that year's summer Army Learn to Row Courses. Blessed with outstanding weather, enthusiasm and a full complement of coaches the novices quickly progressed from their initial daily capsizes into the River Thames into tanned athletes, working together with real purpose. Their transformation was evident at the 2006 Joint Services Regatta when, despite training for only two weeks, their superior fitness and desire saw them dispatch RN and RAF novice crews that had many times their experience. The final novice race of the day perfectly encapsulated this, as the REME Novice Men's Eight initially fell behind to a well-drilled RAF crew and had to fight back inch by inch for 1,500m before winning by a canvas in the final sprint for the line. Overall, at that Joint Services Regatta, the REME crews won more events than the entire RN contingent and three times as many events as the next Corps.

Notable REME Rowers
Andy Galloway (retired Recovery Mechanic) earned this recognition as a notable REME rower, as he has helped Major Mike Schofield RE hold Army Rowing together throughout his service and civilian career, as well as winning at the Joint Services Regatta almost every year he has competed. He coached REME crews in his own time, and has continued to compete in winning Masters Crews for Christchurch Rowing Club. Without his support and continuity, REME rowing would have struggled.

Other Notable Successes by REME Rowers
Other notable successes by REME rowers include:
- 2005–2014 Henley Royal Regatta, at least one REME rower was a member of a qualifying Army Crew

- 2006 National Championships, Bronze Medal Coxed Four
- 2007 Kingston Head, Winner Men's Eight
- 2007 Head of the River Race, Army crew finished 12th with REME crew members
- 2012 Joint Services Regatta, REME Winners Quadruple Sculls
- 2012 Joint Services Regatta, REME making up 5 of the 9 members of the victorious Army Men's Eight
- 2013 and 2014 Joint Services Regatta, REME Winners Coxed Four and Coxed Pair.

RUGBY

Rugby Union

In the early 1990s, there was some decline in REME Arborfield, a team that had grown many of the talented players that the Corps had seen in the 1970s and 1980s, and it was removed from League 3 South in 1991. New talent was coming in and, under the watchful eye of Captain Dennis Prowse REME, young players continued to be developed. As a result, throughout the mid-1990s, some two-thirds of the Army Colts 1st XV and a large proportion of the Army Under 21 Team was made up of young REME talent.

As we moved through the early-1990s, the mix of talented youth and wily experience made competition for places in the Corps team fierce, and the Bowen Cup (SEE v SEME) became the opportunity for many to prove their worth. As an end-of-season climax, fuelled by 'black hand v technician' rivalry, the game was not for the faint-hearted and tested the mettle of some of the key rugby stalwarts of the time. These included: Major Brian McCall REME (more recently President of REME Rugby), the late Staff Sergeant Seymour Wilson, Staff Sergeant Pete Lockitt (a regular member of the Combined Services and Army Squads), Warrant Officer Class 2 Keith Sked (Corps Captain and subsequently Director REME Rugby Union), Warrant Officer Class 1 Keith Bartlett and Warrant Officer Class 1 Jack Mouncey who championed the 2nd XV players of SEE.

At the start of the 1990s, although there were no Army League/Merit Table rankings, REME was undefeated for some years enjoying a high reputation. As rugby was becoming more professional in approach, Major Prowse was appointed the first Director of REME Rugby and set the strategic vision for Corps rugby. Behind the scenes, Miss Teresa Gillespie, a long-standing supporter, continued to deal with the administration. Given the quality of REME players, a number of whom were also on contracts at clubs such as Harlequins, Coventry and Wakefield, and with a vibrant fixtures list, this set the conditions for the Corps to take the newly-formed Merit Table by storm in the late-1990s.

From 1999 to 2002, REME basked in glory as Merit Table Winners and also Inter-Corps Champions. Performance in military competition was reinforced by performance in civilian competitions and successful tours to Folkestone, the 'Akrotiri 10s' in Cyprus, and the 'Loulé 15s' in Portugal emphasised the prominence of Corps rugby. Having coached the Corps Team, as well as Reading, the Combined Services Under 21 Team and Surrey County Under 16 Team, Major Prowse hung up his boots in 2002 and, thanks to his effective succession planning, Major Keith Sked REME and Warrant Officer Class 1 Steve Powley slipped seamlessly into the REME Director of Rugby and Head Coach appointments respectively. Having set the bedrock, REME rugby continued to flourish.

One Club, Two Codes, Seven Teams
In 2005, under the Directorship of Major Pat Burns REME, and under the team management of Major Ewen Cameron REME and Head Coach Major Dave Hammond REME, REME rugby set the future for Corps-level rugby across the Army. Up to this point, rugby union and rugby league had existed as separate organisations, and had been managed and funded independently. This was all to change. Having impressed the Chairman of REME Rugby with his vision for the future, Major Burns set about unifying the codes with Major Rich Naivalurua REME. Together, they developed a structure that represented all aspects of the game. By drawing on the best practice and experience of all involved with both rugby union and rugby league codes, REME rugby led the way for an organisation off the field and, needless to say, success followed on the field.

In 2010, Major Cameron took over as the Director and REME rugby's reputation as a force to be reckoned with grew, running seven teams in the UK and Germany, and with over 200 men and women having represented the Corps. The men's team continued to compete for the lead of the Merit Table and, in 2011 and 2013, topped the Merit Table and completed those seasons as Inter-Corps Champions. The 'Corps 7s' and the Pegasus Trophy provided showcase events for wider Corps participation. The staging of both during the Corps Weekend in 2012 attracted huge support, and inspired an increase in potential Corps players and support of REME rugby.

The REME rugby tour ethos was rekindled and ambitious large-scale overseas tours were undertaken with REME men touring South Africa in 2006, New Zealand in 2009 and Texas in 2012. These have been a fantastic success and the tours enabled Corps representatives to participate and rekindle the rugby connections made through the years. More widely, Corps rugby continued to fly the flag internationally and, in 2011, at the 'Akrotiri International 10s Tournament' in Cyprus there were three REME teams appearing in the Cup, Plate and Bowl Finals.

Further afield, REME players representing the Army made decisive contributions in winning the Defence World Cup in Australia and New Zealand (run alongside the Rugby World Cup). Of special note is Corporal Ceri Cummings, who, as a dual cap for rugby league and rugby union, was also named Man of the Tournament in the Defence Rugby World Cup (which the British Army won), and was then subsequently selected for the Northern Hemisphere in the 'Help 4 Heroes Rugby Match', along with some real legends of the game.

REME Germany

Throughout the 1990s, REME rugby in Germany flourished and, due to the drive and influence of Major Nigel Williams REME, established a firm base in Osnabruck, around 12 Armoured Workshop REME and, subsequently, 1 Battalion REME. Competition on the Corps circuit was fierce and the fixtures between REME Germany (REME(G)) and the Royal Signals for the Cathedral Cup and the RLC for the Ellis Cup were fierce competitions. The team comprised a fine balance of experience and youth, with the likes of Warrant Officer Class 2 Ian Davies, Sergeant 'H' Harrison and Corporals Dai Dalton and Ted Heath, and this vibrant mix made the Corps a force to be reckoned with.

Throughout the seasons, dominance of the Corps Championships varied but the coaching staff of Sergeant Paul 'Taff' Andrews and then subsequently Staff Sergeant 'Pip' Piper brought the best out of the players and nurtured many to go on to representative level. The REME(G) front row of Corporal Axel Rees, Captain Arwyn Lewis REME and Corporal Dougie Hinds were selected to represent BAOR/BA(G) (British Army (Germany)) after demolishing the Royal Signals front row, much to the annoyance of their coach, Major Andy Hickling. A BA(G) tour to New Zealand and Fiji in 1997 was the reward on which the Corps was represented by Captain Lewis, Corporals Phil Davies and Colin Brookes.

For many, the season's finale was the 'Aarhus 15s Tournament' and the 'Aalborg 7s'. At both events, the Corps could be relied upon to give a good account of itself both on and off the field, and Sergeant Tony Oakley was always on hand to ensure everything was kept above board.

Success continued into the late-1990s under the direction of Major Russ Booth REME and Captain 'Geordie' Wright-Rivers REME with a win over REME UK in the Pegasus Trophy and successive wins in the Ellis Cup against the old enemy the RLC. As a result of these successes, Captain Wright-Rivers was selected to be Director of Rugby for the BA(G) representative side over the period 2000 to 2003.

As with the majority of sports in Germany, the intensity of operations and drawdown saw REME(G) rugby slow down apace. The team managed one more victory in the Ellis Cup in 2009 and, in 2010, reached the Plate Final of the 'Akrotiri 10s' competition.

In 2015, the decision was taken to call an end to the REME(G) rugby side given the ever-reducing numbers of REME soldiers in Germany. In April that year, the team embarked upon a farewell tour to Seattle (USA) and, following training and practice matches with the Seattle Saracens, the then US Champions, the tour concluded with a narrow defeat against a tough Tacoma side.

The REME(G) rugby team's final match was in June 2015 when the last Pegasus Trophy match was contested in Paderborn against REME UK with the result being a wholly acceptable draw before the trophy, and REME(G) rugby, was retired.

REME Women's Rugby

REME women's rugby got off the ground in 2004 under the direction of Major Neil 'Shaky' Graham REME. Having been involved with men's Corps rugby for a number of years, he decided to put together a women's team in order to take part in the 'Akrotiri 10s'. With drive and enthusiasm, the team and the support went from strength to strength but as most of the women had never played before and had to be 'home grown' it took a couple of seasons to build them up. They learnt the hard way, suffering regular and substantial defeats in the early years, but remained undaunted, and having achieved their first win against the Royal Signals, there was no looking back.

After just a couple of seasons, the winning ways continued and the REME Women's Team maintained their presence at the top of the Inter-Corps Championships. In 2010, Major Steve Bridges REME took over as Team Manager and Warrant Officer Class 1 'Mitch' Mitchell as Head Coach. As the success in military competition continued, this was reinforced by success in civilian competitions, most notably winning the 'Bournemouth 7s' in 2011. The Corps-level performance was ultimately reflected on the bigger stage and soon the REME presence within the Army and Combined Services for both rugby union and rugby league was established. By 2013, six REME women formed the backbone of the Army side, and this season saw Corporal Rosie Haigh selected as Captain of not only the Army Team but also the Combined Services Team, and she has subsequently earned her a place in the England Academy.

Rugby League

It would seem that the first formal Army inter-unit match was hosted in 1993 by 4 Armoured Workshop REME (shortly before becoming 3 Battalion REME). The former Commanding Officer recalls:

> 'I was asked by some members of the unit whether they could play league rugby against some like-minded souls in another unit. I checked with the chain of command whose feathers seemed ruffled. They explained that rugby league was not an official Army sport and had never been played in the Army, that the matter should perhaps be run past Public Relations in MoD. After more in that vein, I said that I was primarily interested in satisfying myself that there would be no problem with insurance, and that unless I was ordered not to allow it the match would go ahead. I wasn't, it did, and the game did not see the end of civilisation as we know it'.

Other Army units started playing rugby league, and it became an official Army sport in 1994, with REME sportsmen having been key contributors ever since.

REME Veterans

The REME Veterans Team under the management of Warrant Officer Class 1 'Monster' Howard had their first run out in 2010, and is made up from all standards of rugby players, Army Veterans, ex-Corps and unit-level players. This is a team in which old friendships form the backbone.

A REME Veterans match is now a precursor to the main Corps fixtures, and as the likes of Major Jamie McMeechan REME, Warrant Officer Class 2 Abel Mataintini refuse to grow old gracefully, this will continue. Undaunted enthusiasm has brought unrivalled success most notably in the 2012 'Corps 7s', when they won the Plate Competition by proving once more that youth and fitness are no match for experience and cunning.

Representative Honours
Throughout the mid-1990s and into the 2000s, the Corps had a glut of Army and Combined Services players. Combined Services and Army Team regulars of Major McCall, Captain John Morgan REME and Captain Graham Morgan REME (Corps Captains all), with Staff Sergeant Steve Powley, Staff Sergeant Jon Murley (Corps Captain), Staff Sergeant Paul Simon, Staff Sergeant Paul 'Fred' Oakes, Corporal Ken Ferdinand, Corporal Paul Jinks and Lance Corporal Mick Watson hot on their heels. These players continued to maintain a strong Corps presence in the Army Senior Squad, a trend that has continued to the present day.

More recently, Corporals Ceri Cummings and Tom Chennell have made a significant contribution to both the Army and Combined Services, with Corporals Mundy, Titchard-Jones, Fisher, Jackson, Shaw, and Lance Corporal Komasavi representing the Corps at Army level. On the women's side, Warrant Officer Class 2 Caroline Wilde, Sergeant Rosie Haigh, Corporals Barnard, Metters, Roberts, and Lance Corporal Lewer, and Craftsman Marsh, have gained representative honours for both rugby union and rugby league. At the veterans' level, Major Cameron, Warrant Officers Class 1 Howard, Mitchell, and Thomas, and Sergeant Reffell have been stalwarts representing both the Army and Combined Services Teams.

Other Notable Achievements
Beyond REME rugby activities, members of the Corps have maintained considerable influence and made significant contributions to Army and Combined Services rugby through representation in key management positions. These include: Staff Sergeant Axel Rees (Head Coach, Army Rugby Union), Captain Burnie Burnard REME (Assistant Army Coach), Major Naivalurua (Director Army Rugby League), Colonel Andy Allen (late REME) (Chairman Army XXXV), Major Quant REME (Secretary Army XXXV), Captain Geordie Wright-Rivers (Director of Rugby BA(G) after Major Quant), Staff Sergeant 'Tiny' Baker (Head Coach

Army XXXV), Brigadier Allan Thomson (late REME) (Director Army Rugby Coaching), Lieutenant Colonel Lewis (Secretary Army Rugby Coaching), Lieutenant Colonel Dave Edmondson REME (Chairman Army Referees Society), Major Cameron (Secretary Army Referees Society). Furthermore, in recognition of their contribution to REME rugby, Brigadier McCall and Major Cameron have been awarded Corps Lifetime Achievement Awards.

SAILING

Sailing is a recognised Army and Corps sport, and genuine adventurous training pursuit, that contributes to the rich fabric of Service life. It enhances the robustness of officers and soldiers by providing character-forming opportunities for team and leadership development in challenging, adventurous environments. The REME Sailing Club (formerly REME Yacht Club) is still dedicated to providing those opportunities for all Corps personnel, including serving members, retired members, dependents and veterans. Throughout all its disciplines, REME sailing is a key part of Corps life. It is one of the very few military clubs that can offer everything from simple paddle boarding to international offshore racing, and all by the utilisation of its own high-quality and well-maintained sailing equipment.

Offshore Sailing

Since the early-1990s, the Corps has operated two Hallberg-Rassy yachts (HR 31, HR 34 and most recently HR 342), named 'Seahorse' and 'Lillibulero' respectively. Initially, these were replaced every four years but as prices rose and REME's finances shrunk, ownership was extended from four to eight years, each hull being replaced every four years. 'Master Craftsman', the Westerly Sealord purchased for REME 50 went round the Atlantic circuit again in 1994/1995 before being sold.

    The creation of the Army Offshore Sailing Centre (AOSC) allowed the Corps to join other clubs affiliated to the Army Sailing Association (ASA) at Royal Clarence Yard, Gosport. The Corps remained here until the winter of 1999/2000 when the AOSC relocated to Dolphin Pool, Fort Blockhouse in association with the Royal Navy Sailing Association (RNSA). The move to the AOSC's current facilities in Sword Building took place in 2012 and were formally opened in May 2013. The close association with RNSA encouraged Major Mike Barham REME in 2005 to oversee the purchase and campaigning of a Sonata sports boat,

'Artel', in the RNSA Wednesday evening series as well as other events in the Solent. She was replaced in 2007 by the acquisition of a Hunter 707, 'Artificer', after which began a close relationship with Southampton UOTC who regularly sailed her.

Entries in the Fastnet Race continued on and off, led by Major Steve Taylor REME, racing both Nicholson 55 and Challenge 67 yachts. 2007 was a notable year, as REME's entry won both Inter-Services Trophies for the first time and finished 20th overall in IRC (a system of handicapping sailboats and yachts for the purpose of racing) in a Challenger 67, named 'Endeavour'. (**See Plate 66**) UK end-of-season REME Yacht Club rallies continued in the autumn of each year but, from 2007, they followed a Solent-based Sail Training Week (STW). Changes to the qualifications awarded by the Royal Yachting Association (RYA) instructors on such events made the viability of STWs questionable. This unfortunately led to STWs in Germany becoming regattas with no formal qualifications being awarded.

Another innovation from Major Barham was Exercise CHANNEL PICKLE, an adventurous sail training expedition in November each year for those soldiers on Phase 2 Training on a Nicholson 55 yacht. Named after HMS Pickle, the vessel that brought news of Admiral Nelson's death to England after Trafalgar, the exercise started in 2003 and has run every year since.

Notable REME Offshore Sailors

HRH The Princess Royal presented Major Alan Johnson REME with a Lifetime Commitment Award in 2007 and, in 2008, an Outstanding Commitment Award to Major Barham for their contributions to the REME Yacht Club and offshore sailing. (**See Plate 67**)

Another REME sailor, Lieutenant Colonel (Retd) Syd Thomas, was presented with a Lifetime Commitment Award in 2011 for services to both Services and Cardiff Bay Yacht Club racing. A number of ex-REME personnel joined the Joint Services Adventurous Sail Training Centre after retiring from the Army in the 2000s. Of these, ex-Staff Sergeant Vaughan Marsh is notable. He rose from Staff Skipper in 2005 to Fleet Operations Manager and Training Officer, before moving to the RYA in May 2013 as Chief Instructor Sail Cruising. Other REME sailors have continued to make a significant contribution to Army offshore sailing over the past two decades. Successes have included contributing to Army wins in the Services Offshore Regattas in 2004 and 2010 and Royal Ocean Racing Club series events. In 2014, two REME sailors, Major Will Naylor

REME and Captain Phil Caswell REME took part in the Round Britain and Island Race as part of the six-man Army team achieving second in class in this gruelling event.

Dinghy Sailing
Until the 2000s, the predominant teaching, cruising and racing dinghy for REME was the universally renowned Bosun dinghy of which the Corps had a small fleet located at Theale near Arborfield. Its stability and robustness made it the perfect all-rounder and was used for many years until new and exciting hull and sail designs became more readily available. Better and cheaper manufacturing costs allowed for the development of lightweight fibreglass hydrodynamic (flat run aft) planing boats such as the Laser II. Keeping up with the latest hull designs, and combined with asymmetric gennakers (a large headsail), the REME Yacht Club reduced its displacement-hulled Bosun fleet and purchased new dinghies such as the Laser II, RS 400, Laser Stratos and Laser 2000. By the mid-2000s, the thermoplastic plastic constructed Laser Pico completed the new REME fleet, as its trainer for RYA Level 1 and 2 qualifications.

Lance Corporals Nolson and Nellyer representing REME and the Army at the Laser 2000 National Championships, Pwllheli 2009

Throughout the 1990s, the Corps developed many new sailors by running numerous RYA courses at Theale. A small cohort of instructors, led by Major Chris Jones REME, taught all levels of sailing from Basic and Advanced through to Instructor. This reached a pinnacle in 1998, when the Corps became a certified RYA Teaching Establishment in its own right. Unfortunately, this ran for only a few years as the operational pressures of the 2000s led to fewer instructors and administrators being available to manage and run the centre. All dinghy training thereafter came under the auspice of the Berkshire Sail Training Centre, which was also based at Theale.

Keelboat racing remained very popular with the Corps and hit an all-time peak in 1997, when 18 three-man crews turned up for the Sea View Regatta, held annually on the Isle of Wight. For many years, the Sea View Regatta was the highlight of the dinghy season and, due to the yacht-like nature of the Mermaid keelboat, it attracted a host of offshore sailors as well. Sadly, additional expenses, rising costs, an increase in overseas operations and the prolific growth of more radical sports saw the Keelboat racing days of the Corps dwindle. After a brief spell with the Island Sailing Club at Cowes sailing Sonars, the last event (to date) took place in 2011 in the Western Solent (Lymington) with racing conducted in SB3 Sports Boats. This was a class of boat that the Corps had recently purchased with the drive of Major Barham. A lifting-fin keeled one-design boat, the REME SB3 (later re-designated SB20) was named 'Sail Army Engineering' and soon began competing in regional (including Cowes Week), national, European and even World Championships events, skippered predominately by Major Barham, Warrant Officer Class 2 Ray Olive and Captain Chris Haugvik REME.

Team Racing has been the pinnacle of dinghy sailing for many years within the Corps, Army, Services and civilian circuits. A unique combination of boat handling, speed control and an interpretation of the rules creates very exciting racing. It is probably the only sailing competition, which regularly sees the lead boat turning around and sailing back round the course. Over the period, the Corps was extremely fortunate to have two of the most pre-eminent Team Racers in the Army, Colonel Nick Ross and Colonel Bruce Burnett (both late REME). Needless to say, when they teamed up to race in inter-Corps, ASA or inter-Services competitions they usually swept the board. After their retirement, the Corps Team was Captained by Captain Andy Snell REME but, most recently, by Captain Haugvik.

Notable REME Dinghy Sailors

As explained in Volume 2 of Craftsman of the Army, Colonels Ross and Burnett have been two of the most superlative REME dinghy and keelboat sailors. Colonel Ross retired from the Army in 2002, but not before achieving great success at all levels of competition. His record of winning the many and various individual sailing trophies in REME and Army sailing is unsurpassed. He won the REME Sea View Trophy on 10 occasions, the ASYC Gold Cup five times, the ASA's Sea View Trophy twice, the Warminster Trophy, Laser II Cup, the ASA's Individual Dinghy Trophy, the Inter-Corps and Inter-Services Team Racing Championships (many times), as well as the Coningham Cup (Sea View Inter-Services Team Racing) nine times in a single decade.

He complemented his amazing racing pedigree through his support to REME and Army sailing by means of appointments. After fulfilling the role of ASA Dinghy Secretary, he became the ASA's Rear Commodore (Dinghies) between 1992 and 1998, fostering sailing Army wide. He continued sailing in and captaining the team, whilst discharging his Flag Officer's duties – no mean feat. In his last few years, his contribution to sailing extended beyond the Corps and the Services by coaching the GB Racing Team, becoming a member of the UK Team Racing Association Committee and Chairman of the RYA's Team Racing Committee.

Colonel Burnett came from a similar sailing background to that of Colonel Ross. Captaining his university team whilst at Cambridge, he declined the opportunity to compete at the World Laser Championships in 1973 (after successfully qualifying) to commission into REME, after which, he began a distinguished military racing career. A REME, Army and Combined Services Team Captain, Colonel Burnett also won the REME Sea View Keelboat Regatta on eight occasions over a 14-year period, as well as the Tibble Trophy, Gold Cup, Coningham Cup and countless Inter-Corps and Inter-Services Team Racing Competitions.

Other successes outside the Army included, becoming the National Champion in the National Swallow Keelboat Class (an Olympic class from 1948) in 2000. REME appointments included Dinghy Secretary, Rear Commodore (Dinghies) and RYC Principle Secretary but later he took over the post of ASA Rear Commodore (Dinghies) from Colonel Ross, which he held for eight years. Notably, the ASA Rear Commodore (Dinghies) Flag Officer's position was then handed over to Colonel Alex Tucker (late AAC but originally a REME sailor), which he held for six years, true testament to the calibre and influence REME has had over Army sailing throughout the past three decades.

Windsurfing

Windsurfing equipment has changed enormously over the last two decades. The introduction of carbon fibre masts and 3D sail design has improved sail response; meanwhile, the boards themselves are lighter, shorter and wider. In the early-2000s, the Army followed international sailing by introducing 'Formula Boards'. With a width of one metre and 1.5 metres shorter than the old 'longboards', they were capable of higher speeds and carrying very large sails.

Early in the period, the Corps was performing very well on long boards with Dave Tindall winning the Army Championships in 1993 and 1996, Neil Curry and Brian Grieves competing on the national circuit in 1994, and REME winning the Army Team Championships in 1995. In 1996, Dave Tindall was joined on the Inter-Services heavyweight podium by Brian Grieves, who remained dominant in windsurfing until his retirement in 2007.

In the lightweight category, Tim Sands and Ron Moles were frequently on the Army podium. REME's depth of competent sailors brought frequent Inter-Corps Series first or second places. That depth being generated through training camps and activities led by the likes of Jon Uttley, the first RYA windsurfer trainer in the Corps. In 1998, three REME sailors attended the world longboard championships with Brian Grieves (34th), Steve Myers (57th) and Mark Borley (63rd). REME remained competitive on the introduction of Formula Boards, with prizes also being taken by Jed Cunningham (who also represented the Army at international level) and Steve Myers (who led a major Army windsurfing expedition to Hawaii and kept the Renesse Competition (Holland) running).

Overseas trips proved popular, with training camps at Lake Garda in 2005 and Dahab in 2006, 2007 and 2008. These locations were ideal to practice the free-ride skills needed in the increasingly popular slalom and master blaster type races. More important, they encouraged younger soldiers who were much needed to replace a number of REME windsurfers retiring and deploying on frequent operational tours. These retirements included Neil Curry, who received an ASA Outstanding Achievement Award for 21 years' service to Army windsurfing.

The growth in novices was further aided by some enthusiastic Senior Non-Commissioned Officer instructors at SEME and SEAE who, though not gladiators on the race scene, contributed a huge amount. In 2006, Neil Vidot won the Army Novice Championships and was the first person to go on to win the Inter-Services Novice Championships since 1989 (Dave Tindall). REME won the Army Novice Championships again in 2007 and

2010. The financial crisis and changes in exchange rates made overseas training very expensive and a Weymouth-based camp was conducted in 2010.

Corps windsurfing success continued after 2006 with second place in the Inter-Corps Series being a regular occurrence. Jon Leng and Paul Finn were both sailing well and represented the Army. In 2008, Army windsurfing moved from Netley to Thorney Island, which was less windsurf friendly due to the tidal mud flats and absence of family camping facilities that had been a key part of REME social sailing and the REME Yacht Club BBQ. Racing became concentrated at Hayling Island, with further changes being made to the format to encourage more sailors to compete, taking into account the fact that increasing numbers of sailors were less experienced. As at 2015, REME continues to maintain a strong position in Army windsurfing, winning the Inter-Corps Series and having four sailors in the top 12 at the 2014 Army Championships.

Kitesurfing

Kitesurfing came into the mainstream in 1999, when windsurfing manufacturers started producing commercial equipment. Constant improvements in safety equipment and kite designs meant that the sport was easier and more forgiving to beginners and, from 2000 onwards, participation in the sport has increased considerably. There are now a number of different disciplines being developed including freestyle, wave riding and racing. The Army has concentrated on freestyle and started to introduce racing from 2014.

In 2008, REME took the lead in developing kitesurfing as an Army sport with initial efforts concentrated on gaining recognised status. Major Martyn Jones REME and Warrant Officer Class 1 Sammy Samanjoul focused on junior development, instructor training and the start of a pool of regular participants. Major Jones and Major Jim Edwards RE organised the first Army Championships in 2009 at Rhosneigr (Wales), which significantly emphasised that the fledgling sport could attract a large number of competitors across the Corps and Army. The majority of participants were REME with Captain Mark Jeffery REME winning the novice competition.

From 2009 to 2012, the number of participants increased with overseas trips to Hurghada (Egypt) and the Cape Verde Islands (West Africa). REME was instrumental in starting the annual Inter-Services Competition in 2012, which has now grown to one of the largest kitesurfing competitions in UK.

An annual development camp was started at Newgale (Wales), which increased participation at the junior level. This camp also introduced Corporal Adam Hogarth and Lance Corporal James Matthews, who had regular success at the Inter-Services Competition and are usually seen on the podium.

Army and REME kitesurfing are now firmly established at Thorney Island and the Army is recognised as accredited British Kitesurfing Association trainers. The UK centre runs beginner and instructor courses throughout the year, but courses are also accredited in Cyprus at Lemmings Beach.

REME Sailing Club

REME sailing provides the variety and reward necessary to inspire and maintain enthusiasm for military life, particularly in the gaps between military commitments, exercises and in supporting de-compression. Over the past two decades, operational challenges have taken their toll on the support to all sport within the Corps. However, now with the future amalgamation of the REME training schools at Lyneham, there is a great opportunity to develop an inland sailing centre of excellence, where young soldiers can be introduced, gain entry-level qualifications, be developed by the Corps instructors, learn to race and then move into Army and Combined Services Squads.

SQUASH

Squash is an individual game on court and a team game off it. The same ethos that personnel display through their core values are brought to the fore in one of the most demanding and physical sports soldiers can participate in.

For the last 23 years, REME squash has taken great strides forward, both in the number of players and the success enjoyed by individuals and teams alike. The grass roots involvement has continued to expand with personnel encouraged to enter civilian squash leagues if they want to bring their playing standard to a level at which they can represent the Corps and the Army. Staff Sergeant Lenny Westover runs the Army Berkshire Premier League side with the team maintaining a good position within the strong league. The Army has an Army Development Team in the Wiltshire League, with various REME players representing the Army including Corporal Warren Mitchell and Corporal Gibson. The annual

REME Championships (traditionally held in November) are a mixture of individual and team competitions (minor and major units), from which the Corps team is selected for the Inter-Corps Championships later in the same month.

The Corps team has enjoyed limited but high profile success at both Army and Combined Services levels. Major Gary Clarke (REME before commissioning and transferring to the AGC) was the Army Individual Champion from 1994 to 2001 and the Inter-Services Champion in 2006. His success has been emulated in more recent years by Staff Sergeant Westover, who has been the Army Under 25 Champion (1999 and 2000) and Men's Individual Champion (2005, 2009 and 2012). In 2014, he crowned his playing career by becoming the second REME player to lift the coveted Inter-Services Championship Trophy. Other notable contributions have come from Craftsman Cotton who was the 1992 Army Squash Under 25 Champion followed by Sergeant Fraser White who was also the Under 25 Champion in 2004 and 2006. Lieutenant Colonel Phil Croager REME enjoyed success with the Army team, winning the Inter-Services Veterans Team in 2009 and again in 2012. This was followed in 2014 by the Over 45 Trophy.

The two technical training schools continue to be a source of quality squash players with SEME winning the major unit trophy no less than 15 times between 1992 and 2015. Staff Sergeant Ritchie Fewtrell is the current talent scout, and regularly drags 'volunteers' along to squash development days organised by Warrant Officer Class 2 Craig Lilley. These development days are run in both Harrogate and Aldershot with the aim of Corps regulars getting together for training and passing on their expertise to emerging players. The REME Open Champion Trophy has been sewn up by Staff Sergeant Westover since 2008 (there were thoughts about donating it to him), but preceding him were: Warrant Officer Class 2 John Mayhew in 2007, Major Croager in 2005 and 2006, Corporal Westover from 2002 to 2004, Staff Sergeant Al Jobes in 2001, Staff Sergeant Gary Clarke from 1996 to 2000, Captain Croager in 1995, Captain Tam Tervitt REME in 1994 and Corporal Gary Clarke who won from 1989 to 1992.

The REME Team has had mixed fortunes over the years, but is now experiencing a resurgence. Some 10 years ago, the team had strength in all playing positions but, over the years, various members of the team have come to the end of their military careers and playing for the team. Despite this challenge, the team had continued to produce the results when competing against other Corps teams and finishing third was a regular occurrence. Unfortunately, the team was finally relegated to Division 2, four years ago after nearly 20 years of continuous representation at the highest level.

Now, with a great deal of time and investment in junior players, and the successful turnout for the 2014 REME Championships, we are starting to see a new generation of squash player coming forward to help return the team to its former glory days.

In 2014, the Corps entered two teams into the Inter-Corps Championships. The A Team captained by Staff Sergeant Westover convincingly won Division 2, after completing a clean sweep across the board. The B Team, under Captain Dean Eamer REME, gained promotion from Division 3, narrowly missing out on outright victory by a single game. The second team has had an absence of several years, as a lack of quality players prevented a team being entered.

2015 will see REME squash saying goodbye to Colonel Alistair Duncan (late REME), who has been the Chairman for the last eight years. His predecessors (all late REME) were: Colonel Clive Ward (2002 to 2006), Colonel Stuart Cameron (2000 to 2001), Colonel Roger Owen (1995 to 1999), Colonel Tony Meagher (1993 to 1994) and Colonel Rob Lucas (1991 to 1992).

Corps members have also made progress towards their England coaching qualifications, whilst ensuring that up-and-coming players are drafted into the Army Development Team. This team regularly plays in the Wiltshire League and players experience a far higher level of squash than they would at unit level.

STRENGTH SPORTS

These are fledgling REME sports, which have successfully advanced as a result of the enthusiasm and ability of the key players involved.

Strongman (Strong Soldier)

REME Strong Soldier is for both male and female REME personnel. It was officially 'born' in 2013, when the sport gained 'other sport' status with the REME Sports Association. The Chairman was Warrant Officer Class 1 Porter, an experienced powerlifter and strongman, who had competed for many years in both military and civilian competitions. He achieved many podium finishes, including first place in the highly-regarded Chase Competition and second place at the Welsh Open.

The Secretary, Warrant Officer Class 2 Cooper, has been an integral part of bringing the sport of strongman and strongwoman to REME and Armed Forces communities. He has competed in a number of civilian competitions, including Yorkshire's Strongest Man and the Southern Qualifiers for Britain's Natural Strongest Man in the Under 105kg category.

The Treasurer was Staff Sergeant Wall, who had been competing at strongman and powerlifting events since 2012. Warrant Officer Class 1 France, Warrant Officer Class 2 Cooper, and Sergeant Slinger were other key competitors who represented REME at Forces Strongman Championships.

REME Strongest Soldier was incorporated into Forces Strongman, which held up to five competitions each year. An annual REME Championships, to determine the strongest REME soldiers, was inaugurated in May 2014 at 10 Battalion REME at Bordon. It was anticipated that the move of REME Phase 2 Training to Lyneham would facilitate the administration and growth of the sport in the longer term.

Powerlifting

Powerlifting was not a REME sport in its own right, although it was hoped that, in 2015, it would join strongman as a recognised sport within the Strong Soldier Division. It had been an Army sport for several years, which was in no small measure due to the contribution of REME personnel, who have competed at Army, Combined Services, national and even international standards since 2003.

Powerlifting came onto the REME scene when the then Sergeant Neil Thomas broke a Guinness World Record in January 2003, whilst on his Artificer Weapons Course – a record for a Serviceman that still stood at the time of writing. Following his success, permission was granted for Staff Sergeant Thomas to complete his trade training early and depart for New Zealand to compete at the World Uniformed Services Games. And to this day, he remains the only individual, who, technically, was presented with his artificer scroll on a beach south of the equator. On return, he achieved the recognition of powerlifting as a sport within the Army and across the three Services. From 2003 to 2007, he was Secretary and, in 2008, became the Chairman of Army Powerlifting. Through Major Neil Thomas (now AGC), REME can claim to be directly involved with the establishment of the sport in the Armed Forces. At the time of writing, Major Thomas was Vice President of the World Federation, President of the British Association, and still Chairman of Combined Services, a position held for the previous six years.

Staff Sergeant Madronal Army Champion 2005 – 75kg Category

The early years of the sport saw individuals competing in many unit-level and Army events. From 2004 onwards, REME saw individuals competing within the national framework with Major Thomas and Captain Seb Madronal REME the main achievers. In 2005, Major Thomas won his first World Bench Press Championships. In 2006, REME finished runner-up to the RE Team at the Army Championships. Antwerp in 2007, saw double success for Major Thomas and Captain Madronal at the World Single Lift Championships, whilst Corporal Kim Zilke and Major Thomas represented England at the European Championships in Como (Italy). In 2007, 7 Battalion REME become the Army Bench Press Champions and the Corps became Army Team Champions, something replicated in 2008.

Since then, the sport has grown but with success coming to individuals more than the Corps as a whole. By 2015, Sergeant Simon Robb had become the most dominant force within the Army and Combined Services, and was selected to compete at the National Championships and to obtain selection to compete for England at the 2015 World Championships. Captain Madronal was still competing at national level, albeit as a veteran, and had also qualified as a national-level referee. Craftsman Oliver Boulton had been selected to represent the Army at numerous Combined Services Championships and has been part of the men's team for three years, all of those being victorious for the Army. At the time of writing, REME personnel and teams were dominating the Services powerlifting scene, with further talent having emerged, including Corporal Robert Adkins and Lance Corporal Rebecca Jones.

SWIMMING AND WATER POLO

Swimming and water polo team strength during the mid-1990s was on the increase, with Corps numbers for the UK, ATRA (Army Training and Recruitment Agency) and BAOR teams breaking 50 swimmers each. This rise continued while the likes of Brigadier Martin Boswell (late REME), Major Jim Fenwick REME, Captain Joe Eggert REME and Major Ian Corroyer REME headed up their respective teams. Every year, REME battalions, workshops, LADs and training organisations were able to enter teams into the divisional events and, if successful, this would lead on to competing at district and then Army-level events. It would be at this time that a number of the younger swimmers would be selected for Army Team training. It was common to see Sergeant John Scott, Craftsman Neil Graham and Sergeant Phil Stockwell on the selection list each year for both swimming and water polo disciplines.

Towards the late-1990s, Major Corroyer became the Secretary for this sport while Staff Sergeant John Scott ran swimming and water polo within ATRA. In 1999, there were huge successes at all levels. Divisional and district wins led to a place at the Army Inter-Unit Finals and a first for any REME unit. The Army Inter-Unit Shield was theirs and remained so for the next few years. This same year also saw a win at the Inter-Corps Championships, the first in 10 years. Staff Sergeant John Scott now took on the role of Secretary and inter-Corps organiser, while the teams continued to enjoy successes at all levels and including water polo, which now saw some younger swimmers take a big interest in what was traditionally an older player team game. Corporals Ben Young, Neil Graham, Si Naylor and Roy Illingworth were the mainstay of any water polo squad, regularly training with the Army team and playing at Combined Services level.

Women's swimming was now also on the up and, by 2005, a core of 25 women swimmers was now common at Corps events but less so at smaller inter-unit meetings. The same was seen throughout other Army and Corps teams. Warrant Officer Class 2 Simon Parsons and Major Laura White REME have made huge advances in increasing the popularity of swimming and water polo among the women of the Corps and numbers training and competing are still on the up.

It should be noted that the Corps has been running the annual Inter-Corps Swimming and Water Polo Championships, since its inception in 1989, and it now attracts hundreds of competitors to compete in the Aldershot Garrison Swimming Pool. During its first decade, the Championships consisted of just four relay events and a water polo competition. Captain John Scott REME has competed since its start, 27 years ago, and has organised the event for the last 18 years. Its popularity boomed in 2000, when it was expanded into a two-day event, and now 30 games of water polo are regularly played and 63 swimming events competed for, covering all strokes and distances.

TARGET SHOOTING

Small-bore

Target shooting is a test of marksmanship skills, concentration, self-discipline and motivation. It has considerable military training value in improving individual marksmanship ability, while competition helps individuals cope with the pressures and stress inherent in operational shooting. Small-bore target rifle shooting is a recognised Army sport. It is carried out using rifles, which are designed specifically for the sport in accordance with rules laid down by the national shooting body, the National Small-bore Rifle Association, and the International Shooting Sport Federation, the body governing target shooting up to Olympic standard. Shooting is conducted from the prone, standing and kneeling positions indoors at 25 yards and outdoors at 50 metres, and from the prone position outdoors at 100 yards. While the distances aren't great, the precision required is; the '10 ring' at 50 metres is only 10.4 millimetres in diameter for all positions, and the light '.22LR' bullets are deflected by even slight winds.

An accomplished small-bore marksman, Major Dom Lethbridge REME started shooting competitively in 1992. (**See Plate 68**) He has represented the Army since starting the REME Commissioning Course in 2001, and was first selected for the Combined Services in 2005. Appointed discipline Captain for the REME Rifle Association in 2007, Major Lethbridge secured funding for and established the Corps Centre of Excellence at Bordon, directly resulting in increased Corps participation and now reflected in a significant REME presence in Army representative teams.

He took on Captaincy of the Army Small-bore Target Rifle Team in 2011, and has Captained the Combined Services against the English

Small-bore Shooting Union. At the time of writing, Major Lethbridge has been five times Army Champion, twice winner of the Wilkinson Sword for the Combined Services Individual Champion, and holds the Inter-Services Three Positions (prone, standing and kneeling) and Inter-Services Aggregate Trophies. He competes regularly for civilian rifle clubs and his home county of Suffolk, and in 2013 was runner-up in the Army Sportsman of the Year Awards.

WINTER SPORTS

During the 1990s, the Corps continued to run the REME Alpine Skiing Championships from the Fellhorn area in Bavaria, later moving to Jungholz to bring both the alpine and langlauf competitors together. Building on the success of the Corps Championships, the REME Alpine and Snowboarding Race Training Camp in Stubai (Austria) was launched in 2000. Exercise SUPREME GLACIER grew in popularity over the next 15 years, providing multidiscipline instruction and race training for alpine, snowboard and Telemark (named after the Telemark region of Norway, where the discipline originated) disciplines. The training camp delivers focused coaching to prepare participants for onward competition at divisional and Army championships.

In 2002, the Corps Winter Sports Championships relocated from the REME facilities in Bavaria to Les Contamines (France) to bring all three disciplines together into a single family event at the end of each winter season. The resort was chosen as a proven one, that could raise the standard and professionalism of alpine, Nordic and snowboarding racing within the Corps. With the addition of Telemark events in 2012, Les Contamines served the needs of the Corps well for 12 years, providing multidiscipline championships for all standards. In 2014, the Corps successfully delivered its winter sports championships in two locations, Stubai Glacier (Austria) and Sjusjøen, north of Lillehammer (Norway), with great success. There were 1,370 personnel competing in REME winter sports activities, which truly encompasses the REME winter sport ethos of 'sport for all'. This new home for REME winter sports continues to be developed with the aim of recreating combined championships from 2017.

Alpine Skiing

The popularity of the REME facilities in Bavaria and the long-standing Corps winter sports philosophy of 'skiing for all', remains the envy of many across the Army. To build on this success, in 2008, the Corps Committee created three winter sports committees to focus on maximising sporting talent from across the disciplines of alpine, Nordic and snowboarding. With the creation of the REME Alpine Committee, came the birth of the REME Alpine Ski Squad, a centrally-managed collection of the very best skiers from across REME. These carefully selected athletes receive equipment, clothing and focused high-level race training, in order to deliver two unit teams to compete in the Army Alpine Championships each year. Any member of the Corps can be selected for the squad and earn their REME Winter Sports Jumper. Members of the squad are rotated through two centres of excellence, in order to maintain two ski teams representing REME at the Army Alpine Championships each year. The results of the REME teams in the period 2008/2009 to 2014/2015 are shown in Figure 29.1 (at the end of this Chapter).

Nordic Skiing

Nordic Skiing in REME encompasses the separate international winter sports disciplines of cross country skiing and biathlon, as well as the Military Patrol Race. Prior to 2009, it was considered a sport but, in 2009, the demanding combination of physical endurance and sprint, and the leadership and personal discipline required to operate and train in austere and unforgiving conditions were fully recognised as individual military training.

Whilst Nordic skiing continued to be well supported throughout the 1990s, a step change in the approach to training occurred under Major Ian Duncan REME and Warrant Officer Class 2 Mick Bartlett. In 2004, a Corps Nordic training camp was established in Scandinavia. Initially in Norway, then Sweden, and finally settling in Sjusjøen (Norway) from 2007 onwards. In 2005, 2 Close Support Battalion REME was established as the Corps team and 10 Training Regiment as the feeder team for novice skiers, with appropriate resources allocated. This strategy change resulted in a steady increase in levels of participation and performance across the Corps, with Warrant Officer Class 1 Dave Butters, a three times Corps Champion, instrumental in early talent identification and training.

CORPS SPORTING AND ADVENTUROUS ACTIVITIES

Lance Corporal Gleave in his Great Britain strip

From 2010, multiple REME teams were competing strongly in the divisional and Army Championships, culminating in 2 Close Support Battalion REME achieving second place in both the 1 (UK) Division and Army/National Biathlon Championships in 2012 and 1 Close Support Battalion winning the 1 (UK) Division Championships and coming second in the Army/National Biathlon Championships in 2015. In 2010, Corporal Carl Gibson became the first REME soldier to win the British Biathlon Union Club Championships and he raced for the Great Britain Biathlon Team at the Biathlon World Championships in Khanty-Mansiysk (Russia) in 2012. Lance Corporal Alex Gleave was selected for the Great Britain Biathlon Team in 2013 and raced in the International Biathlon Union World Cup and for Great Britain over the 2014/2015 Season. Corporal Sean Bowen was selected for the Great Britain Biathlon Team in 2014.

Snowboarding
It was another bone-chilling cold day on the Stubai Glacier in December 2001, when an intrepid collection of REME snowboarders pioneered the first Corps Championships alongside the Royal Engineers and Army Medical Services. Such was the success of that event, and the subsequent interest shown from across the Corps, that the following year Warrant

Officer Class 2 Del Elesmore and Corporal John Craig organised the first stand-alone REME Snowboarding Championships; a competition that has endured, with increasing popularity, ever since.

For those unfamiliar with the world of snowboarding or even winter sports, a little introduction may be needed if only to emphasise the rapid growth of this challenging sport. Born in the mid-1960s, competitions flourished through the 1970s and 1980s and, with growing popularity, it became an Olympic winter sport in 1998. The first Army Snowboarding Championships followed a year later in 1999. Despite its relative youth, snowboarding as a competitive sport within the Army appears to have been the fastest growing Army sport of the last decade, bar none.

The typical competition consists of several disciplines, some of which are very familiar to the skiing fraternity, others (Boardercross or Boarder X) are more akin to a cross between a wrestling match and a BMX race.

The Parallel Giant Slalom discipline is very familiar to all winter sports enthusiasts, racing through gates down a fixed course. In this version, riders race head-to-head on two identical slalom courses set side-by-side, competing on a knock-out basis.

In Boardercross, four riders of varying ability race down a narrow course, similar to a motocross course, with banked corners, turning gates, bumps and jumps. Rules are practically unheard of other than 'start' and 'finish'. In other words, a certain amount of 'interaction' between riders is tolerated, even expected. The top two riders of each race go through to the next round.

In Slopestyle, individuals descend a straight-line course of jumps of varying sizes, rails and boxes (down which one can slide in any orientation including on one's face, backside or stomach if it goes wrong). Points are scored for style, difficulty, height and overall impression.

One of the undoubted attractions of snowboarding is that it incorporates many of the qualities required in military life. Each soldier benefits from the hard physical and mental challenges of this sport. They learn to push themselves to their physical limits, to understand and be comfortable with being outside their 'comfort zone' and to strive to improve. In 2008, REME snowboarding greatly benefitted from the establishment of a dedicated committee, initially led by (then) Major Fraser-Hitchen REME and supported by the likes of Captain Peter Bramwell REME, Captain Mark Greensmith REME, Lieutenant Simon Nicholson REME, Warrant Officer Class 2 'Jono' Johnson and Sergeant Matt Phillips.

Most notably, it has not taken the Corps long to establish itself as one of, if not, the best in the Army. Holding the title of Army Champions, no less than nine times between 2001 and 2014, the Corps Team has finished in the top two and, occasionally, the top three, every single season. A further accolade and testament to the development of REME riders, has been the selection of at least one or more riders to represent the Army at the Inter-Services Ski and Snowboard Championships in every season since its inception.

Other notable achievements in this period include Lance Corporal Natt Baker qualifying for the British Championships in Boardercross and Captain Simon Nicholson's selection for the GB Boardercross Squad in 2010. Corporal Mark Blackbourn was also selected for the British Championships in 2014, and finished seventh in Boardercross.

REME snowboarding is very junior compared to the more established disciplines, but it undoubtedly punches well above its weight at Army and tri-Service level. Interest in the sport is still exceptionally high amongst junior soldiers, as it brings a sense of cohesion, fun and challenge in a relaxed and inviting atmosphere.

Telemark Skiing

Since its formation in 2010, REME Telemark strategy has been to provide the opportunity for 10% of the Corps to try (taster, formal course or expedition participant) Telemark skiing. Whether accomplished downhill skiers, proficient snowboarders, Nordic gladiators or novice sliders, during Exercise SUPREME GLACIER/SNOW SPANNER each year the REME Telemark Committee has created the opportunity for REME soldiers to try and learn a physically challenging and exciting skill, in a controlled sporting/expeditionary environment.

The successive Chairman (Colonels Jeanne Ebling and Rod Williams (both late REME) and, currently, Lieutenant Colonel Alistair Bryant REME) have ensured there are consistently improving Telemark skiing opportunities. This has meant harnessing an enthusiastic, determined and diverse team to provide challenging, novel and enjoyable training, whilst encouraging taster entry to the sport to develop an emerging cross country and racing capability.

In November 2014, on Exercise SUPREME GLACIER in Austria, 24 Royal Marine and 12 REME soldiers, received formal Telemark instruction over two weeks. This culminated in two formal races (Telemark Classic and Parallel Sprint) with 20 to 25 competitors in each race. On

Exercise GROUSE in the Allgäu (Germany) in February 2015, an eight-man preparatory expedition training camp was held. This included mountain cross and back country touring training, as well as avalanche awareness, transceiver use, group management and general winter mountain safety. This camp was planned in direct support of the high-profile exciting Telemark Expedition in 2016 to highlight the challenging diversity of the discipline, and to exploit media awareness to grow interest within the Corps.

ADVENTUROUS ACTIVITIES

Adventurous training is an integral part of military training, which provides Services personnel with the opportunity to participate in and gain qualifications in a range of activities. It has been defined by MoD as:

> 'Challenging outdoor training for Services personnel in specified adventurous activities that incorporates controlled exposure to risk, in order to develop: leadership; teamwork; physical fitness; moral and physical courage; as well as other personal attributes and skills that are vital to the delivery of Operational Capability'.

There is no fixed template for what comprises adventurous training. An adventurous training package may be tacked onto a broader training exercise or deployment, or it may be a standalone exercise, and it may be a one-off or a routinely repeated exercise. An adventurous training exercise may comprise a single activity, such as paragliding, or a combination of several. Typical adventurous training activities include: trekking, climbing, winter sports, parachuting (or paragliding), sailing, kayaking and other water sports. Many sports described in this Chapter have been carried out as adventurous training activities, and so much of the picture of REME adventurous training has already been covered.

Adventurous training activities are often not mandatory. The extent to which they are engaged in, and the quality of the training tend to reflect the initiative and enthusiasm of the organisers. As members of REME tend to have ample initiative and enthusiasm, it is not surprising that the Corps has made a fulsome contribution to Army adventurous training. Whilst the Army supports adventurous training, some of the more interesting and challenging exercises would not be possible without supplementary funding. As a Corps, REME has been willing to dip into its funds to meet the funding gap. For example, in 2012, the Corps provided some £73,000 to support 163 adventurous training activities in which 1,711 members of the Corps participated. Clearly, it is not possible in this Chapter to provide details of all the adventurous activities REME personnel have been involved in, but REME's commitment to adventurous training over the years has been well illustrated by the story of its facilities in Bavaria.

REME Adventurous Training Centre 1992–2015
By the mid-1990s, most 'regimental' ski huts had closed, as they were no longer being publicly funded under the Exercise SNOW QUEEN scheme. Adventurous training needs were to be met by the publicly-funded lodge in the Allgäu area. REME recognised the need to continue to run its own facility in the area, and identified a suitable lodge, Berghaus Lieb, which nestled high on the hillside above the picturesque hamlet of Gunzesried-Säge (Bavaria). This was initially rented in 1992 by the Commander Equipment Support 1 (UK) Division for the benefit of REME personnel. This was followed by a long-term rental and the development of the lodge into the REME Adventurous Training Centre (ATC).

As such, it soon came to be regarded as 'one of the jewels in the Corps crown'. Initially, it was supported by Corps funds but, in due course, it was to become a financially self-sustaining facility. During this time, the Corps continued to launch its summer and winter adventurous training needs from the 52-bed facility. The REME ATC provided units with the ability to deliver their own adventurous training by conducting hill walking, canoeing, rock climbing, white water rafting, paragliding, mountain biking and many other challenging pursuits throughout the summer months. During the winter months, the REME ATC was dedicated to alpine skiing, which also included giving REME families based in Germany, the ability to attend family skiing packages at a very affordable cost. (**See Plate 69**)

The Strategic Defence and Security Review of 2010 and the plan for Army 2020 undermined the financial viability of both the REME ATC and the REME Hotel (see Chapter 27 ('Other Corps Institutions, Facilities and Activities')). This was linked to issues related to the withdrawal from Germany, restrictions on the use of military staff in management roles, as well as tax issues related to changes in the Status of Forces Agreement. It resulted in the Corps terminating its lease on the facility in 2015.

Whilst the end of this era is a sad one for those who enjoyed the facilities provided, it is by no means the end of the story. At the time of writing, the REME Executive Committee was determined to facilitate a sustainable adventurous training solution for REME in the Army 2020 timeframe. Research has already been conducted with a view to providing a commercially-operated facility in regions of known interest to the Corps, possibly of a modular design, which can be expanded as necessary to meet the demands of the Corps.

The Rory Cape Memorial Award
The Rory Cape Memorial Award was instituted in 1974, with a bequest from the family, to commemorate Captain Rory Cape REME who took part in many adventurous activities before his tragic death from cancer in 1972. The aim of this prestigious award is to encourage and further the interests of adventurous and enterprising activities within the Corps. The award is made annually to the REME officer or soldier who is considered to have made the most outstanding contribution to adventurous or enterprising activities during the past year.

There is no fixed template for deciding the award. It may reflect personal achievement, as in the case Major Shenton, described earlier in this Chapter. It may reflect cumulative efforts, as in the case of Major Mark Smyth REME who organised and took part in a number of high-level mountaineering expeditions. It may also reflect the contribution made to helping others develop their skills, as in the case of Warrant Officer Class 1 David Lynch who was himself involved in skiing instruction and, over time, had personally enabled about 1,200 soldiers to experience winter adventurous training activities. An annual award is not made unless it relates to an activity of the highest merit, so the one thing that all the award winners have in common is that of exceptional achievement in the field of adventurous and enterprising activities. The winners of the Rory Cape Memorial Award between 1994 and 2014 are shown in Figure 29.2 (at the end of this Chapter).

Centre of Excellence	Team result at Army Championships	Competed at Inter-Services Championships	Awarded Corps Colours	Other Achievements
2008/2009				
3 CS Bn REME	7th	Cpl M Atkinson Cpl Franey	SSgt Packham Cpl M Atkinson Cpl Franey	
7 CS Bn REME	2nd			
2009/2010				
3 CS Bn REME	5th	Cpl M Atkinson Cpl Franey	Capt Mackay Sgt Gaskell	Army Female: Cpl Franey
7 CS Bn REME	4th			
2010/2011				
3 CS Bn REME	2nd		Maj Rogers SSgt Edwards Cpl Whiteley	Army Novice: Cpl Davis Army Junior: Cfn Kear Rory Cape: Maj Rogers
7 CS Bn REME	6th			
2011/2012				
3 CS Bn REME	3rd	Capt Thomas LCpl S Atkinson	Capt Thomas LCpl S Atkinson Cpl Earl-Mitchell	Army Junior: Cfn Kear
7 CS Bn REME	2nd			
2012/2013				
3 CS Bn REME	4th	SSgt M Atkinson LCpl S Atkinson LCpl Barron Cfn Kear	Cpl Clark Cpl Barron Cfn Kear Cfn Dillon	
7 CS Bn REME	2nd			
2013/2014				
3 CS Bn REME	2nd	Cpl S Atkinson Cpl Barron LCpl Orton	SSgt J Bennett LCpl Orton	
7 CS Bn REME	4th			

2014/2015			
3 CS Bn REME	Disqualified	Capt Thomas LCpl Hayes LCpl Orton	Capt Odling Sgt Spencer-Fleet Cpl Macdonald Cpl Hughes LCpl Hayes
5 FS Bn REME	2nd		

Figure 29.1: REME at the Army Alpine Championships

Year	Award Winner
1994	Col S J Abate
1995	Maj G F Tanner
1996	WO2 N Rennie
1997	WO2 M Brazier
1998	Capt S S Wetherall
1999	WO2 I Forbes
2000	WO2 M I Smith
2001	Maj M Smyth
2002	Maj N B Weller
2003	WO1 A C Thomas
2004	WO1 S R Willson
2005	WO1 S A Mansfield
2006	WO1 D Lynch
2007	Not awarded
2008	SSgt J Westlake
2009	Not awarded
2010	Maj A J Rogers
2011	Maj R K Shenton
2012	Not awarded
2013	Not awarded
2014	Not awarded

Figure 29.2: Winners of the Rory Cape Memorial Award 1994 to 2011

APPENDIX A

KEY CORPS POST-HOLDERS AND AWARDS

Colonel in Chief
Field Marshal His Royal Highness The Prince Philip, Duke of Edinburgh
KG KT OM GBE AC QSO psc(n)

Master General REME
Lieutenant General A C Figgures CB CBE DSc MA(Hons) MBA CEng FREng FIMechE FRAes FIET FCGI MAPD rcds hcsc psc+ me

Colonels Commandant as at 1 August 2016

Maj Gen	S M	Andrews	CBE	Appointed 1 Mar 10
Lt Gen	P W	Jaques	CBE	Appointed 1 Mar 12
Maj Gen	J McN R	Henderson	CB	Appointed 1 Jun 14
Maj Gen	R M B	Nitsch	CB	Appointed 1 Jun 14
Brig	M J	Boswell		Appointed 1 Oct 15
Maj Gen	P N Y M	Sanders	DSO CBE	Appointed 1 Jul 16
Maj Gen	M J	Gaunt		Appointed 1 Jul 16

Former Colonels Commandant (in post from 1993 – as at 1 August 2016)

				From	To
Maj Gen	C	Tyler	CB	14 Feb 89	14 Feb 94
Maj Gen	D	Shaw	CB CBE	01 Jan 91	31 Dec 95
Maj Gen	G M	Hutchinson	CB	01 Apr 91	31 Mar 96
Gen	Sir Rupert	Smith	KCB DSO OBE QGM	1 Nov 92	31 Oct 97
Maj Gen	M S	Heath	CB CBE	14 Feb 94	13 Feb 99
Maj Gen	J F J	Johnston	CB CBE	1 Mar 93	29 Feb 00
Maj Gen	P J G	Corp	CB	1 Jan 96	31 Dec 00
Maj Gen	A G	Sharman	CBE	01 Apr 96	31 Mar 02
Maj Gen	D J M	Jenkins	CB CBE	1 Nov 97	31 Oct 02
Maj Gen	P V R	Besgrove	CBE	14 Feb 99	13 Feb 04
Maj Gen	L D	Curran	CB	1 Mar 00	28 Feb 05
Lt Gen	D L	Judd	CB	1 Jan 01	31 Dec 08
Brig	R J	Croucher	CBE	1 Oct 01	31 Jan 04
Lt Gen	A C	Figgures	CB CBE	10 Apr 02	31 Mar 11
Gen	Sir Peter	Wall	KCB CBE	1 Nov 02	01 Nov 09
Brig	S J	Tetlow	MBE	1 Feb 04	31 Jan 08
Maj Gen	M	Huntley	CB	1 Feb 04	28 Feb 10
Brig	N T S	Williams	MBE	1 Feb 08	31 Jan 11
Maj Gen	T N	Tyler	CB	1 Mar 05	28 Feb 12
Maj Gen	I C	Dale	CBE	1 Jan 09	31 Dec 13
Brig	B W	McCall		1 Feb 11	31 Jan 14
Maj Gen	K E	Ferguson		1 Apr 11	31 Mar 16
Gen	Sir Christopher	Deverell	KCB MBE	1 Nov 09	1 Jul 16

Three-Star Officers Appointed between 1 January 1993 and 1 August 2016

Lt Gen	A C	Figgures	CB CBE	DCDS (Eqpt Capability)	19 Jun 06
Lt Gen	P W	Jaques	CBE	Chief of Materiel (Land)	8 Mar 16
Lt Gen	D L	Judd	CB	Dep Comd Jt Forces HQ Brunssum	3 May 04

Two-Star Officers Appointed between 1 January 1993 and 1 August 2016

Maj Gen	S M	Andrews	CBE	Dir Strat & Change HQ Surgeon Gen	30 Jun 09
Maj Gen	M A	Armstrong		Dir Svc Del DIO HQ Army	1 Apr 14
Maj Gen	P V R	Besgrove	CBE	DGES(A) Mar 97/ACOS J1 AFSOUTH Jan 00	24 Jun 96
Maj Gen	P J G	Corp	CB	DGES(A)	18 Jun 93
Maj Gen	L D	Curran	CB	President OB	22 Dec 98
Maj Gen	I C	Dale	CBE	DG Land Eqpt DE&S	15 Sep 08
Maj Gen	J McN R	Henderson	CB	GOC British Forces Germany	24 Aug 12
Maj Gen	M	Huntley	CBE	DG Log (Land)	4 Nov 02
Maj Gen	G I	Mitchell	MBE	Dir DCDC	19 Apr 16
Maj Gen	R M B	Nitsch	CBE	GOC Sp Comd, (Dir Army Pers Jun 15)	30 Aug 13
Maj Gen	A G	Sharman	CBE	DGLS	1 Jul 95
Maj Gen	T N	Tyler	CBE	DAG & DGSC(A) (DG Log Land/QMG Feb 06)	17 Apr 04
Maj Gen	M L	Wildman	CBE	DG WFM	Oct 99

Directors of Electrical and Mechanical Engineering (Army)

Brig	R J	Croucher	ADC	Apr 99	Mar 02
Brig	S	Tetlow	MBE ADC	Mar 05	May 05
Brig	N T S	Williams	MBE ADC	May 05	Dec 07
Brig	B W	McCall	ADC	Dec 07	Dec 10
Brig	M J	Boswell	ADC	Dec 10	Apr 12

Regimental Colonels and Colonels REME

Col	A G	Platt		Regt Col	1993–1995
Col	A H	Millington		Regt Col	1995–1997
Col	R M	Joy		Regt Col	1997–2000
Col	R B	Peregrine		Regt Col	2000–2002
Col	P T	McCarthy		Regt Col	2002–2004
Col	N	Moore	MBE	Regt Col	2004–2006
Col	J	Mulroy		Regt Col	2006–2006
Col	R N H	Bennett	MVO	Regt Col	2006–2008
Col	M L	Court		Regt Col	2008–2011
Col	I P	Gibson	ADC	Regt Col	2011–2012
Col	I P	Gibson	ADC	Col REME	2012–2013
Col	D G	Scott	ADC	Col REME	2013

Corps Secretaries

Brig	M W	Clark		1993	1995
Col	D R	Axson		1995	2002
Brig	A D	Ball	CBE	2002	2013
Col	S A M	Jarvis		2013	2013
Lt Col	M	Tizard		2013	2014
Lt Col	W J R	Barclay		2013	2016

KEY CORPS POST-HOLDERS AND AWARDS

Corps Artificer Sergeant Majors

Date	Incumbent
2003	WO1 (ASM) J P Swan
2003–2004	WO1 (ASM) C J Howell BSc MCMI
2004–2005	WO1 (ASM) B D Lamont IEng MIIE
2005–2008	WO1 (CASM) J W Walker MEng BSc(Hons) IEng MIET
2008–2010	WO1 (CASM) J M Murley IEng MIET MCGI
2010–2012	WO1 (CASM) S J Jones BSc(Hons) IEng MIET
2012–2014	WO1 (CASM) M G Mason IEng MSOE MCGI MCMI
2014–2016	WO1 (CASM) L J Condron IEng MIMechE MCMI
2016	WO1 (CASM) R J Bateman IEng MSOE MIRTE CMgr

Territorial Army Key Posts

Brigadiers

Brig	Celia	Harvey	OBE QVRM TD	Asst Comd HQ FTC	Serving
Brig	Bill	O'Leary	QVRM TD DL	ADMwS APC	Serving

Colonel REME TA (or Colonel REME Reserves)

Col	George Illingworth	TD	1995–1998
Col	Tom Gillanders	TD	1998–2001
Col	John Harvey	TD	2001–2004
Col	Andy Ewens	TD	2004–2007
Col	Vince Mifsud	OBE TD	2007–2010
Col	Mandie Cran		2010–2013
Col	Ian Adkins	(Col REME Reserves)	2013

Operational Awards for Gallant and Distinguished Service

Date	Rank	Name	Previous Award	Theatre
	**Conspicuous Gallantry Cross (CGC)**				
28 Feb 08	Cpl	Adam W Miller	Citation Chapter 9	Iraq
	**The Most Excellent Order of the British Empire (Military Division) Third Class or Commander (CBE)**				
11 May 92	Col	Peter V R Besgrove		NI
08 May 98	Brig	Andrew C Figgures		FRY
	**Military Cross (MC)**				
31 Oct 03	Sgt	Craig G J Comber	Citation Chapter 8	Iraq
19 Jul 07	SSgt	Christopher B Lyndhurst	Citation Chapter 9	Iraq
19 Jul 07	LCpl	Paul C Wilson	Citation Chapter 9	Iraq
28 Feb 08	Lt Col	Robert C Fram	Citation Chapter 9	Iraq
25 Jul 08	Cpl	Richard S Street	Citation Chapter 11	Afghanistan
	**Queen's Gallantry Medal (QGM)**				
12 Oct 93	Cpl	C G Tierney		NI
10 Nov 95	WO2	R W Wells	BEM	NI
	**The Most Excellent Order of the British Empire (Military Division) Fourth Class or Officer (OBE)**				
21 Nov 94	Capt	M Savage		NI
08 May 95	Maj	P H K Miller		NI
08 May 95	Cpl	B W Carruthers		Rwanda
10 Nov 95	Maj	P D Phillips		NI
10 Nov 95	Sgt	J M Mackie		FRY
13 May 97	Maj	A U Campbell		NI
13 May 97	SSgt	I W Purchase		NI

KEY CORPS POST-HOLDERS AND AWARDS

Date	Rank	Name	Previous Award	Theatre
08 May 98	Sgt	P J Long		NI
08 May 98	Capt	S R Mason		NI
29 Oct 99	Maj	J Power		NI
03 Nov 00	Maj	R M B Nitsch		FY Albania
03 Nov 00	Cpl	K Fitzgerald		FY Albania
30 Oct 01	WO1	A J R Boyle		FY
19 Apr 02	Capt	D J Bailey REME (V)		FY
29 Oct 02	Sgt	P R Cutler		Afghanistan
31 Oct 03	Cpl	J P Fleming		Iraq
31 Oct 03	Maj	F J Pettifer		Sp to Op TELIC
09 Nov 05	SSgt	N D Allcock		Iraq
15 Dec 06	Maj	D J Eastman		Afghanistan
28 Feb 08	Capt	R L Earl		Afghanistan
06 Mar 09	SSgt	J P Guthrie		Afghanistan
		Queen's Commendation for Bravery (QCB)		
08 May 98	Cpl	C G Tierney		NI
09 Sep 05	Sgt	P M Caress		UK Exercise (Eagles Eye)
09 Sep 05	Sgt	G W Mather		UK Exercise (Eagles Eye)
24 Mar 06	Cpl	J M Hughes		Non-Combatant Gallantry
06 Mar 09	Cpl	G M Jones		Iraq
25 Mar 11	Cfn	R Bowden		Rest of World
30 Sep 11	LCpl	J D Taberner		Miscellaneous

Date	Rank	Name	Previous Award	Theatre
	Queen's Commendation for Valuable Service (QCVS)				
10 Nov 95	Capt	N J P Sharples		FRY
10 Nov 95	Cfn	J E Flux		FRY
10 May 96	Sgt	N C Kerr		NI
08 Nov 96	Sgt	S Belson		NI
08 Nov 96	SSgt	M J Phillips		FRY
13 May 97	WO2	P M Feeney		NI
13 May 97	WO2	R J Simpson		NI
05 Dec 97	Lt Col	R A Martin		FRY
05 Dec 97	A/WO1	P G Pinchard		NI
08 May 98	WO2	A J Parkinson		NI
19 Oct 98	Maj	P G Mitchell		FRY
07 May 99	SSgt	M J Farley		NI
29 Oct 99	Capt	D J Bailey REME (V)		FRY
31 Dec 99	SSgt	P J Carney		Kosovo/Mac
14 Apr 00	Col	S J S Cameron		FRY
14 Apr 00	WO2	C Darroch		FRY
14 Apr 00	Cpl	M E Grason		FRY
14 Apr 00	Maj	G B Hills		FRY
03 Nov 00	WO1	S P March		NI
06 Apr 01	Capt	R F Casey REME (V)		FRY
30 Oct 01	Maj	P T Gooderson		Sierra Leone
19 Apr 02	Maj	T J McClung		NI
29 Apr 03	WO2	J V F Voss		NI

Date	Rank	Name	Previous Award	Theatre
30 Sep 03	Lt Col	E C Feldmanis		NI
31 Oct 03	Cfn	A L Marshall		Iraq
31 Oct 03	Capt	L Rosie		Iraq
31 Oct 03	WO1	L Sankey		Iraq
31 Oct 03	WO2	J R Scott		Iraq
31 Oct 03	Sgt	A L Tyler		Iraq
31 Oct 03	Cpl	D E Williams		Iraq
23 Apr 04	Sgt	S H Brown		NI
23 Apr 04	SSgt	S R Peacock		Iraq
07 Sep 04	Maj Gen	A C Figgures	CBE	Iraq
19 Jul 07	Maj	A Burton		NI
19 Jul 07	SSgt	D Devlin		NI
19 Jul 07	SSgt	P Harland		Iraq
25 Jul 08	Cpl	G D Wilson		Iraq
11 Sep 09	SSgt	J S Reeves		Afghanistan
25 Mar 11	Sgt	R McClenaghan		Rest of World
30 Sep 11	Cpl	M J P Downes		Afghanistan
30 Sep 11	Brig	R M B Nitsch	MBE	Afghanistan
30 Sep 11	LCpl	P T Quinn		Afghanistan
23 Mar 12	LCpl	D Lavery REME (V)		Afghanistan
23 Mar 12	SSgt	M A Lovell		Afghanistan

APPENDIX B
TERMINOLOGY AND ACRONYMS

TERMINOLOGY

Ranks

The following is a list of ranks in reverse order of seniority with an explanation of some of the terminology used. For example, OF1 is NATO terminology, which indicates rank equivalence between Services and between countries.

Officers
- **Second Lieutenant (OF1).** Correct abbreviation '2Lt', but Lieutenant is sometimes abbreviated as 'Lieut'
- **Lieutenant (OF1).** Abbreviation 'Lt'
- **Captain (OF2).** Abbreviation 'Capt'. A Capt doing a staff job would normally be graded a Staff Officer Grade 3 (SO3)
- **Major (OF3).** Abbreviation 'Maj'. A Maj doing a staff job would normally be graded a Staff Officer Grade 2 (SO2)
- **Lieutenant Colonel (OF4).** Abbreviation 'Lt Col'. A Lt Col doing a staff job would normally be graded a Staff Officer Grade 1 (SO1)
- **Colonel (OF5).** Abbreviation 'Col'
- **Brigadier (OF6).** Abbreviation 'Brig'. A Brig would normally fill a post at 'one-star' level, and, generally, doing a staff job has the word 'Director' in the job title
- **Major General (OF7).** Abbreviation 'Maj Gen'. A Maj Gen would normally fill a post at 'two-star' level, often with the words 'Director General' (DG) in the job title
- **Lieutenant General (OF8).** Abbreviation 'Lt Gen'.

Other Ranks
- **Craftsman.** Abbreviation 'Cfn', equivalent to Private, Trooper, Rifleman in other arms and services
- **Lance Corporal.** Abbreviation 'LCpl'
- **Corporal.** Abbreviation 'Cpl'
- **Sergeant.** Abbreviation 'Sgt'

TERMINOLOGY AND ACRONYMS

- **Staff Sergeant.** Abbreviation 'SSgt'. Some SSgts have qualified as artificers and are then sometimes referred to as 'tiffies'
- **Warrant Officer Class 2.** Abbreviation 'WO2'. This rank normally comes with an indication (in brackets) of the expertise of the individual. Thus a WO2 qualified as an artificer would have the suffix (Artificer Quartermaster Sergeant) abbreviated as WO2 (AQMS), and often referred to as 'Q'. A Company Sergeant Major would be WO2 (CSM) and a Company Quartermaster Sergeant would be WO2 (CQMS), and often referred to as 'the CSM' or 'CQMS' respectively
- **Warrant Officer Class 1.** Abbreviation 'WO1'. The rank is normally similarly qualified to a WO2; an artificer would be (Artificer Sergeant Major) abbreviated as WO1 (ASM), and often referred to as 'the ASM'. A Regimental Sergeant Major would be abbreviated as WO1 (RSM) and generally referred to as 'the RSM'.

REME UNITS

REME units are divided into first and second line units as is explained in some detail in Chapter 2 ('The Fundamentals and Organisation to 2010'). The following paragraphs provide a basic guide.

First Line
This refers to REME personnel embedded in a non-REME unit, who provide repair and recovery support up to Level 2. Around two-thirds of REME is at first line. The embedded elements vary greatly in size from a single attached tradesman, to a full sub-unit, which may be commanded by a Captain or even a Major in the case of the larger sub-units. The larger sub-units usually have the words 'Light Aid Detachment' (LAD) or 'Regimental Workshop' (Regt Wksp) in their title.

Second Line
Second line REME units provide a deeper level of technical support. Prior to the Logistic Support Review (LSR) (Chapter 2 refers), all REME second line units had the words 'Workshop REME' in their title. This was confusing as second line units included both large workshops, which were classed as 'major units' (commanded by Lieutenant Colonels), and smaller units that were classed as 'independent sub-units' (commanded by Majors).

Post-LSR, most REME second line resources were concentrated in major units commanded by Lieutenant Colonels, and had the words 'Battalion REME' in their unit title. The battalions were divided into sub-units called 'companies' (coy) in line with general Army practice. Some second line resources did not go into the battalions, but instead went into 'Logistic' battalions in the form of sub-units (companies) commanded by Majors. Their parent battalions provided both Equipment Support (ES) and Logistic Support (such as supply and transport).

The primary role of the REME sub-unit was not to provide first line support for its own unit, but to provide second line support for the formation its battalion supported. The term 'ES' refers to a support function, which embraces more than purely engineering. 'REME' is the capbadged organisation from which the technical and engineering staff come. In practice, 'ES' and 'REME' are closely interlinked, and at unit level the terms were often used interchangeably without confusion.

ACRONYMS

A Vehicle	Armoured Vehicle
AAC	Army Air Corps
AATAM	All Arms Tactical Aide Memoire
ABEO	A vehicle mounted mesh system, which replaces bar armour (and is lighter/easier to fit and caused less problems)
ABRO	Army Base Repair Organisation (an agency formed from the former REME base repair organisation)
ABTF	Airborne Task Force
ACA&I	Army Competent Advisor and Inspector (formerly CAA&I)
ACFC	Artificer Command and Field Course (Phases 1, 2, 3)
ACGS	Assistant Chief of the General Staff
ACM	Army Commitment Matrix
ADOC	Army Department of Operations and Commitments
AEO	Aeronautical Engineering Officer
AER	Army Emergency Reserve – amalgamated as part of the Territorial and Army Volunteer Reserve (T&AVR) in 1967
AETW	Aircraft Engineering Training Wing (formerly at Middle Wallop)
AFV	Armoured Fighting Vehicle
AIEFSO	Accident Investigation and Engineering Flight Safety Officer
AITO	Army Individual Training Organisation
AM	Availability Management (Branch at HQ LAND)
ANA	Afghan National Army
ANCOP	Afghan National Civil Order Police – something of an elite force within the ANP (higher literacy, better trained, more deployable)
ANP	Afghan National Police
ANSF	Afghan National Security Forces
AO	Area of Operations
AOA	Aircraft Operating Authority (for example, Comd 1 Arty Bde for UAS)
AOP	Air Observation Post
APC	Army Personnel Centre (based in Glasgow), or Armoured Personnel Carrier
APOD	Aerial Port of Debarkation or Air Port of Debarkation
AQMS	Artificer Quartermaster Sergeant
AR	Army Reserve
ARIB	Afghanistan Roulement Infantry Battalion

ARRC	Allied Rapid Reaction Corps (NATO organisation set up after the Cold War – with its HQ in Bielefeld (Germany))
ARRV	Armoured Repair and Recovery Vehicle based on a main battle tank chassis
ARV	Armoured Repair Vehicle
ASB	Artificer Selection Board
ASCLB	Artificer Selection Course Loading Board
ASM	Artificer Sergeant Major (Warrant Officer Class 1)
ATFC	Army Technical Foundation College – REME soldiers go on the 'Technical Stream' at ATFC Winchester
ATPMV	All-terrain Protected Mobility Vehicle
ATRA	Army Training and Recruitment Agency
ATSA	Army Technical Support Agency
ATV	All-Terrain Vehicle, also known as Quad Bike
AUP	Afghan Uniformed Police
AVLB	Armoured Vehicle Launched Bridge
AVRE	Armoured Vehicle Royal Engineers
B Vehicle	Essentially a wheeled military vehicle
BAG	Battalion Artillery Group (Afghanistan)
BARMA	Operation BARMA is the name for IED mine-clearing operations/procedures
BATUK	British Army Training Unit Kenya
BCCS	Basic Close Combat Skills
BCR	Battle Casualty Replacement
BDR	Battle Damage Repair – techniques for repairing damaged equipment that would not normally be applied in peacetime situations
BG	Battle Group – battalion-sized grouping of sub-units/attached elements from different Arms (for example, two tank squadrons and two companies of armoured infantry plus supporting recce)
BGTI	Battlegroup Thermal Imaging System
BIH	Bosnian Army (largely Muslim)
BiH	State of Bosnia-Herzegovina (often informally called just Bosnia)
B-ISTAR	Base Intelligence, Surveillance, Target Acquisition, and Reconnaissance – this includes electro-optical systems mounted in towers to cover the area around a bases in hostile territory
BITE	Built-in Test Equipment

TERMINOLOGY AND ACRONYMS

Bn	Battalion (major unit, normally 400 – 700 strong commanded by a Lieutenant Colonel)
BRAC/T	Base Realignment and Closure/Transition Plan – in Afghanistan from 2012
BRF	Brigade Reconnaissance Force (Afghanistan)
BRV	Beach Recovery Vehicle
BSG	Brigade Support Group – grouping of logistic and other support elements in direct support of a brigade
BSN	Camp Bastion (Afghanistan – once a MOB, became a JOB)
BTEC	Business and Technology Education Council
BTO	Battalion Technical Officer
BUF	Basic Unit Fleet – formerly Unit Holdings; equipment held at unit level to deliver effective individual training and meet other essential ongoing requirements
C Vehicle	Plant (mostly of a specialist nature used by the Royal Engineers)
CAA&I	DEME(A) had a role as a Competent Army Authority and Inspectorate
CALFEX	Combined Arms Live Fire Exercise
CAN	Camp Abu Naji (Base in Maysan Province near Al Amarah in Iraq)
CASEVAC	Casualty Evacuation
CASREP	Casualty Report – in the case of equipment casualties this is often used to mean 'task'
CBA	Combat body armour
CD CSS	Capability Directorate Combat Service Support
CDM	Chief of Defence Materiel – Head of DE&S
CEG	Career Employment Group
CES	Complete Equipment Schedule – list of the all items that go with an equipment to make it operationally usable (for example, tools, shovels, electronic items, jacks)
CESTA	Centralised Equipment Support Technical Area (within COB on Operation TELIC – Iraq)
CF	Combined Forces – new name for battlegroups in Afghanistan (2010)
CFX	Confirmatory Field Exercise (confirms readiness training)
CGS	Chief of the General Staff (professional head of the Army)
CH	Chieftain – British main battle tank, which preceded Challenger
CHARV	Chieftain Armoured Recovery Vehicle

CHARRV	Chieftain Armoured Repair and Recovery Vehicle
CHE	Controlled Humidity Environment
CIED	Counter Improvised Explosive Device
CIM	Capability Integration Manager
CIMIC	Civil Military Cooperation
CIS	Command and Information Systems
CJO	Three-star Chief of Joint Operations at PJHQ
CLB	Casualty Locating Beacon
CLM	Command, Leadership and Management
CLP	Combat Logistic Patrol
CLR RM	Commando Logistic Regiment Royal Marines
CLS	Contractor Logistic Support
CLV	Command and Liaison Vehicle
CMO	Civil Military Operation
CO	Commanding Officer of a unit (normally a Lieutenant Colonel for Field Army units)
COB	Contingency Operating Base (Iraq)
COE	Contemporary Operating Environment (term coined during operations in Afghanistan for that type of operational environment)
COMBRITFOR	Commander British Forces
CONDO	Contractors Deployed on Operations
Coy	Company (sub-unit, normally about 100 strong commanded by a Major)
CP	Control Point (Afghanistan), or Check Point, Command Post
CPA	Coalition Provisional Authority – set up in Iraq in 2003
CPPRF	Containerised Power Pack Repair Facility
CQMS	Company Quartermaster Sergeant
CR 1 and 2	Challenger 1 and 2 – British main battle tank with 120mm gun
CRARRV	Challenger Armoured Repair and Recovery Vehicle
CS	Close Support
CSA	Customer-Supplier Agreement
CSIF	Centralised Servicing and Inspection Facility
CSS	Combat Service Support (embraces both ES and Log Sp functions)
CSSG(G)	Combat Service Support Group (Germany) – a grouping of largely Germany-based support units (such as REME, logistics, medical, RMP), which provides support for a deployed force, renamed 102 Log Bde in 1999

TERMINOLOGY AND ACRONYMS

CSSG(UK)	Combat Service Support Group (UK) – a grouping of UK-based support units (such as REME, logistics, medical, RMP), which provides support for a deployed force, renamed 101 Log Bde on 1 June 1999
CSSTAT	Combat Service Support Training and Advisory Team – formed early 2010 to support deployments to Afghanistan
CST	Combat Support Tankers
CT	Collective Training
CT 1 – 3	Collective Training Levels 1 to 3 – linked to Campaign Force Operations and Readiness Mechanism Cycle
CTO	Collective Training Objectives
CTS	Crew Training School
CVR(T)	Combat Vehicle Reconnaissance (Tracked)
CWWO	Corps Welfare Warrant Officer (established 2010)
DACP	Defence Acquisition Change Programme (dates not known – certainly going in 2008)
DARA	Defence Aviation Repair Agency
DCAE	Defence College of Aeronautical Engineering
DCC	Dismounted Close Combat
DCEME	Defence College of Electro-Mechanical Engineering formed 1 April 2004 with its Headquarters based at HMS SULTAN, Gosport, which drew together technical training organisations from all three Services – as described in Chapter 23
DCMT	Defence College of Management and Technology – formed 2004 based in Shrivenham
DCOMD	Deputy Commander
DCTT	Defence College of Technical Training
DE&S	Defence Equipment and Support – formed in 2007 when the DLO and DPA merged
DEME(A)	Director Electrical and Mechanical Engineering (Army)
DES	Director Equipment Support (one-star posts in HQ DGES(A))
DFID	UK Department for International Development set up in 1997
DG	Director General
DGATR	Director General Army Training and Recruiting
DGEME	Director General Electrical and Mechanical Engineering
DGES(A)	Director General Equipment Support (Army)
DIANA	Digital and Analogue Test Equipment
DIO	Defence Infrastructure Organisation
DLO	Defence Logistic Organisation (2000 – 2007)

DLTP	Defence Logistics Transformation Programme – subsumed a number of 'improve logistics' programmes/studies including the DLO Change Programme and the End-to-End Study
DMS	Deployable Machine Shop
DOAST	Desired Order of Arrival Staff Table – staff table for a deployment showing the order in which various elements of a force are wanted to arrive, it is a guide to movement planners on the loading/scheduling of ships/aircraft so that what arrives first is what is needed first
DPA	Defence Procurement Agency
DPA	Defence Planning Assumption
DPTA	Drawsko Pomorskie Training Area (western Poland)
DRACAS	Data Reporting Analysis Corrective Action System (linked to WFM programme – aim to identify £55m savings)
DRO	Divisional Recovery Officer
DROPS	Dismountable Rack Offload and Pickup System
DSAE	Defence School of Aeronautical Engineering
DSEME	Defence School of Electronic and Mechanical Engineering – a joint organisation formed on 1 April 2004, which subsumed SEME and SEAE
DSG	Defence Support Group (Defence base repair organisation that took over the ABRO)
DSTL	Defence Science and Technology Laboratory
DTA	Defence Technical Academy (planned to be built at RAF St Athan)
DTR	Defence Training Review
DTT	Defence Technical Training site – planned to be at Lyneham
DTTCP	Defence Technical Training Change Programme
E&MA	Engines and Major Assemblies (for example, engines, gearboxes and power packs for A Vehicles)
EC	Equipment Care
ECC	Equipment Capability Customer
ECCP	Equipment Casualty Clearing Point
ECI	Equipment Condition (or Care) Inspection
ECM	Electronic Counter Measures (includes equipment used to give protection against remotely detonated IEDs)
ECM (FP)	Electronic Counter Measures (Force Protection) – for example, suites fitted to vehicles, wearable ECM (including anti-sniper)
EMA	Ease of Maintenance Assessment

TERMINOLOGY AND ACRONYMS

EME	Electrical and Mechanical Engineer(ing) – also common term for officer commanding a LAD
EngO	Engineering Officer – an accredited status for both TA and Regular officers – intended to lead to CEng
EOD	Explosive Ordnance Disposal
EPLS	Enhanced Palletised Load System – new DROPS
ERV	Electronic Repair Vehicle
ES	Equipment Support
ESPO	Engineering Support Planning Officer
ES Sqn	Equipment Support Squadron
ESS	Equipment Sustainability System (as in Camp Bastion) repair facilities operated initially by KBR, then taken over by the DSG
ESSPA	Equipment Support Spares Procurement Agency
E-SPIRE	Enhanced Sight Periscope Infrared Equipment
F&S	Finance and Secretariat – civil servants who deal with budgetary and financial matters as well as general administration
FAHALAWAL	Operation FAHALAWAL name for rehabilitation exercises in Afghanistan
FAS	Future Army Structure (work during period between Iraq invasion and SDSR 2010)
FAS-NS	Future Army Structure – Next Steps
FCO	Foreign and Commonwealth Office
FDDOL	Force Driving Defence Operational Liability – fleet requirement defined by Defence Planning Assumption (DPA) scales of effort, readiness and concurrency; it must also equip Permanently Committed Forces (PCF), enable sustainability and essential requirements for the generation of FE (Force Elements) and/or FE@R to meet DPAs
FET	Force Equipment Table – document allocating forces from various formations etc to a particular operation or exercise
FG	Force Generation
FIP	Fuel Injection Pump
FIST	Future Integrated Soldier Technology – name for programme to provide future personal weapons and equipment
FMECA	Failure Modes Effects and Criticality Analysis
FOB	Forward Operating Base
FOE	Forecast of Events
FORM	Force Operational Readiness Mechanism (son of FRC)

Fortress	Name for SV(R) fitted with Theatre Entry Standard (UOR) kit
FR	Force Reconnaissance (as in FR Sqn in Afghanistan)
FRC	Force Readiness Cycle, or Full Regeneration Capability (first provided in Camp Bastion with the DSG in charge)
FRES	Future Rapid Effects System
FRT	Forward Repair Team – usually based on a single vehicle, which also carries an engine or major assembly needed to repair an equipment in situ; it is usually but not necessarily associated with the repair of armoured vehicles (or aircraft)
FS	Force Support
FSIAB	Fitter Section in a Box – ISO platform transported 'bouncy castle' with power and facilities used for repairs in Afghanistan
FSR	Field Service Representative – civilian support staff, for example, in Afghanistan – especially for new equipment
FTX	Field Training Exercise (or Final Test Exercise)
FV432	The FV432 is the Armoured Personnel Carrier (APC) variant of the British Army's FV430 series of Armoured Fighting Vehicles (AFVs)
FV434	The FV434 is the Armoured Repair Vehicle (ARV) variant of the British Army's FV430 series of AFVs
FVRDE	Fighting Vehicles Research and Development Establishment
FYROM	Former Yugoslav Republic of Macedonia
GDLS:FPE	General Dynamics Land Systems: Force Protection Europe
GLOC	Ground Line of Communication – 'roads' to the uninitiated
GM	Ground Manoeuvre (for example, brigades – term used in force development work)
GMLRS	Guided MLRS (MLRS that fires guided munitions)
GPATE	General Purpose Automatic Test Equipment
GPMG	General Purpose Machine Gun (7.62 mm belt-fed machine gun – often called the 'gimpy')
GPS	Global Positioning System
GPTIRF	General Purpose Thermal Imaging Repair Facility
GS	General Support
HET	Heavy Equipment Transporter (son of tank transporter)
HFT	Hybrid Foundation Training
HIDAS	Helicopter Integrated Defensive Aids Suite
HLB	Higher Level Budget
HNC	Higher National Certificate

HND	Higher National Diploma
HQ LAND	Headquarters Land Command
HQ JFSp(A)	Headquarters Joint Force Support (Afghanistan) – one-star HQ – manages support for UK forces in Afghanistan
HUMINT	Human intelligence (intelligence gained from people)
HVO	Croatian Force in Bosnia (sometimes allied with the BIH against the Serbs, but not consistently so)
IDF	Ineffective Direct Fire
IED	Improvised Explosive Device
IFV	Infantry Fighting Vehicle
IHLB	Intermediate Higher Level Budget (major segment within a HLB)
ILS	Integrated Logistic Support
ILSM	Integrated Logistic Support Manager
IMV	Infantry Mobility Vehicle
IPR	Intellectual Property Rights
IPT	Integrated Project Team (multidisciplinary team responsible for procuring equipment or supporting it in service)
IR	Individual Reinforcement (or Replacement)
IRC	Interim Regeneration Capability (within ESS system)
ISAF	International Security and Assistance Force – the NATO organisation responsible for, inter alia, coordinating NATO's support in Afghanistan
ISB	Intermediate Staging Base
ISD	In-Service Date
ISI	Interim Safety Inspection – including those carried out every 21 days on equipments in Afghanistan not operating from bases
ISRD	In-Service Reliability Demonstration
IST	Intimate Support Team – a bespoke grouping of ES personnel set up to do a particular task, and exists only until the task has been completed; the manpower will frequently be drawn from REME battalions, but could also come from LADs
ISTAR	Intelligence, Surveillance, Target Acquisition, and Reconnaissance
ITD	Individual Training Directive
ITO	The Army's Individual Training Organisation
ITP	Individual Training Package
IUAS	Integrated Unmanned Aerial Systems

JAG	Joint Aviation Group (for example, in Camp Bastion Afghanistan)
JAMES	Joint Asset Management and Engineering Solution – deployable IT system to give asset visibility (and inclusion of engineering data)
JCLM	Junior Command, Leadership and Management
JDOA	Joint Desired Order of Arrival
JHF(K)	Joint Helicopter Force deployed to support training in Kenya (use Puma helicopters to scare off game)
JFLogC	Joint Force Logistic Component
JFSp(A)	Joint Force Support (Army) – the Army support element in Afghanistan
JHF	Joint Helicopter Force – tri-Service battlefield helicopter force (with its HQ collocated with LAND Command) of all battlefield helicopters
JHF(A)	Joint Helicopter Force (Afghanistan)
JOA	Joint Operational Area (for example, Bosnia and Kosovo combined)
JOB	Joint Operating Base
JOES	Junior Officers Equipment Support Course
JRRF	Joint Rapid Reaction Force
JSAT	Joint Services Adventure Training
JSCSC	Joint Services Command and Staff College – formed 1998 at Shrivenham
KAF	Kandahar Airfield
KBR	An American engineering, procurement, and construction company (formerly Kellogg Brown and Root)
KFOR	NATO Kosovo Force
KLA	Kosovo Liberation Army
KSF	Kuwait Support Facility
LAD	Light Aid Detachment
LCMR	Lightweight Counter Mortar Radar
LEAN or Lean	Lean management is an approach to running an organisation that supports the concept of continuous improvement, a long-term approach to work that systematically seeks to achieve small, incremental changes in processes to improve efficiency and quality
LEC	Locally Employed Civilians/Contractors
LFG	Lightweight Field Generator

TERMINOLOGY AND ACRONYMS

LFR	Land Fleet Requirement (post SDSR 2010) – the total equipment/vehicle fleet required for land forces
LIRC	UOR for Lightweight Intimate Recovery Capability – to allow protected recovery at the lighter end of the scale from the SV(R) – especially for urban tasks
L of C or LOC	Line of Communication
LROD	Aluminium cage armour used to protect against shaped charge weapons – developed by BAE and much lighter than the steel armour used previously
LRU	Line Replaceable Unit – technically speaking any assembly replaced to make an equipment fit, but the term is generally used in connection with electronic 'black boxes'
LSA	Logistic Support Analysis (to support ILS planning)
LSR	Logistic Support Review or Logistic Support Regiment
LWC	Land Warfare Centre – based at Warminster
MAG	Maintenance Advisory Group
MAS	Manned Aerial Surveillance
MASU	Mobile Air Support Unit
MATTs	Military Annual Training Tests
MCCP	Movement Control Check Point
MDBF	Mean Distance Between Failures
MERT	Medical Emergency Response Teams
MGO	Master General of the Ordnance – ancient title – senior Army officer responsible for the procurement of equipment
MGREME	Master General REME (instituted 2012 with demise of DEME(A) post)
MIS	Management Information System
MLRS	Multiple Launch Rocket System
MM/FH	Ratio of Maintenance Man-hours to Flying-hours (for aircraft)
MND(SE)	Multinational Division (South East) – UK-led organisation controlling Southern Zone in Iraq in 2003
MOB	Main Operating Base (Afghanistan)
MoD	Ministry of Defence
MoD PE	Ministry of Defence (Procurement Executive)
MP&GS	REME's Manpower and Gapping Strategy for manning units
MPV	Mine Protected Vehicle
MRAP	Mine Resistant Ambush Protected
MRCOA	Military Registered Civilian Owned Aircraft

MRX	Mission Rehearsal Exercise (before an operational tour – for aircraft workshops and so is aviation terminology)
MSA	Mission Specific Assessment (of training to take on a specific mission)
MSG	Maintenance Support Group (Germany and UK)
MSR	Main Supply Route
MST	Mission Specific Training – this includes an element of REME maintainer training aligned to specific missions
MTI	Military Training Instructor (roles that tradesmen can fill)
NAFEC	Naval Air Facility El Centro – US fixed/rotary wing facility used by AAC
NARO	Naval Aircraft Repair Organisation
NCO	Non-Commissioned Officer – Junior NCO (JNCO) up to the rank of Corporal, Senior NCO (SNCO) Sergeant and above
NDA(N) or (S)	Nad-e-Ali (North) or (South) – operational areas north and west of Lashkar Gah in Afghanistan
NED	Non-Executive Director
NES(N) or (S)	Nahr-e-Saraj (North) or (South) – operational areas near Gereshk in Afghanistan
NFF	No fault found
NGO	Non-Government Organisation
NMS	New Management Strategy
NSC(A)	National Support Command (Afghanistan)
NSE	National Support Element (grouping of units and organisations, which provides second and third line support to a force deployed on operations)
NTM	Notice to move
NTM-A	NATO Training Mission Afghanistan
O&D	Organisation (or Operations) and Deployment
OC	Officer Commanding a sub-unit (such as a platoon or company)
OET	Operational Equipment Table – items of equipment held in a theatre that get handed over to units whilst they are on tour
OJAR	Officer's Joint Appraisal Report
OMLT	Operational Mentoring and Liaison Team
OPP Trades	Operational Pinch Point Trades
OPR	Off Platform Repair (for example, the repair of power packs and 'black boxes' removed from equipments for second line repair)

TERMINOLOGY AND ACRONYMS

OPS	Operational Performance Standard (requirement for REME Career Employment Groups)
OTEP	Operational Training Equipment Pool
OTX	Overseas Training Exercise
PAAB	Potential Artificer Assessment Board
PB	Patrol Base
PCF	Permanently Committed Forces (reflected in Defence Planning Assumptions)
PDS	Post-Design Services – investigations and modifications normally carried out on an equipment after it had entered service
PDT	Pre-Deployment Training Package
PEP	Priming Equipment Packs – pre-scaled deployment packs, including ES items, to support 30 days on operations
PFA	Personal Fitness Assessment
PFI	Private Finance Initiative
PID	Positive Identification (required, for example, in Afghanistan before engagement with long range systems)
PJHQ	Permanent Joint HQ – established at Northwood after the first Gulf War to control all UK military operations
PM	Protected Mobility
PMAG	Provisional Military Advisory Group (Afghanistan)
PNVS	Pilot Night Vision Sensor
POGO	Proof of Good Order (for example, ensuring equipments being brought back from Afghanistan are clear of biological and other hazards)
POR	Post Operational Report
PP	Power pack – usually refers to the PP of an armoured vehicle, which consists of an engine and gearbox combined in a unit that can be quickly and easily replaced to repair the armoured vehicle
PPP	Public-Private Partnership
PPRF	Power Pack Repair Facility
PPV	Protected Patrol Vehicle (for example, Mastiff)
PRE	Periodic REME Examination
PRT	Provincial Reconstruction Team (working in Afghanistan)
PRU	Personnel Recovery Unit (regional units, established as part of the Army's response to casualties in Afghanistan)
PSI	Permanent Staff Instructor (such as in a TA unit)

PV	Private Venture
QMG	Quartermaster General – ancient role – senior officer responsible for equipment and materiel
QRD	Quartermaster Readiness Date
QRF	Quick Reaction Force
RA	Royal Artillery, often referred to as 'Gunners'
RAC	Royal Armoured Corps
RAJA	REME Association Job Agency
RAOC (E)	Royal Army Ordnance Corps (Engineering)
RASC	Royal Army Service Corps
RCT	Royal Corps of Transport
RE	Royal Engineers, often referred to as 'Sappers'
RLC	Royal Logistic Corps
REME	Corps of Royal Electrical and Mechanical Engineers
RMRO	REME Manning and Records Office
ROG	Rear Operations Group ('son of Rear Party', those left behind when, for example, a REME battalion deploys on a tour – trains BCRs, supports equipment left behind)
RP&C	Route Proving and Clearance – Talisman operations by Royal Engineers
RPG	Rocket Propelled Grenade
RQMS	Regimental Quartermaster Sergeant
RRF	Rapid Reaction Force
RRFLG	Rapid Reaction Force Logistic Group – to support the UN RRF in Bosnia
RSOI	Reception Staging and Orientation Package – for those arriving in theatre to 'fine tune' their training to their specific AO
RSOM	Reception Staging and Onward Movement (of an expeditionary force)
RTMC	Reserves (later Reinforcement) Training and Mobilisation Centre established at Chilwell (1999)
RWS	Remote Weapon System
SA80	Originally termed 'Small Arms for the 1980s' – in service from 1985 to the present day – it is a family of assault weapons for the British Army, comprising the Individual Weapon (IW) and Light Support Weapon (LSW)
SAAE	School of Army Aeronautical Engineering (at Arborfield)

TERMINOLOGY AND ACRONYMS

SADCHAP	Size, Access, Defence, Concealment, Hardstanding, Accommodation, Position (checklist of points to consider when siting a REME unit)
SCE	Service Children's Education
SCIAD	Scientific Advisor – MoD scientific staff attached, including those attached to the Equipment Capability Branch in Afghanistan
SCLM	Senior Command, Leadership and Management
SDR 98	Strategic Defence Review 1998
SDSR 2010	Strategic Defence and Security Review 2010 – Coalition Government Review
SEAE	School of Electronic and Aeronautical Engineering
SEME	School of Electrical and Mechanical Engineering
SFA	Security Force Assistance
SFA-AT	ISAF Security Force Assistance Advisor Team
SJAR	Soldier's Joint Appraisal Report
SLA	Service Level Agreement (customer-supplier) or Single (soldier) Living Accommodation
SLB	Shaibah Logistic Base (handed back to Iraqi Army in late-2006)
SLDT	Self-Loading Dump Truck
SLOC	Surface Lines of Communication
SLTS	Second Line Test Stations (for example, for repair of ECM equipments)
SME	Subject Matter Expert
SNUT	Soldiers Not Under Training (soldiers in training organisations waiting for courses to start – primarily Phase 2 Training)
SOP	Standard Operating Procedure
SOSI	System of Systems Integrator
SQEP	Suitably Qualified and Experienced Personnel – concept partly driven by the Haddon-Cave Review
SRF	Sight Repair Facility
SSR	Security Sector Reform – Iraq – REME repaired/recovered SSR vehicles
STA	Surveillance and Target Acquisition
STANTA	Stanford Training Area – Middle Eastern village training scenario
STTE	Special Tools and Test Equipment
SVIED	Suicide Vest Improvised Explosive Device (US Army slang)

SVRM	Suicide and Vulnerability Risk Management Policy
TADS	Target Acquisition and Designation System
TAT	Transaction Assurance Team (inspectors of vehicles coming out of theatre at the end of operations in Iraq)
TDT	Training Development Team
TECHEVAL	Technical Evaluation
TEQS	REME TA Education Qualification Scheme – aimed at giving a Level 2 NVQ and Level 2 Technical Certificate
TERS	Theatre Equipment Redeployment System – set up to manage return of equipment from Iraq
TES	Technical Enabling Services (organisation set up to provide technical support to both the DLO and DPA), or Tactical Effects Simulation (type of field exercise), or Tactical Engagement Simulation
TEU	Essentially a 20-foot ISO container
TFH	Task Force Helmand – the main British Army combat component in Helmand – based on a brigade
TiC	Troops in Contact (needing aviation or other support)
TLCM	Through Life Capability Management
TNA	Training Needs Analysis
TNTLS	Tactical Navigation and Target Location System
TOA	Transition of Authority (for an operational area)
TPDP	Trade Proficiency Development Booklet
T-PLS	Threshold Palletised Load System
TQM	Total Quality Management
TRP	Theatre Redeployment Pool
TS Spec	Technical Support Specialist – REME role formed 1 April 2008 from former Technical Storemen, Regimental Specialists and some REME Unspecified/E2 Drivers
TSS	Technical Support Specialist
TST	Technical Support Team
TSU	Transition Support Unit (for example, TSU NES (Nahr-e-Saraj Afghanistan)
TSV	Tactical Support Vehicle
TTP	Tactics, Techniques and Procedures
TUAS	Tactical Unmanned Air Systems
TXS	Theatre Exit Standards – laid down by Army HQ for equipment coming back from, for example, Afghanistan

TERMINOLOGY AND ACRONYMS

UAS	Unmanned Aerial System
UAV	Unmanned Aerial Vehicles
UNHCR	United Nations High Commission for Refugees
UNPROFOR	United Nations Protection Force – UNPROFOR 1 was the multinational force set up to help protect the delivery of aid in Bosnia by the UNHCR and others
UOR	Urgent Operational Requirement (for equipment, or items/kits to enhance/protect equipment)
USMC	US Marine Corps
USUR	Urgent Statement of User Requirement (new terminology – Afghanistan era)
VMA	Vehicle Mechanic A repairs A Vehicles
VMB	Vehicle Mechanic B repairs B Cehicles
VSEL	Vickers Shipbuilding and Engineering Limited
WCSP	Warrior Capability Sustainment Programme
WFI	War Fighting Increment (increments of manpower and equipment to bring a unit from its peacetime establishment to its full war fighting strength)
WFM	Whole Fleet Management
WHG	Warthog (PM vehicle) as in WHG Group in Afghanistan
WMD	Weapons of Mass Destruction – nuclear, chemical and biological weapons
WMIK	Weapons Mounted Installation Kit
WO	Warrant Officer (Class 2 and Class 1)
WR	Warrior vehicle – family of tracked AFVs originally developed to replace the older FV430 series of vehicles
WR510	Warrior Infantry Fighting Vehicle carrying infantry sections
WR512	Warrior Mechanised Combat Repair Vehicle
WR513	Warrior Mechanised Recovery Vehicle (Repair)

INDEX

Abate Col S J, 606
Abbott Lt Col J, 100
Abdullah II King of Jordan, 515
Adams Capt H, 551–2
Adkins Col I, 328–9, 611
Adkins Cpl R, 595
Alanbrooke Viscount, 513
Alexander Capt F, 544
Alexander Gen Viscount, 2
Allawi Ayad, 122
Allcock SSgt N D, 613
Allen Col A, 298, 582
Allenby K, 564
Allison Miss J, 504
al-Sadr Muqtada, 120 122, 128
al-Sistani Grand Ayatollah Ali, 122
Altass Craig, 569
Altass Tony, 569
Ames Sgt R, 573
Anderson Maj Andy, 538
Andrews Maj Gen S, 496, 607, 609
Ansell Col D, 559
Anthistle Col A, 442
Armstrong Maj Gen M, 106, 609
Arnold Maj M, 291
Ashton Capt R, 231
Ashurst Cfn 'Ashy', 535
Aspray Maj R, 286–7
Atherton, 536
Atkinson LCpl S, 605
Atkinson SSgt M, 605
Axson Col D, 438, 441, 610

Bailey Capt D, 613–14
Baker LCpl N, 601
Ball Brig A, 381, 392, 438, 441–2, 443, 483, 485, 610
Ballard Mr N, 512
Barclay Lt Col W, 441–2, 610
Barham Maj M, 583–4, 586, Plate 67
Barnard Cpl, 582
Barnes Cpl, 493
Barron LCpl, 605
Bartlett WO1 K, 577
Bartlett WO2 M, 598
Bartolini WO1 M, 568
Bass Capt S, 546
Bate WO2 C, 548
Bateman WO1 (CASM) R, 611
Baxter Mr B, 499–500, Plate 52
Beaumont Cpl, 540–1

Beaven Mr P, 512
Beeken Maj P, 520
Beer Maj M, 548
Beharry Pte, 128
Belgum Lt Col G, 141
Bell Maj, Plate 8
Belson Sgt S, 614
Bennett Col R, 493, 610
Bennett SSgt J, 605
Besgrove Maj Gen P, 368, 370, 427, 500, 608–609, 612
Betteridge Lt Col A, 422
bin Laden Osama, 160
Birrell Lt Col A, Plate 8
Blackbourn Cpl M, 601
Blair Tony, 79, 91, 322, 375, 432
Booth Lt Col A, 392
Booth Maj R, 580
Booth Ms J, 503
Booty Cfn R, 549
Borley Mark, 588
Boswell Brig M, 29, 40, 428, 432–3, 443, 526, 595, 607, 610
Boulton Cfn O, 594–5
Bowden Cfn R, 613
Bowen Cpl S, 599
Boyle WO1 A J R, 613
Bradley Sgt J, 107–108
Braithwaite Cpl R, 569
Bramwell Capt P, 600
Brazier WO2 M, 606
Bremer Paul, 121
Bridges Maj S, 581
Brierley Maj P, 52–3
Brittain Col J, 163
Brookes Cpl C, 580
Brooks SSgt C, 177
Brown Col P, 47
Brown Cpl, 137–8
Brown Cpl K, 212
Brown Gordon, 322, 375, 432
Brown Maj M, 521
Brown Sgt S, 615
Brown WO 2, 559–60
Bryant Lt Col A, 601
Bulmer Col M, 538
Bunyard Maj T, 564
Burn LCpl, 148
Burnett Col B, 586–7
Burns Maj P, 578
Burton Maj A, 615

INDEX

Bush President George W, 91, 98, 118, 122
Butler Brig E (late Royal Green Jackets), 173, 175
Butler Maj J, 567–8
Butters WO1 D, 598
Byng WO2, 290

Callaway Capt, 321
Cambridge Mr T, 524
Cameron Col S, 592, 614
Cameron Maj E, 578, 582–3
Campbell Maj A, 537, 612
Capper Col M, 381, 383, 392
Caress Sgt P, 613
Carey Brig M, 283
Cargill Cpl J, 540
Carney Capt, 107
Carney SSgt P ,614
Carpenter Cpl 'Chippie', 146
Carruthers Cpl B, 612
Carter WO2 M, 558
Case Lt Col R, 570
Casey Capt R, 614
Caswell Capt P, 585
Caswell SSgt S, 563
Caswell WO2, 571
Chennell Cpl T, 582
Chidgey WO1, 546
Christie Cfn, 540–1
Clark Brig M, 610
Clark Cpl, 605
Clark Gen (US) W, 82
Clarke Maj (AGC) G (ex-REME), 591
Clarke SSgt Gary, 591
Cleasby Lt Col I, 442, 500, 504
Colclough Maj (RAPTC) M, 555
Combellack LCpl B, 536
Comber Sgt C, 111–12, 507, 612
Condron WO1 (CASM) L, 611
Cook Steph, 564
Cook WO1 S, 575
Cooper Maj, Plate 39
Cooper WO2, 593
Corner WO2 R, 535–6
Corp Maj Gen P, 354, 356, 358, 368, 608–609
Corroyer Capt I, 595
Cotton Cfn, 591
Cotty, 569
Court Col M, 234–5, 610
Cowan Lt Gen S (late Royal Signals), 365, 369–70
Craig Capt A, 175
Craig Cpl J, 600
Cran Col M, 327–8, 443, 611
Crawford Lt Col J, 294
Creak Capt (AGC) J (ex-REME), 541–4

Crichard Lt Col G, 479, 531
Crilley Lt G, 193
Croager Lt Col P, 591
Croucher Brig R, xiv, 370, 427–8, 608, 610
Cryer Capt M, 550
Cummings Cpl C, 579, 582
Cunningham Jed, 588
Curran Maj Gen L, 608–609
Currie Capt H, 568
Curry Lt Col N, 442, 588
Cutler Sgt P, 613
Cyrans WO1, 546

Dale Maj Gen I, 125, 374, 496, 608–609
Daley SSgt, 547
Dalton Cpl D, 579
Darroch WO2 C, 614
Davies Cpl P, 580
Davies Lt Col P, 289
Davies WO2 D, 558
Davies WO2 I, 579
Davis Cpl, 605
Davison Mr C, 293, 439, 442–3
Dawson Maj I, 535, 538
Dean Cpl, 565
Denton Capt P, 535
Deverell Gen Sir Christopher (late Royal Tank Regiment), 608
Devlin SSgt D, 615
Dillon Cfn, 605
Dinsdale Mr S, 512
Dixon WO1, 546
Dixon WO2 I, 548
Dorward Col M, 467
Dower P, 555
Dowling Sgt M, 507
Downes Cfn 'Digger', 535
Downes Cpl M, 615
Drew Brig J, 386–8, 488–90, 492
Drysdale WO1, 175
Duncan Col A, 257, 443, 592
Duncan Maj I, 48, 598
Dunne Mr P, 391, 518
Durand Maj (Canada) B, 558
Durham Mr D, 494, 512
Dyas WO1 B, 573

Eade Mr C, 537
Eamer Capt D, 592
Earl Capt R, 613
Eastman Maj D, 171, 613
Ebling Col J, 601
Eddy Maj (Canada) R, 557
Edmondson Maj D, 103
Edwards Lt Col J, 503, 538–40, 557
Edwards Sgt (RLC) 'Taff', 534

Edwards SSgt, 605
Edwin WO2 M, 518
Egan Col D, 469–71
Eggert Capt J, 595
Eggleton WO1 S, 567, 569
Eldred Mr P, 499
Elesmore WO2 D, 600
Elford Cdre (RN) D, 479
Ellis Sgt D, 51
Elmes Capt, 139
Evans Angela, Plate 56
Ewens Col A, 611

Farish LCpl, 551, 571
Farley SSgt M, 614
Farley WO1, 134
Feeney WO2 P, 614
Feldmanis Lt Col E, 615
Fenn Cfn R, 518
Fenwick Maj J, 595
Ferdinand Cpl K, 582
Ferguson Maj Gen K, 72, 608
Field Lt, 571
Figgures Lt Gen A, 6, 31, 374, 383, 485, 607–609, 612, 615, Plate 8
Finn Paul, 589
Fisher Cpl, 582
Fitzgerald Cpl K, 613
Fleming Cpl J, 613
Fletcher Lt Col P, 546
Flux Cfn J, 614
Forbes WO2 I, 606
Fordham Jay, 133
Found Cfn A, 216
Fountain Capt I, 538, 540
Fox Capt J, 503, 540, 550, 564–6
Fram Lt Col R, 149–50, 505, 612
France WO1, 593
Franey Cpl, 605
Frapwell Sgt S, 539
Fraser-Hitchen Col A, 147, 154, 238, 550, 600
Friend WO2, 318
Frost Mr R, 525

Gallagher Capt I, 538
Gallagher SSgt N, 518
Galloway Andy, 576
Gardiner Cpl, 493
Gardiner Cpl D, 574
Garner Lt Gen (US) Jay, 121
Garrett Cpl J (James), 113
Garrett Cpl J (Jason), 507
Garson SSgt, 135
Gaskell Sgt, 605
Gatward Lt Col R, 392
Gaunt Maj Gen M, 199, 209, 607
Getty Cpl, 223

Gibson Col I, 443, 524, 526, 610
Gibson Cpl C, 590, 599
Gillanders Col T, 611
Gillespie Miss T, 577
Gilliam Maj D, 499
Gillies Lt Col T, 557–8
Gleave LCpl A, 599
Gooderson Maj P, 614
Gordon, 569
Gorse WO1 G, 567, 569
Gowing Mr P, 392
Gowlett 2Lt, 135
Gracianio SSgt J, 558
Graham Cpl N, 595
Graham Maj N, 580
Graham SSgt T, 567
Grant Lt Gen S (late Royal Engineers), 370
Grason Cpl M, 614
Gray Col P, 314–16
Gray Mr B, 376
Green, 569
Green Mr D, 506, Plate 55
Green Wg Cdr (RAF) A, 517–18
Greensmith Capt M, 600
Grieves B, 588
Guthrie SSgt J, 613
Gwilliam Cfn R, 539

Haddon-Cave Mr C, 291, 293, 431–2, 439
Haggerty WO1 P, 549
Haigh Cpl R, 581–2
Haines Mr A, 519, Plate 58
Hall Cpl K, 563
Hall SSgt B, 559–60, 562–3
Hammond Maj D, 578
Hanks Cfn, 535
Harding Maj P, 150
Harkness The Rev J, 509
Harland SSgt P, 615
Harrison Sgt 'H', 579
Harrold Sgt G, 557
Harrow SSgt J, 546–7
Harvey Brig C, 611
Harvey Col J, 307, 313–14, 611
Haughton WO1 (Army Sgt Maj) G, 527–8
Haugvik Capt, 586
Hawker Cpl N, 568–9
Hayes LCpl, 606
Hazel WO1 H, 213
Heard WO2 H, 535–6
Heath Cpl Ted, 579
Heath Maj Gen M, 350, 354, 358, 361, 368, 608
Heelis Maj M, 58–9
Henderson Maj Gen J, 101, 163, 607, 609
Henderson Maj R, 504
Heseltine Mr M, 360

INDEX

Hestleton Neil, 569
Hestleton Sgt Daz, 568–9
Hickling Maj (Royal Signals) A, 579
Hill Maj S, 231
Hills Maj G, 614
Hinds Cpl D, 579
Hinson Capt Gino, 539
Hirst Lt Col D, 531
Hirst Maj I, 437
HM The Queen, 6, 31, 441, 484–5, 492, 552, Plate 38
Hogarth Cpl A, 590
Holden Maj G, 53
Holder Mr R, 392
Hole WO1 S, 548–9
Holford Col S, 550
Holman Maj J, 520
Holmes Cfn, 551–2
Hood LCpl, 565
Horne Maj J, 573
Houghton Lt J, 548
Howard WO1 'Monster', 581–2
Howell WO1 C, 611, Plate 56
HRH Prince Michael of Kent, 527
HRH The Countess of Wessex, 516
HRH The Prince Philip, x–xi, 428, 440, 482, 489–90, 493, 495, 500, 519, 607, Plates 50–2, 58
HRH The Princess Royal, 584, Plate 67
Hughes Cfn, 194
Hughes Col G, 442
Hughes Cpl, 606
Hughes Cpl J M, 613
Hunt Cpl S, 568–9
Huntley Maj Gen M, 254, 370, 374, 493, 608–609
Hutchins LCpl, 222
Hutchinson Maj Gen M, 608

Illingworth Col G, 304, 611
Illingworth Cpl R, 595
Isbister SSgt J, 540
Izzard Capt W, 319

Jackson Cpl, 582
Jackson Lt Gen Sir Mike (late Parachute Regiment), 80, 82
Jaques Lt Gen P W, 607, 609
Jarvis Col S, 441, 472, 610
Jefferis Cfn J, 539
Jeffery Capt M, 589
Jenkins Maj Gen D, 608
Jinks Cpl P, 582
Jobes SSgt A, 591
John, 569
Johns Mr Ted, 567
Johnson Maj A, 584

Johnson WO2 'Jono', 600
Johnston Cfn, 222
Johnston Maj Gen J, 502, 608
Jones Brig R, 283, 362
Jones Cpl G M, 613
Jones LCpl R, 595
Jones Lt Col B, Plate 8
Jones Maj C, 586
Jones Maj M, 589
Jones Mr R, 498, 500, Plate 52
Jones V, 540
Jones WO1 (CASM) S, 611, Plate 56
Jones WO2 R, 550
Joy Col M, 538
Joy Col R M, 428, 437, 610
Joyce Capt C, 291
Judd Lt Gen D L, 370, 608–609

Karzai Hamid, 161, 163
Kear Cfn, 605
Kemp LCpl Y, 539
Kennedy Cfn, 551–2
Kerr Sgt N, 614
Keymer Lt Col D, 500
Keymer Mrs C, 499–500
Kitchen WO1 S, 527
Knaggs Col C (late Irish Guards), 173
Knapman Mr C, 392
Knight Maj D, 511
Komasavi LCpl, 582
Kristensen SSgt G, 549

Lamont Capt S, 539
Lamont WO1 B, 611, Plate 56
Langmead, 569
Laughton Capt S, 573
Lavery LCpl D, 615
Lawson Capt, Plate 39
Le Var Dr R, 510, 512–13
Le Var Lt Col Larry, 499–500, 509–13, Plate 52
Leach Maj M, 559–60
Learmont Gen Sir John (late Royal Artillery), 360
Leibrick Sgt A, 540
Leng Jon, 589
Lethbridge Maj D, 596–7, Plate 68
Lewer LCpl, 582
Lewis Capt A, 579–80
Lihou Cfn, 54
Lilley WO2 C, 591
Lloyd AVM (RAF), 479
Loader Lt Col P, 224, 270
Lockitt SSgt P, 577
Logan Sgt, 131
Long Sgt P J, 613
Longfellow Cfn M, 536

Longford Mr C, 392
Longmore Col P, 526
Lorimer Brig J (late Parachute Regiment), 192
Lovell SSgt M A, 546, 615
Lucas Col R, 592, Plate 39
Lucas LCpl P, 537
Lynch SSgt T, 536–7
Lynch WO1 D, 604, 606
Lyndhurst SSgt C B, 130–1, 612

Macdonald Cpl, 606
MacDonald Sgt N, 559
Mack Capt Sandy, 568–9
Mackay Capt, 605
Mackie Sgt J, 612
Madronal Capt S, 594
Mansfield WO1 S, 606
March WO1 S P, 614
Maric Cpl Z, 565
Marsh Cfn, 582
Marsh SSgt V, 584
Marshall Cfn A, 615
Martin, 569
Martin Lt Col R A, 614
Martin WO2, 569
Marven Cpl K, 109–11, 316
Mason Capt S, 613
Mason WO1 (CASM) M G, 611
Massey Brig (late Royal Corps of Transport), 534
Mather Sgt G W, 613
Matthew Lt Col T, 392
Matthews LCpl J, 590
Matthews WO1, 551–2, 565
May-Miller WO1, 569
McCall Brig B W, 428, 577, 582–3, 608, 610
McCarthy Col P T, 442, 610
McClenaghan Sgt R, 615
McClung Maj T J, 614
McCreesh Maj D, 534–5, 538, 540
McGeever SSgt P, 545–6
McIvor Cfn M, 539
McKenzie LCpl, 537
McKenzie SSgt A, 559
McLoughlin WO2 K, 51
Meagher Col A, 592
Metcalfe Maj Gen V, 487
Metters Cpl, 582
Mifsud Col V, 321, 611
Miller Cpl A W, 147–9, 507, 612
Miller Maj P H K, 612
Millington Col A, 500, 610, Plate 52
Mills SSgt D, 546
Minett, 536
Mitchell Cpl W, 590
Mitchell Maj Gen G I, 538, 609
Mitchell Maj P G, 476, 614

Mitchell WO1 'Mitch', 538, 581
Moffat Capt C, 537–8, 540
Moles Ron, 588
Monkhouse WO2, 318
Montgomery FM Viscount, xiv
Moore Col N, 610
Moore Mr P, 390
Moorhouse Maj D, 162
Moran Cfn J, 539
More WO1, 152
Morelli LSgt V, 108
Morgan Capt G, 582
Morgan Capt J, 582
Morgan Maj O, 518
Mortimer Capt (RLC), 197–8
Mosedale Mr A, 392
Moss SSgt B, 564
Mouncey WO1 J, 577
Mulholland Maj, Plate 8
Mulroy Col J, 550, 610
Mundy Cpl, 582
Murfin WO2 S, 575
Murley WO1 (CASM) J, 582, 611, Plate 56
Murray Cpl K, 568–9
Murrison Dr A, 525
Myers Steve, 588

Naivalurua Maj R, 578, 582
Natalie Cfn, 565
Naylor Cpl S, 595
Naylor Maj W, 584
Nicholls WO2 J, 533
Nicholson Lt S, 600–601
Nicholson Sgt 'Nico', 538
Nitsch Maj Gen R M B, 607, 609, 613, 615
Noble Mr R, 517–18
Noke Capt P, 202
Nolan Maj M, 295
Nunn SSgt D, 535

O'Brien LCpl, 571
O'Donoghue Gen Sir Kevin (late Royal Engineers), 365, 373–4
O'Neill WO2 A, 559, 560, 562
Oakes Col M, 575
Oakes SSgt P, 582
Oakley Sgt A, 580
Obama President B, 182, 220
Odling Capt, 139, 606
O'Leary Brig W, 611, Plate 39
Orton LCpl, 605–606
Owen Col R, 592
Owen Cpl S, 563

Packham SSgt, 605
Paice Mr E, 521

INDEX

Palmer Brig J, 500, Plate 52
Parkinson WO2 A J, 614
Parsons WO2 S, 177, 595
Patey Capt G, 558
Patey Maj M, 524, 526
Peacock SSgt S R, 615
Pendlington Col M, 125, 139, 141, 443, 479, 525, 531
Penrose LCpl, 130
Peregrine Col R, xiv, 387, 420, 610
Perry Capt R, 550
Peters Capt A, 232
Petraeus Lt Gen (US) D, 122–3
Pettifer Maj F, 613
Phillips Maj P D, 612
Phillips Sgt M, 600
Phillips SSgt M J,614
Philp Col A, 428
Phipps Lt Col A, 392
Pinchard WO1 P G, 614
Pink Mr Malcolm, 501
Pinkney LCpl, 212
Piper SSgt 'Pip', 579
Platt Capt A, 214
Platt Col A G, 484, 610
Pledger AM (RAF) M, 373
Porter WO1, 592
Power Maj J, 125, 613
Powley WO1 S, 578, 582
Prince John, 381
Proctor Capt D, 538
Prowse Maj D, 577–8
Purchase SSgt I W, 612
Pyott Cpl M, 225

Quinn Capt F, 564–5
Quinn LCpl P T, 615
Quinn Lt Col L E, 443

Ramsden Cfn, 571
Rees Carla, 512
Rees Cpl A, 579, 582
Reeves SSgt J S, 615
Reffell WO1, 582
Reid Dr J, 165
Rennie WO2 N, 606
Reynolds Capt P, 559–61
Reynolds Maj F, 511
Rhodes SSgt W, 568
Rickard Brig R, 383, 389, 475
Ringrose Maj M C, 442
Robb Sgt S, 594
Roberts Cpl, 582
Robertson Cpl, 216
Robertson Cpl 'Gaz', 201
Robertson Sgt M, 550
Rodolfo Cfn, 130

Rogers Maj A J, 605–606
Rogers Maj D, 538
Rosie Capt L, 615
Ross Col N, 586–7
Ross LCpl B, 539
Rouse Col J, 115
Rudge WO1, 571
Rumsfeld Secretary of Defense (US) D, 92, 118, 121, 245

Samanjoul WO1 Sammy, 589
Sanders Maj Gen P (late Royal Green Jackets), 607
Sands Tim, 588
Sankey WO1 L, 615
Sapsford Sgt, 129
Savage Capt M, 612
Saville Col J, 309, 312, 465
Sayer Capt T, 63–5
Sayer WO2 C, 559–61
Schofield Maj (RE) M, 576
Scott Capt J, 595–6
Scott Col D G, 176, 179, 531, 610
Scott WO2 J, 615
Selby Brig M, 538, 564
Sergeant LCpl G, 518
Sharman Maj Gen A G, 356, 608, 609
Sharples Maj N, 323, 614
Shaw Cpl, 582
Shaw John, 538
Shaw Maj Gen D, 608
Shenton Maj R K, 543, 604, 606
Shewry Lt Col P, 141
Sibbons Col M, 503
Simon SSgt P, 582
Simons Cpl J, 114, 507
Simpson Brig I, 77, 486
Simpson WO2 R J, 614
Sked WO1 K, 577–8
Skivington Mrs Z, 520
Skivington WO2 G, 465
Slinger Sgt, 593
Smith Gen Sir Rupert (late Parachute Regiment), 608
Smith Lt Col M, 573
Smith Lt Col P W, 443
Smith Sgt S, 535, 540
Smith WO2 M I, 606
Smyth Maj M, 604, 606
Snell Capt A, 586
Spencer-Fleet Sgt, 606
Stanley Cfn, 571
Stewart Lt Col R (Bob) (late 1 Cheshire), 58
Steyn Capt J, 290
Stockbridge Mr M, 382, 392
Stockwell Sgt P, 595
Stones WO2, 571

Stradins Lt Col P, 531
Street Cpl R S, 180, 507, 612
Stuart Maj A, 142
Summerfield, 569
Sutton Capt M, 212–13
Swan Paddy, 538
Swan WO1 J, 611, Plate 56
Sykes LCpl, 130

Taberner LCpl J D, 613
Tanner Maj G F, 606
Taylor Cpl R, 558
Taylor LCpl M, 533
Taylor Maj S, 584
Teare Lt Col A, 526
Tervitt Capt T, 591
Teskey Maj A, 174
Tester Cfn, 571
Tetlow Brig S J, 428, 430, 442, 608, 610
Thatcher The Rev S, 493, 513
Thomas Capt, 605
Thomas Lt Col S, 584
Thomas Maj (AGC) N, 593–4
Thomas WO1, 582
Thomas WO1 A, 605–606
Thompson WO1 C, 557
Thomson Col A, 209, 583
Thomson Cpl 'Tommo', 535
Tierney Cpl C G, 612–13
Tindall Dave, 588
Titchard-Jones Cpl, 582
Tizard Lt Col M, 441, 524, 526, 567–9, 610
Trussler Sgt A, 534
Turner AVM (RAF), 479
Twinn SSgt R, 177–8
Tyler Maj Gen C, 608, Plate 39
Tyler Maj Gen T N, 374, 519, 608, 609, Plate 58
Tyler Sgt A L, 615

Vidot Neil, 588
Voss WO2 J V F, 614

Walker Lt Gen Sir Michael (late Royal Anglian), 70
Walker SSgt, 541
Walker WO1 (CASM) J W, 611, Plate 56
Wall Gen Sir Peter (late Royal Engineers), 565, 608
Wall LCpl C, 536, 540
Wall SSgt, 593

Ward Col C, 256–7, 428, 592
Ward Cpl, 138
Warner Lt Col S, 193
Watson Cpl M, 582
Webber Brig S, 488
Weller Maj N B, 606
Wells WO2 R W, 612
Westlake SSgt J, 606
Westover SSgt L, 590–2
Wetherall Capt S S, 606
Wharmby Lt Col (RLC) M, 49
White Cpl C, 195
White Maj, 571–2
White Maj L, 595
White Sgt F, 591
Whiteley Cpl, 605
Whiteside Peter, 564
Whittaker SSgt, 202
Whittle Lt, 49
Whittle Sgt C, 129
Whittle Capt H, 540
Wilde WO2 C, 582
Wildman Maj Gen M L, 609
Williams Brig N, 71, 428, 430, 488, 608, 610
Williams Capt D, 615
Williams Col R, 293, 296, 439, 443, 519, 601
Williams Lt Col B, 381, 392
Williams Maj N, 579
Williams Sgt C, 546
Willshire Capt D, 538, 540
Willson WO1 S, 606
Wilson Capt M, 565
Wilson Cpl G D, 615
Wilson LCpl P, 137–8, 612
Wilson SSgt S, 577
Winthrop Lt Col I, 231
Wise Lt Col P, 318
Wolfendale Capt D, 515
Wood LCpl 'Bri', 536
Wood SSgt G, 536–7
Woodhouse SSgt D, 548
Woolley WO1 A, 539
Workman Lt Col A, 538
Worrall Mr J, 520
Worrell Maj D, 146
Wright-Rivers Capt 'Geordie', 580, 582

Young Cpl B, 595
Youngs WO2, 138

Zilke Cpl K, 594